普通高等教育"十一五"国家级规划教材

新世纪高等院校英语专业本科生系列教材(修订版)

总主编 戴炜栋

西方思想经典

Heritage of Western Intellectual Tradition: A Sourcebook

朱 刚

上海外语教育出版社
外教社 SHANGHAI FOREIGN LANGUAGE EDUCATION PRESS

图书在版编目（ＣＩＰ）数据

西方思想经典 / 朱刚编著. -- 上海：上海外语教育
出版社, 2016 (2023重印)
　新世纪高等院校英语专业本科生系列教材. 修订版
　ISBN 978-7-5446-3278-2

　Ⅰ.①西… Ⅱ.①朱… Ⅲ.①英语－高等学校－教材
②思想史－西方国家 Ⅳ.①H319.4：B

中国版本图书馆CIP数据核字（2013）第050136号

出版发行：上海外语教育出版社
　　　　　（上海外国语大学内）　邮编：200083
电　　话：021-65425300（总机）
电子邮箱：bookinfo@sflep.com.cn
网　　址：http://www.sflep.com
责任编辑：钱明丹

印　　刷：上海信老印刷厂
开　　本：787×1092　1/16　印张35.5　字数921千字
版　　次：2016 年 6 月第 1 版　2023 年 12 月第 6 次印刷

书　　号：ISBN 978-7-5446-3278-2 / B • 0029
定　　价：55.00 元
本版图书如有印装质量问题，可向本社调换
质量服务热线：4008-213-263

新世纪高等院校英语专业本科生系列教材编委会

主任：戴炜栋

委员：（以姓氏笔画为序）

王守仁	南京大学	张维友	华中师范大学
王守元	山东大学	何兆熊	上海外国语大学
王 蔷	北京师范大学	杨信彰	厦门大学
申 丹	北京大学	宋渭澄	南京国际关系学院
石 坚	四川大学	杜瑞清	西安外国语学院
史志康	上海外国语大学	汪榕培	大连外国语学院
冯建文	兰州大学	姚乃强	解放军外国语学院
朱永生	复旦大学	胡文仲	北京外国语大学
刘世生	清华大学	顾大僖	上海师范大学
刘海平	南京大学	秦秀白	华南理工大学
庄智象	上海外国语大学	徐青根	苏州大学
李 力	西南师范大学	陶 洁	北京大学
李绍山	解放军外国语学院	黄国文	中山大学
李悦娥	山西大学	黄源深	上海外贸学院
张少雄	中南大学	蒋洪新	湖南师范大学
张伯香	武汉大学	程爱民	南京师范大学
张绍杰	东北师范大学	廖七一	四川外国语学院
张春柏	华东师范大学		

总　序

　　随着改革开放的日趋深入，社会各界对外语人才的需求持续增长，我国英语专业的招生规模逐年扩大，教学质量不断提高。英语专业本科生教育的改革、学科建设及教材的出版亦取得了巨大的成绩，先后出版了一系列在全国有影响的精品教材。21世纪的到来对英语人才的培养提出了更高的标准，同时也为学科建设和教材编写提出了新的要求。随着中国加入世界贸易组织，社会需要的不是仅仅懂英语的毕业生，而是思维科学、心理健康、知识面广博、综合能力强，并能熟练运用英语的高素质的专门人才。由于中学新的课程标准的颁布，中学生英语水平逐年提升，英语专业本科生入学时的基础和综合素质也相应提高。此外，大学英语（公外）教育的迅猛发展，学生英语能力的提高，也为英语专业学生的培养提出了严峻的挑战和更新更高的要求。这就规定了21世纪的英语教学不是单纯的英语培训，而是英语教育，是以英语为主体，全面培养高素质的复合型人才。教材的编写和出版也应顺随这种潮流。

　　为了迎接时代的挑战，作为我国最大的外语教材和图书出版基地之一的上海外语教育出版社（外教社）理应成为外语教材出版的领头羊。在充分调研的基础上，外教社及时抓住机遇，于新世纪之初约请了全国25所主要外语院校和教育部重点综合大学英语院系的50多位英语教育家，在上海召开了"全国高等院校英语专业本科生系列教材编写委员会会议"。代表们一致认同了编写面向新世纪教材的必要性、可行性和紧迫性，并对编写思想、教材构建、编写程序等提出了建议和要求。而后，外教社又多次召开全国和上海地区的专家、学者会议，撰写编写大纲、确定教材类别、选定教材项目、讨论审核样稿。经过一年多的努力，终于迎来了第一批书稿。

　　这套系列教材共分语言知识和语言技能、语言学与文学、语言与文化、人文科学、测试与教学法等几个板块，总数将超过150余种，可以说几乎涵盖了当前我国高校英语专业所开设的全部课程。编写内容深入浅出，反映了各个学科领域的最新研究成果；编写体例采用国家最新有关标准，力求科学、严谨，满足各门课程的具体要求；编写思想上，除了帮助学生打下扎实的语言基本功外，还着力培养学生分析问题、解决问题的能力，提高学生的人文、科学素养，培养健康向上的人生观，使学生真正成为我国21世纪所需要的外语专门人才。

　　本套教材编写委员会由我国英语界的知名人士组成，其中多数是在各个领域颇有建树的专家，不少是高等学校外语专业教学指导委员会的委员。教材作者均由编写委员会的专家在仔细审阅样稿后商定，有的是从数名候选人中遴选，总体上代表了中国英语教育的发展方向和水平。

　　鉴于该套教材编写理念新颖、特色明显、体系宏大、作者权威，国家教育部已经将其列入了"十一五"重点教材规划项目。我们相信，继"高等院校英语语言文学专业研究生系列教材"之后，外教社该套教材的编写和出版，不仅会满足21世纪英语人才的培养需要，其前瞻性、先进性和创新性也将为外语乃至其他学科教材的编写开辟一条新的思路，拓展一片新的视野。

戴炜栋

上海外国语大学校长

Heritage of Western Intellectual Tradition　A Sourcebook

前　言

　　南京大学外国语学院英语系自 2000 年起在英语专业高年级开设必修课"西方思想经典"和"中国思想经典"，两课入选"江苏省优秀课程群"。

　　"中国思想经典"的授课内容是源远流长的以儒家（含儒、道、墨、法、佛等各家）为代表的中国传统文化，包括二十世纪新儒学和现当代西方儒学研究。该课的宗旨就是让英语专业的学生能够熟练流利地用英语表述中国文化与思想经典。

　　"西方思想经典"则是本教材的内容，从古希腊罗马一直讲到二十世纪，旨在使英语专业的本科生打下初步的西学基础，以便能够深入地了解西方文化。

　　西方人文思潮是西方文明数千年发展的积累，是西方文化的精华。学习西方思想文化典籍，可以拓宽英语专业本科生在西方文化、科学、哲学、美学等人文、社会、自然科学领域里的知识，加深对欧美文化的了解，增加对欧美人文脉络的总体把握，也是英语专业其他专业课程的高度凝练：通过用英语表述西方文化传统和中华文化精髓，在更高层次上加强"听说读写译"英语语言基本功，提高跨文化交际的能力。

　　西方思想原著的文字比较艰涩，内容比较生疏，这些文字和思想常常博大精深，涉及到人类知识的多个方面。要和这些思想形成交流和对话，需要学习者有较好的知识结构，具备一定的知识储备，还需要逐步提高理解和领悟能力，养成良好的归纳总结和逻辑分析的习惯。通过本课程的学习，这些素质可以得到进一步的加强。

　　英语专业学生对西方人文思潮比较生疏，加上阅读量比较大，语言比较艰涩，阅读起来会有费时费力的感觉，尤其在最初的几个星期。

　　下面的一些建议或许对学习本教材有帮助：

　　端正态度：具备阅读西方思想经典的能力是英语专业的专业特征之一，英语专业的同学对此要有足够的认识，树立起充分的信心；

　　讲究方法：精读和泛读相结合。善于抓住文章的中心论点，对部分段落和词句要反复研读，仔细思考，和作者产生思想互动；其他的部分只需了解大意，没有必要过分依赖字典（本教材提供了尽可能多的注释，以帮助理解，提高阅读速度）；

　　提高效率：阅读量大，时间有限，要注意提高阅读效率，提高时间段的信息获取量和接受量，注意不断加以改进和提高；

　　抓住关键：善于抓住关键词句，发言和写作时加以论述，忌讳泛泛而谈；

　　动手动脑：利用图书馆和网络，消化吸收阅读的文字，养成写作的习惯，产生自己的思想。阅读时做少量的读书笔记，记下书中重要的观点、自己的想法、遇到的问题；

善于交流：学习中遇到的困难、产生的想法，要不失时机地向老师和同学提出，课堂上积极发言，参与讨论，争取不断有所收获。

在介绍西方思想的同时，本教材提供相应的中国人文背景，这也是本教材的主要特色：连接古今，打通中西，帮助学生在跨时代、跨语境、跨文化、跨知识领域的环境下领会与把握中西文化的精髓，中西对比，融会贯通，在这个基础上了解知识的形成过程，进行批判性思考，提高在国际化环境下使用双语在较高层次进行文化沟通、思想交流的能力。有如钱钟书先生在《管锥编》"前言"中所说：研习中西，贵在"打通"，从这个意义上来说，"打通"仍然是研习外国语言文化的最高境界。

1935年时的中央大学外国文学系的培养目标，就是"研究各国文学及其民族思想之表现，以激发独立进展之精神，并培养为中国民族宣达意志之人才"。清华"国学"研究院的四大导师（王国维、梁启超、陈寅恪、赵元任）皆谙熟国史，精通外文，采用"中西并举、贯穿融会、为我所用"的治学方法，"复以本民族命运为重，孜孜寻求中国兴衰之原因"。陈寅恪先生的"中体西用资循诱"，吴宓先生的"择善而从，比较出新"，钱钟书先生的中西"打通"，这些对外国思想文化的认识，其立意之高，境界之高，目标之高，依然值得我们借鉴。

本教材是南京大学英语系数年教学经验的积累，在编写过程中得到很多同行的指点与同学的帮助。杨金才教授在使用本教材中提出很多宝贵建议，任裕海副教授在审读时做了重要的批改和更正，博士生孙希佳、张宇做了认真细致的校读，使用本教材的七年里本科生们做了很多精彩的课堂报告与演示，其中的部分内容已经体现在本教材中。上海外语教育出版社谢宇女士和本教材的责任编辑钱明丹在教材编写过程中提出了诸多宝贵意见和建议。在此谨对以上人员表示衷心的感谢。由于教材内容涉及西方人文传统的方方面面，编者受知识和能力的局限，理解上和语言表述中难免会有错误或不恰当之处，请专家和读者提出宝贵意见。

编者

2007 年 9 月

Heritage of Western Intellectual Tradition　A Sourcebook

INTRODUCTION

… the past as past is gone, save for esthetic enjoyment and refreshment, while the present is with us. Knowledge of the past is significant only as it deepens and extends our understanding of the present. (John Dewey: *Liberalism and Social Action*)

I am only a child playing on the beach, while vast oceans of truth lie undiscovered before me. (Isaac Newton)

I was aware that the reading of all good books is indeed like a conversation with the noblest men of past centuries who were the authors of them, nay a carefully studied conversation, in which they reveal to us none but the best of their thoughts. (René Descartes: *Discourse on Method*)

Definition of key terms:

"Western" refers to countries in Europe and the US; "thought" stands for humanistic ideas as they appear in works of religion, political science, economics, philosophy, science, etc.; and "heritage" represents the recognized classics or canon.

Aims of the textbook:

This textbook chooses to examine in a roughly chronological order about three dozens of major in the West thinkers starting from the dawn of its civilization to the contemporary world. The chief objective of the textbook is to acquaint students with some enduring ideas from the Western intellectual history, and discuss with them some influential speculations on the nature of man, society, religion, science, and art. It will concentrate on a number of questions, such as the position of man in nature, the relation of God and man, the advancement of human understanding, and the nature of human existence. These questions and more have inspired intellectual inquiries in the Western world for over two thousand years and have contributed a great deal to the development of its civilization. They are of general interest to art students and are of special help to students working in language and culture.

How to read:

A distinctive feature of this textbook is that students are required to learn how to make comparisons of Sino-Western heritages through critical thinking and how to appreciate both

Chinese and Western cultures in a cross-cultural historical context. To this end, texts from Chinese and Western cultures are put together to observe the intricacies, and comparisons between ideas of different historical times and geographical locations are strongly encouraged. The textbook is a compilation of selected excerpts intended for close reading and class discussion. Students are, however, encouraged to find the complete works in the library or through the Internet and read after class.

Division of each unit:

The textbook contains sixteen units. Each unit is made up of four parts: basic texts for close reading, compare with China, supplementary reading, and questions for discussion. To ensure a smooth reading, each unit starts with a guide to pronunciation and brief introductions to the texts selected. "Key Concepts" are provided at the end of each text to facilitate understanding. Major ideas in the basic text are highlighted for easy identification, though students are encouraged to find their own important quotes in the text. It is suggested that class discussions should be centered around the "Key Concepts" and the boldfaced sentences in the text, in connection with references to the other texts in "Compare with China" and "Supplementary Reading." Connection building across historical moments and cultural matrices proves to be an effective way for reading and comprehension.

Teaching requirements:

Good preview, close reading of key paragraphs, and participation in class discussion.

CONTENTS

Unit 1 The Christian Bible **1**

Genesis 2

Exodus 7

Gospel According to Matthew 12

Acts of the Apostles 18

Compare with China

  1. Chinese Creation Stories 24

  2. 汉译《圣经》之考察 28

Supplementary Reading

  1. Is Religion Just Organized Superstition? Is Superstition Always

  Religious? 32

  2. How Is Science Different from Religion? 33

  3. Why I Am Not a Christian 35

Questions for Discussion 39

Unit 2 Greek & Roman Sages (1) **41**

Socrates: The Apology 42

Plato: The Republic 58

Compare with China

  1. Axial Age 65

  2. 苏格拉底与孔子的言说方式比较 66

Supplementary Reading

  雅典凭什么判苏格拉底死刑 67

Questions for Discussion 69

Heritage of Western Intellectual Tradition   A Sourcebook

Unit 3 Greek & Roman Sages (2) 70

Aristotle: The Politics 71

Cicero: On the Laws 83

Compare with China

Great Learning and *The Mean* 94

Supplementary Reading

Marcus Tullius Cicero Quotes 97

Questions for Discussion 98

Unit 4 Medieval Christian Church Fathers 99

St. Augustine: The Enchiridion 100

Thomas Aquinas: Summa Contra Gentiles 110

Compare with China

Neo-Confucianism and Later Confucian Philosophy 120

Supplementary Reading

1. Common Characteristics of Scholasticism 123

2. St. Thomas Aquinas 128

Questions for Discussion 130

Unit 5 Renaissance Adventurers 131

Christopher Columbus: Journal and Letter 132

Nicolò Machiavelli: *The Prince* 141

Compare with China

The Rise and Fall of 15th Century Chinese Seapower 154

Supplementary Reading

1. No Cheers for Columbus 161

2. Conservatives Hail for Columbus 162

Questions for Discussion 164

Unit 6 Religious Reformation 165

Desiderius Erasmus: A Pilgrimage for Religion's Sake 166

Martin Luther: An Open Letter to the Christian Nobility 176

John Calvin: Institutes of the Christian Religion 186

Heritage of Western Intellectual Tradition A Sourcebook

Compare with China

Wang Yangming and Matteo Ricci's Progression to China 195

Supplementary Reading

Excerpts of the 95 Theses 199

Questions for Discussion 203

Unit 7 Modern Scientific Thinking (1) 204

Francis Bacon: Novum Organum 205

René Descartes: Discourse on Method 211

Compare with China

Matteo Ricci: The Art of Printing 223

Supplementary Reading

Calculating Machines in China and Europe in the 17th Century — The

Western View 225

Questions for Discussion 227

Unit 8 Modern Scientific Thinking (2) 228

Galileo Galilei: Letter to the Grand Duchess Christina 229

Isaac Newton: The Mathematical Principles of Natural Philosophy 242

Optics 245

Compare with China

Development of Science in Ancient China 248

Supplementary Reading

Critical Thinking 252

Questions for Discussion 254

Unit 9 Modern Political Science 256

Thomas Hobbes: Leviathan 257

John Locke: Of Civil Government 270

Compare with China

1. Confucianism and Human Dignity: Toward a Balanced View of

Rights and Duty 283

2. Locke Talking about China and the Chinese 286

Heritage of Western Intellectual Tradition   A Sourcebook

Supplementary Reading

   1. Political Controversies in the 17th Century England 288

   2. Charles I: Speech Before Execution (January 30, 1649) 295

Questions for Discussion 297

Unit 10 Classical Liberalism 298

Adam Smith: An Inquiry into the Nature and Causes of the Wealth

of Nations 299

John Stuart Mill: On Liberty 308

Compare with China

   1. Western Images of China 322

   2. Qianlong Meets Macartney: Collision of Two World Views 327

Supplementary Reading

   1. The Declaration of Independence 331

   2. United Nations Universal Declaration of Human Rights (1948) 336

Questions for Discussion 339

Unit 11 Anti-Liberalism 340

Jean-Jacques Rousseau: A Discourse on the Moral Effects of the

Arts and Sciences 341

Friedrich Nietzsche: The Will to Power 356

Compare with China

From Western Liberalism to Asian Communitarianism 366

Supplementary Reading

   1. Edmund Burke: Reflections on the Revolution in France 369

   2. Declaration of the Rights of Man and of the Citizen 374

Questions for Discussion 377

Unit 12 Evolutionists 378

Thomas Malthus: An Essay on the Principle of Population 379

Charles Darwin: The Origin of Species (1859) 392

Charles Darwin: The Descent of Man 402

Compare with China

The Warning Voice of Social Darwinism in Early 20th Century China ... 405

Heritage of Western Intellectual Tradition　A Sourcebook

Supplementary Reading

    1. Autobiography of Charles Darwin 410

    2. Piltdown Man Forgery 415

Questions for Discussion 416

Unit 13 Socialism and Communism 417

    Karl Marx and Friedrich Engels: Manifesto of the Communist Party 418

    Eduard Bernstein: Evolutionary Socialism 431

Compare with China

    1. Karl Marx on China 435

    2. 《共产党宣言》在中国的早期翻译、出版和传播 442

Supplementary Reading

    1. Study Guide for *The Communist Manifesto* 444

    2. V. I. Lenin: Marxism and Revisionism 447

Questions for Discussion 450

Unit 14 Early 20th Century: Man & Society 452

    Sigmund Freud: An Outline of Psychoanalysis 453

    John Dewey: Liberalism and Social Action 460

Compare with China

    John Dewey as a Learner in China 471

Supplementary Reading

    1. Freud on the Couch 478

    2. Early Education in China 482

Questions for Discussion 484

Unit 15 Science & Religion 485

    Bertrand Russell: A Free Man's Worship 486

    Alfred North Whitehead: Science and the Modern World (1925) 495

Compare with China

    Bertrand Russell: Chinese and Western Civilization Contrasted 504

Supplementary Reading

    Alfred North Whitehead on Education 512

Questions for Discussion 517

Heritage of Western Intellectual Tradition — A Sourcebook

Unit 16 Man & Woman: Modern Existence 518

Jean-Paul Sartre: Existentialism 520

Simone de Beauvoir: The Second Sex 528

Compare with China

The First Glimpses of China 537

Supplementary Reading

1. Existentialism 541

2. Virginia Woolf: A Room of One's Own 544

Questions for Discussion 550

Heritage of Western Intellectual Tradition A Sourcebook

UNIT 1

The Christian Bible

Pretest

- What do you know about the Christian Bible?
- Why is the Bible so significant to so many people in the world?
- What are the messages conveyed through the creation story and the Exodus?

What You Will Learn in This Unit

- Some knowledge about the Christian Bible;
- Important sections from the Bible; and
- Chinese creation stories.

Learn to Pronounce

Apostle /əˈpɒsl/ 使徒，耶稣的十二门徒
Ananias /ˌænəˈnaɪəs/ 亚拿尼亚
Damascus /dəˈmɑːskəs/ 大马士革
Ethiopia /ˌiːθɪˈəʊpjə/ 埃塞俄比亚
Euphrates /juːˈfreɪtɪz/ 幼发拉底河
Exodus /ˈeksədəs/ 出埃及记
Genesis /ˈdʒenɪsɪs/ 创世记
Gospel /ˈgɒspəl/ （圣经）福音书
Israelite /ˈɪzrɪəlaɪt/ 犹太人
Jacob /ˈdʒeɪkəb/ 雅各

Jerusalem /dʒeˈruːsələm/ 耶路撒冷
Jesus /ˈdʒiːzəs/ 耶稣
Judaism /ˈdʒuːdeɪɪzəm/ 犹太教
Matthew /ˈmæθjuː/ 马太
Moses /ˈməʊzɪz/ 摩西
Nazareth /ˈnæzərɪθ/ 拿撒勒
Pharaoh /ˈfeərəʊ/ （古埃及）法老
Saul /sɔːl/ 扫罗
Sinai /ˈsaɪnaɪ/ 西奈

Introduction

Christianity is the world's most popular religion as roughly 33% of the world population is believed to be Christians (roughly, Muslims take up 18%, Hindus 16%, Buddhists 6%, Chinese traditional religions 4%, and atheists 16%). The Christian Bible, also called the Holy Bible, the Sacred Book or Scriptures of Judaism and of Christianity, is the most widely distributed book in human history. Literature, art, and music of Western culture are deeply indebted to biblical themes, motifs, and images. Translations of the Bible helped the development of Western vernacular languages. The word "Bible" derived through Latin from the Greek *biblia,* or "books," the diminutive form of *byblos,* the word for "papyrus" or "paper," exported from the ancient Phoenician port city of Biblos. The Jewish Bible or the Hebrew Scriptures contains 39 books originally written in Hebrew. The Christian Bible comprises of two parts, the Old Testament and the New Testament. In 1382 the first complete English Bible appeared in manuscript by the English reformer John Wycliffe (1328–1384), whose goal was to liberate the Bible from its possession and use by clergy alone to the hands of the laity. The controversy over the Bible, or Biblical Criticism, gave rise to two branches of modern learning: exegesis (critical interpretation) and hermeneutics (the science of interpretive principles).

The Old Testament, used by Roman Catholics, contains the Bible of Judaism plus 7 other books and additions to these books. The Old Testament used by the Protestants is limited to the 39 books of the Jewish Bible. It was written originally in Hebrew during 1200 to 100 BCE[1]. The word "testament" derives from the Latin word for "covenant," and the term "Old Testament" was said to be devised by a Christian, Melito of Sardis, at about AD 170 to distinguish between the "Old Covenant" that God made with Israel and the "New Covenant" established through Jesus Christ. The first 6 books of the Old Testament tell how Israelites became a people and settled in the Promised Land, an area roughly corresponding to present day Palestine, and the following 7 books are a continuation of their story on this Land. The last 11 books contain poetry, theology, and some additional historical works. The style of the Old Testament includes narratives, poetic works, prophetic works, law, and apocalypses.

Genesis*

The English title is derived from *genesis kosmou* (Greek, "origin of the cosmos"). The book falls into two parts: chapters 1–11 are concerned with the primeval history of humankind and contain stories

---

1   **BCE:** before the Common Era

*   Selected here are the first three chapters of the Genesis.

about the first man and the first woman, and the first covenant made by God with humanity in the person of Noah; chapters 12–50 are mainly an account of the lives of the Hebrew patriarchs Abraham, Isaac, and Jacob, or a history of the origins of the Hebrew nation. The basic aim of Genesis is to relate creation and history to God, and, specifically, to explain the role of Israel in the world. Genesis is still regarded by many as a literal account of the Creation but most see it as myth or legend expressive merely of tribal beliefs, superstitions, and mores, though archaeological investigations have revealed that events, places, and persons in Genesis most probably have basis in historical fact.

In the beginning God created the heaven and the earth. And the earth was without form, and void; and darkness was upon the face of the deep. And the Spirit of God moved upon the face of the waters. And God said, "Let there be light": and there was light. And God saw the light, that it was good: and God divided the light from the darkness. And God called the light Day, and the darkness he called Night. And the evening and the morning were the first day.[1]

And God said, "Let there be a firmament[2] in the midst of the waters, and let it divide the waters from the waters." And God made the firmament, and divided the waters which were under the firmament from the waters which were above the firmament: and it was so. And God called the firmament Heaven. And the evening and the morning were the second day.

And God said, "Let the waters under the heaven be gathered together unto one place, and let the dry land appear": and it was so. And God called the dry land Earth; and the gathering together of the waters called he Seas: and God saw that it was good. And God said, "Let the earth bring forth grass, the herb yielding seed,[3] and the fruit tree yielding fruit after his kind, whose[4] seed is in itself, upon the earth": and it was so. And the earth brought forth grass, and herb yielding seed after his kind, and the tree yielding fruit, whose seed was in itself, after his kind: and God saw that it was good. And the evening and the morning were the third day.

And God said, "Let there be lights in the firmament of the heaven to divide the day from the night; and let them be for signs, and for seasons, and for days, and years: And let them be for lights in the firmament of the heaven to give light upon the earth": and it was so. And God made two great lights; the greater light to rule the day, and the lesser light to rule the night: he made the stars also. And God set them in the firmament of the heaven to give light upon the earth. And to rule over the day and over the night, and to divide the light from the darkness: and God saw that it was good. And the evening and the morning were the fourth day.

Creation of Adam by Michelangelo

---

1 **Let there be ... the first day.:** Pay attention to diction and sentence structure, all typical of the Biblical style.
2 **firmament:** vault or expanse of the heavens; the sky
3 **herb yielding seed:** grammatically, herb which yields seed
4 "Whose" modifies "fruit."

And God said, "Let the waters bring forth abundantly the moving creature that hath life, and fowl[1] that may fly above the earth in the open firmament of heaven." And God created great whales, and every living creature that moveth, which the waters brought forth abundantly, after their kind, and every winged fowl after his kind: and God saw that it was good. And God blessed them, saying, "Be fruitful, and multiply, and fill the waters in the seas, and let fowl multiply in the earth." And the evening and the morning were the fifth day.

And God said, "Let the earth bring forth the living creature after his kind, cattle, and creeping thing, and beast of the earth after his kind": and it was so. And God made the beast of the earth after his kind, and cattle after their kind, and every thing that creepeth upon the earth after his kind: and God saw that it was good.

And God said, "Let us make man in our[2] image, after our likeness: and let them have dominion over the fish of the sea, and over the fowl of the air, and over the cattle, and over all the earth, and over every creeping thing that creepeth upon the earth." So God created man in his own image, in the image of God created he him[3]: male and female created he them. And God blessed them, and God said unto them, "Be fruitful, and multiply, and replenish[4] the earth, and subdue it: and have dominion over the fish of the sea, and over the fowl of the air, and over every living thing that moveth upon the earth."

And God said, "Behold, I have given you every herb bearing seed, which is upon the face of all the earth, and every tree, in the which is the fruit of a tree yielding seed; to you it shall be for meat. And to every beast of the earth, and to every fowl of the air, and to every thing that creepeth upon the earth, wherein there is life, I have given every green herb for meat": and it was so. And God saw every thing that he had made, and, behold, it was very good. And the evening and the morning were the sixth day.

Thus the heavens and the earth were finished, and all the host of them. And on the seventh day God ended his work which he had made; and he rested on the seventh day from all his work which he had made. And God blessed the seventh day, and sanctified[5] it: because that in it he had rested from all his work which God created and made.[6]

God planted Eden and put Adam & Eve there.

These are the generations[7] of the heavens and of the earth when they were created, in the

---

1 **fowl:** bird

2 The plural "our" referring to the singular God indicates, in Christian doctrine, the unity of the Father, Son and Holy Spirit as one God in three persons, i.e. the Trinity. It may also indicate the "royal we", used by kings and queens to indicate his / her royal superiority, while the Chinese kings tend to use the singular (孤家) to the same effect.

3 **created he him:** he, God; him, man

4 **replenish:** produce a new stock

5 **sanctify:** make holy

6 **because that in ... and made.:** This relates to concepts such as the sabbath day, the sabbatical year and the sabbatical leave.

7 "Generation" means "creation."

day that the LORD God made the earth and the heavens. And every plant of the field before it was in the earth, and every herb of the field before it grew: for the LORD God had not caused it to rain upon the earth, and there was not a man to till the ground. But there went up a mist from the earth, and watered the whole face of the ground. And the LORD God formed man of the dust of the ground, and breathed into his nostrils the breath of life; and man became a living soul.

And the LORD God planted a garden eastward in Eden; and there he put the man whom he had formed. And out of the ground made the LORD God to grow every tree that is pleasant to the sight, and good for food; the tree of life also in the midst of the garden, and the tree of knowledge of good and evil. And a river went out of Eden to water the garden[1]; and from thence it was parted, and became into four heads. The name of the first is Pison: that is it which compasseth the whole land of Havilah, where there is gold; and the gold of that land is good: there is bdellium (宝石) and the onyx (玛瑙) stone. And the name of the second river is Gihon: the same is it that compasseth the whole land of Ethiopia. And the name of the third river is Hiddekel: that is it which goeth toward the east of Assyria[2]. And the fourth river is Euphrates. **And the LORD God took the man, and put him into the garden of Eden to dress it and to keep it. And the LORD God commanded the man, saying, "Of every tree of the garden thou mayest freely eat: But of the tree of the knowledge of good and evil, thou shalt not eat of it: for in the day that thou eatest thereof thou shalt surely die.[3]"**

And the LORD God said, "It is not good that the man should be alone; I will make him an help meet[4] for him." And out of the ground the LORD God formed every beast of the field, and every fowl of the air; and brought them unto Adam to see what he would call them: and whatsoever Adam called every living creature, that was the name thereof. And Adam gave names to all cattle, and to the fowl of the air, and to every beast of the field; but **for Adam there was not found an help meet for him. And the LORD God caused a deep sleep to fall upon Adam, and he slept: and he took one of his ribs, and closed up the flesh[5] instead thereof. And**

Serpent tempts Eve.

the rib, which the LORD God had taken from man, made he a woman,[6] and brought her unto the man. And Adam said, "This is now bone of my bones, and flesh of my flesh: she shall be called Woman, because she was taken out of Man. Therefore shall a man leave his father and his mother, and shall cleave unto[7] his wife: and they shall be one flesh." And they were both naked, the man and his wife, and were not ashamed.

1　**water the garden:** Notice here water stands for life, as it does elsewhere in the world.

2　**Assyria:** ancient country of Asia, extending from the northern border of present-day Iraq south to the mouth of the Little Zab River in the northern part of Iraq, including the valley of the Tigris River.

3　**Of every tree of the garden ... surely die.:** This is one of the controversial statements in the Bible and leads to questions like "Where does evil come from?" and "Why man is forbidden to know?"

4　**meet:** mate, meaning God will make for the man a helper as his partner

5　**closed up the flesh:** the flesh filled up

6　"Adam" in Hebrew means "man" or "mankind," while "Eve" has to do with "life" or "living."

7　**cleave unto:** cling or stick to

Now the serpent[1] was more subtil than any beast of the field which the LORD God had made. And he said unto the woman, "Yea, hath God said, 'Ye shall not eat of every tree of the garden'?" And the woman said unto the serpent, "We may eat of the fruit of the trees of the garden: But of the fruit of the tree which is in the midst of the garden, God hath said, 'Ye shall not eat of it, neither shall ye touch it, lest ye die.'" **And the serpent said unto the woman, "Ye shall not surely die[2]: For God doth know that in the day ye eat thereof, then your eyes shall be opened, and ye shall be as gods, knowing good and evil.[3]" And when the woman saw that the tree was good for food, and that it was pleasant to the eyes, and a tree to be desired to make one wise, she took of the fruit thereof, and did eat, and gave also unto her husband with her and he did eat.** And the eyes of them both were opened, and they knew that they were naked; and they sewed fig leaves together, and made themselves aprons.

And they heard the voice of the LORD God walking in the garden in the cool of the day: and Adam and his wife hid themselves from the presence of the LORD God amongst the trees of the garden. And the LORD God called unto Adam, and said unto him, "Where art thou?" And he said, "I heard thy voice in the garden, and I was afraid, because I was naked; and I hid myself." And he said, "Who told thee that thou wast naked? Hast thou eaten of the tree, whereof I commanded thee that thou shouldest not eat?" And the man said, "The woman whom thou gavest to be with me, she gave me of the tree, and I did eat." And the LORD God said unto the woman, "What is this that thou hast done?" And the woman said, "The serpent beguiled[4] me, and I did eat." And the LORD God said unto the serpent, "Because thou hast done this, thou art cursed above all cattle, and above every beast of the field; upon thy belly shalt thou go, and dust shalt thou eat all the days of thy life: And I will put enmity between thee and the woman, and between thy seed and her seed; it shall bruise thy head, and thou shalt bruise his heel." **Unto the woman he said, "I will greatly multiply thy sorrow and thy conception; in sorrow thou shalt bring forth children; and thy desire shall be to thy husband, and he shall rule over thee." And unto Adam he said, "Because thou hast hearkened[5] unto the voice of thy wife, and hast eaten of the tree, of which I commanded thee, saying 'Thou shalt not eat of it': cursed is the ground for thy sake; in sorrow shalt thou eat of it all the days of thy life; thorns also and thistles shall it bring forth to thee; and thou shalt eat the herb of the field; in the sweat of thy face shalt thou eat bread, till thou return unto the ground; for out of it wast thou taken: for dust thou art, and unto dust shalt thou return."** And Adam called his wife's name Eve; because she was the mother of

Adam and Eve leaving the Garden of Eden

---

1   **serpent:** snake. "Snake" in Hebrew means "sly," punning with another word meaning "naked."
2   **shall not surely die:** 不一定会死
3   **For God doth know that ... good and evil.:** Pay attention to the sarcastic tone here: everything so absolute in God's statements is made uncertain to appeal to the inquisitive nature in man — you may very well ask: is this nature also made by God ?
4   **beguile:** deceive
5   **hearken:** hark or listen

all living. Unto Adam also and to his wife did the LORD God make coats of skins, and clothed them.

And the LORD God said, "Behold, the man is become as one of us, to know good and evil: and now, lest he put forth his hand, and take also of the tree of life, and eat, and live for ever[1]": Therefore the LORD God sent him forth from the garden of Eden, to till the ground from whence he was taken. So he drove out the man; and he placed at the east of the garden of Eden Cherubim, and a flaming sword which turned every way, to keep the way of the tree of life.

Key Concepts

create the heaven and the earth	Spirit of God
Eden	the serpent
know good and evil	tree of knowledge of good and evil
make man in our image	tree of life

Exodus*

Exodus is the second book of the Bible. It was so named because it relates the departure of the Israelites from Egypt and their wanderings through the desert up to Mount Sinai (西奈山). The deliverance from Egyptian slavery and the making of the covenant between God and the Israelites at Sinai have been of central significance to Judaism, as nearly all subsequent Jewish religious and civil life has been based on attempts to observe and obey the words of God at Sinai. Exodus was traditionally ascribed to Moses, but most scholars believe it was compiled by the priesthood around 550 BC.

Moses by Michelangelo

In the third month, when the children of Israel were gone forth out of the land of Egypt, the same day came they into the wilderness of Sinai. For they were departed from Rephidim[2], and

---

1   **the man is become ... live for ever:** Compare with similar legends in Chinese mythology, the Monkey in *Pilgrims to the West*, for instance, has challenged the "royal authority" by tasting the forbidden elixir (长生不老药) in Heaven.

*   The selection contains chapters 19, 20, and 21.

2   **Rephidim:** one of the places visited by the Israelites during their wandering. At Rephidim, the Israelites found no water to drink, and in distress they blamed Moses for their troubles. God commanded Moses to strike a certain "rock in Horeb," which caused a stream to flow from it, providing enough water for all of the people.

were come to the desert of Sinai, and had pitched in the wilderness; and there Israel camped before the mount. And Moses[1] went up unto God, and the LORD called unto him out of the mountain, saying, "Thus shalt thou say to the house of Jacob, and tell the children of Israel; **'Ye have seen what I did unto the Egyptians, and how I bare you on eagles' wings, and brought you unto myself. Now therefore, if ye will obey my voice indeed, and keep my covenant, then ye shall be a peculiar treasure unto me above all people: for all the earth is mine: And ye shall be unto me a kingdom of priests[2], and an holy nation.** These are the words which thou shalt speak unto the children of Israel."

And Moses came and called for the elders of the people, and laid before their faces all these words which the LORD commanded him. And all the people answered together, and said, "All that the LORD hath spoken we will do." And Moses returned the words of the people unto the LORD. And the LORD said unto Moses, "Lo, I come unto thee in a thick cloud, that the people may hear when I speak with thee, and believe thee for ever." And Moses told the words of the people unto the LORD.

And the LORD said unto Moses, "Go unto the people, and sanctify[3] them to day and to morrow[4], and let them wash their clothes. And be ready against the third day: for the third day the LORD will come down in the sight of all the people upon mount Sinai. And thou shalt set bounds unto the people round about, saying, 'Take heed to yourselves, that ye go not up into the mount, or touch the border of it: whosoever toucheth the mount shall be surely put to death: There shall not an hand touch it, but[5] he shall surely be stoned, or shot through[6]; whether it be beast or man, it shall not live: when the trumpet soundeth long, they shall come up to the mount.'"

And Moses went down from the mount unto the people, and sanctified the people; and they washed their clothes. And he said unto the people, "Be ready against the third day: come not at[7] your wives."

---

1   **Moses:** Moses was born during 1292–1225 BCE, 400 years after Jacob went to Egypt with 70 Hebrews to settle in Goshen. As the Pharaoh was afraid that Hebrews might outnumber Egyptians, he ordered Hebrew women to drown all male babies in the Nile. Moses' mother floated him on the Nile in a tiny basket, but he was picked up by Pharaoh's daughter. The princess gave him a name in Hebrew, meaning "son drawn in water," yet her Hebrew was so poor as to use the active voice "son drawing" out of water, a role he was to play for his blood kinsmen. Moses is often regarded as one of the few great intellectuals, as he conceived laws to be equally applicable to everyone, and a religion to be spiritual and practical guide to a better life.

2   **a kingdom of priests:** It is interesting to notice how the ideal Christian state is composed of here. Compare with the Confucian state and Plato's.

3   **sanctify:** purify or consecrate

4   **to day and to morrow:** today and tomorrow

5   **not ... but:** whenever

6   **shot through:** shot through with arrows

7   **come not at:** keep away from

And it came to pass on the third day in the morning, that there were thunders and lightnings, and a thick cloud upon the mount, and the voice of the trumpet exceeding loud; so that all the people that was in the camp trembled. And Moses brought forth the people out of the camp to meet with God; and they stood at the nether[1] part of the mount. And mount Sinai was altogether on a smoke, because the LORD descended upon it in fire: and the smoke thereof ascended as the smoke of a furnace, and the whole mount quaked greatly. And when the voice of the trumpet sounded long, and waxed louder and louder, Moses spake and God answered him by a voice. **And**

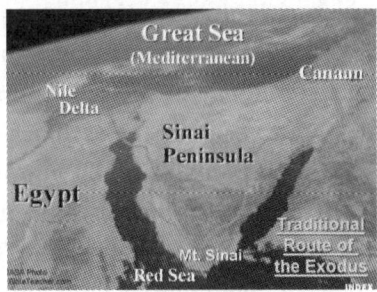

Route of the Exodus

the LORD came down upon mount Sinai, on the top of the mount: and the LORD called Moses up to the top of the mount; and Moses went up. And the LORD said unto Moses, "Go down, charge the people, lest they break through unto the LORD to gaze, and[2] many of them perish. And let the priests also, which come near to the LORD, sanctify themselves, lest the LORD break forth upon them[3]." And Moses said unto the LORD, "The people cannot come up to mount Sinai: for thou chargedst us, saying, 'Set bounds about the mount, and sanctify it.'" And the LORD said unto him, "Away, get thee down, and thou shalt come up, thou, and Aaron[4] with thee: but let not the priests and the people break through to come up unto the LORD, lest he break forth upon them." So Moses went down unto the people, and spake unto them.

And God spake all these words, saying, **"I am the LORD thy God, which have brought thee out of the land of Egypt, out of the house of bondage. Thou shalt have no other gods before me. Thou shalt not make unto thee any graven image[5], or any likeness of any thing that is in heaven above, or that is in the earth beneath, or that is in the water under the earth: Thou shalt not bow down thyself to them, nor serve them: for I the LORD thy God am a jealous God[6], visiting the iniquity[7] of the fathers upon the children unto the third and fourth generation of them that hate me[8]; And shewing mercy unto thousands of them that love me, and keep my commandments. Thou shalt not take the name of the LORD thy God in vain; for the LORD will not hold him guiltless that taketh his name in**

---

1 **nether:** lower

2 **and:** or

3 **break forth upon them:** break out against them

4 **Aaron:** Moses' elder brother, the patriarchy of the Jewish priesthood

5 **graven image:** image that is engraved, idol

6 **a jealous God:** a God who tolerates no rivals

7 **iniquity:** wickedness, injustice

8 **visiting the iniquity ... that hate me:** namely, I shall bring punishment on those who hate me and on their descendants down to the third and fourth generation

Heritage of Western Intellectual Tradition — A Sourcebook

vain[1]. **Remember the sabbath day, to keep it holy. Six days shalt thou labour, and do all thy work: But the seventh day is the sabbath of the LORD thy God; in it thou shalt not do any work, thou, nor thy son, nor thy daughter, thy manservant, nor thy maidservant, nor thy cattle, nor thy stranger that is within thy gates[2]. For in six days the LORD made heaven and earth, the sea, and all that in them[3] is, and rested the seventh day: wherefore the LORD blessed the sabbath day, and hallowed it. Honour thy father and thy mother: that thy days may be long upon the land which the LORD thy God giveth thee. Thou shalt not kill. Thou shalt not commit adultery. Thou shalt not steal. Thou shalt not bear false witness against thy neighbour. Thou shalt not covet thy neighbour's house, thou shalt not covet thy neighbour's wife, nor his manservant, nor his maidservant, nor his ox, nor his ass, nor any thing that is thy neighbour's.**

...

"Now these are the judgments which thou shalt set before them.

"If thou buy an Hebrew servant, six years he shall serve: and in the seventh he shall go out free for nothing. If he came in by himself, he shall go out by himself: if he were married, then his wife shall go out with him. If his master have given him a wife, and she have born him sons or daughters[4]; the wife and her children shall be her master's, and he shall go out by himself.

And if the servant shall plainly say, 'I love my master, my wife, and my children; I will not go out free': Then his master shall bring him unto the judges; he shall also bring him to the door, or unto the door post; and his master shall bore his ear through with an awl; and he shall serve him for ever.

departure of the Israelites from Egypt to Mount Sinai

"And if a man sell his daughter to be a maidservant, she shall not go out as the menservants do. If she please not her master, who hath betrothed her to himself, then shall he let her be redeemed: to sell her unto a strange nation he shall have no power, seeing[5] he hath dealt deceitfully with her. And if he have betrothed her unto his son, he shall deal with her after the manner of daughters. If he take him[6] another wife; her food, her raiment, and her duty of marriage, shall he not diminish. And if he do not these three unto her, then shall she go out free without money[7].

---

1 **taketh his name in vain:** make wrongful use of his name
2 **stranger that is within thy gates:** the foreigners who live in your country
3 **them:** heaven and earth, the sea
4 **she have born him sons or daughters:** Pay attention to the subjunctive mood.
5 **seeing:** because, considering that
6 **him:** his son
7 **money:** paid for redemption

"He that smiteth a man, so that he die, shall be surely put to death. And if a man lie not in wait, but God deliver him into his hand[1]; then I will appoint thee a place whither he shall flee. But if a man come presumptuously upon his neighbour to slay him with guile; thou shalt take him from mine altar, and he may die.

"And he that smiteth his father, or his mother, shall be surely put to death.

"And he that stealeth a man, and selleth him, or if he be found in his hand[2], he shall surely be put to death.

"And he that curseth his father, or his mother, shall surely be put to death.

"And if men strive together, and one smite another with a stone, or with his fist, and he die not, but keepeth his bed[3]: If he rise again, and walk abroad upon his staff, then shall he that smote him be quit[4]: only he shall pay for the loss of his time, and shall cause him to be thoroughly healed.

"And if a man smite his servant, or his maid, with a rod, and he die under his hand; he shall be surely punished. Notwithstanding, if he continue a day or two, he shall not be punished: for he is his money.

"If men strive, and hurt a woman with child, so that her fruit depart from her, and yet no mischief follow: he shall be surely punished, according as the woman's husband will lay upon him; and he shall pay as the judges determine. And if any mischief follow, then thou shalt give life for life, Eye for eye, tooth for tooth, hand for hand, foot for foot, Burning for burning, wound for wound, stripe for stripe."

Key Concepts

holy nation	sabbath day
jealous God	Thou shalt not …
land of Egypt	thunders and lightnings
miracles and wonders and signs	wilderness of Sinai

The New Testament is the second and smaller of the two major divisions of the Christian Bible, containing 27 documents written within 100 years between AD 50 and 150, handed down in Greek.

---

1 **if a man lie ... his hand:** if a man kills accidentally
2 **he be found in his hand:** he keeps him as his servant
3 **keepeth his bed:** has to stay in bed
4 **quit:** not guilty

It tells the fulfillment of the promise of the Old Testament and interprets the new covenant between God and the followers of the Christ through the life and death of Jesus. It contains a variety of writings: Gospels, recollections, historical narrative, Epistles or letters of advice, and apocalyptic descriptions. Gospels are not biography, although bearing resemblance to biographies of heroes in the Greco-Roman world. They comprise of a series of individual accounts of acts or sayings, each having a kind of completeness, but arranged to create a cumulative effect.

Gospel According to Matthew*

The four Gospels in the New Testament contain stories of the life and teachings of Christ. Matthew is made up of eight fairly distinct sections: five discourses of Jesus Christ, each introduced by a narrative concerning deeds of Jesus, an introductory narrative followed by two culminating narratives. The influence of *Matthew* on Christianity has been dominant ever since its composition. Besides its theological importance in the formulation of doctrine, such well-known sections as the Beatitudes, the Lord's Prayer, and the passion stories are widely known and frequently read.

The Sermon on the Mount

And seeing the multitudes, he went up into a mountain: and when he was set, his disciples came unto him: And he opened his mouth, and taught them, saying, **"Blessed are the poor in spirit: for theirs is the kingdom of heaven. Blessed are they that mourn: for they shall be comforted. Blessed are the meek: for they shall inherit the earth. Blessed are they which do hunger and thirst after[1] righteousness: for they shall be filled. Blessed are the merciful: for they shall obtain mercy. Blessed are the pure in heart: for they shall see God. Blessed are the peace-makers: for they shall be called the children of God. Blessed are they which are persecuted for righteousness' sake: for theirs is the kingdom of heaven. Blessed are ye, when men shall revile[2] you, and persecute you, and shall say all manner of evil against you falsely, for my sake. Rejoice, and be exceeding glad: for great is your reward in heaven: for so persecuted they[3] the prophets which were before you.[4]**

---

* Taken from Chapters 5, 6 and 7. Matthew, one of the twelve disciples of Jesus Christ, is said to preach fifteen years in Judaea after Christ's ascension and he then carried the Gospel to Ethiopia where he was murdered.

1 **do hunger and thirst after:** pursue earnestly

2 **revile:** curse, use abusive language

3 **so persecuted they:** they so persecuted

4 **Rejoice, and be ... before you.:** Compare with the Old Testament style. Do you see any remarkable differences?

"Ye are the salt of the earth: but if the salt have lost his[1] savour, wherewith shall it be salted? It is thenceforth good for nothing, but to be cast out, and to be trodden under foot of men. Ye are the light of the world. A city that is set on a hill cannot be hid. Neither do men light a candle, and put it under a bushel[2], but on a candlestick; and it giveth light unto all that are in the house. Let your light so shine before men, that they may see your good works, and glorify your Father which is in heaven.

"Think not that I am come to destroy the law, or the prophets: **I am not come to destroy, but to fulfil. For verily I say unto you, till heaven and earth pass, one jot or one tittle shall in no wise pass from the law, till all be fulfilled. Whosoever therefore shall break one of these least[3] commandments, and shall teach men so, he shall be called the least in the kingdom of heaven: but whosoever shall do and teach them, the same shall be called great in the kingdom of heaven.** For I say unto you, that except your righteousness shall exceed the righteousness of the scribes[4] and Pharisees[5], ye shall in no case enter into the kingdom of heaven.

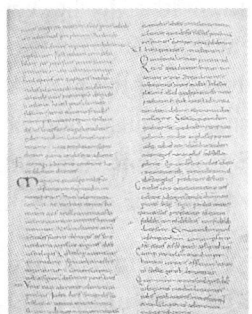

Book of Matthew in Latin, c.830

"Ye have heard that it was said by them of old time[6], Thou shalt not kill; and whosoever shall kill shall be in danger of the judgment: But I say unto you, that whosoever is angry with his brother without a cause shall be in danger of the judgment: and whosoever shall say to his brother, 'Ra-ca[7],' shall be in danger of the council: but whosoever shall say, 'Thou fool,' shall be in danger of hell fire. Therefore if thou bring thy gift to the altar, and there rememberest that thy brother hath ought[8] against thee; Leave there thy gift before the altar, and go thy way; first be reconciled to thy brother, and then come and offer thy gift. Agree with thine adversary quickly, whiles thou art in the way with him; lest at any time the adversary deliver thee to the judge, and the judge deliver thee to the officer, and thou be cast into prison. Verily I say unto thee, Thou shalt by no means come out thence, till thou hast paid the uttermost farthing[9].

"Ye have heard that it was said by them of old time, Thou shalt not commit adultery: But I say unto you, That whosoever looketh on a woman to lust after her hath committed adultery with

---

1 **his:** its
2 **put it under a bushel:** not that the expression "hide light under a bushel" is now used as an idiom, meaning to avoid letting people know that you are good at something
3 **least:** least important
4 **scribes:** Jews in ancient times who make and keep records
5 **Pharisees:** a group within Palestinian Judaism noted for their punctilious observance of laws regarding ritual purity, cleansings and food; self-righteous people
6 "Ye have heard that it was said by them of old time" suggests an exclamation based on the Old Testament.
7 **Ra-ca:** a word to show disrespect
8 **ought:** anything
9 **uttermost farthing:** debt of the smallest value

her already in his heart. And if thy right eye offend thee, pluck it out, and cast it from thee: for it is profitable for thee that one of thy members should perish, and not that thy whole body should be cast into hell. And if thy right hand offend thee, cut it off, and cast it from thee: for it is profitable for thee that one of thy members should perish, and not that thy whole body should be cast into hell. It hath been said, Whosoever shall put away his wife, let him give her a writing of divorcement: But I say unto you, That whosoever shall put away his wife, saving for[1] the cause of fornication, causeth her to commit adultery: and whosoever shall marry her that is divorced committeth adultery.

"Again, ye have heard that it hath been said by them of old time, Thou shalt not forswear thyself, but shalt perform unto the Lord thine oaths[2]. But I say unto you, Swear not at all; neither by heaven; for it is God's throne: Nor by the earth; for it is his footstool: neither by Jerusalem; for it is the city of the great King. Neither shalt thou swear by thy head, because thou canst not make one hair white or black. But let your communication be, Yea, yea; Nay, nay[3]: for whatsoever is more than these cometh of evil[4].

The Crucifixion of Jesus

"Ye have heard that it hath been said, An eye for an eye, and a tooth for a tooth. But I say unto you, That ye resist not evil: but whosoever shall smite thee on thy right cheek, turn to him the other also. And if any man will sue thee at the law, and take away thy coat, let him have thy cloke also. And whosoever shall compel thee to go a mile, go with him twain[5]. Give to him that asketh thee, and from him that would borrow of thee turn not thou away[6].

"Ye have heard that it hath been said, Thou shalt love thy neighbour, and hate thine enemy. But I say unto you, Love your enemies, bless them that curse you, do good to them that hate you, and pray for them which despitefully use you, and persecute you; That ye may be the children of your Father which is in heaven: for he maketh his sun to rise on the evil and on the good, and sendeth rain on the just and on the unjust. For if ye love them which love you, what reward have ye? Do not even the publicans[7] the same? And if ye salute your brethren only, what do ye more than others? Do not even the publicans so? Be ye therefore perfect, even as your Father which is in heaven is perfect.

---

1 **saving for:** except for
2 **perform ... thine oaths:** honor your promise; thine: your
3 **Yea, yea; Nay, nay:** literally, yes is yes, no is no.
4 **whatsoever is more ... of evil:** anything more than this comes from the evil
5 **twain:** two miles
6 **from him ... thou away:** do not turn those away who come to borrow money from you
7 **publicans:** tax collectors

"Take heed that ye do not your alms before men, to be seen of them[1]: otherwise ye have no reward of your Father which is in heaven. Therefore when thou doest thine alms do not sound a trumpet before thee, as the hypocrites do in the synagogues[2] and in the streets, that they may have glory of men. Verily I say unto you, they have their reward. But when thou doest alms, let not thy left hand know what thy right hand doeth: That thine alms may be in secret: and thy Father which seeth in secret himself shall reward thee openly.

"And when thou prayest, thou shalt not be as the hypocrites are: for they love to pray standing in the synagogues and in the corners of the streets, that they may be seen of men[3]. Verily I say unto you, They have their reward. But thou, when thou prayest, enter into thy closet, and when thou hast shut thy door, pray to thy Father which is in secret; and thy Father which seeth in secret shall reward thee openly. But when ye pray, use not vain repetitions, as the heathen do: for they think that they shall be heard for their much speaking[4]. Be not ye therefore like unto them[5]: for your Father knoweth what things ye have need of, before ye ask him. **After this manner therefore pray ye: Our Father which art in heaven, Hallowed be thy name. Thy kingdom come. Thy will[6] be done in earth, as it is in heaven. Give us this day our daily bread. And forgive us our debts, as we forgive our debtors. And lead us not into temptation, but deliver us from evil: For thine is the kingdom, and the power, and the glory, for ever. Amen.**

"For if ye forgive men their trespasses, your heavenly Father will also forgive you: But if ye forgive not men their trespasses, neither will your Father forgive your trespasses.

"Moreover when ye fast, be not, as the hypocrites, of a sad countenance: for they disfigure their faces, that they may appear unto men to fast. Verily I say unto you, They have their reward. But thou, when thou fastest, anoint thine head, and wash thy face; that thou appear not unto men to fast, but unto thy Father which is in secret: and thy Father, which seeth in secret, shall reward thee openly.

"Lay not up for yourselves treasures upon earth, where moth (蛀虫) and rust doth corrupt, and where thieves break through and steal: But lay up for yourselves treasures in heaven, where neither moth nor rust doth corrupt, and where thieves do not break through nor steal: For where your treasure is, there will your heart be also. The light of the body is the eye: if therefore thine eye be single[7], thy whole body shall be full of light. But if thine eye be evil, thy whole body shall be full of darkness. If therefore the light that is in thee be

---

1   **Take heed that ... to be seen of them:** Make certain you do not perform your religious duties in public so that people will see what you do; alms: charitable donations of money or food to the poor
2   **synagogues:** buildings for Jewish assembly
3   **they may be seen of men:** everyone will see them
4   **much speaking:** unnecessary repetition
5   **Be not ye therefore like unto them:** Do not therefore behave like them
6   **will:** intention
7   **single:** earnest, healthy

darkness, how great[1] is that darkness!

"No man can serve two masters: for either he will hate the one, and love the other; or else he will hold to the one, and despise the other. Ye cannot serve God and mammon[2]. Therefore I say unto you, Take no thought for your life, what ye shall eat, or what ye shall drink; nor yet for your body, what ye shall put on. Is not the life more than meat, and the body than raiment? Behold the fowls of the air: for they sow not, neither do they reap, nor gather into barns; yet your heavenly Father feedeth them. Are ye not much better than they? **Which of you by taking thought can add one cubit unto his stature[3]? And why take ye thought for raiment? Consider the lilies of the field, how they grow; they toil not, neither do they spin: And yet I say unto you, That even Solomon[4] in all his glory was not arrayed like one of these.** Wherefore, if God so clothe the grass of the field, which to day is, and to morrow is cast into the oven, shall he not much more clothe you, O ye of little faith? Therefore take no thought, saying, What shall we eat? or, What shall we drink? or, Where- withal shall we be clothed? (For after all these things do the Gentiles[5] seek:) for your heavenly Father knoweth that ye have need of all these things. But seek ye first the kingdom of God, and his righteousness; and all these things shall be added unto you. Take therefore no thought for the morrow: for the morrow shall take thought for the things of itself. Sufficient unto the day is the evil thereof.[6]

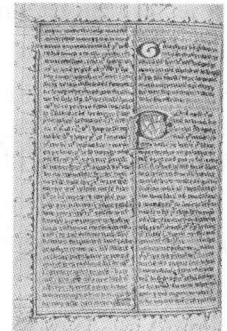

Wyclif New Testament, c.1420

"**Judge not, that ye be not judged. For with what judgment ye judge, ye shall be judged: and with what measure ye mete, it shall be measured to you again**[7]. And why beholdest thou the mote[8] that is in thy brother's eye, but considerest not the beam[9] that is in thine own eye? Or how wilt thou say to thy brother, Let me pull out the mote out of thine eye; and, behold, a beam is in thine own eye? Thou hypocrite, first cast out the beam out of thine own eye; and then shalt thou see clearly to cast out the mote out of thy brother's eye.

"Give not that which is holy unto the dogs, neither cast ye your pearls before swine, lest they trample them under their feet, and turn again and rend[10] you.

"**Ask, and it shall be given you; seek, and ye shall find; knock, and it shall be opened**

---

1 **great:** serious

2 **mammon:** personification of wealth and miserliness

3 **add one cubit unto his stature:** make oneself look more magnificent

4 **Solomon:** King of Israel (d. 930 BC), noted for his wisdom

5 **Gentiles:** non-Jewish people

6 **Sufficient unto ... thereof.:** Today's trouble is enough for today.

7 **with what measure ... you again:** namely, the measure you give will be the measure you get

8 **mote:** speck

9 **beam:** log

10 **rend:** attack

unto you: **For every one that asketh receiveth; and he that seeketh findeth; and to him that knocketh it shall be opened. Or what man is there of you, whom if his son ask bread, will he[1] give him a stone? Or if he ask a fish, will he give him a serpent? If ye then, being evil, know how to give good gifts unto your children, how much more shall your Father which is in heaven give good things to them that ask him? Therefore all things whatsoever ye would that men should do to you, do ye even so to them[2]: for this is the law and the prophets.**

"Enter ye in the strait[3] gate: for wide is the gate, and broad is the way, that leadeth to destruction, and many there be which go in thereat[4]: Because strait is the gate, and narrow is the way, which leadeth unto life, and few there be that find it.

"Beware of false prophets, which come to you in sheep's clothing, but inwardly they are ravening[5] wolves. Ye shall know them by their fruits. Do men gather grapes of thorns, or figs of thistles[6]? Even so every good tree bringeth forth good fruit; but a corrupt tree bringeth forth evil fruit. A good tree cannot bring forth evil fruit, neither can a corrupt tree bring forth good fruit. Every tree that bringeth not forth good fruit is hewn down, and cast into the fire. Wherefore by their fruits ye shall know them.

"Not every one that saith unto me, Lord, Lord, shall enter into the kingdom of heaven; but he that doeth the will of my Father which is in heaven. Many will say to me in that day, Lord, Lord, have we not prophesied in thy name? And in thy name have cast out devils? And in thy name done many wonderful works? And then will I profess unto them, I never knew you: depart from me, ye that work iniquity.

"Therefore whosoever heareth these sayings of mine, and doeth them, I will liken him unto a wise man, which built his house upon a rock: And the rain descended, and the floods came, and the winds blew, and beat upon that house and it fell not: for it was founded upon a rock. And every one that heareth these sayings of mine, and doeth them not, shall be likened unto a foolish man, which built his house upon the sand: And the rain descended, and the floods came, and the winds blew, and beat upon that house; and it fell: and great was the fall of it." And it came to pass, when Jesus had ended these sayings, the people were astonished at his doctrine: For he taught them as one having authority, and not as the scribes.

---

1   **he:** the father

2   **Therefore all things ... so to them:** So whatever you wish that men would do to you, do so to them. "Even" means "equally." 比较《论语・颜渊》: "己所不欲，勿施于人。"

3   **strait:** narrow

4   **many there be which go in thereat:** many people enter by it

5   **ravening:** ravenous

6   **gather grapes ... of thistles:** namely, gather grapes from thorns, or figs from thistles

Key Concepts

Blessed are the ...   peace
forgive   reward
house upon a rock   salt and light
lay up treasures   straight gate
love

Acts of the Apostles*

Acts of the Apostles is the fifth book of the New Testament. Sometimes called the Gospel of the Spirit, the Acts tells of the development of the Christian church under the impulse of the Holy Spirit. Covering a period of roughly 30 years, the book gives valuable insights into the Jewish Christian church in Palestine. Particularly notable are the numerous speeches made by the dominant characters.

And when the day of Pentecost[1] was fully come, they[2] were all with one accord in one place. And suddenly there came a sound from heaven as of a rushing mighty wind, and it filled all the house where they were sitting. And there appeared unto them cloven tongues like as of fire, and it sat upon each of them[3]. And they were all filled with the Holy Ghost, and began to speak with other tongues, as the Spirit gave them utterance. And there were dwelling at Jerusalem Jews, devout men, out of every nation under heaven. Now when this was noised abroad[4], the multitude came together, and were confounded, because that every man heard them speak in his own language. And they were all amazed and marvelled, saying one to another, "Behold

Descent of the Holy Spirit

---

* Taken from Chapters 2, 7, 9 and 10. Apostles, meaning messengers or people sent, refer especially to the twelve disciples of Christ sent forth to preach the Gospel, with some others to replace Judas.

1　**Pentecost**（五旬节）**:** festival held by the Jews in May or June in commemoration of God's giving of the Law to Moses on Mount Sinai

2　**they:** the disciples

3　**there appeared ... each of them:** Then they saw what looked like tongues of fire which spread out and touched each person there; cloven: split, partly divided

4　**when this was noised abroad:** when this sound was widely heard

are not all[1] these which speak Galilaeans? And how hear we every man in our own tongue, wherein we were born? Parthians, and Medes, and Elamites, and the dwellers in Mesopotamia, and in Judaea, and Cappadocia, in Pontus, and Asia, Phrygia, and Pamphylia, in Egypt, and in the parts of Libya about Cyrene, and strangers of Rome, Jews and proselytes, Cretes and Arabians, we do hear them speak in our tongues the wonderful works of God[2]." And they were all amazed, and were in doubt, saying one to another, "What meaneth this? Others mocking said, These men are full of new wine."

But Peter, standing up with the eleven, lifted up his voice, and said unto them, "Ye men of Judaea, and all ye that dwell at Jerusalem, be this known unto you, and hearken to my words: For these are not drunken, as ye suppose, seeing it is but the third hour of the day. But this is that which was spoken by the prophet Joel[3]; 'And it shall come to pass in the last days,' saith God, 'I will pour out of my Spirit upon all flesh: and your sons and your daughters shall prophesy, and your young men shall see visions, and your old men shall dream dreams: And on my servants and on my handmaidens I will pour out in those days of my Spirit; and they shall prophesy. And I will shew wonders in heaven above, and signs in the earth beneath; blood, and fire, and vapour of smoke: The sun shall be turned into darkness, and the moon into blood, before that great and notable day of the Lord come. And it shall come to pass, that whosoever shall call on the name of the Lord shall be saved.' Ye men of Israel, hear these words; Jesus of Nazareth, a man approved of God[4] among you by miracles and wonders and signs, which God did by him in the midst of you, as ye yourselves also know: Him, being delivered by the determinate counsel and fore-

Stephen the First Martyr

knowledge of God, ye have taken, and by wicked hands have crucified and slain[5]: Whom God hath raised up, having loosed the pains of death: because it was not possible that he should be holden of it[6]. For David speaketh concerning him, 'I foresaw the Lord always before my face, for he is on my right hand, that I should not be moved[7]. Therefore did my heart rejoice, and my tongue was glad; moreover also my flesh shall rest in hope: Because thou wilt not leave my soul in hell, neither wilt thou suffer thine Holy One to see corruption. Thou hast made known to me the ways of life; thou shalt make me full of joy with thy countenance.' Men and brethren, let me

---

1 **not all:** partial negation here

2 **speak in our tongues ... of God:** speak about … the wonderful things God has done

3 **Joel:** Hebrew prophet, nothing is known about him except that he wrote one of 12 short prophetic books in the Old Testament.

4 **a man approved of God:** a man attested to you by God

5 **Him, being delivered by ... crucified and slain:** In accordance with his own plan God had already decided that Jesus would be handed over to you; and you killed him by letting sinful men crucify him.

6 **be holden of it:** be held in the power of death

7 **moved:** shaken

Heritage of Western Intellectual Tradition — A Sourcebook

freely speak unto you of the patriarch David, that he is both dead and buried, and his sepulchre[1] is with us unto this day. Therefore being a prophet, and knowing that God had sworn with an oath to him, that of the fruit of his loins, according to the flesh, he would raise up Christ to sit on his throne[2]; He seeing this before spake of the resurrection of Christ, that his soul was not left in hell, neither his flesh did see corruption. This Jesus hath God raised up, whereof we all are witnesses. Therefore being by the right hand of God exalted, and having received of[3] the Father the promise of the Holy Ghost, he hath shed forth this, which ye now see and hear. For David is not ascended into the heavens: but he saith himself, 'The Lord said unto my Lord[4], "Sit thou on my right hand, until I make thy foes thy footstool."' Therefore let all the houses of Israel know assuredly, that God hath made that same Jesus, whom ye have crucified, both Lord and Christ."

Now when they heard this, they were pricked in their heart, and said unto Peter and to the rest of the apostles, "Men and brethren, what shall we do?" Then Peter said unto them, "Repent, and be baptized every one of you in the name of Jesus Christ for the remission of sins, and ye shall receive the gift of the Holy Ghost. For the promise is unto you, and to your children, and to all that are afar off, even[5] as many as the LORD our God shall call." And with many other words did he testify and exhort, saying, "Save yourselves from this untoward[6] generation."

Then they that gladly received his word were baptized: and the same day there were added unto them about three thousand souls.

…

Ye stiffnecked and uncircumcised in heart and ears, ye do always resist the Holy Ghost: as your fathers did, so shall ye. Which of the prophets have not your fathers persecuted? And they have slain them which shewed before of the coming of the Just One[7]; of whom ye have been now the betrayers and murderers: Who have received the law by the disposition of angels, and have not kept it."

Conversion of Saul on the Road to Damascus

When they heard these things, they were cut to the heart, and they gnashed on him with their teeth. But he, being full of the Holy Ghost, looked up stedfastly into heaven, and saw the glory of God, and Jesus standing on the right hand of God, and said, "Behold, I see the heavens opened, and the Son of man standing on the right hand of God." Then they cried out with a loud voice, and

---

1   **sepulchre:** tomb
2   **that of the fruit ... on his throne:** that he would make one of David's descendants a king just as David was
3   **of:** from
4   **The Lord said unto my Lord:** namely, God says to Jesus Christ
5   **even:** the same
6   **untoward:** corrupt, wicked
7   **And they have ... the Just One:** and they killed those who announced beforehand the coming of the Righteous One

stopped their ears[1], and ran upon him with one accord, And cast him out of the city, and stoned him: and the witnesses laid down their clothes at a young man's feet, whose name was Saul. And they stoned Stephen, calling[2] upon God, and saying, "Lord Jesus, receive my spirit." And he kneeled down, and cried with a loud voice, "Lord, lay not this sin to their charge." And when he had said this, he fell asleep. And Saul was consenting unto[3] his death.

…

And Saul, yet breathing out threatenings and slaughter against the disciples of the Lord, went unto the high priest, And desired of him letters to Damascus to the synagogues, that if he found any of this way, whether they were men or women, he might bring them bound unto Jerusalem. And as he journeyed, he came near Damascus: and suddenly there shined round about him a light from heaven: And he fell to the earth, and heard a voice saying unto him, "Saul, Saul, why persecutest thou me?" And he said, "Who art thou, Lord?" And the Lord said, "I am Jesus whom thou persecutest: it is hard for thee to kick against the pricks[4]." And he trembling and astonished said, "Lord, what wilt thou have me to do?" And the Lord said unto him, "Arise, and go into the city, and it shall be told thee what thou must do." And the men which journeyed with him stood speechless, hearing a voice, but seeing no man. And Saul arose from the earth; and when his eyes were opened, he saw no man: but they led him by the hand, and brought him into Damascus. And he was three days without sight, and neither did eat nor drink.

And there was a certain disciple at Damascus, named Ananias; and to him said the Lord in a vision, "Ananias." And he said, "Behold, I am here, Lord." And the Lord said unto him, 'Arise, and go into the street which is called Straight, and enquire in the house of Judas for one called Saul, of Tarsus: for, behold, he prayeth, And hath seen in a vision a man named Ananias coming in, and putting his hand on him, that he might receive his sight." Then Ananias answered, "Lord, I have heard by many of this man[5], how much evil he hath done to thy saints at Jerusalem: And here he hath authority from the chief priests to bind all that call on thy name.[6]" But the Lord said unto him, "Go thy way: for he is a chosen vessel unto me[7], to bear my name[8] before the Gentiles, and kings, and the children of Israel: For I will show him how great things he must suffer for my name's sake." And Ananias went his way, and entered into the house; and putting his hands on him said, "Brother Saul, the Lord, even Jesus, that appeared unto thee in the way as thou camest,

---

1   **stopped their ears:** would not listen
2   **calling:** Stephen calling
3   **was consenting unto:** was happy to see
4   **kick against the pricks:** struggle against fate
5   **I have heard by many of this man:** split proposition: I have heard ... of this man.
6   **And here he hath ... on thy name.:** And he has come to Damascus with authority from the chief priests to arrest all who worship you.
7   **vessel unto me:** instrument of mine
8   **bear my name:** carry my name

hath sent me, that thou mightest receive thy sight, and be filled with the Holy Ghost." And immediately there fell from his eyes as it had been scales[1]: and he received sight forthwith, and arose, and was baptized. And when he had received meat, he was strengthened.

Then was Saul certain days with the disciples which were at Damascus. And straightway he preached Christ in the synagogues, that he is the Son of God. But all that heard him were amazed, and said; "Is not this he that destroyed them which called on this name in Jerusalem, and came hither for that intent, that he might bring them bound unto the chief priests?[2] " But Saul increased the more in strength, and confounded the Jews which dwelt at Damascus, proving that this is very Christ[3].

...

There was a certain man in Caesarea called Cornelius, a centurion of the band called the Italian band. A devout man, and one that feared God with all his house, which gave much alms to the people, and prayed to God always. He saw in a vision evidently about the ninth hour of the day an angel of God coming in to him, and saying unto him, "Cornelius." And when he looked on him, he was afraid, and said, 'What is it, Lord?" And he said unto him, "Thy prayers and thine alms are come up for a memorial before God[4]. And now send men to Joppa, and call for one Simon,

Peter's Vision

whose surname is Peter: He lodgeth with one Simon a tanner, whose house is by the sea side: he shall tell thee what thou oughtest to do." And when the angel which spake unto Cornelius was departed, he called two of his household servants, and a devout soldier of them that waited on him continually; And when he had declared all these things unto them, he sent them to Joppa.

On the morrow, as they went on their journey, and drew nigh unto the city, Peter went up upon the housetop to pray about the sixth hour: And he became very hungry, and would have eaten: but while they made ready, he fell into a trance, And saw heaven opened, and a certain vessel descending unto him, as it had been a great sheet knit at the four corners, and let down to the earth: Wherein were all manner of fourfooted beasts of the earth, and wild beasts, and creeping things, and fowls of the air. And there came a voice to him, Rise, Peter; kill, and eat. But Peter said, Not so, Lord; for I have never eaten any thing that is common or unclean. And the voice spake unto him again the second time, What God hath cleansed, that

---

1 **there fell from his eyes as it had been scales:** something like scales fell from his eyes
2 **came hither ... the chief priests:** came here for the purpose of arresting those people and taking them back to the chief priests
3 **this is very Christ:** Jesus is Christ
4 **come up for a memorial before God:** God is pleased with your prayers and works of charity, and is ready to answer you.

call not thou common[1]. This was done thrice: and the vessel was received up again into heaven.

Now while Peter doubted in himself what this vision which he had seen should mean, behold, the men which were sent from Cornelius had made enquiry for Simon's house, and stood before the gate, And called, and asked whether Simon, which was surnamed Peter, were lodged there. While Peter thought on the vision, the Spirit said unto him, Behold, three men seek thee. Arise therefore, and get thee down, and go with them, doubting nothing: for I have sent them. Then Peter went down to the men which were sent unto him from Cornelius; and said, Behold, I am he whom ye seek: what is the cause wherefore ye are come? And they said, Cornelius the centurion, a just man, and one that feareth God, and of good report among all the nation of the Jews, was warned from God by an holy angel to send for thee into his house, and to hear words of thee. Then called he them in, and lodged them. And on the morrow Peter went away with them, and certain brethren from Joppa accompanied him. And the morrow after they entered into Caesarea. And Cornelius waited for them, and had called together his kinsmen and near friends. And as Peter was coming in, Cornelius met him, and fell down at his feet, and worshipped him. But Peter took him up, saying, Stand up; I myself also am a man. And as he talked with him, he went in, and found many that were come together. And he said unto them, Ye know how that it is an unlawful thing for a man that is a Jew to keep company, or come unto one of another nation[2]; but God hath shewed me that I should not call any man common or unclean. Therefore came I unto you without gainsaying, as soon as I was sent for: I ask therefore for what intent ye have sent for me? And Cornelius said, Four days ago I was fasting until this hour; and at the ninth hour I prayed in my house, and, behold, a man stood before me in bright clothing, And said, Cornelius, thy prayer is heard, and thine alms are had in remembrance in the sight of God. Send therefore to Joppa, and call hither Simon, whose surname is Peter; he is lodged in the house of one Simon a tanner by the seaside: who, when he cometh, shall speak unto thee. Immediately therefore I sent to thee; and thou hast well done that thou art come[3]. Now therefore are we all here present before God, to hear all things that are commanded thee of God[4].

Then Peter opened his mouth, and said, "Of a truth I perceive that God is no respecter of persons[5]: But in every nation he that feareth him, and worketh righteousness, is accepted with him. The word which God sent unto the children of Israel, preaching peace by Jesus Christ: (he is Lord of all:) That word, I say, ye know, which was published[6] throughout all Judaea, and began from Galilee, after the baptism which John preached; How God anointed Jesus of Nazareth with the Holy Ghost and with power: who went about doing good, and healing all that were

---

1　**that call not thou common:** Do not consider anything unclean that God has declared clean.

2　**it is an unlawful thing ... another nation:** it is unlawful for a Jew to associate with or to visit anyone from another nation

3　**thou hast well done that thou art come:** you have been kind enough to come

4　**that are commanded thee of God:** that the Lord has recommented you to say

5　**Of a truth ... of persons:** I truly understand that God shows no partiality.

6　**published:** spread

Heritage of Western Intellectual Tradition — A Sourcebook

oppressed of the devil; for God was with him. And we are witnesses of all things which he did both in the land of the Jews, and in Jerusalem; whom they slew and hanged on a tree: Him God raised up the third day, and shewed him openly; Not to all the people, but unto witnesses chosen before of God, even to us, who did eat and drink with him after he rose from the dead. And he commanded us to preach unto the people, and to testify that it is he which was ordained of God to be the Judge of quick[1] and dead. To him give all the prophets witness, that through his name whosoever believeth in him shall receive remission of sins."

While Peter yet spake these words, the Holy Ghost fell on all them which heard the word. And they of the circumcision which believed were astonished, as many as came with Peter, because that on the Gentiles also was poured out the gift of the Holy Ghost.[2] For they heard them speak with tongues[3], and magnify God. Then answered Peter, "Can any man forbid water, that these should not be baptized, which have received the Holy Ghost as well as we?" And he commanded them to be baptized in the name of the Lord.

Key Concepts

baptize

healing

made Jesus both Lord and Christ

miracles and wonders and signs

Peter with the eleven

rose from the dead

vision

Compare with China

1. Chinese Creation Stories

There are various creation stories apart from the Christian one in the Bible — in fact each country in Asia, even each ethnic group in an Asian country, has its own myth of how man and universe were created. The following is a Chinese myth of creation, which has become a collective memory of the nation. Compare this myth with the Christian myth to find the differences and similarities.

---

1 **quick:** living

2 **And they of the circumcision ... the Holy Ghost.:** The circumcised Jewish believers who had come with Peter were amazed because God had poured out his gift of the Holy Spirit on the Gentiles also.

3 **speak with tongues:** speak with dialects

Pan Gu 盘古 Created Earth and Heavens

In the beginning, the heavens and earth were still one and all was chaos. The universe was like a big black egg, carrying Pan Gu inside itself. After 18 thousand years Pan Gu woke from a long sleep. He felt suffocated[1], so he took up a broad ax and wielded it with all his might to crack open the egg. The light, clear part of it floated up and formed the heavens, the cold, turbid[2] matter stayed below to form the earth. Pan Gu stood in the middle, his head touching the sky, his feet planted on the earth. The heavens and the earth began to grow at a rate of ten feet per day, and Pan Gu grew along with them. After another 18 thousand years, the sky was higher, the earth thicker, and Pan Gu stood between them like a pillar 9 million *li* in height so that the sky and the earth would never join again.

When Pan Gu died, his breath became the wind and clouds, his voice the rolling thunder. One eye became the sun and another the moon. His body and limbs turned to five big mountains and his blood formed the roaring water. His veins became stretching roads and his muscles fertile land. The innumerable stars in the sky came from his hair and beard, and flowers and trees from his skin and the fine hairs on his body. His marrow turned to jade and pearls. His sweat flowed like the good rain and sweet dew that nurtured all things on the earth. According to some versions of the Pan Gu legend, his tears flowed to make rivers and radiance of his eyes turned into thunder and lightning. When he was happy the sun shone, but when he was angry black clouds gathered in the sky. One version of the legend has it that the fleas and lice[3] on his body became the ancestors of mankind.

女娲

Nuwa 女娲 Makes Men

Nuwa was the goddess who separated the heaven from the Earth, creating the Divine Land (China). She was the original ancestor of the Chinese nation. According to legend, Nuwa was the younger sister of Emperor Fuxi 伏羲 (said to have lived during the third millennium BC) and she herself was an empress.

The historical records say: Nuwa had the surname Feng; she had the body of a snake, a human head and the virtue of a divine being. She was also known as Mixi. The name Nuwa first appeared in one of the Elegies[4] of Chu entitled *Tian Wen*:

> Nuwa loved peace and delighted in making things. She moulded figures from the yellow earth and gave them life and the ability to bear children: this is how humanity was created. When demons fought a terrible war, they broke the pillars which held the

---

1   **suffocated:** having difficulty breathing
2   **turbid:** thick, muddy
3   **lice:** singular louse, small insects living on bodies of animals and human beings
4   **elegy:** song for the dead

Heritage of Western Intellectual Tradition   A Sourcebook

heavens up. The firmament cracked open and the human world was put in mortal peril.

To save the lives of those she had created, Nuwa worked unceasingly, melting down the five-coloured stones to mend the breach. When the firmament was whole again, Nuwa, exhausted[1] by her toil, lay down on the earth and was transformed into a vast mountain range. In this way, she nurtured the growth of the Chinese nation by providing a rich and fertile land. This tale is known as "Nuwa Mending the Firmament."

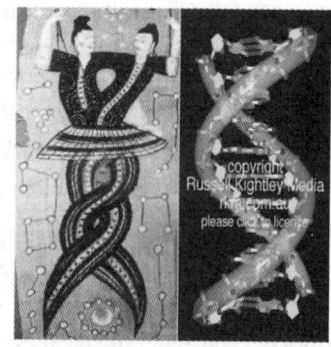

DNA double helix, discovered in 1953, resembles the picture of Fuxi and Nuwa, unearthed in Tulufan, hence the cover for the first issue of UNESCO's International Social Science Journal, Chinese edition, 1983

Amongst China's ethnic minorities, another story has survived concerning how Emperor Fuxi came to take his sister Nuwa as his bride. This tale is known as "Marriage of a Brother and a Sister."

The ferocious[2] God of Thunder was captured by Fuxi's father and imprisoned deep within a mountain cave. No one was allowed to visit him. Fuxi and Nuwa could no longer bear to hear the Thunder God's pitiable entreaties[3] for water, but they

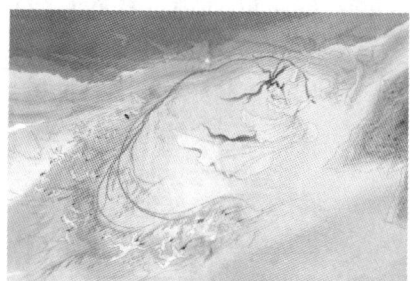

Nuwa makes men

dared not bring him any water. Eventually, the two of them shed tears which the god drank out of their cupped hands. The Thunder God was so strengthened by the tears that he burst out of his mountain prison. To repay Fuxi and Nuwa for their part in the rescue, the Thunder God pulled a long canine[4] tooth from his mouth and gave it to them saying: "In three days, mankind will suffer a terrible calamity[5]. You may use this tooth to keep yourselves safe from harm."

Having said this, the Thunder God leaped into the sky and disappeared.

Three days later, the sky was filled with thunder and lightning. A tremendous storm broke out. Rain fell incessantly and the flood waters rose; huge waves swept across the earth and the entire human race was destroyed. As the flood began, the Thunder God's tooth transformed itself into a boat. Safe aboard this vessel, Fuxi and his sister rode the waves and drifted with the tides. Only when the waters had subsided did Fuxi and Nuwa realise that they alone had survived the

---

1 **exhausted:** very tired
2 **ferocious:** fierce, savage
3 **entreaty:** earnest request
4 **canine:** of dog
5 **calamity:** great misfortune or disaster

desolation[1]. When they had grown into adults, Fuxi and Nuwa became husband and wife in order to bear descendants and establish a new human race.

This second story reflects the custom of intermarriage between blood relations in ancient China. It also shows why Nuwa is known as the mother of the Chinese nation.

It is said that there were no men when the sky and the Earth were separated. It was Nuwa who made men by moulding yellow clay. The work was so taxing that her strength was not equal to it. So she dipped a rope into the mud and then lifted it. The mud that dripped from the rope also became men. Those made by moulding yellow clay were rich and noble, while those made by lifting the rope were poor and low. — from《太平御览》(*Taiping Anthologies for the Emperor*)

Nuwa Mending the Sky

In ancient times, the four corners of the sky collapsed and the world with its nine regions split open. The sky could not cover all the things under it, nor could the Earth carry all the things on it. A great fire raged and would not die out; a fierce flood raced about and could not be checked. Savage beasts devoured innocent people; vicious birds preyed on the weak and old.

Nuwa traveling on a thunder-chariot

Then Nuwa melted rocks of five colours and used them to mend the cracks in the sky. She supported the four corners of the sky with the legs she had cut off from a giant turtle. She killed the black dragon to save the people of Jizhou, and blocked the flood with the ashes of reeds.

Thus the sky was mended, its four corners lifted, the flood tamed, Jizhou pacified, and harmful birds and beasts killed, and the innocent people were able to live on the square Earth under the dome of the sky. It was a time when birds, beasts, insects and snakes no longer used their claws or teeth or poisonous stings, for they did not want to catch or eat weaker things.

Nuwa's deeds benefited the heavens above and the Earth below. Her name was remembered by later generations and her light shone on every creation.

Now she is said to be traveling on a thunder-chariot drawn by a two-winged dragon and two green hornless dragons, with auspicious[2] objects in her hands and a special mattress underneath, surrounded by golden clouds, a white dragon leading the way and a flying snake following behind.

Floating freely over the clouds, she takes ghosts and gods to the ninth heaven and had an audience with the Heavenly Emperor at Lin Men, where she rested in peace and dignity under the

---

1 **desolation:** wretchedness, ruin
2 **auspicious:** suggesting a successful future

emperor. She never boasted of her achievements, nor does she try to win any renown; she wanted to conceal her virtues, in line with the ways of the universe.

2. 汉译《圣经》之考察

Since Columbus discovered the New World by the end of the 15th century, in the name of the Christian God, the Christian West had been sending its missionaries to other parts of the world. In this process of Christian colonization, the translation of the Bible played a significant role. The following is an account of Bible translation in China, which carries a special meaning if put in the context of China's opening up to the West.

开封犹太人读经图

亚历山大东征把希腊文化带到了东方，希腊化时代（前323—前30年）不同程度地影响到近东各个民族，其中意义最大的莫过于犹太文化希腊化。生活在亚历山大里亚城的很多犹太作家只用希腊语写作，因此必须把希伯来文《圣经》译成希腊文，这样犹太人才能看懂。于是出现了《圣经》的"七十子译本"（Septuagint）。据说约在前3世纪到前2世纪期间，以色列12支派的72位学者应托勒密王朝之请，在亚历山大里亚每人独居一室，进行翻译，最后各人译文竟彼此一字不差，故称"七十子译本"。到公元一世纪已流传至巴勒斯坦，成为基督教最早应用的旧约《圣经》，现在仍为希腊正教会的通行本。这是《圣经》翻译的开始。

今日普遍使用的中文《圣经》，是国语和合本《圣经》（简称"和合本"）。这部为学者所赞赏的百万字译著，已有80多年的历史，却鲜有人知道它的来历。今天所见最早的汉译《圣经》是18世纪的，可稽考的汉译工作却可追溯到7世纪的唐朝。也许还有更早的译本，均未经证实。

唐以前基督教是否传入中国，至今尚无确切的史料来说明，以下几种说法可供参考。

多马、巴多罗买传入说。最早提及基督教传入中国的西方人士，是古罗马的阿诺比尤斯（Arnobius），他于公元300年左右写的《驳斥异教论》中说："传教工作可以说是遍及印度、赛里斯（Seres，中国包括其中）、波斯和米底斯"。一同来东方传福音的有多马和巴多罗买二人，多马去了印度，而巴多罗买则来到中国；**基督徒逃难说**。公元65年，罗马皇帝尼禄迫害基督徒，70年耶路撒冷被毁，四散逃难的基督徒部分来到东方，侨居中国。这三种传说都指东汉明帝永平年间的事情。这时期的基督徒多为犹太人，福音主要靠口传，新约《圣经》尚未诞生，旧约《圣经》被带来中国不是没有可能。

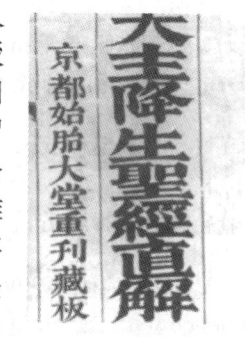

犹太人来华侨居，已有很长的历史，有始于周、汉、唐等不同说法。根据史料，唐朝已有相当数目的犹太人在中国居住。犹太人起初自称"一赐乐业"（"以色列"之音译），做

礼拜时戴着蓝色帽子，因此也被称为"蓝帽回回"（戴白帽的回教徒称为"白帽回回"）。最著名的犹太人聚居地是河南开封，设有犹太会堂，称西那高刻（Synagogue）。17世纪有天主教学者来开封访问研究，证实会堂中存在一部年代达五、六百年之久的《摩西五经》。可惜19世纪中叶的战乱使这珍贵典籍流失无存。犹太侨民是否将《摩西五经》译成中文，已难以证实。

叙利亚传教士传入说。东汉时代，有叙利亚教士二人，藉学习养蚕冶丝之名，来到中国传教。

三国孙吴时传入说。明朝洪武年间在江西得大铁十字架，上铸赤乌年号（238–250）。铁十字架上书："四海庆安澜，铁柱宝光留十字；万民怀大泽，金炉香篆蔼千秋"。假如铁十字架真是基督教遗物，那么可以想见基督教在公元三世纪的中国就已经存在。

传说毕竟不是史实，不能作为历史研究的依据。基督教传入中国的年代，有据可考的年代是公元635年（贞观九年）。

可稽考的《圣经》汉译

7世纪的唐朝，经济繁荣，泱泱大国，对域外文化兼容并蓄，一般认为基督教就是这时传入中国的。公元635年，基督教聂斯托利派传教士阿罗本（Alopen）从波斯抵达西安传教译经，时称景教。根据公元1625年在西安出土的"大秦景教流行中国碑"所记，其中有"真经"、"旧法"、"翻经建寺"等语，证实在唐朝时已有翻译圣经之举，并有一部份译本出版与流传，但并非全译，译本亦已失传。

元朝时，天主教方济各会派（Franciscan）传教士到中国传教。孟高维诺（Montecorvino）主教于1305年从北京寄给罗马教皇的信中说："现在我已将全部新约和诗篇译成中文，并请人用最优美书法抄写完毕。"一般认为孟高维诺曾把新约和《圣咏集》（即《诗篇》）译成"鞑靼人通用的语言"，不过也有人疑为汉文。马可·波罗在《马可·波罗游记》中也提及在大汗宫中见过"四本福音的圣经"，只是没有说明是否用中文写成。意大利托钵僧卡皮泥在1245年奉教皇因诺森四世之命，出使元朝，他不但看见中国有新旧约圣经，也看见教堂和敬拜活动。

马礼逊的译经活动

以上是基督教在中国的早期活动，也是汉译《圣经》有据可考的时期。可惜的是，唐、元译本皆未流传后世。

明以来的《圣经》汉译

明清以降，大批传教士来华，尤其是英、美教士十分热心译经工作，影响颇大。在天主教方面有利玛窦的"祖传天主十诫"、巴设的白话文四福音、保罗书信及希伯来书、阳玛诺的《天主降生圣经直解》、贺清泰的《古新圣经》等。其中《巴设译本》可能成为后人马士曼和马礼逊译经时的蓝本。到18世纪末，随着基督新教来华，圣经汉译可谓百花齐放了。

1、马士曼（Joshua Marshman）、拉沙（Joannes Lassar）译本。第一本汉译《圣经》，是根

据拉丁文在印度完成的。译者马士曼、拉沙前后花了 16 年翻译《圣经》,《新约》于 1811 年出版,并于 1822 年在印度塞兰普尔出版《新旧遗诏全书》。然而这本《圣经》很可能没有流传到中国。

从事汉语圣经修订工作的传教士

2、马礼逊(Robert Morrison)、米怜(William Milne)译本。第一个在中国把《圣经》完整地译成汉语的是马礼逊。1810 年和 1811 年,马礼逊先后译成了《使徒行传》和《路加福音》;1813 年将新约翻了出来,并于次年在广州出版,一共排印了 2000 部,工本费共用去 3818 元西班牙银币。随后与米怜合作翻译旧约,于 1819 年完成旧约的汉译工作,在伦敦皇家亚洲学院的资助下于 1823–1824 年在南洋马六甲出版圣经全书,并印了阐述圣经的单张,取名为《神天圣书》,线装 21 卷。此次译经工作,有中国人参与。旅居伦敦的华人杨三德(译音)为马礼逊抄录巴设译稿,同时也指导马氏学习中文;印书工人梁发 1810 年起在马六甲英华书院与米怜共同印刷圣经。梁发后来成为第一位华人牧师。另外广州耶稣会士袁光明(译音)、李十公、陈老宜等人曾从旁协助。

3、麦都思(Walter Henry Medhurs)、郭实猎译本。本书其实是由一个四人小组合作的产物。新约称为《新遗诏书》,1837 年出版,石印;旧约于 1838–1840 之间在香港出版,名为《新旧遗诏圣书》。新约的翻译多由麦都思负责,其实是修订马礼逊、米怜的译本。郭实猎后来又将新约译本修改出版,名为《救世主耶稣新遗诏书》,1840 年出版。本书为太平天国所翻印,不过甚多修改。1847 年,洪秀全连续两个星期去新教教士罗孝全处听课,第一次看到了《圣经》译本,可能是郭实猎的译本。根据郭实猎的称法,太平军将新约和旧约称为“遗书”,后面再加“圣书”二字。太平军用“天国”来表示其所建立的朝代。据说,这词来自郭实猎所译福音书中马太所指的天国。在太平天国的大力推广下,《圣经》普遍流传,地位空前高涨。据说洪秀全手下有 500 人从事圣经的汉译和改编工作。外国宣教团体认为福音遍传中国的时机已到,立即发起捐献运动,要为中国印刷一百万本新约圣经。还在上海设立了一个印刷厂,专门印刷出版圣经。大英圣书公会所捐得款项,足够该会在华事工未来 20 年之经费。

4、代表译本。《南京条约》签订后,清廷被迫开放五口。英、美各传教机构于 1843 年在香港成立委员会,修订已有的中文《圣经》译本,由各地传教士分五组译出新约初稿,交代表委员会审阅。旧约部分不再由各地传教士参与其事,而由来自广州、厦门、上海等地的代表组成的委员会进行翻译。由于意见分歧,委员会陷于分裂,后分成两个团体各自工作。一个团体由麦都思、米怜、施敦力(John Stronach)和理雅各(James Legge)组成,于 1853 年完成旧约译稿,1854 年出版。1855 年又与代表委员会译本《新约圣经》合订在上海出版,仍称代表委员会译本《圣经全书》。人称“上帝”版。该版得到王韬润色。裨治文(Elijah Coleman Bridgeman)和克陛存(Michael Simpson Culbertson)因为不赞成委员会所采用之文言文体和“上帝”译名,两人另行翻译新旧约全书,相继于 1859 年和 1862 年完成,交给上海华美圣经会 1863 年出版——古汉语“神”版,亦称裨治文译本。

印刷好了的苗文圣经

以上均为文言文译本,当时称“文理”译本,或“深文理”译本,至 1877 年已有 11 种之多。

　　5、和合译本。1890 年，新教传教士在上海召开大会议决定出版一本全国通用的中文圣经，以求减少版本过多而造成的译文混乱现象，务求做到文笔流畅而又忠于原文。次年，共成立了三个《圣经》重译委员会，分别负责三种不同文体的版本：文理、浅文理，以及国语(或官话)。全部翻译历时 27 年，其中以"国语和合译本"最受欢迎，成为今日绝大多数教会采用的标准译本。

　　国语译本从动工(1906)到出版(1919)仍在世上的，只有富善(Chauncey Goodrich)一人。富善在中国传道前后 60 年之久，其中 29 年用在译经工作上。新约重译工作在狄考文支持下进行，于 1907 年出版官话和合译本新约。该译本译文准确，但文字不够流畅，此后又屡经修订，至《圣经全书》出版时，与初版相比，改动甚多。旧约重译工作在富善支持下进行，并议定五点译经原则，如译文必须切合原文，必须是通用的白话文，不使用地方方言，而又便于上口诵读等。旧

和合译本委员会

约译成历时 13 载，于 1919 年初与新约合订出版官话和合译本《新旧约全书》，有"神"和"上帝"两种版本。该版本逐渐取代了《圣经》的其他中译本，为中国教会普遍接受。这也是外国传教士在华集体翻译的最后一版中文《圣经》。

　　国语译本受到教会好评，被誉为最佳白话文模范作品。它不但满足了近代中国教会的需要，更成为白话文运动的先锋。为了向不讲普通话的中国人传福音，教士们将中文《圣经》再改写成各地方言。这些方言译本种类很多，如上海、福州、宁波等方言。方言译本多采用汉字译音，少数为传教士创造的罗马字母拼音，后一方法后来成为汉语拼音的滥觞。另外还出版过不少少数民族语言的版本。其中最早的满文译本于 1822 年出版，另有朝鲜文译本、蒙文译本、苗文译本等。特别值得一提，在《圣经》未被译成民族语言之前，不少少数民族只有语言而无文字，所以他们中有不少用《圣经》翻译使用的注音字母为其文字，有的甚至沿用至今。

　　再看看东正教方面的译本。满清政府于雍正五年(1727)正式批准俄国东方教会(即希腊教会)在中国设立教会，原意为方便俄国使节人员礼拜，东正教士正式开始向中国传教。来自俄国的东正教士当中有不少专门从事汉学研究，著述甚多。其中有高理主教于 1864 年着手将新约圣经由希腊原文译成中文，又经巴拉第主教修订，正式成书。目前保存的版本 1864 年在北京印刷。

　　上面提到的这些译本都是外国传教士翻译的。中国基督徒也在动手翻译圣经。如金陵神学院教师朱宝惠与赛兆祥于 1929 年合译出版《新约全书》；王宣忱自行翻译，于 1933 年在青岛出版重译本《新约全书》；1946 年燕京大学宗教学院出版了吕振中的《新译的新旧约全书》；陆亨理和郑寿麟博士从希腊文和希伯来文直接翻译新约和《诗篇》。新约定名为《国语新旧库译本新约全书》，于 1939 年出版。新约及《诗篇》的第三版合订试验本，于 1958 年在香港出版。

　　有人统计迄今为止世界上《圣经》的各种版本有 1600 多种，仅在中国的发行量就已达 3 亿余部，而每年又有新的译本。(自陈恒，有删节)

Supplementary Reading

To many students, superstition, religion and science are quite different categories; but to some, there might be intricate connections among the three. The author of the following two essays give an explanation by drawing some demarcation lines between them. Do you agree with him?

1. Is Religion Just Organized Superstition? Is Superstition Always Religious?

Is there a real connection between religion and superstition? Some, particular adherents of various religious faiths, will often argue that the two are fundamentally different types of beliefs. Those who stand outside of religion, however, will notice some very important and fundamental similarities which bear closer consideration. Obviously, not everyone who is religious is also superstitious and not everyone who is superstitious is also religious. A person can faithfully attend church services all life without giving a second thought to a black cat walking in front of them. On the other hand, a person who completely rejects any religion whatsoever may consciously or unconsciously avoid walking under a ladder — even if there is no one on the ladder who might drop something.

If neither necessarily leads to the other, it might be easy to conclude that they are different types of beliefs. Moreover, because the very label "superstition" seems to include a negative judgment of irrationality, childishness, or primitiveness, it is understandable that religious believers wouldn't want their own faiths to be categorized with superstitions.

We must, nevertheless, acknowledge that the similarities are not superficial. For one thing, both superstition and traditional religions are non-materialistic in nature. They do not conceive of the world as a place controlled by sequences of cause and effect between matter and energy. Instead, they presume the added presence of immaterial forces which influence or control the course of our lives. Furthermore, there is also the appearance of a desire to provide meaning and coherence to otherwise random and chaotic events. If we get hurt in an accident, it might be attributed to a black cat, to spilling salt, to failing to pay sufficient honor to our ancestors or perform the appropriate sacrifices to the spirits, etc. There seems to be a genuine continuum between what we tend to call "superstition" and the ideas in animistic[1] religions. In both cases, people are expected to avoid certain actions and perform other actions in order to ensure that they do not fall victim to the unseen forces at work in our world. In both cases, the very idea that such unseen forces are at work seems to stem (at least in part) both from a desire to explain otherwise random events and from a desire to have some means of affecting those events.

---

1 **animistic:** believing in the existence of spiritual beings

These are all important psychological benefits often used to explain the reason why religion exists and why religion persists. They are also reasons for the existence and persistence of superstition. It seems reasonable to argue, then, that while superstition may not be a form of religion, it does spring from some of the same basic human needs and desires as religion does. Thus, a greater understanding of how and why superstition develops can be useful in gaining a better understanding and appreciation of religion. (Adapted from Austin Cline)

2. *How Is Science Different from Religion?*

People frequently confuse science with the theories *of* science. They are separate things. Science is a process for generating ideas about nature. All too often I receive an email from someone proclaiming science "false." Those who understand science know that it is nonsense to make such claims. Since it is a method to produce theories, it only makes sense to call a theory of science true or false but not science itself. Theories may come and go with experimental results but the methodologies of science are going to stay the same.

The most important part of the definition of science is the Scientific Method. It is what makes science so good at allowing us to understand our world. The Greeks thought that they figure everything out by pure thought, that is, by philosophy alone. Maybe, but given that people can and do come up with wrong ideas, it is better to have some type of filter to detect fallacious reasoning. The Scientific Method acts as this filter by telling us to check our theories with observations. The Scientific Method can be described by a series of steps:

1. Identify a problem.
2. Make a hypothesis concerning the problem.
3. Do an experiment to test your hypothesis.
4. Draw a conclusion from the experiment.
5. If your hypothesis agrees with your conclusion, go back to step 3. If your hypothesis disagrees with your conclusion, go back to step 2.

Some of the words used in science are used differently than in everyday language. This simple fact is the solution to much confusion layman have about science. The word "hypothesis," as used above in the Scientific Method, means, "a tentative assumption made in order to draw out and test its logical or empirical consequences," i.e., it is an educated guess to explain a phenomenon. When a hypothesis agrees well with experiments, we gain confidence that it is in some way "correct" and we distinguish these hypotheses from their less valuable counterparts by referring to them as a "theory." When one speaks of a theory in science, one means, "a plausible or scientifically acceptable general principle or body of principles offered to explain phenomena." Notice that this definition is different from how the word is sometimes used in everyday speech. There it can mean an unproved assumption. This is opposite to the sense in which a scientist would use the word! In science, an unproved assumption would better be called a hypothesis. It is a very common mistake to confuse these two meanings of the word "theory," which is reflected when people say, "It's only

Heritage of Western Intellectual Tradition   A Sourcebook

a theory," in regards to the theory of evolution or the Big Bang[1].

Now that we have discussed what science is, we can discuss religion. What is religion? In the broadest sense, it is "a cause, principle, or system of beliefs held to with ardor and faith." A system of beliefs can be personal but more often people tend to subscribe to the system of beliefs advocated by a particular religion or denomination[2]. These beliefs by definition are held with ardor and faith, which will lead us to our first difference between science and religion. "Faith" is "firm belief in something for which there is no proof/complete trust" or "belief without doubt or question." Or in the Bible's own words, "Now faith is the substance of things hoped for, the evidence of things not seen." Warning alarms should be sounding in your head right now! Having belief in something with no proof begs that one ask oneself how you can justify that belief in the first place. Furthermore, given the obvious fact that humans can and do believe in false ideas (e.g., the Catholic Church once believed the Earth was at the center of the universe), how can a rational person ever believe in something without doubt or question? A rational, reasonable person should not and could not. The Scientific Method demands that we be prepared to reject a hypothesis or belief but faith requires us to hold a belief with certainty. Thus at the heart of the conflict between science and religion is the conflict between faith and reason. At the most fundamental level, science and religion are incompatible because of the latter's requirement of faith.

Science encourages questioning of its theories whereas religion presents its "theories" as truth. It is only by questioning our ideas that false ideas can be discovered and replaced with better ones. As I already mentioned, human reasoning is not perfect and thus subject to error. This is the motivation behind us continually checking our theories. Science is designed to detect faulty theories through experimentation, so science is self-repairing. For a great example of this in action is the famous Curtis-Shapely debate.[3]

Faith is not the beautiful testament to our convictions that churches would lead you to believe. Faith is an attempt to keep you and your ideas static. It is an attempt to control your mind by eliminating your questioning. Those who reject faith and embrace reason are called Freethinkers. We call ourselves that because we encourage the questioning of ideas. Perhaps the most well-known incidence displaying the dangers of faith involved the Catholic church and Galileo. One of the many discoveries Galileo had made with his telescope was that the planet Jupiter had four moons that revolve around it and that the planet Venus undergoes phases similar to those of the

---

1 **Big Bang:** a currently accepted explanation of the beginning of the universe. This theory proposes that the universe was once extremely compact, dense, and hot. A cosmic explosion called the big bang occurred about 10 billion to 20 billion years ago, and the universe has since been expanding and cooling. There are scientists who question the validity of this theory.

2 **denomination:** religious sect

3 Harlow Shapley (1885–1972) argued in 1920 that the Universe is composed of many galaxies like our own, identified by astronomers of his time as "spiral nebulae." But Heber Doust Curtis (1872–1942) argued that these "spiral nebulae" were just nearby gas clouds, and that the Universe was composed of only one big Galaxy.

moon. This did several things. First, it proved that there was more than one point in the solar system that things revolved around and also it strongly suggested that Venus orbited the sun. Now the Church as this time advocated the Aristotelian view that everything revolved around the earth as opposed to the Copernican theory that says the planets go around the sun. When church authorities learned that Galileo published the book *Dialogue* that supported the Copernican theory, they had him arrested and put on trial. Galileo's defense was simple enough: they could look through his telescope and his accusers could see for themselves the truth. However, they *refused* to do this because they believed that the very act of looking through the telescope would undermine their faith! Galileo was found guilty and sentenced to house arrest. (Adapted from Austin Cline)

3. *Why I Am Not a Christian* *

The Nobel laureate Bertrand Russell is often known for his radical ideas and unconventional behaviour, especially his critical attitudes toward Christianity, which finds its expression in the following excerpts of an essay.

As your Chairman has told you, the subject about which I am going to speak to you tonight is "Why I Am Not a Christian." Perhaps it would be as well, first of all, to try to make out what one means by the word *Christian*. It is used these days in a very loose sense by a great many people. Some people mean no more by it than a person who attempts to live a good life. In that sense I suppose there would be Christians in all sects and creeds; but I do not think that that is the proper sense of the word, if only because it would imply that all the people who are not Christians — all the Buddhists, Confucians, Mohammedans, and so on — are not trying to live a good life. I do not mean by a Christian any person who tries to live decently according to his lights. I think that you must have a certain amount of definite belief before you have a right to call yourself a Christian. The word does not have quite such a full-blooded meaning now as it had in the times of St. Augustine and St. Thomas Aquinas[1]. In those days, if a man said that he was a Christian it was known what he meant. You accepted a whole collection of creeds which were set out with great precision, and every single syllable of those creeds you believed with the whole strength of your convictions.

What Is a Christian?

Nowadays it is not quite that. We have to be a little more vague in our meaning of Christianity. I think, however, that there are two different items which are quite essential to anybody calling himself a Christian. The first is one of a dogmatic (教条的) nature — namely, that you must

***

* This is a selection from the lecture delivered by Bertrand Russell on March 6, 1927, to the National Secular Society, South London Branch, at Battersea Town Hall.
1 For St. Augustine and St. Thomas Aquinas, see Unit 4.

believe in God and immortality. If you do not believe in those two things, I do not think that you can properly call yourself a Christian. Then, further than that, as the name implies, you must have some kind of belief about Christ. The Mohammedans, for instance, also believe in God and in immortality, and yet they would not call themselves Christians. I think you must have at the very lowest the belief that Christ was, if not divine, at least the best and wisest of men. If you are not going to believe that much about Christ, I do not think you have any right to call yourself a Christian. Of course, there is another sense, which you find in *Whitaker's Almanack*[1] and in geography books, where the population of the world is said to be divided into Christians, Mohammedans, Buddhists, fetish worshipers, and so on; and in that sense we are all Christians. The geography books count us all in, but that is a purely geographical sense, which I suppose we can ignore. Therefore I take it that when I tell you why I am not a Christian I have to tell you two different things: first, why I do not believe in God and in immortality; and, secondly, why I do not think that Christ was the best and wisest of men, although I grant him a very high degree of moral goodness.

The Existence of God

To come to this question of the existence of God: it is a large and serious question, and if I were to attempt to deal with it in any adequate manner I should have to keep you here until Kingdom Come[2], so that you will have to excuse me if I deal with it in a somewhat summary fashion. You know, of course, that the Catholic Church has laid it down as a dogma that the existence of God can be proved by the unaided reason. That is a somewhat curious dogma, but it is one of their dogmas. They had to introduce it because at one time the freethinkers adopted the habit of saying that there were such and such arguments which mere reason might urge against the existence of God, but of course they knew as a matter of faith that God did exist. The arguments and the reasons were set out at great length, and the Catholic Church felt that they must stop it. Therefore they laid it down that the existence of God can be proved by the unaided reason and they had to set up what they considered were arguments to prove it. There are, of course, a number of them, but I shall take only a few.

A newspaper clipping from the London Evening News on September 18, 1961 following Russell and Edith's completion of one-week prison sentence for anti-nuclear demonstration

The First-cause Argument

Perhaps the simplest and easiest to understand is the argument of the First Cause. (It is maintained that everything we see in this world has a cause, and as you go back in the chain of causes further and further you must come to a First Cause, and to that First Cause you give the

---

1   *Whitaker's Almanack:* a reference book published annually in the United Kingdom
2   **Kingdom Come:** a Biblical allusion, meaning here "the next world"

name of God.) That argument, I suppose, does not carry very much weight nowadays, because, in the first place, cause is not quite what it used to be. The philosophers and the men of science have got going[1] on cause, and it has not anything like the vitality it used to have; but, apart from that, you can see that the argument that there must be a First Cause is one that cannot have any validity. I may say that when I was a young man and was debating these questions very seriously in my mind, I for a long time accepted the argument of the First Cause, until one day, at the age of eighteen, I read John Stuart Mill's *Autobiography*[2], and I there found this sentence: "My father taught me that the question 'Who made me?' cannot be answered, since it immediately suggests the further question 'Who made god?'" That very simple sentence showed me, as I still think, the fallacy (谬论) in the argument of the First Cause. If everything must have a cause, then God must have a cause. If there can be anything without a cause, it may just as well be the world as God, so that there cannot be any validity in that argument. It is exactly of the same nature as the Hindu's view, that the world rested upon an elephant and the elephant rested upon a tortoise; and when they said, "How about the tortoise?" the Indian said, "Suppose we change the subject." The argument is really no better than that. There is no reason why the world could not have come into being without a cause; nor, on the other hand, is there any reason why it should not have always existed. There is no reason to suppose that the world had a beginning at all. The idea that things must have a beginning is really due to the poverty of our imagination. Therefore, perhaps, I need not waste any more time upon the argument about the First Cause.

The Character of Christ

I now want to say a few words upon a topic which I often think is not quite sufficiently dealt with by Rationalists[3], and that is the question whether Christ was the best and the wisest of men. It is generally taken for granted that we should all agree that that was so. I do not myself. I think that there are a good many points upon which I agree with Christ a great deal more than the professing Christians do. I do not know that I could go with Him all the way, but I could go with Him much further than most professing Christians can. You will remember that He said, "Resist not evil: but whosoever shall smite thee on thy right cheek, turn to him the other also." That is not a new precept or a new principle. It was used by Lao-tse and Buddha some 500 or 600 years before Christ, but it is not a principle which as a matter of fact Christians accept. I have no doubt that the present prime minister[4], for instance, is a most sincere Christian, but I should not advise any of you to go and smite him on one cheek. I think you might find that he thought this text was intended in a figurative sense.

Then there is another point which I consider excellent. You will remember that Christ said,

---

1   **got going:** started discussion
2   For John Stuart Mill, see Unit 10.
3   **Rationalists:** Rationalism was a reflection of Enlightenment on theology in the late 17th and 18th centuries. It introduced a critical spirit by insisting that traditional beliefs be examined in the light of reason and science, and rejected revelation, miracles, and the specific dogmatic teachings.
4   **Stanley Baldwin (1867–1947):** British statesman, twice prime minister (1923–1929, 1935–1937)

"Judge not lest ye be judged." That principle I do not think you would find was popular in the law courts of Christian countries. I have known in my time quite a number of judges who were very earnest Christians, and none of them felt that they were acting contrary to Christian principles in what they did. Then Christ says, "Give to him that asketh of thee, and from him that would borrow of thee turn not thou away." That is a very good principle.

Your Chairman has reminded you that we are not here to talk politics, but I cannot help observing that the last general election was fought on the question of how desirable it was to turn away from him that would borrow of thee, so that one must assume that the Liberals and Conservatives of this country are composed of people who do not agree with the teaching of Christ, because they certainly did very emphatically turn away on that occasion.

Then there is one other maxim of Christ which I think has a great deal in it, but I do not find that it is very popular among some of our Christian friends. He says, "If thou wilt be perfect, go and sell that which thou hast, and give to the poor." That is a very excellent maxim, but, as I say, it is not much practised. All these, I think, are good maxims, although they are a little difficult to live up to. I do not profess to live up to them myself; but then, after all, it is not quite the same thing as for a Christian.

Fear, the Foundation of Religion

Religion is based, I think, primarily and mainly upon fear. It is partly the terror of the unknown and partly, as I have said, the wish to feel that you have a kind of elder brother who will stand by you in all your troubles and disputes. Fear is the basis of the whole thing — fear of the mysterious, fear of defeat, fear of death. Fear is the parent of cruelty, and therefore it is no wonder if cruelty and religion have gone hand in hand. It is because fear is at the basis of those two things. In this world we can now begin a little to understand things, and a little to master them by help of science, which has forced its way step by step against the Christian religion, against the churches, and against the opposition of all the old precepts. Science can help us to get over this craven (怯懦的) fear in which mankind has lived for so many generations. Science can teach us, and I think our own hearts can teach us, no longer to look around for imaginary supports, no longer to invent allies in the sky, but rather to look to our own efforts here below to make this world a better place to live in, instead of the sort of place that the churches in all these centuries have made it.

What We Must Do

We want to stand upon our own feet and look fair and square at the world — its good facts, its bad facts, its beauties, and its ugliness; see the world as it is and be not afraid of it. Conquer the world by intelligence and not merely by being slavishly subdued by the terror that comes from it. The whole conception of God is a conception derived from the ancient Oriental despotisms[1]. It is

---

1   **ancient Oriental despotisms:** this statement, perceived today, is problematic for its obvious Orientalist perspective: the Western God is oppressive because it comes from the East.

a conception quite unworthy of free men. When you hear people in church debasing(贬低) themselves and saying that they are miserable sinners, and all the rest of it, it seems contemptible and not worthy of self-respecting human beings. We ought to stand up and look the world frankly in the face. We ought to make the best we can of the world, and if it is not so good as we wish, after all it will still be better than what these others have made of it in all these ages. A good world needs knowledge, kindliness, and courage; it does not need a regretful hankering after the past or a fettering of the free intelligence by the words uttered long ago by ignorant men. It needs a fearless outlook and a free intelligence. It needs hope for the future, not looking back all the time toward a past that is dead, which we trust will be far surpassed by the future that our intelligence can create.

Questions for Discussion

1. What does "covenant" mean? Describe the old covenant and the new.
2. What is the meaning of the "original sin"?
3. Do you think God is justified in his punishment of man?
4. Discuss the image of Eve, and of Adam if you like, from the feminist perspective if possible.
5. Are there differences between the God in the Old Testament and Jesus in the New Testament?
6. What is the significance of the Ten Commandments, or the Decalogue (the Greek for "ten words") as ethical standards for the Hebrews?
7. Comment on the following statement:
   "The history in the Bible often is reliable, but that is a far cry from complete accuracy; after all, accuracy was not a purpose of a biblical writer. In Scripture we encounter a view *about* History, not researched history." (Samuel Sandmel, *The Enjoyment of Scripture*)
8. Nuwa and the God of the Hebrew Bible bear no resemblance to each other, but the Chinese and Hebrew creation myths have a good number of points in common:
   a. Humans created on the final day of creation: On the first day, Nuwa created chickens; on the second, dogs; on the third, sheep; on the fourth, pigs; on the fifth, horses; on the sixth, humans. God created humans last on a separate day.
   b. Humans created in the deity's own image: Nuwa, inspired by her own reflection in the yellow river, decided to make clay models in her image. "And God said, Let us make man in our own image, after our likeness ..." (Genesis 1:1-26).
   c. Humans created out of the earth: Nuwa used a vine to scatter the unformed lumps of clay, which fell to the ground and took the form of humans. "And the LORD God formed men of the dust of the ground ..." (Genesis 2:7).

d. Humans given the divine command to reproduce: Nuwa gave her creations the institution of marriage so that they could propagate themselves. "… and God said unto them, Be fruitful, and multiply, and replenish the earth …" (Genesis 1:28).

e. The creator-deity stopping the great flood: Water poured down from the sky because a fight between two gods had damaged the foundation of the heavens. Humans were being drowned in the flood when Nuwa patched up the sky with colored stones and stopped the deluge. "… and God made a wind to pass over the earth, and the waters assuaged." (Genesis 8:1).

f. The rainbow as a sign that all was well after the rain: The rainbow is the colored stones that Nuwa is said to use to patch the sky. "And God said ... I do set my bow in the cloud, and it shall be for a token of a covenant between me and the earth ..." (Genesis 9:12).

Comment on these similarities and differences and more in the creation story between the Chinese legend and the Western Bible.

9. Identify the following Biblical allusions:

a. … no woman was ever nearer to her mate than I am: ever more absolutely bone of his bones, and flesh of his flesh.
    — C. Brontë, *Jane Eyre*

b. How like Eve's apple doth thy beauty grow,
    If thy sweet virtue answer not thy show!
    — W. Shakespeare, *Sonnet* 93

c. Forbidden fruit is sweet. (English proverb)

d. Life is real — life is earnest —
    And the grave is not its goal:
    Dust thou art, to dust returnest,
    Was not spoken of the soul.
    — H. Longfellow, *A Psalm of Life*

e. When Adam delved and Eve span
    Who was then a gentleman?
    — John Ball

10. What is Bertrand Russell's attitude towards religion? Is he serious? Why is he not a Christian? What does he mean when he says that we "ought to stand up and look the world frankly in the face"?

11. "Religion is the sigh of the oppressed creature, the feeling of a heartless world, and the soul of soulless circumstances. It is the opium of the people." This is the famous statement made about religion in general and Christianity in particular by Karl Marx in *Critique of Hegel's Philosophy of Right*. What is Marx talking about? In what sense is religion "the opium of the people"?

UNIT 2

Greek & Roman Sages (1)

Pretest

- What do you know about the Greek & Roman thinkers?
- What is the significance of their ideas?
- Which one of them do you like best or know most, and why?

What You Will Learn in This Unit

- Two of the greatest men of thought in ancient Greece: Socrates and Plato;
- Their ideas concerning man, nature, and wisdom; and
- The "Axial Age" in ancient Greece and China.

Learn to Pronounce

Apollo /əˈpɒləʊ/ 阿波罗

Athens /ˈæθɪnz/ 雅典

Delphi /ˈdelfaɪ/ 特尔斐

den /den/ 洞穴

hemlock /ˈhemlɒk/ 一种毒药

Memorabilia /ˌmemərəˈbɪlɪə/ 大事记

Plato /ˈpleɪtəʊ/ 柏拉图

Pythagoras /paɪˈθægərəs/ 毕达哥拉斯

Socrates /ˈsɒkrətiːz/ 苏格拉底

Tiber /ˈtaɪbə/ 台伯河

Trojan /ˈtrəʊdʒən/ 特洛伊的

Troy /ˈtrɒɪ/ 特洛伊

Xenophon /ˈzenəfən/ 色诺芬

Introduction

Temple of Athena Nike, built around 420 BC, is an excellent example of a classical temple, with ionic columns and a frieze around the top.

After the Dark Age (1000–750? BC) and the Archaic Age (750–480 BC), the ancient Greek civilization witnessed the most famous period called the Classical Age (480–323 BC), known as the cradle of Western civilization. Macedonian kings, Philip II and his son Alexander the Great (356–323 BC) turned the formerly weak kingdom into an international superpower. The mountainous kingdom of Macedonia eventually became the leader of Greece and conqueror of the Persian Empire. Unlike most other peoples of the time, Greeks of the Classical Age usually were not ruled by kings. Greek communities treasured the freedom to govern by themselves, although they argued about the best way to do that and often warred against each other. During this period, ancient Greeks reached their highest prosperity and produced amazing cultural accomplishments. Greek philosophy at the time formed the basis of all later philosophical speculation in the Western world. The idea of "searching into myself and other men" for Socrates was organized by Plato into a systematic philosophy. Plato discarded the objects of the real world as being merely shadows of eternal Forms or Ideals, the object of true knowledge. The goal of the philosopher, he said, is to know the eternal Forms and to instruct others in that knowledge.

Socrates: The Apology

Socrates of Athens (c.469–399 BC), the first of the great trio of ancient Greeks who laid the philosophical foundations of Western culture, is known for "bringing down philosophy from heaven to earth" (Cicero). His mother Phaenarete was a "midwife" by profession, a term Socrates used to describe himself for bringing out knowledge within man. His outward appearance is grotesque: stout and not tall, with prominent eyes, snub nose, broad nostrils, and wide mouth. But he is "all glorious within": for his record of endurance against a self-imposed life of hardships, for his civil disobedience of the oligarchy(寡头政府) of the Thirty Tyrants to arrest Leon in 404 BC, and for his resistance during 406–405 BC against the unconstitutional condemnation of the generals by a collective verdict. Like the Chinese sage Confucius, he called to pursue philosophy, devoting himself to teaching and self-examination, since he believed vice is a result of ignorance whereas virtue of knowledge means knowing right and acting rightly. He had the sense of mission, and the way he fulfilled it is through talking to young men of promise, politicians, poets, and artisans in streets, marketplace, and gymnasia about notions of right and wrong. He claimed he was testing the oracle of Apollo at Delphi that he was the wisest of men because he took it the mission from God to make his fellowmen aware of their ignorance. He had strong belief in God as ruler of the world. He was obedient to laws of Athens, though he steered clear of politics. But in 399 BC he was charged with neglecting gods of the state, introducing new divinities, and corrupting morals of the young from loyalty to principles of democracy. As a man of principle he refused to compromise. Angered jury voted for death penalty. Rejecting planned escape, he fulfilled the sentence by drinking hemlock. Socrates wrote no books and established no regular school. Information about him comes chiefly from the dialogues of Plato and in the Memorabilia of Xenophon.

Socrates: How you, O Athenians, have been affected by my accusers, I cannot tell; but I know that they almost made me forget who I was, so persuasively did they speak; and yet they have hardly uttered a word of truth. But of the many falsehoods told by them, there was one which quite amazed me; I mean when they said that you should be upon your guard and not allow yourselves to be deceived by the force of my eloquence. To say this, when they were certain to

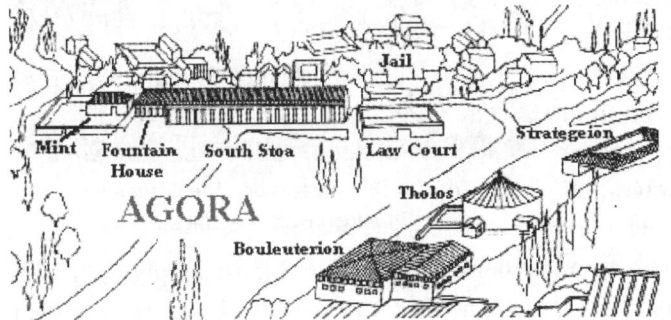

be detected as soon as I opened my lips and proved myself to be anything but a great speaker, did indeed appear to me most shameless, unless by the force of eloquence they mean the force of truth; for if such is their meaning, I admit that I am eloquent. But in how different a way from theirs! Well, as I was saying, they have scarcely spoken the truth at all; but from me you shall hear the whole truth[1]: not, however, delivered after their manner in a set oration duly ornamented with words and phrases. No, by heaven! But I shall use the words and arguments which occur to me at the moment; for I am confident in the justice of my cause: at my time of life I ought not to be appearing before you, O men of Athens, in the character of a juvenile orator, let no one expect it of me. And I must beg of you to grant me a favor: If I defend myself in my accustomed manner, and you hear me using the words which I have been in the habit of using in the agora[2], at the tables of the money-changers, or anywhere else, I would ask you not to be surprised, and not to interrupt me on this account. For I am more than seventy years of age, and appearing now for the first time in a court of law, I am quite a stranger to the language of the place; and therefore I would have you regard me as if I were really a stranger, whom you would accuse if he spoke in his native tongue, and after the fashion of his country[3]: Am I making an unfair request of you? Never mind the manner, which may or may not be good; but think only of the truth of my words, and give heed to that: let the

---

1 **they have scarcely … whole truth:** Pay attention to how Socrates goes about to define "truth."

2 **agora:** marketplace

3 **I would have … his country:** Pay attention to the way Socrates argues: I am one of you (people in the agora), not them (officials, judges).

Heritage of Western Intellectual Tradition   A Sourcebook

speaker speak truly and the judge decide justly.

And first, I have to reply to the older charges and to my first accusers, and then I will go on to the later ones. For of old I have had many accusers, who have accused me falsely to you during many years; and I am more afraid of them than of Anytus[1] and his associates, who are dangerous, too, in their own way. But far more dangerous are the others, who began when you were children, and took possession of your minds with their falsehoods, telling of one Socrates, a wise man, who speculated about the heaven above, and searched into the earth beneath, and made the worse appear the better cause. The disseminators (传播者) of this tale are the accusers whom I dread; for their hearers are apt to fancy that such inquirers do not believe in the existence of the gods. And they are many, and their charges against me are of ancient date, and they were

made by them in the days when you were more impressionable than you are now, in childhood, or it may have been in youth, and the cause when heard went by default[2], for there was none to answer. And hardest of all, I do not know and cannot tell the names of my accusers; unless in the chance case of a Comic poet. All who from envy and malice (怨恨) have persuaded you, some of them having first convinced themselves, all this class of men are most difficult to deal with;

Theatre Dionysus where The Clouds by Aristophanes was staged

for I cannot have them up here, and cross-examine them, and therefore I must simply fight with shadows[3] in my own defense, and argue when there is no one who answers. I will ask you then to assume with me, as I was saying, that my opponents are of two kinds; one recent, the other ancient: and I hope that you will see the propriety of my answering the latter first, for these accusations you heard long before the others, and much oftener.

Well, then, I must make my defense, and endeavor to clear away in a short time, a slander which has lasted a long time. May I succeed, if to succeed be for my good and yours, or likely to avail me in my cause. The task is not an easy one; I quite understand the nature of it. And so leaving the event with God, in obedience to the law[4] I will now make my defense.

I will begin at the beginning, and ask what is the accusation which has given rise to the slander of my person, and in fact has encouraged Meletus[5] to prefer this charge against me. Well, what do the slanderers say? They shall be my prosecution and I will sum up their words in an

---

1 **Anytus:** one of Socrates' prosecutors
2 **went by default:** did not appear
3 **fight with shadows:** What is this "fight with shadows"? What is Socrates implicitly attacking here?
4 **in obedience to the law:** For the same reason of "obeying the law," Socrates chose to die rather than a planned escape.
5 **Meletus:** another of Socrates' prosecutors

affidavit[1]: "Socrates is an evil-doer, and a curious person, who searches into things under the earth and in heaven, and he makes the worse appear the better cause; and he teaches the aforesaid doctrines to others." Such is the nature of the accusation: it is just what you have yourselves seen in the comedy of Aristophanes[2], who has introduced a man whom he calls Socrates going about and saying that he walks in air and talking a deal of nonsense concerning matters of which I do not pretend to know either much or little, not that I mean to speak disparagingly(说坏话)of any one who is a student of natural philosophy. I should be very sorry if Meletus could bring so grave a charge against me. But the simple truth is, O Athenians, that I have nothing to do with physical speculations: many of those here present are witnesses to the truth of this, and to them I appeal. Speak then, you who have heard me, and tell your neighbors whether any of you have ever known me hold forth in few words or in many upon such matters ... You hear their answer. And from what they say of this part of the charge you will be able to judge of the truth of the rest.

As little foundation is there for the report that I am a teacher, and take money; this accusation has no more truth in it than the other. Although, if a man were really able to instruct mankind, to receive money for giving instruction would, in my opinion, be an honor to him. There is Gorgias of Leontium, and Prodicus of Ceos, and Hippias of Elis,[3] who go the round of the cities, and are able to persuade the young men to leave their own citizens by whom they might be taught for nothing, and come to them whom they not only pay, but are thankful if they may be allowed to pay them. There is at this time a Parian philosopher residing in Athens, of whom I have heard; and I came to hear of him in this way: I came across a man who has spent a world of money on the Sophists[4], Callias, the son of Hipponicus, and knowing that he had sons, I asked him: 'Callias,' I said, 'if your two sons were foals[5] or calves there would be no difficulty in finding some one to put over them; we should hire a trainer of horses, or a farmer probably, who would improve and perfect them in their own proper virtue and excellence; but as they are human beings, whom are you thinking of placing over them? Is there any one who understands human and political virtue? You must have thought about the matter, for you have sons; is there any one?' 'There is,' he said. 'Who is he?' said I, 'and of what country? and what does he charge?' 'Evenus the Parian,' he replied, 'he is the man, and his charge is five minae[6].' Happy is Evenus, I said to myself, if he really has this wisdom, and teaches at such a moderate charge. Had I the same, I should have been very proud and conceited; but the truth is that I have no knowledge of the kind.

1　**affidavit:** written statement as oath
2　**Aristophanes (448?－385 BC):** Athenian playwright, one of the greatest writers of comedy in literary history, whose *The Clouds* (423 BC) satirizes Socrates' ideas for opposing to the interests of the state.
3　**Gorgias (c. 485－c. 380 BC):** Greek rhetorician and Sophistic philosopher; **Prodicus** and **Hippias** are also leading 5th-century Sophists.
4　**Sophists** (meaning in Greek "master craftsman" or "man of wisdom"): originally, name applied by the ancient Greeks to learned men, in the 5th century BC, to itinerant teachers who provided instruction in higher branches of learning for a fee
5　**foal:** young horse
6　**mina:** (*pl.* minae) unit of money in ancient Greece

Heritage of Western Intellectual Tradition　A Sourcebook

I dare say, Athenians, that some one among you will reply, 'Yes, Socrates, but what is the origin of these accusations which are brought against you; there must have been something strange which you have been doing? All these rumors and this talk about you would never have arisen if you had been like other men: tell us, then, what is the cause of them, for we should be sorry to judge hastily of you.' Now I regard this as a fair challenge, and I will endeavor to explain to you the reason why I am called wise and have such an evil fame. Please to attend then. And although some of you may think that I am joking, I declare that I will tell you the entire truth. Men of Athens, this reputation of mine has come of a certain sort of wisdom which I possess. If you ask me what kind of wisdom, I reply, wisdom such as may perhaps be attained by every man, for to that extent I am inclined to believe that I am wise; whereas the persons of whom I was speaking have a superhuman wisdom, which I may fail to describe, because I have it not myself; and he who says that I have, speaks falsely, and is taking away my character. And here, O men of Athens, I must beg you not to interrupt me, even if I seem to say something extravagant. **For the word which I will speak is not mine. I will refer you to a witness who is worthy of credit; that witness shall be the God of Delphi, he will tell you about my wisdom, if I have any, and of what sort it is. You must have known Chaerephon; he was early a friend of mine, and also a friend of yours, for he shared in the recent exile of the people, and returned with you. Well, Chaerephon, as you know, was very impetuous[1] in all his doings, and he went to Delphi and boldly asked the oracle to tell him whether, as I was saying, I must beg you not to interrupt, he asked the oracle to tell him whether any one was wiser than I was, and the Pythian prophetess[2] answered, that there was no man wiser.** Chaerephon is dead himself; but his brother, who is in court, will confirm the truth of what I'm saying.

Why do I mention this? Because I am going to explain to you why I have such an evil name. When I heard the answer, I said to myself, What can the god mean? and what is the interpretation of his riddle? for I know that I have no wisdom, small or great. What then can he mean when he says that I am the wisest of men? And yet he is a god, and cannot lie; that would be against his nature. After long consideration, I thought of a method of trying the question. I reflected that if I could only find a man wiser than myself, then I might go to the god with a refutation in my hand. I should say to him, 'Here is a man who is wiser than I am; but you said that I was the wisest.' Accordingly I went to one who had the reputation of wisdom, and ob-

Delphi was considered by the ancients to be the center of the world. Private citizens and public officials would come to consult the oracle there, who was said to speak the words of the good Apollo.

served him, his name I need not mention; he was a politician whom first among I selected for

---

1   **impetuous:** acting on impulse; Chaerephon (c. 450–399 BC) was a loyal friend and follower of Socrates.

2   **the Pythian prophetess:** In Homeric legend Apollo was primarily a god of prophecy. His most important oracle was at Delphi, the site of his victory over the Python, the fabled serpent. He sometimes gave the gift of prophecy to mortals whom he loved.

examination, and the result was as follows: When I began to talk with him, I could not help thinking that he was not really wise, although he was thought wise by many, and still wiser by himself; and thereupon I tried to explain to him that he thought himself wise, but was not really wise; and the consequence was that he hated me, and his enmity was shared by several who were present and heard me. **So I left him, saying to myself, as I went away: conceit of Man, although I do not suppose that either of us knows anything really beautiful and good, I am better off than he is, for he knows nothing, and thinks that he knows; I neither know nor think that I know. In this latter particular, then, I seem to have slightly the advantage of him.** Then I went to another who had still higher pretensions to wisdom, and my conclusion was exactly the same. Whereupon I made another enemy of him, and of many others besides him.[1]

Then I went to one man after another, being not unconscious of the enmity which I provoked, and I lamented and feared this: but necessity was laid upon me, the word of God, I thought, ought to be considered first. And I said to myself, I must go to all who appear to know, and find out the meaning of the oracle. And I swear to you, Athenians, by the dog I swear! for I must tell you the truth, **the result of my mission was just this: I found that the men most in repute were all but the most foolish; and that others less esteemed were really wiser and better.** I will tell you the whole of my wanderings and of the 'Herculean' labors[2], as I may call them, which I en-

Pythia the female medium in contact with Apollo at Delphi. Her name was taken from the dragon, Python, whose slaying by Apollo established the holy shrine in Apollo's name.

dured only to find at last the oracle irrefutable. After the politicians, I went to the poets; tragic, dithyrambic[3], and all sorts. And there, I said to myself, you will be instantly detected; now you will find out that you are more ignorant than they are. Accordingly, I took them some of the most elaborate passages in their own writings, and asked what was the meaning of them, thinking that they would teach me something. Will you believe me? I am almost ashamed to confess the truth, but I must say that there is hardly a person present who would not have talked better about their poetry than they did themselves. Then I knew that not by wisdom do poets write poetry, but by a sort of genius and inspiration; they are like diviners or soothsayers who also say many fine things, but do not understand the meaning of them. The poets appeared to me to be much in the

---

1   **Then I went to another … besides him.:** Pay attention to the edge of irony in Socrates' negative definition of "wisdom": I am wiser only because I know I am not wise.

2   **'Herculean' labors:** Hercules is son of Zeus, noted for his strength and his many legendary exploits. Hera, the jealous wife of Zeus, sent a fit of madness upon Hercules during which he killed his wife and children. He was told by the oracle at Delphi that he should purge himself by becoming the servant of his cousin Eurystheus, king of Mycenae, who devised as a penance the twelve difficult tasks, hence the "Labors of Hercules."

3   **dithyrambic:** usually short poem in an inspired wild irregular strain

same case; and I further observed that upon the strength of their poetry they believed themselves to be the wisest of men in other things in which they were not wise. So I departed, conceiving myself to be superior to them for the same reason that I was superior to the politicians.

At last I went to the artisans; I was conscious that I knew nothing at all, as I may say, and I was sure that they knew many fine things; and here I was not mistaken, for they did know many things of which I was ignorant, and in this they certainly were wiser than I was. But I observed that even the good artisans fell into the same error as the poets; because they were good workmen they thought that they also knew all sorts of high matters, and this defect in them overshadowed their wisdom; and therefore I asked myself on behalf of the oracle, whether I would like to be as I was, neither having their knowledge nor their ignorance, or like them in both; and I made answer to myself and to the oracle that I was better off as I was.[1]

This inquisition has led to my having many enemies of the worst and most dangerous kind, and has given occasion also to many calumnies[2]. **And I am called wise, for my hearers always imagine that I myself possess the wisdom which I find wanting[3] in others: but the truth is, O men of Athens, that God only is wise; and by his answer he intends to show that the wisdom of men is worth little or nothing; he is not speaking of Socrates, he is only using my name by way of illustration, as if he said, O men, he is the wisest, who, like Socrates, knows that his wisdom is in truth worth nothing.** And so I go about the world, obedient to the god, and search and make enquiry into the wisdom of any one, whether citizen or stranger, who appears to be wise; and if he is not wise, then I show him that he is not wise; and my occupation quite absorbs me, and I have no time to give attention to any public matter of interest or to any concern of my own, but I am in utter poverty by reason of my devotion to the god[4].

There is another thing — young men of the richer classes, who have not much to do, come about me of their own accord; they like to hear the pretenders examined, and they often imitate me, and proceed to examine others; there are plenty of persons, as they quickly discover, who think that they know something, but really know little or nothing; and then those who are examined by them, instead of being angry with themselves are angry with me: this confounded Socrates, they say; this villainous mis-

The Acropolis hill, so called the "Sacred Rock" of Athens, is the most important site of the city.

leader of youth!, and then if somebody asks them, Why, what evil does he practice or teach? they

---

1 Read the whole paragraph to bear in mind that Socrates is often regarded by contemporary critics as the first "intellectual" in the West, one who is extraordinarily independent in thinking and action, a naysayer.

2 **calumny:** slander

3 **wanting:** lacking

4 **I am in … to the god:** Socrates was known for his poverty: he wore no shoes nor shirts, and whether winter or summer he wore the same coat. "A slave who was made to live so would run away."

do not know, and can't tell; but in order that they may not appear to be at a loss, they repeat the ready-made charges which are used against all philosophers about teaching things up in the clouds and under the earth, and making the worse appear the better cause; for they do not like to confess that their pretense of knowledge has been detected, which is the truth; and as they are numerous and ambitious and energetic, and are drawn up in battle array and have persuasive tongues, they have filled your ears with their loud and inveterate[1] calumnies. And this is the reason why my three accusers, Meletus and Anytus and Lycon, have set upon me; Meletus, who has a quarrel with me on behalf of the poets; Anytus, on behalf of the craftsmen and politicians; Lycon, on behalf of the rhetoricians: and as I said at the beginning, I cannot expect to get rid of such a mass of calumny all in a moment. And this, O men of Athens, is the truth and the whole truth; I have concealed nothing, I have dissembled[2] nothing. And yet, I know that my plainness of speech makes them hate me, and what is their hatred but a proof that I am speaking the truth? Hence has arisen the prejudice against me; and this is the reason of it, as you will find out either in this or in any future enquiry.

...

Some one will say: And are you not ashamed, Socrates, of a course of life which is likely to bring you to an untimely end[3]? To him I may fairly answer: There you are mistaken: a man who is good for anything ought not to calculate the chance of living or dying; he ought only to consider whether in doing anything he is doing right or wrong, acting the part of a good man or of a bad. Whereas, upon your view, the heroes who fell at Troy were not good for much, and the son of Thetis[4] above all, who altogether despised danger in comparison with disgrace; and when he was so eager to slay Hector,

Socrates and His Students by Johann Friedrich Greuter

his goddess mother said to him, that if he avenged his companion Patroclus, and slew Hector, he would die himself, 'Fate,' she said, in these or the like words, 'waits for you next after Hector;' he, receiving this warning, utterly despised danger and death, and instead of fearing them, feared rather to live in dishonor, and not to avenge his friend. 'Let me die forthwith,' he replies, 'and be avenged of my enemy, rather than abide here by the beaked ships, a laughing-stock and a burden of the earth.' Had Achilles any thought of death and danger? For wherever a man's place is,

---

1 **inveterate:** long-established
2 **dissemble:** hide, distort
3 **untimely end:** unnatural death
4 **the son of Thetis:** Achilles, greatest of the Greek warriors in the Trojan War. The River Styx made him invulnerable except for the heel by which his mother held him. Achilles fought many battles during the 10-year siege of Troy. When Patroclus, Achilles' friend and companion, was killed by the Trojan prince Hector, Achilles returned to battle, slew Hector, and dragged his body in triumph behind his chariot. He later was mortally wounded in the heel by Paris.

Heritage of Western Intellectual Tradition   A Sourcebook

whether the place which he has chosen or that in which he has been placed by a commander, there he ought to remain in the hour of danger; he should not think of death or of anything but of disgrace. And this, O men of Athens, is a true saying.

...

Men of Athens, do not interrupt, but hear me; there was an understanding between us that you should hear me to the end: I have something more to say, at which you may be inclined to cry out; but I believe that to hear me will be good for you, and therefore I beg that you will not cry out. I would have you know, that if you kill such a one as I am, you will injure yourselves more than you will injure me. Nothing will injure me, not Meletus nor yet Anytus, they cannot, for a bad man is not permitted to injure a better than himself. I do not deny that Anytus may, perhaps, injure me; and he may imagine, and others may imagine, that he is inflicting a great injury: but there I do not agree. For the evil of doing as he is doing, the evil of unjustly taking away the life of another, is greater far[1].

And now, Athenians, I am not going to argue for my own sake, as you may think, but for that you may not sin against the God by condemning me, who am his[2] gift to you. For if you kill me you will not easily find a successor to me, who, if I may use such a ludicrous[3] figure of speech, am a sort of gadfly[4], given to the state by God; and the state is a great and noble steed who is tardy in his motions owing to his very size, and requires to be stirred into life. I am that gadfly which God has attached to the state, and all day long and in all places am always fastening upon you, arousing and persuading and reproaching you. You will not easily find another like me, and therefore I would advise you to spare me. I dare say that you may feel out of temper (like a person who is suddenly awakened from sleep), and you think that you might easily strike me dead as Anytus advises, and then you would sleep on for the remainder of your lives, unless God in his care of you sent you another gadfly. When I say that I am given to you by God, the proof of my

Socrates wandering in Athens

mission is this: if I had been like other men, I should not have neglected all my own concerns or patiently seen the neglect of them during all these years, and have been doing yours, coming to you individually like a father or elder brother, exhorting you to regard virtue; such conduct, I say, would be unlike human nature. If I had gained anything, or if my exhortations had been paid, there would have been some sense in my doing so; but now, as you will perceive, not even the impudence of my accusers dares to say that I have ever exacted or sought pay of any one; of that they have no witness. And I have a sufficient witness to the truth of what I say, my poverty.

---

1 **greater far:** far greater injury

2 **his:** God's

3 **ludicrous:** ridiculous

4 **gadfly:** horse or cow fly. Discuss this analogue to find its implication here in relation to broader issues such as the function of intellectuals in society.

Some one may wonder why I go about in private giving advice and busying myself with the concerns of others, but do not venture to come forward in public and advise the state. I will tell you why. You have heard me speak at sundry times and in diverse places of an oracle or sign[1] which comes to me, and is the divinity which Meletus ridicules in the indictment. This sign, which is a kind of voice, first began to come to me when I was a child; it always forbids but never commands me to do anything which I am going to do. This is what deters me from being a politician. And rightly, as I think. For I am certain, O men of Athens, that if I had engaged in politics, I should have perished long ago, and done no good either to you or to myself. And do not be offended at my telling you the truth: for the truth is, that no man who goes to war with you or any other multitude, honestly striving against the many lawless and unrighteous deeds which are done in a state, will save his life; he who will fight for the right, if he would live even for a brief space, must have a private station and not a public one.

I can give you convincing evidence of what I say, not words only, but what you value far more, actions. Let me relate to you a passage of my own life which will prove to you that I should never have yielded to injustice from any fear of death, and that 'as I should have refused to yield' I must have died at once. I will tell you a tale of the courts, not very interesting perhaps, but nevertheless true. The only office of state which I ever held, O men of Athens, was that of senator: the tribe Antiochis, which is my tribe, had the presidency at the trial of the generals who had not taken up the bodies of the slain[2] after the battle of Arginusae; and you proposed to try them in a body, contrary to law, as

1938 年 7 月，陶行知参观雅典苏格拉底石牢，在石牢门前静坐五分钟并题诗："这位老人家，为何也坐牢？欢喜说真话，假人都烦恼。"

you all thought afterwards; but at the time I was the only one of the Prytanes[3] who was opposed to the illegality, and I gave my vote against you; and when the orators threatened to impeach and arrest me, and you called and shouted, I made up my mind that I would run the risk, having law and justice with me, rather than take part in your injustice because I feared imprisonment and death. This happened in the days of the democracy. But when the oligarchy of the Thirty was in power, they sent for me and four others into the rotunda[4], and bade us bring Leon the Salaminian from Salamis, as they wanted to put him to death. This was a specimen of the sort of commands which they were always giving with the view of implicating as many as possible in their crimes; and then I showed, not in word only but in deed,

---

1 **speak at sundry times and in diverse places of an oracle or sign:** split proposition here: speak … of an oracle or sign

2 **who had not … the slain:** who did not take back the bodies of the dead

3 **Prytane:** Greek word *prytaneum*, the name given to the headquarters of the executive, here the governing body

4 **rotunda:** round building

that, if I may be allowed to use such an expression, I cared not a straw[1] for death, and that my great and only care was lest I should do an unrighteous or unholy thing. For the strong arm of that oppressive power did not frighten me into doing wrong; and when we came out of the rotunda the other four went to Salamis and fetched Leon, but I went quietly home. For which I might have lost my life, had not the power of the Thirty shortly afterwards come to an end. And many will witness to my words.

Now do you really imagine that I could have survived all these years, if I had led a public life, supposing that like a good man I had always maintained the right and had made justice, as I ought, the first thing? No indeed, men of Athens, neither I nor any other man. But I have been always the same in all my actions, public as well as private, and never have I yielded any base compliance[2] to those who are slanderously termed my disciples, or to any other. Not that I have any regular disciples. But if any one likes to come and hear me while I am pursuing my mission, whether he be young or old, he is not excluded. Nor do I converse only with those who pay; but any one, whether he be rich or poor, may ask and answer me and listen to my words; and whether he turns out to be a bad man or a good one, neither result can be justly imputed[3] to me; for I never taught or professed to teach him anything. And if any one says that he has ever learned or heard anything from me in private which all the world has not heard, let me tell you that he is lying.

But I shall be asked, why do people delight in continually conversing with you? I have told you already, Athenians, the whole truth about this matter: they like to hear the cross-examination of the pretenders to wisdom; there is amusement in it. Now this duty of cross-examining other men has been imposed upon me by God; and has been signified to me by oracles, visions, and in every way in which the will of divine power was ever intimated[4] to any one. This is true, O Athenians; or, if not true, would be refuted. If I am or have been corrupting the youth, those of them who are now grown up and have become sensible that I gave them bad advice in the days of their youth should come forward as accusers, and take their revenge; or if they do not like to come themselves, some of their relatives, fathers, brothers, or other kinsmen, should say what evil their families have suffered at my hands. Now is their time. Many of them I see in the court. There is Crito, who is of the same age and of the same deme[5] with myself, and there is Critobulus his son, whom I also see. Then again there is Lysanias of Sphettus, who is the father of Aeschines, he is present; and also there is Antiphon of Cephisus, who is the father of Epigenes; and there are the brothers of several who have associated with me. There is Nicostratus the son of Theosdotides, and the brother of Theodotus (now Theodotus himself is dead, and therefore he, at any rate, will not seek to stop him); and there is Paralus the son of Demodocus, who had a brother Theages; and Adeimantus the son of Ariston, whose brother Plato is present; and Aeantodorus, who is the brother of Apollodorus, whom I also see. I might mention a great many others, some of whom

---

1 **not a straw:** not at all
2 **compliance:** submission
3 **impute:** regard as the outcome of
4 **intimate:** give hint to
5 **deme:** town

Meletus should have produced as witnesses in the course of his speech; and let him still produce them, if he has forgotten, I will make way for him. And let him say, if he has any testimony of the sort which he can produce. Nay, Athenians, the very opposite is the truth. For all these are ready to witness on behalf of the corrupter[1], of the injurer of their kindred, as Meletus and Anytus call me; not the corrupted youth only, there might have been a motive for that, but their uncorrupted elder relatives. Why should they too support me with their testimony? Why, indeed, except for the sake of truth and justice, and because they know that I am speaking the truth, and that Meletus is a liar.

Well, Athenians, this and the like of this is all the defense which I have to offer. Yet one word more. Perhaps there may be some one who is offended at me, when he calls to mind how he himself on a similar, or even a less serious occasion, prayed and entreated (恳求) the judges with many tears, and how he produced his children in court, which was a moving spectacle, together with a host of relations and friends; whereas I, who am probably in danger of my life, will do none of these things. The contrast

Socrates teaching in Athens

may occur to his mind, and he may be set against me, and vote in anger because he is displeased at me on this account. Now if there be such a person among you[2], mind, I do not say that there is, to him I may fairly reply: My friend, I am a man, and like other men, a creature of flesh and blood, and not 'of wood or stone,' as Homer says; and I have a family, yes, and sons, O Athenians, three in number, one almost a man, and two others who are still young; and yet I will not bring any of them hither in order to petition you for an acquittal. And why not? Not from any self-assertion or want[3] of respect for you. Whether I am or am not afraid of death is another question, of which I will not now speak. But, having regard to public opinion, I feel that such conduct would be discreditable to myself, and to you, and to the whole state. One who has reached my years, and who has a name for wisdom, ought not to demean himself. Whether this opinion of me be deserved or not, at any rate the world has decided that Socrates is in some way superior to other men. And if those among you who are said to be superior in wisdom and courage, and any other virtue, demean themselves in this way, how shameful is their conduct! I have seen men of reputation, when they have been condemned, behaving in the strangest manner: they seemed to fancy that they were going to suffer something dreadful if they died, and that they would be immortal if you only allowed them to live; and I think that such are a dishonor to the state, and that any stranger coming in would have said of them that the most eminent men of Athens, to whom the Athenians themselves give honor and command, are no better than women. And I say that these things ought not to be done by those of us who have a reputation; and if they are done, you ought not to permit them; you ought rather to show that you are far more disposed to

---

1   **on behalf of the corrupter:** i.e., to support me — Socrates is charged with corrupting the young

2   **if there be such a person among you:** Socrates uses the subjunctive mood.

3   **want:** lack, neglect

condemn the man who gets up a doleful scene and makes the city ridiculous, than him who holds his peace[1].

But, setting aside the question of public opinion, there seems to be something wrong in asking a favor of a judge, and thus procuring an acquittal, instead of informing and convincing him. For his duty is, not to make a present of justice[2], but to give judgment; and he has sworn that he will judge according to the laws, and not according to his own good and pleasure; and we ought not to encourage you, nor should you allow yourselves to be encouraged, in this habit of perjury[3], there can be no piety in that. Do not then require me to do what I consider dishonorable and impious and wrong, especially now, when I am being tried for impiety on the indictment of Meletus. For if, O men of Athens, by force of persuasion and entreaty I could overpower your oaths, then I should be teaching you to believe that there are no gods, and in defending should simply convict myself of the charge of not believing in them. But that is not so, far otherwise. For I do believe that there are gods, and in a sense higher than that in which any of my accusers believe in them. And to you and to God I commit my cause, to be determined by you as is best for you and me. (*Socrates was found guilty by 281 votes to 220, and in a second vote condemned to death[4].*)

...

Not much time will be gained, O Athenians, in return for the evil name which you will get from the detractors[5] of the city, who will say that you killed Socrates, a wise man; for they will call me wise even although I am not wise when they want to reproach you. If you had waited a little while, your desire would have been fulfilled in the course of nature. For I am far advanced in years, as you may perceive, and not far from death. I am speaking now only to those of you who have condemned me to death. And I have another thing to say to them[6]: You think that I was convicted through deficiency of words — I mean, that if I had thought fit to leave nothing undone, nothing unsaid, I might have gained an acquittal. Not so; the deficiency which led to my conviction was not of words — certainly not. But I had not the boldness or impudence or inclination to address you as you would have liked me to address you, weeping and wailing and lamenting, and saying and doing many things which you have been accustomed to hear from

---

1   **you are far more ... holds his peace:** i.e. more likely to condemn A, not B

2   **For his duty is, not to make a present of justice:** A judge is not supposed to give justice as a present.

3   **perjury:** making false statement

4   *second vote condemned to death*: It was customary for the guilty to suggest an alternative punishment, payment of a fine, for instance. But Socrates rose to address the tribunal: he should be declared a civic benefactor and given an annual pension as a reward to his services to Athenian youth. Meanwhile, he agreed to pay a token fine of one mina. Upon acquittal, he would return to his old way of life. The tribunal was enraged, and sentenced him to death in the second vote. Even then, a voluntary withdrawal from the accused would change the mind of the prosecutors. But Socrates forced the issue by refusing to do anything "involving the least shade of compromise."

5   **detractor:** person who questions the value of

6   **them:** the detractors

others, and which, as I say, are unworthy of me. But I thought that I ought not to do anything common or mean in the hour of danger: nor do I now repent of the manner of my defence, and I would rather die having spoken after my manner, than speak in your manner and live. For neither in war nor yet at law ought any man to use every way of escaping death. For often in battle there is no doubt that if a man will throw away his arms, and fall on his knees before his pursuers, he may escape death; and in other dangers there are other ways of escaping death, if a man is willing to say and do anything. The difficulty, my friends, is not in avoiding death, but in avoiding unrighteousness; for that runs faster than death. I am old and move slowly, and the slower runner[1] has overtaken me, and my accusers are keen and quick, and the faster runner[2], who is unrighteousness, has overtaken them. And now I depart hence condemned by you to suffer the penalty of death, and they, too, go their ways condemned by the truth to suffer the penalty of villainy and wrong; and I must abide by my award — let them abide by theirs. I suppose that these things may be regarded as fated, — and I think that they are well.

And now, O men who have condemned me, I would fain[3] prophesy to you; for I am about to die, and that is the hour in which men are gifted with prophetic power. And I prophesy to you who are my murderers, that immediately after my death punishment far heavier than you have inflicted on me will surely await you. Me you have killed because you wanted to escape the accuser[4], and not to give an account of your lives. But that will not be as you suppose: far otherwise. For I say that there will be more accusers of you than there are now; accusers whom hitherto I have restrained: and as they are younger they will be more severe with you, and you will be more offended at them. For if you think that by killing men you can avoid the accuser censuring your lives, you are mistaken; that is not a way of escape which is either possible or honorable; the easiest and noblest way is not to be crushing others, but to be improving yourselves. This is the prophecy which I utter before my departure, to the judges who have condemned me.

Socrates calmly drinking hemlock

Friends, who would have acquitted me, I would like also to talk with you about this thing which has happened, while the magistrates are busy, and before I go to the place at which I must die. Stay then awhile, for we may as well talk with one another while there is time. You are my friends, and I should like to show you the meaning of this event which has happened to me. O my judges — for you I may truly call judges — I should like to tell you of a wonderful circumstance. Hitherto the familiar oracle within me has constantly been in the habit of opposing me even about trifles, if I was going to make a slip or error about anything; and now as you see there has come

---

1   **slower runner:** death
2   **faster runner:** unrighteousness
3   **fain:** with pleasure
4   **accuser:** Socrates

Heritage of Western Intellectual Tradition — A Sourcebook

upon me that which may be thought, and is generally believed to be, the last and worst evil. But the oracle made no sign of opposition, either as I was leaving my house and going out in the morning, or when I was going up into this court, or while I was speaking, at anything which I was going to say; and yet I have often been stopped in the middle of a speech; but now in nothing I either said or did touching this matter has the oracle opposed me. What do I take to be the explanation of this? I will tell you. I regard this as a proof that what has happened to me is a good, and that those of us who think that death is an evil are in error. This is a great proof to me of what I am saying, for the customary sign would surely have opposed me had I been going to evil and not to good.

Let us reflect in another way, and we shall see that there is great reason to hope that death is a good, for one of two things: — either death is a state of nothingness and utter unconsciousness, or, as men say, there is a change and migration of the soul from this world to another. Now if you suppose that there is no consciousness, but a sleep like the sleep of him who is undisturbed even by the sight of dreams, death will be an unspeakable gain. For if a person were to select the night in which his sleep was undisturbed even by dreams, and were to compare with this the other days and nights of his life, and then were to tell us how many days and nights he had passed in the course of his life better and more pleasantly than this one, I think that any man, I will not say a private man, but even the great king, will not find many such days or nights, when compared with the others.[1] Now if death is like this, I say that to die is gain; for eternity is then only a single night. But if death is the journey to another place, and there, as men say, all the dead are, what good, O my friends and judges, can be greater than this? If indeed when the pilgrim arrives in the world below, he is delivered from the professors of justice[2] in this world, and finds the true judges who are said to give judgment there, Minos and Rhadamanthus and Aeacus and Triptolemus,[3] and other sons of God who were righteous in their own life, that pilgrimage will be worth making. What would not a man give if he might converse with Orpheus and Musaeus and Hesiod and Homer[4]? Nay, if this be true, let me die again and again. I, too, shall have a wonderful interest in a place where I can converse with Palamedes, and Ajax the son of Telamon,[5] and other heroes of old, who have suffered death

---

1 **if a person were to select ... with the others:** Namely, compared with other days and nights, this undisturbed night (death) is obviously far better.

2 **the professors of justice:** namely, one who professed that he possesses justice

3 **Minos:** legendary ruler of Crete in Greek mythology. Minos was the son of Zeus, father of the gods, and of the princess Europa. He was widely considered a just ruler; **Rhadamanthus:** son of Zeus and Europa and brother of Minos; **Aeacus:** son of the nymph Aegina and Zeus, father of Peleus and grandfather of Achilles. Aeacus ruled over his people with such justice that after his death he became one of the three judges of the underworld; and **Triptolemus:** the original priest of the grain goddess Demeter.

4 **Orpheus:** in Greek mythology, poet and musician, son of the muse Calliope and Apollo, god of music, or Oeagrus, king of Thrace; **Hesiod (c. 800 BC):** Greek poet, who occupies a unique place in Greek literature both for his moral precepts and for his highly personal tone.

5 **Palamedes:** in Greek mythology, the inventor of writing; **Ajax:** mighty warrior in the Trojan War; **Telamon:** king of Salamís, the son of Aeacus, king of Aegina, and the father of the hero and warrior Ajax the Greater.

through an unjust judgment; and there will be no small pleasure, as I think, in comparing my own sufferings with theirs. Above all, I shall be able to continue my search into true and false knowledge; as in this world, so also in that; I shall find out who is wise, and who pretends to be wise, and is not. What would not a man give, O judges, to be able to examine the leader of the great Trojan expedition; or Odysseus or Sisyphus[1], or numberless others, men and women too! What infinite delight would there be in conversing with them and asking them questions! For in that world they do not put a man to death for this; certainly not. For besides being happier in that world than in this, they will be immortal, if what is said is true.

Wherefore, O judges, be of good cheer about death, and know this of a truth — that no evil can happen to a good man, either in life or after death. He and his are not neglected by the gods; nor has my own approaching end happened by mere chance. But I see clearly that to die and be released was better for me; and therefore the oracle gave no sign. For which reason also, I am not angry with my accusers, or my condemners; they have done me no harm, although neither of them meant to do me any good; and for this I may gently blame them.

Still I have a favor to ask of them. When my sons are grown up, I would ask you, O my friends, to punish them; and I would have you trouble them, as I have troubled you, if they seem to care about riches, or anything, more than about virtue; or if they pretend to be something when they are really nothing, — then reprove them, as I have reproved you, for not caring about that for which they ought to care, and thinking that they are something when they are really nothing. And if you do this, I and my sons will have received justice at your hands.

The hour of departure has arrived, and we go our ways — I to die, and you to live. Which is better God only knows.

Key Concepts

corrupting the youth	knowledge
force of eloquence	mission
gadfly	riddle
God of Delphi	truth
impiety	wisdom
justice	word of truth

---

1 **Sisyphus:** in Greek mythology, king of Corinth, son of Aeolus, king of Thessaly. Sisyphus saw the god Zeus carry off the beautiful maiden Aegina and told her father what he had witnessed. Enraged with Sisyphus, Zeus condemned him for eternity to roll to the top of a steep hill a stone that always rolled down again.

Plato: The Republic*

Plato (c. 428–c. 347 BC), Greek philosopher, second of the great trio of ancient Greeks, was born to an aristocratic family in Athens. The young man of political ambitions was disillusioned by the political leadership in Athens and eventually became a disciple of Socrates, whose death he witnessed. In 387 BC he established the Academy in Athens, the first "European university" where Aristotle studied and kings "sent for advice on laws and government." Like his master, Plato worked in dialogue form: philosophical ideas discussed and criticized in the context of a conversation or debate involving two or more persons. He wrote 35 such dialogues, following the pattern of "ignorance → assistance → questions → knowledge → beginning of wisdom." The ideas in these dialogues are Plato's, although Socrates is the main character. For Plato, knowledge should be certain and infallible, and genuinely real as contrasted with appearance. Hence his theory of Forms or Ideas arranged hierarchically, the supreme Form being Form of the Good. His ideal state is composed of three classes: merchant class, military class, philosopher-kings, determined by education that begins and ends with one's whole life. Plato's ideal educational system is so structured as to produce

philosopher-kings. Literature, therefore, has no place in Plato's state since artistic creation is rooted in inspired madness. His essentially antagonistic view of art and the artist, however, does allow for religious and moralistic kinds of art.

AND now, I said, let me show in a figure how far our nature is enlightened or unenlightened: — **Behold! Human beings living in an underground den, which has a mouth open towards the light and reaching all along the den; here they have been from their childhood, and have their legs and necks chained so that they cannot move, and can only see before them, being prevented by the chains from turning round their heads. Above and behind them a fire is blazing at a distance, and between the fire and the prisoners there is a raised way**; and you will see, if you look, a low wall built along the way, like the screen which marionette[1] players have in front of them, over which they show the puppets.

I see.

And do you see, I said, men passing along the wall carrying all sorts of vessels, and statues and figures of animals made of wood and stone and various materials, which appear over the

---

* Selected from Book VII where Socrates is speaking to Glaucon. Unlike Socrates, Plato's dialogues, more detailed and sophisticated, move beyond ethical questions (who are wise) into metaphysics and epistemology (nature of wisdom). It is probably because of this that the American transcendentalist Ralph Waldo Emerson (1803–1882) agreed with Omar Khayyam (c. 1050–1122): "Burn the libraries, for their value is in this book."

1 **marionette:** puppet moved by string on stage. Compare this with the modern leather silhouette or shadow play, where the movement of the artificial objects maneuvered by persons are projected onto a screen.

wall? Some of them are talking, others silent.

You have shown me a strange image, and they are strange prisoners.

Like ourselves, I replied; and they see only their own shadows, or the shadows of one another, which the fire throws on the opposite wall of the cave?

True, he said; how could they see anything but the shadows if they were never allowed to move their heads?

And of the objects which are being carried in like manner they would only see the shadows?

Yes, he said.

And if they were able to converse with one another, would they not suppose that they were naming what was actually before them?

Very true.

And suppose further that the prison had an echo which came from the other side, would they not be sure to fancy when one of the passers-by spoke that the voice which they heard came from the passing shadow?

No question, he replied.

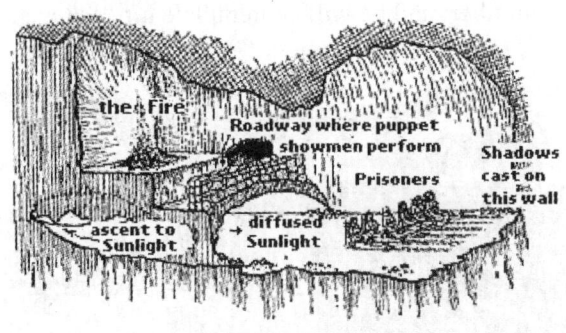

Plato's Cave

To them, I said, the truth would be literally nothing but the shadows of the images.

That is certain.

And now look again, and see what will naturally follow if the prisoners are released and disabused[1] of their error. At first, when any of them is liberated and compelled suddenly to stand up and turn his neck round and walk and look towards the light, he will suffer sharp pains; the glare will distress him, and he will be unable to see the realities of which in his former state he had seen the shadows; and then conceive some one saying to him, that what he saw before was an illusion, but that now, when he is approaching nearer to being and his eye is turned towards more real existence, he has a clearer vision, — what will be his reply? And you may further imagine that his instructor is pointing to the objects as they pass and requiring him to name them, — will he not be perplexed? Will he not fancy that the shadows which he formerly saw are truer than the objects which are now shown to him?

---

1 **disabuse:** correct

Far truer.

And if he is compelled to look straight at the light, will he not have a pain in his eyes which will make him turn away to take in the objects of vision which he can see, and which he will conceive to be in reality clearer than the things which are now being shown to him?

True, he now.

And suppose once more, that he is reluctantly dragged up a steep and rugged ascent, and held fast until he's forced into the presence of the sun himself, is he not likely to be pained and irritated? When he approaches the light his eyes will be dazzled, and he will not be able to see anything at all of what are now called realities.

Not all in a moment, he said.

He will require to grow accustomed to the sight of the upper world. And first he will see the shadows best, next the reflections of men and other objects in the water, and then the objects themselves; then he will gaze upon the light of the moon and the stars and the spangled heaven; and he will see the sky and the stars by night better than the sun or the light of the sun by day?

Certainly.

Last of all he will be able to see the sun, and not mere reflections of him in the water, but he will see him in his own proper place, and not in another; and he will contemplate him as he is.[1]

Certainly.

He will then proceed to argue that this is he[2] who gives the season and the years, and is the guardian of all that is in the visible world, and in a certain way the cause of all things which he and his fellows have been accustomed to behold?

Plato's underground den illustrated

Clearly, he said, he would first see the sun and then reason about him.

And when he remembered his old habitation, and the wisdom of the den and his fellow-prisoners, do you not suppose that he would felicitate himself on the change, and pity them?

Certainly, he would.

And if they were in the habit of conferring honours among themselves on those who were

---

1 **Last of all he will be … as he is.:** Here Plato alludes to the five stages of coming to terms with truth.
2 **he:** namely, the Sun

quickest to observe the passing shadows and to remark which of them went before, and which followed after, and which were together; and who were therefore best able to draw conclusions as to the future, do you think that he would care for such honours and glories, or envy the possessors of them? Would he not say with Homer, "Better to be the poor servant of a poor master, and to endure anything, rather than think as they do and live after their manner?"

Yes, he said, I think that he would rather suffer anything than entertain these false notions and live in this miserable manner.

Imagine once more, I said, such a one coming suddenly out of the sun to be replaced in his old situation; would he not be certain to have his eyes full of darkness?

To be sure, he said.

And if there were a contest, and he had to compete in measuring the shadows with the prisoners who had never moved out of the den, while his sight was still weak, and before his eyes had become steady (and the time which would be needed to acquire this new habit of sight might be very considerable) would he not be ridiculous? Men would say of him that up he went and down he came without his eyes; and that it was better not even to think of ascending; and if any one tried to loose another and lead him up to the light, let them only catch the offender, and they would put him to death[1].

No question, he said.

This entire allegory, I said, you may now append[2], dear Glaucon, to the previous argument; the prison-house is the world of sight, the light of the fire is the sun, and you will not misapprehend me if you interpret the journey upwards to be the ascent[3] of the soul into the intellectual world according to my poor belief, which, at your desire, I have expressed whether rightly or wrongly God knows. **But, whether true or false, my opinion is that in the world of knowledge the idea of good appears last of all, and is seen only with an effort; and, when seen, is also inferred to be the universal author of all things beautiful and right, parent of light and of the lord of light in this visible world, and the immediate source of reason and truth in the intellectual; and that this is the power upon which he who would act rationally, either in public or private life must have his eye fixed.**

I agree, he said, as far as I am able to understand you.

Moreover, I said, you must not wonder that those who attain to this beatific vision[4] are unwilling to descend to human affairs; for their souls are ever hastening into the upper world where they desire to dwell; which desire of theirs is very natural, if our allegory may be trusted.

---

1   **they would put him to death:** an allusion, probably, to the death of Socrates
2   **append:** add
3   **ascent:** climb, rise
4   **attain to this beatific vision:** arrive at this saintly revelation

Yes, very natural.

And is there anything surprising in one who passes from divine contemplations to the evil state of man, misbehaving himself in a ridiculous manner; if, while his eyes are blinking and before he has become accustomed to the surrounding darkness, he is compelled to fight in courts of law, or in other places, about the images or the shadows of images of justice, and is endeavouring to meet the conceptions of those who have never yet seen absolute justice?

Anything but surprising, he replied.

Anyone who has common sense will remember that the bewilderments of the eyes are of two kinds, and arise from two causes, either from coming out of the light or from going into the light, which is true of the mind's eye, quite as much as of the bodily eye; and he who remembers this when he sees any one whose vision is perplexed and weak, will not be too ready to laugh; he will first ask whether that soul of man has come out of the brighter light, and is unable to see because unaccustomed to the dark, or having turned from darkness to the day is dazzled by excess of light. And he will count the one happy in his condition and state of being, and he will pity the other; or, if he have a mind to laugh at the soul which comes from below into the light, there will be more reason in this than in the laugh which greets him who returns from above out of the light into the den[1].

That, he said, is a very just distinction.

But then, if I am right, certain professors of education must be wrong when they say that they can put a knowledge into the soul which was not there before, like sight into blind eyes.

They undoubtedly say this, he replied.

Whereas, our argument shows that the power and capacity of learning exists in the soul already[2]; and that just as the eye was unable to turn from darkness to light without the whole body, so too the instrument of knowledge can only by the movement of the whole soul be turned from the world of becoming into that of being, and learn by degrees to endure the sight of being, and of the brightest and best of being, or in other words, of the good.

Very true.

And must there not be some art which will effect conversion in the easiest and quickest manner; not implanting the faculty of sight, for that exists already, but has been turned in the wrong direction, and is looking away from the truth?

Yes, he said, such an art may be presumed.

---

1   **or, if he have a mind ... into the den:** Comparatively he who laughs when seeing a soul coming from darkness into the light will be more justifiable.

2   **the power and capacity of learning exists in the soul already:** Compare with Socrates, who has the same belief in man's knowledge within, to be brought out by "midwives" like himself.

And whereas the other so-called virtues of the soul seem to be akin to bodily qualities, for even when they are not originally innate[1] they can be implanted later by habit and exercise, wisdom more than anything else contains a divine element which always remains, and by this conversion is rendered useful and profitable; or, on the other hand, hurtful and useless. Did you never observe the narrow intelligence flashing from the keen eye of a clever rogue[2] — how eager he is, how clearly his paltry[3] soul sees the way to his end; he is the reverse of blind, but his keen eyesight is forced into the service of evil, and he is mischievous in proportion to his cleverness.

Very true, he said.

But what if there had been a circumcision[4] of such natures in the days of their youth; and they had been severed from those sensual pleasures, such as eating and drinking, which, like leaden weights, were attached to them at their birth, and which drag them down and turn the vision of their souls upon the things that are below — if, I say, they had been released from these impediments and turned in the opposite direction, the very same faculty in them would have seen the truth as keenly as they see what their eyes are turned to now.

Very likely.

Yes, I said; and there is another thing which is likely. Or rather a necessary inference from what has preceded, that neither the uneducated and uninformed of the truth, nor yet those who never make an end of their education, will be able ministers of State; not the former, because they have no single aim of duty which is the rule of all their actions, private as well as public; nor the latter, because they will not act at all except upon compulsion, fancying that they are already dwelling apart in the islands of the blest.

Very true, he replied.

Then, I said, the business of us who are the founders of the State will be to compel the best minds to attain that knowledge which we have already shown to be the greatest of all — they must continue to ascend until they arrive at the good; but when they have ascended and seen enough we must not allow them to do as they do now.

What do you mean?

I mean that they remain in the upper world: but this must not be allowed; they must be made to descend again among the prisoners in the den, and partake of[5] their labours and honours, whether they are worth having or not.

---

1   **innate:** inborn, inherent
2   **rogue:** rascal
3   **paltry:** worthless, contemptible
4   **circumcision:** surgical removal of the foreskin of males, here act of separation
5   **partake of:** take part in, become involved with

But is not this unjust? He said; ought we to give them a worse life, when they might have a better?

You have again forgotten, my friend, I said, the intention of the legislator, who did not aim at making any one class in the State happy above the rest; the happiness was to be in the whole State, and he held the citizens together by persuasion and necessity, making them benefactors of the State, and therefore benefactors of one another; to this end he created them, not to please themselves, but to be his instruments in binding up the State.

True, he said, I had forgotten.

Observe, Glaucon, that there will be no injustice in compelling our philosophers to have a care and providence[1] of others; we shall explain to them that in other States, men of their class are not obliged to share in the toils of politics: and this is reasonable, for they grow up at their own sweet will, and the government would rather not have them. Being self-taught, they cannot be expected to show any gratitude for a culture which they have never received. But we have brought you into the world to be rulers of the hive, kings of yourselves and of the other citizens, and have educated you far better and more perfectly than they have been educated, and you are better able to share in the double duty. **Wherefore each of you, when his turn comes, must go down to the general underground abode, and get the habit of seeing in the dark. When you have acquired the habit, you will see ten thousand times better than the inhabitants of the den, and you will know what the several images are, and what they represent, because you have seen the beautiful and just and good in their truth. And thus our State which is also yours will be a reality, and not a dream only, and will be administered in a spirit unlike that of other States, in which men fight with one another about shadows only and are distracted in the struggle for power, which in their eyes is a great good[2]. Whereas the truth is that the State in which the rulers are most reluctant to govern is always the best and most quietly governed, and the State in which they are most eager, the worst[3].**

Quite true, he replied.

And will our pupils, when they hear this, refuse to take their turn at the toils of State, when they are allowed to spend the greater part of their time with one another in the heavenly light?

---

1   **providence:** careful preparation for the future
2   **men fight with … is a great good:** Compare this idea of shadow with Taoist conceptions of emptiness, though the argument behind may be very different.
3   **the State in which … the worst:** Also compare the Daoist idea of good governance ("*wuwei*"), the 18th century liberalism (Adam Smith's hands off policy in Unit 10) and the idea of "he governs best who governs least" in the 19th century transcendentalism.

Impossible, he answered; for they are just men, and the commands which we impose upon them are just; there can be no doubt that every one of them will take office as a stern necessity, and not after the fashion of our present rulers of State.

Yes, my friend, I said; and there lies the point. You must contrive for your future rulers another and a better life than that of a ruler, and then you may have a well-ordered State; for only in the State which offers this, will they rule who are truly rich, not in silver and gold, but in virtue and wisdom, which are the true blessings of life. Whereas if they go to the administration of public affairs, poor and hungering after their own private advantage, thinking that hence they are to snatch the chief good, order there can never be[1]; for they will be fighting about office, and the civil and domestic broils[2] which thus arise will be the ruin of the rulers themselves and of the whole State.

Most true, he replied.

Key Concepts

allegory

becoming/being/the good

darkness and light

education

eyes and vision

knowledge

puppet show

shadows

underground den

Compare with China

1. Axial Age

Karl Jaspers[3] created the term "Axial Age" of human civilization for the period 800–200 BC exemplified by the world's greatest spiritual leaders in *The Origin and Goal of History*:

The most extraordinary events are concentrated in this period. Confucius and Lao-tse were living in China, all the schools of Chinese philosophy came into being, including

---

1 **order there can never be:** there can never be order

2 **broil:** quarrel

3 **Karl Jaspers (1883–1969):** German philosopher and one of the originators of existentialism, whose work influenced modern theology and psychiatry as well as philosophy.

Heritage of Western Intellectual Tradition   A Sourcebook

those of Mo-ti（墨子）, Chuang-tse（庄子）, Lieh-tsu（列子）and a host of others; India produced the Upanishads（《奥义书》）and Buddha（佛陀）and, like China, ran the whole gamut of philosophical possibilities down to scepticism, to materialism, sophism and nihilism（虚无主义）; in Iran Zarathustra（琐罗亚斯德）taught a challenging view of the world as a struggle between good and evil; in Palestine the prophets made their appearance, from Elijah（以利亚）, by way of Isaiah（以赛亚）and Jeremiah（耶利米）to Deutero-Isaiah（以赛亚后续者）; Greece witnessed the appearance of Homer, of the Philosophers — Parmenides（巴门尼德）, Heraclitus（赫拉克利特）and Plato — of the tragedians, Thucydides（修昔底德）and Archimedes（阿基米德）. Everything implied by these names developed during these few centuries almost simultaneously in China, India, and the West, without any one of these regions knowing of the others.

Please review what you have read and learned about Confucius, Mencius and Lao-tse and make comparisons with Socrates, Plato and Aristotle.

What do you have to say about such coincidences in history?

What are the major similarities and differences among those great thinkers of human civilization?

2. 苏格拉底与孔子的言说方式比较

This is a comparison, from the perspective of a Chinese scholar, between the discourses of Socrates and Confucius, the two founding fathers of philosophy in the two great civilizations. There tends to be misinterpretation whenever East and West are brought together, but what is more important is your own findings through such a comparison.

　　苏格拉底常被誉为"西方的孔子"，而且与孔子一样，也没有留下自己亲自撰写的著作，而只有由弟子们所记述的言论；在孔子，这是由于他"述而不作"，在苏格拉底则是由于他认为自己的使命是通过谈话启发人们去关心和思考真理、追求智慧；两人都以口头对话的形式阐述了自己的思想，且都把关注的重点集中于伦理道德问题。孔子和苏格拉底可说是中西方传统言说标准的确立者。然而，苏格拉底把言说的标准最终确立于言说本身，孔子则把言说标准放在言说之外，从而最终取消了言说的标准。

　　在言说的性质上，只有苏格拉底对话才真正具有对话的性质，孔子的对话其实并不是真正的对话，而是类似于"教义问答"的权威对话和独白，问者所起的作用只是提起话头和等待教导。与孔子在对话中的"诲人不倦"的"答疑解惑者"形象不同，苏格拉底在对话中多半是以提问者的身份出现，他的对手才是问题的解释者和回答者。但全部对话的灵魂恰好是提问者而不是回答者，是针对回答的提问才使问题变得更清楚了。然而，苏格拉底并不以全知者自居，有一种开放的心态。所以在对话中并没有任何预设的前提，一个问题将引出什么样的回答并不是预先策划好的，而是临场发挥的，只有话语本身的逻辑在把言谈导向某个越来越清晰的方向。苏格拉底相信，话语有其自身的标准(逻各斯)，但这标准不是他所独有的，而是人人固有的理性，这理性即使是他自己一个人所发现和自觉到的，也要由别人嘴里说出的话语来证实其普遍性。

与此相反，孔子虽然并不认为自己"生而知之"，而是"学而知之"，但在对话中，他是以"学成者"的身分高居于他人之上的，而对学生，凡是需要知道的他全知道，凡是他不知道的都是不必知道的。他教导学生说："诲女知之乎！知之为知之，不知为不知，是知也"，但至少他认为自己所知的那一点是不可怀疑的，必须"笃信好学，守死善道"，却从未考虑过是否会有自以为知其实却并不知的情况，后面这种情况正是苏格拉底对自己的知和那些号称有知识的人("智者")的知都抱怀疑态度的根本原因；所以孔子的"知其不知"与苏格拉底的"自知其无知"本质上是完全不同的，后者是对自己已有的知的一种反思态度，它导致把对话作为双方一起探求真知识的过程，前者则把对话看作传播已知知识的场所。孔子对自己也不知的东西的确是坦然承认的，但那只是因为他不认为这些知识是必须知道的。(自邓晓芒，有删节)

Supplementary Reading

The following essay tries to tell us that the death of Socrates is to be understood in its original context, which the author tries to present and explain to his readers. Things were more complicated 2500 years ago in Athens, the essay says, than what we tend to take it today. However, the grandeur of Socrates as a man of thinker is by no means diminished, even though his conviction was "justifiable," as the essay seems to explain.

雅典凭什么判苏格拉底死刑

公元前三九九年，哲学家苏格拉底被雅典的一个人民法庭判处死刑。其时，雅典人正在装点海船，准备次日前往提洛岛祭祀阿波罗神。

传说当初雅典王子提修斯自愿作为七对被迫献给米诺牛的雅典童男童女之一，前往克里特岛，决心解脱强加在雅典人身上的诅咒。在临行之前，雅典人许愿说，如若他们安全返还，将每年前往提洛岛祭祀阿波罗神。对此种神圣的宗教祭祀活动，城邦依例认真对待。为确保城市洁净，一律暂缓处决死囚。苏格拉底乃被投入监狱，等待祭祀结束后处决。其间，弟子们轮流探监，陪伴老师度过最后的日子。于是，便有了柏拉图记载苏氏狱中言论的那几篇著名的对话录。约摸一个月后，这位年已七旬的哲人遣退妻儿，在众位弟子面前饮下毒鸩，从容就死。

在苏格拉底一案中，一方是追求真理、舍生取义的伟大哲人，另一方则是以民主自由为标榜、被视为民主政治源头的雅典城邦。孰是孰非，谁善谁恶，不那么泾渭分明，成了现代人心里一个难以解开的结。

　　然而，对雅典人来说，这桩案子根本就不成为一个问题，因为整个案件完全是依照雅典城邦的法律来审判的。起诉苏格拉底的三人都是雅典公民，以美莱特斯为首，依法提起公诉。审判的程序同样复杂而民主。不同于现代，雅典的法庭不设法官，只设主持官，负责组织审判并维持法庭的秩序，判决的权力则在陪审团。陪审团成员从公民群体中抽签产生。审判苏格拉底一案的陪审团由五百人组成，显然不是一件什么了不起的大案。较大的案件会有多达二千人的陪审团，而重大的案件则往往由公民大会直接审判。

　　法庭上的审判同样不同于现代，先是由原告和被告分别为自己辩护，并进行举证。之后陪审团举行第一次投票，决定被告是否有罪。如果被告获得的票数占多数，他即获得清白之名。但案子并未就此完结，还要看原告获得票数的多寡。如果他获得的票数不到总票数的五分之一，就要遭到处罚。这条措施是为了防止有人恶意诬告。如若出现有罪和无罪的票数相等的情况，则被告无罪释放。如果判定被告有罪，则由原告和被告本人分别提出具体的刑罚，再由陪审团投票选取其中之一作为最终的判罚。苏格拉底在第一轮投票中以二百八十票对二百二十票被判有罪，随后提出的对自己的处罚又近乎玩笑，先是说自己非但无罪，反而于城邦有功，理应得到城邦的礼遇，后又提出罚款一百德拉克玛了事。由于此一刑罚太不合情理，反而迫使部分本来同情他的陪审员转向选择原告提出的刑罚，最后以三百六十票对一百四十票被判死刑。

　　用现代人的眼光来看，苏格拉底的罪名似乎是莫须有的，没有确凿的犯罪行为，其言论也没有导致直接的伤害。但在雅典，对犯罪行为的认定不同于现代。无论什么指控，无论犯罪行为是否确凿，也无论是否造成直接的伤害，只要陪审团投票认定，罪名即告成立。

　　因为唯一的标准是陪审团的投票，又没有权威的刑侦机构对事实进行科学的甄别，所以当事人的辩护就变得至关重要。辩护辞往往都是事先写好的，或自己写的，或请专业的高手代写的。于是，法庭辩护就成了演说术的一个重要组成部分。这些辩辞不仅讨论案件本身，而且往往对自己的贡献或品德大大夸耀一番，以博得陪审团的同情。

　　或许又有人会问，对于像苏格拉底这样一位大哲学家，雅典人似乎没有表现出应有的对权威人士的尊敬，仅以区区罪名，即判以极刑。殊不知，在雅典是不存在任何个人权威的。既没有知识的权威，也没有道德的权威，甚至没有政治的权威。唯有一个权威，那就是人民的权威。苏格拉底虽然是一位名人，但他的名气更多地来自于他的怪诞。在喜剧家阿里斯托芬的笔下《云》一剧），苏格拉底在空中行走，行动怪异。他的哲学不过是诡辩之术。现实中的苏格拉底也许并非如此，但阿里斯托芬的喜剧则是在雅典最大节日之一的戏剧节上隆重上演，到场观看的雅典人多达近二万人，无疑会给许多的雅典人留下深刻的印象，无疑会影响到时隔二十四年之后的审判。

　　对苏格拉底的审判，当然还有一个更为深层的原因。古代希腊的民主政治同现代世界形形色色的民主政治殊为不同。在古希腊文中，"民主政治"（demokratia）一词由"人民"（demos）和"统治"（kratos）复合而成。显而易见，民主政治即人民的统治，强调的是公民的广泛参与和直接管理，以及公民在政治生活中近乎绝对的平等权利。值得注意的是，"人民"是一个集合名词，它体现作为一个整体的公民群体，个人完全被隐去了。在现代的民主政治中，个体一面从属于群体，一面却享有作为个体的独立性，享有自由。但在古希腊，个体是完全从属于群体的，群体的意志和利益高于其它一切，为此可以牺牲个体的利益和权利。雅典一条独特的法律即最好地说明了这一点。依法雅典人每年可以放逐一位政治领袖，由公民大会投票选出。因以破碎陶片充作选票，而得名"陶片放逐法"。投票时只要在陶片上刻上名字即可。无需过失，也无需罪行，只要获得票数超过六千，即遭流放。

　　如果以现代人的眼光看，这纯属对个人自由与权利的践踏。但在雅典，像底米斯托克利等一批最著名的政治家都在流放之列。这就是说，在古代希腊，个人是没有现代意义上的自由的。既没有脱离群体的自由，也没有言论的自由。苏格拉底的言论明确表示出他对"人民"这个群体的轻蔑，想要同它保持距离。同时在"人民"看来，他的言行实际上已经造成了某种伤害，因为他的弟子参与了推翻民主政治的活动。他的被处死，其实在情理之中。(自黄洋，有删节)

Questions for Discussion

1. What is Socrates' way of argument?
2. Why is this "way" of argument influential to late-comers, especially to sceptics?
3. What is knowledge, according to Plato?
4. Based on the teaching of the Allegory of the Cave, what can we do that is analogous to turning our heads and seeing the causes of the shadows? What is necessary for us to achieve this reflective understanding?
5. Comment on the importance of the idea of "Form".
6. How does Plato look upon "politics"?
7. What are the qualities of a Ruler, according to Plato?
8. Do you see any similarity between the wisdom of the Greek sages and that of the Chinese?

Heritage of Western Intellectual Tradition　A Sourcebook

UNIT 3

Greek & Roman Sages (2)

Pretest

- What do you know about Aristotle, last of the great trio of the ancient Greek philosophers?
- What is the significance of the Roman thinkers at the time?
- Do you see any connection between the ancient Greek and Roman civilizations?

What You Will Learn in This Unit

- One more of the great ancient Greek philosopher, Aristotle and the Roman orator Cicero;
- Their ideas concerning man, nature, and political system; and
- The "Great Mean" in ancient Greece and China.

Learn to Pronounce

Aeneas /ɪˈniːəs/ 埃涅阿斯

Antony /ˈæntənɪ/ 安东尼

aristocracy /ˌærɪsˈtɒkrəsɪ/ 贵族统治

Aristotle /ˈærɪstɒtl/ 亚里士多德

Caesar /ˈsiːzə/ 凯撒

Cicero /ˈsɪsərəʊ/ 西赛罗

Hellenic /heˈliːnɪk/ 希腊人的

Homer /ˈhəʊmə/ 荷马

Lyceum /laɪˈsɪəm/ 逍遥学派

Macedonia /ˌmæsɪˈdəʊnɪə/ 马其顿王国

Octavian /ɒkˈteɪvɪən/ 屋大维

oligarchy /ˈɒlɪgɑːkɪ/ 寡头统治

oratory /ˈɒrətərɪ/ 演讲术

Peripatetic /ˌperɪpəˈtetɪk/ 逍遥学校

Pompey /ˈpɒmpɪ/ 庞培

Remus /ˈriːməs/ 瑞摩斯

rhetoric /ˈretərɪk/ 修辞学

Romulus /ˈrɒmjʊləs/ 罗穆卢斯

Introduction

Like Plato, Aristotle took form as a distinguishing property of objects, but, unlike Plato, he seemed to be much more interested in this form as an independent existence apart from the objects in which it is found. Hence the meticulous studies he had made on concrete objects of his interest, as may be found in his discussion of forms of government in the following excerpt. His material universe consists of four elements, fire, air, earth, and water, plus a fifth, the constituent of the heavenly bodies "above" the moon. The intuitive(直觉的)hypotheses of the ancient Greeks foreshadowed many theories of modern science, and many of their moral ideas have been incorporated into Chris-

By 100 BC, Roman culture slowly took hold in many of Rome's conquered territories. The Temple of Jupiter in Lebanon was built after the Romans took control in 64 BC.

tian moral doctrine. Their political ideas influenced modern political leaders, too.

The city-states of ancient Greece fell to Roman conquerors in 146 BC. Roman myth traces Rome's origins to Romulus, son of Mars and descendent of Aeneas, who brought his people to Italy after the city of Troy burned. Romulus and his twin brother Remus were thrown into the Tiber by their grand uncle, but were washed ashore and suckled by a she-wolf who became the symbol of Rome. Romulus and Remus founded Rome in 753 BC, and Romulus killed Remus to become the city's first king, giving it his name. By 338 BC, two years before Alexander the Great became the king, the Roman Republic (from the Latin *res publica*, or "that which belongs to the people") had conquered her Latin neighbours to grow from a small city of 10,000 into a great cosmopolitan metropolis of 1 million whose empire of 15 million subjects encompassed the entire Mediterranean basin, thanks to its professional, highly-trained, rigorously disciplined citizen-soldiers. The Romans invaded Greece in 197 BC and two years later placed Greek cities under Roman protection. The Roman world contributed Jesus to Western civilization, but an equally important contribution is the Roman laws, military art, and civil administration. Both the empire and the church led the Western world. But the success of Roman imperialism also brought in the century of civil war that destroyed the Republic. Cicero fought valiantly for 20 years to stabilize the government and preserve the Republic by bringing responsible citizens together against dangerous demagogues and potential military tyrants. In the end, however, he failed.

Aristotle: The Politics*

Aristotle (384–322 BC), Greek philosopher and scientist, son of a physician to the royal court, was

---

* Aristotle abandoned Platonic dialogues as the style is too restrictive, to favour expository treatises with greater intellectual intensity and logical intricacy. He emphasizes more on definition, like what he is doing in this treatise on politics, which, based on his study of 158 constitutions of Greek city-states, argues for constitutional government and respect for law, a combination of aristocracy and democracy.

born at Stagira in Macedonia. At 17 he went to Athens to study at Plato's Academy, and remained there for about 20 years, first as student and then as teacher, the "mind" of the Academy, as Plato called him. In 345 BC he went to Pella, the Macedonian capital, to be the tutor for the king's young son Alexander, later known as Alexander the Great. He returned to Athens in 335 BC to establish his own school, the Lyceum, or Peripatetic ("walking" or "strolling") school with spacious gardens. Aristotle is an erudite man, and his thought covers wide areas like logic, epistemology, metaphysics, ethics, physics, biology, zoology, psychology, literary theory, and politics. Hence Darwin's remark that the intellectual heroes of his own time "were mere schoolboys compared to old Aristotle." One greatest difference between Aristotle and Plato is that, to use an analogy, one stresses on biology whereas the other on mathematics. That is, Aristotle studies the "built-in specific pattern" of each individual in its development and growth toward proper self-realization as a specimen of its type. Science studies general kinds, but these kinds find their existence in particular individuals. Science and philosophy, therefore, must balance. With the fall of the Roman Empire, most of Aristotle's works were lost in the West, and others were preserved by Arabic, Syriac, and Jewish scholars. In the 13th century, the Latin West renewed its interest in Aristotle, and St. Thomas Aquinas found in it a philosophical foundation for Christian thought. And by the end of the 17th century, Western culture was almost "entirely Aristotelian." Aristotle wrote 170 books, 47 of which still exist more than two thousand years later.

BOOK I

Every state is a community of some kind, and every community is established with a view to some good; for mankind always act in order to obtain that which they think good. But, if all communities aim at some good, the state or political community, which is the highest of all, and which embraces all the rest, aims at good in a greater degree than any other, and at the highest good.

Some people think that the qualifications of a statesman, king, householder, and master are the same, and that they differ, not in kind, but only in the number of their subjects. For example, the ruler over a few is called a master; over more, the manager of a household; over a still larger number, a statesman or king, as if there were no difference between a great household and a small state. The distinction which is made between the king and the statesman is as follows: When the government is personal, the ruler is a king; when, according to the rules of the political science, the citizens rule and are ruled in turn, then he is called a statesman.

But all this is a mistake; for governments differ in kind, as will be evident to any one who considers the matter according to the method which has hitherto guided us[1]. As in other depart-

---

1   **according to the method which has hitherto guided us:** Aristotle is known for a special method he developed, the deductive (演绎的) reasoning with a system of syllogistic logic (三段论): two valid propositions (the major and minor premises 大小前提) give rise to a third and equally valid proposition (the conclusion). This deductive method was picked up by theologians in the Middle Ages as the basis of Scholasticism (see Unit 4), to be replaced in Renaissance with a more inductive (归纳的) method developed by people like Francis Bacon and René Descartes (see Unit 7). And the interest in "method" reached a peak in the 20th century.

ments of science, so in politics, the compound should always be resolved into the simple elements or least parts of the whole. We must therefore look at the elements of which the state is composed, in order that we may see in what the different kinds of rule differ from one another, and whether any scientific result can be attained about each one of them.[1]

He who thus considers things in their first growth and origin, whether a state or anything else, will obtain the clearest view of them. In the first place there must be a union of those who cannot exist without each other; namely, of male and female, that the race may continue (and this is a union which is formed, not of deliberate purpose, but because, in common with other animals and with plants, mankind have a natural desire to leave behind them an image of themselves), and of natural ruler and subject, that both may be preserved. For that which can foresee by the exercise of mind is by nature intended to be lord and master, and that which can with its body give effect to such foresight is a subject, and by nature a slave; hence master and slave have the same interest.[2] Now nature has distinguished between the female and the slave. For she is not niggardly[3], like the smith who fashions the Delphian knife[4] for many uses; she makes each thing for a single use, and every instrument is best made when intended for one and not for many uses. But among barbarians no distinction is made between women and slaves, because there is no natural ruler among them: they are a community of slaves, male and female. Wherefore the poets say,

It is meet that Hellenes should rule over barbarians;

as if they thought that the barbarian and the slave were by nature one.

Out of these two relationships between man and woman, master and slave, the first thing to arise is the family, and Hesiod is right when he says,

First house and wife and an ox for the plough,

Socrates and Plato

for the ox is the poor man's slave. The family is the association established by nature for the supply of men's everyday wants, and the members of it are called by Charondas[5] "companions of the cupboard," and by Epimenides the Cretan[6], "companions of the manger[7]." But when several families are united, and the association

---

1 **We must therefore ... one of them.:** Compare with Plato's *Republic* to see the different ways in which a state is being studied, which may help to illustrate the differences between the two Greek philosophers.

2 **For that which ... the same interest.:** Aristotle is criticized for his idea of slavery as natural rather than cultural, although it may not be fair to expect him to think otherwise (cf. the Confucian idea of a ruler who exercises his mind 劳心者治人).

3 **niggardly:** giving unwillingly

4 **Delphian knife:** an instrument that could serve other purposes than that of a knife

5 **Charondas:** a 6th century BC Sicilian lawgiver, whose laws were admired by Aristotle

6 **Epimenides the Cretan:** a 6th century BC philosopher, known for his famous utterance, "All Cretans are liars," which gave rise to a paradox — As he himself was a Cretan, he would be a liar if he were telling the truth.

7 **manger:** long box for horses to feed from

aims at something more than the supply of daily needs, the first society to be formed is the village. And the most natural form of the village appears to be that of a colony from the family, composed of the children and grandchildren, who are said to be suckled "with the same milk." And this is the reason why Hellenic states were originally governed by kings; because the Hellenes were under royal rule before they came together, as the barbarians still are. Every family is ruled by the eldest, and therefore in the colonies of the family the kingly form of government prevailed because they were of the same blood. As Homer says:

Each one gives law to his children and to his wives.

For they lived dispersedly, as was the manner in ancient times. Wherefore men say that the Gods have a king, because they themselves either are or were in ancient times under the rule of a king. For they imagine, not only the forms of the Gods, but their ways of life to be like their own.

When several villages are united in a single complete community, large enough to be nearly or quite self-sufficing, the state comes into existence, originating in the bare needs of life, and continuing in existence for the sake of a good life. And therefore, if the earlier forms of society are natural, so is the state, for it is the end of them, and the nature of a thing is its end. For what each thing is when fully developed, we call its nature, whether we are speaking of a man, a horse, or a family. Besides, the final cause and end of a thing is the best, and to be self-sufficing is the end and the best.

...

Hence it is evident that the state is a creation of nature, and that man is by nature a political animal[1]. And he who by nature and not by mere accident is without a state, is either a bad man or above humanity; he is like the

Tribeless, lawless, hearthless one,

whom Homer denounces — the natural outcast is forthwith a lover of war; he may be compared to an isolated piece at draughts.

Now, that man is more of a political animal than bees or any other gregarious[2] animals is evident. Nature, as we often say, makes nothing in vain, and man is the only animal whom she has endowed with the gift of speech. And whereas mere voice is but an indication of pleasure or pain, and is therefore found in other animals (for their nature attains to the perception of pleasure and pain and the intimation of them to one another, and no further), the power of speech is intended to set forth the expedient[3] and inexpedient, and therefore likewise the just and the unjust. And it is a characteristic of man that he alone has any sense of good and evil, of just and unjust,

---

1   **man is by nature a political animal:** This is an often quoted statement, though what Aristotle means may be different from its present day usage.

2   **gregarious:** living in company with others

3   **expedient:** useful

and the like, and the association of living beings who have this sense makes a family and a state.

Further, the state is by nature clearly prior to the family and to the individual, since the whole is of necessity prior to the part; for example, if the whole body be destroyed, there will be no foot or hand, except in an equivocal sense, as we might speak of a stone hand[1]; for when destroyed the hand will be no better than that. But things are defined by their working and power; and we ought not to say that they are the same when they no longer have their proper quality, but only that they have the same name. The proof that the state is a creation of nature and prior to the individual is that the individual, when isolated, is not self-sufficing; and therefore he is like a part in relation to the whole. But he who is unable to live in society, or who has no need because he is sufficient for himself, must be either a beast or a god: he is no part of a state. **A social instinct is implanted in all men by nature, and yet he who first founded the state was the greatest of benefactors. For man, when perfected, is the best of animals, but, when separated from law and justice, he is the worst of all; since armed injustice is the more dangerous, and he is equipped at birth with arms, meant to be used by intelligence and virtue, which he may use for the worst ends. Wherefore, if he has not virtue, he is the most unholy and the most savage of animals, and the most full of lust and gluttony[2]. But justice is the bond of men in states, for the administration of justice, which is the determination of what is just, is the principle of order in political society.**[3]

...

BOOK III

Having determined these questions, we have next to consider whether there is only one form of government or many, and if many, what they are, and how many, and what are the differences between them.

A constitution is the arrangement of magistracies[4] in a state, especially of the highest of all. The government is everywhere sovereign in the state, and the constitution is in fact the government. For example, in democracies the people are supreme, but in oligarchies, the few; and, therefore, we say that these two forms of government also are different: and so in other cases.

First, let us consider what is the purpose of a state, and how many forms of government there are by which human society is regulated. We have already said, in the first part of this treatise, when discussing household management and the rule of a master, that **man is by nature a political animal. And therefore, men, even when they do not require one another's help,**

---

1 **stone hand:** namely, not hand of a body or person
2 **gluttony:** habit of eating and drinking more than is needed
3 **But justice is the bond ... in political society.:** Aristotle is obviously one of the first political scientists, if we compare him with, say Machiavelli and Hobbes (see Unit 5 and Unit 9), in terms of state and politics.
4 **magistracy:** area for civil administration

desire to live together; not but that they are also brought together by their common interests in proportion as they severally[1] attain to any measure of well-being. This is certainly the chief end, both of individuals and of states. And also for the sake of mere life (in which there is possibly some noble element so long as the evils of existence do not greatly overbalance the good) **mankind meet together and maintain the political community. And we all see that men cling to life even at the cost of enduring great misfortune, seeming to find in life a natural sweetness and happiness.**

There is no difficulty in distinguishing the various kinds of authority; they have been often defined already in discussions outside the school. The rule of a master, although the slave by nature and the master by nature have in reality the same interests, is nevertheless exercised primarily with a view to the interest of the master, but accidentally considers the slave, since, if the slave perish, the rule of the master perishes with him. On the other hand, the government of a wife and children and of a household, which we have called household

Raphael's School of Athens (ca. 1510)

management, is exercised in the first instance for the good of the governed or for the common good of both parties, but essentially for the good of the governed, as we see to be the case in medicine, gymnastic (训练), and the arts in general, which are only accidentally concerned with the good of the artists themselves. For there is no reason why the trainer may not sometimes practice gymnastics, and the helmsman[2] is always one of the crew. The trainer or the helmsman considers the good of those committed to his care. But, when he is one of the persons taken care of, he accidentally participates in the advantage, for the helmsman is also a sailor, and the trainer becomes one of those in training. And so in politics: when the state is framed upon the principle of equality and likeness, the citizens think that they ought to hold office by turns. Formerly, as is natural, every one would take his turn of service; and then again, somebody else would look after his interest, just as he, while in office, had looked after theirs. But nowadays, for the sake of the advantage which is to be gained from the public revenues (税收) and from office, men want to be always in office. One might imagine that the rulers, being sickly, were only kept in health while they continued in office; in that case we may be sure that they would be hunting after places. The conclusion is evident: that governments which have a regard to the common interest are constituted in accordance with strict principles of justice, and are therefore true forms; but those which regard only the interest of the rulers are all defective and perverted forms, for they are despotic, whereas a state is a community of freemen.

Having determined these points, we have next to consider how many forms of government there are, and what they are; and in the first place what are the true forms, for when they are

---

1 **severally:** respectively

2 **helmsman:** man at the wheel to direct the course of a ship

determined the perversions of them will at once be apparent. The words constitution and government have the same meaning, and the government, which is the supreme authority in states, must be in the hands of one, or of a few, or of the many. The true forms of government, therefore, are those in which the one, or the few, or the many, govern with a view to the common interest; but governments which rule with a view to the private interest, whether of the one or of the few, or of the many, are perversions. For the members of a state, if they are truly citizens, ought to participate in its advantages. Of forms of government in which one rules, we call that which regards the common interests, kingship or royalty; that in which more than one, but not many, rule, aristocracy; and it is so called, either because the rulers are the best men, or because they have at heart the best interests of the state and of the citizens. But when the citizens at large administer the state for the common interest, the government is called by the generic name — a constitution. And there is a reason for this use of language. One man or a few may excel in virtue; but as the number increases it becomes more difficult for them to attain perfection in every kind of virtue, though they may in military virtue, for this is found in the masses. Hence in a constitutional government the fighting-men have the supreme power, and those who possess arms are the citizens.

Of the above-mentioned forms, the perversions are as follows: of royalty, tyranny; of aristocracy, oligarchy[1]; of constitutional government, democracy[2]. For tyranny is a kind of monarchy which has in view the interest of the monarch only; oligarchy has in view the interest of the wealthy; democracy, of the needy: none of them the common good of all.

But there are difficulties about these forms of government, and it will therefore be necessary to state a little more at length the nature of each of them. For he who would make a philosophical study of the various sciences, and does not regard practice only, ought not to overlook or omit anything, but to set forth the truth in every particular. Tyranny, as I was saying, is monarchy exercising the rule of a master over the political society; oligarchy is when men of property have the government in their hands; democracy, the opposite, when the indigent[3], and not the men of property, are the rulers. And here arises the first of our difficulties, and it relates to the distinction drawn. For democracy is said to be the government of the many. But what if the many are men of property and have the power in their hands? In like manner oligarchy is said to be the government of the few; but what if the poor are fewer than the rich, and have the power in their hands because they are stronger? In these cases the distinction which we have drawn between these different forms of government would no longer hold good.

Suppose, once more, that we add wealth to the few and poverty to the many, and name the governments accordingly — an oligarchy is said to be that in which the few and the wealthy, and a democracy that in which the many and the poor are the rulers — there will still be a difficulty. For, if the only forms of government are the ones already mentioned, how shall we describe

---

1   **oligarchy:** government by a small group of all-powerful people
2   **democracy:** Here the idea of democracy, as we shall see, carries a negative implication.
3   **indigent:** the poor

Heritage of Western Intellectual Tradition   A Sourcebook

those other governments also just mentioned by us, in which the rich are the more numerous and the poor are the fewer, and both govern in their respective states?

The argument seems to show that, whether in oligarchies or in democracies, the number of the governing body, whether the greater number, as in a democracy, or the smaller number, as in an oligarchy, is an accident due to the fact that the rich everywhere are few, and the poor numerous. But if so, there is a misapprehension (误解) of the causes of the difference between them. For the real difference between democracy and oligarchy is poverty and wealth. Wherever men rule by reason of their wealth, whether they be few or many, that is an oligarchy, and where the poor rule, that is a democracy. But as a fact the rich are few and the poor many; for few are well-to-do, whereas freedom is enjoyed by all, and wealth and freedom are the grounds on which the oligarchical and democratical parties respectively claim power in the state.

...

Our conclusion, then, is that political society exists for the sake of noble actions, and not of mere companionship. Hence they who contribute most to such a society have a greater share in it than those who have the same or a greater freedom or nobility of birth but are inferior to them in political virtue; or than those who exceed them in wealth but are surpassed by them in virtue.

From what has been said it will be clearly seen that all the partisans of different forms of government speak of a part of justice only.

There is also a doubt as to what is to be the supreme power in the state: Is it the multitude? Or the wealthy? Or the good? Or the one best man? Or a tyrant? Any of these alternatives seems to involve disagreeable consequences. If the poor, for example, because they are more in number, divide among themselves the property of the rich — is not this unjust? No, by heaven (will be the reply), for the supreme authority justly willed it. But if this is not injustice, pray what is? Again, when in the first division all has been taken, and the majority divide anew the property of the minority, is it not evident, if this goes on, that they will ruin the state? Yet surely, virtue is not the ruin of those who possess her, nor is justice destructive of a state; and therefore this law of confiscation (没收) clearly cannot be just. If it were, all the acts of a tyrant must of necessity be just; for he only coerces other men by superior power, just as the multitude coerce[1] the rich. But is it just then that the few and the wealthy should be the rulers? And what if they, in like manner, rob and plunder the people — is this just? If so, the other case will likewise be just. But there can be no doubt that all these things are wrong and unjust.

...

In all sciences and arts the end is a good, and the greatest good and in the highest degree a good in the most authoritative of all — this is the political science of which the good is justice, in other words, the common interest. All men think justice to be a sort of equality; and to a certain

---

1   **coerce:** use force to make obedient

extent they agree in the philosophical distinctions which have been laid down by us about Ethics. For they admit that justice is a thing and has a relation to persons, and that equals ought to have equality. But there still remains a question: equality or inequality of what? Here is a difficulty which calls for political speculation. For very likely some persons will say that offices of state ought to be unequally distributed according to superior excellence, in whatever respect, of the citizen, although there is no other difference between him and the rest of the community; for that those who differ in any one respect have different rights and claims. But, surely, if this is true, the complexion or height of a man, or any other advantage, will be a reason for his obtaining a greater share of political rights. The error here lies upon the surface, and may be illustrated from the other arts and sciences. When a number of flute players are equal in their art, there is no reason why those of them who are better born should have better flutes given to them; for they will not play any better on the flute, and the superior instrument should be reserved for him who is the superior artist. If what I am saying is still obscure, it will be made clearer as we proceed. For if there were a superior flute-player who was far inferior in birth and beauty, although either of these may be a greater good than the art of flute-playing, and may excel flute-playing in a greater ratio than he excels the others in his art, still he ought to have the best flutes given to him, unless the advantages of wealth and birth contribute to excellence in flute-playing, which they do not. Moreover, upon this principle any good may be compared with any other. For if a given height may be measured wealth and against freedom[1], height in general may be so measured. Thus if A excels in height more than B in virtue, even if virtue in general excels height still more, all goods will be commensurable[2]; for if a certain amount is better than some other, it is clear that some other will be equal. But since no such comparison can be made, it is evident that there is good reason why in politics men do not ground their claim to office on every sort of inequality any more than in the arts. For if some be slow, and others swift, that is no reason why the one should have little and the others much; it is in gymnastics contests that such excellence is rewarded. Whereas the rival claims of candidates for office can only be based on the possession of elements which enter into the composition of a state. And therefore the noble, or free-born, or rich, may with good reason claim office; for holders of offices must be freemen and taxpayers: a state can be no more composed entirely of poor men than entirely of slaves. But if wealth and freedom are necessary elements, justice and valor are equally so; for without the former qualities a state cannot exist at all, without the latter not well.

If the existence of the state is alone to be considered, then it would seem that all, or some at least, of these claims are just; but, if we take into account a good life, then, as I have already said, education and virtue have superior claims[3]. As, however, those who are equal in one thing ought

---

1   **may be measured wealth and against freedom:** may be measured against wealth and freedom

2   **commensurable:** measurable with the same standard

3   **education and virtue have superior claims:** Aristotle attaches great importance to education. To him, education must be a public matter, since it is intimately intertwined with the health of the constitutions. Education must also teach how to rule and be ruled in turn, which requires nurturing well-ordered characters governed by reason and cultivating virtue. Cf. Confucian emphasis on education and virtue as superior claims (both living almost at the same time).

Heritage of Western Intellectual Tradition   A Sourcebook

not to have an equal share in all, nor those who are unequal in one thing to have an unequal share in all, it is certain that all forms of government which rest on either of these principles are perversions[1]. All men have a claim in a certain sense, as I have already admitted, but all have not an absolute claim. The rich claim because they have a greater share in the land, and land is the common element of the state; also they are generally more trustworthy in contracts. The free claim under the same tide as the noble; for they are nearly akin. For the noble are citizens in a truer sense than the ignoble, and good birth is always valued in a man's own home and country. Another reason is, that those who are sprung from better ancestors are likely to be better men, for nobility is excellence of race. Virtue, too, may be truly said to have a claim, for justice has been acknowledged by us to be a social virtue, and it implies all others. Again, the many may urge their claim against the few; for, when taken collectively, and compared with the few, they are stronger and richer and better. But, what if the good, the rich, the noble, and the other classes who make up a state, are all living together in the same city? Will there, or will there not, be any doubt who shall rule? No doubt at all in determining who ought to rule in each of the above-mentioned forms of government. For states are characterized by differences in their governing bodies — one of them has a government of the rich[2], another of the virtuous, and so on. But a difficulty arises when all these elements co-exist. How are we to decide? Suppose the virtuous to be very few in number: may we consider their numbers in relation to their duties, and ask whether they are enough to administer the state, or so many as will make up a state? Objections may be urged against all the aspirants to political power. For those who found their claims on wealth or family might be thought to have no basis of justice; on this principle, if any one person were richer than all the rest, it is clear that he ought to be ruler of them. In like manner he who is very distinguished by his birth ought to have the superiority over all those who claim on the ground that they are freeborn. In an aristocracy, or government of the best, a like difficulty occurs about virtue; for if one citizen be better than the other members of the government, however good they may be, he too, upon the same principle of justice, should rule over them. And if the people are to be supreme because they are stronger than the few, then if one man, or more than one, but not a majority, is stronger than the many, they ought to rule, and not the many.

All these considerations appear to show that none of the principles on which men claim to rule and to hold all other men in subjection to them are strictly right. To those who claim to be masters of the government on the ground of their virtue or their wealth, the many might fairly answer that they themselves are often better and richer than the few — I do not say individually, but collectively. And another ingenious objection which is sometimes put forward may be met in a similar manner. Some persons doubt whether the legislator who desires to make the justest laws ought to legislate with a view to the good of the higher classes or of the many, when the case which we have mentioned occurs. Now what is just or right is to be interpreted in the sense of "what is equal"; and that which is right in the sense of being equal is to be considered with reference to the advantage of the state, and the common good of the citizens. And a citizen is one who shares in governing and being governed. He differs under different forms of government,

---

1 **perversion:** distortion, falsification
2 **government of the rich:** namely, governed by the rich

but in the best state he is one who is able and willing to be governed and to govern with a view to the life of virtue.

BOOK IV

We have now to inquire what is the best constitution for most states, and the best life for most men, neither assuming a standard of virtue which is above ordinary persons, nor an education which is exceptionally favored by nature and circumstances, nor yet an ideal state which is an aspiration only, but having regard to the life in which the majority are able to share, and to the form of government which states in general can attain. As to those aristocracies, as they are called, of which we were just now speaking, they either lie beyond the possibilities of the greater number of states, or they approximate to the so-called constitutional government, and therefore need no separate discussion. And in fact the conclusion at which we arrive respecting all these forms rests upon the same grounds. **For if what was said in the *Ethics* is true, that the happy life is the life according to virtue lived without impediment, and that virtue is a mean[1], then the life which is in a mean, and in a mean attainable by every one, must be the best. And the same principles of virtue and vice are characteristic of cities and of constitutions; for the constitution is in a figure the life of the city.**

Now in all states there are three elements: one class is very rich, another very poor, and a third in a mean. It is admitted that moderation and the mean are best, and therefore it will clearly be best to possess the gifts of fortune in moderation; for in that condition of life men are most ready to follow rational principle. But he who greatly excels in beauty, strength, birth, or wealth, or on the other hand who is very poor, or very weak, or very much disgraced, finds it difficult to follow rational principle. Of these two the one sort grow into violent and great criminals, the others into rogues[2] and petty rascals. And two sorts of offenses correspond to them, the one committed from violence, the other from roguery. Again, the middle class is least likely to shrink from rule, or to be over-ambitious for it; both of which are injuries to the state. Again, those who have too much of the goods of fortune, strength, wealth, friends, and the like, are neither willing nor able to submit to authority. The evil begins at home; for when they are boys, by reason of the luxury in which they are brought up, they never learn, even at school, the habit of obedience. On the other hand, the very poor, who are in the opposite extreme, are too degraded. So that the one class cannot obey, and can only rule despotically[3]; the other knows not how to command and must be ruled like slaves. Thus arises a city, not of freemen, but of masters and slaves, the one despising, the other envying; and nothing can be more fatal to friendship and good fellowship in

---

1 **virtue is a mean:** It is interesting to notice the "mean" mentioned here and discussed in the "Doctrine of the Mean" in the *Nicomachean Ethics*, and the similar idea in Confucianism in terms of " 中庸 ". Discuss the similarity and difference. The *Nicomachean Ethics* examines the nature of happiness, asserting that human happiness derives from "self-sufficiency," by which Aristotle means the application of reason to fulfill one's innate abilities.

2 **rogue:** rascal, vagabond（流浪汉）

3 **rule despotically:** rule like a tyrant who uses unlimited power cruelly

states than this: for good fellowship springs from friendship; when men are at enmity (敵意) with one another, they would rather not even share the same path. But a city ought to be composed, as far as possible, of equals and similars; and these are generally the middle classes. Wherefore the city which is composed of middle-class citizens is necessarily best constituted in respect of the elements of which we say the fabric of the state naturally consists. And this is the class of citizens which is most secure in a state, for they do not, like the poor, covet their neighbors' goods; nor do others covet theirs, as the poor covet the goods of the rich; and as they neither plot against others, nor are themselves plotted against, they pass through life safely. Wisely then did Phocylides[1] pray — "Many things are best in the mean; I desire to be of a middle condition in my city[2]."

Thus it is manifest that the best political community is formed by citizens of the middle class, and that those states are likely to be well-administered in which the middle class is large, and stronger if possible than both the other classes, or at any rate than either singly; for the addition of the middle class turns the scale, and prevents either of the extremes from being dominant. Great then is the good fortune of a state in which the citizens have a moderate and sufficient property; for where some possess much, and the others nothing, there may arise an extreme democracy, or a pure oligarchy; or a tyranny may grow out of either extreme — either out of the most rampant democracy, or out of an oligarchy; but it is not so likely to arise out of the middle constitutions and those akin to them. I will explain the reason of this hereafter, when I speak of the revolutions of states. The mean condition of states is clearly best, for no other is free from faction; and where the middle class is large, there are least likely to be factions and dissensions. For a similar reason large states are less liable to faction than small ones, because in them the middle class is large; whereas in small states it is easy to divide all the citizens into two classes who are either rich or poor, and to leave nothing in the middle. And democracies are safer and more permanent than oligarchies, because they have a middle class which is more numerous and has a greater share in the government; for when there is no middle class, and the poor greatly exceed in number, troubles arise, and the state soon comes to an end. A proof of the superiority of the middle class is that the best legislators have been of a middle condition; for example, Solon[3], as his own verses testify; and Lycurgus[4], for he was not a king; and Charondas[5], and almost all legislators.[6]

---

1 **Phocylides:** a 6th century BC Greek poet, whose gnomic (aphoristic) verses exist in fragments

2 **middle condition in my city:** The idea of the middle class being the backbone of a society is also found in Confucius, who advocates property and education as prerequisites for a citizen. Cf. 子曰："庶矣哉！"有曰："既庶矣，又何加焉？"曰："富之。"曰："既富矣，又何加焉？"曰："教之。"(《论语》13:9)

3 **Solon (638?–559? BC):** Athenian statesman and legislator, considered the founder of Athenian democracy

4 **Lycurgus (c. 396–c. 325 BC):** Athenian financier, statesman, and orator, pupil of Plato and most famous for his administration of Athenian finances from 338 to 326 BC

5 **Charondas:** a 6th century BC Sicilian lawgiver, whose laws, admired by Aristotle, were used at the time in cities of Sicily and Italy

6 **A proof of ... all legislators.:** Aristotle, though, was never sure if such a government was a reality. He left Athens in 323 BC when Alexander died and he was denounced for impiety, for fear that Athenian justice would "sin twice against philosophy" (he was referring to Socrates). The next year he died in Chalcis, his mother's homeland.

Key Concepts

constitution	moderation/mean
government	royalty/aristocracy/constitutional government
justice	statesman
justice and law	tyranny/oligarchy/democracy
Lyceum	virtue

Cicero: On the Laws

Cicero (Marcus Tullius, 106–43 BC), Roman statesman, lawyer, scholar, and writer of philosophical and political treatises, is remembered as the greatest Roman orator and innovator of the Ciceronian rhetoric. As a youth he studied law, oratory, literature, and philosophy in Rome. After brief military service and three years' experience as a lawyer, he traveled to Greece and Asia to continue his studies. He returned to Rome in 77 BC and began his political career by aligning himself with Pompey the Great. In 74 BC he entered the Senate and was forced into exile in 58 BC as he refused to make peace with Caesar. He returned to Rome in 50 BC and joined Pompey, Caesar's archrival. After Pompey was defeated by Caesar in 48 BC, Cicero accepted Caesar's overtures of political friendship. After Caesar's assassination in 44 BC, Cicero returned to politics and supported Caesar's adopted son, Octavian, later the emperor Augustus, in a power struggle with the Roman consul Marc Antony. When Antony and Octavian reconciled, Antony immediately proscribed Cicero. Cicero was caught by Antony's soldiers and died bravely on December 7, 43 BC. His head and hands  were nailed to the Rostra from which he had so often moved the crowd. Fulvia, Antony's wife, drove pins through his tongue which had so often pierced other Romans. Cicero's writing covers numerous subjects of intellectual interest, and he creates a rich prose style that has exercised a pervasive influence on all the literary languages of Europe. Outstanding are the treatises *On the Republic, On the Laws, On Duty,* and *On the Nature of the Gods.* The three persons in the selection below represent Cicero (Marcus) and his two brothers.

MARCUS: The whole subject of universal law and jurisprudence (司法体系) must be comprehended in this discussion, in order that this which we call civil law, may be confined in some one small and narrow space of nature. For we shall have to explain the true nature of moral justice, which must be traced back from the nature of man. And laws will have to be considered

Heritage of Western Intellectual Tradition   A Sourcebook

by which all political states should be governed. And last of all, shall we have to speak of those laws and customs of nations which are framed for the use and convenience of particular countries (in which even our own people will not be omitted), which are known by the title of civil laws.

QUINTUS: You take a noble view of the subject, my brother, and go to the fountainhead[1], in order to throw light on the subject of our consideration; and those who treat civil law in any other manner, are not so much pointing out the paths of justice as those of litigation (诉讼).

MARCUS: That is not quite the case, my Quintus. **It is not so much the science of law that produces litigation, as the ignorance of it.** But more of this by-and-by. At present let us examine the first principles of Right.

Now, many learned men have maintained that it springs from law. I hardly know if their opinion be not correct, at least according to their own definition; for "law," say they, "is the highest reason implanted in nature, which prescribes those things which ought to be done, and forbids the contrary." And when this same reason is confirmed and established in men's minds, it is then law.

They therefore conceive that prudence is a law, whose operation is to urge us to good actions, and restrain us from evil ones. And they think, too, that the Greek name for law, which is derived from the word, to distribute, implies the very nature of the thing, that is, to give every man his due. The Latin name, *lex*, conveys the idea of selections, *a legendo*. According to the Greeks, therefore, the name of law implies an equitable distribution: according to the Romans, an equitable selection. And, indeed, both characteristics belong peculiarly to law.

And if this be a correct statement, which it seems to me for the most part to be, then the origin of right is to be sought in the law. For this is the true energy of nature, this is the very soul and reason of a wise man, and the test of virtue and vice. But since all this discussion of ours relates to a subject, the terms of which are of frequent occurrence in the popular language of the citizens, we shall be sometimes obliged to use the same terms as the vulgar, and to call that law, which in its written enactments sanctions what it thinks fit by special commands or prohibitions.

Let us begin, then, to establish the principles of justice on that supreme law, which has existed from all ages before any legislative enactments were drawn up in writing, or any political governments constituted.

QUINTUS: That will be more convenient, and more sensible with reference to the subject of the discussion which we have determined on.

MARCUS: Shall we, then, seek for the origin of justice at its fountainhead? when we have

---

1 **go to the fountainhead:** you are going to deal with the basic of the science of law

discovered which, we shall be in no doubt to what these questions which we are examining ought to be referred.

QUINTUS: Such is the course I would advise.

ATTICUS: I also subscribe to your brother's opinion.

MARCUS: Since, then, we wish to maintain and preserve the constitution of that republic which Scipio[1], in those six books which I have written under that title, has proved to be the best, and **since all our laws are to be accommodated to the kind of political government there described, we must also treat of the general principles of morals and manners, and not limit ourselves on all occasions to written laws; but I purpose to trace back the origin of right from nature itself, who will be our best guide in conducting the whole discussion.**

ATTICUS: You will do right, and when she is our guide it is absolutely impossible for us to err.

MARCUS: Do you then grant, my Atticus (for I know my brother's opinion already), that the entire universe is regulated by the power of the immortal Gods, that by their nature, reason, energy, mind, divinity, or some other word of clearer signification, if there be such, all things are governed and directed? for if you will not grant me this, that is what I must begin by establishing.

ATTICUS: I grant you all you can desire. But owing to this singing of birds and babbling of water, I fear my fellow-learners can scarcely hear me.

MARCUS: You are quite right to be on your guard; for even the best men occasionally fall into a passion, and they will be very indignant if they hear you denying the first article of this notable book, entitled "The Chief Doctrines of Epicurus[2]," in which he says "that God takes care of nothing, neither of himself nor of any other being!"

Pompey the Great, Cicero and Julius Caesar

ATTICUS: Pray proceed, for I am waiting to know what advantage you mean to take of the concession I have made you.

MARCUS: I will not detain you long. This is the bearing which they have on our subject. **This animal — prescient[3], sagacious[4], complex, acute, full of memory, reason, and counsel, which we call man — has been generated by the supreme God in a most transcendent condition. For he is the only crea-**

---

1 **Scipio Africanus the Younger (c. 185–129 BC):** Roman general, adopted grandson of Scipio the Elder
2 **Epicurus (341–270 BC):** 伊壁鸠鲁，Greek philosopher whose followers are known as "philosophers of the garden," as he gave instruction in the garden of his home
3 **prescient:** knowing about future
4 **sagacious:** showing good judgment

ture among all the races and descriptions of animated beings who is endued with superior reason and thought, in which the rest are deficient. And what is there, I do not say in man alone, but in all heaven and earth, more divine than reason, which, when it becomes right and perfect, is justly termed wisdom?

There exists, therefore, since nothing is better than reason, and since this is the common property of God and man, a certain aboriginal rational intercourse（交流）between divine and human natures. But where reason is common, there right reason must also be common to the same parties; and since this right reason is what we call law, God and men must be considered as associated by law. Again, there must also be a communion of right where there is communion of law. And those who have law and right thus in common, must be considered members of the same commonwealth.

And if they are obedient to the same rule and the same authority, they are even much more so to this one celestial regency（天朝）, this divine mind and omnipotent deity（万能的神祇）. So that the entire universe may be looked upon as forming one vast commonwealth of Gods and men. And, as in earthly states certain ranks are distinguished with reference to the relationships of families, according to a certain principle which will be discussed in its proper place, that principle, in the nature of things, is far more magnificent and splendid by which men are connected with the Gods, as belonging to their kindred[1] and nation.

For when we are reasoning on universal nature, we are accustomed to argue (and indeed the truth is just as it is stated in that argument) that in the long course of ages, and the uninterrupted succession of celestial revolutions, there arrived a certain ripe time for the sowing of the human race; and when it was sown and scattered over the earth, it was animated by the divine gift of souls. And as men retained from their terrestrial origin those other particulars by which they cohere together, which are frail and perishable, their immortal spirits were ingenerated[2] by the Deity. From which circumstance

Cicero, standing left, publicly exposed Catalin, seated lower right, for his plot of an armed rebellion.

it may be truly said, that we possess a certain consanguinity[3], and kindred, and fellowship with the heavenly powers. And among all the varieties of animals, there is not one except man which retains any idea of the Divinity. And among men themselves, there is no nation so savage and ferocious as not to admit the necessity of believing in a God, however ignorant they may be of what sort of God they ought to believe in[4]. From whence we conclude that every man must recognise a Deity, who has any recollection and knowledge of his own origin.

---

1 **kindred:** people with relationship by birth
2 **ingenerate:** produce within, innate
3 **consanguinity:** relationship by blood
4 **however ignorant ... to believe in:** split prep., namely, however ignorant ... of what sort of God ...

Now, the law of virtue is the same in God and man, and in no other disposition besides them. This virtue is nothing else than a nature perfect in itself, and wrought up to the most consummate excellence. There exists, therefore, a similitude[1] between God and man. And as this is the case, what connection can there be which concerns us more nearly, and is more certain?

Since, then, the Deity has been pleased to create and adorn man to be the chief and president of all terrestrial creatures, so it is evident, without further argument, that human nature has also made very great advances by its own intrinsic energy; that nature, which without any other instruction than her own, has developed the first rude principles of the understanding, and strengthened and perfected reason to all the appliances of science and art[2].

ATTICUS: Oh ye immortal Gods! to what a distance back are you tracing the principles of justice! However, you are discoursing in such a style that I will not show any impatience to hear what I expect you to say on the Civil Law. But I will listen patiently, even if you spend the whole day in this kind of discourse; for assuredly these, which perhaps you are embracing in your argument for the sake of others, are grander topics than even the subject itself for which they prepare the way.

MARCUS: You may well describe these topics as grand, which we are now briefly discussing. But of all the questions which are ever the subject of discussion among learned men, there is none which it is more important thoroughly to understand than this, that man is born for justice, and that law and equity have not been established by opinion, but by nature[3]. This truth will become still more apparent if we investigate the nature of human association and society.

For there is no one thing so like or so equal to another, as in every instance man is to man[4]. And if the corruption of customs, and the variation of opinions, did not induce an imbecility[5] of minds, and turn them aside from the course of nature,[6] no one would more nearly resemble than all men would resemble all men. Therefore, whatever definition we give of man, will be applicable to the whole human race. And this is a good argument that there is no dissimilarity of kind among men; because if this were the case, one definition could not include all men.

In fact, reason, which alone gives us so many advantages over beasts, by means of which we conjecture, argue, refute, discourse, and accomplish and conclude our designs, is assuredly

---

1   **similitude:** resemblance
2   **the Deity has … science and art:** Does this eulogy of man sound familiar? Cf. Shakespeare in *Hamlet*: What a piece of work is a man!/How noble in reason!/How infinite in faculty!/…the beauty of the world! The paragon of animals!
3   **man is born … but by nature:** Cf. The inborn wisdom of man for Socrates and Plato (see Unit 2). Reformists like Martin Luther and John Calvin would also welcome this notion of an inborn wisdom and justice (see Unit 6).
4   **man is to man:** man is so like or so equal to man
5   **imbecility:** stupidity
6   **And if the corruption … course of nature:** Compare this notion of culture/nature with Jean-Jacques Rousseau in *A Discourse on the Moral Effects of the Arts and Sciences* (see Unit 12).

Heritage of Western Intellectual Tradition   A Sourcebook

common to all men; for the faculty of acquiring knowledge is similar in all human minds, though the knowledge itself may be endlessly diversified. By the same senses we all perceive the same objects, and those things which move the senses at all, do move in the same way the senses of all men. And those first rude elements of intelligence which, as I before observed, are the earliest developments of thought, are similarly impressed upon all men; and that faculty of speech which is the interpreter of the mind, agrees in the ideas which it conveys, though it may differ in the words by which it expresses them. And therefore there exists not a man in any nation, who, if he adopts nature for his guide, may not arrive at virtue.[1]

The Roman Forum of the Empire

Nor is this resemblance which all men bear to each other remarkable in those things only which are in accordance with right reason, but also in errors. For all men alike are captivated by pleasure, which, although it is a temptation to what is disgraceful, nevertheless bears some resemblance to natural good; for, as by its delicacy and sweetness it is delightful, it is through a mistake of the intellect adopted as something salutary(有益的).

And by error scarcely less universal, we shun death as if it were a dissolution of nature, and cling to life because it keeps us in that existence in which we were born. Thus, likewise, we consider pain as one of the greatest evils, not only on account of its present asperity[2], but also because it seems the precursor of mortality. Again, on account of the apparent resemblance between renown with honour, those men appear to us happy who are honoured, and miserable who happen to be inglorious. In like manner our minds are all similarly susceptible of inquietudes[3], joys, desires, and fears; nor if different men have different opinions, does it follow that those who deify dogs and cats, do not labour under superstition equally with other nations, though they may differ from them in the forms of its manifestation.

Again, what nation is there which has not a regard for kindness, benignity, gratitude, and mindfulness of benefits? What nation is there in which arrogance, malice, cruelty, and unthankfulness, are not reprobated and detested? And while this uniformity of opinions proves that the whole race of mankind is united together, the last point is that a system of living properly makes men better. If what I have said meets your approbation[4], I will proceed; or if any doubts occur to you, we had better clear them up first.

ATTICUS: There is nothing which strikes us, if I may reply for both of us.

---

1 **And therefore there … arrive at virtue.:** It may also be interesting if you compare this idea of an internal virtue with the *xin* (mind) school of Neo-Confucianism of Wang Yangming (1472–1529).

2 **asperity:** harshness

3 **inquietude:** anxiety

4 **approbation:** approval

MARCUS: **It follows, then, that nature made us just that we might share our goods with each other, and supply each other's wants. You observe in this discussion, whenever I speak of nature, I mean nature in its genuine purity, but that there is, in fact, such corruption engendered by evil customs, that the sparks, as it were, of virtue which have been given by nature are extinguished, and that antagonist vices arise around it and become strengthened[1].**

But if, as nature prompts them to, men would with deliberate judgments, in the words of the poet, "being men, think nothing that concerns mankind indifferent to them[2]," then would justice be cultivated equally by all. **For to those to whom nature has given reason, she has also given right reason, and therefore also law, which is nothing else than right reason enjoining what is good, and forbidding what is evil. And if nature has given us law, she hath also given us right. But she has bestowed reason on all, therefore right has been bestowed on all.**[3] And therefore did Socrates deservedly execrate[4] the man who first drew a distinction between utility and nature, for he used to complain that this error was the source of all human vices, to which this sentence of Pythagoras[5] refers — "The things belonging to friends are common" — and that other, "Friendly equality." From whence it appears, that when a wise man has displayed this benevolence which is so extensively and widely diffused[6] towards one who is endowed with equal virtue, then that phenomenon takes place which is altogether incredible to some people, but which is a necessary consequence, that he loves himself not more dearly than he loves his friends.

...

MARCUS: It is therefore an absurd extravagance (胡言) in some philosophers to assert, that all things are necessarily just which are established by the civil laws and the institutions of nations. Are then the laws of tyrants just, simply because they are laws? Suppose the thirty tyrants of Athens[7] had imposed certain laws on the Athenians? or suppose again that these Athenians were delighted with these tyrannical laws, would these laws on that account have been considered just? For my own part, I do not think such laws deserve any greater estimation than that passed during our own interregnum[8], which ordained that the dictator should be empowered to put to

---

1   **antagonist vices arise ... strengthened:** Again compare this notion of culture/nature with Jean-Jacques Rousseau in *A Discourse on the Moral Effects of the Arts and Sciences*. see Unit 12.

2   **think nothing ... indifferent to them:** take everything seriously

3   **But she has bestowed ... on all.:** The idea of reason being implanted in man by nature is picked up and further elaborated by the church fathers, though for a different purpose. See Thomas Aquinas in Unit 4.

4   **execrate:** express hatred of

5   **Pythagoras (582?–500? BC):** 毕达哥拉斯，Greek philosopher and the first "true" mathematician, whose doctrines strongly influenced Plato

6   **diffuse:** spread

7   **thirty tyrants of Athens:** a group of Athenian oligarchs in the 4th century BC, organized into a council, who ruthlessly overturned democratic laws and institutions and executed opposition leaders

8   **interregnum:** period between the end and beginning of sovereign's reign

Heritage of Western Intellectual Tradition   A Sourcebook

death with impunity[1] whatever citizens he pleased, without hearing them in their own defence.

For there is but one essential justice which cements society, and one law which establishes this justice. This law is right reason, which is the true rule of all commandments and prohibitions. Whoever neglects this law, whether written or unwritten, is necessarily unjust and wicked.

But if justice consists in submission to written laws and national customs, and if, as the same school affirms, everything must be measured by utility alone, he who thinks that such conduct will be advantageous to him will neglect the laws, and break them if it is in his power. And the consequence is, that real justice has really no existence if it have[2] not one by nature, and if that which is established as such on account of utility is overturned by some other utility.

But if nature does not ratify law, then all the virtues may lose their sway[3]. For what becomes of generosity, patriotism, or friendship? Where will the desire of benefitting our neighbours, or the gratitude that acknowledges kindness, be able to exist at all? For all these virtues proceed from our natural inclination to love mankind. And this is the true basis of justice, and without this not only the mutual charities of men, but the religious services of the Gods, would be at an end; for these are preserved, as I imagine, rather by the natural sympathy which subsists between divine and human beings, than by mere fear and timidity.

But if the will of the people, the decrees of the senate, the adjudications[4] of magistrates, were sufficient to establish rights, then it might become right to rob, right to commit adultery, right to substitute forged (伪造的) wills, if such conduct were sanctioned by the votes or decrees of the multitude. But if the opinions and suffrages of foolish men had sufficient weight to outbalance the nature of things, then why should they not determine among them, that what is essentially bad and pernicious should henceforth pass for good and beneficial? Or why, since law can make right out of injustice, should it not also be able to change evil into good?

But we have no other rule by which we may be capable of distinguishing between a good or a bad law than that of nature. Nor is it only right and wrong which are discriminated by nature,

The Colosseum, Rome (A.D. 80)

but generally all that is honourable is by this means distinguished from all that is shameful; for common sense has impressed in our minds the first principles of things, and has given us a general acquaintance with them; by which we connect with virtue every honourable quality, and with vice all that is disgraceful[5].

---

1 **impunity:** exempting from punishment
2 **have:** should have
3 **sway:** control, influence
4 **adjudication:** judgment
5 **with vice all that is disgraceful:** we connect with vice all that is disgraceful

Heritage of Western Intellectual Tradition   A Sourcebook

But to think that these differences exist only in opinion, and not in nature, is the part of an idiot. For even the virtue of a tree or a horse, in which expression there is an abuse of terms, does not exist in our opinion only, but in nature; and if that is the case, then what is honourable and disgraceful must also be discriminated by nature.

For if opinion could determine respecting the character of universal virtue, it might also decide respecting particular or partial virtues. But who will dare to determine that a man is prudent and cautious, not from his general conduct, but from some external appearances? For virtue evidently consists in perfect reason, and this certainly resides in nature. Therefore so does all honour and honesty in the same way.

...

But we are often too much disturbed by the dissensions of men and the variation of opinions. And because the same thing does not happen with reference to our senses, we look upon them as certain by nature. Those objects indeed, which sometimes present to us one appearance, sometimes another, and which do not always appear to the same people in the same way, we term fictions of the senses; but it is far otherwise. For neither parent, nor nurse, nor master, nor poet, nor drama, deceive our senses; nor do popular prejudices seduce them[1] from the truth. But all kinds of snares are laid for the mind, either by those errors which I have just enumerated, which, taking possession of the young and uneducated, imbue them deeply, and bend them any way they please; or by that pleasure which is the imitator of goodness, being thoroughly and closely implicated with all our senses — the prolific mother of all evils. For she so corrupts us by her blandishments[2], that we no longer perceive some things which are essentially excellent because they have none of this deliciousness and pruriency[3].

It follows that I may now sum up the whole of this argument by asserting, as is plain to every one from these positions which have been already laid down, that all right and all that is honourable is to be sought for its own sake. In truth, all virtuous men love justice and equity for what they are in themselves; nor is it like a good man to make a mistake, and love that which does not deserve their affection. Right, therefore, is desirable and deserving to be cultivated for its own sake; and if this be true of right, it must be true also of justice. What then shall we say of liberality[4]? Is it exercised gratuitously[5], or does it covet some reward and recompense? If a man does good without expecting any recompense for his kindness, then it is gratuitous: if he does expect compensation, it is a mere matter of traffic[6]. Nor is there any doubt that he who truly deserves the reputation of a generous and kindhearted man, is thinking of his duty, not of his interest. In the same way the virtue of justice demands neither emolument[7] nor salary, and there-

---

1   **them:** senses
2   **blandishment:** flattery
3   **pruriency:** desirability
4   **liberality:** generosity
5   **gratuitously:** doing good without payment
6   **traffic:** exchange
7   **emolument:** profit

fore we desire it for its own sake. And the case of all the moral virtues is the same, and so is the opinion of them.

Besides this, if we weigh virtue by the mere utility and profit that attend it, and not by its own merit, the one virtue which results from such an estimate will be in fact a species of vice. For the more a man refers all his actions especially to his own advantage, the further he recedes from probity[1]; so that they who measure virtue by profit, acknowledge no other virtue than this, which is a kind of vice. For who can be called benevolent, if no one ever acts kindly for the sake of another? And where are we to find a grateful person, if those who are disposed to be so can find no benefactor to whom they can show gratitude? What will become of sacred friendship, if we are not to love our friend for his own sake with all our heart and soul, as people say? if we are even to desert and discard him, as soon as we despair of deriving any further assistance or advantage from him. What can be imagined more inhuman than this conduct? But if friendship ought rather to be cultivated on its own account, so also for the same reason are society, equality, and justice desirable for their own sakes. If this be not so, then there can be no such thing as justice at all; for the most unjust thing of all is to seek a reward for one's just conduct.

What then shall we say of temperance, sobriety, continence, modesty, bashfulness, and chastity? Is it the fear of infamy, or the dread of judgments and penalties, which prevent men from being intemperate and dissolute? Do men then live in innocence and moderation, only to be well spoken of, and to acquire a certain fair reputation? Modest men blush even to speak of indelicacy[2]. And I am greatly ashamed of those philosophers, who assert that there are no vices to be avoided but those which the laws have branded with infamy. For what shall I say? Can we call those persons truly chaste, who abstain from adultery merely for the fear of public exposure, and that disgrace which is only one of its many evil consequences? For what can be either praised or blamed with

Cicero: The good of the people is the chief law.

reason, if you depart from that great law and rule of nature, which makes the difference between right and wrong? Shall corporal defects, if they are remarkable, shock our sensibilities, and shall those of the soul make no impression on us? — of the soul, I say, whose turpitude[3] is so evidently proved by its vices. For what is there more hideous than avarice, more brutal than lust, more contemptible than cowardice, more base than stupidity and folly? Well, then, are we to call those persons unhappy, who are conspicuous for one or more of these, on account of some injuries, or disgraces, or sufferings to which they are exposed, or on account of the moral baseness of their sins? And we may apply the same test in the opposite way to those who are distinguished for their virtue.

Lastly, if virtue be sought for on account of some other things, it necessarily follows that

---

1 **probity:** righteousness, honesty
2 **indelicacy:** immodesty
3 **turpitude:** wickedness

there is something better than virtue. Is it money, then? is it fame, or beauty, or health? all of which appear of little value to us when we possess them; nor can it be by any possibility certainly known how long they will last. Or is it (what it is shameful even to utter) that basest of all, pleasure? Surely not; for it is in the contempt and disdain of pleasure that virtue is most conspicuous .... But the real state of the case is, that since law ought to be both a correctress of vice and a recommender of virtue, the principles on which we direct our conduct ought to be drawn from her. And, thus it comes to pass wisdom is the mother of all the virtuous arts, from the love of which the Greeks have composed the word Philosophy; and which is beyond all contradiction the richest, the brightest, and the most excellent of the gifts which the Gods have bestowed on the life of mankind. For wisdom alone has taught us, among other things, the most difficult of all lessons, namely, *to know ourselves*, a precept so forcible and so comprehensive, that it has been attributed not to a man, but to the God of Delphi himself[1].

For he who knows himself must in the first place be conscious that he is inspired by a divine principle. And he will look upon his rational part as a resemblance to some divinity consecrated within him, and will always be careful that his sentiments as well as his external behavior be worthy of so inestimable a gift of God.[2] And after he has thoroughly examined himself and tested himself in every way, he will become aware what signal advantages he has received from nature at his entrance into life, and with what infinite means and appliances he is furnished for the attainment and acquisition of wisdom, since in the very beginning of all things, he has, as it were, the intelligible principles of things delineated, as it were, on his mind and soul, by the enlightening assistance of which, and the guidance of wisdom, he sees that he shall become a good and consequently a happy man.

For what can be described or conceived more truly happy than the state of that man, whose mind having attained to an exact knowledge and perception of virtue, has entirely discarded all obedience to and indulgence of the body, and has trampled on voluptuousness[3] as a thing unbecoming the dignity of his nature, and has raised himself above all fear of death or pain; who maintains a benevolent intercourse with his friends, and has learnt to look upon all who are united to him by nature as his kindred; who has learnt to preserve piety and reverence towards the Gods and pure religion; and who has sharpened and improved the perceptions of his mind, as well as of his eyesight, to choose the good and reject the evil, which virtue from its foreseeing things is called Prudence?[4]

When this man shall have surveyed the heavens, the earth, and the seas, and studied the

---

1　**the most difficult ... Delphi himself:** This refers to the admonition "*Gnothi se auton*" ("Know Thyself") inscribed on the Sun god Apollo's Oracle of Delphi temple.

2　**For he who knows himself ... of God.:** Cf. Men's resemblance to God found in Genesis: And God said, "Let us make man in our image, after our likeness."

3　**voluptuousness:** sensual pleasure

4　**For what can be ... called Prudence?:** Grammatically the paragraph is a long sentence: What can be described or conceived more truly happy than the state of that man ...?

nature of all things, and informed himself from whence they have been generated, to what state they will return, and of the time and manner of their dissolution, and has learnt to distinguish what parts of them are mortal and perishable, and what divine and eternal — when he shall have almost attained to a knowledge of that Being who superintends and governs these things, and shall look on himself as not confined within the walls of one city, or as the member of any particular community, but as a citizen of the whole universe, considered as a single Commonwealth: amid such a grand magnificence of things as this, and such a prospect and knowledge of nature, what a knowledge of himself, O ye immortal Gods, will a man arrive at![1]

Key Concepts

civil laws	right reason
essential justice	universal law
evil customs	universal nature
law of nature	virtue
moral justice	written laws
origin of justice	

Compare with China

Great Learning and The Mean

Study the following ideas of the mean（中庸）as expressed in Confucius and Aristotle. For Confucius, *zhong* means centrality or equilibrium, *yong* normality, *mean* the fundamental moral, idea of moderation, balance, and suitableness, and *cheng* stands for sincerity or truthfulness, involving moral integrity, and relation of human beings to the universe. *The Mean* expresses, in this sense, in psychological and metaphysical terms the same progression from the individual self to world order and unity that the *Great Learning*（《大学》）expresses in social and political terms.

天命之谓性，率性之谓道，修道之谓教。

道也者，不可须臾离也，可离非道也。是故君子戒慎乎其所不睹，恐惧乎其所不闻。莫见乎隐，莫显乎微，故君子慎其独也。

喜怒哀乐之未发谓之中，发而皆中节谓之和。中也者，天下之大本也；和也者，天下

---

1   **When this man ... arrive at!:** Again a long sentence: When this man shall have surveyed ... when he shall have almost attained ... what a knowledge of himself ... will a man arrive at!

之达道也。致中和，天地位焉，万物育焉。

仲尼曰，"君子，中庸；小人，反中庸。君子之中庸也，君子而时中。小人之中庸也，小人而无忌惮也。"

子曰："中庸其至矣乎！民鲜能久矣。道之不行也，我知之矣：知者过之；愚者不及也。道之不明也，我知之矣：贤者过之；不肖者不及也。人莫不饮食也。鲜能知味也。道其不行矣夫。"

What Heaven has conferred is called NATURE; an accordance with this nature is called PATH of duty; the regulation of this path is called INSTRUCTION.

The path may not be left for an instant. If it could be left, it would not be the path. On this account, the superior man does not wait till he sees things, to be cautious, nor till he hears things, to be apprehensive. There is nothing more visible than what is secret, and nothing more manifest than what is minute. Therefore the superior man is watchful over himself, when he is alone.

While there are no stirrings of pleasure, anger, sorrow, or joy, the mind may be said to be in the state of EQUILIBRIUM. When those feelings have been stirred, and they act in their due degree, there ensues what may be called the state of HARMONY. This EQUILIBRIUM is the great root from which grow all the human actings in the world, and this HARMONY is the universal path which they all should pursue. Let the states of equilibrium and harmony exist in perfection, and a happy order will prevail throughout heaven and earth, and all things will be nourished and flourish.

Chung-ni said, "The superior man embodies the course of the Mean; the mean man acts contrary to the course of the Mean. The superior man embodies the course of the Mean because he is a superior man, and so always maintains the Mean. The mean man acts contrary to the course of the Mean because he is a mean man, and has no caution."

The Master said, "Perfect is the virtue which is according to the Mean! Rare have they long been among the people, who could practice it! I know how it is that the path of the Mean is not walked in: — The knowing go beyond it, and the stupid do not come up to it. I know how it is that the path of the Mean is not understood: — The men of talents and virtue go beyond it, and the worthless do not come up to it. There is no body but eats and drinks. But they are few who can distinguish flavours. Alas! How is the path of the Mean untrodden!"

"故君子和而不流；强哉矫。中立而不倚；强哉矫。国有道，不变塞焉；强哉矫。国无道，至死不变；强哉矫。"

"Therefore, the superior man cultivates a friendly harmony, without being weak. — How firm is he in his energy! He stands erect in the middle, without inclining to either side. — How firm is he in his energy! When good principles prevail in the government of his country, he does not change from what he was in retirement. — How firm is he in his energy! When bad principles prevail in the country, he maintains his course to death without changing. — How firm is he in his energy!"

"君子素其位而行，不愿乎其外。素富贵，行乎富贵；数贫贱，行乎贫贱；素夷狄，行乎夷狄；素患难，行乎患难。君子无入而不自得焉。"

"The superior man does what is proper to the station in which he is; he does not desire to go beyond this. In a position of wealth and honor, he does what is proper to a position of wealth and honor. In a poor and low position, he does what is proper to a poor and low position. Situated among barbarous tribes, he does what is proper to a situation among barbarous tribes. In a position of sorrow and difficulty, he does what is proper to a position of sorrow and difficulty. The superior man can find himself in no situation in which he is not himself."

The following is Aristotle's idea of the mean, as is expressed in *The Doctrine of the Mean* (*Nichomachean Ethics*《尼各马可伦理学》, II.6–7):

We may safely assert that the virtue (*areté*) or excellence of a thing causes that thing both to be itself in good condition and to perform its function well. By an equal or fair amount I understand a mean amount, or one that lies between excess and deficiency. By the absolute mean, or mean relative to the thing itself, I understand that which is equidistant from both extremes, and this is one and the same for all. Virtue, then, has to deal with feelings or passions and with outward acts, in which excess is wrong and deficiency also is blamed, but the mean amount is praised and is right — both of which are characteristics of virtue. Virtue, then, is a kind of moderation.

Aristotle's virtue of moderation can be summarized in the following charter:

Vice of Deficiency	Virtuous Mean	Vice of Excess
Cowardice	Courage	Rashness
Insensibility	Temperance	Intemperance
Illiberality	Liberality	Prodigality
Pettiness	Munificence	Vulgarity
Humble-mindedness	High-mindedness	Vain-glory
Want of ambition	Right ambition	Over-ambition
Spiritlessness	Good temper	Irascibility
Surliness	Friendly civility	Obsequiousness
Ironical depreciation	Sincerity	Boastfulness
Boorishness	Wittiness	Buffoonery
Shamelessness	Modesty	Bashfulness
Callousness	Just resentment	Spitefulness

Supplementary Reading

Marcus Tullius Cicero Quotes

The following are statements made by Cicero, sometimes witty and sometimes profound, which might be more profitably read with the witticism of people like Michel Eyquem de Montaigne (1533–1592), French essayist and Francis Bacon, English essayist (See Unit 7).

I criticize by creation, not by finding fault.

What is so beneficial to the people as liberty, which we see not only to be greedily sought after by men, but also by beasts, and to be preferred to all things.

Philosophy, rightly defined, is simply the love of wisdom.

Friendship improves happiness and abates[1] misery, by the doubling of our joy and the dividing of our grief.

Friendship renders prosperity more brilliant, while it lightens adversity[2] by sharing it and making its burden common.

The more laws, the less justice.

The foundation of justice is good faith.

Every evil in the bud is easily crushed: as it grows older, it becomes stronger.

These studies are a spur to the young, a delight to the old; an ornament in prosperity, a consoling refuge in adversity; they are pleasure for us at home, and no burden abroad; they stay up with us at night, they accompany us when we travel, they are with us in our country visits.

My precept to all who build, is, that the owner should be an ornament to the house, and not the house to the owner.

A good deed in the wrong place is like an evil deed.

The mind of each man is the man himself.

The noblest spirit is most strongly attracted by the love of glory.

What greater and better gift can we offer the republic than to teach and to instruct our

---

1　**abate:** make less, reduce
2　**adversity:** unfavorable situation, hostility

Heritage of Western Intellectual Tradition　A Sourcebook

young?

I prefer the most unfair peace to the most righteous war.

The greater the difficulty, the greater the glory.

If only every man would make proper use of his strength and do his utmost, he need never regret his limited ability.

A room without books is like a body without a soul.

A mental stain can neither be blotted out by the passage of time nor washed away by any waters.

Questions for Discussion

1. What is Aristotle's idea concerning political right?
2. What is Aristotle's understanding of human nature? What does he mean when he says that man is a political animal? What are the elements which make us "political animals"?
3. Discuss ways Aristotle talks about politics, which lead to the development of political science.
4. What is the "law" meant in Cicero's essay?
5. *"It is not so much the science of law that produces litigation, as the ignorance of it."* What is more important, to Cicero, than litigation? Why doesn't Cicero think much about litigation?
6. How do Cicero's laws differ from the "laws" we mean today?
7. Compare the Greek trio with Cicero.
8. Compare the idea of the "mean" in Aristotle and Confucius.

UNIT 4

Medieval Christian Church Fathers

Pretest

- What do you know about Scholasticism and the Middle Ages?
- What do you know about St. Augustine and Thomas Aquinas?
- What are the messages conveyed through the works of the two people?

What You Will Learn in This Unit

- Some knowledge about the church fathers of the Middle Ages;
- Important sections from St. Augustine and Thomas Aquinas; and
- Revival of Christianity in Europe and of Confucianism in China.

Learn to Pronounce

Constantine the Great /ˈkɒnstəntaɪn/ 君士坦丁
大帝

Dualism /ˈdjuːəlɪzəm/ 二元论

Manichaeism /ˈmænɪkiːɪzəm/ 摩尼教

Manichean /ˌmænɪˈkɪən/ 摩尼教徒 / 摩尼教的

Mohammed /məʊˈhæmed/ 穆罕默德 (伊斯兰教
创始人)

Monistic /mɒˈnɪstɪk/ 一神论的 / 一元论的

pantheistic /ˌpænθiːˈɪstɪk/ 泛神论的

Patristic era /pəˈtrɪstɪk/ 教父时代

Pharoah /ˈfeərəʊ/ 埃及法老

schism /ˈsɪzəm/ 教派 (林立)

scholasticism /skəˈlæstɪsɪzəm/ 经院哲学

St. Augustine /ɔːˈɡʌstiˈ(ː)n/ 圣奥古斯丁

St. Thomas Aquinas /əˈkwaɪnəs/ 圣托马
斯·阿奎那

theist /ˈθiːɪst/ 有神论者

theology /θiˈɒlədʒɪ/ 神学

Thomism /ˈtəʊmɪzm/ 托马斯主义

Introduction

The Middle Ages, period in the history of Europe that lasted from about 350 to 1450, may be further divided into the Early Middle Ages (350–1050), the High Middle Ages (1050–1300), and the Late Middle Ages (1300–1450). By the end of the Middle Ages, many modern European states had taken shape, and the precursors of many modern institutions, such as universities and bodies of representative government, were created. At the beginning of the 4th century, Constantine the Great moved the capital of the Empire from Rome to Constantinople and declared toleration for Christianity. In 391 Christianity became the official religion of the Roman Empire. From the 3rd through the 5th century, churchmen developed ideas about Christian doctrines

Constantine the Great, the first emperor of Rome to convert to Christianity

in sermons, treatises, and biblical commentaries, and established a standardized body of Christian teaching. Some of these authors came to be known as Fathers of the Church, and their writings called patristic literature. Christianity was understood and interpreted in many different ways in this period. For example, Fathers argued frequently and sometimes violently about the nature of Christ and the nature of the Trinity. The most important and influential of them was Saint Augustine, whose most famous book was *The City of God* (413–426). The period extending from the beginning of Christian speculation to the time of St. Augustine is known as the Patristic era in philosophy and theology. In general, that era inclined to Platonism and underestimated the importance of Aristotle. The Fathers strove to construct on Platonic principles a system of Christian philosophy. They relied more on spiritual intuition than on dialectical proof for the establishment and explanation of the highest truths of philosophy. Then came scholasticism, the philosophic and theological movement that attempted to use natural human reason, in particular, the philosophy and science of Aristotle, to understand the supernatural content of Christian revelation. It was dominant in the medieval Christian schools and universities of Europe from about the middle of the 11th century to the middle of the 15th century. The ultimate ideal of the movement was to integrate into an ordered system both the natural wisdom of Greece and Rome and the religious wisdom of Christianity. Scholasticism culminated in St. Thomas Aquinas, the Prince of Scholastics. Being one of the greatest synthesizers of Aristotle with Christian theology, he was recognized by the Roman Catholic Church as its foremost Western philosopher and theologian.

St. Augustine: The Enchiridion*

Saint Augustine (Aurelius Augustinus, 354– 430), greatest of the Latin Fathers and one of the most

---

* Sometime in 421, Augustine received a request from one Laurentius, a Christian layman, who wanted a handbook (*enchiridion*) that would sum up the essential Christian teaching in the briefest possible form. The shortest complete summary of the Christian faith, Augustine said, is that God is to be served by man in faith, hope, and love. Acknowledging that this answer might indeed be too brief, he proceeds to expand it in an essay, a "conscious effort of the theological magistrate of the Western Church to stand on final ground of testimony to the Christian truth." This "Enchiridion" or "manual" is a bold expression at the time of what we tend to accept as common talks today.

eminent Western Doctors of the Church. Inspired by the Roman orator and statesman Cicero, the 19-year-old student became an earnest seeker after truth or "philosophy" with a conviction of the superiority of reason rather than authority. From 373 until 382, he experimented with several philosophical systems, such as Manichaeism and skepticism before finally becoming a Christian on a dramatic occasion when one day, according to his own account in *Confessions*, he had a mystical experience: he was weeping uncontrollably in the garden for his "earthly appetite" which prevented his conversion (his famous prayer "Give me chastity and continence, only not yet"), when he seemed to hear a voice, like that of a child, repeating, "tolle, lege: tolle, lege (take up and

read)." He interpreted this as a divine exhortation to open the Scriptures and read the first passage he happened to see. It was Romans 13:13–14, where he read: "put on the Lord Jesus Christ, and make no provision for the flesh, to gratify its desires." He immediately resolved to embrace Christianity and was baptized on Easter Eve in 387 by St. Ambrose, bishop of Milan and the most eminent Christian churchman of the day. Shortly after his Baptism, Augustine left Milan with his devout mother and a small party of friends to return to North Africa. He became bishop of Hippo in 396, an office he held until his death. It was a period of political and theological unrest[1], when the barbarians sacked Rome in 410, and schism and heresy threatened the church. Augustine threw himself into the theological battles and developed his doctrines of original sin and divine grace, divine sovereignty, and predestination, which found a ready acceptance in the Roman Catholic Church and later in Protestant theology, and was regarded as the greatest theologian since St. Paul. The best-known work of Augustine is his autobiographical *Confessions* (c. 400) and *The City of God* (413–

26), an answer to the charge that Rome was being punished by the ancient gods of the city for deserting them. John Calvin and Martin Luther, leaders of the Reformation, were both close students of Augustine, the inspiration of the Protestant Reformation.

The Triumph of St. Augustine 1664 Museo del Prado, Madrid

> *God's judgments upon fallen men and angels. The death of the body is man's peculiar punishment.*

… Now the evils I have mentioned are common to all who for their wickedness have been justly condemned by God, whether they be men or angels. But there is one form of punishment peculiar to man — the death of the body. God had threatened him with this punishment of death if he should sin, leaving him indeed to the freedom of his own will, but yet commanding his obedience under pain of

---

1 The late 15th century theology was Pelagian（贝拉基教义）: no original sin and no need for divine grace and redemption, and man was to earn hid salvation by his own efforts. This doctrine was formulated by Romano-British monk Pelagius, who went to Rome about 390, appalled by the lax morals of Roman Christians, and preached Christian asceticism. He argued that the corruption of the human race is due to bad examples and habits, and that true grace lies in the natural gifts of humanity, including free will, reason, and conscience (Stoicism). Starting in 412, St. Augustine wrote to develop his own subtle formulation of the relation of human freedom to divine grace against the Pelagian doctrine of human moral autonomy. As a result Pelagius was accused of heresy.

death; and He placed him amid the happiness of Eden, as it were in a protected nook[1] of life, with the intention that, if he preserved his righteousness, he should thence ascend to a better place.

Through Adam's sin his whole posterity were corrupted, and were born under the penalty of death, which he had incurred.

Thence, after his sin, he was driven into exile, and by his sin the whole race of which he was the root was corrupted in him, and thereby subjected to the penalty of death. And so it happens that all descended from him, and from the woman who had led him into sin, and was condemned at the same time with him, — being the offspring of carnal[2] lust on which the same punishment of disobedience was visited, — were tainted with the original sin, and were by it drawn through divers errors and sufferings into that last and endless punishment which they suffer in common with the fallen angels, their corrupters and masters, and the partakers of their doom. And thus "by one man sin entered into the world, and death by sin[3]; and so death passed upon all men, for that all have sinned." By "the world" the apostle[4], of course, means in this place the whole human race.

The state of misery to which Adam's sin reduced mankind, and the restoration effected through the mercy of God.

Thus, then, matters stood. The whole mass of the human race was under condemnation, was lying steeped and wallowing[5] in misery, and was being tossed from one form of evil to another, and, having joined the faction of the fallen angels, was paying the well-merited penalty of that impious rebellion. For whatever the wicked freely do through blind and unbridled lust, and whatever they suffer against their will in the way of open punishment, this all evidently pertains to the just wrath of God. But the goodness of the Creator never fails either to supply life and vital power to the wicked angels (without which[6] their existence would soon come to an end); or, in the case of mankind, who spring from a condemned and corrupt stock, to impart form and life to their seed, to fashion their members, and through the various seasons of their life, and in the different parts of the earth, to quicken their senses, and bestow upon them the nourishment they need. For He judged it better to bring good out of evil, than not to permit any evil to exist. And if He had determined that in the case of men, as in the case of the fallen angels, there should be no restoration to happiness, would it not have been quite just, that the being who rebelled against God, who in the abuse of his freedom spurned and transgressed the command of his Creator when he could so easily have kept it, who defaced[7] in himself the image of his Creator by stubbornly turning away from His light, who by an evil use of his free-will broke away from his

---

1 **nook:** special place

2 **carnal:** sensual

3 **death by sin:** death entered into the world by sin

4 **apostle:** i.e., St. Paul

5 **wallow:** indulge

6 **which:** God's goodness

7 **deface:** destroy

wholesome bondage to the Creator's laws, — would it not have been just that such a being should have been wholly and to all eternity deserted by God, and left to suffer the everlasting punishment he had so richly[1] earned? Certainly so God would have done, had He been[2] only just and not also merciful, and had He not designed that His unmerited mercy should shine forth the more brightly in contrast with the unworthiness of its objects.

...

Men are not saved by good works, nor by the free determination of their own will, but by the grace of God through faith.[3]

But this part of the human race to which God has promised pardon and a share in His eternal kingdom, can they be restored through the merit of their own works? God forbid. **For what good work can a lost man perform, except so far as he has been delivered from perdition[4]? Can they do anything by the free determination of their own will? Again I say, God forbid. For it was by the evil use of his free-will that man destroyed both it[5] and himself. For, as a man who kills himself must, of course, be alive when[6] he kills himself, but after he has killed himself ceases to live, and cannot restore himself to life; so, when man by his own free-will sinned, then sin being victorious over him, the freedom of his will was lost. "For of whom a man is overcome, of the same is he brought in bondage."[7]** This is the judgment of the Apostle Peter. **And as it is certainly true, what kind of liberty, I ask, can the bond-slave possess, except when it pleases him to sin? For he is freely in bondage who does with pleasure the will of his master. Accordingly, he who is the servant of sin is free to sin. And hence he will not be free to do right, until, being freed from sin, he shall begin to be the servant of righteousness. And this is true liberty, for he has pleasure in the righteous deed; and it is at the same time a holy bondage, for he is obedient to the will of God.** But whence[8] comes this liberty to do right to the man who is in bondage and sold under sin, except he be redeemed by Him who has said, "If the Son shall make you free, ye shall be free indeed"? And before this redemption is wrought in a man, when he is not yet free to do what is right, how can he talk of the freedom of his will and his good works, except he be inflated by that foolish pride of boasting which the apostle restrains when he says, "By grace are ye saved, through faith."

Faith itself is the gift of God; and good works will not be wanting in those who believe.

---

1   **richly:** abundantly, referring to the crimes man has committed as a result of the original sin
2   **had He been:** subjunctive, if He had been
3   **Men are not saved by ... God through faith.:** This section must have a strong appeal to Martin Luther and John Calvin. See Unit 5.
4   **perdition:** destruction
5   **it:** his free-will
6   **when:** before, at the time when
7   **"For of whom ... brought in bondage.":** From Peter 2, 2:19. Man is overwhelmed by somebody and then becomes his slave.
8   **whence:** (from) where

And lest men should arrogate[1] to themselves the merit of their own faith at least, not understanding that this too is the gift of God, this same apostle, who says in another place that he had "obtained mercy of the Lord to be faithful," here also adds: "and that not of yourselves; it is the gift of God: not of works, lest any man should boast." And lest it should be thought that good works will be wanting in those who believe, he adds further: "For we are His workmanship, created in Christ Jesus unto good works, which God hath before ordained that we should walk in them."[2] We shall be made truly free, then, when God fashions us, that is, forms and creates us anew, not as men — for He has done that already — but as good men, which His grace is now doing, that we may be a new creation in Christ Jesus, according as it is said: "Create in me a clean heart, O God."[3] For God had already created his heart, so far as the physical structure of the human heart is concerned; but the psalmist[4] prays for the renewal of the life which is still lingering in his heart.

The freedom of the will is also the gift of God, for God worketh in us both to will and to do.

And further, should any one be inclined to boast, not indeed of his works, but of the freedom of his will, as if that first merit belong[5] to him, this very liberty of good action being given to him as a reward he had earned, let him listen to this same preacher of grace, when he says: "For it is God which worketh in you, both to will and to do of His own good pleasure"; and in another place: "So, then, it is not of him that willeth, nor of him that runneth, but of God that showeth mercy." Now as, undoubtedly, if a man is of the age to use his reason, he cannot believe, hope, love, unless he will to do so, nor obtain the prize of the high calling of God unless he voluntarily run for it; in what sense is it "not of him that willeth, nor of him that runneth, but of God that showeth mercy," except that, as it is written, "the preparation of the heart is

The Conversion of St. Augustine

from the Lord"? Otherwise, if it is said, "It is not of him that willeth, nor of him that runneth, but of God that showeth mercy," because it is of both, that is, both of the will of man and of the mercy of God, so that we are to understand the saying, "It is not of him that willeth, nor of him that runneth, but of God that showeth mercy," as if it meant the will of man alone is not sufficient, if the mercy of God go not with in, — then it will follow that the mercy of God alone is not sufficient, if the will of man go not with it; and therefore, if we may rightly say, "it is not of man that willeth, but of God that showeth mercy," because the will of man by itself is not enough, why may we not also rightly put it in the converse way: "It is not of God that showeth mercy, but of man that willeth," because the mercy of God by itself does not suffice? Surely, if no Christian will dare to say this, "It is not of God that showeth mercy, but of man that willeth," lest he should

---

1   **arrogate:** claim without reason
2   **"For we are His workmanship ... walk in them.":** From Ephesians 2:10. **in them:** in good works
3   **"Create in me a clean heart, O God.":** from Psalms 51:10
4   **the psalmist:** It usually refers to David as the creator of the psalms.
5   **belong:** should belong

openly contradict the apostle, it follows that the true interpretation of the saying, "It is not of him that willeth, nor of him that runneth, but of God that showeth mercy," is that the whole work belongs to God, who both makes the will of man righteous, and thus prepares it for assistance, and assists it when it is prepared. For the man's righteousness of will precedes many of God's gifts, but not all; and it must itself be included among those which it does not precede. We read in Holy Scripture, both that God's mercy "shall prevent me," and that His mercy "shall follow me." It prevents the unwilling to make him willing; it follows the willing to make his will effectual. Why are we taught to pray for our enemies, who are plainly unwilling to lead a holy life, unless that God may work willingness in them? And why are we ourselves taught to ask that we may receive, unless that He who has created in us the wish, may Himself satisfy the wish[1]? We pray, then, for our enemies, that the mercy of God may prevent them, as it has prevented us: we pray for ourselves that His mercy may follow us.

Men, being by nature the children of wrath, needed a Mediator[2]. In what sense God is said to be angry.

And so the human race was lying under a just condemnation, and all men were the children of wrath. Of which wrath it is written: "All our days are passed away in Thy wrath; we spend our years as a tale that is told." Of which wrath also Job says: "Man that is born of a woman is of few days, and full of trouble." Of which wrath also the Lord Jesus says: "He that believeth on the Son hath everlasting life: and he that believeth not the Son shall not see life; but the wrath of God abideth on him[3]." He does not say it will come, but it "abideth on him." For every man is born with it; wherefore the apostle says: "We were by nature the children of wrath, even[4] as others." Now, as men were lying under this wrath by reason of their original sin, and as this original sin was the more heavy and deadly in proportion to the number and magnitude of the actual sins which were added to it,

14th century French manuscript of City of God, illustrating the fall of the rebel angels

there was need for a Mediator, that is, for a reconciler, who, by the offering of one sacrifice, of which all the sacrifices of the law and the prophets were types[5], should take away this wrath. Wherefore the apostle says: "For if, when we were enemies, we were reconciled to God by the death of His Son, much more, being reconciled, we shall be saved by His life." Now when God is said to be angry, we do not attribute to Him such a disturbed feeling as exists in the mind of an angry man; but we call His just displeasure against sin by the name "anger," a word transferred by analogy from human emotions. But our being reconciled to God through a Mediator, and receiving the Holy Spirit, so that we who were enemies are made sons ("For as many as are led

---

1 **may Himself satisfy the wish:** if He Himself may satisfy the wish

2 **mediator:** one who goes in between to bring about reconciliation

3 **the wrath of God abideth on him:** he must endure God's wrath and remain under God's punishment

4 **even:** same

5 **types:** variations

by the Spirit of God, they are the sons of God"): this is the grace of God through Jesus Christ our Lord.

...

Christ, who was Himself free from sin, was made sin for us, that we might be reconciled to God.

Begotten and conceived, then, without any indulgence of carnal lust, and therefore bringing with Him no original sin, and by the grace of God joined and united in a wonderful and unspeakable way in one person with the Word, the Only-begotten of the Father, a son by nature, not by grace, and therefore having no sin of His own; nevertheless, on account of the likeness of sinful flesh in which He came, He was called sin, that He might be sacrificed to wash away sin. For, under the Old Covenant, sacrifices for sin were called sins. And He, of whom all these sacrifices were types and shadows, was Himself truly made sin. Hence the apostle, after saying, "We pray you in Christ's stead, be ye reconciled to God," forthwith adds: "for He hath made Him to be sin for us who knew no sin; that we might be made the righteousness of God in Him." He does not say, as some incorrect copies read, "He who knew no sin did sin for us," as if Christ had Himself sinned for our sakes; but he says, "Him who knew no sin," that is, Christ, God, to whom we are to be reconciled, "hath made to be sin for us," that is, hath made Him a sacrifice for our sins, by which we might be reconciled to God. He, then, being made sin, just as we are made righteousness (our righteousness being not our own, but God's, not in ourselves, but in Him); He being made sin, not His own, but ours[1], not in Himself, but in us, showed, by the likeness of sinful flesh in which He was crucified, that though sin was not in Him, yet that in a certain sense He died to sin, by dying in the flesh which was the likeness of sin; and that although He Himself had never lived the old life of sin, yet by His resurrection He typified our new life springing up out of the old death in sin.

Truth and anger of God

...

By the sacrifice of Christ all things are restored, and peace is made between earth and heaven.

And, of course, the holy angels, taught by God, in the eternal contemplation of whose truth their happiness consists[2], know how great a number of the human race are to supplement their ranks[3], and fill up the full tale of their citizenship. Wherefore the apostle says, that "all things are gathered together in one in Christ, both which are in heaven and which are on earth." The things which are in heaven are gathered together when what was lost therefore in the fall of the angels

---

1 **not His own, but ours:** not His own sin, but our sin

2 **in the eternal ... consists:** The happiness of the angels lies in their timeless meditation on God's truth.

3 **to supplement their ranks:** to fill up the vacancies left by the rebel angels, God created men

is restored from among men; and the things which are on earth are gathered together, when those who are predestined to eternal life are redeemed from their old corruption. And thus, through that single sacrifice in which the Mediator was offered up, the one sacrifice of which the many victims under the law were types, heavenly things are brought into peace with earthly things, and earthly things with heavenly. Wherefore, as the same apostle says: "For it pleased the Father that in Him should all fullness dwell: and, having made peace through the blood of His cross, by Him to reconcile all things to Himself: by Him, I say, whether they be things in earth or things in heaven."

...

Predestination to eternal life is wholly of God's free grace.

And, moreover, who will be so foolish and blasphemous as to say that God cannot change the evil wills of men, whichever, whenever, and wheresoever He chooses, and direct them to what is good? But when He does this He does it of mercy; when He does it not, it is of justice that He does it not; for "He hath mercy on whom He will have mercy, and whom He will He hardeneth[1]." And when the apostle said this, he was illustrating the grace of God, in connection with which he had just spoken of the twins in the womb of Rebecca[2], "who being not yet born, neither having done any good or evil, that the purpose of God according to election might stand, not of works, but of Him that calleth, it was said unto her, The elder shall serve the younger." And in reference to this matter he quotes another prophetic testimony: "Jacob have I loved, but Esau have I hated." But perceiving how what he had said might affect those who could not penetrate by their understanding the depth of this grace: "What shall we say then?" he says: **"Is there unrighteousness with God? God forbid." For it seems unjust that, in the absence of any merit or demerit from good or evil works, God should love the one and hate the other.** Now, if the apostle had wished us to understand that there were future good works of the one, and evil works of the other, which of course God foreknew, he would never have said, "not of works," but, "of future works," and in that way would have solved the difficulty, or rather there would then have been no difficulty to solve. As it is, however, after answering, "God forbid;" that is, God forbid that there should be unrighteousness with God; he goes on to prove that there is no unrighteousness in God's doing this, and says: "For He saith to Moses, I will have mercy on whom I will have mercy, and I will have compassion on whom I will have compassion." **Now who but a fool would think that God was unrighteous, either in inflicting penal justice on those who earned it, or in extending mercy to the unworthy?** Then he draws his conclusion: "So then it is not of him that willeth, nor of him that runneth, but of God that showeth mercy."

1　**"He hath mercy on whom ...":** "God has mercy on anyone he wishes, and he makes stubborn anyone he wishes"; **whom He will He hardeneth:** he hardens those whom he will (from Romans 9:18)

2　**Rebecca:** the young woman who became the wife of Isaac, son of Abraham by Sarah, and gave birth to two sons, Esau and Jacob (Genesis 25:19–34), with very different temperaments. God said to her, "Two nations are in thy womb, and two manner of people shall be separated from thy bowels; and the one people shall be stronger than the other people; and the elder shall serve the younger."

Thus both the twins were born children of wrath, not on account of any works of their own, but because they were bound in the fetters of that original condemnation which came through Adam. But He who said, "I will have mercy on whom I will have mercy," loved Jacob of His undeserved grace, and hated Esau of His deserved judgment. And as this judgment was due to both, the former learnt from the case of the latter that the fact of the same punishment not falling upon himself gave him no room to glory in any merit of his own, but only in the riches of the divine grace; because "it is not of him that willeth, nor of him that runneth, but of God that showeth mercy." And indeed the whole face, and, if I may use the expression, every lineament[1] of the countenance[2] of Scripture conveys by a very profound analogy this wholesome warning to every one who looks carefully into it, that he who glories should glory in the Lord.

As God's mercy is free, so His judgments are just, and cannot be gainsaid[3].

Now after commending the mercy of God, saying, "So it is not of him that willeth, nor of him that runneth, but of God that showeth mercy," that he might commend His justice also (for the man who does not obtain mercy finds, not iniquity[4], but justice, there being no iniquity with God), he immediately adds: "For the scripture saith unto Pharoah, Even for this same purpose have I raised thee up, that I might show my power in thee, and that my name might be declared throughout all the earth." And then he draws a conclusion that applies to both, that is, both to His mercy and His justice: "Therefore hath He mercy on whom He will have mercy, and whom He will He hardeneth." "He hath mercy" of His great goodness, "He hardeneth" without any injustice; so that neither can he that is pardoned glory[5] in any merit of his own, nor he that is condemned complain of anything but his own demerit. For it is grace alone that separates the redeemed from the lost, all having been involved in one common perdition[6] through their common origin. Now if any one, on hearing this, should say, "Why doth He yet find fault? for who hath resisted His will"? as if a man ought not to be blamed for being bad, because God hath mercy on whom He will have mercy, and whom He will He hardeneth, God forbid that we should be ashamed to answer as we see the apostle answered: "Nay, but, O man, who art thou that repliest against God? Shall the thing formed say to Him that formed it, Why hast Thou made me thus? Hath not the potter power over the clay, of the same lump to make one vessel[7] unto honour, and another unto dishonour?" Now some foolish people think that in this place the apostle had no answer to give; and for want of a reason to render, rebuked[8] the presumption of his interrogator. **But there is great weight in**

---

1 **lineament:** distinctive feature

2 **countenance:** face

3 **gainsaid:** denied

4 **iniquity:** wickedness

5 **so that neither can he that is pardoned glory:** so that neither can he ... glory

6 **perdition:** fall

7 **vessel:** container（器皿）. Have you noticed the biblical analogy drawn between men and vessels? Discuss the underlying meanings of such an analogy. Do you find any similar analogy in Chinese culture?

8 **rebuke:** blame

this saying: "Nay, but, O man, who art thou?" and in such a matter as this it suggests to a man in a single word the limits of his capacity[1], and at the same time does in reality convey an important reason. For if a man does not understand these matters, who is he that he should reply against God? And if he does understand them, he finds no further room for reply. For then he perceives that the whole human race was condemned in its rebellious head by a divine judgment so just, that if not a single member of the race had been redeemed[2], no one could justly have questioned the justice of God; and that it was right that those who are redeemed should be redeemed in such a way as to show, by the greater number who are unredeemed and left in their just condemnation, what the whole race deserved, and whither[3] the deserved judgment of God would lead even the redeemed, did not His undeserved mercy interpose[4], so that every mouth might be stopped of those who wish to glory in their own merits[5], and that he that glorieth might glory in the Lord.

...

There is no ground in Scripture for the opinion of those who deny the eternity of future punishments.

It is in vain, then, that some, indeed very many, make moan over the eternal punishment, and perpetual, uninterrupted torments of the lost, and say they do not believe it shall be so; not, indeed, that they directly oppose themselves to Holy Scripture, but, at the suggestion of their own feelings, they soften down everything that seems hard, and give a milder turn to statements which they think are rather designed to terrify than to be received as literally true. For "Hath God," they say, "forgotten to be gracious? hath He in anger shut up His tender mercies?" Now, they read this in one of the holy psalms. But without doubt we are to understand it as spoken of those who are elsewhere called "vessels of mercy," because even they are freed from misery not on account of any merit of

No denying of the eternity of future punishments

their own, but solely through the pity of God. Or, if the men we speak of insist that this passage applies to all mankind, there is no reason why they should therefore suppose that there will be an end to the punishment of those of whom it is said, "These shall go away into everlasting punishment;" for this shall end in the same manner and at the same time as the happiness of those of whom it is said, "but the righteous unto life eternal." But let them suppose,

---

1 **it suggests to a man in a single word the limits of his capacity:** it suggests ... the limits of his capacity

2 **redeemed:** saved

3 **whither:** to where

4 **did not His undeserved mercy interpose:** if without the intervention of God's mercy and salvation which men do not deserve; **interpose:** intervene

5 **did not His undeserved ... their own merits:** His undeserved mercy did not interpose, so that every mouth of those who wish to glory in their own merits might be stopped.

if the thought gives them pleasure, that the pains of the damned are, at certain intervals, in some degree assuaged. For even in this case the wrath of God, that is, their condemnation (for it is this, and not any disturbed feeling in the mind of God that is called His wrath), abideth[1] upon them; that is, His wrath, though it still remains, does not shut up His tender mercies; though His tender mercies are exhibited, not in putting an end to their eternal punishment, but in mitigating, or in granting them a respite[2] from, their torments; for the psalm does not say, "to put an end to His anger," or, "when His anger is passed by," but "in His anger." Now, if this anger stood alone, or if it existed in the smallest conceivable degree, yet to be lost out of the kingdom of God, to be an exile from the city of God, to be alienated from the life of God, to have no share in that great goodness which God hath laid up for them that fear Him, and hath wrought out for them that trust in Him, would be a punishment so great, that, supposing it to be eternal, no torments that we know of, continued through as many ages as man's imagination can conceive, could be compared with it.

Key Concepts

carnal lust	merit of one's own works
free determination of the will	the just wrath of God
gift of God	the original sin
God's mercy and grace	predestination
Mediator	punishment

Thomas Aquinas: Summa Contra Gentiles*

Saint Thomas Aquinas (1225–1274), Prince of Scholastics and most important figure in medieval Scholastic philosophy, is one of the greatest synthesizers of Aristotle and Christian theology. Thomism refers both to the doctrinal system of St. Thomas Aquinas and to the explanations and developments made by his followers. Aquinas was educated at the Benedictine monastery of Monte Cassino and at University of Naples. Ordained a priest at about 1250, he began teaching at University of Paris in 1252. In 1256 he was awarded a doctorate in theology and appointed professor of philosophy. Pope

---

1 **abideth:** bears

2 **respite:** postponement

* Literally, "Summary against the Gentiles (intellectual Muslims)," where Thomas Aquinas tries to build the consonance between philosopher's quest for mundane truth based on reason and Christian's quest for divine truth based on revelation.

Alexander IV summoned him to Rome in 1259 to be his adviser and lecturer to the papal court. St. Augustine had dominated Western thought arguing against sense experience. Early in the 13th century Aristotle was made available, but theologians regarded him with suspicion and leaned toward the more traditional Christian Neoplatonism. However, Aquinas insisted that the truths of faith and those of sense experience are fully compatible and complementary — not a dualistic recognition of each, but a unity of them as the "emanation of the Divine Being." To reach understanding of the highest truths, the aid of revelation is needed in matters of religion. St. Thomas was an extremely prolific author with about 80 works ascribed to him. The two most important are *Summa Contra Gentiles* (*On the Truth of the Catholic Faith,*1261–1264) and *Summa Theologica* (*Summary Treatise of Theology*, 1265–1273). Aquinas was canonized by Pope John XXII in 1323 and proclaimed a Doctor of the Church by Pope Pius V in 1567. In 1879 Pope Leo XIII made Thomism a model of Catholic thought.

CHAPTER III

In What Way It Is Possible to Make Known the Divine Truth

Since, however, not every truth is to be made known in the same way, and *it is the part of an educated man to seek for conviction in each subject, only so far as the nature of the subject allows*, as the Philosopher[1] most rightly observes as quoted by Boethius[2], it is necessary to show first of all in what way it is possible to make known the aforesaid truth.

Now in those things which we hold about God there is truth in two ways. For certain things that are true about God wholly surpass the capability o human reason, for instance that God is three and one: while there are certain things to which even natural reason can attain, for instance that God is[3], that God is one, and others like these, which even the philosophers proved demonstratively of God, being guided by the light of natural reason.

That certain divine truths wholly surpass the capability of human reason, is most clearly evident. For since the principle of all the knowledge which the reason acquires about a thing, is the understanding of that

Summa contra gentiles, Florence, 1521

---

1   **the Philosopher:** i.e., Aristotle

2   **Boethius (c. 480–524):** 波爱修，Roman philosopher and statesman, was made a consul in 510 and, accused of plotting treason, was executed. During imprisonment he wrote *The Consolation of Philosophy* (c. 523), which, though written by a non-Christian, contained elements of Christian ethics highly regarded in Europe during medieval times.

3   **that God is:** namely, that God "exists"

Heritage of Western Intellectual Tradition   A Sourcebook

thing's essence, because according to the Philosopher's teaching the principle of a demonstration is *what a thing is*, it follows that our knowledge about a thing will be in proportion to our understanding of its essence. Wherefore, if the human intellect comprehends the essence of a particular thing, for instance a stone or a triangle, no truth about that thing will surpass the capability of human reason. **But this does not happen to us in relation to God, because the human intellect is incapable by its natural power of attaining to the comprehension of His essence: since our intellect's knowledge, according to the mode of the present life, originates from the senses: so that things which are not objects of sense cannot be comprehended by the human intellect, except in so far as knowledge of them is gathered from sensibles. Now sensibles cannot lead our intellect to see in them[1] what God is, because they are effects unequal to the power of their cause. And yet our intellect is led by sensibles to the divine knowledge so as to know about God that He is, and other such truths, which need to be ascribed to the first principle[2]. Accordingly some divine truths are attainable by human reason, while others altogether surpass the power of human reason.**

Again. The same is easy to see from the degrees of intellects. For if one of two men perceives a thing with his intellect with greater subtlety, the one whose intellect is of a higher degree understands many things which the other is altogether unable to grasp; as instanced in a yokel[3] who is utterly incapable of grasping the subtleties of philosophy. Now the angelic intellect surpasses the human intellect more than the intellect of the cleverest philosopher surpasses that of the most uncultured. For an angel knows God through a more excellent effect than does man, for as much as the angel's essence, through which he is led to know God by natural knowledge, is more excellent than sensible things, even than the soul itself, by which the human intellect mounts to the knowledge of God. And the divine intellect surpasses the angelic intellect much more than the angelic surpasses the human. **For the divine intellect by its capacity equals the divine essence, wherefore God perfectly understands of Himself what He is, and He knows all things that can be understood about Him: whereas the angel knows not what God is by his natural knowledge, because the angel's essence, by which he is led to the knowledge of God, is an effect unequal to the power of its cause. Consequently an angel is unable by his natural knowledge to grasp all that God understands about Himself: nor again is human reason capable of grasping all that an angel understands by his natural power. Accordingly just as a man would show himself to be a most insane fool if he declared the**

Three disadvantages preventing men from discovering truth by reason (Francesco Solimena)

---

1   **them:** objects of sense
2   **the first principle:** Aristotle in his *Metaphysics* demonstrates the existence of a Prime Mover as the First Principle of all things.
3   **yokel:** simple-minded countryman

assertions of a philosopher to be false because he was unable to understand them, so, and much more, a man would be exceedingly foolish, were he to suspect of falsehood the things revealed by God through the ministry of His angels, because they cannot be the object of reason's investigations.

Furthermore. The same is made abundantly clear by the deficiency which every day we experience in our knowledge of things. For we are ignorant of many of the properties of sensible things, and in many cases we are unable to discover the nature of those properties which we perceive by our senses. Much less therefore is human reason capable of investigating all the truths about that most sublime essence.

With this the saying of the Philosopher is in accord where he says that *our intellect in relation to those primary things which are most evident in nature is like the eye of a bat* in *relation to the sun.*

To this truth Holy Writ[1] also bears witness. For it is written (Job xi. 7): *peradventure thou wilt comprehend the steps of God and wilt find out the Almighty perfectly?* and (xxxvi. 26) *Behold God is great, exceeding our knowledge,* and (I Cor. Xiii. 9): *we know in part.*

Therefore all that is said about God, though it cannot be investigated by reason, must not be forthwith rejected as false, as the Manicheans[2] and many unbelievers have thought.

CHAPTER IV

That the Truth about Divine Things which Is Attainable by Reason
Is Fittingly Proposed to Man As an Object of Belief

While then the truth of the intelligible things of God is twofold, one to which the inquiry of reason can attain, the other which surpasses the whole range of human reason, both are fittingly proposed by God to man as an object of belief. We must first show this with regard to that truth which is attainable by the inquiry of reason, lest it appears to some, that since it can be attained by reason, it was useless to make it an object of faith by supernatural inspiration. **Now three disadvantages would result if this truth were left solely to the inquiry of reason. One is that few men would have knowledge of God: because very many are hindered from gathering the fruit of diligent inquiry, which is the discovery of truth, for three reasons.** Some indeed on account of an indisposition[3] of temperament, by reason of which many are naturally indisposed[4] to knowledge: so that no efforts of theirs would enable them to reach to the attain-

---

1   **writ:** written order; **Holy Writ:** Holy Bible
2   **Manichean:** ancient religion named for its founder the Persian sage Mani (c. 216–76?), presented a major challenge to Christianity for several centuries with a dualistic division of the universe into good and evil. The human race is a result of this perpetual struggle, with the human soul to be redeemed from its imprisonment in the evil of the human body.
3   **indisposition:** slight illness
4   **indisposed:** unwilling

Heritage of Western Intellectual Tradition   A Sourcebook

ment of the highest degree of human knowledge, which consists in knowing God. Some are hindered by the needs of household affairs. For there must needs be among men some that devote themselves to the conduct of temporal affairs, who would be unable to devote so much time to the leisure of contemplative research as to reach the summit of human inquiry, namely the knowledge of God. And some are hindered by laziness. For in order to inquire the knowledge of God in those things which reason is able to investigate, it is necessary to have a previous knowledge of many things: since almost the entire consideration of philosophy is directed to the knowledge of God: for which reason metaphysics, which is about divine things, is the last of the parts of philosophy to be studied. Wherefore it is not possible to arrive at the inquiry about the aforesaid truth except after a most laborious study: and few are willing to take upon themselves this labour for the love of a knowledge, the natural desire for which has nevertheless been instilled into the mind of man by God.

The second disadvantage is that those who would arrive at the discovery of the aforesaid truth would scarcely succeed in doing so after a long time. First, because this truth is so profound, that it is only after long practice that the human intellect is enabled to grasp it by means of reason. Secondly, because many things are inquired before hand, as stated above. Thirdly, because at the time of youth, the mind, when tossed about by the various movements of the passions, is not fit for the knowledge of so sublime a truth, whereas *calm gives prudence and knowledge,* as stated in *7 Phys.* Hence mankind would remain in the deepest darkness of ignorance, if the path of reason were the only available way to the knowledge of God: because the knowledge of God which especially makes men perfect and good, would be acquired only by the few, and by these only after a long time.

The third disadvantage is that much falsehood is mingled with the investigations of human reason, on account of the weakness of our intellect in forming its judgments, and by reason of the admixture of phantasms. Consequently many would remain in doubt about those things even which are most truly demonstrated, through ignoring the force of the demonstration: especially when they perceive that different things are taught by the various men who are called wise. Moreover among the many demonstrated truths, there is sometimes a mixture of falsehood that is not demonstrated, but assumed for some probable or sophistical[1] reason which at times is mistaken for a demonstration. Therefore it was necessary that definite certainty and pure truth about divine things should be offered to man by the way of faith.

Accordingly the divine clemency (仁慈) has made this salutary[2] commandment, that even some things which reason is able to investigate must be held by faith: so that all may share in the knowledge of God easily, and without doubt or error.

Hence it is written (Eph. iv. 17, 18): That *henceforward you walk not as also the Gentiles walk in the vanity of their mind, having their understanding darkened*: and (Isa. liv. 13): *All thy*

---

1 **sophistical:** that of sophism
2 **salutary:** having good effect

children shall be taught of the Lord.

CHAPTER V

That Those Things Which Cannot Be Investigated by Reason
Are Fittingly Proposed to Man as an Object of Faith

It may appear to some that those things which cannot be investigated by reason ought not to be proposed to man as an object of faith: because divine wisdom provides for each thing according to the mode of its nature. We must therefore prove that it is necessary also for those things which surpass reason to be proposed by God to man as an object of faith.

Divine intellect equals divine essence (Carlo Crivelli)

For no man tends to do a thing by his desire and endeavour unless it be previously known to him. Wherefore since man is directed by divine providence to a higher good than human frailty can attain in the present life, as we shall show in the sequel[1], it was necessary for his mind to be bidden to something higher than those things to which our reason can reach in the present life, so that he might learn to aspire, and by his endeavours to tend to something surpassing the whole state of the present life. And this is especially competent to the Christian religion, which alone promises goods spiritual and eternal: for which reason it proposes many things surpassing the thought of man: whereas the old law which contained promises of temporal things, proposed few things that are above human inquiry. It was with this motive that the philosophers, in order to wean[2] men from sensible pleasures to virtue, took care to show that there are other goods of greater account than those which appeal to the senses, the taste of which things affords much greater delight to those who devote themselves to active or contemplative virtues.

Again it is necessary for this truth to be proposed to man as an object of faith in order that he may have truer knowledge of God. For then alone do we know God truly, when we believe that He is far above all that man can possibly think of God, because the divine essence surpasses man's natural knowledge, as stated above. Hence by the fact that certain things about God are proposed to man, which surpass his reason[3], he is strengthened in his opinion that God is far above what he is able to think.

There results also another advantage from this, namely, the checking of presumption which

---

1   **in the sequel:** later on

2   **wean:** cause to keep away

3   **which surpass his reason:** cf. The first statement in the Taoist Holy Writ *Daodejing*: The Way that can be spoken of is not the constant Way; The name that can be named is not the constant name (道可道非常道，名可名非常名). It might be more interesting if we compare it with the version in the bamboo clips from Guodian (1993): The Way can be spoken, but that is not the Way people usually refer to; The name can be named, but that is not the name people usually give.

is the mother error. For some there are who[1] presume so far on their wits that they think them-selves capable of measuring the whole nature of things by their intellect, in that they esteem all things true which they see, and false which they see not. Accordingly, in order that man's mind might be freed from this presumption, and seek the truth humbly, it was necessary that certain things far surpassing his intel-lect should be proposed to man by God.

Yet another advantage is made apparent by the words of the Philoso-pher (10 *Ethic.*). For when a certain Simonides[2] maintained that man should neglect the knowledge of God, and apply his mind to human affairs, and declared that *a man ought to relish[3] human things, and mortal things*: the Philosopher contradicted him, saying that *a man ought to devote himself to immortal and divine things as much as he can.* Hence he says (*11 De Anima.*) that though it is but little that we perceive of higher substances, yet that little is more loved and desired than all the knowledge we have of lower

divine essence surpassing man's knowledge (Joos van Ghent)

substances. He says also (*2 De Coelo et Mundo*) that when questions about the heavenly bodies can be answered by a short and probable solution, it happens that the hearer is very much rejoiced. All this shows that however imperfect the knowledge of the highest things may be, it bestows very great perfection on the soul: and consequently, although human reason is unable to grasp fully things that are above reason, it nevertheless acquires much perfection, if at least it hold things, in any way whatever, by faith.

Wherefore it is written (Eccles. iii. 25): *many things are shown to thee above the understand-ing of men,* and (I Cor. ii. 10, 11): *The things … that are of God no man knoweth, but the Spirit of God: but to us God hath revealed them by His Spirit.*

CHPTER VI

That It Is Not a Mark of Levity[4] to Assent to the Things That Are of Faith, Although They Are Above Reason

Now those who believe this truth, *of which reason affords a proof,* believe not lightly, as though *following foolish fables* (2 Pet. i. 16). For divine Wisdom Himself, Who knows all things most fully, designed to reveal to man *the secrets of God's wisdom*: and by suitable arguments proves His presence, and the truth of His doctrine and inspiration, by performing works surpass-

---

1 **For some there are who:** For there are some who
2 **a certain Simonides:** referring probably to Simonides of Ceos (c. 556–468 BC), Greek court poet, most of whose works do not survive
3 **relish:** like, enjoy
4 **levity:** lack of seriousness

ing the capability of the whole of nature, namely, the wondrous healing of the sick[1], the raising of the dead to life[2], a marvelous control over the heavenly bodies, and what excites yet more wonder, the inspiration of human minds, so that unlettered and simple persons are filled with the Holy Ghost, and in one instant are endowed with the most sublime wisdom and eloquence. And after considering these arguments, convinced by the strength of the proof, and not by the force of arms, nor by the promise of delights, but — and this is the greatest marvel of all — amidst the tyranny of persecutions, a countless crowd of not only simple but also of the wisest men, embraced the Christian faith, which inculcates[3] things surpassing all human understanding, curbs the pleasures of the flesh, and teaches contempt of all worldly things. That the minds of mortal beings should assent to such things, is both the greatest of miracles, and the evident work of divine inspiration, seeing that they despise visible things and desire only those that are invisible. And that this happened not suddenly nor by chance, but by the disposition of God, is shown by the fact that God foretold that He would do so by the manifold oracles of the prophets, whose books we hold veneration[4] as bearing witness to our faith. This particular kind of proof is alluded to in the words of Heb. ii, 3, 4: *Which,* namely the salvation of mankind, *having begun to be declared by them that heard Him, God also bearing witness by signs and wonders, and divers … distributions of the Holy Ghost.*

Now such a wondrous conversion of the world to the Christina faith is a most indubitable[5] proof that such signs did take place, so that there is no need to repeat them, seeing that there is evidence of them in their result. For it would be the most wondrous sign of all if without any wondrous signs the world were persuaded by simple and lowly men to believe things so arduous, to accomplish things so difficult, and to hope for things so sublime. Although God ceases not even in our time to work miracles through His saints in confirmation of the faith.

In this 15th-century Italian painting, parents were taking their children to see a teacher who employed the concepts of reason and revelation to teach their students how to think.

On the other hand those who introduced the errors of the sects proceeded in contrary

---

1 **the wondrous healing of the sick:** "And Jesus went about all Galilee … healing all manner of sickness and all manner of disease among the people. And his fame went throughout all Syria: and they brought unto him all sick people that were taken with divers diseases and torments, and those which were possessed with devils, and those which were lunatic, and those that had the palsy; and he healed them." (Matthew 4, 23–24)

2 **the raising of the dead to life:** "Jesus … cometh to the grave. It was a cave, and a stone lay upon it. Jesus said, Take ye away the stone. Martha, the sister of him that was dead, saith unto him, Lord, by this time he stinketh: for he hath been dead four days. Jesus … cried with a loud voice, Lazarus, come forth. And he that was dead came forth, bound hand and foot with graveclothes … Jesus saith unto them, Loose him, and let him go." (John 11, 38–44)

3 **inculcate:** repeat firmly and instill

4 **veneration:** high respect

5 **indubitable:** that cannot be doubted

fashion, as instanced by Mohammed[1], who enticed[2] peoples with the promise of carnal pleasures, to the desire of which the concupiscence[3] of the flesh instigates. He also delivered commandments in keeping with his promises, by giving the reins to carnal pleasure, wherein it is easy for carnal men to obey: and the lessons of truth which he inculcated were only such as can be easily known to any man of average wisdom by his natural powers: yea rather the truths which he taught were mingled by him with many fables and most false doctrines. Nor did he add any signs of supernatural agency, which alone are a fitting witness to divine inspiration, since a visible work that can be from God alone, proves the teacher of truth to be invisibly inspired: but he asserted that he was sent in the power of arms, a sign that is not lacking even to robbers and tyrants. Again, those who believed in him[4] from the outset were not wise men practiced in things divine and human, but beastlike men who dwelt in the wilds, utterly ignorant of all divine teaching; and it was by a multitude of such men and the force of arms that he impelled others to submit to his law.

Lastly, no divine oracles or prophets in a previous age bore witness to him; rather did he corrupt almost all the teaching of the Old and New Testaments by a narrative replete[5] with fables, as one may see by a perusal of his law. Hence by a cunning device, he did not commit the reading of the Old and New Testament Books to his followers, lest he should thereby be convicted of falsehood. Thus it is evident that those who believe his words believe lightly.

CHAPTER VII

That the Truth of Reason Is Not in Opposition to the Truth of the Christina Faith

Now though the aforesaid truth of the Christian faith surpasses the ability of human reason, nevertheless those things which are naturally instilled in human reason cannot be opposed to this truth. For it is clear that those things which are implanted in reason by nature, are most true, so much so that it is impossible to think them to be false. Nor is it lawful to deem false that which is held by faith, since it is so evidently confirmed by God. Seeing then that the false alone is opposed to the true, as evidently appears if we examine their definitions, it is impossible for the aforesaid truth of faith to be contrary to those principles which reason knows naturally[6].

---

1   **Mohammed or Muhammad, Mahomet (c. 570–632):** founder of Islam, whose prophetic teachings became the basis of Islamic civilization

2   **entice:** tempt

3   **concupiscence:** lust

4   **those who believed in him:** Bear in mind Aquinas' attack on Islam: Aristotle was rediscovered largely due to Arab scholars for their preservation and introduction of Aristotle's works.

5   **replete:** filled with

6   **reason knows naturally:** Compare with Cicero's discussion of the relation between natural law and civil law in Unit 3.

Again. The same thing which the disciple's mind receives from its teacher is contained in the knowledge of the teacher, unless he teach insincerely, which it were wicked to say of God. Now the knowledge of naturally known principles is instilled into us by God, since God Himself is the author of our nature. Therefore the divine Wisdom also contains these principles. Consequently whatever is contrary to these principles, is contrary to the divine Wisdom; wherefore it cannot be from God. Therefore those things which are received by faith from divine revelation cannot be contrary to our natural knowledge.

Moreover. Our intellect is stayed by contrary arguments, so that it cannot advance to the knowledge of truth. Wherefore if conflicting knowledges were instilled into us by God, our intellect would thereby be hindered from knowing the truth. And this cannot be ascribed to God.

Furthermore. Things that are natural are unchangeable so long as natural remains. Now contrary opinions cannot be together in the same subject. Therefore God does not instill into man any opinion or belief contrary to natural knowledge.

Hence the Apostle says (Rom. x. 8): T*hy word is nigh thee even in thy heart and in thy mouth. This is the word of faith which we preach.* Yet because it surpasses reason some look upon it as though it were contrary thereto; which is impossible.

This is confirmed also by the authority of Augustine who says *That which truth shall make known can nowise be in opposition to the holy books whether of the Old or of the New Testament.*

From this we may evidently conclude that whatever arguments are alleged against the teachings of faith, they do not rightly proceed from the first self-evident principles instilled by nature. Wherefore they lack the force of demonstration, and are either probable or sophistical arguments, and consequently it is possible to solve them.

Key Concepts

divine intellect	natural power
divine knowledge	object of faith
divine truths	revelation
divine wisdom	sensibles
human reason	truth of reason
natural knowledge	truth of faith

Heritage of Western Intellectual Tradition   A Sourcebook

Heritage of Western Intellectual Tradition   A Sourcebook

Compare with China

Neo-Confucianism and Later Confucian Philosophy

While St. Augustine and Thomas Aquinas were trying to lay the theological foundation for the modern Christianity, Chinese Buddhists at the time were also trying to legitimize and institutionalize（体制化） Buddhism in China. There are huge differences among these two groups of religious people, to be sure, but there might also be instances of relevance and connection between them. Discuss and comment.

The Middle Ages saw the revival of Christianity and its establishment as the dominant religion in Europe, thanks to efforts made by people like St. Augustine and Thomas Aquinas. Starting almost at the same period in Chinese intellectual history was the revival of Confucianism and its establishment as the dominant ideology in face of challenges from Taoism and Buddhism. Try to read the following essay in connection with what was happening for Christianity in the Middle Ages in Europe.

Li Ao asks for Buddhist scripts

Renaissance of Confucianism during late Tang dynasty

The renaissance of Confucianism was a direct reaction against the long prevailing of Taoism since the end of the Han dynasty and the power of Buddhism during the time of North-South division and early Tang dynasty. Tang scholars saw not only their own position as state advisors endangered, but they were afraid of the influence of the foreign religion of Buddhism on Chinese tradition and its government. Buddhism is a religion with a complex metaphysical philosophy, an aspect that the old Confucianism ignores. The aim of Tang and Song Confucian writers was to find a system that was able to explain universe and man in a way that could rival the sophisticated Buddhist philosophy.

The most important Tang scholars defending Confucianism against the influence of Taoism and Buddhism were Han Yu 韩愈 (768–824) and Li Ao 李翱 (772–841). Han, a great essayist of his time, vehemently argued against Buddhism and proposed to go back to the roots of human ethics in Confucian classics. His main concern about Buddhism was that the foreign religion was egalitarian[1] and did not observe the proper relation between the senior and the junior, to the effect of endangering social order. In his essay "Sourcing the way" 原道, he wrote that humanity 仁 and righteousness 义 indicate the way for all under Heaven, unlike the "way" of Taoism and Buddhism where everybody is seeking his own salvation. Li Ao studied the Buddhist philosophy in order to

---

1 **egalitarian:** equality-minded. Compare, if you can, Han Yu's anti-egalitarianism with the similar attitude of the Roman Catholicism during the Reformation.

be able to attack it. His most important writing is *Revival of Human Nature*复性书, with the implication of "Revival of Confucianism." Both Han Yu and Li Ao adopted the teachings of Mencius, but they developed the old philosopher to a more complex stage in terms of human behaviour.

Early Song Neo-Confucianists

It took time for the early re-interpreters of Confucianism to gain ground. The early Song writer Ouyang Xiu欧阳修(1007–72) believed that the traditional Confucian classics were the best means for the education of officials and making of policies. A similar view was held by Sima Guang司马光(1019–86) who wrote the *Comprehensive Mirror Providing Material for Governance* 《资治通鉴》, a historiography with a style oriented from the classical *Annals of Lu Spring and Autumn*《吕氏春秋》.

Also going back to the old classics was Zhou Dunyi周敦颐(1017–73). Basing on the classic *Book of Changes*《易经》, he wrote *Explanation of the Diagram of Highest Extreme*《太极图說》 and traced all existing phenomena like seasons, the Five Elements and the active and inactive principles of *yin* and *yang*阴阳, back to a source of deep silence and motionlessness无极. More important for Confucian thinking is his book *Comprehensive Book of Changes*《易通》, where motionlessness being the source of everything is the basis for achieving sincerity诚 and for being a saint圣人. Sincerity, in terms of non-acting无为, determines good善 or bad恶. Virtue德 is expressed as love or humanity爱/仁, properness or righteousness宜, order or rituals理/礼, comprehending or knowing通/智, keeping or trusting守/信. Through human relationship (*yang*) and righteousness (*yin*), order理 is brought to people, and harmony和 to the empire.

Zhang Zai張載(1020–77) further developed the metaphysical background for the Confucian revival. Based on the *Book of Changes* and the *Doctrine of the Mean*, he postulated in *Correcting the Ignorant*正蒙 that the basic component of the universe is odem or breath气 which he called "Great Emptiness"太虚, a substance to give shape to everything. Every being possessing the Great Emptiness has the potential for a virtuous person. In *Western Inscriptions*西铭 he stresses the unity of Heaven天, Earth地 and all beings. Human nature finds its source in Heaven and is therefore equally good in everyone. The individual difference in character is due to the "quality of substantiation" 气质, and a bad substantiation can be led to its good origin by proper education and self-control.

The brothers Cheng Hao程顥(1032–85) and Cheng Yi程颐(1033–1107) further developed these Proto[1]-Neo-Confucian thoughts by trying to remove the Taoist influence. Referring to Confucian classics such as the *Analects* and the *Great Learning*, they took order理 as the never changing base of universe, providing breath气 ranging from positive阳 to negative阴 to form everything. Consequently, human nature should be good because it is given by the universal order, and the transformation into a being can vary as a result of breath. The good man has to observe the Heavenly path of universal order.

---

1   **proto:** primal, original

Zhu Xi and his philosophy of universal order and human nature

The greatest synthesizer of Neo-Confucianism is Zhu Xi 朱熹(1130–1200), also called "Master Zhu" 朱子, as his philosophy the "Teachings of the Order" 理学 became orthodox in the Yuan Dynasty. Zhu Xi held that the source of universe is the Heavenly Order 天理, also called the Highest Extreme 太极, which in combination with universal breath gives shape to everything. Hence the same order with different shapes 理一分殊. Or in Zhu Xi's own words, "taking water out of a river with a bowl or a bucket, you obtain different measures of water." Zhu Xi was the most important Confucian scholar in his time after Confucius and Mencius, and his interpretation had been the orthodox exegesis[1] of Confucian texts until the end of the Chinese feudal empire.

朱熹

Lu Jiuyuan, Wang Yangming and the philosophy of the mind

Lu Jiuyuan 陆九渊(1139–91) took a somewhat different approach from the metaphysics of Zhu Xi. While still sticking to the idea of the universal order 理/道, Lu laid emphasis on individual enlightenment with this order. The importance of heart or mind 心, in other words, is equal to that of the universal order, as it is a reflection of the natural pattern. At this point, Lu contradicts Zhu Xi who believes that the will and temperament of man 情/欲 destroys this natural order in human nature. The Universal Order, Lu seems to argue, can only be actualized in one's mind, which is dependent of sensual perception. Lu's philosophy or the "Philosophy of the Mind" 心学 gained an upper hand in its struggle with the disciples of Zhu Xi, thanks to its chief adherent the Ming Dynasty philosopher Wang Yangming.

Lu Jiuyuan

Wang Yangming 王阳明(1472–1529), the last great Neo-Confucianist, was deeply influenced by Lu Jiuyuan. With traces of Buddhist and Taoist thinking, he focused on the relationship between the mind 心, temperament of man 情 and human nature 性. While in Zhu Xi the mind is a subjective phenomenon that stands against the objective and all-embracing universal order 理, for Wang all virtue and righteousness of the mind corresponds with the universal order and is bound to it. Human nature is neutral, neither good nor bad, and is likewise connected to the universal order. This immanent[2] positive character of a human being enables it to recognize and distinguish good and bad by his innate knowledge 致良知. This innate[3] knowledge of perfection leads naturally to right behaviour: knowing and acting cannot be separated as Zhu insists then can, as the human mind and the universal order cannot exist without each other.

---

1 **exegesis:** exposition, explanation
2 **immanent:** inherent
3 **innate:** possessed from birth

Heritage of Western Intellectual Tradition   A Sourcebook

Supplementary Reading

1. Common Characteristics of Scholasticism

Scholasticism, a term coming from "Scholar" or Aristotle, refers to a theological movement that intends to integrate into an ordered system both the natural wisdom of Greece and Rome and the religious wisdom of Christianity. It was dominant in the medieval Christian Europe from the mid 11th century to the mid 15th century, and served to initiate the Enlightenment movement that followed it. But is it not dead, as its "characteristics" may still be found in philosophical and theological inquiries of today in the West. Read the following essay and see if you disagree with its author.

Differing much among themselves, and fighting one another vigorously, the Schoolmen still make one school of philosophy, and present a united front against adversaries. They are all orthodox, in the Roman Catholic sense; they are all dualist; they are all optimist (taking a cheerful view of the world and of the competency of human reason); they are all static, or feudal, believing in a fixed hierarchy[1] of beings.

1. Orthodoxy. The Schoolmen were Churchmen, faithful to the Church they served. Their every page testifies to their zeal for orthodoxy. If some were less orthodox[2] than others, they were also less scholastic. They speculated with considerable freedom, but always laboured to make out their speculations to be in harmony with the teachings of Mother Church, and really at heart desired that they should be so. It would not be fair to accuse any of them of heresy, even though it might appear that this or that utterance, pursued through all its consequences, should end in contradicting one or other of the dogmas of faith. The author had no mind to follow his statement so far, and would not have owned that it led so far. Still it would not be right to regard Scholastic Philosophy as a series of mere corollaries[3] drawn from articles of faith, mere dictates of dogmatic theology. The subtlety and variety of Scholastic disputation suffices to set aside such a view. As the application was pressed and followed on, the Schoolmen travelled wide of one another, nor did the Church intervene to bring them together, so long as the dogma from whence they started was not plainly denied. Philosophy, as such, is not founded upon dogma and revelation. It has its own principles, which are truths of intuitive[4] reason; and it proceeds upon facts of experience. To take an example from Scholasticism: its central tenet of the composition of all things out of matter and form has nothing to do with theology. The theory of matter and form is due to Aristotle — clearly no Catholic. Many Catholic philosophers have rejected and do reject matter and form. It is an open issue in philosophy, independent of faith; and there are many

---

1 **hierarchy:** order or grades of importance
2 **orthodox:** generally approved and accepted
3 **corollary:** natural sequence or outcome
4 **intuitive:** immediate understanding without conscious reasoning

such.

2. Dualism. All philosophers draw some distinction between the mind and the world which it cognizes[1]; also, if they be theists, between God and the world. But many, perhaps most modern philosophers, will not allow this distinction to be a clear and deep line of cleavage. They dream of God and the world, they dream of the subject perceiving and the object perceived, meeting in what they call "a higher unity." That is to say, modern philosophy is idealistic, monistic[2], pantheistic. Such, eminently, Scholasticism was not. To every genuine Schoolman, God was "high above all nations," so high that the world in comparison with God cannot be said to be at all. In the sense in which God is, the world is not. As God is above the world, so the world is beyond and independent of the know-

Trained in scholasticism and disillusioned with ecclesiastical abuses, John Wycliffe sponsored translation of Bible into English. Here, Wycliffe is reading his translation to English nobleman John of Gaunt, far right.

ing mind of man. The most pronounced feature of all Scholastic treatises is their pronounced objectivity. The Scholastic mind was bent on being, not on forms of thought or constraining needs of believing.

3. Optimism. The Schoolman is a cheerful man: he has a serene confidence in two things; (1) the competence of the human mind to attain to truth with certitude; (2) the general goodness of Being, and of the tendencies of things. He never asked himself whether life were worth living. With him it was an axiom that Being is good, and Living Being still better, for there was more of Being in it. The Schoolman venerated faith, but he maintained that there was also a natural, or rational, knowledge of God; and that sundry truths of religion could be established by philosophical argument.

4. Static. Modern philosophy is the philosophy of change, of phenomena, of perpetual flux. Scholasticism is the philosophy of permanent substantial being. Not that the Schoolmen ignored change, but by preference they rested upon complete existences and achieved results, e.g. a perfect morality and a full-grown society, not the development of either. One word on Evolution. The Schoolman, with Aristotle, believed in abiogenesis[3], the development of maggots[4] and reptiles[5] and fish out of mud and decaying matter. They believed in the ontogenetic[6] evolution of the human embryo[7] from mere vegetative life to the life of a brute animal, and thence to the life of a

---

1   **cognize:** have knowledge
2   **monistic:** metaphysical and theological view that there is only one principle or essence in the Universe, to be distinguished from dualism and pluralism
3   **abiogenesis:** generation of life from non-living matter
4   **maggot:** larva
5   **reptile:** cold-blooded crawling animal
6   **ontogenetic:** origin and development of an individual organism from embryo to adult
7   **embryo:** early stage offspring before birth

Heritage of Western Intellectual Tradition   A Sourcebook

rational being. St. Thomas teaches what is called ontogenetic evolution, the evolution of the individual perfect animal from a lower form. Of phylogenetic[1] evolution, or the evolution of species, he seems never to have thought. St. Thomas, with Aristotle, points out a static series of gradations, or what has been termed "evolution in co-existence" in the following passage: "A wonderful chain of beings is revealed to our study. The lowest member of the higher genus is always found to border close upon the highest member of the lower genus. Thus some of the lowest members of the genus[2] of animals attain to little beyond the life of plants; certain shell-fish, for example, have only the sense of touch, and are attached to the ground like plants. Hence Dionysius[3] says: 'Divine Wisdom has joined the ends of the higher to the beginnings of the lower'" (Contra Gentiles, ii. 68). He has in view the series: plant, animal, man, angel. But he did not derive plant, animal, and man from a common ancestor.

Scholasticism is known for its rigorous reading of the Scripture

Revival of Scholasticism

1. *The Revival of the Seventeenth Century.*

The one hundred and fifty years from the middle of the sixteenth to the end of the seventeenth century is known in history as the period of the Counter-Reformation. During that period the Catholic Church consolidated her position in the countries that remained to her after the great revolt, and planted herself by vast missionary efforts in new lands. In Spain and Italy she quite recovered, and even improved upon, the position that had been hers in the Middle Ages. With this revival of Catholicism, the dying embers of Scholasticism were kindled into a new glow in the countries just named. Two Religious Orders, the Dominicans and the Jesuits, brought their schools to a level which recalled the brighter days of the now decadent University of Paris.

Scholastic and modern philosophy differ in their orientation. Not every reference to God can be said to belong to (dogmatic or revealed) theology. God is to some extent known by reason; and to that extent He is an object, nay a principal object, of philosophy. Scholasticism, then, and the philosophy of our day differ in this, that Scholasticism is ever referring to God, modern philosophy has for its centre, man. In which particular, perhaps, it may be found that modern philosophy stands to Scholasticism as geocentrism[4] to heliocentrism[5] in astronomy.

---

1   **phylogenetic:** evolutionary development and history of a species or higher taxonomic grouping of organisms
2   **genus:** class
3   **St. Dionysius of Alexandria** (狄奥尼修斯)**:** often known as Dionysius the Great (c.190–c.264), a Christian theologian
4   **geocentrism:** belief that the earth is the center of the universe
5   **heliocentrism:** belief that the sun is the center of the universe

Heritage of Western Intellectual Tradition   A Sourcebook

2. *The Leonine Revival of 1879.*

Leo XIII made two big pronouncements: one on Civil Government, the Labour Question, and Socialism; the other on Scholastic Philosophy, notably the philosophy of the greatest of the Schoolmen, St. Thomas Aquinas. The Pope deplores the decay of philosophy, even in the Catholic schools, since the sixteenth century. Philosophy has become a house of confusion, every man babbling his own conceits; nothing remains fixed and certain, there is no foothold for science to climb by. "We all see how the society of the family and of the State itself is endangered by the pest of perverse opinions. Society would be much more peaceful and far more safe if in our Universities and Schools there were taught a sounder doctrine, more in accordance with the teaching of the Church. Such a doctrine is found in the volumes of Thomas Aquinas. Thomas's arguments on the true notion of liberty, now running into license, on the divine origin of every sort of authority, on laws and their force, on the paternal and equable rule of the Sovereign Pontiffs[1], on obedience to higher powers, on mutual charity amongst all men, and the like subjects, all these his arguments are fraught with[2] mighty and invincible strength for the overthrow of those principles of new-invented law, which are plainly perilous to the order of society and the public safety."

3. *The Future of Scholasticism.*

These wishes and commands of Leo XIII have been repeated by his successor, Pius X. Will they be ever carried out to any considerable extent? Will Scholasticism ever overleap the walls of the Seminaries? Will it remain a philosophy for the clergy only, a vestibule[3] to dogmatic theology for those whose profession it is to be theologians, or will it largely imbue[4] the Catholic laity[5] also? Will it take a hold upon the universities? Will it ever colour, as Kant[6] and Hegel[7] at this day colour, the thought of the writers in our magazines? Any ordinary educated man who spent a week with St. Thomas, Duns Scotus[8], and Suárez[9], would come out crying: "No chance; Scholastic tomes are only less archaic than Babylonian bricks; Scholasticism is as the traceable old bed of a river, which the water once filled, but to which it will never return; the current of modern thought has turned irrevocably another way." On the other hand a great thinker has

---

1   **pontiff:** pope
2   **fraught with:** full of
3   **vestibule:** entrance
4   **imbue:** inspire
5   **laity:** layman
6   **Immanuel Kant (1724–1804):** German philosopher, considered by many Western scholars as the most influential thinker of modern times
7   **Georg Wilhelm Friedrich Hegel (1770–1831):** German idealist philosopher, one of the most influential thinkers of the 19th century
8   **John Duns Scotus (c.1266–1308):** Scottish theologian and philosopher, founder of a school of Scholasticism known as Scotism
9   **Francisco Suárez (1548–1617):** Spanish Jesuit theologian and philosopher, who made a major contribution to the philosophy of law

written: "If ever there was a power on earth who has had an eye for the times, who has confined himself to the practicable, and has been happy in his anticipations, whose words have been facts and whose commands prophecies, such is he in the history of ages who sits from generation to generation in the chair of the Apostles." Nevertheless, a little further on, the same writer adds: "The past never returns." We may therefore augur two facts for the future: (1) Scholasticism will return; (2) It will not return as it was in the Middle Ages. In other words, what will come back will be Neo-Scholasticism.

Saint Anselm of Canterbury (c. 1033–1109),was regarded as Father of early Scholasticism

Like a thirteenth-century church, a parish (教区) church still, in daily use; an ancient monument, and something besides; a present-day house of prayer, answering to the needs of a twentieth-century congregation, and for that purpose refitted, repaired, and restored, Scholasticism must be vindicated[1] from the ravages of time[2], it must remain essentially the building that it was; but it must receive new furniture, and be enlarged to take in new discoveries. And whatever there is in it, old indeed, but proved to be inconsistent with truth, must be removed. The reader has much misread Scholastic philosophy, if he takes it to be one and the same with the deposit[3] of Catholic faith. Scholasticism is not "the faith once given to the saints." It is a product of human reason, like any other philosophy. It has not come down from heaven, but man made it, and man may change it. It is irreformable, to a Catholic, only so far as its conclusions happen to coincide with dogmas taught by the Church. Hence there is no impiety in the idea of a Neo-Scholasticism. We are not called upon simply to re-echo St. Thomas, or any other mediaeval doctor, piling up quotations, adding nothing and altering nothing. St. Thomas himself did not go to work in that way upon his predecessors, no, not even upon Aristotle. We are called upon to follow a living, not a dead Thomas; to say now what St. Thomas would say, were he now alive.

Scholasticism in the Middle Ages, as we have seen, was a clerical philosophy. Dante[4], indeed, is an instance of an illustrious[5] layman, highly conversant[6] with Scholasticism; but the students who thronged[7] the halls of mediaeval Paris and Oxford, intent upon philosophy, were chiefly clerics. Philosophy, like so many other things, has been laicised[8] since then. Will Scholasticism ever be laicized, or will it remain a property of the Seminary?

The future of Scholasticism is an interesting study, because upon Scholasticism, to all

---

1   **vindicate:** prove that someone is free from guilt or blame
2   **the ravages of time:** the damage or destructive effects caused by time
3   **deposit:** accumulation, storage
4   **Dante Alighieri (1265–1321):** Italian poet, best known for his epic masterpiece, *The Divine Comedy*
5   **illustrious:** distinguished
6   **conversant:** having a knowledge of
7   **throng:** come in crowds
8   **laicize:** become a laic or layman

appearance, so at least Popes have thought, depends in great measure the hopes of the Roman Catholic Church ever recovering the ascendancy which she has lost over the intellect of mankind. (Adapted from http://www.nd.edu/Departments/Maritain/etext/scholas4.htm)

2. *St. Thomas Aquinas*

"He will enter the Order of Friars Preachers[1], and so great will be his learning and sanctity that in his day no one will be found to equal him."

According to legend, these are the words of a lowly hermit to St. Thomas Aquinas's mother, shortly before the Catholic saint's birth in 1225. Aquinas, born to a count and countess in Roccasecca, Italy, would go on to achieve a state of religious learning so profound that no one could match his religious and intellectual abilities.

At age five, the young St. Thomas was introduced to the Benedictine monks of Monte Cassino for training. While receiving instruction there, St. Thomas was noted for his diligence and prayer, and even his advanced questions, such as "What is God?"

In 1236 the Abbot of Monte Cassino, knowing that this small boy deserved better instruction than his community could provide, sent him to the University of Naples where in a matter of months St. Thomas reportedly began to surpass his professors in knowledge and understanding.

After he had received the habit of the Order of St. Dominic around 1243, his mother, Countess of Teano, having barely seen her child after he was sent to Monte Cassino, conspired[2] to kidnap St. Thomas and tempt him to leave the religious life and return to his family. While St. Thomas was under the Countess's control at the fortress of San Giovanni, she sent an impure woman to tempt him to abandon his religious celibacy[3], but St. Thomas drove the temptress out of his cell with a brand from the fire.

While he was in captivity for over a year, St. Thomas's sister provided the young scholar with copies of the Holy Scriptures, Aristotle's *Metaphysics*, and the *Sentences* of Peter Lombard[4]. When he was released, the Dominicans rejoiced[5] at the intellectual progress St. Thomas had made while imprisoned.

Despite his family's protests, St. Thomas continued to pursue membership in the Domini-

---

1 **Friars Preachers or Dominicans:** members of the Order of Preachers, a Roman Catholic religious order founded in 1214 by Spanish theologian Saint Dominic (c. 1170–1221), for the purpose of counteracting, by means of preaching, teaching, and the example of austerity, the heresies prevalent at the time
2 **conspire:** secretly plan
3 **celibacy:** living unmarried, here chastity
4 **Peter Lombard (c. 1100–1160):** Italian theologian and bishop of Paris, whose *Four Books of Sentences* became the standard theological text of the Middle Ages
5 **rejoice:** feel great happiness

can Order, finally becoming a member of the Order of Friars Preachers. The Order sent him to study with St. Albert the Great[1] in Cologne and at the University of Paris.

Despite his imposing large build, St. Thomas remained devotedly humble. His peers at the University of Paris referred to him as the "dumb ox," because of his size and meek humbleness to present his knowledge in front of others. However, after a brilliant defence of a difficult thesis in class, his teacher exclaimed, "We call this young man a dumb ox, but his bellowing in doctrine will one day resound throughout the world."

By 1250, St. Thomas had been ordained[2] to the priesthood and was now preaching to packed crowds in churches in Germany, France, and Italy. People came from miles around to hear his brilliant interpretations of the Scripture. In 1257, St. Thomas, coincidentally in the same year as the other great theologian St. Bonaventure[3], received his doctorate in Theology from the University of Paris.

As his fame grew, his life became increasingly hectic[4]. He was simultaneously praying, preaching, teaching, writing, and journeying … while also writing his famous book the *Summa Theologica*. He was in tremendous demand: people flocked to hear his sermons, the Pope demanded his presence in Rome, and Paris claimed the "dumb ox" as its own.

However, his busy life soon caught up with him. By 1273, St. Thomas was experiencing regular religious ecstasies[5] and visions[6]. After the Eucharist in a Naples Church, he was reported to have been contacted by Jesus himself. Three of the brethren[7] reported hearing a booming heavenly voice resound, "Thou has written well of me, Thomas; what reward wilt thou have?" St. Thomas replied, "None other than thyself, Lord."

Soon after, St. Thomas ceased his work on the *Summa Theologica*, citing the impossibilities of ever truly interpreting the word of God. In 1274, Pope Gregory X called for a general council of the Church at Lyons and St. Thomas, while en route[8], fell ill near Terracina and was taken in by local Cistercian monks. He died on March 7 of that year at the age of 49.

After his death, his body was given to the Dominican Church at Toulouse, where a shrine was erected. However, it was later destroyed during the French Revolution. As a precaution, his

---

1   **St. Albertus Magnus (c. 1200 – 1280):** called Albert the Great, known as doctor universalis for his wide interest in natural science. He was especially noted for introduction of Greek and Arabic science and philosophy to the medieval world.
2   **ordain:** officially make someone a priest
3   **St. Bonaventure (c. 1217 – 1274):** Christian theologian and minister general of the Franciscans, called the Seraphic Doctor, especially noted for spiritual writings
4   **hectic:** full of excitement without rest
5   **ecstasy:** great joy
6   **vision:** object seen in the mind's eye
7   **brethren:** brothers
8   **en route:** on the way

Heritage of Western Intellectual Tradition   A Sourcebook

body was later moved to the Church of St. Sernin in Toulouse with his left arm sent to the Cathedral of Naples and his right arm to the Dominican Church of S. Maria Sopra Minerva in Rome.

St. Thomas was canonized by Pope John XXII on July 18, 1323, and was proclaimed Doctor of the Church by Pope Pius V in 1567, becoming the patron saint[1] of all Catholic universities and students worldwide. St. Thomas' feast day[2] is celebrated internationally on January 28. (Adapted from D. J. Kennedy)

Questions for Discussion

1. In what sense is Man's death justifiable/unjustifiable?
2. In what sense is this "law" related to Stoicism?
3. How do "mercy" and "justice" coexist?
4. Why do the Church Fathers take pains to convince us that man is not able to be self-reliant?
5. Why is reason alone unreliable, to Aquinas?
6. Why is the "way" important to Aquinas?
7. There were people, both in the Christian West and in China, who argued that human nature is benevolent (Pelagianism[3] and Mencius [人性之善也，犹水之就下也]) and those who argue that human nature is malevolent (St. Augustine and Xunzi ["人之性，恶；其善者，伪也。"《荀子·性恶》)]). What is the possible consequence for such a difference? How may such a difference affect the mentality of the two cultures?
8. What is Scholasticism? How do you understand Scholasticism as an intellectual movement?
9. How do you evaluate the Church Fathers? What can we make out of them in the 21st century in China?

---

1 **patron saint:** saint regarded as a special protector
2 **feast day:** religious anniversary for celebration
3 **Pelagianism:** theological doctrine propounded by Pelagius, British monk, and condemned as heresy by the Roman Catholic Church in A.D. 416. It denied original sin and affirmed the ability of humans to be righteous by the exercise of free will.

Unit 5

Renaissance Adventurers

Pretest

- What do you know about Columbus and Machiavelli, and the time they lived in?
- What do you think *The Prince* meant at the time and means to us today?
- What is the message conveyed through Columbus' journals and letters?

What You Will Learn in This Unit

- Some knowledge about the late Renaissance Europe;
- Passages from Columbus' journals and letters and *The Prince*; and
- Chinese seafaring in the 15th century.

Learn to Pronounce

Antigua /æn'ti:gə/ 安提瓜岛

Borgia /'bɒdʒə/ 博尔吉亚家族

Byzantine /bɪ'zæntaɪn/ 拜占庭

Christopher Columbus /kə'lʌmbəs/ 哥伦布

Constantinople /ˌkɒnstæntɪ'nəupl/ 君士坦丁堡

Florence /'flɔːrəns/ 佛罗伦萨

Florentine /'flɒrəntaɪn/ 佛罗伦萨人，佛罗伦萨的

Guadeloupe /ˌgwadə'luːp/ 瓜德罗普

Hannibal /'ænɪbəl/ 汉尼拔

Honduras /hɒn'djuərəs/ 洪都拉斯

indigenous /ɪn'dɪdʒɪnəs/ 土著的

Jamaica /dʒə'meɪkə/ 牙买加

Machiavelli /ˌmækɪə'velɪ/ 马基雅维利

Medici /'medɪtʃiː/ 意大利美第奇家族

Muslim /'muzlɪm/ 穆斯林

Ottoman /'ɒtəmən/ 奥斯曼帝国

Puerto Rico /'pwɜːtəu 'riːkəu/ 波多黎各

Trinidad /'trɪnɪdæd/ 特立尼达

Panama /ˌpænə'mɑː/ 巴拿马

raison d'état /re'zuŋ 'detrə/ 存在的目的或理由

realpolitik /reɪ'ɑːlpəulɪ'tiːk/ 现实政治

Introduction

The 15th century was one of change and adventure. The late Middle Ages and early Renaissance were marked by spiritual unrest and innovation which were to end in the Protestant Reformation. The new national identities would lead to the triumph of the modern nation-state. The continual expansion of trade and finance would lay the groundwork for the revolutionary transformation of the European economy. Many of these turbulent events were driven by centuries of conflict between Christians and Muslims. The event that had the most far-reaching effects on Europe in the 15th century was that of the fall of the city of Constantinople[1] to the Muslim Ottoman Empire. Constantinople had been the capital of the Orthodox Christian Byzantine Empire for centuries, and it was an important center for trade between Europe and Asia. In 1453 the Ottoman Empire, which had already conquered much of southeastern Europe, captured the city, closing an important trade route from Europe to the East. Europeans longed for a sea route to Asia that would allow them to bypass the Muslims and purchase Asian products directly. In addition, European princes and kings quickly realized that the first nation to find such a route could become very wealthy by monopolizing the highly profitable Asian trade. The first European nation to begin actively seeking a sea route to Asia was Portugal, which began exploring the western coast of Africa, hoping to find a route to the riches of Asia by going around the southern tip of the continent. Other nations, not wanting to be left behind, began sponsoring voyages of exploration as well. Into this world, full of the excitement of exploration and discovery, Christopher Columbus was born.

The 16th century saw political unrest in Italy, as various states on the Italian Peninsula fell prey to armies from the more centralized countries of the north. The Italian states in 1507 were controlled by France, Spain, and Germany. In 1499 King Louis XII of France subjugated Milan. Rivalry between Charles V, the Holy Roman emperor, and King Francis I of France led to another French invasion of Italy in 1524. The Spanish Charles V took control of Milan in 1535, which remained a Spanish possession for almost 200 years. During the 18th century Italy still remained divided and controlled by foreigners. Until 1748 it was the site of a succession of European wars. The Peace of Utrecht (1713) transferred Spain's holdings in Italy to the Austrians, who exercised dominion in the peninsula throughout most of the second half of the 18th century. It is against this background that Machiavelli's *Prince* is to be read and understood.

Christopher Columbus: Journal and Letter

Christopher Columbus (1451–1506), Italian-born explorer, is widely thought to have been the first

---

1   **Constantinople:** modern Istanbul, the largest city in Turkey and the only city in the world sitting astride two continents — Europe and Asia. The city was renamed Constantinople by Roman emperor Constantine the Great in the 4th century as eastern part of the Roman Empire, and served as the capital of the Byzantine Empire which survived after the breakup of the Western Empire until it was captured by the Ottomans in the 15th century and made the capital of the Ottoman Empire.

European to sail across the Atlantic Ocean and make landfall on the American continent in an attempt to find a shorter route to India and China. Columbus based his calculations for the journey on Biblical

scripture, specifically the Books of Esdras[1] in the Apocrypha. On August 3, 1492, Columbus departed from Palos de la Frontera, Spain, with three ships in search of a westward route to Asia. He made four voyages between 1492 and 1504 from Spain to lands he later called the "New World." On his first voyage, he explored parts of Cuba and Hispaniola in 1492 and 1493. From 1493 to 1496, he continued with 17 vessels to explore those regions and also ventured to Guadeloupe, Antigua, Puerto Rico and Jamaica. On his third voyage, from 1498 to 1500, he sailed to Trinidad along the northern coast of South America. On his final journey in 1502, he embarked with four ships to explore the coast of Central America, including Honduras and Panama. He returned to Spain in 1504 and died two years later. Columbus was not the first European to reach the Americas — vikings from Scandinavia had briefly settled on the North American coast, in what is now Newfoundland, Canada, in the late 10th or early 11th century. However, Columbus' explorations had a profound impact on the world. They led directly to the opening of the western hemisphere to European colonization; to large-scale exchanges of plants, animals, cultures, and ideas between the two worlds; and, on a darker note, to the deaths of millions of indigenous American peoples from war, forced labor, and disease.

PROLOGUE[2]

Because, most Christian and very exalted and very excellent and very powerful Princes, King and Queen of the Spains and of the Islands of the Sea, our Lords, in this present year of 1492 after your Highnesse had made an end to the war of the Moors, who[3] were reigning in Europe, and having finished the war in the very great city of Granada, where in this present year on the 2nd day of the month of January, I saw the Royal banners of your Highnesses placed by force of arms on the towers of the Alhambra, which is the fortress of the said City[4]: and I saw the Moorish King come out to the gates of the City and kiss the Royal hands of your Highnesses, and the hands of the Prince, my Lord: and then in that present month, because of the information which I had given your Highnesses about the lands of India[5], and about a Prince who is called Great Khan（可汗）, which means in our Romance language, King of Kings, — how he and his predecessors had many times sent to Rome to beg for men learned in our Holy Faith that they might be instructed therein, and that the Holy Father had never furnished them, and so, many peoples believing in idolatries[6]

1　**Books of Esdras:** considered part of the Old Testament Apocrypha (Greek "hidden things"), an appendix to the Catholic Bible

2　Christopher Columbus wrote this at the beginning of the first voyage.

3　**who:** King and Queen of Spain. Pay attention to the elegant style and the long, involved sentences.

4　**the said City:** namely, the "city of Granada" in southern Spain, capital of Granada Province. Granada was founded in the 8th century by the Moors. Between 1036 and 1234, it was a part of Moorish Spain and then the capital of the kingdom of Granada until the Spanish conquest of the kingdom in 1492.

5　**India:** actually North America

6　**idolatry:** worship of idols

and receiving among themselves sects of perdition[1], were lost: — your Highnesses, as Catholic Christians and Princes, loving the Holy Christian faith and the spreading of it, and enemies of the sect of Mahomet[2] and of all idolatries and heresies, decided[3] to send me, Christopher Columbus, to the said regions of India, to see the said Princes and the peoples and lands, and learn of their disposition, and of everything, and the measures which could be taken for their conversion to our Holy Faith: and you ordered that I should not go to the east by land, by which it is customary to go,

Columbus takes leave of Ferdinand V and Isabella.

but by way of the west, whence until to-day we do not know certainly that any one has gone. So that, after having banished all the Jews from all your Kingdoms and realms, in the same month of January, your Highnesses ordered me to go with a sufficient fleet to the said regions of India: and for that purpose granted me great favours and ennobled me, that from then henceforward I might entitle myself *Don*[4] and should be High Admiral of the Ocean-Sea[5] and Viceroy[6] and perpetual Governor of all the islands and continental land which I might discover and acquire, and which from now henceforward might be discovered and acquired in the Ocean-Sea, and that my eldest son should succeed in the same manner, and thus from generation to generation for ever after: and I started from the city of Granada on Saturday, the 12th day of the month of May in the same year 1492: I came to the village of Palos, which is a sea-port, where I fitted out three vessels, very suitable for a similar undertaking: and **I left the said port, well supplied with a large quantity of provisions and with many seamen, on the 3rd day of the month of August in the said year on a Friday at the half hour before sunrise, and took my way to the Canary Islands of your Highnesses, which are in the said Ocean-Sea, in order to set out on my voyage from there and sail until I arrived at the Indies, and make known the message of your Highnesses to those Princes, and fulfil the commands which had thus been given me: and for this purpose, I decided to write everything I might do and see and which might take place on this voyage, very punctually from day to day, as will be seen henceforth.** Also, Lords and Princes, besides describing each night what takes place during the day, and during the day, the sailings of the night, I propose to make a new chart for navigation, on which I will locate all the sea and the lands of the Ocean-Sea, in their proper places, under their winds[7]; and further, to compose a book and show everything by means of drawing, by the latitude from

---

1 **perdition:** ruin, damnation
2 **Mahomet or Mohammed:** Western forms of Arabic Muhammad (c. 570–632), founder of the Islamic religion
3 The subject of "decided" is "your Highnesses."
4 **Don:** noble title of Spain
5 **the Ocean-Sea:** namely, the Atlantic
6 **Viceroy:** governor
7 **under their winds:** direction of the wind

the equator and by longitude from the west, and above all, it is fitting that I forget sleep, and study the navigation diligently, in order to thus fulfil these duties, which will be a great labour.

Letter[1]

Sir:

As I know that you will have pleasure of the great victory which our Lord hath given me in my voyage, I write you this, by which you shall know that, in twenty days I passed over to the Indies with the fleet which the most illustrious King and Queen, our Lords, gave me: where I found very many islands peopled with inhabitants beyond number. And, of them all, I have taken possession for their Highnesses, with proclamation and the royal standard displayed; and I was not gainsaid[2]. On the first which I found, I put the name San Salvador, in commemoration of His High Majesty, who marvellously hath given all this: the Indians call it Guanahani. The second I named the Island of Santa Maria de Concepcion, the third Ferrandina, the fourth Isabella, the fifth La Isla Juana [Cuba]; and so for each one a new name. When I reached Juana, I followed its coast westwardly, and found it so large that I thought it might be the mainland province of Cathay. And as I did not thus find any towns and villages on the seacoast, save small hamlets with the people whereof I could not get speech, because they all fled away forthwith, I went on farther in the same direction, thinking I should not miss of great cities or towns. And at the end of many leagues, seeing that there was no change, and that the coast was bearing me northwards, whereunto my desire was contrary since the winter was already confronting us, I formed the purpose of making from thence to the South, and as the wind also blew against me, I determined not to wait for other weather and turned back as far as a port agreed upon; from which I sent two men into the country to learn if there were a king, or any great cities. They travelled for three days, and found interminable[3] small villages and a numberless population, but nought[4] of ruling authority; wherefore they returned. I understood sufficiently from other Indians whom I had already taken, that this land, in its continuousness, was an island; and so I followed its coast eastwardly for a hundred and seven leagues as far as where it terminated; from which headland I saw another island to the east, ten or eight leagues distant from this, to which I at once gave the name La Spañola. And I proceeded thither, and followed the northern coast, as with La Juana, eastwardly for a hundred and seventy-eight great leagues in a direct easterly course, as with La Juana. The which, and all the others, are very large to an excessive degree, and this extremely so. In it, there are many havens on the seacoast, incomparable with any others that I know in Christendom, and plenty of rivers so good and great that it is a marvel. The lands thereof are high, and in it are very many ranges of hills, and most lofty mountains incomparably beyond the Island of Centrefrei; all most beautiful in a thousand shapes, and all accessible, and full of trees of a thousand kinds, so lofty that they seem to reach the sky.

---

1 This "Letter" was written when the first voyage was about to come to a close.
2 **gainsay:** deny. Pay attention to the colonial expressions Columbus uses in this letter.
3 **interminable:** endless
4 **nought:** nothing

Heritage of Western Intellectual Tradition   A Sourcebook

And I am assured that they never lose their foliage; as may be imagined, since I saw them as green and as beautiful as they are in Spain during May. And some of them were in flower, some in fruit, some in another stage according to their kind. And the nightingale was singing, and other birds of a thousand sorts, in the month of November, round about the way that I was

First encounter of Columbus and indigenous peole

going. There are palm-trees of six or eight species, wondrous to see for their beautiful variety; but so are the other trees, and fruits, and plants therein. There are wonderful pinegroves, and very large plains of verdure[1], and there is honey, and many kinds of birds, and many various fruits. In the earth there are many mines of metals; and there is a population of incalculable number. **Spañola is a marvel; the mountains and hills, and plains and fields, and land, so beautiful and rich for planting and sowing, for breeding cattle of all sorts, for building of towns and villages.** There could be no believing, without seeing, such harbours as are here, as well as the many and great rivers, and excellent waters, most of which contain gold[2]. In the trees and fruits and plants, there are great differences from those of Juana. **In this, there are many spiceries, and great mines of gold and other metals. The people of this island, and of all the others that I have found and seen or not seen, all go naked, men and women, just as their mothers bring them forth; although some women cover a single place with the leaf of a plant, or a cotton something which they make for that purpose. They have no iron or steel, nor any weapons; nor are they fit thereunto; not because they be not a well-formed people and of fair stature, but that they are most wondrously timorous[3].** They have no other weapons than the stems of reeds in their seeding state, on the end of which they fix little sharpened stakes. Even these, they dare not use; for many times has it happened that I sent two or three men ashore to some village to parley[4], and countless numbers of them sallied[5] forth, but as soon as they saw those approach, they fled away in such wise[6] that even a father would not wait for his son. And this was not because any hurt had ever been done to any of them: — on the contrary, at every headland where I have gone and been able to hold speech with them, I gave them of everything which I had, as well cloth as many other things, without accepting aught[7] therefor; but such they are, incurably timid. It is true that since they have

---

1 **verdure:** green vegetation
2 **gold:** Pay attention to this word as it frequently appears in this short letter. Other important words include "land," "faith," "desired," "profit", etc.
3 **timorous:** timid
4 **parley:** have talks
5 **sally:** go out
6 **wise:** manner
7 **aught:** anything

become more assured, and are losing that terror, they are artless and generous with what they have, to such a degree as no one would believe but he who had seen it. Of anything they have, if it be asked for, they never say no, but do rather invite the person to accept it, and show as much lovingness as though they would give their hearts. And whether it be a thing of value, or one of little worth, they are straightways[1] content with whatsoever trifle of whatsoever kind may be given them in return for it[2]. I forbade that anything so worthless as fragments of broken platters[3], and pieces of broken glass, and strapbuckles, should be given them; although when they were able to get such things they seemed to think they had the best jewel in the world, for it was the hap[4] of a sailor to get, in exchange for a strap, gold to the weight of two and a half castellanos[5], and others much more for other things of far less value; while for new blancas they gave every thing they had, even though it were the worth of two or three gold castellanos, or one or two arrobas[6] of spun cotton. They took even pieces of broken barrel-hoops[7], and gave whatever they had, like senseless brutes; insomuch that it seemed to me ill. I forbade it, and **I gave gratuitously a thousand useful things that I carried, in order that they may conceive affection, and furthermore may be made Christians; for they are inclined to the love and service of their Highnesses and of all the Castilian nation[8], and they strive to combine in giving us things which they have in abundance, and of which we are in need.** And they know no sect, or idolatry; save that they all believe that power and goodness are in the sky, and they believed very firmly that I, with these ships and crew, came from the sky; and in such opinion, they received me at every place where I landed, after they had lost their terror. And this comes not because they are ignorant; on the contrary, they are men of very subtle wit, who navigate all those seas, and who give a marvellously good account of everything — but because they never saw men wearing clothes or the like of our ships. And as soon as I arrived in the Indies, in the first island that I found, I took some of them by force, to the intent that they should learn our speech and give me information of what there was in those parts. And so it was, that very soon they understood us and we them, what by speech or what by signs; and those Indians have been of much service. To this day I carry them with me who are still of the opinion that I come from heaven, as

Columbus set sail from Palos de la Frontera, Spain.

---

1   **straightways:** immediately
2   **it:** anything they have
3   **platter:** large shallow plate
4   **hap:** luck
5   **castellano:** gold coin issued by Fernando III, King of Castile and Leon (1119–1252)
6   **arroba:** Spanish weight for about 25.36 pounds
7   **barrel-hoop:** band put around a barrel
8   **Castilian nation:** Castile, former kingdom in Spain. In 1469, the marriage of Ferdinand II of Aragón and Isabella I of Castile led to the union of the two kingdoms and, eventually, of all Spain.

Heritage of Western Intellectual Tradition   A Sourcebook

appears from much conversation which they have had with me. And they were the first to proclaim it wherever I arrived; and the others went running from house to house and to the neighbouring villages, with loud cries of "Come! come to see the people from heaven!" Then, as soon as their minds were reassured about us, every one came, men as well as women, so that there remained none behind, big or little; and they all brought something to eat and drink, which they gave with wondrous lovingness. They have in all the islands very many canoes[1], after the manner of rowing-galleys[2], some larger, some smaller; and a good many are larger than a galley of eighteen benches. They are not so wide, because they are made of a single log of timber, but a galley could not keep up with them in rowing, for their motion is a thing beyond belief. And with these, they navigate through all those islands which are numberless, and ply[3] their traffic. I have seen some of those canoes with seventy and eighty men in them, each one with his oar. In all those islands, I saw not much diversity in the looks of the people, or in their manners and language; but they all understand each other, which is a thing of singular towardness[4] for what I hope their Highnesses will determine, as to making them conversant with our holy faith, unto which they are well disposed. I have already told how I had gone a hundred and seven leagues, in a straight line from West to East, along the seacoast of the Island of Juana; according to which itinerary, I can declare that that island is larger than England and Scotland combined; as, over and above those hundred and seven leagues, there remains for me, on the western side, two provinces whereto I did not go — one of which they call Anan, where the people are born with tails — which provinces cannot be less in length than fifty or sixty leagues, according to what may be understood from the Indians with me, who know all the islands. This other, Española, has a greater circumference than the whole of Spain from Colibre in Catalunya, by the seacoast, as far as Fuente Ravia in Biscay; since, along one of its four sides, I went for a hundred and eight-eight great leagues in a straight line from West to East. **This is a land to be desired, — and once seen, never to be relinquished (放弃) — in which — although, indeed, I have taken possession of them all for their Highnesses, and all are more richly endowed than I have skill and power to say, and I hold them all in the name of their Highnesses who can dispose thereof as much and as completely as of the kingdoms of Castile — in this Española, in the place most suitable and best for its proximity to the gold mines, and for traffic with the continent, as well on this side as on the further side of the Great Can, where there will be great commerce and profit,** I took possession of a large town which I named the city of Navidad. And I have made fortifications there, and a fort which by this time will have been completely finished and I have left therein men enough for such a purpose, with arms and artillery, and provisions for more than a year, and a boat, and a man who is master of all sea-craft for making others; and great friendship with the King of that land, to such a degree that he prided himself on calling and holding me as his brother. And even

---

1 **canoe:** light boat
2 **galley:** flat, single-decked ship
3 **ply:** go to and fro
4 **a thing of singular towardness:** something very apparent

though his mind might change towards attacking those men, neither he nor his people know what arms are, and go naked. As I have already said, they are the most timorous creatures there

On October 12, 1492, Columbus made first landfall in the Bahamas and renamed the island San Salvador (Holy Savior).

are in the world, so that the men who remain there are alone sufficient to destroy all that land, and the island is without personal danger for them if they know how to behave themselves. It seems to me that in all those islands, the men are all content with a single wife; and to their chief or king they give as many as twenty. The women, it appears to me, do more work than the men. Nor have I been able to learn whether they held personal property, for it seemed to me that whatever one had, they all took shares of, especially of eatable things. Down to the present, I have not found in those islands any mon-

strous men, as many expected, but on the contrary all the people are very comely; nor are they black like those in Guinea, but have flowing hair; and they are not begotten[1] where there is an excessive violence of the rays of the sun. It is true that the sun is there very strong, notwithstanding that it is twenty-six degrees distant from the equinoctial line. In those islands, where there are lofty mountains, the cold was very keen there, this winter; but they endure it by being accustomed thereto, and by the help of the meats which they eat with many and inordinately hot spices. Thus I have not found, nor had any information of monsters, except of an island which is here the second in the approach to the Indies, which is inhabited by a people whom, in all the islands, they regard as very ferocious[2], who eat human flesh. These have many canoes with which they run through all the islands of India, and plunder and take as much as they can. They are no more ill-shaped than the others, but have the custom of wearing their hair long, like women; and they use bows and arrows of the same reed-stems, with a point of wood at the top, for lack of iron which they have not. Amongst those other tribes who are excessively cowardly, these are ferocious; but I hold them as nothing more than the others. These are they who have to do with the women of Matremonio — which is the first island that is encountered in the passage from Spain to the Indies — in which there are no men. Those women practise no female usages, but have bows and arrows of reeds such as above mentioned; and they arm and cover themselves with plates of copper of which they have much. In another island, which they assure me is larger than Española, the people have no hair. In this, there is incalculable gold; and concerning these and the rest I bring Indians with me as witnesses. And in conclusion, to speak only of what has been done in this voyage, which has been so hastily performed, their Highnesses may see that I shall give them as much gold as they may need, with very little aid which their Highnesses will give me; spices and cotton at once, as much as their Highnesses will order to be

---

1 **begotten:** born
2 **ferocious:** fierce, savage

shipped, and as much as they shall order to be shipped of mastic[1], — which till now has never been found except in Greece, in the island of Xio, and the Seignory[2] sells it for what it likes; and aloe[3]-wood as much as they shall order to be shipped; and slaves as many as they shall order to be shipped — and these shall be from idolaters. And I believe that I have discovered rhubarb and cinnamon[4], and I shall find that the men whom I am leaving there will have discovered a thousand other things of value; as I made no delay at any point, so long as the wind gave me an opportunity of sailing, except only in the town of Navidad till I had left things safely arranged and well established. And in truth I should have done much more if the ships had served me as well as might reasonably have been expected. This is enough; and thanks to eternal God our Lord who gives to all those who walk His way, victory over things which seem impossible; and this was signally one such, for although men have talked or written of those lands, it was all by conjecture[5], without confirmation from eyesight, importing just so much that the hearers for the most part listened and judged that there was more fable in it than anything actual, however trifling. **Since thus our Redeemer has given to our most illustrious King and Queen, and to their famous kingdoms, this victory in so high a matter, Christendom should take gladness therein and make great festivals, and give solemn thanks to the Holy Trinity for the great exaltation they shall have by the conversion of so many peoples to our Holy faith; and next for the temporal benefit which will bring hither refreshment and profit, not only to Spain, but to all Christians.** This briefly, in accordance with the facts. Dated on the caravel[6], off the Canary Islands, the 15 February of the year 1493. At your command,

The Admiral

Key Concepts

great mines of gold and other metals

island/seacoast/tribe

name (places)

people from heaven

proclamation

spread the Holy Christian faith

take possession for

the royal standard displayed

timid

---

1 **as much as they shall order to be shipped of mastic:** as much of mastic as they shall order to be shipped; **mastic**（乳香）**:** aromatic resinous exudate from mastic trees used for pastry making, drinks, baked goods, chewing gum, cosmetics such as toothpaste, lotions for the hair and skin

2 **Seignory:** authority of a feudal lord

3 **aloe**（芦荟）**:** plant with sharp pointed leaves

4 **rhubarb**（大黄）**and cinnamon**（桂皮）**:** garden plants used for spice

5 **conjecture:** guess, idea with no facts as proof

6 **caravel:** small sailing ship

Nicolò Machiavelli: *The Prince**

Nicolò Machiavelli (1469–1527), Italian writer, statesman, and political theorist, came from a wealthy and prominent house in Florence some 20 years later than Columbus. In the years when young  Florentines crowded to the lectures of Politian[1], Machiavelli learned chiefly by himself at home. With the first downfall of the Medici[2] in Florence in 1494, he was appointed Chancellor and Secretary to the Second Chancery, the Ten of Liberty and Peace under the free Republic of Florence. He took a leading part in the affairs of the Republic until 1512, when the Medici returned to power, and Machiavelli lost his office. Shortly after this he was accused of complicity against the Medici, imprisoned, and put to question by torture. After release, he retired to his small property near Florence at the age of 43, and devoted himself to literature. In 1525 the Medici were once more banished. Machiavelli returned, hoping to secure his former office of secretary. Unhappily he was taken ill soon after he reached Florence and died there. His major work *The Prince* attracted much criticism for its amoral cynicism. Erasmus, for one, wrote *The Education of a Christian Prince* 5 years later in 1518 as a response to *The Prince*, saying a ruler should have a moral obligation to his people and devote his every waking moment to the economic, cultural, social improvement of the masses. However, readers of today should bear in mind that Machiavelli summarily wrote his treatise in response to a balkanized and eruptive state which Machiavelli was much a part. It is also a reflection on the rational, original thought of the author, as well as a reflection of the classical education he received in his youth. It is a clarion call of nationalism in face of factions and foreign invasion, and of rationality in a political atmosphere full of pseudo-virtuosity with little traces of religious orientation. And his idea of statism is the first landmark for modern concept of *raison d'état* and *realpolitik*.

Chapter XIV   That Which Concerns a Prince on the Subject of the Art of War

A prince ought to have no other aim or thought, nor select anything else for his study, than war and its rules and discipline; for this is the sole art that belongs to him who rules, and it is of such force that it not only upholds those who are born princes, but it often enables men to rise

---

*   *The Prince* (1532): based on the despotism and tyranny of Cesare Borgia (whom he observed closely in 1502 when sent as an envoy to Rome), argues that a ruler is not bound by traditional ethical norms and should be concerned only with acquiring and maintaining political power. The idealism of the medieval Christian king and Renaissance humanism is gone, to be replaced by the gloomy realities of human nature. For this the mild-tempered man of classic scholar was called "old Nick" by the British historian Thomas Babington Macaulay (1800–1859), a term synonymous with deceit, immorality, craftiness and "devil."

1   **Politian (full name Angelo Poliziano, 1454–1494):** Italy's leading humanist scholar of Greek and Latin at the time, who attracted pupils from all the cities of Italy and from distant parts of Europe, including Michelangelo

2   **Medici:** a banking family which virtually ruled Florence from 1434 to 1494. They were overthrown by the republic in 1494, but restored to power in 1512, and from 1537 became hereditary dukes of Florence.

from a private station to that rank. And, on the contrary, it is seen that when princes have thought more of ease than of arms they have lost their states. And the first cause of your losing it is to neglect this art; and what enables you to acquire a state is to be master of the art. Francesco Sforza[1], through being martial, from a private person became Duke of Milan; and the sons, through avoiding the hardships and troubles of arms, from dukes became private persons. For among other evils which being unarmed brings you, it causes you to be despised, and this is one of those ignominies against which a prince ought to guard himself, as is shown later on. Because there is nothing proportionate between the armed and the unarmed; and it is not reasonable that he who is armed should yield obedience willingly to him who is unarmed, or that the unarmed man should be secure

Map of Italy under foreign occupation in 1500

among armed servants. Because, there being in the one disdain and in the other suspicion, it is not possible for them to work well together. And therefore a prince who does not understand the art of war, over and above the other misfortunes already mentioned, cannot be respected by his soldiers, nor can he rely on them. He ought never, therefore, to have out of his thoughts this subject of war, and in peace he should addict himself more to its exercise than in war; this he can do in two ways, the one by action, the other by study.

As regards action, he ought above all things to keep his men well organized and drilled, to follow incessantly the chase[2], by which he accustoms his body to hardships, and learns something of the nature of localities, and gets to find out how the mountains rise, how the valleys open out, how the plains lie, and to understand the nature of rivers and marshes, and in all this to take the greatest care. Which knowledge is useful in two ways. Firstly, he learns to know his country, and is better able to undertake its defence; afterwards, by means of the knowledge and observation of that locality, he understands with ease any other which it may be necessary for him to study hereafter; because the hills, valleys, and plains, and rivers and marshes that are, for instance, in Tuscany[3], have a certain resemblance to those of other countries, so that with a knowledge of the aspect of one country one can easily arrive at a knowledge of others. And the prince that lacks this skill lacks the essential which it is desirable that a captain should possess, for it teaches him to surprise his enemy, to select quarters[4], to lead armies, to array the battle, to besiege towns to advantage.

Philopoemen[5], Prince of the Achaeans, among other praises which writers have bestowed on

---

1   **Francesco Sforza (1401–1466):** Duke of Milan, founder of the Sforza dynasty of Milan

2   **the chase:** hunted animal

3   **Tuscany:** region in northern Italy

4   **quarters:** lodgings

5   **Philopoemen (253–182 BC?):** Greek general who crushed the Spartans at Mantinea in 208 BC and defeated Nabis, tyrant of Sparta, in 192 BC

Heritage of Western Intellectual Tradition   A Sourcebook

him, is commended because in times of peace he never had anything in his mind but the rules of war; and when he was in the country with friends, he often stopped and reasoned with them: "If the enemy should be upon that hill, and we should find ourselves here with our army, with whom would be the advantage? How should one best advance to meet him, keeping the ranks[1]? If we should wish to retreat, how ought we to pursue?" And he would set forth to them, as he went, all the chances that could befall an army; he would listen to their opinion and state his, confirming it with reasons, so that by these continual discussions there could never arise, in times of war, any unexpected circumstances that he could not deal with.

But to exercise the intellect the prince should read histories, and study there the actions of illustrious men, to see how they have borne[2] themselves in war, to examine the causes of their victories and defeat, so as to avoid the latter and imitate the former; and above all do as an illustrious man did, who took as an exemplar one who had been praised and famous before him, and whose achievements and deeds he always kept in his mind, as it is said Alexander the Great imitated Achilles, Caesar Alexander, Scipio Cyrus[3]. And whoever reads the life of Cyrus, written by Xenophon[4], will recognize afterwards in the life of Scipio how that imitation was his glory, and how in chastity, affability[5], humanity, and liberality Scipio conformed to those things which have been written of Cyrus by Xenophon. A wise prince ought to observe some such rules, and never in peaceful times stand idle, but increase his resources with industry in such a way that they may be available to him in adversity, so that if fortune chances it may find him prepared to resist her blows.

Chapter XV   Concerning Things for Which Men, and Especially Princes, Are Praised or Blamed

It remains now to see what ought to be the rules of conduct for a prince towards subject and friends. And as I know that many have written on this point, I expect I shall be considered presumptuous in mentioning it again, especially as in discussing it I shall depart from the methods of other people. But, it being my intention to write a thing which shall be useful to him who apprehends it, **it appears to me more appropriate to follow up the real truth of the matter than the imagination of it; for many have pictured republics and principalities which in fact have never been known or seen, because how one lives is so far distant from how one**

---

1   **keep the ranks:** remain in battle line

2   **borne:** shown

3   **Caesar Alexander, Scipio Cyrus:** Caesar imitated Alexander, Scipio imitated Cyrus. **Alexander the Great (356 –323 BC):** king of Macedonia, conqueror of the Persian Empire, a great military genius; Achilles in Greek mythology is the greatest of the Greek warriors in the Trojan War; **Gaius Julius Caesar (100–44 BC):** Roman general and statesman, who laid the foundations of the Roman imperial system; **Scipio Africanus the Elder (c. 234–183 BC):** one of the most famous generals of ancient Rome, hero of the Second Punic War between Carthage and Rome; **Cyrus the Great (c. 600–530 BC):** king of Persia. When Babylon, Egypt, Lydia, and the city-state of Sparta in Greece combined against him, he conquered Lydia in 546 BC, and in 539 BC the kingdom of Babylon fell to Cyrus.

4   **Xenophon (c. 430 –c. 355 BC):** Greek historian, soldier, and essayist, whose works contribute greatly to knowledge of Greece and Persia in the 4th century BC

5   **affability:** pleasantness of manner

Heritage of Western Intellectual Tradition   A Sourcebook

ought to live, that he who neglects what is done for what ought to be done, sooner effects his ruin than his preservation; for a man who wishes to act entirely up to his professions of virtue[1] soon meets with what destroys him among so much that is evil.

Hence it is necessary for a prince wishing to hold his own to know how to do wrong, and to make use of it or not according to necessity. Therefore, putting on one side imaginary things concerning a prince, and discussing those which are real, I say that all men when they are spoken of, and chiefly princes for being more highly placed, are remarkable for some of those qualities which bring them either blame or praise; and thus it is that one is reputed liberal, another miserly, using a Tuscan term (because an avaricious person in our language is still he who desires to possess by robbery, whilst we call one miserly who deprives himself too much of the use of his own); one is reputed generous, one rapacious[2]; one cruel, one compassionate; one faithless, another faithful; one effeminate and cowardly, another bold and brave; one affable[3], another haughty; one lascivious[4], another chaste; one sincere, another cunning; one hard, another easy; one grave, another frivolous[5]; one religious, another unbelieving, and the like. And I know that every one will confess that it would be most praiseworthy in a prince to exhibit all the above qualities that are considered good; but because they can neither be entirely possessed nor observed, for human conditions do not permit it, **it is necessary for him to be sufficiently prudent that he may know how to avoid the reproach of those vices which would lose him his state; and also to keep himself, if it be possible, from those which would not lose him it[6]; but this not being possible, he may with less hesitation abandon himself to them.** And again, he need not make himself uneasy at incurring a reproach for those vices without which the state can only be saved with difficulty, for if everything is considered carefully, it will be found that something which looks like virtue, if followed, would be his ruin; whilst something else, which looks like vice, yet followed brings him security and prosperity.

Chapter XVI   Concerning Liberality and Meanness

Commencing then with the first of the above-named characteristics, I say that it would be well to be reputed liberal. Nevertheless, liberality exercised in a way that does not bring you the reputation for it, injures you; for if one exercises it honestly and as it should be exercised, it may not become known, and you will not avoid the reproach of its opposite. Therefore, any one wishing to maintain among men the name of liberal is obliged to avoid no attribute of magnificence; so that a prince thus inclined will consume in such acts all his property, and will be compelled in the end, if he wish to maintain the name of liberal, to unduly weigh down his people[7], and tax them, and do everything he

---

1 **it appears to me ... professions of virtue:** another trace of Marchiavellianism: extreme pragmatism where the end justifies the means since in his world of politics, it is success that counts, not virtue.
2 **rapacious:** greedy
3 **affable:** friendly
4 **lascivious:** lustful
5 **frivolous:** not serious
6 **it:** his state
7 **compelled in the end, if he wish to maintain the name of liberal, to unduly weigh down his people:** compelled ... to unduly weigh down his people

can to get money. This will soon make him odious to his subjects, and becoming poor he will be little valued by any one; thus, with his liberality, having offended many and rewarded few, he is affected by the very first trouble and imperiled by whatever may be the first danger; recognizing this himself, and wishing to draw back from it, he runs at once into the reproach of being miserly.

Therefore, a prince, not being able to exercise this virtue of liberality in such a way that it is recognized, except to his cost, if he is wise he ought not to fear[1] the reputation of being mean, for in time he will come to be more considered than if liberal, seeing that with his economy his revenues are enough, that he can defend himself against all attacks, and is able to engage in enterprises without burdening his people; thus it comes to pass that he exercises liberality towards all from whom he does not take, who are numberless, and meanness towards those to whom he does not give, who are few.

We have not seen great things done in our time except by those who have been considered mean; the rest have failed. Pope Julius the Second[2] was assisted in reaching the papacy by a reputation for liberality, yet he did not strive afterwards to keep it up, when he made war on the King of France; and he made many wars without imposing any extraordinary tax on his subjects, for he supplied his additional expenses out of his long thriftiness. The present King of Spain would not have undertaken or conquered in so many enterprises if he had been reputed liberal. A prince, therefore, provided that he has not to rob his subjects, that he can defend himself, that he does not become poor and abject, that he is not forced to become rapacious, ought to hold of little account a reputation for being mean, for it is one of those vices which will enable him to govern.

And if any one should say: Caesar obtained empire by liberality, and many others have reached the highest positions by having been liberal, and by being considered so, I answer: Either you are a prince in fact, or in a way to become one. In the first case this liberality is dangerous, in the second it is very necessary to be considered liberal; and Caesar was one of those who wished to become pre-eminent in Rome; but if he had survived after becoming so, and had not moderated his expenses, he would have destroyed his government. And if any one should reply: Many have been princes, and have done great things with armies, who have been considered very liberal, I reply: Either a prince spends that which is his own or his subjects' or else that of others. In the first case he ought to be sparing, in the second he ought not to neglect any opportunity for liberality. And to the prince who goes forth with his army, supporting it by pillage, sack, and extortion[3], handling that which belongs to others, this liberality is necessary, otherwise he would not be followed by soldiers. And of that which is neither yours nor your subjects' you can be a ready giver, as were

---

1   **a prince ... if he is wise he ought not to fear:** a prince … ought not to fear
2   **Julius II (1443–1513):** pope (1503–1513), a powerful ruler as well as greatest art patron among the popes in the Renaissance period
3   **pillage, sack, and extortion:** plunder by force

Heritage of Western Intellectual Tradition   A Sourcebook

Cyrus, Caesar, and Alexander; because it does not take away your reputation if you squander that of others, but adds to it; it is only squandering your own that injures you.

And there is nothing which wastes so rapidly as liberality, for even whilst you exercise it you lose the power to do so, and so become either poor or despised, or else, in avoiding poverty, rapacious and hated. And a prince should guard himself, above all things, against being despised and hated; and liberality leads you to both. Therefore it is wiser to have a reputation for meanness which brings reproach without hatred, than to be compelled through seeking a reputation for liberality to incur a name for rapacity which begets reproach with hatred.

Chapter XVII   Concerning Cruelty and Clemency, and Whether It Is Better to Be Loved Than Feared

Cesare Borgia (c. 1476–1507), Italian soldier, and politician

Coming now to the other qualities mentioned above, I say that every prince ought to desire to be considered clement and not cruel. Nevertheless he ought to take care not to misuse this clemency. Cesare Borgia[1] was considered cruel; notwithstanding, his cruelty reconciled the Romagna[2], unified it, and restored it to peace and loyalty. And if this be rightly considered, he will be seen to have been much more merciful than the Florentine people, who, to avoid a reputation for cruelty, permitted Pistoia[3] to be destroyed. Therefore a prince, so long as he keeps his subjects united and loyal, ought not to mind the reproach of cruelty; because with a few examples he will be more merciful than those who, through too much mercy, allow disorders to arise, from which follow murders or robberies; for these are wont to injure the whole people, whilst those executions which originate with a prince offend the individual only.

And of all princes, it is impossible for the new prince to avoid the imputation of cruelty, owing to new states being full of dangers. Hence Virgil[4], through the mouth of Dido, excuses the inhumanity of her reign owing to its being new, saying:

"Res dura, et regni novitas me talia cogunt Moliri, et late fines custode tueri."

---

1   **Cesare Borgia:** Italian military leader and illegitimate son of Rodrigo Borgia, later Pope Alexander VI. He was notorious for licentious habits and violent temper, but was also a patron of artists, including Leonardo da Vinci. His political astuteness led Machiavelli to cite him as an example of the new "Prince."

2   **Emilia-Romagna:** region in north central Italy

3   **Pistoia:** a city in central Italy, capital of Pistoia Province in Tuscany Region, largely destroyed during the rioting between the Cancellieri and Panciatichi factions in 1502 and 1503

4   **Virgil (70–19 BC):** Roman poet, author of the *Aeneid*, the most influential work of literature produced in ancient Rome. In the *Aeneid*, Dido, queen of Carthage, fell in love with Aeneas and was driven to suicide when Aeneas, warned by Jupiter, left her to continue on his destined mission to found Rome. The line reads: "… against my will, my fate, A throne unsettled, and an infant state, Bid me defend my realms with all my pow'rs, And guard with these severities my shores."

Nevertheless he ought to be slow to believe and to act, nor should he himself show fear, but proceed in a temperate manner with prudence and humanity, so that too much confidence may not make him incautious and too much distrust render[1] him intolerable.

Upon this a question arises: whether it be better to be loved than feared or feared than loved? It may be answered that one should wish to be both, but, because it is difficult to unite them in one person, it is much safer to be feared than loved, when, of the two, either must be dispensed with[2]. Because this is to be asserted in general of men, that they are ungrateful, fickle, false, cowardly, covetous, and as long as you succeed they are yours entirely; they will offer you their blood, property, life, and children, as is said above, when the need is far distant[3]; but when it approaches they turn against you. And that prince who, relying entirely on their promises, has neglected other precautions, is ruined; because friendships that are obtained by payments, and not by greatness or nobility of mind, may indeed be earned, but they are not secured, and in time of need cannot be relied upon; and men have less scruple[4] in offending one who is beloved than one who is feared, for love is preserved by the link of obligation which, owing to the baseness of men, is broken at every opportunity for their advantage; but fear preserves you by a dread of punishment which never fails.

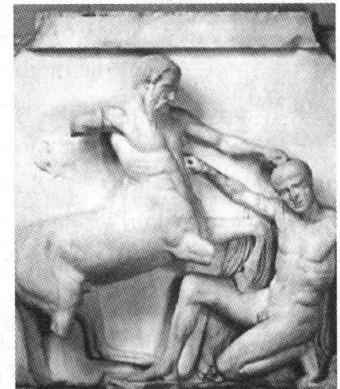

The battle between the centaurs and their neighbors the Lapiths who invited them to a wedding feast but the centaurs attempted to carry off the bride and other women

Nevertheless a prince ought to inspire fear in such a way that, if he does not win love, he avoids hatred; because he can endure very well being feared whilst he is not hated, which will always be as long as he abstains from the property of his citizens and subjects and from their women. But when it is necessary for him to proceed against the life of someone, he must do it on proper justification and for manifest cause, but above all things he must keep his hands off the property of others, because men more quickly forget the death of their father than the loss of their patrimony[5]. Besides, pretexts for taking away the property are never wanting[6]; for he who has once begun to live by robbery will always find pretexts for seizing what belongs to others; but reasons for taking life, on the contrary, are more difficult to find and sooner lapse. But when a prince is with his army, and has under control a multitude of soldiers, then it is quite necessary for him to disregard the reputation of cruelty, for without it he would never hold his army united or disposed to its duties.

---

1   **too much distrust render:** too much distrust may not render
2   **when, of the two, either must be dispensed with:** if one could only keep one of the two
3   **when the need is far distant:** when they do not really need to offer their blood, property, life, and children
4   **scruple:** hesitation caused by uneasiness of conscience
5   **patrimony:** inherited property
6   **wanting:** lacking

Among the wonderful deeds of Hannibal[1] this one is enumerated: that having led an enormous army, composed of many various races of men, to fight in foreign lands, no dissensions arose either among them or against the prince, whether in his bad or in his good fortune. This arose from nothing else than his inhuman cruelty, which, with his boundless valour, made him revered and terrible in the sight of his soldiers, but without that cruelty, his other virtues were not sufficient to produce this effect. And short-sighted writers admire his deeds from one point of view and from another condemn the principal cause of them. That it is true his other virtues would not have been sufficient for him may be proved by the case of Scipio, that most excellent man, not only of his own times but within the memory of man, against whom, nevertheless, his army rebelled in Spain; this arose from nothing but his too great forbearance, which gave his soldiers more license than is consistent with military discipline. For this he was upbraided in the Senate by Fabius Maximus[2], and called the corrupter of the Roman soldiery. The Locrians[3] were laid waste by a legate[4] of Scipio, yet they were not avenged by him, nor was the insolence[5] of the legate punished, owing entirely to his easy nature. Insomuch that someone in the Senate, wishing to excuse him, said there were many men who knew much better how not to err than to correct the errors of others. This disposition, if he had been continued in the command, would have destroyed in time the fame and glory of Scipio; but, he being under the control of the Senate, this injurious characteristic not only concealed itself, but contributed to his glory.

Returning to the question of being feared or loved, I come to the conclusion that, men loving according to their own will and fearing according to that of the prince, a wise prince should establish himself on that which is in his own control and not in that of others; he must endeavour only to avoid hatred, as is noted.

Chapter XVIII   Concerning the Way in Which Princes Should Keep Faith[6]

Every one admits how praiseworthy it is in a prince to keep faith, and to live with integrity and not with craft. Nevertheless our experience has been that those princes who have done great things have held good faith of little account, and have known how to circumvent[7] the intellect of men by craft, and in the end have overcome those who have relied on their word. You must know there are two ways of contesting, the one by the law, the

---

1   **Hannibal (247–183 BC):** Carthaginian general, best known for his march on Rome from Spain across the Alps in 218–217 BC

2   **Fabius Maximus (c. 275–203 BC):** Quintus Fabius Maximus Verrucosus, called "Cunctator" (the Deplayer), Roman statesman and general

3   **Locrians:** Hellenic tribe settled in Greek mainland

4   **legate:** ambassador

5   **insolence:** offence, rudeness

6   This chapter is the most controversial and provocative of *The Prince*.

7   **circumvent:** get the better of, defeat

other by force; the first method is proper to men, the second to beasts; but because the first is frequently not sufficient, it is necessary to have recourse to the second. Therefore it is necessary for a prince to understand how to avail himself of the beast and the man. This has been figuratively taught to princes by ancient writers, who describe how Achilles and many other princes of old were given to the Centaur Chiron[1] to nurse, who brought them up in his discipline; which means solely that, as they had for a teacher one who was half beast and half man, so it is necessary for a prince to know how to make use of both natures, and that one without the other is not durable. **A prince, therefore, being compelled knowingly to adopt the beast, ought to choose the fox and the lion[2]; because the lion cannot defend himself against snares and the fox cannot defend himself against wolves.** Therefore, it is necessary to be a fox to discover the snares and a lion to terrify the wolves. Those who rely simply on the lion do not understand what they are about. Therefore a wise lord cannot, nor ought he to, keep faith when such observance may be turned against him, and when the reasons that caused him to pledge it exist no longer. If men were entirely good this precept would not hold, but because they are bad, and will not keep faith with you, you too are not bound to observe it with them. Nor will there ever be wanting to a prince legitimate reasons to excuse this non-observance. Of this endless modern examples could be given, showing how many treaties and engagements have been made void and of no effect through the faithlessness of princes; and he who has known best how to employ the fox has succeeded best.

But it is necessary to know well how to disguise this characteristic, and to be a great pretender and dissembler[3]; and men are so simple, and so subject to present necessities, that he who seeks to deceive will always find someone who will allow himself to be deceived. One recent example I cannot pass over in silence. Alexander the Sixth[4] did nothing else but deceive men, nor ever thought of doing otherwise, and he always found victims; for there never was a man who had greater power in asserting, or who with greater oaths would affirm a thing, yet would observe it less; nevertheless his deceits always succeeded according to his wishes, because he well understood this side of mankind.

Therefore it is unnecessary for a prince to have all the good qualities I have enumerated, but it is very necessary to appear to have them. And I shall dare to say this also, that to have them and always to observe them is injurious, and that to appear to have them is useful; to appear merciful, faithful, humane, religious, upright, and to be so, but with a mind so framed that should you require not to be so, you may be able and know how to change to the opposite.

---

1 **Centaur Chiron:** in Greek mythology, one of the centaurs noted for his goodness and wisdom, under whom some Greek heroes, including Achilles and Jason, were put for education. Centaurs were a race of monsters usually represented as human down to the waist, with the lower torso and legs of a horse, characterized by savageness and violence and often portrayed as followers of Dionysus for drunkenness and lust.

2 **choose the fox and lion:** This is typical of Machiavellianism: strong enough to fight, yet smart enough to avoid traps.

3 **dissembler:** one who hides one's real feeling

4 **Alexander VI (c. 1431–1503):** pope (1492–1503), noted for his worldliness and corruption

And you have to understand this, that a prince, especially a new one, cannot observe all those things for which men are esteemed, being often forced, in order to maintain the state, to act contrary to fidelity, friendship, humanity, and religion. **Therefore it is necessary for him to have a mind ready to turn itself accordingly as the winds and variations of fortune force it, yet, as I have said above, not to diverge from the good if he can avoid doing so, but, if compelled, then to know how to set about[1] it.**

...

CHAPTER XXV   What Fortune Can Effect in Human Affairs and How to Withstand Her

It is not unknown to me how many men have had, and still have, the opinion that the affairs of the world are in such wise governed by fortune and by God that men with their wisdom cannot direct them and that no one can even help them; and because of this they would have us believe that it is not necessary to labour[2] much in affairs, but to let chance govern them. This opinion has been more credited in our times because of the great changes in affairs which have been seen, and may still be seen, every day, beyond all human conjecture. Sometimes pondering over this, I am in some degree inclined to their opinion. Nevertheless, not to extinguish our free will, I hold it to be true that Fortune is the arbiter of one-half of our actions, but that she still leaves us to direct the other half, or perhaps a little less.

I compare her to one of those raging rivers, which when in flood overflows the plains, sweeping away trees and buildings, bearing away the soil from place to place; everything flies before it, all yield to its violence, without being able in any way to withstand it; and yet, though its nature be such, it does not follow therefore that men, when the weather becomes fair, shall not make provision, both with defences and barriers, in such a manner that, rising again, the waters may pass away by canal, and their force be neither so unrestrained nor so dangerous. So it happens with fortune, who shows her power where valour has not prepared to resist her, and thither she turns her forces where she knows that barriers and defences have not been raised to constrain her.

And if you will consider Italy, which is the seat of these changes, and which has given to them their impulse, you will see it to be an open country without barriers and without any defence. For if it had been defended by proper valour, as are Germany, Spain, and France, either this invasion would not have made the great changes it has made or it would not have come at all. And this I consider enough to say concerning resistance to fortune in general.

But confining myself more to the particular, I say that a prince may be seen happy to-day and ruined to-morrow without having shown any change of disposition or character. This, I believe, arises firstly from causes that have already been discussed at length, namely, that the prince who

---

1 **set about:** engage oneself with
2 **labour:** think and manipulate

relies entirely on fortune is lost when it changes. I believe also that he will be successful who directs his actions according to the spirit of the times, and that he whose actions do not accord with the times will not be successful. Because men are seen, in affairs that lead to the end which every man has before him, namely, glory and riches, to get there by various methods; one with caution, another with haste; one by force, another by skill; one by patience, another by its opposite; and each one succeeds in reaching the goal by a different method. One can also see of two cautious men the one attain his end, the other fail; and similarly, two men by different observances are equally successful, the one being cautious, the other impetuous[1]; all this arises from nothing else than whether or not they conform in their methods to the spirit of the times. This follows from what I have said, that two men working differently bring about the same effect, and of two working similarly, one attains his object and the other does not.

Changes in estate[2] also issue from this, for if, to one who governs himself with caution and patience, times and affairs converge in such a way that his administration is successful, his fortune is made; but if times and affairs change, he is ruined if he does not change his course of action. But a man is not often found sufficiently circumspect[3] to know how to accommodate himself to the change, both because he cannot deviate from what nature inclines him to do, and also because, having always prospered by acting in one way, he cannot be persuaded that it is well to leave it; and, therefore, the cautious man, when it is time to turn adventurous, does not know how to do it, hence he is ruined; but had he changed his conduct with the times fortune would not have changed.

Pope Julius the Second went to work impetuously in all his affairs, and found the times and circumstances conform so well to that line of action that he always met with success. Consider his first enterprise against Bologna[4], Messer Giovanni Bentivogli[5] being still alive. The Venetians were not agreeable to it, nor was the King of Spain, and he had the enterprise still under discussion with the King of France; nevertheless he personally entered upon the expedition with his accustomed boldness and energy, a move which made Spain and the Venetians stand irresolute and passive, the latter from fear, the former from desire to recover the kingdom of Naples; on the other hand, he drew after him the King of France, because that king, having observed the movement, and desiring to make the Pope his friend so as to humble the Venetians, found it impossible to refuse him. Therefore Julius with his impetuous action accomplished what no other pontiff with simple human wisdom could have done; for if he had waited in Rome until he could get away, with his plans arranged and everything fixed, as any other pontiff would have done, he would never have succeeded. Because the King of France would have made a thousand excuses, and the others

---

1   **impetuous:** acting on impulse
2   **estate:** condition
3   **circumspect:** cautious
4   **Bologna:** city in northern Italy, capital of Bologna Province
5   **Messer Giovanni Bentivogli (1438–1508):** ruler of Bologna from 1462 to 1506. Machiavelli's strong condemnation of conspiracies may have got its edge from his own recent experience (February 1513), when he had been arrested and tortured for his alleged complicity in the Boscoli conspiracy.

Heritage of Western Intellectual Tradition   A Sourcebook

would have raised a thousand fears.

I will leave his other actions alone, as they were all alike, and they all succeeded, for the shortness of his life did not let him experience the contrary; but if circumstances had arisen which required him to go cautiously, his ruin would have followed, because he would never have deviated from those ways to which nature inclined him.

I conclude, therefore that, fortune being changeful and mankind steadfast in their ways, so long as the two are in agreement men are successful, but unsuccessful when they fall out. For my part I consider that it is better to be adventurous than cautious, because fortune is a woman, and if you wish to keep her under it is necessary to beat and ill-use her; and it is seen that she allows herself to be mastered by the adventurous rather than by those who go to work more coldly. She is, therefore, always, woman-like, a lover of young men, because they are less cautious, more violent, and with more audacity command her.

Chapter XXVI　An Exhortation to Liberate Italy from the Barbarians

Having carefully considered the subject of the above discourses, and wondering within myself whether the present times were propitious[1] to a new prince, and whether there were elements that would give an opportunity to a wise and virtuous one to introduce a new order of things which would do honour to him and good to the people of this country, it appears to me that so many things concur to favour a new prince that I never knew a time more fit than the present.

And if, as I said, it was necessary that the people of Israel should be captive so as to make manifest the ability of Moses[2]; that the Persians should be oppressed by the Medes so as to discover the greatness of the soul of Cyrus[3]; and that the Athenians should be dispersed to illustrate the capabilities of Theseus[4]: then at the present time, in order to discover the virtue of an Italian spirit, it was necessary that Italy should be reduced to the extremity that she is now in, that she should be more enslaved than the Hebrews, more oppressed than the Persians, more scattered than the Athenians; without head, without order, beaten, despoiled, torn, overrun; and to have endured every kind of desolation.

Although lately some spark may have been shown by one, which made us think he was ordained by God for our redemption, nevertheless it was afterwards seen, in the height of his career, that fortune rejected him; **so that Italy, left as without life, waits for him who shall yet heal her**

1　**propitious:** favourable

2　**Moses:** living around 1200 BC, Hebrew prophet and lawgiver, and founder of Israel. See Unit 1.

3　**Cyrus the Great (c. 600 – 530 BC):** king of Persia (550 – 530 BC), became ruler of the Persian district (subject to the Medes) of Anshan in about 558 BC, and led a rebellion against the Medes that resulted in the overthrow of the Median Empire in 550 BC.

4　**Theseus:** in Greek mythology, king of Athens, the greatest Athenian hero known for his wisdom and generosity as well as his love of danger and adventure

wounds and put an end to the ravaging and plundering of Lombardy[1], to the swindling and taxing of the kingdom and of Tuscany, and cleanse those sores that for long have festered. **It is seen how she entreats God to send someone who shall deliver her from these wrongs and barbarous insolencies[2]. It is seen also that she is ready and willing to follow a banner if only someone will raise it.**

Machiavelli's tomb at Santa Croce, Florence

Nor is there to be seen at present one in whom she can place more hope than in your illustrious house[3], with its valour and fortune, favoured by God and by the Church of which it is now the chief, and which could be made the head of this redemption. This will not be difficult if you will recall to yourself the actions and lives of the men I have named. And although they were great and wonderful men, yet they were men, and each one of them had no more opportunity than the present offers, for their enterprises were neither more just nor easier than this, nor was God more their friend than He is yours.

With us there is great justice, because that war is just which is necessary, and arms are hallowed when there is no other hope but in them. Here there is the greatest willingness, and where the willingness is great the difficulties cannot be great if you will only follow those men to whom I have directed your attention. Further than this, how extraordinarily the ways of God have been manifested beyond example: the sea is divided, a cloud has led the way, the rock has poured forth water, it has rained manna[4], everything has contributed to your greatness; you ought to do the rest. God is not willing to do everything, and thus take away our free will and that share of glory which belongs to us.

And it is not to be wondered at if none of the above-named Italians have been able to accomplish all that is expected from your illustrious house; and if in so many revolutions in Italy, and in so many campaigns, it has always appeared as if military virtue were exhausted, this has happened because the old order of things was not good, and none of us have known how to find a new one. And nothing honours a man more than to establish new laws and new ordinances when he himself was newly risen. Such things when they are well founded and dignified will make him revered and admired, and in Italy there are not wanting opportunities to bring such into use in every form.

Here there is great valour in the limbs whilst it fails in the head. Look attentively at the duels and the hand-to-hand combats, how superior the Italians are in strength, dexterity, and subtlety.

---

1   **Lombardy:** region in northern Italy

2   **insolency:** insult, offence

3   **your illustrious house:** referring to Giuliano de Medici, who had just been created a cardinal by Leo X, to be elected Pope as Clement VII in 1523

4   **manna:** a Biblical allusion for food provided by God for the Israelites during their 40 years in the wilderness (Exodus 16:31–35)

But when it comes to armies they do not bear comparison, and this springs entirely from the insufficiency of the leaders, since those who are capable are not obedient, and each one seems to himself to know, there having never been any one so distinguished above the rest, either by valour or fortune, that others would yield to him. Hence it is that for so long a time, and during so much fighting in the past twenty years, whenever there has been an army wholly Italian, it has always given a poor account of itself; the first witness to this is Il Taro, afterwards Allesandria, Capua, Genoa, Vaila, Bologna, Mestri[1].

If, therefore, your illustrious house wishes to follow these remarkable men who have re-deemed their country, it is necessary before all things, as a true foundation for every enterprise, to be provided with your own forces, because there can be no more faithful, truer, or better soldiers. And although singly they are good, altogether they will be much better when they find themselves commanded by their prince, honoured by him, and maintained at his expense. Therefore it is necessary to be prepared with such arms, so that you can be defended against foreigners by Italian valour.

Key Concepts

by force/by skill	love/fear
craft	prince
cruelty/clemency	security/prosperity
fox/wolf	spirit of the times
law/force	the art of war
liberality/meanness	vices/virtues

Compare with China

The Rise and Fall of 15th Century Chinese Seapower

While overseas expansion and internal political strife was ransacking much of Europe in the 15th and 16th centuries, a similar but in many ways different situation found itself in China. The Ming Dynasty reunited what is now called China proper after almost 400 years of foreign incursion and occupation, and the Emperor Zhu Di is noted for dispatching his Admiral Zheng He on expeditions to the south seas. Unlike the colonial mission of Columbus, Zheng He's seven maritime[1] expeditions

---

1 **Allesandria, Capua, Genoa, Vaila, Bologna, Mestri:** names of the towns and cities of Italy

from 1405 to 1433 improved the communication between China and other coastal states. It also indicates, as the following essay shows, the national strength of China when compared with the Renaissance Europe.

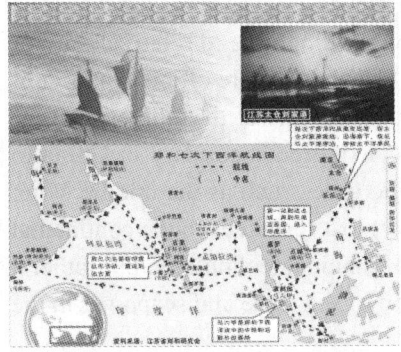

郑和下西洋：人类航海史上的伟大壮举

Over fifty years before the first intrepid[2] Portuguese caravels[3] inspired by Prince Henry the Navigator[4] traversed[5] the southern tip of Africa to first enter the Indian Ocean in 1488, fleets of hundreds of immense Chinese junks sent by the Ming Emperor Zhu Di traversed from the China Sea past Sumatra to Ceylon, India, Arabia and East Africa. Seven epic Chinese naval expeditions from 1405 to 1433 explored and brought under the Chinese tributary[6] system the vast periphery[7] of the Indian Ocean. However, less than a century after this Chinese maritime high water mark, it was a crime to even go to sea from China in a multi-masted ship. How could an empire have such a dramatic shift in nautical[8] policy? Jared Diamond[9] postulated that the rapid demise[10] of Chinese seapower and ocean-going maritime technology was a result of a political power struggle between two factions of the Chinese court, combined with an overwhelming political unity. One decision stopped fleets over the whole of China. He further postulated that the decision became irreversible due to the loss of shipyards capable of turning out ships that would prove the folly of that temporary decision. Politically fragmented Europe thus had the advantage, in Diamond's view, of enabling multiple and continual opportunities for continuing and expanding overseas exploration. For instance, Christopher Columbus, an Italian by birth, succeeded on his fifth try convincing Spain to support his western explorations, after failure to convince the King of Portugal, the Duke of Medina-Sedona, the Count of Medina-Celi, and an initial, rejected proposal to the King and Queen of Spain.

Professor Diamond's thesis is perhaps over-simple. I postulate several interrelated reasons for the demise of China's initially promising ocean-going technology and policies. One element of the interrelated reasons is the centralization argument that China had centralized political unification that ultimately hindered[11] broader based support for a long term maritime policy. Another

---

1   **maritime:** connected with sea
2   **intrepid:** fearless
3   **caravel:** light ship
4   **Prince Henry the Navigator (1394–1460):** Portuguese prince and patron of explorers. He sponsored many exploratory expeditions along the West African coast. His patronage led to the development of the Portuguese caravel and improved navigational instruments and the advancement of cartography（地图绘制）.
5   **traverse:** travel across
6   **tributary:** paying contribution to a ruler
7   **periphery:** external boundary
8   **nautical:** of navigation
9   **Jared Diamond:** professor of geography and physiology at UCLA
10 **demise:** decline
11 **hinder:** prevent from happening

Heritage of Western Intellectual Tradition   A Sourcebook

reason is that there was a struggle in the Imperial court between the Confucian courtiers and the palace eunuchs[1], with seapower losing in parallel with its eunuch sponsors. Third there was an internal Chinese court policy struggle between competing theories of the commercial and technology benefits of foreign trade, against the benefits in social purity of isolationism. Isolationism won. Fourth, the navy had become dependent in the 15th century on a meager[2] set of maritime missions that were overly fragile and thus the Chinese navy was vulnerable to relatively minor changes in the strategic situation. The completion of the Grand Canal as a more efficient and safer means of grain transport is the primary event that engendered the demise of the Chinese ocean-going navy. And finally, that maritime threats were always considered secondary in China to continental or land-based threats, and thus in difficult economic times such as the middle Ming dynasty, the maritime solutions to national security (i.e. the navy) lost resources to the continental solutions (i.e. the army). I further argue that it was not a lack of nautical technology, but rather a combination of the above factors that caused a Chinese rejection of sea trade and seapower in the mid-15th century.

Marco Polo journeyed to the court of the Mongol ruler Kublai Khan in 1275, and returned to his native Venice in 1295. His account has become one of the most famous travel guides in history.

The Yuan (Mongol) dynasty of the 13th and 14th centuries maintained the large fleet, sent emissaries[3] to Sumatra 苏门答腊, Ceylon 锡兰, and southern India to establish influence, and Yuan merchants gradually took over the spice trade from the Arabs. It was the Yuan ships of this era that Marco Polo[4] saw and reported, consisting of four-masted ocean-going junks with sixty individual cabins for merchants, up to 300 crew and watertight bulkheads[5]. The Yuan dynasty greatly favored sea power (somewhat at the expense of lake and river combatants, which had been developing human-powered paddlewheel ships up until this period). However, while the Yuan achieved greater foreign contacts and overseas trading success, Khubilai Khan failed spectacularly in his two massive maritime expeditions against Japan (1274 and 1281), and also in expeditions against the Liu Ch'iu (Ryukyu) Islands. A major feature of the Mongol rule of the Yuan dynasty was a dramatic lessening of Confucian influence in the Imperial court, and a great opening to foreign influences.

The early Ming emperors inherited much of the Yuan maritime technology and policy. There were huge ocean-going warships, large ocean capable cargo ships, a regular coastal grain delivery system transporting grain from the southern provinces to the northern ones, and considerable foreign contacts, primarily in south east Asia but extending to Ceylon and India. However, two other dynamics[6] were at work. First, the Ming dynasty was continually working to restore her

1 **eunuchs:** castrated men in court service
2 **meager:** poor
3 **emissary:** messenger
4 **Marco Polo (1254–1324):** Venetian traveler and author, whose account of his travels and experiences in China offered Europeans a firsthand view of Asian lands and stimulated interest in Asian trade
5 **watertight bulkhead:** waterproof partition separating the compartments in a ship
6 **dynamics:** forces that produce change

native culture after a century-long of foreign rule. The Grand Canal, initially completed during the Sui dynasty (6th century AD), with a vast remodelling and extension to the new northern capital at Peking during the Yuan (13th century), was initially in disrepair due to the extensive conflict between the Yuan and Ming. The early Ming saw the rebuilding and improvement of the Grand Canal and other canals, paved highways, bridges, defenses, temples, shrines and walled cities. Second, the Ming administration was being restructured, with a resurgence[1] of Confucian scholars as senior officials and a great development in the use of eunuchs in high office as well. These two categories of high officials were in considerable conflict throughout the Ming period. The Confucians were generally ascendant, but during the rule of the third Ming Emperor, Zhu Di, the eunuch administrators and warriors were greatly trusted and given great power. Many of the eunuch administrators had been loyal retainers to Zhu Di in the frontier wars and the rebellion for decades, whereas the Confucian administrators and warrior princes had defended the old, recently defeated regime.

Gavin Menzies argued that Zheng He discovered the world in 1421. After the book, it's "virtually impossible to still argue that Columbus discovered America, that Cook found Australia or that Magellan was the first to circumnavigate the world."

In the case of the Ming Indian Ocean expeditions, the Emperor Zhu Di chose as his agent and leader of the expeditions the eunuch Admiral Zheng He. Born 1372 into a Muslim family named Ma in Yunnan, he was taken at age ten into the Ming service, and subsequently castrated at age thirteen and placed into the household of the twenty-five year old Prince of Yan, Zhu Di, the fourth son of the first Ming emperor. Over the next ten years, from Yunnan to the northern frontier, Ma He (who was to be given the name Zheng He when the prince became emperor) served in the field doing frontier defense with Prince Zhu Di. The large, commanding and battle experienced eunuch distinguished himself during Prince Zhu Di's bid for the throne, in both the 1399 defense of Beiping and the final campaign of 1402 to capture Nanjing.

In 1403 the new emperor Zhu Di issued orders to begin construction of an imperial fleet of warships and support ships to visit ports in the China seas and the Indian Ocean. The fleet was larger than required to reopen trade with the southern and western regions, but such magnificence might well convince any foreign ruler harboring the deposed Chinese emperor of Zhu Di's strength. And foreign trade, such as that which had occurred fifty years previously under the Yuan dynasty, might well help a treasury depleted by a long civil war.

At the time of the Ming Indian Ocean voyages, Chinese ocean-going technology was somewhat superior to the European, with the exception of navigation. In ship size, the Chinese had by far the larger ships. The largest ships of the Zheng He expeditions were about 500 feet long. The dimension of the ships given in Chinese histories was always subject to the accusation of

1 **resurgence:** revival

Heritage of Western Intellectual Tradition   A Sourcebook

exaggeration. However, in 1962, an actual rudder post of one of Zheng He's treasure ships was discovered at the site of one of the Ming shipyards near Nanking. This timber was 36.2 feet long,

and when reverse engineered to typical proportions, this yields a ship length of 480 to 536 feet, depending upon different assumptions about the draught. In comparison, the ocean-going European ships of this period were considerably smaller, more typically 100 feet long (i.e. 1500 tons for Zheng He and perhaps 300 tons for the Portuguese explorers). The Chinese had been using multi-masted ships for several centuries, while the Portuguese had just in the past century developed this innovation with their new, secret design caravel.

Zheng He and his fleet

In summary, before the 15th century, the Chinese were ahead in oceangoing ship technology, with larger compartmented ships and efficient fore-and-aft lugsails on multiple masts. In the 15th century, the Chinese and the Europeans were in rough overall parity[1]. The Chinese were ahead in ship size and hull construction, and the Portuguese were ahead in the arts of navigation, and there was parity in sail technology (the Chinese with battened[2] lugsails, the Portuguese with lateen sails[3]). Neither had a distinct overall advantage. Both were technologically capable of great voyages of discovery, mercantile[4] enterprise, and colonization. In tracing the developments, what is distinctive is that the rate of progress in nautical technology of the West was considerably faster than that of the East. By the 16th century, the West was clearly superior in ocean-going maritime technology (especially considering the regression[5] that occurred in China due to policy influences).

Chinese seapower progress was most substantial during the Sung and the Yuan dynasties, when the motive was the expansion of trade. The Sung were driven into a southern power base, and deprived of the greater agricultural tax revenues[6] of the north, sought maritime trade to fill the gap. The Yuan were foreign rulers, without the fear of foreign contamination[7] so common to indigenous[8] Chinese ruling lines, and valued trade as demonstrated by the opening of both overland and maritime trade routes. The zenith[9] of Chinese seapower was reached during the Ming dynasty, but it was fleeting and carried by the momentum of opportunities created by the earlier Sung and Yuan maritime advances. The Ming maritime effort was primarily prestige[10] and diplomacy. In

1   **parity:** equality
2   **battened:** nailed and strengthened with boards
3   **lateen sail:** triangular sails on a long yard
4   **mercantile:** commercial
5   **regression:** backward movement
6   **revenue:** income
7   **contamination:** influence
8   **indigenous:** native
9   **zenith:** highest point
10   **prestige:** respect, recognition

Heritage of Western Intellectual Tradition   A Sourcebook

Yuan times, the tax income from ship duties essentially paid the costs of maritime activities. In the early Ming period, excessive, empire-wide taxation developed a fleet that was magnificent but overly expensive for the limited benefits gained. The tributary revenues of the Ming Indian Ocean treasure fleet flowed straight to the emperor for the construction of palaces and temples, far removed from the maritime shipyards. In effect, it was over-taxation, with the Ming maritime organization set up to take the blame. In Europe, the maritime structure was initially governmental, but the continuing long term effort was generally mercantile. Companies were set up, groups of individuals invested in colonies in expectation of personal profit. The Spanish in Central and South America, the Portuguese in Brazil, Africa and the Indian Ocean, the Dutch in Africa and India and the English in North America and the Indian subcontinent all shared this aggressive mercantile nature. The British East India Company, so powerful for centuries with its own sepoy army[1] and Bombay Marine, is merely the most famous and most powerful of a host of lesser yet effective Western merchant corporations dedicated to the expanse of trade. The West also had the impetus[2] of a centuries long and bitter war versus Islam. By aggressive exploration and exploitation, the Portuguese could hope to gain an alternative and lucrative[3] sea-route to the East Indies and also take the Islamic competitors from the rear.

Alfred Thayer Mahan, an American naval officer of the late 18th , early 19th centuries, suggested that the growth of the British Empire was predicated on[4] her command of the seas. Mahan perceived that seapower was developed by the combination of (1) geographic position, (2) physical conformation[5], (3) extent of territory, (4) number of population, (5) character of the people, and (6) character of the government. While China is blessed with plenty of territory and a large population, her geographic position is to be largely surrounded by land, with sea trade routes not particularly convenient, with most of the people far from the sea (the exception being the south coastal Chinese), and with governments through the ages generally disinterested in the seapower or ocean commerce. In a few periods of history, Chinese governments have managed (Sung and Yuan dynasties) to fight these natural factors. However, when it comes down to either army or navy, or either agricultural or maritime trade, in China the army/agriculture side has always won. The navy/maritime trade aspect is a luxury to be discarded in China when the strategic situation is deteriorating[6] and resources are limited.

The debate within the Ming dynasty in the early 15th century was between the Confucian scholar officials and the eunuch administrators, with topics of domestic agriculturalism versus sea-borne trade, canal transport versus coastal transport, and cultural purity through isolationism versus cultural improvement through extensive foreign contacts. The Chinese were cultur-

---

1　**sepoy army:** Indian soldiers
2　**impetus:** drving force or impulse
3　**lucrative:** profitable
4　**was predicated on:** was founded or based on
5　**conformation:** structure
6　**deteriorate:** become worse

Heritage of Western Intellectual Tradition　A Sourcebook

ally inclined to be disinterested in non-Chinese products and ideas, with a few notable exceptions. And the Confucian ideals had longer powers of persuasion than any temporary good eunuch leadership, especially since the eunuch system more often than not created abuses. In 1411 the important Grand Canal was fully repaired and brought to full capacity in all seasons by an improved water supply at the summit section. After the efficiency of the inland canal grain transport route had been proven in supplying the northern capital, the coastal grain transport service was abolished in 1415, while thousands of new canal sailing barges were constructed. Finally, challenges on the northern border from the Mongols became more serious, and they required investment in land power (army, land defenses) for survival. Zhu Di, who had created the treasure fleet, himself diminished the sea service after the fifth expedition that was conducted from 1416 to 1419 due to these pressures. Zhu Zhanji the fifth Ming emperor commissioned[1] Zheng He to accomplish one final, seventh treasure ship expedition in 1430, for increased prestige and restoration of the tribute trade. This was the largest expedition, with 300 ships and 27,500 men. However, Confucian courtiers and a general trend towards a sterile conventionalized version of Neo-Confucianism, very idealistic in metaphysics, led to a widespread loss of interest in geographical science and maritime techniques. The introspective[2] culture of the Middle and Late Ming periods was one cause of many for a decline in many branches of science and technology.

The navy collapsed. By 1474 it was down to one third of its Early Ming size. By 1503 the navy was down to one tenth of its Early Ming size, desertions were widespread and the corps of shipwrights disintegrated. Sailors were sent inland to support the Grand Canal, and loss of prestige for the navy precluded effective recruitment[3]. The anti-maritime party grew more powerful and made its power known through imperial edicts[4]. In 1500 it was made a capital offense[5] for a Chinese to go to sea in a ship with more than two masts without special permission. A ruling of 1525 authorized officials to destroy the larger classes of ships. China entered a xenophobic[6] isolationist phase similar to (but less intense than) that which closed Japan for two centuries. The navy and Chinese-borne overseas trade was gone. The motives of the Western sea explorers and the Eastern treasure fleets were very different. The Chinese were essentially on a dignified tour of the civilized world, initially perhaps in a search for the deposed emperor, but ultimately for the rich gifts of tribute and for the prestige. The Europeans, on the other hand, were engaged in their bitter war with Islam and working for profit. De Zurara, chronicler of Prince Henry the Navigator, lists these motives for Prince Henry in priority order: (1) Cosmographical knowledge, (2) Profit of traffic, (3) Commerce, (4) War

---

1 **commission:** give authority to

2 **introspective:** inward looking

3 **precluded effective recruitment:** prevented the navy from successfully hiring new members

4 **imperial edicts:** orders proclaimed by the emperor

5 **capital offense:** punishment by death

6 **xenophobic:** hating foreigners

Heritage of Western Intellectual Tradition   A Sourcebook

versus Islam, (5) Missionary zeal, and (6) the Prince's famous horoscope[1]. There were great economic considerations for the Europeans. In China, the economic considerations were reserved for the inland activities; overseas activities were wanton expenses without sufficient return demonstrated to warrant[2] continuation. The Europeans were in competition with Islam and with each other; the Chinese acknowledged no competitors. In summary, the precipitous[3] fall of Chinese seapower in the 15th century is not surprising. It was fragile even in its time of greatest glory during the treasure ship expeditions of the early Ming dynasty. As Ming China settled down into the more typical Chinese isolationist philosophy, increased efficiency of inland transport (notably an all weather capable Grand Canal) enabled a turning away from the sea and the coast line, and a reliance on a semi-static coastal militia vice[4] a mobile sea-striking arm. (Adapted from Michael L. Bosworth)

Supplementary Reading

1. No Cheers for Columbus

Though Columbus' discovery of America is celebrated in the West, it is a controversy to non-Westerners, especially to native Americans, in the age of post-colonialism. The following essay is an expression of such sentiments.

(AP. 12 October 2002) Venezuelan President Hugo Chavez（查维斯）urged Latin Americans on Saturday not to celebrate Columbus Day[5], saying the 1492 discovery of the Americas triggered[6] a 150-year "genocide[7]" of native Indians by foreign conquerors who behaved "worse than Hitler." The President signed a decree Saturday changing the name of Venezuela's "Columbus Day" to *Día de la Resistencia Indígena* (Day of Indigenous Resistance) in honor of the nation's indigenous groups. Wearing traditional brightly colored dresses adorned with feathers and beads, representatives of local indigenous communities gathered outside the presidential office to applaud the decree.

1　**horoscope:** a forecast of a person's future based on a diagram showing the relative positions of the stars and planets at that person's birth
2　**warrant:** guarantee
3　**precipitous:** steep, drastic
4　**vice:** in place of
5　**Columbus Day:** celebrated on the second Monday in October
6　**trigger:** cause to happen
7　**genocide:** killing of a race by mass murder

"Christopher Columbus was the spearhead of the biggest invasion and genocide ever seen in the history of humanity," the populist president told a meeting in Caracas of representatives of Indian peoples from across the continent.

Columbus Day on Oct. 12 is celebrated as a holiday in the United States and several Latin American nations, but Chavez said it should be remembered as the "Day of Indian Resistance."

"We Venezuelans, we Latin Americans, have no reason to honor Columbus," he added.

The Venezuelan leader said Spanish, Portuguese and other foreign conquerors had massacred South America's Indian inhabitants at an average rate of roughly "one every 10 minutes." He described Spanish conquistadors like Hernan Cortes[1] and Francisco Pizarro[2], as "worse than Hitler." He said even the continent's geographical names, like America and Venezuela, were imposed by foreigners.

The Monastery of Jeronimos was built in 1498 as a monument to the 15th-century navigators who discovered the sea route to India.

The Venezuelan leader hailed as heroes Indian chiefs who had fought against the invaders, such as Guaicaipuro[3] who resisted the Spanish founders of Caracas, and American Indian chief Sitting Bull[4], who defeated U.S. Gen. George Armstrong Custer at the Battle of Little Bighorn in 1876.

"Long live Sitting Bull!" Chavez declared, drawing applause from his audience, many of whom wore traditional native clothes and head-dresses. There are approximately 350,000 indigenous peoples from 28 distinct ethnic groups in this South American country of 24 million. Most Venezuelans are considered to be "meztizo," a mix of Spanish, African, and native indigenous bloodlines.

2. *Conservatives Hail for Columbus*

In decades past, Columbus Day was an occasion to honor the courageous explorer who discovered America, and to rejoice in the spread of Western civilization across a savage wilderness.

---

1   **Hernan Cortes (1485–1547):** Spanish explorer and conqueror of the Aztec Empire of Mexico

2   **Francisco Pizarro (c. 1476–1541):** Spanish conqueror and governor of Peru (1532–1541)

3   **Guaicaipuro (c. 1530–1568):** native Venezuelan chief who formed a powerful coalition of different tribes during 16th century against the Spanish conquest of Venezuelan territory when the Spaniards discovered gold in the area and started to exploit the mines. Guaicaipuro attacked, forcing the Spanish to leave, and became the central figure in the uprising of all the native tribes, until he was killed by Spanish troops.

4   **Sitting Bull (native American name Tatanka Yotanka, c. 1831–1890):** native American leader of the Sioux, exiled, imprisoned and finally got killed for his anti-settlement activity

In recent years, however, the advocates of multiculturalism and "political correctness[1]" have succeeded in portraying Columbus and the Europeans who followed him to the New World as brutal conquerors whose genocidal assault destroyed a pristine[2] Indian paradise. As a result, Columbus Day has become an occasion for protests by Indians, vandalism[3] of Columbus statues, and an incessant drumbeat of guilt and apology, especially in the public schools.

In his book, "The Enemies of Christopher Columbus," Thomas A. Bowden discusses and refutes a variety of "politically correct" criticisms of Christopher Columbus and the civilization that he brought with him to a new continent. Columbus Day, he maintains, should call forth a celebration of the core values of Western civilization — reason, science, technology, progress, capitalism, individual rights, law, and the selfish pursuit of individual happiness here on earth — at a time when such a celebration is desperately needed, to defend those great values against assault by America's declared enemies.

Here is an excerpt from the book:

Savagery and civilization cannot co-exist in the same geographical area. Civilized people must be able to depend on their neighbors to understand and obey the principles of individual rights as expressed in written laws that define land boundaries, enforce contracts, and protect personal property. Primitive peoples, who have not yet reached the concept of a universal moral law governing all human beings as individuals, cannot act on such principles or be relied upon to obey such laws. Lacking the ability to rule their lives by reason, savages inevitably succumb to a whole range of non-rational influences — such as fear, superstition, drug-induced hallucinations[4], hatred of outsiders, revenge, or lust for conquest — that propel them onto the warpath at unpredictable intervals. The Europeans, in establishing their settlements in the New World, found themselves enmeshed[5] in precisely this conflict between civilization and barbarism. Hence they confronted a fundamental choice: to marshal[6] their superior powers and displace the Indians, or else turn around and sail home.

In that context, the European immigrants had an absolute right to settle America and displace the Indians — by force when necessary. However, to the extent that individual Indians (such as Pocahontas[7], who married an Englishman) were capable of grasping and abiding by the principles

---

1　**political correctness:** PC was a spontaneous declaration in the 1980s that particular ideas, expressions and behaviour in regards to race, sex, culture and body had to be reconsidered from the perspective of multiculturalism. Some of PC's ideas have been accepted by the legislature and people who transgress will be punished.

2　**pristine:** primitive, unspoiled

3　**vandalism:** destruction, damage

4　**hallucination:** state of drunkenness or illusion

5　**enmeshed:** involved, caught

6　**marshal:** display, organize

7　**Pocahontas (c. 1595–1617):** daughter of the Native American chief Powhatan, is said to have saved the life of Captain John Smith in 1608, though historians doubt the story. She was captured by the English in 1612, converted to Christianity and took the name Rebecca. In 1614 she married John Rolfe, one of the colonists.

Heritage of Western Intellectual Tradition　A Sourcebook

of civilized behavior, they should have been permitted and encouraged to become full citizens with full rights.

Columbus should be honored, for in so doing, we honor Western civilization. But the critics do not want to bestow such honor, because their real goal is to denigrate[1] the values of Western civilization and to glorify the primitivism, mysticism, and collectivism embodied in the tribal cultures of American Indians. They decry[2] the glorification of the West as "cultural imperialism" and "Eurocentrism." We should, they claim, replace our reverence for Western civilization with multiculturalism, which regards all cultures (including vicious tyrannies) as morally equal. In fact, they aren't. Some cultures are better than others: a free society is better than slavery; reason is better than brute force as a way to deal with other men; productivity is better than stagnation[3]. In fact, Western civilization stands for man at his best.

Questions for Discussion

1. What is the significance of Christopher Columbus' discovery of America?
2. What can you find in Columbus' Letter?
3. What are the similarity and difference between Columbus and Zheng He?
4. How do you like Machiavelli and his *The Prince*?
5. Comment on *The Prince* as a treatise of political science.
6. How do you explain the fact that Renaissance writers should have so different opinions on man and human nature?
7. In what sense is Machiavelli justifiable?
8. Comment on this statement in *The Prince* with cynical realism: "men more quickly forget the death of their father than the loss of their patrimony."
9. Put Columbus and Machiavelli in the broader context of religious reformation and Renaissance, what do you have to say?

---

1 **denigrate:** defame
2 **decry:** make less valuable, belittle
3 **stagnation:** becoming sluggish, inactive

UNIT 6

Religious Reformation

Pretest

- What do you know about the Reformation or Counter Reformation?
- State briefly the causes of the Reformation.
- Compare Martin Luther and John Calvin.

What You Will Learn in This Unit

- Some knowledge about the Christian Reformation;
- Important selections from Desiderius Erasmus, Martin Luther and John Calvin; and
- Revival of Confucianism in China.

Learn to Pronounce

Anglican Church /ˈæŋglɪkən/ 英国国教
Basel /ˈbɑːzl/ 巴塞尔（瑞士城市）
Erasmus /iˈræzməs/ of Rotterdam /ˈrɒtədæm/ 依拉斯姆斯
Geneva /dʒɪˈniːvə/ 日内瓦（瑞士城市）
John Calvin /ˈkælvɪn/ 约翰·加尔文
liturgy /ˈlɪtə(ː)dʒɪ/ 礼拜仪式

Martin Luther /ˈluːθə/ 马丁·路德
Presbyterianism /ˌprezbɪˈtɪərɪənɪzm/ 长老会制
Protestantism /ˈprɒtɪstəntɪzm/ 基督教新教
Wittenberg /ˈwɪtnbəg/ 维滕贝格（德国城市）

Introduction

The 15th century was an era of change and adventure, especially so in terms of the religious ferment that took place in the Western church, which extended into the 16th century with far-reaching political, economic, and social effects. Over the centuries, the church, particularly the office of the papacy, had become deeply involved in the political life of Western Europe. The resulting intrigues and political manipulations, combined with the church's increasing power and wealth, contributed to the bankruptcy of the church as a spiritual force. Abuses such as the sale of indulgences (or spiritual privileges) and relics and the corruption of the clergy exploited the pious and further undermined the church's spiritual authority. In the 16th century, Erasmus of Rotterdam was the chief proponent of liberal Catholic reform to attack moral abuses and popular superstitions in the church and urge the imitation of Christ. Martin Luther claimed that what distinguished himself from previous reformers was that while they attacked corruption in the life of the church, he went to the theological root of the problem — the perversion of the church's doctrine of redemption and grace. In Basel, Calvin brought out the first edition of his *Institutes of the Christian Religion* in 1536, the first extensive, systematic, theological treatise of the new reform movement. Calvin agreed with Luther's teaching on justification by faith (因信称义). However, he found a more positive place for law within the Christian community than Luther did in his concern to distinguish sharply between law and gospel. In England the Reformation's roots were primarily political rather than religious. Henry VIII, incensed by Pope Clement VII's refusal to grant him a divorce, repudiated papal authority and in 1534 established the Anglican Church with the king as its supreme head. In spite of its political implications, Henry's reorganization of the church permitted the beginning of religious reform in England, which included the preparation of a liturgy in English, *The Book of Common Prayer*. In Scotland, John Knox, who spent time in Geneva and was greatly influenced by John Calvin, led the establishment of Presbyterianism, which made possible the eventual union of Scotland with England.

Desiderius Erasmus: A Pilgrimage for Religion's Sake*

Desiderius Erasmus (c.1466–1536), Dutch writer, scholar, and Prince of the Humanists, is renowned for his profound influence on the intellectual life of Renaissance Europe. Born in Rotterdam out of wedlock, the illegitimate son received the best education of his day in monastic schools. At 9 he was sent to the school of the celebrated humanist Hegius at Deventer, where his taste for humanism was

---

* Pay attention to the sarcasm in "pilgrimage" (Catholic formalism) and "religion" (Is it really for religious sake?). This lively piece criticizes blind worship of Mary instead of God, because perhaps, being the sister of mercy, she would grant things that God himself wouldn't allow. Erasmus also ridicules the overelaboration of church buildings during his time in contrast to the good church of "small chapel built on a wooden platform," together with other perversities of a formalistic Scholasticism: fasts, pilgrimages, veneration of saints and their relics. This worldliness, the craving for wealth, rapacity, pomp, contrasts markedly with Christ's practical lay piety.

awakened — he changed his Christian name "Herasmus" to "Desiderius Erasmus" meaning "the desired beloved" for his love of Greek and Latin, and by 10 he could read difficult works in Latin with

ease. When Erasmus entered the monastery, his monastic superiors became "barbarians" for discouraging his classical studies (some of them could not even utter a simple Latin verb in daily prayers). He was ordained a priest in 1492 and studied Scholastic philosophy and Greek at the University of Paris, chief seat of scholastic learning of the time. Finding religious life uncongenial, he received papal dispensation to live and dress as a secular scholar. Erasmus felt called upon to free scholarship from the rigidity and formalism of medieval traditions, and was convinced that what was needed to regenerate Europe was sound learning. He maintained correspondence with more than 500 men of the highest importance in politics and thought, including Thomas More, lord chan-

cellor of England. The famous satire *The Praise of Folly* (1509) advocates a return to simple Christian ethics by ironically praising foolish activities of the day and attacking superstitious religious practices and the vanity of Church leaders. Its keen cultural critique was soon echoed in the works of More and Rabelais. We have to bear in mind that Erasmus belonged to the renaissance humanism, not the frontline Reformation nor Counter Reformation, but a middle-of-the-road man for his moderation and good sense[1]. His satire was not directed against the Church but at those who were debasing the holiness of the Church and weakening Christian tradition. After his death, his writings were put on the index of prohibited books (catalog listing books dangerous to faith and morals under penalty of excommunication if read), but the immense number of editions and translations of his books has proved the popularity of his writing.

Menedemus: What marvel is this? Don't I see my neighbor Ogygius, whom nobody's laid eyes on for six whole months? I heard he was dead. It's his very self, unless I'm losing my mind completely. I'll go up to him and say hello. — Greetings, Ogygius.

Ogygius: Same to you, Menedemus.

Men.:   Where in the world do you return from, safe and sound? A sad rumor spread here that you'd sailed in Stygian waters[2].

Ogyg.:   No, thank heaven; I've seldom enjoyed better health.

Men.:   I hope you'll always be able to refute silly rumors of that sort! **But what's this fancy outfit? You're ringed with scallop shells[3], choked with tin and leaden images on every side, decked out with straw necklaces, and you've snake eggs[3] on your arms.**

---

1   **moderation and good sense:** As early as 1517 Luther said of Erasmus: "My liking for Erasmus declines from day to day. …The human is of more value to him than the Divine. … The times are now dangerous, and I see that a man is not a more sincere or a wiser Christian for all that he is a good Greek or Hebrew scholar." Luther felt hurt, moreover, by the cool and reserved manner in which Erasmus passed judgment on his writings. Nevertheless, Erasmus always opposed any persecution of Luther, and burned the Bull of excommunication(逐出教会) in open defiance of Pope Leo X.

2   **Stygian waters:** in Greek mythology, the River Styx, the entrance to the underworld, often described as the boundary river over which the aged ferryman Charon transported the shades of the dead. Pay attention to the intentional mixture of Greek and Christian elements.

3   **scallop shells:** 扇贝壳; **snake eggs:** beads; They are traditional symbols of pilgrims.

Heritage of Western Intellectual Tradition   A Sourcebook

Ogyg.: I've been on a visit to St. James of Compostella[1] and, on my way back, to the famous Virgin-by-the-Sea[2], in England; or rather I revisited her, since I had gone there three years earlier.

Men.:   Out of curiosity, I dare say.

Ogyg.: On the contrary, out of devotion.

Men.:   Greek letters[3], I suppose, taught you that devotion.

Ogyg.: My wife's mother had bound herself by a vow that if her daughter gave birth to a boy and he lived, I would promptly pay my respects to St. James and thank him in person.

Men.:   Did you greet the saint only in your own name and your mother-in-law's?

Ogyg.: Oh, no, in the whole family's.

Men.:   Well, I imagine your family would have been no less safe even if you had left James ungreeted. But do please tell me: what answer did he make when you thanked him?

pilgrim accessories

Ogyg.: None, but he seemed to smile as I offered my gift, nodded his head slightly, and at the same time held out these scallop shells.

Men.:   Why does he give these rather than something else?

Ogyg.: Because he has plenty of them; the sea nearby supplies them.

Men.:   **Generous saint, who both delivers those in labor[4] and gives presents to callers!** But what new kind of vowing is this, that some lazy person lays the work on others? If you bound yourself by a vow that, should your affairs prosper, I would fast twice a week, do you think I'd do what you had vowed?

the Cathedral of Santiago de Compostella, the ultimate goal of the pilgrimage

Ogyg.: No, I don't, even if you'd sworn in your own name. For you enjoy mocking the saints. But she's my mother-in-law; custom had to be kept. You're acquainted with women's whims, and besides I had an interest in it too.

---

1   **St. James of Compostella:** the Cathedral of Santiago de Compostella in Galicia in northwestern Spain, where according to legend the remains of the apostle St. James were buried
2   **Virgin-by-the-Sea:** the village of Walsingham in Norfolk, England, which, due to the vision of Lady Richeldis de Faverches, became one of the greatest pilgrimage sites in all of Europe in the Middle Ages
3   **Greek letters:** the Bible
4   **delivers those in labor:** helps women with childbirth, midwife. Notice the sarcasm.

Men.:   If you hadn't kept her vow, what risk would there have been?

Ogyg.:   The saint couldn't have sued me at law, I admit, but he could have been deaf thereafter to my prayers or secretly have brought some disaster upon my family. You know the ways of the mighty.

Men.:   Tell me, how is the excellent James?

Ogyg.:   Much colder than usual.

Men.:   Why? Old age?

Ogyg.:   Joker! You know saints don't grow old. But this new-fangled[1] notion that pervades the whole world results in his being greeted more seldom than usual. And if people do come, they merely greet him; they make no offering at all, or only a very slight one, declaring it would be better to contribute that money to the poor.

Men.:   A wicked notion!

Ogyg.:   And thus so great an apostle[2], accustomed to shine from head to foot in gold and jewels, now stands a wooden figure with hardly a tallow candle to his name.

         …

Men.:   But what fortune brought you back to England?

Ogyg.:   An unexpectedly favorable breeze carried me there, and I had virtually promised the Virgin-by-the-Sea that I would pay her another visit in two years.

Men.:   What were you going to ask of her?

Ogyg.:   Nothing new, just the usual things: family safe and sound, a larger fortune, a long and happy life in this world, and eternal bliss in the next.

Men.:   Couldn't the Virgin Mother here at home see to those matters? At Antwerp[3] she has a church much grander than the one by the sea.

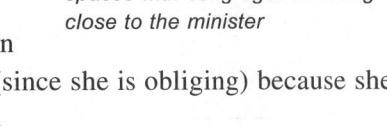
Protestant church in the 16th century preferred empty, open spaces with congregation sitting close to the minister

Ogyg.:   I can't deny that, but different things are bestowed in different places, either because she prefers this or (since she is obliging) because she accommodates herself to our feelings in this respect.

---

1 **new-fangled:** newly-created
2 **so great an apostle:** St. James
3 **Antwerp:** busy port and financial center in northern Belgium, famous for its diamond industry

Heritage of Western Intellectual Tradition   A Sourcebook

Men.: I've often heard about James, but I beg you to describe for me the domain of the Virgin-by-the-Sea.

Ogyg.: Well, I'll do the best I can in brief. She has the greatest fame throughout England, and you would not readily find anyone in that island who hoped for prosperity unless he greeted her annually with a small gift, according to his means[1].

Men.: Where does she live?

Ogyg.: By the northwest coast of England, only about three miles from the sea. The village has scarcely any means of support apart from the tourist trade. There's a college of canons[2], to whom, however, the Latins add the title of Regulars: an order midway between monks and the canons called Seculars.

Men.: You tell me of amphibians, such as the beaver.

Ogyg.: Yes, and the crocodile. But details aside, I'll try to satisfy you in a few words. In unfavorable matters, they're canons; in favorable ones, monks.

Men.: So far you're telling me a riddle.

Ogyg.: But I'll add a precise illustration. **If the Roman pontiff assailed all monks with a thunderbolt[3], then they'd be canons, not monks. Yet if he permitted all monks to take wives, then they'd be monks.**

Men.: Strange favors. I wish they'd take mine, too.

Ogyg.: But to get to the point. This college depends almost entirely on the Virgin's generosity for its support. The larger gifts are reserved, to be sure, but any small change, anything of trifling value, goes toward feeding the community and their head, whom they call the prior.

Men.: Do they live holy lives?

Ogyg.: They're not without praise. They're richer in piety than income. The church is fine and splendid[4], but the Virgin doesn't dwell there; in honor of her Son she yields that to him. She has her own church, that she may be on the right of her Son.

---

1 **means:** wealth
2 **canons:** Christian priests with special duties in a cathedral or members of certain Roman Catholic orders
3 **thunderbolt:** excommunication, which is a biblical allusion to the thunderbolt God uses to hit Satan and his rebel angels
4 **fine and splendid:** again the sarcasm in expressions like "without praise," "richer in piety than income" and "fine and splendid"

Men.:   The right? Which direction does the Son face, then?

Ogyg.:   I'm glad you remind me. When he faces west he has his mother on his right; when he turns to the east she's on his left. However, she doesn't dwell here, either, for the building is not yet finished, and the place is quite airy — windows and doors open, and Ocean, father of the winds, nearby.

Men.:   Too bad. So where does she live?

Ogyg.:   In that church, which as I said is unfinished, is a small chapel built on a wooden platform. Visitors are admitted through a narrow door on each side. There's very little light: only what comes from tapers（细蜡烛）, which have a most pleasing scent.

Men.:   All this is appropriate to religion.

Ogyg.:   Yes, and if you peered inside, Menedemus, you would say it was the abode of the saints, so dazzling is it with jewels, gold, and silver[1].

Men.:   You make me impatient to go there.

Ogyg.:   You won't regret the trip.

Men.:   Is there no holy oil there?

Ogyg.:   Silly! That oil exudes only from the tombs of saints, such as Andrew and Catherine[2]. Mary isn't buried.

Men.:   My mistake, I admit. But finish your story.

Ogyg.:   As the cult spreads more widely, different things are displayed in different places.

Men.:   In order, perhaps, that the giving may be more generous; as it is said, "Loot quickly comes when sought by many hands."

Ogyg.:   And custodians[3] are always present.

Men.:   Some of the canons?

Ogyg.:   **No, they're not used, lest on a favorable opportunity for religious devotion they might stray from devoutness, and while honoring the Virgin pay too little regard to their own virginity. Only in the interior chapel, which I said is the inner sanctum of the Holy Virgin, a canon stands by the altar.**

---

1   **dazzling is it with jewels, gold, and silver:** "perversities of a formalistic Scholasticism"

2   **Andrew and Catherine:** St. Andrew is one of the twelve apostles of Jesus Christ; St. Catherine is a virgin and martyr in the 4th century.

3   **custodian:** a person with responsibility for taking care of something

Heritage of Western Intellectual Tradition   A Sourcebook

Men.:   What for?

Ogyg.:   To receive and keep the offering.

Men.:   Do people contribute whether they want to or not?

Ogyg.:   Not at all, but a certain sense of duty impels some to give when a person is standing by; they wouldn't give if no one were present to watch them. Or sometimes they give more liberally than they would otherwise.

Men.:   That's human nature. I'm no stranger to it.

Ogyg.:   Nay, there are some so devoted to the Most Holy Virgin that while they pretend to lay an offering on the altar, they steal, with astonishing nimbleness, what somebody else had placed there.

Men.:   Suppose there's no witness: would the Virgin strike them dead on the spot?

Ogyg.:   Why would the Virgin do that, any more than does the heavenly Father himself, whom men aren't afraid to rob of treasures, even digging through the church wall for the purpose?

Men.:   I can't tell which to be the more astonished at, their impious audacity or God's mildness.

Ogyg.:   Then, on the north side — not of the church (don't mistake me) but of the wall enclosing the whole area adjacent to the church — is a certain gateway. It has a tiny door, the kind noblemen's gates have, so that whoever wants to enter must first expose his shins to danger and then stoop besides.

Men.:   Certainly it wouldn't be safe to go at an enemy through such a door.

Ogyg.:   Right. The custodian told me that once a knight on horseback escaped through this door from the hands of an enemy who was on the point of overtaking him in his flight. In despair he commended[1] himself then and there to the Holy Virgin, who was close by. For he had determined to take refuge at her altar if the door was open. And mark this wonder: suddenly the knight was entirely within the churchyard and the other man outside, furious.

Men.:   And was this wondrous tale of his believed?

Ogyg.:   Of course.

Men.:   A rational chap like you wouldn't accept it so easily.

Ogyg.:   He showed me on the door a copper plate, fastened by nails, containing a likeness of the knight who was saved, dressed in the English fashion of that period as we see it in old pictures — and if pictures don't lie, barbers had a hard time in those days, and so did weavers and dyers.

---

1 **commend:** entrust, commit

Men.:   How so?

Ogyg.:   Because the knight was bearded like a goat, and his clothing didn't have a single pleat and was so tight that it made the body itself thinner. There was another plate, too, showing the size and shape of the shrine.

Saint Pete's Basilica, commissioned by Pope Julius II, supervised by Michelangelo in 1546

Men.:   You had no right to doubt after that!

Ogyg.:   Beneath the little door was an iron grating[1], admitting you only on foot. It was not seemly[2] that a horse should afterward trample the spot the horseman had consecrated to the Virgin.

Men.:   And rightly consecrated.

Ogyg.:   To the east is a small chapel, filled with marvels. I betake myself to it. Another custodian receives us. After we've prayed briefly, we're immediately shown the joint of a human finger (the largest of three). I kiss it and then ask whose relics these are, "Saint Peter's," he says. "Not the apostle Peter's?" "Yes." Then looking at the great size of the joint, which might have been a giant's, I said, "Peter must have been an extremely big man." At this one of my companions burst into a loud laugh, which annoyed me no end, for if he had been quiet the attendant would have kept none of the relics from our inspection. However, we appeased him with some coins.

In front of the little building was a structure that during the wintertime (he said), when everything was covered by snow, had been brought there suddenly from far away. Under this were two wells, filled to the top. They say the stream of water is sacred to the Holy Virgin. It's a wonderfully cold fluid, good for headache and stomach troubles.

Men.:   If cold water cures headache and stomach troubles, oil will put out fire next.

Ogyg.:   You're hearing about a miracle, my good friend — besides, what would be miraculous about cold water quenching thirst?

Men.:   Clearly this is only one part of the story.

Ogyg.:   That stream of water, they declared, suddenly shot up from the ground at the command of the Most Holy Virgin. Inspecting everything carefully, I inquired how many years it was since the little house had been brought there. "Some ages," he replied. "In any event," I said, "the walls don't look very old." He didn't dissent. "Even these wooden posts don't look old." He didn't deny they had been placed there recently, and the fact was self-

---

1   **grating:** framework of metal bars
2   **seemly:** suitable and polite

Heritage of Western Intellectual Tradition   A Sourcebook

evident. "Then," I said, "the roof and thatch of the horse seem rather recent." He agreed. "Not even these crossbeams, nor the very rafters supporting the roof, appear to have been put here many years ago." He nodded. "But since no part of the building has survived, how is it known for certain," I asked, "that this is the cottage brought here from so far away?"

Men.:   How did the attendant get out of that tangle, if you please?

Ogyg.:   Why, he hurriedly showed us an old, worn-out bearskin fastened to posts and almost laughed at us for our dullness in being slow to see such a clear proof. So, being persuaded, and excusing our stupidity, we turned to the heavenly milk of the Blessed Virgin.

Men.:   **O Mother most like her Son! He left us so much of his blood on earth; she left so much of her milk that it's scarcely credible a woman with only one child could have so much, even if the child had drunk none of it.**

Ogyg.:   The same thing is said about the Lord's Cross, which is exhibited publicly and privately in so many places that if the fragments were joined together they'd seem a full load for a freighter. And yet the Lord carried his whole cross.

Men.:   Doesn't it seem amazing to you, too?

Ogyg.:   Unusual, perhaps, but by no means amazing, since the Lord, who multiplies these things as he wills, is omnipotent.

Men.:   You explain it reverently, but for my part I'm afraid many such affairs are contrived for profit.

Ogyg.:   I don't think God will stand for anybody mocking him in that way.

Men.:   On the contrary, though Mother and Son and Father and Spirit are robbed by the sacrilegious, sometimes they don't even bestir themselves slightly enough to frighten off the criminals by a nod or a noise. So great is the mildness of divinity.

Ogyg.:   That's true. But hear the rest. This milk is kept on the high altar, in the midst of which is Christ; on the right, for the sake of honor, is his Mother. For the milk represents his Mother.

Men.:   So it's in plain sight.

Ogyg.:   Enclosed in crystal, that is.

Men.:   Therefore liquid.

Ogyg.:   What do you mean, liquid, when it flowed fifteen hundred years ago? It's hard: you'd say powdered chalk, tempered with white of egg.

Men.:   Why don't they display it exposed?

Ogyg.:   To save the virginal milk from being defiled by the kisses of men.

Men.:   Well said, for in my opinion there are those who would bring neither clean nor chaste mouths to it.

Ogyg.:   When the custodian saw us, he rushed up, donned[1] a linen vestment, threw a sacred stole[2] round his neck, prostrated himself devoutly, and adored. Next he held out the sacred milk for us to kiss. We prostrated ourselves devoutly on the lowest step of the altar and, after first saluting Christ, uttered to the Virgin a short prayer I had prepared for this occasion: "Virgin Mother, who hast had the honor of suckling at thy maidenly breast the Lord of heaven and earth, thy Son Jesus, we pray that, cleansed by his blood we may gain that blessed infancy of dovelike simplicity which, innocent of all malice, deceit, and guile, longs without ceasing for the milk of gospel doctrine until it attains to the perfect man, to the measure of the fulness of Christ, whose blessed company thou enjoyest forever, with the Father and Holy Spirit. Amen."

Men.:   Certainly a devout intercession.[3] What effect did it have?

Ogyg.:   **Mother and Son both seemed to nod approval, unless my eyes deceived me. For the sacred milk appeared to leap up, and the Eucharistic elements[4] gleamed somewhat more brightly. Meanwhile the custodian approached us, quite silent, but holding out a board like those used in Germany by toll collectors on bridges.**

Key Concepts

generous saint	prayer
greedy boards	religious devotion
heretics	toll collectors
marvels	tourist trade
pilgrimage	Virgin Mother

---

1   **donned:** wore
2   **stole:** strip of silk worn by priests during services
3   **intercession:** prayer on behalf of another
4   **Eucharistic elements:** bread and wine consecrated and consumed during the Holy Communion. Theological interpretations vary from the literal transformation of the elements into the body and blood of Christ, to symbolism representing the real presence of Christ and a simple memorial meal.

Heritage of Western Intellectual Tradition   A Sourcebook

Martin Luther: An Open Letter to the Christian Nobility

Martin Luther (1483 – 1546), German theologian and religious reformer, initiated the Protestant Reformation which led up to new trends in social, political, and educational thought. Luther descended from peasantry. At 17 he enrolled at the University of Erfurt where he talked long and seriously enough to be nicknamed "the Philosopher." Hans Luther intended his son to become a lawyer, but in the summer of 1505, he suddenly abandoned his studies, sold his books, and entered the Augustinian monastery in Erfurt. He later related that on July 2, 1505 when he was returning from a visit he was overtaken by a thunderstorm and cried out in terror, "Help, St. Anne, and I'll become a monk."[1] In November 1510, on behalf of seven Augustinian monasteries, he made a visit to Rome, where he was shocked by the worldliness of the Roman clergy. Seven years later this 34-year-old stocky man in a monk's cassock nailed a paper to the door of the Castle Church, which was the bulletin board of the University of Wittenberg. It was the eve of All Saints' Day, Oct. 31, 1517. The Ninety-Five Theses opposed the manner in which indulgences（赎罪券）were being sold in order to raise money for the building of Saint Peters in Rome, which led to his condemnation and excommunication in January 1521. He refused firmly to recant. The Elector Frederick the Wise of Saxony protected him by confining him to the Wartburg castle, where he began his translation of the New Testament from Erasmus' Greek text into German — it has been said that he would still be a great shaper of the modern world had he done nothing else — the Lutheran churches of the world listed 72.5 million members in the mid-20th century. "The Open Letter" came at a time when the situation was desperate. As a last resort, Luther turned to temporal authorities who had a voice in the imperial diet. It is believed to be Luther's greatest work. The first 4,000 copies were followed less than a week by the need for the second edition. It is a "connecting link between the thought of the Middle Ages and that of modern times, prophetic of the new age, but showing how closely the new is bound up with the old." Luther died on Feb. 18, 1546 and was buried in the Castle Church at Wittenberg where he had posted the Ninety-Five Theses.

To His Most Illustrious and Mighty Imperial Majesty[2], and to the Christian Nobility of the German Nation,

Doctor Martin Luther

Grace and power from God, Most Illustrious Majesty, and most gracious and dear Lords.

---

1 **"Help, St. Anne, and I'll become a monk.":** The 22-year-old young man must have taken this experience as a divine revelation because that year he suddenly had a keen awareness of death: two of his brothers got killed by plague, and one close friend died suddenly.

2 **To His Most … Imperial Majesty:** Luther here was appealing to the imperial power after Pope Leo X, the Council of Constance and canon law (church law) rejected him. But when he found that they had all failed, he could only rely on the Holy Scriptures as ultimate authority.

It is not out of sheer forwardness or rashness that I, a single, poor man, have undertaken to address your worships. The distress and oppression which weigh down all the Estates of Christendom, especially of Germany, and which move not me alone, but everyone to cry out time and again, and to pray for help, have forced me even now to cry aloud that God may inspire some one with His Spirit to lend this suffering nation a helping hand. Oft times the councils made some presence at reformation[1], but their attempts have been cleverly hindered by the guile of certain men and things have gone from bad to worse. I now intend, by the help of God, to throw some light upon[2] the wiles and wickedness of these men, to the end[3] that when they are known, they may not henceforth be so hurtful and so great a hindrance. God has given us a noble youth[4] to be our head and thereby has awakened great hopes of good in many hearts; wherefore it is meet[5] that we should do our part and profitably use this time of grace.

Birth-place of Martin Luther (the third house on right-hand side)

In this whole matter the first and most important thing is that we take earnest heed[6] not to enter on[7] it trusting great might[8] or in human reason, even though all power in the world were ours; for God cannot and will not suffer a good work to be begun with trust in our own power or reason. Such works[9] He crushes ruthlessly to earth, as it (Ps. 33:16) is written in the xxxiii Psalm, "There is no king saved by the multitude of an host: a mighty man is not delivered by much strength." On this account, I fear, it came to pass of old[10] that the good Emperors Frederick I[11] and II and many other German emperors were shamefully oppressed and trodden under foot by the popes, although all the world feared them[12]. It may be that they relied on own might more than on God, and therefore they had to fall. In our own times, too, what was it that raised the blood-thirsty Julius II[13] to such heights? Nothing else, I fear, except that France, the Germans and Venice

---

1 **made some presence at reformation:** heard and discussed issues concerning reformation

2 **throw some light upon:** try to explain to you

3 **to the end:** to the effect, for the purpose

4 **noble youth:** Jesus Christ

5 **meet:** proper

6 **take earnest heed:** be watchful, be careful

7 **enter on:** start doing

8 **trusting great might:** trusting in great might

9 **works:** man's conscious efforts. Luther was alluding to the indulgencies bought for remissions by the pope of all the penalties of purgatory, which, Luther believd, had been imposed on sinners by the pope.

10 **came to pass of old:** happened in the past

11 **Frederick I:** called Frederick Barbarossa (c. 1123–1190), Holy Roman Emperor and King of Germany (1152–1190), whose grandson Frederick II (1194–1250) was Holy Roman Emperor (1215–1250)

12 **all the world feared them:** Here, as elsewhere in the essay, Luther is tactfully foregrounding the discord between the Pope and the secular leaders.

13 **Julius II (1443–1513):** made pope (1503–1513)

Heritage of Western Intellectual Tradition   A Sourcebook

relied (Judges 20:21) upon themselves. The children of Benjamin[1] slew 42,000 Israelites because the latter relied on their own strength.

That it may not so fare[2] with us and our noble young Emperor Charles[3], we must be sure that in this matter are dealing not with men, but with the princes of hell, who can fill the world with war and bloodshed, but whom war and bloodshed do not overcome. We must go at[4] this work despairing of[5] physical force and humbly trusting God; we must seek God's help with earnest prayer, and fix our minds on nothing else than the misery and distress of suffering Christendom, without regard to the deserts of evil men. Otherwise we may start the game with great prospect of success, but when we get well into it the evil spirits will stir up such confusion that the whole world will swim in blood, and yet nothing will come of it. Let us act wisely, therefore, and in the fear of God. The more force we use, the greater our disaster if we do not act humbly and in God's fear. The popes and the Romans have hitherto been able, by the devil's help, to set kings at odds with[6] one another, and they may well be able to do it again, if we proceed by our own might and cunning, without God's help.

I The Three Walls of the Romanists

The Romanists[7], with great adroitness, have built three walls about them, behind which they have hitherto defended themselves in such wise that no one has been able to reform them; and this has been the cause of terrible corruption throughout all Christendom.

Copy of the infamous Indulgence. Salvation was bought and sold like common marketplace commodity.

First, when pressed by the temporal power, they have made decrees and said that the temporal power has no jurisdiction over them, but, on the other hand, that the spiritual is above the temporal power. Second, when the attempt is made to reprove them out of the Scriptures[8], they raise the objection that the interpretation of the Scriptures belongs to no one except the pope. Third, if threatened with a council, they answer with the fable that no one can call a council but the pope.

---

1 **Benjamin:** In the Old Testament (Genesis 42–45), he was the youngest and most beloved son of the patriarch Jacob and was founder of the Israelite tribe of Benjamin.

2 **fare:** get on

3 **Emperor Charles:** namely Charles V (1500–1558), Holy Roman Emperor (1519–1558)

4 **go at:** deal with

5 **despairing of:** giving up vain hope of

6 **at odds with:** fight against

7 **Romanists:** here Roman Catholic authorities, the "pope, bishops, priests and monks" who champion papal supremacy

8 **reprove them out of the Scriptures:** criticize them according to the Bible

In this wise they have slyly stolen from us our three rods, that they may go unpunished, and have ensconced themselves within the safe stronghold of these three walls, that they may practice all the knavery and wickedness which we now see. Even when they have been compelled to hold a council they have weakened its power in advance by previously binding the princes with an oath to let them remain as they are. Moreover, they have given the pope full authority over all the decisions of the council, so that it is all one[1] whether there are many councils or no councils — except that they deceive us with puppet-shows and sham-battles. So terribly do they fear for their skin[2] in a really free council! And they have intimidated kings and princes by making them believe it would be an offense against God not to obey them in all these knavish, crafty deceptions.

Josh. 6:20 Now God help us, and give us one of the trumpets with which the walls of Jericho[3] were overthrown, that we may blow down these walls of straw and paper, and may set free the Christian rods for the punishment of sin, bringing to light the craft and deceit of the devil, to the end that through punishment we may reform ourselves, and once more attain God's favor.

Against the first wall we will direct our first attack.

Disputation on the Power and Efficacy of Indulgences Commonly Known as The 95 Theses (1517)

It is pure invention that pope, bishops, priests and monks are to be called the "spiritual estate"; princes, lords, artisans, and farmers the "temporal estate." That is indeed a fine bit of lying and hypocrisy. Yet no one should be frightened by it; and for this reason — viz.[4], that all Christians are truly of the "spiritual estate," and there is among them no difference at all but that of office, as Paul says in I Corinthians 12:12, We are all one body, yet every member has its own work, where by it serves every other, all because we have one baptism, one Gospel, one faith, and are all alike Christians; for baptism, Gospel and faith alone make us "spiritual" and a Christian people.

But that a pope or a bishop anoints, confers tonsures[5]; ordains, consecrates, or prescribes dress unlike that of the laity, this may make hypocrites and graven images, but it never makes a Christian or "spiritual" man. Through baptism all of us are consecrated to the priesthood, as St. Peter says in I Peter 2:9, "Ye are a royal priesthood, a priestly kingdom," and the book of Revelation says, Rev. 5:10 "Thou hast made us by Thy blood to be priests and kings." For if we had no higher consecration than pope or bishop gives, the consecration by pope or bishop would never

---

1   **all one:** all the same

2   **fear for their skin:** fear for their lives

3   **walls of Jericho:** Jericho, site of the world's earliest known town, scene of famous siege during the Israelite conquest of Canaan, when it is said that the walls fell down at the shout of the army under Joshua.

4   **viz.:** namely

5   **tonsures:** the shaving of the head, especially of a person entering a priesthood or monastic order

make a priest, nor might anyone either say mass or preach a sermon or give absolution. Therefore when the bishop consecrates it is the same thing as if he, in the place and stead of the whole congregation, all of whom have like power, were to[1] take one out of their number and charge him to use this power for the others[2]; just as though ten brothers, all king's sons and equal heirs, were to choose one of themselves to rule the inheritance for them all, — they would all be kings and equal in power, though one of them would be charged with the duty of ruling.

To make it still clearer. If a little group of pious Christian laymen were taken captive and set down in a wilderness, and had among them no priest consecrated by a bishop, and if there in the wilderness they were to agree in choosing one of themselves, married or unmarried, and were to charge him with the office of baptizing, saying mass, absolving and preaching, such a man would be as truly a priest as though all bishops and popes had consecrated him. That is why in cases of necessity any one can baptize and give absolution, which would be impossible unless we were all priests. This great grace and power of baptism and of the Christian Estate they have well-nigh destroyed and caused us to forget through the canon law. It was in the manner aforesaid that Christians in olden days chose from their number bishops and priests, who were afterwards confirmed by other bishops, without all the show which now obtains. It was thus that St. Augustine, Ambrose and Cyprian[3] became bishops.

Since, then, the temporal authorities are baptized with the same baptism and have the same faith and Gospel as we, we must grant that they are priests and bishops, and count their office one which has a proper and a useful place in the Christian community. **For whoever comes out the water of baptism can boast that he is already consecrated priest, bishop and pope, though it is not seemly that every one should exercise the office.** Nay, just because we are all in like manner priests, no one must put himself forward and undertake, without our consent and election, to do what is in the power of all of us. For what is common to all, no one dare take upon himself without the will and the command of the community; and should it happen that one chosen for such an office were deposed for malfeasance[4], he would then be just what he was before he held office. Therefore a priest in Christendom is nothing else than an office-holder. While he is in office, he has precedence; when deposed, he is a peasant or a townsman like the rest. Beyond all doubt, then, a priest is no longer a priest when he is deposed. But now they have invented characters indelebilis[5], and prate[6] that a deposed priest is nevertheless something different from a mere layman. They even dream that a priest can never become a layman, or be anything else than a priest. All this is mere talk and man-made law.

---

1   **as if he, in the place and stead of the whole congregation, all of whom have like power, were to:** as if he … were to

2   **Therefore when … for the others:** Namely, bishop's consecration is no more than a mere selection.

3   **Ambrose and Cyprian:** Saint Ambrose (c. 339–97), one of the most celebrated Fathers of the Church; Saint Cyprian (c. 200–58), leader of the Christian church in Africa

4   **deposed for malfeasance:** removed from office for wrongdoing

5   **indelebilis:** Latin for "eternal"

6   **prate:** talk repeatedly

From all this it follows that there is really no difference between laymen and priests, princes and bishops, "spirituals" and "temporals," as they call them, except that of office and work, but not of "estate"; for they are all of the same estate, — true priests, bishops and popes, — though they are not all engaged in the same work, just as all priests and monks have not the same work. This is the teaching of St. Paul in Romans 12:4 and I Corinthians 12:12, and of St. Peter in I Peter 2:9, as I have said above, viz., that we are all one body of Christ, the Head, all members one of another. Christ has not two different bodies, one "temporal," the other "spiritual." He is one Head, and He has one body.

Title page of Martin Luther's treatise On the Babylonian Captivity of the Church (1520)

Therefore, just as those who are now called "spiritual" — priests, bishops or popes — are neither different from other Christians nor superior to them, except that they are charged with the administration of the Word of God and the sacraments, which is their work and office, so it is with the temporal authorities, — they bear sword and rod with which to punish the evil and to protect the good. A cobbler, a smith, a farmer, each has the work and office of his trade, and yet they are all alike consecrated priests and bishops, and every one by means of his own work or office must benefit and serve every other, that in this way many kinds of work may be done for the bodily and spiritual welfare of the community, even as all the members of the body serve one another.

See, now, how Christian is the decree[1] which says that the temporal power is not above the "spiritual estate" and may not punish it. That is as much as to say that the hand shall lend no aid when the eye is suffering. Is it not unnatural, not to say unchristian, that one member should not help another and prevent its destruction? Verily, the more honorable the member, the more should the others help. **I say then, since the temporal power is ordained of God to punish evil-doers and to protect them that do well, it should therefore be left free to perform it office without hindrance through the whole body of Christendom without respect of persons, whether it affect pope, bishops, priests, monks, nuns or anybody else.** For if the mere fact that the temporal power has a smaller place among The Christian offices than has the office of preachers or confessors, or of the clergy, then the tailors, cobblers, masons, carpenters, pot-boys, tapsters, farmers, and all the secular tradesmen, should also be prevented from providing pope, bishops, priests and monks with shoes, clothing, houses, meat and drink, and from paying them tribute. But if these laymen are allowed to do their work unhindered, what do the Roman scribes mean by their laws, with which they withdraw themselves from the jurisdiction[2] of the temporal Christian power, only so that they may be free to do evil and to fulfill what St. Peter has said: 2. Peter 2:1 "There shall be false teachers among you, and through covetousness shall they with feigned words make merchandise of you."

---

1 **how Christian is the decree:** if the decree sounds like a Christian decree
2 **withdraw themselves from the jurisdiction:** exempt themselves from the authority

Heritage of Western Intellectual Tradition   A Sourcebook

On this account the Christian temporal power should exercise its office without let[1] or hindrance, regardless whether it be pope, bishop or priest whom it affects; whoever is guilty, let him suffer. All that the canon law has said to the contrary is sheer invention of Roman presumption. For Thus saith St. Paul to all Christians: Roman 13:1, 4 "Let every soul (I take that to mean the pope's soul also) be subject unto the higher powers; for they bear not the sword in vain[2], but are the ministers of God for the punishment of evildoers, and for the praise of them that do well." St. Peter also says: 1 Peter 2:13, 15 "Submit yourselves unto every ordinance of man for the Lord's sake, for so is the will of God." He has also prophesied that such men shall come as will despise the temporal authorities; and this has come to pass through the canon law.

So then, I think this first paper-wall is overthrown, since the temporal power has become a member of the body of Christendom, and is of the "spiritual estate," though its work is of a temporal nature. Therefore its work should extend freely and without hindrance to all the members of the whole body; it should punish and use force whenever guilt deserves or necessity demands, without regard to pope, bishops and priests, — let them hail[3] threats and bans as much as they will.

Again, it is intolerable that in the canon law so much importance is attached to the freedom, life and property of the clergy, as though the laity were not also as spiritual as good Christians as they, or did not belong to the Church. Why are your life and limb, your property and honor so free, and mine not? We are all alike Christians, and have baptism, faith, Spirit and all things alike. If a priest is killed, the land is laid under interdict, — why not when a peasant is killed? Whence comes this great distinction between those who are equally Christians? Only from human laws and inventions!

Moreover, it can be no good spirit who has invented such exceptions and granted to sin such license and impunity[4]. For if we are bound to strive against the works and words of the evil spirit, and to drive him out in whatever way we can, as Christ commands His Apostles, ought we, then to suffer it[5] in silence when the pope or his satellites are bent on devilish words and works? Ought we for the sake of men to allow the suppression of divine commandments and truths which we have sworn in baptism to support with life and limb[6]? Of a truth we should then have to answer all the souls[7] that would thereby be abandoned and led astray.

It must therefore have been the very prince of devils who said what is written in the canon law: "If the pope were so scandalously bad as to lead souls in crowds to the devil, yet he could not be deposed." On this accursed and devilish foundation they build at Rome, and think that we should let

---

1 **let:** hindrance

2 **for they bear not the sword in vain:** because their power to punish is real

3 **hail:** send

4 **granted to sin such license and impunity:** granted such license and impunity to sin

5 **it:** evil spirit

6 **life and limb:** continued existence

7 **Of a truth we should then have to answer all the souls:** We should then have to answer all the souls of a truth

all the world go to the devil, rather than resist their knavery. If the fact that one man is set over others were sufficient reason why he should escape punishment, then no Christian could punish another, since Christ commands that every man shall esteem himself the lowliest and the least.

Where sin is, there is no escape from punishment; as St. Gregory[1] also writes that we are

Luther's study at Wartburg where he completed his extraordinary translation of the Bible

indeed all equal, but guilt puts us in subjection one to another. Now we see how they whom God and the Apostles have made subject to the temporal sword deal with Christendom, depriving it of its liberty by their own wickedness, without warrant of Scripture. It is to be feared that this is a game of Antichrist[2] or a sign that he is close at hand.

The second wall is still more flimsy[3] and worthless. They wish to be the only Masters of The Holy Scriptures, even though in all their lives they learn nothing from them. They assume for themselves sole authority, and with insolent juggling of words they would persuade us that the pope, whether he be a bad man or a good man, cannot err in matters of faith, and yet they cannot prove a single letter of it. Hence it comes that so many heretical and unchristian, nay, even unnatural ordinances have a place in the canon law, of which, however, there is no present need to speak. For since they think that the Holy Spirit never leaves them, be they never so unlearned and wicked, they make bold to decree whatever they will. And if it were true, where would be the need or use of Holy Scriptures? Let us burn them, and be satisfied with the unlearned lords at Rome, who are possessed of the Holy Spirit, — although He can possess only pious hearts! Unless I had read it myself, I could not have believed that the devil would make such clumsy pretensions at Rome, and find a following.

But not to fight them with mere words, we will quote the Scriptures. St. Paul says in I Corinthians 14:30: "If to anyone something better is revealed, though he be sitting and listening to another in God's Word, then the first, who is speaking, shall hold his peace and give place." What would be the use of this commandment, if we were only to believe him who does the talking or who has the highest seat? Christ also says in John 6:45, that all Christians shall be taught of God. Thus it may well happen that the pope and his followers are wicked men, and no true Christians, not taught of God, not having true understanding. On the other hand, an ordinary man may have true understanding; why then should we not follow him? Has not the pope erred many times? Who would help Christendom when the pope errs, if we were not to believe another, who had the Scriptures on his side, more than the pope?

---

1   **St. Gregory (540–604):** or Gregory the Great, notable for church reform and wise administration
2   **Antichrist:** chief enemy of Christ. During the Reformation, Luther and other protestant leaders identified the papacy itself as the Antichrist.
3   **flimsy:** light, thin

Heritage of Western Intellectual Tradition   A Sourcebook

Therefore it is a wickedly invented fable, and they cannot produce a letter in defense of it, that the interpretation of Scripture or the confirmation of its interpretation belongs to the pope alone. They have themselves usurped this power; and although they allege that this power was given to Peter[1] when the keys were given to him, it is plain enough that the keys were not given to Peter alone, but to the whole community. Moreover, the keys were not ordained for doctrine or government, but only for the binding and loosing of they arrogate to themselves[2] is mere invention. But Christ's word to Peter, Luke 22:32 "I have prayed for thee that thy faith fail not," cannot be applied to the pope, since the majority of the popes have been without faith, as they must themselves confess. Besides, it is not only for Peter that Christ prayed, but also for all Apostles and Christians, as he says in John 17:9, 20: "Father, I pray for those whom Thou hast given Me, and not for these only, but for all who believe on Me through their word." Is not this clear enough?

Only think of it yourself! They must confess that there are pious Christians among us, who have the true faith, Spirit, understanding, word and mind of Christ. Why, then, should we reject their word and understanding and follow the pope, who has neither faith nor Spirit? That would be to deny the whole faith and the Christian Church. Moreover, it is not the pope alone who is always in the right, if the article of The Creed[3] is correct: "I believe one holy Christian Church"; otherwise the prayer must run: "I believe in the pope at Rome," and so reduce the Christian Church to one man, — which would be nothing else than a devilish and hellish error.

Besides, if we are all priests, as was said above, and all have one faith, one Gospel, one sacrament, why should we not also have the power to test and judge what is correct or incorrect in matters of faith? What becomes of the words of Paul in I Corinthians 2:15: "He that is spiritual judgeth all things, yet he himself is judged of no man," II Corinthians 4:13: "We have all the same Spirit of faith"? Why, then, should not we perceive what squares with faith and what does not, as well as does an unbelieving pope?[4]

All these and many other texts should make us bold and free, and we should not allow the Spirit of liberty, as Paul calls Him, to be frightened off by the fabrications of the popes, but we ought to go boldly forward to test all that they do or leave undone, according to our interpretation of the Scriptures, which rests on faith, and compel them to follow not their own interpretation, but the one that is better. In the olden days Abraham had to listen to Sarah, although she was in more complete subjection to him than we are to anyone on earth.

1　**Peter:** St. Peter, the "Prince of the Apostles", whose peculiar symbols are the keys (Matthew 16:13 – 20)

2　**arrogate to themselves:** claim without right

3　**The Creed:** also called the Apostles' Creed since it is believed to have dated from very early times in the Church, a half century or so from the last writings of the New Testament. The creed could be appealed to as held by the church in all its branches to serve as test of "catholicity" (the universal church of the Lord Jesus Christ).

4　**Why, then, should not we perceive … as well as does an unbelieving pope?:** Why, then, should not we perceive … as well as an unbelieving pope does?

Balaam's ass[1], also, was wiser than the prophet himself. If God then spoke an ass against a prophet, why should He not be able even now to speak by a righteous man against the pope? In like manner St. Paul rebukes St. Peter as a man in error. Therefore it behooves every Christian to espouse the cause of the faith, to understand and defend it, and to rebuke errors.

The third wall falls of itself when the first two are down. For when the pope acts contrary to the Scriptures, it is our duty to stand by the Scriptures, to reprove him, and to constrain him,

Luther on Dec. 10, 1520 burnt the Papal Bull.

according to the word of Christ in Matthew 18:15: "If thy brother sin against thee, go and tell it him between thee and him alone; if he hear thee not, then take with thee one or two more; if he hear them not, tell it to the Church; if he hear not the Church, consider him a heathen." Here every member is commanded to care for every other. How much rather should we do this when the member that does evil is a ruling member, and by his evil-doing is the cause of much harm and offense to the rest! But if I am to accuse him before the Church, I must bring the Church together.

They have no basis in Scripture for their contention that it belongs to the pope alone to call a council or confirm its actions; for this is based merely upon their own laws, which are valid only in so far as they are not injurious to Christendom or contrary to the laws of God. When the pope deserves punishment, such laws go out of force, since it is injurious to Christendom not to punish him by means of a council.

…

Let us, therefore, hold fast to this: No Christian authority can do anything against Christ; as St. Paul says, II Corinthians 13:8: "We can do nothing against Christ, but for Christ." Whatever does aught against Christ is the power of Antichrist and of the devil, even though it were to rain and hail wonders and plagues. Wonders and plagues prove nothing, especially in these last evil times, for which all the Scriptures prophesy false wonders. Therefore we must cling with firm faith to the words of God, and then the devil will cease from wonders.

Thus I hope that the false, lying terror with which the Romans have this long time made our conscience timid and stupid, has been allayed. They, like all of us, are subject to the temporal sword; they have no power to interpret the Scriptures by mere authority, without learning; they have no authority to prevent a council or, in sheer wantonness, to pledge it, bind it, or take away its liberty; but if they do this, they are in truth the communion of Antichrist and of the devil, and have nothing at all of Christ except the name.

---

1 **Balaam's ass:** Balaam in the Old Testament was a Gentile prophet. Balak, king of the Moabites, summoned Balaam to pronounce a curse upon the advancing Israelites and drive them away. Balaam consented to go, but on the way the angel of the Lord met him in the famous incident of the talking ass, after which Balaam became a spokesman for God (Numbers 22:21–35).

Key Concepts

absolution

authority

canon law/human laws

cause of the faith

Christian nobility

human reason

interpretation of the Scriptures

priesthood

reformation

spiritual estate/temporal estate

spiritual power/temporal power

three walls/three rods

John Calvin: Institutes of the Christian Religion*

John Calvin (1509 – 1564), French Protestant theologian and most important figure in the second generation of the Protestant Reformation. Calvinism refers to the theology advanced by Calvin and developed by his followers. Calvin received formal instruction for the priesthood at the University of Paris. His father encouraged him to study law, and he was deeply drawn to classical literature, but in 1532 or 1533 he experienced a "sudden conversion" and turned to theology. His association with Nicholas Cop, newly elected rector of the University of Paris, forced both to flee when Cop announced his support in 1535 of Martin Luther. In 1536 he published the provocative work *Institutes of the Christian Religion,* which thrust him into the forefront of Protestantism as its spokesman. During the same year, when he was making a second escape from France to seek asylum in Basel, Calvin was asked by Guillaume Farel[1] to assist the reformation movement in Geneva. Calvin remained in Geneva until 1538 when the town voted against Farel and asked both to leave. In 1541 Genevans asked him to return and lead them again in reforming the church. He remained in that city for the rest of his life, to be an organizer of

---

*   French King Francis I wrote to justify his persecution of French Protestants, and in answer to this Calvin wrote in 1536 the 1st edition of *Institutes of the Christian Religion.*

1   **Guillaume Farel (1489–1565):** French reformer and preacher who played a major role in the introduction of the Reformation into Switzerland. In 1523 he was expelled from France for his Protestant views. He continued to preach reform in Basel, Switzerland. In 1532 he went to Geneva, where his preaching and public disputations helped bring about the triumph of Protestantism, which the town council formally adopted in 1535.

a model Protestant society and virtual ruler of a theocratic city-state. He tried to improve the harsh quality of life in the city threatened by Catholic armies. He supported good hospitals, a proper sewage system, development of a municipal school system for all children, and special care for the poor and infirm. There was complaint for his being too repressive and harsh in his "Holy Commonwealth." Calvin used state power to reinforce doctrinal conformity: hundreds of citizens were banished on moral grounds, and Servetus, a Spanish refugee, was burned at the stake for denying the doctrine of the Trinity. In this sense Calvin was a man of the Middle Ages. But he contributed a systematic statement of the Protestant doctrine: in addition to the Lutheran justification by faith and supreme authority of the Bible for Christian faith, he emphasized the omnipotence and sovereignty of God with sternest predestination, austere moral ideals and religious intolerance. When Calvin died, he was buried in an unmarked grave in Geneva.

By the Fall and Revolt of Adam the Whole Human Race Was Delivered to the Curse, and Degenerated from Its Original Condition; the Doctrine of Original Sin

It was not without reason that the ancient proverb so strongly recommended to man the knowledge of himself[1]. For if it is deemed disgraceful to be ignorant of things pertaining to the business of life, much more disgraceful is self-ignorance, in consequence of which we miserably deceive ourselves in matters of the highest moment, and so walk blindfold.

But the more useful the precept is, the more careful we must be not to use it preposterously[2], as we see certain philosophers have done. For they, when exhorting man to know himself, state the motive to be, that he may not be ignorant of his own excellence and dignity. They wish him to see nothing in himself but what will fill him with vain confidence, and inflate him with pride.

But self-knowledge consists in this. First, When reflecting on what God gave us at our creation, and still continues graciously to give, we perceive how great the excellence of our nature would have been had its integrity remained, and, at the same time, remember that we have nothing of our own, but depend entirely on God, from whom we hold at pleasure whatever he has seen it meet to bestow; secondly, When viewing our miserable condition since Adam's fall, all confidence and boasting are overthrown, we blush for shame, and feel truly humble. For as God at first formed us in his own image, that he might elevate our minds to the pursuit of virtue, and the contemplation of eternal life, so to prevent us from heartlessly burying those noble qualities which distinguish us from the lower animals, it is of importance to know that we were endued with reason and intelligence, in order that we might cultivate a holy and honourable life, and regard a blessed immortality as our destined aim.

At the same time, **it is impossible to think of our primeval dignity without being imme-**

---

1 **knowledge of himself:** referring to the admonition "*Gnothi se auton*" ("Know Thyself") inscribed on the sun god Apollo's Oracle of Delphi temple

2 **preposterously:** unreasonably

diately reminded of the sad spectacle of our ignominy[1] and corruption, ever since we fell from our original in the person of our first parent. In this way, we feel dissatisfied with ourselves, and become truly humble, while we are inflamed with new desires to seek after God, in whom each may regain those good qualities of which all are found to be utterly destitute[2] ...

Calvin in Geneva

As the act which God punished so severely must have been not a trivial fault, but a heinous[3] crime, it will be necessary to attend to the peculiar nature of the sin which produced Adam's fall, and provoked God to inflict such fearful vengeance on the whole human race. The common idea of sensual intemperance[4] is childish. The sum and substance of all virtues could not consist in abstinence from a single fruit amid a general abundance of every delicacy that could be desired, the earth, with happy fertility, yielding not only abundance, but also endless variety.

We must, therefore, look deeper than sensual intemperance. **The prohibition to touch the tree of the knowledge of good and evil was a trial of obedience, that Adam, by observing it, might prove his willing submission to the command of God. For the very term shows the end of the precept to have been to keep him contented with his lot, and not allow him arrogantly to aspire beyond it.** The promise, which gave him hope of eternal life as long as he should eat of the tree of life, and, on the other hand, the fearful denunciation of death the moment he should taste of the tree of the knowledge of good and evil, were meant to prove and exercise his faith. Hence it is not difficult to infer in what way Adam provoked the wrath of God. **Augustine, indeed, is not far from the mark, when he says, (in Psal. 19) that pride was the beginning of all evil, because, had not man's ambition carried him higher than he was permitted, he might have continued in his first estate.**

A further definition, however, must be derived from the kind of temptation which Moses describes. When, by the subtlety of the devil, the woman faithlessly abandoned the command of God, her fall obviously had its origin in disobedience. This Paul confirms, when he says, that, by the disobedience of one man, all were destroyed. At the same time, it is to be observed, that the first man revolted against the authority of God, not only in allowing himself to be ensnared by the wiles of the devil, but also by despising the truth, and turning aside to lies. Assuredly, when the word of God is despised, all reverence for Him is gone. His majesty cannot be duly honoured

---

1 **ignominy:** public shame
2 **destitute:** lacking
3 **heinous:** very wicked
4 **intemperance:** lack of self-control

Heritage of Western Intellectual Tradition   A Sourcebook

among us, nor his worship maintained in its integrity, unless we hang as it were upon his lips[1]. Hence infidelity was at the root of the revolt. **From infidelity, again, sprang ambition and pride, together with ingratitude; because Adam, by longing for more than was allotted him, manifested contempt for the great liberality with which God had enriched him. It was surely monstrous impiety that a son of earth should deem it little to have been made in the likeness, unless he were also made the equal of God**[2]. If the apostasy[3] by which man withdraws from the authority of his Maker, nay, petulantly[4] shakes off his allegiance to him, is a foul and execrable[5] crime, it is in vain to extenuate[6] the sin of Adam. Nor was it simple apostasy. It was accompanied with foul

Church government Calvin established at Geneva

insult to God, the guilty pair assenting to Satan's calumnies[7] when he charged God with malice, envy, and falsehood. In fine[8], infidelity opened the door to ambition, and ambition was the parent of rebellion, man casting off the fear of God, and giving free vent to his lust. Hence, Bernard[9] truly says, that, in the present day, a door of salvation is opened to us when we receive the gospel with our ears, just as by the same entrance, when thrown open to Satan, death was admitted. Never would Adam have dared to show any repugnance[10] to the command of God if he had not been incredulous as to his word. The strongest curb to keep all his affections under due restraint, would have been the belief that nothing was better than to cultivate righteousness by obeying the commands of God, and that the highest possible felicity[11] was to be loved by him. Man, therefore, when carried away by the blasphemies of Satan, did his very utmost to annihilate the whole glory of God.

As Adam's spiritual life would have consisted in remaining united and bound to his Maker, so estrangement from him was the death of his soul. Nor is it strange that he who perverted the whole order of nature in heaven and earth deteriorated his race by his revolt. "The whole creation groaneth," saith St. Paul, "being made subject to vanity, not willingly," (Rom. 8: 20, 22.) If the

---

1   **hang ... upon his lips:** listen wholeheartedly to him
2   **made the equal of God:** see Ezekiel 28, Isaiah 14. The desire to be equal with God is also the reason of Satan's revolt in *Paradise Lost*.
3   **apostasy:** giving up one's religion
4   **petulantly:** unreasonably
5   **execrable:** very bad
6   **extenuate:** make less serious
7   **calumny:** slander
8   **in fine:** in a word
9   **Saint Bernard of Clairvaux (1090–1153):** French abbot and theologian and primary builder of the reforming Cistercian monastic order, declared a Doctor of the Church in 1830
10 **repugnance:** distastefulness
11 **felicity:** happiness

Heritage of Western Intellectual Tradition   A Sourcebook

reason is asked, there cannot be a doubt that creation bears part of the punishment deserved by man, for whose use all other creatures were made. Therefore, since through man's fault a curse has extended above and below, over all the regions of the world, there is nothing unreasonable in its[1] extending to all his offspring. After the heavenly image in man was effaced[2], he not only was himself punished by a withdrawal of the ornaments in which he had been arrayed, viz., wisdom, virtue, justice, truth, and holiness, and by the substitution in their place of those dire pests, blindness, impotence, vanity, impurity, and unrighteousness, but he involved his posterity also, and plunged them in the same wretchedness.

This is the hereditary corruption to which early Christian writers gave the name of Original Sin, meaning by the term the depravation of a nature formerly good and pure. The subject gave rise to much discussion, there being nothing more remote from common apprehension, than that the fault of one should render all guilty, and so become a common sin. This seems to be the reason

Calvin in his study in Geneva

why the oldest doctors of the church only glance obscurely at the point, or, at least, do not explain it so clearly as it required. This timidity, however, could not prevent the rise of a Pelagius[3] with his profane fiction — that Adam sinned only to his own hurt, but did no hurt to his posterity. Satan, by thus craftily hiding the disease, tried to render it incurable. But when it was clearly proved from Scripture that the sin of the first man passed to all his posterity, recourse was had to the cavil[4], that it passed by imitation, and not by propagation[5]. The orthodoxy, therefore, and more especially Augustine, laboured to show, that we are not corrupted by acquired wickedness, but bring an innate corruption from the very womb.

But lest the thing itself of which we speak be unknown or doubtful, it will be proper to define original sin. I have no intention, however, to discuss all the definitions which different writers have adopted, but only to adduce[6] the one which seems to me most accordant with truth. **Original sin, then, may be defined a hereditary corruption and depravity of our nature, extending to all the parts of the soul, which first makes us obnoxious[7] to the wrath of God, and then produces in us works which in Scripture are termed works of the flesh.** This corruption is repeatedly designated by Paul by the term sin, (Gal. 5: 19;) while the works which proceed from it, such as adultery, fornication[8], theft, hatred,

---

1 **its:** the curse's
2 **was effaced:** became indistinct
3 **Pelagius (c. 360–c. 420):** Roman-British monk and theologian who denied St. Augustine's doctrines of predestination and original sin and argues instead that each person possesses free will, hence the possibility of salvation. He was declared heretical by Councils in 416 and 418.
4 **cavil:** finding fault with
5 **propagation:** transmission, multiplication
6 **adduce:** put forward
7 **obnoxious:** very disagreeable
8 **fornication:** voluntary sex between people who are not married to each other

murder, revellings[1], he terms, in the same way, the fruits of sin, though in various passages of Scripture, and even by Paul himself, they are also termed sins.

The two things, therefore, are to be distinctly observed, viz., that being thus perverted and corrupted in all the parts of our nature, we are, merely on account of such corruption, deservedly condemned by God, to whom nothing is acceptable but righteousness, innocence, and purity. This is not liability[2] for another's fault. For when it is said, that the sin of Adam has made us obnoxious to the justice of God, the meaning is not, that we, who are in ourselves innocent and blameless, are bearing his guilt, but that since by his transgression we are all placed under the curse, he is said to have brought us under obligation. Through him, however, not only has punishment been derived, but pollution instilled, for which punishment is justly due. Hence Augustine, though he often terms it another's sin, (that he may more clearly show how it comes to us by descent,) at the same time asserts that it is each individual's own sin. And the Apostle most distinctly testifies, that "death passed upon all men, for that all have sinned," (Rom. 5: 12;) that is, are involved in original sin, and polluted by its stain. Hence, even infants bringing their condemnation with them from their mother's womb, suffer not for another's, but for their own defect. For although they have not yet produced the fruits of their own unrighteousness, they have the seed implanted in them. Nay, their whole nature is, as it were, a seed-bed of sin, and therefore cannot but be odious and abominable to God. Hence it follows, that it is properly deemed sinful in the sight of God; for there could be no condemnation without guilt.

Next comes the other point, viz., that this perversity in us never ceases, but constantly produces new fruits, in other words, those works of the flesh which we formerly described; just as a lighted furnace sends forth sparks and flames, or a fountain without ceasing pours out water. Hence, those who have defined original sin as the want of the original righteousness which we ought to have had, though they substantially comprehend the whole case, do not significantly enough express its power and energy. For our nature is not only utterly devoid of goodness, but so prolific in all kinds of evil, that it can never be idle[3].

Eternal Election, by Which God Has Predestined Some to Salvation, Others to Destruction

The covenant of life is not preached equally to all, and among those to whom it is preached, does not always meet with the same reception. This diversity displays the unsearchable depth of the divine judgment, and is without doubt subordinate to God's purpose of eternal election. But if it is plainly owing to the mere pleasure of God that salvation is spontaneously offered to some, while others have no access to it, great and difficult questions immediately arise, questions which are inexplicable, when just views are not entertained concerning election and predestination. To many this seems a perplexing[4] subject, because they deem it most incongruous[5] that of the great

---

1　**revelling:** excessive merrymaking
2　**liability:** responsibility
3　**idle:** stopping producing evil
4　**perplexing:** puzzling, confusing
5　**incongruous:** contradictory

body of mankind some[1] should be predestinated to salvation, and others to destruction. How ceaselessly they entangle themselves will appear as we proceed. We may add, that in the very obscurity which deters them, we may see not only the utility of this doctrine, but also its most pleasant fruits. We shall never feel persuaded as we ought that our salvation flows from the free mercy of God as its fountain, until we are made acquainted with his eternal election, the grace of God being illustrated by the contrast, viz., that he does not adopt all promiscuously[2] to the hope of salvation, but gives to some what he denies to others.

It is plain how greatly ignorance of this principle detracts from the glory of God, and impairs true humility. But though thus necessary to be known, Paul declares that it cannot be known unless God, throwing works entirely out of view, elect those whom he has predested. His words are, "Even so then at this present time also, there is a remnant[3] according to the election of grace. And if by grace, then it is no more of works: otherwise grace is no more grace. But if it be of works, then it is no more grace: otherwise work is no more work," (Rom. 11: 6.) If to make it appear that our salvation flows entirely from the good mercy of God, we must be carried back to the origin of election, then those who would extinguish it, wickedly do as much as in them lies to obscure what they ought[4] most loudly to extol[5], and pluck up humility by the very roots. Paul clearly declares that it is only when the salvation of a remnant is ascribed to gratuitous election, we arrive at the knowledge that God saves whom he wills of[6] his mere good pleasure, and does not pay a debt, a debt which never can be due.

Those who preclude access, and would not have any one to obtain a taste of this doctrine, are equally unjust to God and men, there being no other means of humbling us as we ought, or making us feel how much we are bound to him. Nor, indeed, have we elsewhere any sure ground of confidence. This we say on the authority of Christ, who, to deliver us from all fear, and render us invincible amid our many dangers, snares and mortal conflicts, promises safety to all that the Father has taken under his protection, (John 10: 26.) From this we infer, that all who know not that they are the peculiar people of God, must be wretched from perpetual trepidation[7], and that those therefore, who, by overlooking the three advantages which we have noted, would destroy the very foundation of our safety, consult ill for themselves and for all the faithful. What? Do we not here find the very origin of the Church, which, as Bernard rightly teaches, (Serm. in Cantic.) could not be found or recognized among the creatures, because it lies hid (in both cases wondrously[8]) within the lap of blessed predestination, and the mass of wretched condemnation?

---

1 **of the great body of mankind some:** some of the great body of mankind
2 **promiscuously:** indiscriminately
3 **remnant:** small part that remains
4 **those who would extinguish it, wickedly do as much as in them lies to obscure what they ought:** those … wickedly do to obscure as much lies in them as possible what they ought …
5 **extol:** praise highly
6 **of:** out of
7 **trepidation:** alarm, terror
8 **wondrously:** as a wonder

But before I enter on the subject, I have some remarks to address to two classes of men.

The subject of predestination, which in itself is attended with considerable difficulty, is rendered very perplexed and hence perilous[1] by human curiosity, which cannot be restrained from wandering into forbidden paths and climbing to the clouds determined if it can that none of the secret things of God shall remain unexplored[2]. When we see many, some of them in other respects not bad men, every where rushing into this audacity[3] and wickedness, it is necessary to remind them of the course of duty in this matter.

First, then, **when they inquire into predestination, let then remember that they are penetrating into the recesses[4] of the divine wisdom, where he who rushes forward securely and confidently, instead of satisfying his curiosity will enter in inextricable labyrinth[5].** For it is not right that man should with impunity[6] pry into things which the Lord has been pleased to conceal within himself, and scan that sublime eternal wisdom which it is his pleasure that we should not apprehend but adore, that therein also his perfections may appear. Those secrets of his will, which he has seen it meet to manifest, are revealed in his word — revealed in so far as he knew to be conducive to[7] our interest and welfare. ...

I admit that profane[8] men lay hold of the subject of predestination to carp[9], or cavil[10], or snarl[11], or scoff[12]. But if their petulance[13] frightens us, it will be necessary to conceal all the principal articles of faith, because they and their fellows leave scarcely one of them unassailed with blasphemy. A rebellious spirit will display itself no less insolently[14] when it hears that there are three persons in the divine essence, than when it hears that God when he created man foresaw every thing that was to happen to him. Nor will they abstain from their jeers when told that little more than five thousand years have elapsed since the creation of the world. For they will ask, why did the power of God slumber so long in idleness? In short, nothing can be stated that they will not assail with derision[15]. To quell their blasphemies, must we say nothing concerning the divinity of

---

1 **perilous:** dangerous
2 **determined if it ... remain unexplored:** determined ... that none of the secret things of God shall remain unexplored
3 **audacity:** boldness
4 **recess:** secret place
5 **inextricable labyrinth:** difficult and entangled situation from which there is no escape
6 **with impunity:** with no punishment
7 **conducive to:** leading to
8 **profane:** worldly
9 **carp:** complaint
10 **cavil:** fault finding
11 **snarl:** growl
12 **scoff:** mock
13 **petulance:** irritation, impatience
14 **insolently:** offensively, contemptuously
15 **derision:** laugh, mocking

the Son and Spirit? Must the creation of the world be passed over in silence? No! The truth of God is too powerful, both here and everywhere, to dread the slanders of the ungodly.

As Augustine powerfully maintains in his treatise, De Bono Perseverantiae. For we see that the false apostles were unable, by defaming and accusing the true doctrine of Paul, to make him ashamed of it. There is nothing in the allegation that the whole subject is fraught with danger to pious minds, as tending to destroy exhortation[1], shake faith, disturb and dispirit the heart. Augustine disguises not that on these grounds he was often charged with preaching the doctrine of predestination too freely, but, as it was easy for him to do, he abundantly refutes the charge. As a great variety of absurd objections are here stated, we have thought it best to dispose of each of them in its proper place. Only I wish it to be received as a general rule, that the secret things of God are not to be scrutinized, and that those which he has revealed are not to be overlooked, lest we may, on the one hand, be chargeable with curiosity, and, on the other, with ingratitude. For it has been shrewdly observed by Augustine, (de Genesi ad Literam, Lib. 5,) that we can safely follow Scripture, which walks softly, as with a mother's step, in accommodation to our weakness. Those, however, who are so cautious and timid, that they would bury all mention of predestination in order that it may not trouble weak minds, with what color, pray, will they cloak their arrogance, when they indirectly charge God with a want of due consideration, in not having foreseen a danger for which they imagine that they prudently provide? Whoever, therefore, throws obloquy[2] on the doctrine of predestination, openly brings a charge against God, as having inconsiderately allowed something to escape from him which is injurious to the Church.

The predestination by which God adopts some to the hope of life, and adjudges others to eternal death, no man who would be thought pious ventures simply to deny; but it is greatly caviled at, especially by those who make prescience[3] its cause.

We, indeed, ascribe both prescience and predestination to God; but we say, that it is absurd to make the latter subordinate to the former. When we attribute prescience to God, we mean that all things always were, and ever continue, under his eye; that to his knowledge there is no past or future, but all things are present, and indeed so present, that it is not merely the idea of them that is before him, (as those objects are which we retain in our memory,) but that he truly sees and contemplates them as actually under his immediate inspection. This prescience extends to the whole circuit of the world, and to all creatures. By predestination we mean the eternal decree of God, by which he determined with himself whatever he wished to happen with regard to every man. All are not[4] created on equal terms, but some are preordained to eternal life, others to eternal damnation; and, accordingly, as each has been created for one or other of these ends, we say that he has been predestinated to life or to death. ...

---

1   **exhortation:** earnest request or persuasion
2   **obloquy:** public shame, abuse
3   **prescience:** foresight, foreknowledge
4   **All are not:** Not all are

We say, then, that Scripture clearly proves this much, that God by his eternal and immutable counsel[1] determined once for all those whom it was his pleasure one day to admit to salvation, and those whom, on the other hand, it was his pleasure to doom to destruction. We maintain that this counsel, as regards the elect, is founded on his free mercy, without any respect to human worth, while those whom he dooms to destruction are excluded from access to life by a just and blameless, but at the same time incomprehensible judgment. In regard to the elect, we regard calling as the evidence of election, and justification as another symbol of its manifestation, until it is fully accomplished by the attainment of glory. But as the Lord seals his elect by calling and justification, so by excluding the reprobate[2] either from the knowledge of his name or the sanctification[3] of his Spirit, he by these marks in a manner discloses the judgment which awaits them. I will here omit many of the fictions which foolish men have devised to overthrow predestination. There is no need of refuting objections which the moment they are produced abundantly betray their hollowness. I will dwell only on those points which either form the subject of dispute among the learned, or may occasion any difficulty to the simple, or may be employed by impiety as specious[4] pretexts for assailing the justice of God.

Key Concepts

Adam's fall/degeneration   original sin
curse/wrath of God   predestination
free will/freedom of choice   prescience
grace   self-knowledge
human nature

Compare with China

Wang Yangming and Matteo Ricci's Progression to China

Jesuit order is a product of the Reformation and Counter Reformation in Europe. But when it reached China in the late 16th century, it also helped the reformation of spirituality there, as the following essay seems to argue, taking the well-known case of Matteo Ricci[1] as an example. Christian missionary, or

---

1 **immutable counsel:** unchangeable advice
2 **reprobate:** people of immoral character
3 **sanctification:** making holy
4 **specious:** seemingly

the forced conversion, is a controversial issue. Read and discuss.

The Jesuit father Matteo Ricci's entrance to China at the end of the 16th century turned a new page in the chronicle of cultural interactions between China and the West. As historical record shows, some 950 years before Ricci, Christianity under the name of *Jing jiao* 景教 or Illustrious Religion already came to China at the time of Emperor Taizong of Tang 唐太宗. Although Emperor Taizong and his court might not know that Nestorian Christianity[2] had been condemned by the Vatican as heretic, they certainly knew that this was a religion foreign and alien, and yet the emperor issued a decree to allow its spread in China. The irony is, however, that the religious freedom the Nestorian Christians enjoyed in China during the Tang did not help it take roots in the Chinese soil, for after two hundred years it was still a minor sect and disappeared altogether soon afterwards.

Matteo Ricci (1552–1610), believed to be the first oil painting by a Chinese painter

It is well-known that during the Yuan Dynasty at the end of the 13th century, when the Mongolians ruled China, Kublai Khan, revered by some Han Chinese *daoxue* scholars 道学家 as a "Great Confucian Master," put the so-called "people with colored eyes" above the Han Chinese, and quite a few Christians became ministers and generals, a situation that made it appear as though the Mongolian court was ready to be converted to Christianity. The Roman Papacy sent out missionaries to China as a sort of spiritual crusaders, among whom one Franciscan father eventually became the archbishop of Xanadu[3], the capital of Yuan. Under the aegis of the Mongolian power, those Christian missionaries expanded their evangelizing activities to southern provinces like Fujian and Zhejiang, which had been the home base of *daoxue* Confucianism during the Southern Song Dynasty. And yet, despite the patronage of the Mongolian rulers, this alien religion from the West, known in Chinese as *Yelikewen jiao* 也里可温教, failed completely in the attempt to forcefully proselytize the Han and the Southern people. When the Southerners rose up in rebellion, the last Mongolian emperor blessed by the Pope's envoy to the Yuan court was driven back to the vast steppes, and the alien creed under his protection soon disappeared in both north and south China.

In comparison, the third attempt at entrance into China by the Christians, notably the Jesuits,

---

1 **Matteo Ricci (1552 – 1610):** Italian Jesuit missionary, who "gave the Chinese their first understanding of the West and provided Europeans with an accurate description of China." In 1583 he settled in Guangdong where he studied Chinese, adopted Chinese dress, and made friends. In 1601 he finally achieved his goal of being admitted to Beijing, the capital, where he preached and taught science to Chinese scholars.

2 **Nestorian Christianity:** the doctrine taught by Nestorius, Bishop of Constantinople (died c.451), later declared heretical, of two persons (one human, one divine) as well as two natures in the incarnate Christ

3 Xanadu, or Zanadu（上都）, was the summer capital of Kublai Khan's Mongol Empire. It is in Inner Mongolia, 275 km north of Beijing. The palace, where Kublai Khan stayed in summer, is 550 metres square, 40% the size of Forbidden City in Beijing.

faced a political obstacle unknown in the first two attempts. The Ming Dynasty turned around to prevent in the strictest measure cult of any kind, even condemning some of Mencius's ideas as anti-Confucian heresy. Religious intolerance hardened into a state policy, and by the time of the mid-Ming Dynasty, the emperor and his ministers became suspicious of anyone coming from overseas as a potential conspirator with the Japanese pirates conspiring with Chinese secret societies. The Ming court did not really close off China because it needed maritime trade to take in large quantities of silver to finance a huge empire, mainly from America then colonized by the Europeans, but in all other areas not related to finance and economy, Ming China was sealed off from the outside world. In the same year when Ricci was born (1552), Francis Xavier, one of the founders of the Society of Jesus, died on the Shangchuan island near the estuary of Zhujiang in bitter disappointment that he had no chance to set foot on the Chinese mainland.

Entering Guangdong in the eleventh year of the Wanli reign during the Ming Dynasty (1583) and died in Beijing in the thirty-eighth year (1610), Ricci spent 28 years in China and laid the foundation for Catholicism to stay active with thousands of followers, uninterrupted in its mission despite the imperial ban during the Qing or even the dissolution of the Society of Jesus in Europe, till right before the Opium Wars. In facing the Ming dignitaries, Ricci could not reveal his true identity as a priest of an alien creed, but had to identify himself as a "scholar from the West" in order to win over the elites in the Chinese empire. And yet, he made the religion from the West taking roots among the Chinese populace under politically unfavorable conditions when Ming China had adopted the policies of guarding itself against alien creeds within and all foreigners from the outside.

First in Europe and then in China, scholars have all tried to solve the riddle of Ricci's success. One must appeal to history itself to exorcize puzzling historical paradoxes. Students of Ricci's mission all put emphasis on his strategies of using his learning for religious purposes, but few have discussed the complementary interrelations of "learning 学 " and "strategy 术 ", or have thoroughly explored the specific intellectual environment in which Ricci made use of those strategies.

In medieval China, it was a tradition that "learning" changed along with "strategies." What is meant by "strategy" here is the strategy to rule, to regulate the political order, to provide psycho-logical and social cohesion, and to guide the behavior of all the subjects, which needs to be justified as a whole in a theoretical interpretation in terms of morality and belief systems. Such theoretical interpretations are the so-called classical studies promoted by the empire from the Han to the Qing Dynasties. Ever since the mid-Western Han Dynasty, when Confucianism became the only doctrine revered as the orthodoxy, generations of monarchs and regents had acknowledged that two ancients, namely Confucius and the Duke of Zhou, had a better understanding of the will of heaven than most later political and cultural elites.

By the mid-Yuan Dynasty, the Mongolian court had made the Four Books, the Confucian classics edited and compiled by Zhu Xi and his followers, the official primary texts for those Han and Southerner Chinese who wanted to secure an office in government service. And yet, all through the Yuan and the Ming Dynasties, another system of Song Confucianism remained active among people in the southern provinces, a school of teaching developed by Lu Jiuyuan, Zhu Xi's contemporary, whose system was predicated on the assumption that "the mind is the principle 心即理". Lu and his followers ridiculed Zhu Xi for his futile counsel of studying the Confucian classics again and again for the discovery of "truth," and they advocated the bold idea that "all the six classics are but notes to elucidate one's self 六经注我". Following such logic, anyone, no matter of what race or ethnicity, can become like a sage once he has fully understood his own mind. If that is the case, then, can the emperor still monopolize the absolute authority of a living sage? From this a series of subversive propositions can be deduced, to the detriment of the old tradition. It is therefore not at all surprising that at the beginning of the 16th century, Wang Shouren 王守仁 could quickly draw a large following when he claimed to have realized that Lu Jiuyuan's teaching of the mind 300 years earlier was truly in conformity with the original ideas of Confucius and Mencius, while Zhu Xi's doctrine, having been modified by the first two emperors of the Ming Dynasty and made into an invisible knife for the killing of the mind, became corrupt and decayed along with the imperial dictatorship in decline.

Matteo Ricci entered China when the ban on the teachings of Wang Yangming had been lifted and those teachings elevated to the status of subclassics for civil examinations. Wang's teachings had reached the zenith of their influence and branched out in society as various schools, characterized by skepticism toward the official doctrines of Neo-Confucianism and the articulation of various eccentric personal views.

For instance, they separated Confucian "learning" from "strategy," and emphasized the superiority of the way of teachers 师道 to that of the monarch 君道, a logical consequence being the demand to change the centralized power of the monarch. Again, Wang Yangming's theory of cultivating one's "good conscience" undoubtedly destabilized a continuous tradition of the Confucianism passed down from Confucius to Zengzi 曾子, Zisi 子思, and Mencius 孟子, a theory constructed by Zhu Xi and sanctioned by the imperial court as the orthodoxy. Ideas like this spread and gradually became a consensus among scholars in culturally important locales in the Chinese empire, and as a result some room was created for the toleration of the transmission of alien cultures outside the traditional mainstream.

Matteo Ricci and Xu Guangqi discussing about Tao, early oil painting

Some basic notions widely acknowledged and accepted by Wang's followers, however, were even more directly favorable at the time for Ricci to spread Western learning and Christian creed. The first was Wang Yangming's reaffirmation of Lu Jiuyuan's proposition that sages could emerge from anywhere, and therefore it was possible to envision Jesus from the West as comparable to Confucius from the East. The second was related to Wang Yangming's anxiety over the purification of the mind, hence the search for the best strategy to remedy people's confused minds. Since Ricci claimed that the "true meaning" of the Western religion was compatible with the original intentions of Confucianism, how could not the followers of Wang's teachings feel exalted at the prospect of having some spiritual auxiliaries in their attempt to revive true Confucianism? And finally, the third was the emphasis Wang's followers put on the way of teachers and of friends 友道,

Heritage of Western Intellectual Tradition   A Sourcebook

which eventually led to a general call for restructuring of the traditional moral relationships, or a reversion of priorities in the moral relationships like that between the monarch and the subjects, for they maintained that likeminded friends coming together willing to help each other would constitute the most reliable foundation for the effective change of social customs, the elimination of evils, and the rectification of errors. They even declared friendship was the leading principle of the five relationships 五伦之纲. Can this be called an early manifestation of the civil consciousness in a modern sense?

We should say that Matteo Ricci was world savvy. Having been trapped in Guangdong for twelve years as a "monk from the West" with very little success in his Christian mission, he changed his costumes and appeared in Nanchang, where Wang Yangming first made his fame, as a "scholar from the West." Immediately he felt much more comfortable in a cultural ambience where Wang's followers had discarded the old order in which one's place of origin and kinship mattered, but took great pleasure in "having friends coming from afar." Ricci wrote his timely *On Friendship*《交友论》 and enjoyed an instant success, while Wang's followers were pleased to find much support in this collection of Western philosophical wisdom, particularly the idea that the monarch and the officials should behave like friends who had common goals and shared their wealth and properties. After that, Ricci used every means to achieve his own goal and tried his best to accommodate to Wang's teachings, making strategies to promote Western

A painting of a Jesuit missionary by a Chinese artist

learning, while taking advantage of Western learning to promote his religion. Eventually Ricci made Christianity a steady religion in China in the third attempt, and created a favorable condition for his successors like Adam Schall von Bell and Ferdinand Verbiest to survive the political crisis in the dynastic change from the Ming to the Qing, and for the Jesuits to engage in their evangelical activities up to the time when the Qing empire suffered defeat from British and French aggression. (Adapted from *Zhu Weizheng*, Trans. Zhang Longxi)

Supplementary Reading

Excerpts of the 95 Theses

The following are excerpts of the 95 Theses Martin Luther nailed on the church door at Wittenburg. Read these theses and try to find how Luther differed from Roman Catholic Church at the time:

1. When our Lord and Master Jesus Christ said, "Repent" (Mt 4:17), he willed the entire life of believers to be one of repentance.

2. This word cannot be understood as referring to the sacrament of penance, that is, confession and satisfaction, as administered by the clergy.

3. Yet it does not mean solely inner repentance; such inner repentance is worthless unless it produces various outward mortification[1] of the flesh.

4. The penalty of sin remains as long as the hatred of self (that is, true inner repentance), namely till our entrance into the kingdom of heaven.

5. The pope neither desires nor is able to remit[2] any penalties except those imposed by his own authority or that of the canons.

6. The pope cannot remit any guilt, except by declaring and show-ing that it has been remitted by God; or, to be sure, by remitting guilt in cases reserved to his judgment. If his right to grant remission in these cases were disregarded, the guilt would certainly remain unforgiven.

20. Therefore the pope, when he uses the words "plenary[3] remis-sion of all penalties," does not actually mean "all penalties," but only those imposed by himself.

21. Thus those indulgence preachers are in error who say that a man is absolved from every penalty and saved by papal indulgences.

Handwriting on the door
Oct. 31, 1517

22. As a matter of fact, the pope remits to souls in purgatory no penalty which, according to canon law, they should have paid in this life.

23. If remission of all penalties whatsoever could be granted to anyone at all, certainly it would be granted only to the most perfect, that is, to very few.

24. For this reason most people are necessarily deceived by that indiscriminate and high-sounding promise of release from penalty.

26. The pope does very well when he grants remission to souls in purgatory, not by the power of the keys[4], which he does not have, but by way of intercession[5] for them.

27. They preach only human doctrines who say that as soon as the money clinks into the money chest, the soul flies out of purgatory.

28. It is certain that when money clinks in the money chest, greed and avarice can be increased; but when the church intercedes, the result is in the hands of God alone.

30. No one is sure of the integrity of his own contrition[6], much less of having received

---

1 **mortification:** overcoming bodily desires
2 **remit:** forgive, excuse
3 **plenary:** ultimate, absolute
4 **power of the keys:** supreme ecclesiastical authority claimed by the pope as the successor of St. Peter, a Biblical allusion to Mathew 16:19 "And I will give thee the keys of the kingdom of heaven: and whatsoever thou shalt bind on earth shall be bound in heaven."
5 **intercession:** prayer or entreaty
6 **contrition:** repentance

plenary remission.

31. The man who actually buys indulgences is as rare as he who is really penitent; indeed, he is exceedingly rare.

32. Those who believe that they can be certain of their salvation because they have indulgence letters will be eternally damned, together with their teachers.

33. Men must especially be on guard against those who say that the pope's pardons are that inestimable gift of God by which man is reconciled to him.

34. For the graces of indulgences are concerned only with the penalties of sacramental satisfaction established by man.

35. They who teach that contrition is not necessary on the part of those who intend to buy souls out of purgatory or to buy confessional privileges preach unchristian doctrine.

36. Any truly repentant Christian has a right to full remission of penalty and guilt, even without indulgence letters.

37. Any true Christian, whether living or dead, participates in all the blessings of Christ and the church; and this is granted him by God, even without indulgence letters.

39. It is very difficult, even for the most learned theologians, at one and the same time to commend to the people the bounty[1] of indulgences and the need of true contrition.

40. A Christian who is truly contrite seeks and loves to pay penalties for his sins; the bounty of indulgences, however, relaxes penalties and causes men to hate them — at least it furnishes occasion for hating them.

41. Papal indulgences must be preached with caution, lest people erroneously think that they[2] are preferable to other good works of love.

42. Christians are to be taught that the pope does not intend that the buying of indulgences should in any way be compared with works of mercy.

43. Christians are to be taught that he who gives to the poor or lends to the needy does a better deed than he who buys indulgences.

45. Christians are to be taught that he who sees a needy man and passes him by, yet gives his money for indulgences, does not buy papal indulgences but God's wrath.

46. Christians are to be taught that, unless they have more than they need, they must reserve enough for their family needs and by no means squander[3] it on indulgences.

---

1 **bounty:** reward

2 **they:** indulgences

3 **squander:** waste

Heritage of Western Intellectual Tradition   A Sourcebook

47. Christians are to be taught that the buying of indulgences is a matter of free choice, not commanded.

48. Christians are to be taught that the pope, in granting indulgences, needs and thus desires their devout prayer more than their money.

49. Christians are to be taught that papal indulgences are useful only if they do not put their trust in them, but very harmful if they lose their fear of God because of them.

50. Christians are to be taught that if the pope knew the exactions[1] of the indulgence preachers, he would rather that the basilica[2] of St. Peter were burned to ashes than built up with the skin, flesh, and bones of his sheep.

51. Christians are to be taught that the pope would and should wish to give of his own money, even though he had to sell the basilica of St. Peter, to many of those from whom certain hawkers[3] of indulgences cajole[4] money.

52. It is vain to trust in salvation by indulgence letters, even though the indulgence commissary[5], or even the pope, were to offer his soul as security.

53. They are the enemies of Christ and the pope who forbid altogether the preaching of the Word of God in some churches in order that indulgences maybe preached in others.

54. Injury is done to the Word of God when, in the same sermon, an equal or larger amount of time is devoted to indulgences than to the Word.

57. That indulgences are not temporal treasures is certainly clear, for many indulgence sellers do not distribute them freely but only gather them.

58. Nor are they the merits of Christ and the saints, for, even without the pope, the latter always work grace for the inner man, and the cross, death, and hell for the outer man[6].

59. St. Lawrence[7] said that the poor of the church were the treasures of the church, but he spoke according to the usage of the word in his own time.

60. Without want of consideration we say that the keys of the church, given by the merits of Christ, are that treasure.

62. The true treasure of the church is the most holy gospel of the glory and grace of God.

---

1   **exaction:** enforced payment
2   **basilica:** church
3   **hawker:** person going from house to house selling goods
4   **cajole:** use deceit to persuade
5   **indulgence commissary:** deputy selling the indulgences
6   **death, and hell for the outer man:** work death, and hell for the outer man
7   **St. Lawrence:** one of the deacons of the Roman Church, died 258

67. The indulgences which the demagogues[1] acclaim as the greatest graces are actually understood to be such only insofar as they promote gain.

68. They are nevertheless in truth the most insignificant graces when compared with the grace of God and the piety of the cross.

71. Let him who speaks against the truth concerning papal indulgences be anathema[2] and accursed.

72. But let him who guards against the lust and license of the indulgence preachers be blessed.

76. We say on the contrary that papal indulgences cannot remove the very least of venial[3] sins as far as guilt is concerned.

77. To say that even St. Peter if he were now pope, could not grant greater graces is blasphemy against St. Peter and the pope.

78. We say on the contrary that even the present pope, or any pope whatsoever, has greater graces at his disposal, that is, the gospel, spiritual powers, gifts of healing, etc., as it is written, 1 Co 12 [:28].

79. To say that the cross emblazoned[4] with the papal coat of arms, and set up by the indulgence preachers is equal in worth to the cross of Christ is blasphemy.

Questions for Discussion

1. Point out criticism / sarcasm made explicitly or implicitly by Erasmus on the Church.
2. Compare the differences / similarities between Augustine, Aquinas and Erasmus.
3. Bertrand Russell commented on Erasmus's neutrality: "He had always been timid, and the times were no longer suited to timid people. For honest men, the only honorable alternatives were martyrdom or victory." Comment on this remark.
4. What caused Martin Luther to protest against the popery in Rome?
5. Why should Luther insist on the right to interpret the Bible?
6. How did Luther argue for his audacity?
7. Why is the original sin so central to Calvin?
8. Does predestination mean that we simply wait for God's judgment and so nothing?
9. How did Calvin illustrate the relationship between prescience and predestination?
10. Discuss the impact of the Reformation on people's mentality.

---

1 **demagogue:** political leader who stirs up people's emotion rather than reason
2 **anathema:** curse of the church
3 **venial:** not serious
4 **emblazoned:** decorated in a noticeable way

UNIT 7

Modern Scientific Thinking (1)

Pretest

- What do you know about Renaissance science and its scientists?
- What is the significance of their ideas, both scientific and humanistic?
- Quote to show which one of them you like best or know most, and why?

What You Will Learn in This Unit

- Two great scientists in Renaissance Europe: Bacon and Descartes;
- Their ideas concerning nature, man, human history, and wisdom; and
- Matteo Ricci on the art of printing in China.

Learn to Pronounce

Athena /əˈθiːnə/ 雅典娜（希腊神话中的智慧、技艺及战争女神）

axiom /ˈæksɪəm/ 公理，格言

Cartesian /kɑːˈtiːzjən/ 笛卡尔（哲学）的，笛卡尔信徒

Cartesianism /kɑːˈtiːzɪənɪzəm/ 笛卡儿哲学

Diana /daɪˈænə/ 狄安娜（罗马神话中的狩猎及月亮女神）

Francis Bacon /ˈbeɪkən/ 培根

indice /ˈɪndɪsiːz/ 指数

Jesuit /ˈdʒezjʊɪt/ 耶稣会信徒

Leibniz /ˈlaɪbnɪtz/ 莱布尼兹

Renaissance /rɪˈneɪsəns, ˈrenəsans/ 文艺复兴

René Descartes /deɪˈkɑːt, dɛkart/ 笛卡儿

Sparta /ˈspɑːtə/ 斯巴达（古希腊城邦）

-204-

Introduction

The emergence of the nation-state, the cleavage of the Christian Church due to the Protestant Reformation, and the overseas expansion of European nation states, especially the Renaissance and its accompanying scientific revolution, all had enormous impact on the 17th century Europe. The spirit of curiosity and experimentation that characterized the Renaissance created a fertile climate for the development of "science." Leonardo da Vinci studied structures and processes of nature in terms of art and science. Important inventions such as gunpowder, printing press, and compass were part of practical results of Renaissance scientific inquiry. Renaissance scholars emphasized concrete experience over abstract theory and tried to observe the natural world carefully, completely, and without preconceived ideas. The chief obstacle to modern science, it seemed, lay in a view of nature based on the ideas of Aristotle and of Christian theologians. The entire physical universe in this view was centered on humankind, and there was a basic purpose to all movement. Gravity was explained as the inclination of all bodies to be at the center of the earth; acceleration was believed to be a consequence of the growing eagerness of a falling body as it moved closer to its natural home. The breakthrough of this view was made by Renaissance science with the introduction of the concept of the universe as an entity that could be approached objectively. The most important belief, common to philosophers and intellectuals of this period was, perhaps, an abiding faith in the power of human reason. If humanity could so unlock the laws of the universe as Newton did, why could it not also discover the laws underlying all of nature and society? People came to assume that through use of reason, an unending progress would be possible — progress in knowledge, in technical achievement, and even in moral values.

Francis Bacon: Novum Organum*

Francis Bacon (1561–1626), statesman, philosopher, master of the English tongue, and pioneer of modern scientific thinking, "the most powerful mind of modern times," is remembered artistically for the sharp worldly wisdom of his essays, politically for his power as a speaker in Parliament and as James I's lord chancellor, and intellectually as an urgent advocate for new ways by which men might establish a legitimate command over nature. Bacon was educated at Trinity College, Cambridge, where he showed distaste for learning based exclusively on citation of authority, chiefly Aristotle. In 1584 he became a member of the Parliament, but lost favor with the queen in 1593 for

---

*　Bacon was one of those who drew our attention to the importance of "method" or "instrument" by which we perceive things (it is not a coincidence that a few years later René Descartes wrote on "ways"). The principles of *Novum Organum* (The New Instrument) include accurate observation and experimentation, calling for abandoning prejudices and preconceived attitudes, which he called idols.

Heritage of Western Intellectual Tradition　A Sourcebook

opposing a bill for royal subsidy. In 1603 he was dubbed by James I, and appointed attorney general in 1613. His political career came to the peak when he was made lord keeper of the great

seal in March 1617 and Lord Chancellor in 1618. Charged by Parliament with accepting bribes in 1621, Bacon confessed to all the 28 charges, resigned the seal of his office and was imprisoned in the Tower of London with a fine of £40,000. He was pardoned in September 1621, but the king prohibited his return to Parliament or the court. Bacon was known for his pen. His writings fall into three categories: philosophical, purely literary, and professional. The best of his philosophical works are *The Advancement of Learning* (1605), and *Novum Organum* (1620). *The New Atlantis* was written in 1614, which did not get into print until 1626. In March 1626, when experimenting with the process of putrefaction, he was seized with a sudden chill and died on April 9, 1626.

Aphorisms[1] Concerning the Interpretation of Nature and the Kingdom of Man

Man, being the servant and interpreter of Nature, can do and understand so much and so much only as he has observed in fact or in thought of the course of nature: beyond this he neither knows anything nor can do anything.

II

Neither the naked hand nor the understanding left to itself can effect much. It is by instruments and helps that the work is done, which[2] are as much wanted for the understanding as for the hand. And as the instruments of the hand either give motion or guide it, so the instruments of the mind supply either suggestions for the understanding or cautions.

III

Human knowledge and human power meet in one[3]; for where the cause is not known the effect cannot be produced. Nature to be commanded must be obeyed; and that which is in contemplation is as the cause is in operation as the rule.

IV

Towards the effecting of works, all that man can do is put together or put asunder natural bodies. The rest is done by nature working within[4].

---

1 **aphorisms:** short, concise, witty, sharp remarks

2 "Which" modifies "instruments and helps."

3 **Human knowledge and human power meet in one:** This reminds us of his famous statement "knowledge is power."

4 **nature working within:** intelligence

VI

It would be an unsound fancy and self-contradictory to expect that things which have never yet been done can be done except by means which have never yet been tried.

XI

As the sciences which we now have do not help us in finding out new works, so neither does the logic which we now have[1] help us in finding out new sciences.

XII

The logic now in use serves rather to fix and give stability to the errors which have their foundations in commonly received notions than to help the search after truth. So it does more harm than good.

XVIII

The discoveries which have hitherto been made in the sciences are such as lie close to vulgar notions, scarcely beneath the surface. **In order to penetrate into the inner and further recesses of nature, it is necessary that both notions and axioms be derived from things by a more sure and guarded way; and that a method of intellectual operation be introduced altogether better and more certain.**

XIX

There are and can be only two ways of searching into and discovering truth. The one flies from the senses and particulars to the most general axioms[2], and from these principles, the truth of which it takes for settled and immovable, proceeds to judgment and to the discovery of middle axioms. And this way is now in fashion. **The other derives axioms from the senses and particulars, rising by a gradual and unbroken ascent, so that it arrives at the most general axioms last of all. This is the true way, but as yet untried.**[3]

XXII

Both ways set out from the senses and particulars, and rest in the highest generations; but the difference between them is infinite. For the one just glances at experiment and particulars in passing, the other dwells duly and orderly among them. The one, again, begins at once by establishing certain abstract and useless generalities, the other rises by gradual steps to that which is prior and better known in the order of nature.

XXXI

It is idle to expect any great advancement in science from the superinducing[4] and engrafting[5] of

---

1   **the logic which we now have:** old (Aristotelian) method
2   **The one flies from ... general axioms:** namely, move directly to the "most general axioms"
3   **There are and can be only two ways ... as yet untrled.:** The two ways are commonly known as deductive and inductive methods respectively, with the first widely used at the time by the Church fathers and Scholasticism.
4   **superinduce:** make continue or induce in addition
5   **engraft:** implant, insert

new things upon old. **We must begin anew from the very foundations, unless we would revolve forever in a circle with mean and contemptible progress.**

XXXV

It was said by Borgia of the expedition of the French into Italy, that they came with Italy, that they came with chalk in their hands to mark out their lodgings, not with arms to force their way in. I in like manner would have my doctrine enter quietly into the minds that are fit and capable of receiving it; for confutations[1] cannot be employed, when the difference is upon first principles and very notions and even upon forms of demonstrations.

XXXVI

Age of Enlightenment

One method of delivery alone remains to us, which is simply this: we must lead men to the particulars themselves, and their series and order; while men on their side must force themselves for awhile to lay their notions by[2] and begin to familiarize themselves with facts.

XXXVII

The doctrine of those who have denied that certainty could be attained at all, has some agreement with my way of proceeding at the first setting out; but they end in being infinitely separated and opposed. For the holders of that doctrine assert simply that nothing can be known; I also assert that not much can be known in nature by the way which is now in use. But then they go on to destroy the authority of the senses and understanding; whereas I proceed to devise and supply helps for the same.

XXXVIII

The idols and false notions which are now in possession of the human understanding, and have taken deep root therein, not only so beset[3] men's minds that truth can hardly find entrance, but even after entrances is obtained, they will again in the very instauration[4] of the science meet and trouble us, unless men being forewarned of the danger fortify themselves as far as may be against their assaults.

XXXIX

There are four classes of Idols which beset men's minds. To these for distinction's sake I have assigned names, — calling the first class *Idols of the Tribe*; the second, *Idols of*

---

1 **confutation:** showing to be wrong
2 **lay ... by:** lay aside, put down
3 **beset:** close in on all sides
4 **instauration:** restoration

the Cave; the third, *Idols of the marketplace*; the fourth, *Idols of the Theatre*.

XL

The formation of ideas and axioms by true induction is no doubt the proper remedy to be applied for the keeping off and clearing away of idols. To point them out, however, if of great use; for the doctrine of Idols is to the Interpretation of Nature what the doctrine of the refutation of Sophisms[1] is to common Logic.

XLI

The Idols of the Tribe have foundation in human nature itself, and in the tribe or race of men. For it is a false assertion that the sense of man is the measures of things. On the contrary, all perceptions as well of the sense as of the mind are according to the measure of the individual and not according to the measure of the universe. And the human understanding is like a false mirror, which, receiving rays irregularly distorts and discolors[2] the nature of things by mingling its own nature with it[3].

XLII

The Idols of the Cave are the idols of the individual man. For every one (besides the errors common to human nature in general) has a cave or den of his own, which refracts[4] and discolours the light of nature; owing either to his own proper and peculiar nature; or to his education and conversation with others; or to the reading of books, and the authority of those whom he esteems and admires; or to the differences of impressions, accordingly as they take place in a mind preoccupied and predisposed or in a mind indifferent and settled; or the like. So that the spirit of man (according as it is meted out[5] to different individuals) is in fact a thing variable and full of perturbation[6], and governed as I were by chance. Whence it was well observed by Heraclitus[7] that men look for sciences in their own lesser worlds, and not in the greater or common world.

XLIII

There are also Idols formed by the intercourse and association of men with each other, which I call Idols of the Marketplace, on account of the commerce and consort[8] of men there. For

---

1   **sophism:** false reasoning intended to deceive. Sophists in ancient Greece referred to learned men and to itinerant teachers who provided instruction for a fee, who were "the first to systematize education."

2   **discolor:** change the color

3   **mingle its own nature with it:** force one's understanding upon things being investigated

4   **refract:** cause light to bend

5   **mete out:** fit, allot

6   **perturbation:** anxiety, confusion

7   **Heraclitus (c. 540–480 BC):** Greek philosopher who believed that fire is the primordial source of matter and that the entire world is in a constant state of change

8   **consort:** association

it is by discourse that men associate; and words are imposed according to the apprehension of the vulgar. And therefore the ill and unfit choice of words wonderfully obstructs the understanding[1]. Nor do the definitions or explanations wherewith in some things learned men are wont[2] to guard and defend themselves, by any means set the matter right.[3] But words plainly force and overrule[4] the understanding, and throw all into confusion, and lead men away into numberless empty controversies and idle fancies.

XLIV

Lastly, there are Idols which have immigrated into men's minds from the various dogmas of philosophies, and also from wrong laws of demonstration. These I call Idols of the Theatre; because in my judgment all the received systems are but so many stage-plays, representing worlds of their own creation after an unreal and scenic fashion. Nor is it only of the systems now in vogue[5], or only of the ancient sects and philosophies, that I speak; for many more plays of the same kind may yet be composed and in like artificial manner set forth; seeing that errors the most widely different have nevertheless causes for the most part alike[6]. Neither again do I mean this only of entire systems, but also of many principles and axioms in science, which by tradition, credulity, and negligence have come to be received.

Key Concepts

commonly received notions

dogma of philosophy

four classes of Idols

general axiom

human knowledge

human power

idols of the Tribe

idols of the Cave

idols of the Market

idols of the Theatre

instruments

interpretation of Nature

sense of man

understanding

---

1 **ill and unfit … the understemding:** Notice Bacon's doubt on language, and compare it with the similar views of Lao-tse in ancient China and deconstructionists in contemporary West.

2 **wont:** accustomed

3 **Nor do the definitions … matter right.:** Nor do the definitions or explanations … set the matter right.

4 **overrule:** decide against

5 **in vogue:** popular, in fashion

6 **errors the most widely … part alike:** namely, errors … have … causes … alike

René Descartes: Discourse on Method*

René Descartes (1596–1650), French philosopher, scientist, and mathematician, sometimes called Father of modern philosophy. He was one of the first to oppose scholastic Aristotelianism by methodically doubting knowledge based on authority, the senses, and reason. He found certainty in the intuition that, when he is thinking, he exists, expressed in the famous statement "I think, therefore I am." At the Jesuit College of La Flèche, the child took classical studies, science, mathematics, and Scholastic philosophy, as well as acting, music, poetry, dancing, riding, and fencing. Because of his weak physical condition, the teachers, upon the order of his physician, reluctantly granted him permission to stay in bed until noon each day, but they were surprised at his progress in study, especially in mathematics. Roman Catholicism exerted a strong influence on Descartes throughout his life, a "most zealous Catholic" as a friend described him. Like Luther, he had a dream on Nov. 10, 1619 where he saw three scenes stand out in sharp focus: strong winds blowing him away from a church structure, thunderstorm roaring in his ears, and an open dictionary containing a poem asking "Which life shall I follow?" This question was to shape his future. From 1619 to 1628, Descartes traveled in northern and southern Europe, saying that he was studying the book of the world. As religious intolerance was mounting in France, he sold his properties and moved to the Netherlands in 1628, where he spent most of his remaining life. It was probably during the first years of his residence in the Netherlands that Descartes wrote his major works, such as *Meditations on First Philosophy* (1641) and *The Principles of Philosophy* (1644). Descartes attempted to apply the rational deductive methods of science, and particularly of mathematics, to philosophy, in contrast to Scholasticism based entirely on views of recognized authorities. Cartesianism constituted a serious threat to established religious authority. In 1663 the Roman Catholic Church placed Descartes' works on the Index of Forbidden Books, and the University of Oxford forbade the teaching of his doctrines. Descartes discovered the fundamental law of reflection: the angle of incidence is equal to the angle of reflection. He systematized analytic geometry. He was the first to use the last letters of the alphabet to designate unknown quantities and the first letters to designate known ones. He also invented the method of indices (as in x^2) to express the powers of numbers.

PART I

Good sense is of all things in the world the most equally distributed, for everybody thinks himself so abundantly provided with it, that even those most difficult to please in all other matters

---

*   *Discourse on Method, Rightly Conducting the Reason and Seeking Truth in the Sciences* is the 4th and final part of *Essais philosophiques* (*Philosophical Essays*), published in 1637. The other parts are: *An Essay on Geometry, Another on Optics, A Third on Meteors.*

Heritage of Western Intellectual Tradition   A Sourcebook

do not commonly desire more of it than they already possess. It is unlikely that this is an error on their part; it seems rather to be evidence in support of the view that the power of forming a good judgment and of distinguishing the true from the false, which is properly speaking what is called Good sense or Reason, is by nature equal in all men. Hence too it will show that the diversity of our opinions does not proceed from some men being more rational than others, but solely from the fact that our thoughts pass through diverse channels[1] and the same objects are not considered by all. For to be possessed of good mental powers is not sufficient; the principal matter is to apply them well. The greatest minds are capable of the greatest virtues, and those who proceed very slowly may, provided they always follow the straight road, really advance much faster than those who, though they run, forsake it.

Lighting upon and pursuing certain paths

For myself I have never ventured to presume that my mind was in any way more perfect than that of the ordinary man; I have even longed to possess thought as quick or an imagination as accurate and distinct, or a memory as comprehensive or ready, as some others. And besides these I do not know any other qualities that make for the perfection of the human mind. For as to reason or sense, inasmuch as it is the only thing that constitutes us men and distinguishes us from the brutes, I would fain[2] believe that it is to be found complete in each individual, and in this I follow the common opinion of the philosophers, who say that the question of more or less occurs only in the sphere of the *accidents* and does not affect the *forms* or *natures* of the *individuals* in the same *species*.

But I shall not hesitate to say that I have had great good fortunate from my youth up, in lighting upon and pursuing certain paths which have conducted me to considerations and maxims from which I have formed a Method, by whose assistance it appears to me I have the means of gradually increasing my knowledge and of little by little raising it to the highest possible point which the mediocrity[3] of my talents and the brief duration of my life can permit me to reach. For I have already reaped from it fruits of such a nature that, even though I always try in the judgments I make on myself to lean to the side of self-depreciation rather than to that of arrogance, and though, looking with the eye of a philosopher on the diverse actions and enterprises of all mankind, I find scarcely any[4] useless, I do not cease to receive extreme satisfaction in the progress which I seem to have already made in the search after truth, and to form such hopes for the future as to venture to believe that, if amongst the occupations of men, simply as men, there is some one in particular that is excellent and important, that is the one which I have selected.

---

1   **channel:** the key word here, meaning "perspective," "approach" or "method"
2   **fain:** willingly
3   **mediocrity:** averageness, ordinariness
4   **diverse actions and enterprises of all mankind, I find scarcely any:** I find scarcely any actions and enterprises of all mankind

It must always be recollected, however, that possibly I deceive myself, and that what I take to be gold and diamonds is perhaps no more than copper and glass. I know how subject we are to delusion in whatever touches ourselves, and also how much the judgments of our friends ought to be suspected when they are in our favour. But in this Discourse I shall be very happy to show the paths I have followed, and to set forth my life as in a picture, so that everyone may judge of it for himself; and thus in learning from the common talk what are the opinions which are held of it[1], a new means of obtaining self-instruction will be reached, which I shall add to those which I have been in the habit of using.

That my design is not here to teach the Method which everyone should follow in order to promote the good conduct of his Reason but only to show in what manner I have endeavored to conduct my own. Those who set about giving precepts must esteem themselves more skillful than those to whom they advance them[2], and if they fall short in the smallest matter they must of course take the blame for it. But regarding this Treatise simply as a history or, if you prefer it, a fable in which, amongst certain things which may be imitated, there are possibly others also which it would not be right to follow, I hope that it will be of use to some without being hurtful to any, and that all will thank me for frankness.

I have been nourished on letters since my childhood, and since I was given to believe that by their means a clear and certain knowledge could be obtained of all that is useful in life[3], I had an extreme desire to acquire instruction. But so soon as I had achieved the entire course of study at the close of which one is usually received into the ranks of the learned, I entirely changed my opinion. **For I found myself embarrassed with so many doubts and errors that it seemed to me that effort to instruct myself had no effect other than the increasing discovery of my own ignorance.** And yet I was studying at one of the most celebrated Schools in Europe, where I thought that there must be men of learning if they were to be found anywhere in the world. I learned there all that others learned; and not being satisfied with the sciences that we were taught, I even read through all the books which fell into my hands, treating of what is considered most curious and rare. Along with this I knew the judgments that others had formed of me, and I did not feel that I was esteemed inferior to my fellow-students, although there were amongst them some destined to fill the places of our masters. And finally our century seemed to me as flourishing, and as fertile in great minds, as any which had preceded. And this made me take the liberty of judging all others by myself and of coming to the conclusion that there was no learning in the world such as I was formerly led to believe it to be.

I did not omit, however, always to hold in esteem those exercises which are the occupation of the Schools. I knew that the Languages which one learns there are essential for the understand-

---

1 **learning from the common talk ... held of it:** learning ... what are the opinions ... of it
2 **them:** precepts
3 **a clear and certain knowledge could be obtained of all that is useful in life:** of all knowledge a clear and certain part that is useful could be obtained

Heritage of Western Intellectual Tradition   A Sourcebook

ing of all ancient literature; that fables with their charm stimulate the mind and histories of memorable deeds exalt it; and that, when read with discretion[1], these books assist in forming a sound judgment. I was aware that the reading of all good books is indeed like a conversation with the noblest men of past centuries who were the authors of them, nay a carefully studied conversation, in which they reveal to us none but the best of their thoughts. I deemed Eloquence to have a power and beauty beyond compare; that Posey[2] has most ravishing[3] delicacy and sweetness; that in Mathematics there are the subtlest discoveries and inventions which may accomplish much, both in satisfying the curious, and in furthering all the arts, and in diminishing man's labour; that those writings that deal with Morals contain much that is instructive, and many exhortations[4] to virtue which are most useful; that Theology points put the way to Heaven; that philosophy teaches us to speak with an appearance of truth on all things, and causes us to be admired by the less learned; that Jurisprudence, Medicine and all other sciences bring honour and riches to those who cultivate them; and finally that it is good to have examined all things, even those most full of superstition and falsehood, in order that we may know their just value, and avoid being deceived by them.

But I considered that had already given sufficient time to languages and likewise even to the readings of the literature of the ancients, both their histories and their fables. For to converse with those of other centuries is almost the same thing as to travel. It is good to know something of the customs of different peoples in order to judge more sanely of our own, and not to think that everything of a fashion not ours is absurd and contrary to reason, as do those who have seen nothing. **But when one employs too much time in traveling, one becomes stranger in one's own country, and when one is too curious about things which were practised in past centuries, one is usually very ignorant about those which are practised in our own time.** Besides, fables make one imagine many events possible which in reality are not so, and even the most accurate of histories, if they do not exactly misrepresent or exaggerate the value of things in order to render them more worthy of being read, at least omit in them all the circumstances which are basest and least notable; and from this fact it follows that what is retained is not portrayed as it really is, and that those who regulate their conduct by examples which they derive from such a source, are liable to fall into the extravagances[5] of the knights-errant[6] of Romance, and form projects beyond their power of performance.

I esteemed Eloquence most highly and I was enamoured of Poesy, but I thought that both were gifts of the mind rather than fruits of study. Those who have the strongest power of reasoning, and who most skillfully arrange their thoughts in order to render them clear and intelligible, have

---

1 **discretion:** prudence, carefulness
2 **posey:** brief verse
3 **ravishing:** charming
4 **exhortation:** earnest demand or request
5 **extravagance:** absurd act
6 **errant:** traveling in search of adventure

the best power of persuasion even if they can but speak the language of lower Brittany[1] and have never learned Rhetoric. And those who have the most delightful original ideas and who know how to express them with the maximum of style and suavity[2], would not fail to be the best poets even if the art of Poetry were unknown to them.

Most of all was I delighted with Mathematics because of the certainty of its demonstrations and the evidence of its reasoning; but I did not yet understand its true use, and, believing that it was of service only in the mechanical arts, I was astonished that, seeing how firm and solid was its basis, no loftier edifice[3] had been reared thereupon. On the other hand I compared the works of the ancient pagans which deal with Morals to palaces most superb and magnificent, which are yet built on sand and mud alone. They praise the virtues most highly and show them to be more worthy of being prized than anything else in the world, but they do not sufficiently teach us to become acquainted with them, and often that which is called by a fine name is nothing but insensibility or pride, or despair, or parricide[4].

I honoured our Theology and aspired as much as anyone to reach to heaven, but having learned to regard it as a most highly assured fact that the road is not less open to the most ignorant than to the most learned, and that the revealed truths which conduct thither are quite above our intelligence, I should not have dared to submit them to the feebleness of my reasonings; and I thought that, in order to undertake to examine them and succeed in so doing, it was necessary to have some extraordinary assistance from above and to be more than a mere man.

René Descartes with his sister Königin Christine

I shall not say anything about Philosophy, but that, seeing that it has been cultivated for many centuries by the best minds that have ever lived, and that nevertheless no single thing is to be found in it which is not subject of dispute, and in consequence which is not dubious, I had not enough presumption to hope to fare[5] better there than other men had done. And also, considering how many conflicting opinions there may be regarding the selfsame matter, all supported by learned people, while there can never be more than one which is true, I esteemed as well-nigh[6] false all that only went as far as being probable.

---

1 **Brittany:** a region in France on a peninsula between the English Channel and the Bay of Biscay, settled c. 500 by Britons driven out of their homeland by the Anglo-Saxons. The region was formally incorporated into France in 1532.

2 **suavity:** elegance, politeness

3 **edifice:** construction, building

4 **parricide:** murder of one's father or ruler

5 **fare:** do

6 **well-nigh:** almost

Then as to the other sciences, inasmuch as they derive their principles from Philosophy, I judged that one could have built nothing solid on foundations so far from firm. And neither the honour nor the promised gain was sufficient to persuade me to cultivate them, for, thanks be to God, I did not find myself in a condition which obliged me to make a merchandise of science for the improvement of my fortune; and, although I did not pretend to scorn all glory like the Cynics[1], I yet had very small esteem for what I could not hope to acquire, excepting through fictitious titles. And, finally, as to false doctrines, I thought that I already knew well enough what they were worth to be subject to deception neither by the promises of an alchemist[2], the predictions of an astrologer, the impostures[3] of a magician, the artifices or the empty boastings of any of those who make a profession of knowing that of which they are ignorant[4].

This is why, as soon as age permitted me to emerge from the control of my tutors, I entirely quitted the study of letters. And resolving to seek no other science than that which could be found in myself, or at least in the great book of the world, I employed the rest of my youth in travel, in seeing courts and armies, in intercourse with men of diverse temperaments and conditions, in collecting varied experiences, in proving myself in the various predicaments[5] in which I was placed by fortune, and under all circumstances bringing my mind to bear on the things which came before it, so that I might derive some profit from my experience. For it seemed to me that I might meet with much more truth in the reasoning that each man makes on the matters that specially concern him, and the issue of which would very soon punish him if he made a wrong judgment, than in the case of those made by a man of letters in his study touching speculations which lead to no result, and which bring about no other consequences to himself excepting that he will be all the more vain the more they are removed from common sense, since in this case it proves him to have employed so much the more ingenuity and skill in trying to make them seem probable. And I always had an excessive desire to learn to distinguish the true from the false, in order to see clearly in my actions and to walk with confidence in this life.

It is true that while I only considered the manners of other men I found in them nothing to give me settled convictions; and I remarked in them almost as much diversity as I had formerly seen in the opinions of philosophers. So much was this the case that the greatest profit which I derived from their study was that, in seeing many things which, although they seem to us very extravagant and ridiculous, were yet commonly received and approved by other great nations, **I learned to believe nothing too certainly of which I had only been convinced by example and custom.** Thus little by little I was delivered from many errors which might have obscured our

Heritage of Western Intellectual Tradition   A Sourcebook

---

1   **Cynics:** members of a school of Greek philosophers founded during the second half of the 4th century BC by people like Diogenes who, known for their eccentricities and insolence, argued for returning to a simple life through self-sufficiency

2   **alchemist:** one who studies alchemy, art in the Middle Ages to change ordinary things into gold

3   **imposture:** deception

4   **subject to deception neither by … they are ignoraut:** Compare this talk of knowledge and wisdom with that by Socrates in Unit 2.

5   **predicament:** unpleasant situation

natural vision and rendered us less capable of listening to Reason. But after I had employed several years in thus studying the book of the world and trying to acquire some experience, I one day formed the resolution of also making myself an object of study and of employing all the strength of my mind in choosing the road I should follow. This succeeded much better, it appeared to me, than if I had never departed either from my country or my books.

PART II

I was then in Germany, to which country I had been attracted by the wars which are not yet at an end[1]. And as I was returning from the coronation[2] of the Emperor to join the army, the setting in of winter detained me in a quarter where, since I found no society to divert me, while fortunately I had also no cares or passions to trouble me, I remained the whole day shut up alone in a stove-heated room, where I had complete leisure to occupy myself with my own thoughts. One of the first of the considerations that occurred to me was that there is very often less perfection in works composed of several portions, and carried out by the hands of various masters, than in those on which one individual alone has worked. Thus we see that buildings planned and carried out by one architect alone are usually more beautiful and better proportioned than those which many have tried to put in order and improve, making use of old walls which were built with other ends in view. In the same way also, those ancient cities which, originally mere villages, have become in the process of time great towns, are usually badly constructed in comparison with those which are regularly laid out on a plain by a surveyor who is free to follow his own ideas. Even though, considering their buildings each one apart, there is often as much or more display of skill in the one case than in the other, the former have large buildings and small buildings indiscriminately placed together, thus rendering the streets crooked and irregular, so that it might be said that it was chance rather than the will of men guided by reason that led to such an arrangement. And if we consider that this happens despite the fact that from all time there have been certain officials who have had the special duty of looking after the buildings of private individuals in order that they may be public ornaments, we shall understand how difficult it is to bring about much that is satisfactory in operating only upon the works of others. Thus I imagined that those people who were once half-savage, and who have become civilized only by slow degrees, merely forming their laws as the disagreeable necessities of their crimes and quarrels constrained them, could not succeed in establishing so good a system of government as those who, from the time they first came together as communities, carried into effect the constitution laid down by some prudent legislator. Thus it is quite certain that the constitution of the true Religion whose ordinances are of God alone is incomparably better regulated than any other. And, to come down to human affairs, I believe that if Sparta[3] was very flourishing in former times, this was not because of the excel-

---

1   **the wars which are not yet at an end:** the Thirty Years' War, a series of European conflicts lasting from 1618 to 1648, fought mainly in Germany but involving most of the countries of western Europe

2   **coronation:** ceremony of crowning a ruler

3   **Sparta:** one of the two leading city-states of ancient Greece, the other being Athens

lence of each and every one of its laws, seeing that many were very strange and even contrary to good morals, but because, being drawn up by one individual, they all tended towards the same end. And similarly I thought that the sciences found in books — in those at least whose reasonings are only probable and which have no demonstrations, composed as they are of the gradually accumulated opinions of many different individuals — do not approach so near to the truth as the simple reasoning which a man of common sense can quite naturally carry out respecting the things which come immediately before him. **Again I thought that since we have all been children before being men, and since it has for long fallen to us to be governed by our appetites and by our teachers (who often enough contradicted one another, and none of whom perhaps counseled us always for the best), it is almost impossible that our judgments should be so excellent or solid as they should have been had we had complete use of our reason since our birth, and had we been guided by its means alone.**

It is true that we do not find that all the houses in a town are razed[1] to the ground for the sole reason that the town is to be rebuilt in another fashion, with streets made more beautiful; but at the same time we see that many people cause their own houses to be knocked down in order to rebuild them, and that sometimes they are forced so to do where there is danger of the houses falling of themselves, and when the foundations are not secure. From such examples I argued to myself that there was no plausibility in the claim of any private individual to reform a state by altering everything, and by overturning it throughout, in order to set it right again. Nor is it likewise probable that the whole body of the Sciences, or the order of teaching established by the Schools, should be reformed. **But as regards all the opinions which up to this time I had embraced, I thought I could not do better than endeavour once for all to sweep them completely away, so that they might later on be replaced, either by others which were better, or by the same, when I had made them conform to the uniformity of a rational scheme. And I firmly believed that by this means I should succeed in directing my life much better than if I had only built on old foundations and relied on principles of which I allowed myself to be in youth persuaded without having inquired into their truth.** For although in so doing I recognized various difficulties, these were at the same time not insurmountable, nor comparable to those which are found in reformation of the most insignificant kind in matters which concern the public. In the case of great bodies it is too difficult a task to raise them again when they are once thrown down, or even to keep them in their places when once thoroughly shaken; and their fall cannot be otherwise than very violent. Then as to any imperfections that they may possess (and the very diversity that is found between them is sufficient to tell us that these in many cases exist) custom has doubtless greatly mitigated[2] them, while it has also helped us to avoid, or insensibly corrected a number against which mere foresight would have found it difficult to guard. And finally the imperfections are almost always more supportable than would be the process of removing them, just as the great roads which wind about amongst the mountains become, because of being frequented, little by

---

1 **raze:** destroy completely
2 **mitigate:** make less severe

little so well-beaten and easy that it is much better to follow them than to try to go more directly by climbing over rocks and descending to the foot of precipices[1].

This is the reason why I cannot in any way approve of those turbulent and unrestful spirits who, being called neither by birth nor fortune to the management of public affairs, never fail to have always in their minds some new reforms. And if **I thought that in this treatise there was contained the smallest justification for this folly, I should be very sorry to allow it to be published. My design has never extended beyond trying to reform my own opinion and to build on a foundation which is entirely my own. If my work has given me a certain satisfaction, so that I here present to you a draft of it, I do not so do because I wish to advise anybody to imitate it.** Those to whom God has been most beneficent in the bestowal of His graces will perhaps form designs which are more elevated; but I fear much that this particular one will seem too venturesome for many. The simple resolve to strip oneself of all opinions and beliefs formerly received is not to be regarded as an example that each man should follow, and the world may be said to be mainly composed of two classes of minds neither of which could prudently adopt it. There are those who, believing themselves to be cleverer than they are, cannot restrain themselves from being precipitate[2] in judgment and have not sufficient patience to arrange their thoughts in proper order; hence, once a man of this description had taken the liberty of doubting the principles he formerly accepted, and had deviated from the beaten track, he would never be able to maintain the path which must be followed to reach the appointed end more quickly, and he would hence remain wandering astray all through his life. Secondly, there are those who having reason or modesty enough to judge that they are less capable of distinguishing truth from falsehood than some others from whom instruction might be obtained, are right in contenting themselves with following the opinions of these others rather than in searching better ones for themselves.

For myself I should doubtless have been of these last if I had never had more than a single master, or had I never known the diversities which have from all time existed between the opinions of men of the greatest learning. But I had been taught, even in my College days, that there is nothing imaginable so strange or so little credible that it has not been maintained by one philosopher or other, and I further recognized in the course of my travels that all those whose sentiments are very contrary to ours are yet not necessarily barbarians or savages, but may be possessed of reason in as great or even a greater degree than ourselves. I also considered how very different the self-same man, identical in mind and spirit, may become, according as he is brought up from childhood amongst the French or Germans, or has passed his whole life amongst Chinese or cannibals. I likewise noticed how even in the fashions of one's clothing the same thing that pleased

---

1　**precipice:** steep rock. It might be worthwhile to take notice of Descartes, political attitudes. Unlike Martin Luther or Galileo, he would not prefer any drastic measures for an evolution. He used Copernican theory, for instance, in *The World,* but when he heard of the conflict between Galileo and the Pope, he decided to submit to ecclesiastical order and not to publish the work. But later this Copernican idea did appear in *Discourse on Method.*

2　**precipitate:** hasty, rash

Heritage of Western Intellectual Tradition — A Sourcebook

us ten years ago, and which will perhaps please us once again before ten years are passed, seems at the present time extravagant and ridiculous. I thus concluded that it is much more custom and example that persuade us than any certain knowledge, and yet in spite of this the voice of the majority does not afford a proof of any value in truths a little difficult to discover, because such truths are much more likely to have been discovered by one man than by a nation. I could not, however, put my finger on a single person whose opinions seemed preferable to those of others, and I found that I was, so to speak, constrained myself to undertake the direction of my procedure.

But like one who walks alone and in the twilight I resolved to go so slowly, and to use so much circumspection[1] in all things, that if my advance was but very small, at least I guarded myself well from falling. I did not wish to set about the final rejection of any single opinion which might formerly have crept into my beliefs without having been introduced there by means of Reason, until I had first of all employed sufficient time in planning out the task which I had undertaken, and in seeking the true Method of arriving at a knowledge of all the things of which my mind was capable.

Among the different branches of Philosophy, I had in my younger days to a certain extent studied Logic; and in those of Mathematics, Geometrical Analysis and Algebra — three arts or sciences which seemed as though they ought to contribute something to the design I had in view. But in examining them I observed in respect to Logic that the syllogisms[2] and the greater part of the other teaching served better in explaining to others those things that one knows (or like the art of Lully[3], in enabling one to speak without judgment of those things of which one is ignorant) than in learning what is new. And although in reality Logic contains many precepts which are very true and very good, there are at the same time mingled with them so many others which are hurtful or superfluous, that it is almost as difficult to separate the two as to draw a Diana[4] or a Minerva[5] out of a block of marble which is not yet roughly hewn. And as to the Analysis of the ancients and the Algebra of the moderns, besides the fact that they embrace only matters the most abstract, such as appear to have no actual use, the former is always so restricted to the consideration of symbols that it cannot exercise the Understanding without greatly fatiguing the Imagination; and in the latter one is so subjected to certain rules and formulas that the result is the construction of an art which is confused and obscure, and which embarrasses the mind, instead of a science which contributes to its cultivation. This made me feel that some other Method must be found, which, comprising the advantages of the three, is yet exempt[6] from their faults. And as a multiplicity of laws often

---

1   **circumspection:** prudence, caution
2   **syllogism:** form of reasoning in which a conclusion is reached from two premises
3   **Raymond Lully (c. 1233–1315):** Spanish philosopher, one of the first scholars in Europe to advocate the study of the Arabic language, also known for his missionary crusades for the conversion of the Muslims
4   **Diana:** goddess of the moon and of the hunt in Roman mythology, counterpart of the Greek goddess Artemis, shown as a young hunter with bow and arrows
5   **Minerva:** goddess of handicrafts, patron of the arts and trades in Roman mythology, counterpart of Greek goddess Athena.
6   **exempt:** free from

Heritage of Western Intellectual Tradition   A Sourcebook

furnishes excuses for evildoing, as a State is hence much better ruled when, having but very few laws, these are most strictly observed; so, instead of the great number of precepts of which Logic is composed, I believed that I should find the four which I shall state quite sufficient, provided that I adhered to a firm and constant resolve never on any single occasion to fail in their observance.

The first of these was to accept nothing as true which I did not clearly recognize to be so: that is to say, carefully to avoid precipitation and prejudice in judgments, and to accept in them nothing more than what was presented to my mind so clearly and distinctly that I could have no occasion to doubt it.

The second was to divide up each of difficulties which I examined into as many parts as possible, and as seemed requisite in order that it might be resolved in the best manner possible.

The third was to carry on my reflections in due order, commencing with objects that were the most simple and easy to understand, in order to rise little by little, or by degrees, to knowledge of the most complex, assuming an order, even if a fictitious one, among those which do not follow a natural sequence relatively to one another.[1]

The last was in all cases to make enumerations so complete and review so general that I should be certain of having omitted nothing.

…

Part IV

For a long time I had remarked that it is sometimes requisite in common life to follow opinions which one knows to be most uncertain, exactly as though they were indisputable, as has been said above. But because in this case I wished to give myself entirely to the search after Truth. I thought that it was necessary for me to take an apparently opposite course, and to reject as absolutely false everything as to which I could imagine the least ground of doubt, in order to see if afterwards there remained anything in my belief that was entirely certain. Thus, because our senses sometimes deceive us, I wished to suppose that nothing is just as they cause us to imagine it to be; and because there are men who deceive themselves in their reasoning and fall into paralogisms[2], even concerning the simplest matters of geometry, and judging that I was as subject to error as was any other, I rejected as false all the reasons formerly accepted by me as demonstrations. And since all the same thoughts and conceptions which we have while awake may also come to us in sleep, without any of them being at that time true, I resolved to assume that everything that ever entered into my mind was no more true than the illusions of my dreams. But immediately afterwards I noticed that whilst I thus wished to think all things false, it was abso-lutely essential that the "I" who thought this should be somewhat, and remarking that this truth "I think, therefore I am" was so certain and so assured that all the most extravagant suppositions

---

1 **The third was … to one another.:** Compare this Cartesian method with that of Bacon's.
2 **paralogism:** that which goes against logic, fallacy

brought forward by the skeptics were incapable of shaking it, I came to the conclusion that I could receive it without scruple[1] as the first principle of the Philosophy for which I was seeking.

And then, examining attentively that which I was, I saw that I could conceive that I had no body, and that there was no world nor place where I might be; but yet that I could not for all that conceive that I was not. On the contrary, I saw from the very fact that I thought of doubting the truth of other things, it very evidently and certainly followed that I was; on the other hand if I had only ceased from thinking, even if all the rest of what I had ever imagined had really existed, I should have no reason for thinking that I had existed. From that I knew that I was a substance the whole essence or nature of which is to think, and that for its existence there is no need of any place, nor does it depend on any material thing; so that this "me," that is to say, the soul by which I am what I am, is entirely distinct from body, and is even more easy to know than is the latter; and even if body were not, the soul would not cease to be what it is.

After this I considered generally what in a proposition is requisite in order to be true and certain; for since I had just discovered one which I knew to be such, I thought that I ought also to know in what this certainty consisted. And having remarked that there was nothing at all in the statement "I think, therefore I am" which assures me of having thereby made a true assertion, excepting that I see very clearly that to think it is necessary to be[2], I came to the conclusion that I might assume, as a general rule, that the things which we conceive very clearly and distinctly are all true — remembering, however, that there is some difficulty in ascertaining which are those that we distinctly conceive.

Following upon this, and reflecting on the fact that I doubted, and that consequently my existence was not quite perfect (for I saw clearly that it was a greater perfection to know than to doubt), I resolved to inquire whence I had learnt to think of anything more perfect than I myself was; and I recognized very clearly that his conception must proceed from some nature which was really more perfect. As to the thoughts which I had of many other things outside of me, like the heavens, the earth, light, heat, and a thousand others, I had not so much difficulty in knowing whence they came, because, remarking nothing in them which seemed to render them superior to me, I could believe that, if they were true, they were dependencies upon my nature, in so far as it possessed some perfection; and if they were not true, that I held them from nought, that is to say, that they were in me because I had something lacking in my nature. But this could not apply to the idea of a Being more perfect than my own, for to hold it from nought would be manifestly impossible; and because it is no less contradictory to say of the more perfect that it is what results from and depends on the less perfect, than to say that there is something which proceeds from nothing, it was equally impossible that I should hold it from myself. In this way it could but follow that it had been placed in me by a Nature which was really more perfect than mine could be, and which even had within itself all the perfections of which I could form any idea — that is to say, to put it in a word, which was God.

---

1 **scruple:** uneasiness of conscience

2 **to be:** here ontological existence

Key Concepts

doubts/ignorance

"I think, therefore I am"

Logic

Mathematics

Method

pursuing certain paths

reason

scholastic Aristotelianism

straight road

Compare with China

The 17th century European scientific revolution went hand in hand with Sino-European cultural exchange, as the following essays show. Compare the development of "science" in the two very different worlds to see if you have any conclusions to draw.

Matteo Ricci: The Art of Printing

One of the first sources of information about China was the Jesuits who served at the Wing court in the sixteenth and seventeenth centuries. Clerics such as Matteo Ricci found much to admire in Chinese civilization. Here Ricci expresses a keen interest in Chinese printing methods, which at that time were well in advance of the techniques used in the West.

The art of printing was practiced in China at a date somewhat earlier than that assigned to the beginning to printing in Europe, which was about 1405. It is quite certain that the Chinese knew the art of printing at least five centuries ago, and some of them assert that printing was known to their people before the beginning of the Christian era, about 50 BCE. Their method of printing differs widely from that employed in Europe, and our method would be quite impracticable for them because of the exceedingly large number of Chinese characters and symbols. At present they cut their characters in a reverse position and in a simplified form, on a comparatively small tablet made for the most part from the wood of the pear tree or the apple tree, although at times the wood of the jujube tree is also used for this purpose.

Their method of making printed books is quite ingenious. The text is written in ink, with a brush made of very fine hair, on a sheet of paper which is inverted and pasted on a wooden tablet. When the paper has become thoroughly dry, its surface is scraped off quickly and with great skill, until nothing but a fine tissue bearing the characters remains on the wooden tablet.

Then, with a steel graver[1], the workman cuts away the surface following the outlines of the characters until these alone stand out in low relief. From such a block a skilled printer can make copies with incredible speed, turning out as many as fifteen hundred copies in a single day. Chinese printers are so skilled in engraving these blocks, that no more time is consumed in making one of them than would be required by one of our printers in setting up a form of type and making the necessary corrections. This scheme of engraving wooden blocks is well adapted for the large and complex nature of the Chinese characters, but I do not think it would lend itself very aptly to our European type which could hardly be engraved upon wood because of its small dimensions.

Their method of printing has one decided advantage, namely, that once these tablets are made, they can be preserved and used for making changes in the text as often as one wishes. Additions and subtractions can also be made as the tablets can be readily patched[2]. Again, with this method, the printer and the author are not obliged to produce here and now an excessively large edition of a book, but are able to print a book in smaller or larger lots sufficient to meet the demand at the time. We have derived great benefit from this method of Chinese printing, as we employ the domestic help in our homes to strike off copies of the books on religious and scientific subjects which we translate into Chinese from the languages in which they were written originally. In truth, the whole method is so simple that one is tempted to try it for himself after once having watched the process. The simplicity of Chinese printing is what accounts for the exceedingly large numbers of books in circulation here and the ridiculously low prices at which they are sold. Such facts as these would scarcely be believed by one who had not witnessed them.

They have another odd method of reproducing reliefs[3] which have been cut into marble or wood. An epitaph, for example, or a picture set out in low relief on marble or on wood, is covered with a piece of moist paper which in turn is overlayed with several pieces of cloth. Then the entire surface is beaten with a small mallet[4] until all the lineaments[5] of the relief are impressed upon the paper. When the paper dries, ink or some other coloring substance is applied with a light touch, after which only the impression of the relief stands out on the original whiteness of the paper. This method cannot be employed when the relief is shallow; or trade in delicate lines. (from *The Diary of Matthew Ricci*, in Matthew Ricci, *China in the Sixteenth Century*, trans Louis Gallagher)

Heritage of Western Intellectual Tradition   A Sourcebook

---

1 **graver:** carver
2 **patch:** make ready for use
3 **relief:** carving or moulding in which a design stands out from surface
4 **mallet:** hammer with a wooden head
5 **lineament:** distinctive feature or detail

Supplementary Reading

Calculating Machines in China and Europe in the 17th Century — The Western View

In their contribution to this conference, BAI Shangshu and Li Di have reported about their rediscovery of ten calculating devices from the late 17th and/or early 18th century in the Beijing Palace Museum. They did outstanding research work on structures and functions, the origins and manufacturing of their discoveries, which are a real treasure in the world-wide history of mechanical.

Many questions about these Beiiing Calculating Machines (BCM) remain open. Obviously there were considerable influences from Europe. One or more machines may even have come from Europe as a gift to the Emperor of China, but it is also obvious that early developments in Chinese mathematics and technology have played an important role in the making of the machine.

The ten machines can be separated into two classes. In the first class, disks or gear wheels are the fundamental means for performing arithmetical operations. The wheels have ten teeth and carry circular representations of the ten digits 0 ... 9. A special one-tooth device handles the carry problem. So these machines can only be used to do basically additions. Subtraction becomes possible well if additional mathematical manipulations (such as 9-complements) are used. Multiplication and division can also be supported if adequate algorithms[1] are applied. However, elementary multiplications of single digits, necessary in these algorithms, have to be done mentally or with Neper's bones[2]. Of course this class corresponds to the Schickard[3] or Pascal[4] type machines.

The second class uses Neper's bones as fundamental means. Basically the devices from this class realise multiplications of multi-digit numbers with one-digit numbers. This class corresponds to similar devices known in Europe as "Schotts Rechen Cylinder."

Areas to be explored for complete information about the BCM

For complete elucidation of all secrets of the BCM one needs detailed information from at least three fields:

a) thorough examination of all the BCM by experts with mathematical, technical, historical

---

1 **algorithm:** process or set of rules used for calculation or problem-solving
2 **Neper's bones:** or Napier's bones, a tool invented in the early 1600s by Scottish mathematician John Napier, which were multiplication tables inscribed on strips of wood or bone. Napier also invented logarithms, which greatly assisted in arithmetic calculations.
3 Wilhelm Schickard (1592–1635) built the first automatic calculator in 1623.
4 **Blaise Pascal (1623–1662):** French mathematician, physicist, and religious philosopher who made contributions to the construction of mechanical calculators

or intercultural knowledge respectively;

b) a survey of the scientific exchange and other activities between Europe and China before and after the reign of Kang Xi;

c) complete information about the history of calculating devices in Europe and in China during the 17th century and early 18th century.

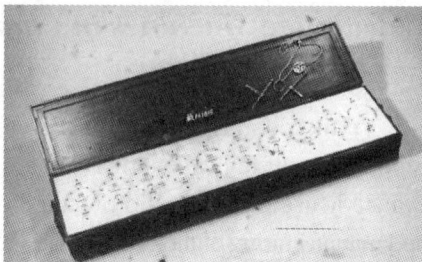

Beijing Disk Calculating Machine

European scholars who lived in China for many years were of great influence in the development of mathematics, astronomy and calendar sciences in China. In 1628 J. Rho translated a book about calculation with Neper's bones (1617) into Chinese. These bones or rods soon became very popular in China, and they were modified and extended by Chinese mathematicians, in particular by Mel Wending who published a book about rod calculation in 1678.

The greatest influence on sciences came from French and German Jesuits who were sent to China after 1685. They certainly carried information about European Disk Calculating Machines (e.g. Pascal) and rod Calculating Machines (e.g. Schott) with them and they kept themselves up to date by corresponding with Jesuits in their home countries. Considering facts such as the possible relations with Leopold, which I mentioned above, it is clear that much more information is necessary about these links.

Kang Xi himself took very great interest in these things and he invited the Western scholars to give lectures to him in the Palace. As a consequence, 53 books on Western sciences were edited by Su li Ching-yün. A well-known link was also Leibniz, who corresponded with J. Bouvet and others in Beijing about the dyadic system, its connections with the hexagrams from the I Ching, about a Chinese Academy of Science and possibly about the Leibniz calculating machine. Leibniz also sent a letter to Emperor Kang Xi with suggestions about this Academy.

H. H. Goldstine mentions that possibly a Leibniz calculating machine was sent to Kang Xi late in the 17th century. No trace can be found of such a gift today, not even in various lists of presents given to Kang Xi.

In the 15th century in Europe the respective algorithm methods of calculation were introduced together with the Indian-Arabian decimal system. The mechanising of these methods by machines or machine-like devices started with two of the most important subroutines: firstly, the digit by digit addition of two multi-digit numbers together with a suitable transport of the carries, and secondly, the multiplication of a multi-digit number with a one-digit number. Subtraction as well as general multiplication and division could then by realised by integrating adequate manual operations.

Pascal (1642) solved the problem of addition with a mechanism of pinwheels. The mechanizing of the multiplication problem mentioned above was solved with a device from Schott (1664). Long before Pascal and Schott, both problems were solved by Schickard (1623) with one machine, or rather two machines in one box. Leibnlz (1672/74) constructed the first machine which completely mechanised all four types of calculation, using teeth-wheels and the stepped-drum mechanism invented by him.

The BDCM No. 141816 has an adding work with teeth-wheels and one-tooth wheels for the carries, which is rather similar to Schickard's work. The display, however, contains 9-complements like Pascal's machine. I could not yet find out if the mechanism can move in both directions, and if not why not. The sketch just displayed, stressing technical aspects instead of chronology, may give some hints as to where to place the BDCM. Obviously there is no direct relation to Schickard, Pascal or Leibniz. So the search for Chinese or European sources of the special features of the Beijing Disk Calculating Machines has to go on. (Adapted from Klaus-D. Graf, Freie Universität Berlin, Institut für Informatik)

Questions for Discussion

1. Why is observation important to Bacon?
2. Comment on "Knowledge Is Power."
3. What are the four "Idols" and why are they the archenemy for Bacon?
4. What is the "method" to Descartes and why is it important?
5. What is the complaint made by Descartes about the weaknesses of the old "method"?

Heritage of Western Intellectual Tradition   A Sourcebook

UNIT 8

Modern Scientific Thinking (2)

Pretest

- What do you know about Renaissance science and its scientists?
- What is the significance of their ideas, both scientific and humanistic?
- Quote to show which one of them you like best or know most, and why?

What You Will Learn in This Unit

- Two more great scientists in Renaissance Europe: Galileo, Newton;
- Their ideas concerning nature, man, human history, and wisdom; and
- Development of science in Ancient China.

Learn to Pronounce

Celestial /sɪˈlestjəl, sɪˈlestʃəl/ 天体的

Copernican /kəʊˈpɜːnɪkən/ 哥白尼的

Galileo Galilei /gælɪˈleɪoʊ/ 伽利略

Inquisition /ɪnkwɪˈzɪʃən/ 宗教法庭

Isaac Newton /ˈnjuːtn/ 牛顿

Johannes Kepler /ˈkeplə/ 开普勒

Jupiter /ˈdʒuːpɪtə/ 木星

Nicholas Copernicus /kəʊˈpɜːnɪkəs/ 哥白尼

pendulum /ˈpendjʊləm/ 钟摆

Ptolemaic /tɒləˈmeɪɪk/ 托勒密的

Ptolemy /ˈtɒlɪmɪ/ 托勒密

Vatican /ˈvætɪkən/ 梵蒂冈，罗马教廷

Galileo Galilei: Letter to the Grand Duchess Christina*

Galileo Galilei (1564 – 1642), Italian mathematician, astronomer and physicist who, with Johannes Kepler, initiated the scientific revolution. Galileo entered the University of Pisa in 1581 to study medicine, where in the first year at the Pisa cathedral he supposedly observed a lamp swinging and found that the lamp always required the same amount of time to complete an oscillation, no matter how large the range of the swing. Later Galileo suggested that the principle of the pendulum might be applied to the regulation of clocks. He left the university without a degree in 1585 for lack of funds, and in 1589 he became professor of mathematics at Pisa, where he is reported to have shown his students the error of Aristotle's belief that bodies of different weights fall at different speeds, by dropping two objects of different weight simultaneously from the Leaning Tower. His contract was not renewed in 1592, probably because he contradicted Aristotelian professors. The same year, he was appointed to the chair of mathematics at the University of Padua. By December 1609, Galileo had built a telescope of 20 times magnification, with which he discovered mountains and craters on the moon. He also discovered the four largest satellites of Jupiter. Florentine priests denounced Galileo's belief in a moving earth as heretical. Galileo wrote a long, open letter on the irrelevance of biblical passages in scientific arguments. Early in 1616, Copernican books were subjected to censorship by edict. Galileo remained silent on the subject for years. *Dialogue on the Two Chief World Systems — Ptolemaic and Copernican* was published at Florence in 1632. The book was greeted with applause from every part of the European continent, but Galileo was summoned to Rome by the Inquisition to stand trial for "grave suspicion of heresy," himself worse "than Luther and Calvin put together." Notwithstanding his pleas of illness and old age, Galileo was compelled to journey to Rome in February 1633 for trial. The sentence was read to him on June 21: he was guilty of having "held and taught" the Copernican doctrine and was ordered to recant. Galileo was sentenced to life imprisonment (swiftly commuted to permanent house arrest). The most dramatic scene took place on June 22, 1633 in Rome where the 70-year-old Galileo kneeling in criminal garb was forced to deny his belief, "I held and believed that the sun is the centre of the world and immovable, and that the earth is not the centre and movable." Rising from his knees at the end of his abjuration, he was said to have murmured, "Still, it moves." The *Dialogue* was ordered to be burned, and the sentence against him was to be read publicly in every university. An investigation was opened in 1979 by Pope John Paul II. In October 1992 a papal commission acknowledged the Vatican's error.

Some years ago, as Your Serene Highness well knows, I discovered in the heavens many things that had not been seen before our own age. The novelty of these things, as well as some

---

* Christina de' Medici (Medici was Italian banking and political family that ruled Florence for almost three centuries), grand duchess of Florence. Remember Martin Luther also appealed to the imperial power for support at the time of crisis (see Unit 6).

consequences which followed from them in contradiction to the physical notions commonly held among academic philosophers[1], stirred up against me no small number of professors — as if I had placed these things in the sky with my own hands in order to upset nature and overturn the sciences[2]. **They seemed to forget that the increase of known truths stimulates the investigation, establishment, and growth of the arts; not their diminution[3] or destruction.**

Showing a greater fondness for their own opinions than for truth, they sought to deny and disprove the new things which, if they had cared to look for themselves, their own senses would have demonstrated to them. To this end they hurled various charges and published numerous writings filled with vain arguments, and they made the grave mistake of sprinkling[4] these with passages taken from places in the Bible which they had failed to understand properly, and which were ill-suited to their purposes.

These men would perhaps not have fallen into such error had they but paid attention to a most useful doctrine of St. Augustine's[5], relative to our making positive statements about things which are obscure and hard to understand by means of reason alone. Speaking of a certain physical conclusion about the heavenly bodies, he wrote: "Now keeping always our respect for moderation in grave piety, we ought not to believe anything inadvisedly[6] on a dubious point, lest in favor to our error we conceive a prejudice against something that truth hereafter may reveal to be not contrary in any way to the sacred books of either the Old or the New Testament."

Galileo's legendary experiment at the Leaning Tower of Pisa. Hence the "Universality of Free Fall" as a cornerstone of modern physics

Well, the passage of time has revealed to everyone the truths that I previously set forth; and, together with the truth of the facts, there has come to light the great difference in attitude between those who simply and dispassionately refused to admit the discoveries to be true, and those who combined with their incredulity some reckless passion of their own. Men who were well grounded in astronomical and physical science were persuaded as soon as they received my first message. There were others who denied them[7] or remained in doubt only because of their novel[8] and unexpected character, and because they had not yet had the opportunity to see for themselves. These men have by degrees come to be satisfied. But some, besides allegiance to their original error, possess I know not what fanciful interest in remaining hostile not so much toward the things in question as toward their

---

1   **notions commonly held among academic philosophers:** cf. Bacon's criticism of the idols
2   **sciences:** Christian sciences
3   **diminution:** diminishing, reduction
4   **sprinkle:** intersperse
5   For St. Augustine, see Unit 4.
6   **inadvisedly:** imprudently
7   **them:** discoveries
8   **novel:** strange

discoverer. No longer being able to deny them, these men now take refuge in obstinate[1] silence, but being more than ever exasperated by that which has pacified[2] and quieted other men, they divert their thoughts to other fancies and seek new ways to damage me.

I should pay no more attention to them than to those who previously contradicted me — at whom I always laugh, being assured of the eventual outcome — were it not that in their new calumnies[3] and persecutions I perceive that they do not stop at proving themselves more learned than I am (a claim which I scarcely contest), but go so far as to cast against me the imputations of crimes which must be, and are, more abhorrent to me than death itself. I cannot remain satisfied merely to know that the injustice of this is recognized by those who are acquainted with these men and with me, as perhaps it is not known to others.

Persisting in their original resolve to destroy me and everything mine by any means they can think of, these men are aware of my views in astronomy and philosophy. They know that as to the arrangement of the parts of the universe, I hold the sun to be situated motionless in the center of the revolution of the celestial orbs while the earth revolves about the sun. They know also that I support this position not only by refuting the arguments of Ptolemy[4] and Aristotle, but by producing many counter-arguments; in particular, some which relate to physical effects whose causes can perhaps be assigned in no other way. In addition there are astronomical arguments derived from many things in my new celestial discoveries that plainly confute the Ptolemaic system while admirably agreeing with and confirming the contrary hypothesis. **Possibly because they are disturbed by the known truth of other propositions of mine which differ from those commonly held, and therefore mistrusting their defense so long as they confine themselves to the field of philosophy, these men have resolved to fabricate[5] a shield for their fallacies out of the mantle of pretended religion and the authority of the Bible.** These they apply with little judgement to the refutation of arguments that they do not understand and have not even listened to.

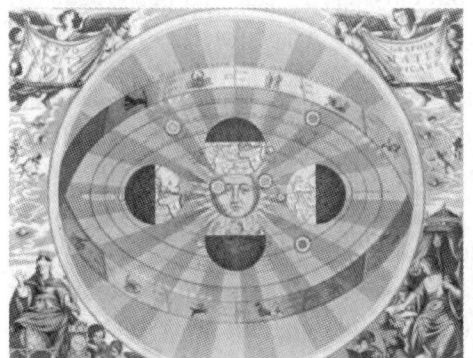

Copernicus' heliocentric model of the solar system challenged Ptolemy's geocentric model, which had been the accepted theory since the 2nd century.

First they have endeavored to spread the opinion that such propositions in general are contrary to the Bible and are consequently damnable and heretical. They know that it is human nature to take up causes whereby a man may oppress his neighbor, no matter how unjustly, rather than those from which a man may receive some just encouragement. Hence

1 **obstinate:** stubborn
2 **pacify:** calm down
3 **calumny:** slander, false statement
4 **Ptolemy (actual name Claudius Ptolemaeus, c. 100 – 170):** astronomer and mathematician, whose astronomical theories dominated scientific thought until the 16th century
5 **fabricate:** make

they have had no trouble in finding men who would preach the damnability and heresy of the new doctrine from their very pulpits[1] with unwonted[2] confidence, thus doing impious and inconsiderate injury not only to that doctrine and its followers but to all mathematics and mathematicians in general. Next, becoming bolder, and hoping (though vainly) that this seed which first took root in their hypocritical minds would send out branches and ascend to heaven, they began scattering rumors among the people that before long this doctrine would be condemned by the supreme authority. They know, too, that official condemnation would not only suppress the two propositions which I have mentioned, but would render damnable all other astronomical and physical statements and observations that have any necessary relation or connection with these.

In order to facilitate their designs, they seek so far as possible (at least among the common people) to make this opinion seem new and to belong to me alone. They pretend not to know that its author, or rather its restorer and confirmer, was Nicholas Copernicus[3]; and that he was not only a Catholic, but a priest and a canon. He was in fact so esteemed by the church that when the Lateran Council under Leo X[4] took up the correction of the church calendar, Copernicus was called to Rome from the most remote parts of Germany to undertake its reform. At that time the calendar was defective because the true measures of the year and the lunar month were not exactly known. The Bishop of Culm, then superintendent of this matter, assigned Copernicus to seek more light and greater certainty concerning the celestial motions by means of constant study and labor. With Herculean[5] toil he set his admirable mind to this task, and he made such great progress in this science and brought our knowledge of the heavenly motions to such precision that he became celebrated as an astronomer. Since that time not only has the calendar been regulated by his teachings, but tables of all the motions of the planets have been calculated as well.

Having reduced his system into six books, he published these at the instance[6] of the Cardinal of Capua and the Bishop of Culm. And since he had assumed his laborious enterprise by order of the supreme pontiff, he dedicated this book *On the celestial revolutions* to Pope Paul III[7]. When printed, the book was accepted by the holy Church, and it has been read and studied by everyone without the faintest hint of any objection ever being conceived against its doctrines. Yet now that manifest experiences and necessary proofs have shown them to be well grounded, persons exist who would strip the author of his reward without so much as looking at his book, and add the shame of having him pronounced a heretic. All this they would do merely to satisfy their personal displeasure conceived without any cause against another man, who has no interest in Copernicus

---

1   **pulpit:** small platform in the church for preaching

2   **unwonted:** unusual

3   **Nicholas Copernicus (1473–1543):** Polish astronomer, best known for his astronomical theory that the sun is at rest near the center of the universe, and that the earth revolves annually around the sun. This is called the heliocentric, or sun-centered, system.

4   **Leo X (1475–1521):** pope from 1513 to 1521

5   **Herculean:** needing great strength or effort

6   **instance:** request

7   **Pope Paul III (1468–1549):** pope (1534–1549) who initiated the Counter Reformation

beyond approving his teachings.

Now as to the false aspersions[1] which they so unjustly seek to cast upon me, I have thought it necessary to justify myself in the eyes of all men, whose judgment in matters of religion and of reputation I must hold in great esteem. I shall therefore discourse of the particulars which these men produce to make this opinion detested[2] and to have it condemned not merely as false but as heretical. To this end they make a shield of their hypocritical zeal for religion. They go about invoking[3] the Bible, which they would have minister to their deceitful purposes[4]. Contrary to the sense of the Bible and the intention of the holy Fathers, if I am not mistaken, they would extend such authorities until even in purely physical matters — where faith is not involved — they would have us altogether abandon reason and the evidence of our senses in favor of some biblical passage, though under the surface meaning of its words this passage may contain a different sense.

Galileo showing his telescope

I hope to show that I proceed with much greater piety than they do, when I argue not against condemning this book[5], but against condemning it in the way they suggest — that is, without understanding it, weighing it, or so much as reading it. For Copernicus never discusses matters of religion or faith, nor does he use argument that depend in any way upon the authority of sacred writings which he might have interpreted erroneously. He stands always upon physical conclusions pertaining to the celestial motions, and deals with them by astronomical and geometrical demonstrations, founded primarily upon sense experiences and very exact observations. He did not ignore the Bible, but he knew very well that if his doctrine were proved, then it could not contradict the Scriptures when they were rightly understood and thus at the end of his letter of dedication, addressing the pope, he said:

If there should chance to be any exegetes[6] ignorant of mathematics who pretend to skill in that discipline, and dare to condemn and censure this hypothesis of mine upon the authority of some scriptural passage twisted to their purpose, I value them not, but disdain their unconsidered judgment. For it is known that Lactantius[7] — a poor mathematician though in other respects a worthy author — writes very childishly about the shape of the earth when he

---

1   **aspersion:** slander
2   **detest:** strongly hate
3   **invoke:** call upon for help
4   **which they would have minister to their deceitful purposes:** they would have the Bible serve their purposes
5   **this book:** Copernicus' *On the celestial revolutions*
6   **exegete:** one who explains the Bible
7   **Lucius Caelius Firmianus Lactantius (c. 240–320):** a native of North Africa, early Christian author who wrote in Latin explaining Christianity in terms that would be pleasant to educated pagans while defending it from pagan philosophers

scoffs[1] at those who affirm it to be a globe. Hence it should not seem strange to the ingenious if people of that sort should in turn deride[2] me. But mathematics is written for mathematicians, by whom, if I am not deceived, these labors of mine will be recognized as contributing something to their domain, as also to that of the Church over which Your Holiness now reigns.

Such are the people who labor to persuade us that an author like Copernicus may be condemned without being read, and who produce various authorities from the Bible, from theologians, and from Church Councils to make us believe that this is not only lawful but commendable. Since I hold these to be of supreme authority I consider it rank temerity[3] for anyone to contradict them — when employed according to the usage of the holy Church. Yet I do not believe it is wrong to speak out when there is reason to suspect that other men wish, for some personal motive, to produce and employ such authorities for purposes quite different from the sacred intention of the holy Church.

Therefore I declare (and my sincerity will make itself manifest) not only that I mean to submit myself freely and renounce any errors into which I may fall in this discourse through ignorance of matters pertaining to religion, but that I do not desire in these matters to engage in disputes with anyone, even on points that are disputable. My goal is this alone; that if, among errors that may abound in these considerations of a subject remote from my profession, there is anything that may be serviceable to the holy Church in making a decision concerning the Copernican system, it may be taken and utilized as seems best to the superiors[4]. And if not, let my book be torn and burnt, as I neither intend nor pretend to gain from it any fruit that is not pious and Catholic. And though many of the things I shall reprove[5] have been heard by my own ears, I shall freely grant to those who have spoken them that they never said them, if that is what they wish, and I shall confess myself to have been mistaken. Hence let whatever I reply be addressed not to them, but to whoever may have held such opinions.

The reason produced for condemning the opinion that the earth moves and the sun stands still is that in many places in the Bible one may read that the sun moves and the earth stands still. Since the Bible cannot err; it follows as a necessary consequence that anyone takes an erroneous and heretical position who maintains that the sun is inherently motionless and the earth movable.

---

1   **scoff:** mock
2   **deride:** laugh at
3   **temerity:** rashness
4   **among errors that ... to the superiors:** Given the difficult situation, Galileo had no intention to insist that the Church adopt the Copernican system. He only wanted to separate purely scientific questions from matters of faith so that rational discussion might remain free. "Galileo did not want the Church to adopt either side of any scientific question and suppress the other as a matter of faith; if the Church were to suppress anything, he wrote, it should forbid any introduction of scriptural authority into debates that could be settled without it, by experience and reason alone."
5   **reprove:** find fault with

With regard to this argument, I think in the first place that it is very pious to say and prudent to affirm that the holy Bible can never speak untruth — whenever its true meaning is understood. But I believe nobody will deny that it is often very abstruse[1], and may say things which are quite different from what its bare words signify. Hence in expounding[2] the Bible if one were always to confine oneself to the unadorned grammatical meaning, one might fall into error. Not only contradictions and propositions far from true might thus be made to appear in the Bible, but even grave heresies and follies. Thus it would be necessary to assign to God feet, hands and eyes, as well as corporeal[3] and human affections, such as anger, repentance, hatred, and sometimes even the forgetting of things past and ignorance of those to come. These propositions uttered by the Holy Ghost were set down in that manner by the sacred scribes in order to accommodate them to the capacities of the common people, who are rude and unlearned. For the sake of those who deserve to be separated from the herd, it is necessary that wise expositors should produce the true senses of such passages, together with the special reasons for which they were set down in these words. This doctrine is so widespread and so definite with all theologians that it would be superfluous to adduce evidence for it.

Galileo facing the Papal Tribunal

Hence I think that I may reasonably conclude that whenever the Bible has occasion to speak of any physical conclusion (especially those which are very abstruse and hard to understand), the rule has been observed of avoiding confusion in the minds of the common people which would render them contumacious[4] toward the higher mysteries. **Now the Bible, merely to condescend to popular capacity, has not hesitated to obscure some very important pronouncements, attributing to God himself some qualities extremely remote from (and even contrary to) His essence.** Who, then, would positively declare that this principle has been set aside, and the Bible has confined itself rigorously to the bare and restricted sense of its words, when speaking but casually of the earth, of water, of the sun, or of any other created thing? Especially in view of the fact that these things in no way concern the primary purpose of the sacred writings, which is the service of God and the salvation of souls — matters infinitely beyond the comprehension of the common people.

This being granted, I think that in discussions of physical problems[5] we ought to begin not from the authority of scriptural passages but from sense-experiences and necessary demonstrations; for the holy Bible and the phenomena of nature proceed alike from the divine Word the former as the dictate of the Holy Ghost and the latter as the observant executrix[6] of God's commands. It is

---

1 **abstruse:** profound
2 **expound:** explain
3 **corporeal:** bodily, physical
4 **contumacious:** stubborn and rebellious
5 **physical problems:** science as opposed to faith
6 **executrix:** female executor

necessary for the Bible, in order to be accommodated to the understanding of every man, to speak many things which appear to differ from the absolute truth so far as the bare meaning of the words is concerned. But Nature, on the other hand, is inexorable[1] and immutable[2]; she never transgresses the laws imposed upon her, or cares a whit[3] whether her abstruse reasons and methods of operation are understandable to men. For that reason it appears that nothing physical which sense-experience sets before our eyes, or which necessary demonstrations prove to us, ought to be called in question (much less condemned) upon the testimony of biblical passages which may have some different meaning beneath their words. For the Bible is not chained in every expression to conditions as strict as those which govern all physical effects; nor is God any less excellently revealed in Nature's actions than in the sacred statements of the Bible. Perhaps this is what Tertullian[4] meant by these words:

"We conclude that God is known first through Nature, and then again, more particularly, by doctrine, by Nature in His works, and by doctrine in His revealed word."

From this I do not mean to infer that we need not have an extraordinary esteem for the passages of Holy Scripture. On the contrary, having arrived at any certainties in physics, we ought to utilize these as the most appropriate aids in the true exposition of the Bible and in the investigation of those meanings which are necessarily contained therein, for these must be concordant[5] with demonstrated truths. I should judge that the authority of the Bible was designed to persuade men of those articles and propositions which[6], surpassing all human reasoning could not be made credible by science, or by any other means than through the very mouth of the Holy Spirit.

Yet even in those propositions which are not matters of faith, this authority ought to be preferred over that of all human writings which are supported only by bare assertions or probable arguments, and not set forth in a demonstrative way. This I hold to be necessary and proper to the same extent that divine wisdom surpasses all human judgment and conjecture[7].

But I do not feel obliged to believe that the same God who has endowed us with senses, reason and intellect has intended us to forego[8] their use and by some other means to give us knowledge which we can attain by them. He would not require us to deny sense and reason in physical matters which are set before our eyes and minds by direct experience or necessary demonstrations. This must be especially true in those sciences of which but

---

1　**inexorable:** unyielding
2　**immutable:** unchangeable
3　**a whit:** the least at all
4　**Tertullian (c. 160–220):** the first important Christian ecclesiastical writer in Latin, known for his blunt sarcasm, epigrammatic phrasing, aggressive partisan spirit, and skillful reasoning
5　**concordant:** in agreement
6　**which:** articles and propositions in the Bible
7　**conjecture:** guess, reflection
8　**forego:** give up

the faintest trace (and that consisting of conclusions[1]) is to be found in the Bible. Of astronomy; for instance, so little is found that none of the planets except Venus are so much as mentioned, and this only once or twice under the name of "Lucifer." If the sacred scribes had had any intention of teaching people certain arrangements and motions of the heavenly bodies, or had they wished us to derive such knowledge from the Bible, then in my opinion they would not have spoken of these matters so sparingly in comparison with the infinite number of admirable conclusions which are demonstrated in that science. Far from pretending to teach us the constitution and motions of the heavens and other stars, with their shapes, magnitudes, and distances, the authors of the Bible intentionally forbore[2] to speak of these things, though all were quite well known to them. Such is the opinion of the holiest and most learned Fathers, and in St. Augustine we find the following words:

"It is likewise commonly asked what we may believe about the form and shape of the heavens according to the Scriptures, for many contend much about these matters. But with superior prudence our authors have forborne to speak of this, as in no way furthering the student with respect to a blessed life — and, more important still, as taking up much of that time which should be spent in holy exercises. What is it to me whether heaven, like a sphere surrounds the earth on all sides as a mass balanced in the center of the universe, or whether like a dish it merely covers and overcasts the earth? Belief in Scripture is urged rather for the reason we have often mentioned; that is, in order that no one, through ignorance of divine passages, finding anything in our Bibles or hearing anything cited from them of such a nature as may seem to oppose manifest conclusions, should be induced to suspect their truth when they teach, relate, and deliver more profitable matters. Hence let it be said briefly, touching the form of heaven, that our authors knew the truth but the Holy Spirit did not desire that men should learn things that are useful to no one for salvation."

The same disregard of these sacred authors toward beliefs about the phenomena of the celestial bodies is repeated to us by St. Augustine in his next chapter. On the question whether we are to believe that the heaven moves or stands still, he writes thus:

Forced recant

"Some of the brethren raise a question concerning the motion of heaven, whether it is fixed or moved. If it is moved, they say, how is it a firmament[3]? If it stands still, how do these stars which are held fixed in it go round from east to west, the more northerly performing shorter circuits near the pole, so that the heaven (if there is another pole unknown to us) may seem to revolve upon some axis, or (if there is no other pole) may be thought to move as a discus[4]? To these men I reply that it would require many subtle and profound reasonings to find out which of these things is actually so; but to undertake this and discuss it is consistent neither with my leisure nor with the duty of those whom

---

1   **conclusion:** statement resulting from reason and logic
2   **forbear:** refrain, hold back
3   **firmament:** heavens, sky
4   **discus:** round plate

I desire to instruct in essential matters more directly conducing to their salvation and to the benefit of the holy Church."

From these things it follows as a necessary consequence that, since the Holy Ghost did not intend to teach us whether heaven moves or stands still, whether its shape is spherical or like a discus or extended in a plane, nor whether the earth is located at its center or off to one side, then so much the less was it intended to settle for us any other conclusion of the same kind. And the motion or rest of the earth and the sun is so closely linked with the things just named, that without a determination of the one, neither side can be taken in the other matters. Now if the Holy Spirit has purposely neglected to teach us propositions of this sort as irrelevant to the highest goal (that is, to our salvation), how can anyone affirm that it is obligatory to take sides on them, that one belief is required by faith, while the other side is erroneous? Can an opinion be heretical and yet have no concern with the salvation of souls? Can the Holy Ghost be asserted not to have intended teaching us something that does concern our salvation? I would say here something that was heard from an ecclesiastic of the most eminent degree: **"That the intention of the Holy Ghost is to teach us how one goes to heaven, not how heaven goes."**

But let us again consider the degree to which necessary demonstrations and sense experiences ought to be respected in physical conclusions, and the authority they have enjoyed at the hands of holy and learned theologians. From among a hundred attestations[1] I have selected the following:

"We must also take heed, in handling the doctrine of Moses, that we altogether avoid saying positively and confidently anything which contradicts manifest experiences and the reasoning of philosophy or the other sciences. For since every truth is in agreement with all other truth, the truth of Holy Writ cannot be contrary to the solid reasons and experiences of human knowledge."

And in St. Augustine we read:

"If anyone shall set the authority of Holy Writ against clear and manifest reason, he who does this knows not what he has undertaken; for he opposes to the truth not the meaning of the Bible, which is beyond his comprehension, but rather his own interpretation, not what is in the Bible, but what he has found in himself and imagines to be there."

This granted, and it being true that two truths cannot contradict one another, it is the function of expositors to seek out the true senses of scriptural texts. These will unquestionably accord with the physical conclusions which manifest sense and necessary demonstrations have previously made certain to us. Now the Bible, as has been remarked, admits in many places expositions that are remote from the signification of the words for reasons we have already given. Moreover, we are unable to affirm that all interpreters of the Bible speak by Divine inspiration for if that were so there would exist no differences among them about the sense of a given passage. **Hence I should**

---

1   **attestation:** witness

think it would be the part of prudence not to permit anyone to usurp[1] scriptural texts and force them in some way to maintain any physical conclusion to be true, when at some future time the senses and demonstrative or necessary reasons may show the contrary. Who indeed will set bounds to human ingenuity[2]? Who will assert that everything in the universe capable of being perceived is already discovered and known? Let us rather confess quite truly that "Those truths which we know are very few in comparison with those which we do not know."

We have it from the very mouth of the Holy Ghost that God delivered up the world to disputations[3], so that man cannot find out the work that God hath done from the beginning even to the end. **In my opinion no one, in contradiction to that dictum[4], should close the road to free philosophizing about mundane[5] and physical things, as if everything had already been discovered and revealed with certainty.** Nor should it be considered rash not to be satisfied with those opinions which have become common. No one should be scorned in physical disputes for not holding to the opinions which happen to please other people best, especially concerning problems which have been debated among the greatest philosophers for thousands of years. One of these is the stability of the sun and mobility of the earth, a doctrine believed by Pythagoras[6] and all his followers, by Heracleides[7] of Pontus (who was one of them), by Philolaus[8], the teacher of Plato, and by Plato himself according to Aristotle. Plutarch[9] writes in his *Life of Numa* that Plato, when he had grown old, said it was absurd to believe otherwise. The same doctrine was held by Aristarchus[10] of Samos, as Archimedes[11] tells us; by Seleucus[12] the mathematician, by Nicetas[13] the philosopher (on the testimony of Cicero), and by many others. Finally this opinion has been amplified[14] and confirmed with many observations and demonstrations by Nicholas Copernicus.

---

1 **usurp:** take illegally

2 **ingenuity:** cleverness, originality

3 **disputation:** controversy, disagreement

4 **dictum:** formal expression

5 **mundane:** this-worldly

6 **Pythagoras (c. 582–500 BC):** Greek philosopher and mathematician, known for the Pythagorean theorem that the square of the hypotenuse of a right triangle is equal to the sum of the squares of the other two sides

7 **Heraclides Ponticus (387–312 BC):** Greek philosopher frequently hailed as the originator of the heliocentric theory. Though this is now generally doubted, he did anticipate the thinking of later astronomers.

8 **Philolaus (c. 480–405 BC):** Greek mathematician and philosopher, a contemporary of Socrates and Democritus

9 **Plutarch (c. 46–120 BC):** Greek biographer and essayist

10 **Aristarchus (c. 310–250 BC):** Greek astronomer who was the first to assert that the earth revolves around the sun

11 **Archimedes (287–212 BC):** Greek mathematician and inventor, who wrote important works on plane and solid geometry, arithmetic, and mechanics. Aristarchus' belief that the earth revolves around the sun is known only through the writings of Archimedes, as none of his own writings has survived.

12 **Seleucus of Seleucia (c. 190 BC–?):** Greek philosopher, the only known philosopher of his time to agree with the heliocentric theory of Aristarchus, which stated that the earth rotated around its own axis which in turn revolved around the sun

13 **Nicetas:** probably a reference to Saint Nicetas the Confessor, bishop of Chalcedon, an ancient maritime town of Bithynia in Asia Minor

14 **amplify:** give fuller information

Heritage of Western Intellectual Tradition A Sourcebook

And Seneca[1], a most eminent philosopher, advises us in his book on comets that we should more diligently seek to ascertain whether it is in the sky or in the earth that the diurnal[2] rotation resides.

Hence it would probably be wise and useful counsel if, beyond articles which concern salvation and the establishment of our Faith, against the stability of which there is no danger whatever that any valid and effective doctrine can ever arise, men would not aggregate[3] further articles unnecessarily. And it would certainly be preposterous[4] to introduce them at the request of persons, who, besides not being known to speak by inspiration of divine grace, are clearly seen to lack that understanding which is necessary in order to comprehend, let alone discuss, the demonstrations by which such conclusions are supported in the subtler sciences. If I may speak my opinion freely, I should say further that it would perhaps fit in better with the decorum[5] and majesty of the sacred writings to take measures for preventing every shallow and vulgar writer from giving to his compositions (often grounded upon foolish fancies) an air of authority by inserting in them passages from the Bible, interpreted (or rather distorted) into senses as far from the right meaning of Scripture as those authors are near to absurdity who thus ostentatiously[6] adorn their writings[7]. Of such abuses many examples might be produced, but for the present I shall confine myself to two which are germane[8] to these astronomical matters. The first concerns those writings which were published against the existence of the Medicean planets[9] recently discovered by me, in which many passages of holy Scripture were cited. Now that everyone has seen these planets, I should like to know what new interpretations those same antagonists[10] employ in expounding the Scripture and excusing their own simplicity. My other example is that of a man who has lately published, in defiance of astronomers and philosophers, the opinion that the moon does not receive its light from the sun but is brilliant by its own nature. He supports this fancy (or rather thinks he does) by sundry[11] texts of Scripture which he believes cannot be explained unless his theory is true; yet that the moon is inherently dark is surely as plain as daylight.

Milton pays a visit to Galileo at the Villa D'Arcetri near Florence

…

1　**Seneca (c. 4–65 BC):** Roman philosopher, dramatist, and statesman, one of the most eminent writers of the Silver Age of Latin literature

2　**diurnal:** occupying one day

3　**aggregate:** collect

4　**preposterous:** completely contrary to reason

5　**decorum:** proper behavior

6　**ostentatiously:** showing for admiration

7　**take measures for preventing ... adorn their writings:** namely, take measures for preventing …vulgar writer from giving air of authority to his compositions

8　**germane:** relevant

9　**Medicean planets:** name given by Galileo to the satellites of Jupiter

10　**antagonist:** opponent

11　**sundry:** various

If in order to banish the opinion in question[1] from the world it were sufficient to stop the mouth of a single man — as perhaps those men persuade themselves who, measuring the minds of others by their own, think it impossible that this doctrine should be able to continue to find adherents — then that would be very easily done. But things stand otherwise. To carry out such a decision it would be necessary not only to prohibit the book of Copernicus and the writings of other authors who follow the same opinion, but to ban the whole science of astronomy. Furthermore, it would be necessary to forbid men to look at the heavens, in order that they might not see Mars and Venus sometimes quite near the earth and sometimes very distant, the variation being so great that Venus is forty times and Mars sixty times as large at one time as at another. And it would be necessary to prevent Venus from being seen round at one time and forked[2] at another, with very thin horns; as well as many other sensory observations which can never be reconciled with the Ptolemaic system in any way, but are very strong arguments for the Copernican. And to ban Copernicus now that his doctrine is daily reinforced by many new observations and by the learned applying themselves to the reading of his book, after this opin- ion has been allowed and tolerated for these many years during which it was less followed and less confirmed[3], would seem in my judgment to be a contravention[4] of truth, and an attempt to hide and suppress her the more as she revealed herself the more clearly and plainly. Not to abolish and censure his whole book, but only to condemn as erroneous this particular proposition, would (if I am not mistaken) be a still greater detriment[5] to the minds of men, since it would afford them occasion to see a proposition proved that it was heresy to believe. And to prohibit the whole science would be to censure a hundred passages of Holy Scripture which teach us that the glory and greatness of Almighty God are marvelously discerned in all his works and divinely read in the open book of heaven …

Therefore let these men begin to apply themselves to an examination of the arguments of Copernicus and others, leaving condemnation of the doctrine as erroneous and heretical to the proper authorities. Among the circumspect[6] and most wise Fathers, and in the absolute wisdom of one who cannot err, they may never hope to find the rash decisions into which they allow them selves to be hurried by some particular passion or personal interest. With regard to this opinion, and others which are not directly matters of faith, certainly no one doubts that the Supreme Pontiff has always an absolute power to approve or condemn; but it is not in the power of any created being to make things true or false, for this belongs to their own nature[7] and to the fact. Therefore in my judgment one should first be assured of the necessary and immutable truth of the

---

1   **the opinion in question:** Copernicus' and Galileo's opinion
2   **forked:** branching out
3   **less followed and less confirmed:** as it is more and more generally accepted
4   **contravention:** opposition, disputation
5   **detriment:** damage
6   **circumspect:** cautious
7   **their own nature:** nature of things

fact, over which no man has power. This is wiser counsel than to condemn either side in the absence of such certainty, thus depriving oneself of continued authority and ability to choose by determining things which are now undetermined and open and still lodged in the will of supreme authority. And in brief, if it is impossible for a conclusion to be declared heretical while we remain in doubt as to its truth, then these men are wasting their time clamoring[1] for condemnation of the motion of the earth and stability of the sun, which they have not yet demonstrated to be impossible or false. ...

Key Concepts

academic philosophers

celestial motions

celestial orb

geocentricism

heavens

heliocentricism

heresies

Nicholas Copernicus

proper authorities

Ptolemy/Aristotle

purely physical matters/faith

Isaac Newton: The Mathematical Principles of Natural Philosophy

Sir Isaac Newton (1642–1727), English mathematician and physicist whose discoveries and theories laid the foundation for much of the progress in science since his time, "the greatest physicist of all time, with the exception of Albert Einstein." He was one of the inventors of calculus (the other being German mathematician G. W. Leibniz). He also solved the mysteries of light and optics, formulated the three laws of motion, and derived from them the law of universal gravitation. Newton's work was vital to the evolution of modern physics. In fact, many of his theories and conclusions remained free of revisions until the 20th century. When Newton was three years old, his widowed mother remarried, leaving him in the care of his grandmother. Eventually his mother, by then widowed a second time, sent him to a grammar school in Grantham. Later he was sent to Trinity College at the University of Cambridge. Newton received his bachelor's degree in 1665 and master's in 1668. He ignored much of the established curriculum of the university to pursue his

---

1   **clamor:** shout

own interests: mathematics and natural philosophy. Proceeding entirely on his own, he investigated the latest developments in mathematics and the new natural philosophy that treated nature
as a complicated machine. Newton is probably best known for discovering universal gravitation,
which explains that all bodies in space and on earth are affected by the force called gravity. He
published this theory in his book *Philosophiae Naturalis Principia Mathematica* in 1687, which
marked a turning point in the history of science. In 1703 the Royal Society elected Newton president,
an office he held for the rest of his life. In addition to science, Newton also showed an interest in
alchemy[1], mysticism, and theology. Many pages of his notes and writings particularly from the later
years of his career are devoted to these topics.

The Rules of Reasoning in Philosophy

RULE I

We are to admit no more causes of natural things than such as are both true and sufficient
to explain their appearances.[2] **To this purpose the philosophers say that Nature does nothing**
in vain, and more is in vain when less will serve; for Nature is pleased with simplicity, and
affects not the pomp[3] of superfluous causes.

RULE II

Therefore to the same natural effects we must, as far as possible, assign the same causes.

As to respiration in a man and in a beast; the descent of stónes in Europe and in America; the
light of our culinary[4] fire and of the sun; the reflection of light in the earth, and in the planets.

RULE III

The qualities of bodies, which admit neither intensification nor remission of degrees, and
which are found to belong to all bodies within the reach of our experiments, are to be esteemed the
universal qualities of all bodies whatsoever.

For since the qualities of bodies are only known to us by experiments, we are to hold for
universal all such as universally agree with experiments; and such as are not liable to diminution
can never be quite taken away. We are certainly not to relinquish[1] the evidence of experiments for

---

1 **alchemy:** ancient chemistry to change metals into gold
2 **We are to admit … their appearances.:** Compare this statement with Bacon's: "Man …can do and understand
   so much and so much only as he has observed in fact or in thought of the course of nature: beyond this he neither
   knows anything nor can do anything."
3 **pomp:** public display
4 **culinary:** relating to cooking

Heritage of Western Intellectual Tradition — A Sourcebook

the sake of dreams and vain fictions of our own devising; nor are we to recede from the analogy of Nature, which is wont to be simple, and always consonant[2] to itself. **We no other way know the extension of bodies than by our senses, nor do these reach it in all bodies; but because we perceive extension in all that are sensible, therefore we ascribe it universally to all others also.** That abundance of bodies are hard, we learn by experience; and because the hardness of the whole arises from the hardness of the parts, we therefore justly infer the hardness of the undivided particles not only of the bodies we feel but of all others. That all bodies are impenetrable[3], we gather not from reason, but from sensation. The bodies which we handle we find impenetrable, and thence conclude impenetrability to be a universal property of all bodies whatsoever. That all bodies are movable, and endowed with certain powers (which we call the inertia) of persevering in their motion, or in their rest, we only infer from the like properties observed in the bodies which we have seen. The extension, hardness, impenetrability, mobility, and inertia of the whole, result from the extension, hardness, impenetrability, mobility, and inertia of the parts; and hence we conclude the least particles of all bodies to be also all extended, and hard and impenetrable, and movable, and endowed with their proper inertia. And this is the foundation of all philosophy. Moreover, that the divided but contiguous[4] particles of bodies may be separated from one another, is matter of observation; and, in the particles that remain undivided, our minds are able to distinguish yet lesser parts, as is mathematically demonstrated. But whether the parts so distinguished, and not yet divided, may, by the powers of Nature, be actually divided and separated from one another, we cannot certainly determine. Yet, had we the proof of but one experiment that any undivided particle, in breaking a hard and solid body, suffered a division, we might by virtue of this rule conclude that the undivided as well as the divided particles may be divided and actually separated to infinity.

Lastly, if it universally appears, by experiments and astronomical observations, that all bodies about the earth gravitate towards the earth, and that in proportion to the quantity of matter which they severally[5] contain; that the moon likewise, according to the quantity of its matter, gravitates towards the earth; that, on the other hand, our sea gravitates towards the moon; and, all the planets one towards another; and the comets in like manner towards the sun; we must, in consequence of this rule, universally allow that all bodies whatsoever are endowed with a principle of mutual gravitation. For the argument from the appearances concludes with more force for the universal gravitation of all bodies than for their impenetrability; of which, among those in the celestial regions, we have no experiments, nor any manner of observation. Not that I affirm gravity to be essential to bodies: by their vis insita[6] I mean nothing but their inertia. This is immutable. Their

---

1   **relinquish:** give up

2   **consonant:** harmonious

3   **impenetrable:** can not be pierced through

4   **contiguous:** touching, neighboring

5   **severally:** each, separately

6   **vis insita:** innate force of matter, "a power of resisting, by which every body … endeavours to persevere in its present state, whether it be of rest, or of moving uniformly forward in a right line."

gravity is diminished as they recede from the earth.[1]

RULE IV

In experimental philosophy we are to look upon propositions inferred by general induction from phenomena as accurately or very nearly true, notwithstanding any contrary hypotheses that may be imagined, till such time as other phenomena occur, by which they may either be made more accurate, or liable to exceptions[2].

Woolsthorpe Manor where Newton was born

This rule we must follow, that the argument of induction may not be evaded by hypotheses.

Optics

All these things being considered, it seems probable to me, that God in the beginning formed matter in solid, massy, hard, impenetrable, moveable particles, of such sizes and figures, and with such other properties, and in such proportion to space, as most conduced[3] to the end for which he formed them; and that these primitive particles, being solids, are incomparably harder than any porous[4] bodies compounded of them; even so very hard, as never to wear or break in pieces; no ordinary power being able to divide what God himself made one in the first creation. While the particles continue entire, they may compose bodies of one and the same nature and texture in all ages: But should they wear away[5], or break in pieces, the nature of things depending on them would be changed. Water and earth, composed of old worn particles and fragments of particles would not be of the same nature and texture now, with water and earth composed of entire particles in the beginning. And therefore, that nature may be lasting, the changes of corporeal things are to be placed only in the various separations and new associations and motions of these

---

1 Here in this paragraph Newton, like Bacon and Descartes, is talking about the "method" he uses in scientific experimentation, though his is a combination of induction and deduction.

2 **liable to exceptions:** namely, less accurate

3 **conduce:** contribute

4 **porous:** full of pores or tiny holes

5 **wear away:** become less strong

permanent particles; compound bodies being apt to break, not in the midst of solid particles, but where those particles are laid together, and only touch in a few points.

The apple tree that inspired Newton to make one of modern science's greatest discoveries (original tree died in 1814, and grafts were planted elsewhere)

It seems to me farther, that those particles have not only a force of inertia accompanied with such passive laws of motion as naturally result from that force, but also that they are moved by certain active principles, such as is that of gravity, and that which causes fermentation[1], and the cohesion[2] of bodies. These principles I consider, not as occult[3] qualities, supposed to result from the specific forms of things, but as general laws of nature, by which the things themselves are formed; their truth appearing to us by phenomena, though their causes be not yet discovered. For these are manifest qualities, and their causes only are occult. **And the *Aristotelians* gave the name of occult qualities, not to manifest qualities, but to such qualities only as they supposed to lie hid in bodies, and to be the unknown causes of manifest effects: Such as would be the causes of gravity, and of magnetic and electric attractions, and of fermentations, if we should suppose that these forces or actions arose from qualities unknown to us, and uncapable of being discovered and made manifest. Such occult qualities put a stop to the improvement of natural philosophy, and therefore of late years have been rejected.**[4] To tell us that every species of things is endowed with an occult specific quality by which it acts and produces manifest effects, is to tell us nothing: **But to derive two or three general principles of motion from phenomena, and afterwards to tell us how the properties and actions of all corporeal things follow from those manifest principles, would be a very great step in philosophy, though the causes of those principles were not yet discovered**: And therefore I scruple[5] not to propose the principles of motion abovementioned, they being of very general extent, and leave their causes to be found out.

Now by the help of these principles, all material things seem to have been composed of the hard and solid particles abovementioned, variously associated in the first creation by the counsel of an intelligent agent[6]. For it became him who created them to set them in order. And

1   **fermentation:** unrest, expansion
2   **cohesion:** sticking together
3   **occult:** hidden
4   **Such occult qualities ... have been rejected.:** Newton is criticizing the mysticism in Scholastic philosophy.
5   **scruple:** hesitate
6   **intelligent agent:** God

if he did so, it's unphilosophical to seek for any other origin of the world, or to pretend that it might arise out of a chaos by the mere laws of nature; though being once formed, it may continue by those laws for many ages. For while comets move in very eccentric[1] orbs in all manner of positions, blind fate could never make all the planets move one and the same way in orbs concentric[1], some inconsiderable irregularities excepted, which may have risen from the mutual actions of comets and planets upon one another, and which will be apt to increase, till this System wants a reformation. Such a wonderful uniformity in the planetary system must be allowed the effect of choice. And so much the uniformity in the bodies of animals, they having generally a right and a left side shaped alike, and on either side of their bodies two legs behind, and either two arms, or two legs, or two wings before their shoulders, a neck running down into a backbone, and a head upon it; and in the head two ears, two eyes, a nose, a mouth, and a tongue, alike situated. Also the first contrivance[2] of those very artificial parts of animals, the eyes, ears, brain, muscles, heart, lungs, midriff, glands, larynx, hands, wings, swimming bladders, natural spectacles[3], and other organs of sense and motion; **and the instinct of brutes and insects, can be the effect of nothing else than the wisdom and skill of a powerful ever-living agent, who being in all places, is more able by his will to move the bodies within his boundless uniform sensorium[4], and thereby to form and reform the parts of the universe, than we are by our will to move the parts of our bodies.** And yet we are not to consider the world as the body of God, or the several parts thereof, as the parts of God. He is a uniform being, void of organs, members or parts, and they are his creatures subordinate to him, and subservient[5] to his will; and he is no more the soul of them, than the soul of man is the soul of the species of things carried through the organs of sense into the place of its sensation, where it perceives them by means of its immediate presence, without the intervention of any third thing. The organs of sense are not for enabling the soul to perceive the species of things in its sensorium, but only for conveying them thither; and God has no need of such organs, he being everywhere present to the things themselves. And since space is divisible *in infinitum*[6], and matter is not necessarily in all places, it may be also allowed that God is able to create particles of matter of several sizes and figures, and in several proportions to space, and perhaps of different densities and forces, and thereby to vary the laws of nature, and make worlds of several sorts in several parts of the universe. At least, I see nothing of contradiction in all this.

---

1   **eccentric:** not having the same center, not circular; **concentric:** having a common center
2   **contrivance:** invention
3   **natural spectacles:** eye-sight
4   **sensorium:** entire sensory system of the body
5   **subservient:** obedient
6   *in infinitum*: endlessly, infinitely

Heritage of Western Intellectual Tradition   A Sourcebook

As in mathematics, so in natural philosophy, the investigation of difficult things by the method of analysis, ought ever to precede the method of composition. This analysis consists in making experiments and observations, and in drawing general conclusions from them by induction and admitting of no objections against the conclusions, but such as are taken from experiments, or other certain truths. For hypotheses are not to be regarded in experimental philosophy. And although the arguing from experiments and observations by induction be no demonstration of general conclusions; yet it is the best way of arguing which the nature of things admits of, and may be looked upon as so much the stronger, by how much the induction is more general. And if no exception occur from phenomena, the conclusion may be pronounced generally. But if at any time afterwards any exception shall occur from experiments, it may then begin to be pronounced with such exceptions as occur. By this way of analysis we may proceed from compounds to ingredients, and from motions to the forces producing them; and in general, from effects to their causes, and from particular causes to more general ones, till the argument ends in the most general. **This is the method of analysis: And the synthesis consists in assuming the causes discovered, and established as principles, and by them explaining the phenomena proceeding from them, and proving the explanations.**

Key Concepts

causes	observation
experimental philosophy	organ of sense
hypothesis	particles
method of analysis	reason/sensation
natural philosophy	simplicity
Nature	

Compare with China

Development of Science in Ancient China

The following timetable shows the approximate progress in the advancement of science in China, and many of its inventions, as we can see, are far ahead that of her European counterparts.

Time lag between some Chinese inventions and their adoption in the West	-1000	-500	0	500	1000	1500	2000
iron plows		• click for text					
cast iron		•					
harness for horses		•					
stirrup			•				
paper		•					
printing – block printing				•			
printing – movable type					•		
porcelain				•			
ship's rudder				•			
compass		•					
crossbow		•					
gunpowder				•			
guns					•		

(www.hyperhistory.com/.../ chinese_inventions.html)

The most valuable Chinese inventions in the history are compass, paper, printing and gun powder. These four inventions have influenced profoundly human life for thousands of years.

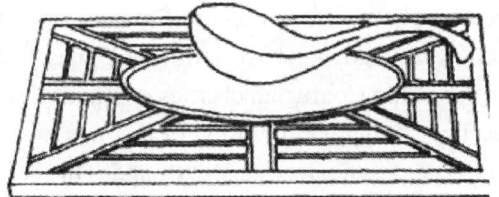

While mining ores and melting copper and iron, people chanced upon a natural magnetite that attracted iron and pointed fixedly north. A compass which uses the nature of a magnetic needle pointing always to the magnetic north due to terrestrial magnetism is an essential tool to determine the location and the direction of a voyager traveling a long distance. Dr. Needham cites one

Sinan (Warring States Period) the earliest guide tool in the world

of the first books to describe the magnetic compass, *Dream Pool Essays* (《梦溪笔谈》 1086) by Shen Kuo in the Song Dynasty, about 100 years earlier than its first record in Europe by Alexander Neekam in 1190. In fact magnetic nature to point to the earthen north was known to the Chinese earlier than to the Europeans. Written in "Lun Heng" (*Discourse Weighed in Balance* 《论衡》), the oldest literature describing the nature of a magnet in the history and written by Wang Chong (王充 c. 27–100) of the Eastern Han are such passages as "lodestone attracts a needle" and "the scoop of Sanam (奚氧)." The book also says that lodestone made in the shape of a scoop is called the scoop of Sanam, and that the head of lodestone placed on the table points to the south. The fact that a magnet means "the stone of Magnesia" indicates that its discovery had been already made before 1,000 BC, but the Chinese used it as a compass for the first time. Compasses contributed greatly to the voyage of the Western vessels all over the earth in the 14th century, whence voyage without them couldn't be imagined. The compass was introduced to the Arab world and Europe during the Northern Song Dynasty (960–1127). Most of today's ships are furnished with the GPS (global positioning system), but when the system is disabled, compasses regain their prestige.

China was the first nation to invent paper. Before its invention, words were written on various natural materials by ancient peoples — on grass stalks by the Egyptians, on earthen plates by the Mesopotamians, on tree leaves by the Indians, on sheepskin by the Europeans and strangest of all, even inscribed on bamboo or wooden strips, tortoise shells or shoulder blades of an ox by the early Chinese. Later, inspired by the process of silk reeling, the people in ancient China succeeded in first making a kind of paper called "bo" out of silk. But its production was expensive due to the scarcity of materials. In the early days of the 2nd century, a court official named Cai Lun produced a new kind of paper from bark, rags, wheat stalks and other materials. It was relatively cheap, light, thin, durable and more suitable for brush writing. Archeological evidence, however, shows that paper was in use two hundred years before then. Either way, the Chinese were significantly ahead of the rest of the world. At the beginning of the 3rd century, the paper making process first spread to Korea and then to Japan. It reached the Arab world in the Tang Dynasty, and Europe in the 12th century. In the 16th century, it went to America by way of Europe and then gradually spread all over the world.

The process of making paper

Before the invention of printing, dissemination of knowledge depended either on word of mouth or handwritten copies of manuscripts. Both took time and were liable to error. Beginning 2,000 years ago in the Western Han Dynasty (206 BC–25 AD), stone-tablet rubbing was in vogue for spreading Confucian classics or Buddhist sutras[1]. This led in the Sui Dynasty (581–618) to the practice of engraving writing or pictures on a wooden board, smearing it with ink and then printing on pieces of paper page-by-page. This became known as block printing. The first book with a verifiable date of printing appeared in China in the year 868, or nearly 600 years before that happened in Europe. In the Tang Dynasty (618–907), this technology was gradually introduced to Korea, Japan, Vietnam, and the Philippines. Yet block printing had its drawbacks. All the boards became useless after the printing was done and a single mistake in carving could ruin a whole block. In 1041–1048 of the Song Dynasty (960–1279), a man named Bi Sheng carved individual characters on identical pieces of fine clay which he hardened by a slow baking process, resulting in pieces of movable type. When the printing was finished, the pieces of type were put away for future use. This technology then spread to Korea, Japan, Vietnam and Europe. Later, German Johann Gutenberg invented movable type made of metal in 1440–1448.[2]

Credit for the invention of gunpowder also goes to ancient China. Ancient necromancers[3] discovered in their practice of alchemy, that an explosion could be induced if certain kinds of ores and fuel were mixed in the right proportions and heated, thus leading to the invention of gunpowder. In the *Collection of the Most Important Military Techniques* (《武经总要》), edited in 1044 by

---

1   **sutra:** records of the oral teachings of Buddha, assembled into Buddhist texts

2   The invention of printing as a practical technology, unlike the other three inventions, could be traced to people outside China. Movable type made from molds was invented separately by the Koreans in the 14th century, for instance, and German printer Johannes Gutenberg (c. 1400–68BC) was considered to be the inventor of Western printing in the use of movable type. But the Chinese were obviously the earliest to make use of it.

3   **necromancer:** person who practices necromancy, or communicating with the dead to learn about future

Zeng Gongliang (曾公亮 998–1078), three formulas for making gunpowder were recorded; an explosive mixture of saltpeter, sulfur and charcoal. Dr. Needham[1] identified these as the earliest formulas of such a kind. The method of powder-making was introduced to the Arab world in the 12th century and to Europe in the 14th. Gunpowder was originally used for making fireworks and its later adaptation revolutionized warfare across the world.

In the field of astronomy, the Chinese were one of the earliest peoples to keep systematic record of their observations of the heavens. Sitings and records of these sitings go back over forty centuries. The Chinese observed sunspots, meteorites, eclipses and comets which they called "guest stars." They also observed rare events such as the splitting of comets as the record of 896 CE from the Tang Dynasty indicates, and meteorite showers. The earliest account of the latter exists in *The Chronicles of Zuo Ming* regarding such a shower in 687 BCE. The Chinese were also one of

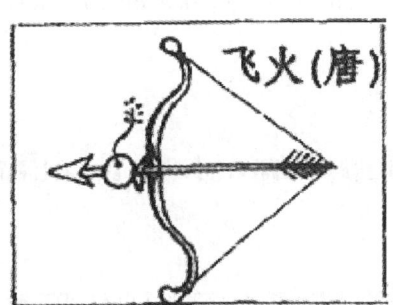

Flying firearrows Tang Dynasty

the earliest people to make star maps: Shi Shen, an astronomer, cataloged an eight-volume series of his observations of the heavens in the 4th century BC. The earliest known Western star maps were made by the Greek astronomer Hiparchus in 2 BC. In addition to their observations and records of the heavens, the Chinese also developed highly sophisticated navigational systems based on the stars. Chinese sailors in the 3rd century BC were already able to find their bearings using the Great Dipper and the North Pole. In conjunction with their observations of the heavens the Chinese also built planetariums, and various instruments including armillaries for measuring the celestial coordinates. Scientists reading the records estimate that the Chinese were probably using an armillary to map the heavens by the 4th century BC. This wood-block printed book from 1633, an expansion of one printed in 1461, illustrates Chinese theories of early astronomy in the Tang (618–907) and Song (960–1279) Dynasties, when there was great interest in celestial phenomena. The armillary sphere shown indicates the motions of the sun and moon, as well as the stars and constellations. Also, the four seasons are arranged in order according to their progressions and retrogradations.

Chinese characters carved in relief on a small block of moistened clay which, hardened by fire, became durable

In Chinese history, the study of astronomy was inseparable from mathematics. From the earliest times, the Chinese, according to Joseph Needham, were far in advance of contemporary civilizations such as those of Egypt, Babylon, Greece and Rome. There is evidence for instance, that the Chinese had mastered the decimal system since the dawn of history. The earliest treatise on mathematics, *Zhoubi Suanjing* was probably written during the Zhou Dynasty between 1030–1022 BCE. During the Han Dynasty (221 BC–220 AD) several mathematical treatises were compiled by distin-

---

1   **Joseph Needham (李约瑟, 1900–1995):** sinologist, best known for his 7 volume *Science and Civilisation in China*

guished mathematicians such as Liu Hui whose *Haidao Suanjing* (*The Sea and Island Mathematical Manual*) appeared sometime around 220 AD. The dual studies in astronomy and mathematics would result in some of the most remarkable inventions including the astronomical clock by the astronomer Su Song over nine hundred years ago. In the 2nd century AD the famous astronomer Shang Heng devised a mobile water-driven globe which revolved in correspondence with the movements of the heavenly bodies.

Supplementary Reading

One peculiarity common to almost all Renaissance and Enlightenment thinkers is the tendency to be observant and analytical. In other words, the age of science and inquiry went hand in hand with a sense of being critical and independent, and the ability to find the "method" for it. The following essay discusses critical thinking as a vital part of university education.

Critical Thinking

Critical thinking is an important and vital topic in modern education. All educators are interested in teaching critical thinking to their students. Many academic departments hope that its professors and instructors will become informed about the strategy of teaching critical thinking skills, identify areas in one's courses as the proper place to emphasize and teach critical thinking, and develop and use some problems in exams that test students' critical thinking skills.

The purpose of specifically teaching critical thinking in the sciences or any other discipline is to improve the thinking skills of students and thus better prepare them to succeed in the world. But, you may ask, don't we automatically teach critical thinking when we teach our subjects, especially mathematics and science, the two disciplines which supposedly epitomize[1] correct and logical thinking? The answer, sadly, is often no. Please consider these two quotations:

"It is strange that we expect students to learn, yet seldom teach them anything about learning."
"We should be teaching students how to think. Instead, we are teaching them what to think."

Perhaps you can now see the problem. All education consists of transmitting to students two different things: (1) the subject matter or discipline content of the course ("what to think"), and (2) the correct way to understand and evaluate this subject matter ("how to think"). We do an excellent job of transmitting the content of our respective academic disciplines, but we often fail to teach students how to think effectively about this subject matter, that is, how to properly understand and evaluate it. This second ability is termed critical thinking.

---

1   **epitomize:** make an epitome or a typical example of

While we as professors have the ability ourselves to think critically (we had to learn these skills to earn advanced degrees in our disciplines), many students — including our own — never develop critical thinking skills. Why? There are a number of reasons. The first goal of education, "what to think," is so traditionally obvious that instructors and students may focus all their energies and efforts on the task of transmitting and acquiring basic knowledge. Indeed, many students find that this goal alone is so overwhelming that they have time for little else. On the other hand, the second goal of education, "how to think" or critical thinking, is often so subtle that instructors fail to recognize it and students fail to realize its absence.

In retrospect, it seems obvious that when the information content of a discipline increases, it becomes even more vital to spend time, not learning more information, but learning methods to acquire, understand, and evaluate this information and the great amount of new information that is not known now but will surely follow. Frankly, it is counterproductive to simply memorize and learn more new and isolated facts when future facts may eventually displace these. Thus, our science education policy has been completely backward, teaching more science facts and less scientific method rather than the converse. The errors of primary and secondary education in math, science, and other disciplines during the last forty years are now well known and are currently being addressed. The latest science books, for example, emphasize critical thinking and the scientific method. They focus on teaching students the proper ways to obtain new reliable knowledge for one's self, not on engendering factual overload.

Definition of Critical Thinking

Critical thinking means correct thinking in the pursuit of relevant and reliable knowledge about the world. Another way to describe it is reasonable, reflective, responsible, and skillful thinking that is focused on deciding what to believe or do. A person who thinks critically can ask appropriate questions, gather relevant information, efficiently and creatively sort through this information, reason logically from this information, and come to reliable and trustworthy conclusions about the world that enable one to live and act successfully in it. Critical thinking is not being able to process information well enough to know to stop for red lights or whether you received the correct change at the supermarket. Such low-order thinking, critical and useful though it may be, is sufficient only for personal survival; most individuals master this. True critical thinking is higher-order thinking, enabling a person to, for example, responsibly judge between political candidates, serve on a murder trial jury, evaluate society's need for nuclear power plants, and assess the consequences of global warming. Critical thinking enables an individual to be a responsible citizen who contributes to society, and not be merely a consumer of society's distractions.

Critical thinking can be described as the scientific method applied by ordinary people to the ordinary world. This is true because critical thinking mimics[1] the well-known method of scientific investigation: a question is identified, a hypothesis formulated, relevant data sought and gathered,

---

1 **mimic:** resemble

Heritage of Western Intellectual Tradition   A Sourcebook

the hypothesis is logically tested and evaluated, and reliable conclusions are drawn from the result. All of the skills of scientific investigation are matched by critical thinking, which is therefore nothing more than scientific method used in everyday life rather than in specifically scientific disciplines or endeavors. It may be that a workable society or culture can tolerate only a small number of critical thinkers, that learning, internalizing, and practicing scientific and critical thinking is discouraged. Most people are followers of authority: most do not question, are not curious, and do not challenge authority figures who claim special knowledge or insight. Most people, therefore, do not think for themselves, but rely on others to think for them. Most people indulge in wishful, hopeful, and emotional thinking, believing that what they believe is true because they wish it, hope it, or feel it to be true. Most people, therefore, do not think critically.

Raymond S. Nickerson (1987), an authority on critical thinking, characterizes a good critical thinker in terms of knowledge, abilities, attitudes, and habitual ways of behaving. Here are some of the characteristics of such a thinker:

organizes thoughts and articulates them concisely and coherently

distinguishes between logically valid and invalid inferences

suspends judgment in the absence of sufficient evidence to support a decision

attempts to anticipate the probable consequences of alternative actions

can structure informally represented problems in such a way that formal techniques, such as mathematics, can be used to solve them

can strip a verbal argument of irrelevancies and phrase it in its essential terms

habitually questions one's own views and attempts to understand both the assumptions that are critical to those views and the implications of the views

is sensitive to the difference between the validity of a belief and the intensity with which it is held

is aware of the fact that one's understanding is always limited, often much more so than would be apparent to one with a noninquiring attitude

Questions for Discussion

1. What is the purpose of Galileo's letter to Christina? How did Galileo go about defending himself?

2. The most influential 20th century German dramatist Bertolt Brecht (1898–1956) wrote *Galileo* shortly after WWII (1947), where Galileo is depicted as one with the responsibility of the intellectual to defend his beliefs in face of opposition from established authorities.

Heritage of Western Intellectual Tradition   A Sourcebook

Discuss Galileo as a modern intellectual.

3. Galileo made major contributions to physics by advancing use of mathematics to understand "how nature is": "Philosophy [science] is written in this grand book, the universe, which stands continually open to our gaze … but this book cannot be understood unless one learns to comprehend the language and read the letters in which it is composed. It is written in the language of mathematics and its characters are triangles, circles and other geometric figures without which it is humanly impossible to understand nature." Comment on this statement of Galileo's.

4. Newton was a figure of undisputed genius and innovation in optics, mechanics and mathematics. What is less well known, however, is that he was devoutly religious and in his view the system of the universe could only proceed from the counsel and dominion of an intelligent and powerful agent. Comment on the role of his religious belief in his scientific research.

5. Comment on the following remark and discuss:

For over two thousand years China held an outstanding record in technological development and the sciences. In China's scientific heyday, however, she was, according to Joseph Needham, "far in advance of contemporary Europe." By the 15th century, however, she went into a decline in terms of making any further advancements in these areas.

UNIT 9

Modern Political Science

Pretest

- What do you know about the English Revolution?
- In what sense is the political science represented by Thomas Hobbes and John Locke meaningful?
- Comment on Locke's ideas concerning the state and the individual.

What You Will Learn in This Unit

- Some knowledge about the Puritan Revolution;
- Important selections from Thomas Hobbes and John Locke; and
- Locke Talking about China and the Chinese.

Learn to Pronounce

automaton /ɔːˈtɒmətən/ 自动装置
Enlightenment /ɪnˈlaɪtənmənt/ 启蒙
John Locke /lɒk/ 洛克
Leviathan /lɪˈvaɪəθən/ 海中怪兽
monarchy /ˈmɒnəkɪ/ 君王政体，君主制
Oliver Cromwell /ˈkrɒmwəl/ 克伦威尔
Presbyterian Scots /ˌprezbɪˈtɪərɪən skɒts/
　信奉基督教长老会的苏格兰人

Puritanism /ˈpjʊərɪtənɪzəm/ 清教主义
regicide /ˈredʒɪsaɪd/ 弑君
royal prerogative /prɪˈrɒgətɪv/ 皇家特权
The Hague /heɪg/ 海牙
Thomas Hobbes /hɒbz/ 霍布斯

Introduction

Political science focuses on the description of the processes by which people and institutions exercise and resist political power, and on an analysis of the formulation of policies, influence of individuals and institutions, and organization of societies. The turbulent period of the Great Britain in the 17th century offered a chance for the development of political science, marked by the English Revolution, also called the Puritan Revolution, from the 1640s to 1660s, plus 40 years as preparation and aftermath of this revolution. It began with the calling of the Long Parliament by King Charles I and proceeded through two civil wars, the trial and execution of the king, the republican experiments of Oliver Cromwell, the restoration of King Charles II, and, ultimately, the Glorious Revolution. The causes of the conflict can be traced to social, economic, constitutional, and religious developments over a century or more. Closer at hand were issues of sovereignty in the English state and Puritanism in the church. Charles's attempt (1637) to impose the Anglican liturgy in Scotland led to the riot in the Presbyterian Scots, whose army occupied the northern counties of England in 1640. English parliament demanded religious and political reform as the price for support of Charles' war against the Scots. The political quarrel became an armed conflict in 1642. Oliver Cromwell led his forces to victory against Charles I. The defeat and subsequent execution of the king left Cromwell as virtual dictator of England. Cromwell died on September 3, 1658, and the drift toward anarchy was halted by General George Monck, commander of the army in Scotland who marched into London with his troops and recalled the Long Parliament, which then restored (May, 1660) Charles II to the throne. The English Revolution was the first of the so-called great revolutions, followed by the Glorious Revolution, so called because, unlike that of 1640 to 1660, it was bloodless and successful: Parliament was sovereign and England prosperous. John Locke's *Two Treatises of Government* (1690) provided an attractive theoretical justification for it. The whole revolution was important because it generated new political and religious ideas and because it extended the English tradition that the government's power should be limited.

Thomas Hobbes: Leviathan*

Thomas Hobbes (1588 – 1679), English philosopher and political theorist, is best known for his

---

*　Leviathan, a Hebrew name for huge monster, is represented in the Bible as crocodile, whale, or sea-serpent. Here it is the symbol of an absolute state. Upon this image Hobbes intends to build a comprehensive theory of government and social structure, "the first great general and comprehensive political philosophy produced by an English thinker."

publications on individual security and the social contract. Hobbes lived during the most tumultuous times in European history, hence his pessimistic theories regarding human nature. Young Thomas

at 4 was able to read and write, at 6 learned Greek and Latin, and at 14 translated Euripides' *Medea* into Latin iambics. At 14 he entered Magdalen College, Oxford, and took a B.A. five years later. But Oxford did not impress him, and he was appalled at the "frequency of insignificant speech" he heard there. Starting from 1609 he made several tours through France and Italy, met and talked with advanced thinkers of the time, including Galileo and Descartes. He wrote a treatise, privately circulated in 1640, *The Elements of Law, Natural and Politic* in defense of the royal prerogative. Fearing that Parliament might have him arrested, he fled to Paris, where he remained in exile for 11 years. His best-known work *Leviathan; or The Matter, Form, & Power of a Commonwealth Ecclesiastical and Civil* (1651) is a forceful exposition of his doctrine of sovereignty. He maintained that a subject had the right to abandon a ruler who could no longer protect him and to transfer his allegiance to one who could; but this statement in Leviathan gave serious offense to Prince Charles' advisers. At the end of 1651, he returned to England and made peace with the new regime. In 1660, when the Commonwealth ended and his former pupil acceded to the throne, Hobbes again came into favor. Hobbes sees people as rational machines governed by passions combined with reason. One passion that never ceases to delight an individual is his superiority over other people. People will by all means compete for this superiority — hence natural right to self-preservation. Security is achieved through the law of nature or good behaviour of his fellows by creating a power sufficient to keep them in awe and to counterbalance the pre-political "state of nature." This power is created if each individual promises every other individual that he will carry out whatever commands some selected person (or an assembly) shall consider necessary for the peace and defense of all. The sovereign's right will be as absolute as its power; it is responsible only to God. It cannot be unjust to its subjects, since they have authorized its actions.

The Introduction

NATURE (the art whereby God hath made and governs the world) is by the art of man, as in many other things, so in this also imitated, that it can make an artificial animal. For seeing life is but a motion of limbs, the beginning whereof is in some principal part within, why may we not say that all *automata* (engines that move themselves by springs and wheels as doth a watch) have an artificial life? For what is the heart, but a *spring*; and the *nerves*, but so many *strings*; and the *joints*, but so many *wheels*, giving motion to the whole body, such as was intended by the Artificer[1]? *Art* goes yet further, imitating that rational and most excellent

---

1 **intended by the Artificer:** just as the art with which God makes man

work of Nature, *man*. **For by art is created that great LEVIATHAN called a COMMONWEALTH, or STATE (in Latin, CIVITAS), which is but an artificial man, though of greater stature and strength than the natural, for whose[1] protection and defence it was intended;** and in which the *sovereignty* is an artificial *soul*, as giving life and motion to the whole body; the *magistrates* and other *officers* of judicature[2] and execution, artificial *joints*; *reward* and *punishment* (by which[3] fastened to the seat of the sovereignty, every joint and member is moved to perform his duty) are the *nerves*, that do the same in the body natural; the *wealth* and *riches* of all the particular members are the *strength*; *salus populi* (the *people's safety*) its *business*; counsellors, by whom all things needful for it to know are suggested unto it, are the *memory*; *equity* and *laws*, an artificial *reason* and *will*; *concord*, *health*; *sedition*[4], *sickness*; and *civil war*, *death*[5]. Lastly, the *pacts* and *covenants*, by which the parts of this body politic were at first made, set together, and united, resemble that fiat[6], or the *Let us make man*, pronounced by God in the Creation.

...

Chapter XIII   Of the Natural Condition of Mankind
as Concerning Their Felicity[7], and Misery

NATURE hath made men so equal in the faculties of body and mind as that, though there be found one man sometimes manifestly[8] stronger in body or of quicker mind than another, yet when all is reckoned[9] together the difference between man and man is not so considerable as that one man can thereupon claim to himself any benefit to which another may not pretend[10] as well as he. For as to the strength of body, the weakest has strength enough to kill the strongest, either by secret machination[11] or by confederacy with others that are in the same danger with himself.

And as to the faculties of the mind, setting aside the arts grounded upon words, and especially that skill of proceeding upon general and infallible rules, called science, which very few have and but in few things, as being not a native faculty born with us, nor attained, as prudence[12], while we look after somewhat else, I find yet a greater equality amongst men than that of strength. For prudence is but experience, which equal time equally bestows on all men in

---

1 **whose:** i.e., man's

2 **judicature:** administration of justice

3 **which:** joints

4 **sedition:** rebellious action

5 *equity* **and** *laws* **... death:** Verb "be" is omitted here.

6 **fiat:** creed, order

7 **felicity:** contentment, happiness

8 **manifestly:** obviously

9 **reckon:** consider

10 **pretend:** claim. Similar claims in man's equality of faculty can be found elsewhere. Cf. Martin Luther and René Descartes.

11 **machination:** evil plot

12 **which very few ... as prudence:** namely, unlike prudence, which is native faculty born with us or can be attained

those things they equally apply themselves unto. That which may perhaps make such equality incredible is but a vain conceit of one's own wisdom, which almost all men think they have in a greater degree than the vulgar; that is, than all men but themselves, and a few others, whom by fame, or for concurring with[1] themselves, they approve. **For such is the nature of men that howsoever they may acknowledge many others to be more witty, or more eloquent or more learned, yet they will hardly believe there be many so wise as themselves; for they see their own wit at hand, and other men's at a distance.** But this proveth rather that men are in that point equal[2], than unequal. For there is not ordinarily a greater sign of the equal distribution of anything than that every man is contented with his share.

The Sea monster Leviathan

From this equality of ability ariseth equality of hope in the attaining of our ends. And therefore if any two men desire the same thing, which nevertheless they cannot both enjoy, they become enemies; and in the way to their end (which is principally their own conservation[3], and sometimes their delectation[4] only) endeavour to destroy or subdue one another. And from hence it comes to pass that where an invader hath no more to fear than another man's single power, if one plant, sow, build, or possess a convenient seat, others may probably be expected to come prepared with forces united to dispossess and deprive him, not only of[5] the fruit of his labour, but also of his life or liberty. And the invader again is in the like danger of another.[6]

And from this diffidence[7] of one another, there is no way for any man to secure himself so reasonable as anticipation; that is, by force, or wiles[8], to master the persons of all men he can so long till he see no other power great enough to endanger him: and this is no more than his own conservation requireth, and is generally allowed. Also, because there be some that, taking pleasure in contemplating their own power in the acts of conquest, which they pursue farther than their security requires, if others, that otherwise would be glad to be at ease within modest bounds, should not by invasion increase their power, they would not be able, long time, by standing only on their defence, to subsist[9]. And by consequence, such aug-

---

1   **concur with:** agree with
2   **equal:** the same
3   **conservation:** here well-being, life
4   **delectation:** enjoyment
5   **deprive him, not only of:** deprive him of not only ...
6   **And the invader again is in the like danger of another.:** Invader himself has the same danger of being deprived of his fruit of labour ...
7   **diffidence:** suspicion
8   **wile:** trick, cunning
9   **they would not ... to subsist:** Namely, those who do not increase their power would not be able to survive because other people have increased their power. **subsist:** survive

mentation[1] of dominion over men being necessary to a man's conservation, it ought to be allowed him.

Again, men have no pleasure (but on the contrary a great deal of grief) in keeping company where there is no power able to overawe them all. For every man looketh that his companion should value him at the same rate he sets upon himself, and upon all signs of contempt or undervaluing naturally endeavours, as far as he dares (which amongst them that have no common power to keep them in quiet is far enough to make them destroy each other), to extort[2] a greater value from his contemners, by damage; and from others, by the example[3].

So that in the nature of man, we find three principal causes of quarrel. First, competition; secondly, diffidence; thirdly, glory.

The first maketh men invade for gain; the second, for safety; and the third, for reputation. The first use violence, to make themselves masters of other men's persons, wives, children, and cattle; the second, to defend them; the third, for trifles, as a word, a smile, a different opinion, and any other sign of undervalue, either direct in their persons or by reflection in their kindred[4], their friends, their nation, their profession, or their name.

Hereby it is manifest that during the time men live without a common power to keep them all in awe, they are in that condition which is called war; and such a war as is of every man against every man[5]. For war consisteth not in battle only, or the act of fighting, but in a tract of time, wherein the will to contend by battle is sufficiently known: and therefore the notion of time is to be considered in the nature of war, as it is in the nature of weather. For as the nature of foul weather lieth not in a shower or two of rain, but in an inclination thereto of many days together: so the nature of war consisteth not in actual fighting, but in the known disposition thereto during all the time there is no assurance to the contrary. All other time is peace.

Whatsoever therefore is consequent to a time of war, where every man is enemy to every man, the same consequent to the time wherein men live without other security than what their own strength and their own invention shall furnish them withal[6]. In such condition there is no place for industry, because the fruit thereof is uncertain: and consequently no culture of the earth; no navigation, nor use of the commodities that may be imported by sea; no commodious[7] building; no instruments of moving and removing such things as require much force; no knowledge of the face of the earth; no account of time; no arts; no letters; no society; and which is worst of all, continual fear, and danger of violent death; and the life of man, solitary, poor, nasty,

---

1 **augmentation:** increase
2 **extort:** obtain by force
3 **the example:** the way he deals with his contemnors
4 **kindred:** relatives
5 **such a war as is of every man against every man:** such as a war of every man against every man is
6 **withal:** with
7 **commodious:** spacious

Heritage of Western Intellectual Tradition   A Sourcebook

brutish, and short.[1]

...

To this war of every man against every man, this also is consequent; that nothing can be unjust. The notions of right and wrong, justice and injustice, have there no place. Where there is no common power, there is no law; where no law, no injustice. Force and fraud[2] are in war the two cardinal[3] virtues. Justice and injustice are none of the faculties neither of the body nor mind[4]. If they were, they might be in a man that were alone in the world, as well as his senses and passions. They are qualities that relate to men in society, not in solitude. It is consequent also to the same condition that there be no propriety, no dominion, no mine and thine distinct[5]; but only that to be every man's that he can get, and for so long as he can keep it. And thus much for the ill condition which man by mere nature is actually placed in; though with a possibility to come out of it, consisting partly in the passions, partly in his reason.

The passions that incline men to peace are: fear of death; desire of such things as are necessary to commodious living; and a hope by their industry to obtain them. And reason suggesteth convenient articles of peace upon which men may be drawn to agreement. These articles are they which otherwise are called the laws of nature, whereof I shall speak more particularly in the two following chapters.

Chapter XIV   Of the First and Second natural Laws, and of Contracts

The right of nature, which writers commonly call *jus naturale*, is the liberty each man hath to use his own power as he will himself for the preservation of his own nature; that is to say, of his own life; and consequently, of doing anything which, in his own judgement and reason, he shall conceive to be the aptest means thereunto.

By liberty is understood, according to the proper signification of the word, the absence of external impediments[6]; which impediments may oft take away part of a man's power to do what he would, but cannot hinder him from using the power left him according as his judgement and reason shall dictate to him.

A law of nature, *lex naturalis*, is a precept, or general rule, found out by reason, by which a man is forbidden to do that which is destructive of his life, or taketh away the means of preserving the same, and to omit that by which he thinketh it[7] may be best preserved. For though

---

1 **In such condition ... and short.:** Compare this gloomy picture of man's nature with that described in people like Machiavelli.

2 **fraud:** deception

3 **cardinal:** chief

4 **none of the faculties neither of the body nor mind:** not the faculties of the body or mind

5 **no mine and thine distinct:** no personal difference

6 **impediment:** hindrance, obstacle

7 **it:** his life

they that speak of this subject use to confound *jus* and *lex*, *right* and *law*, yet they ought to be distinguished, because right consisteth in liberty to do, or to forbear; whereas law determineth and bindeth to one of them: so that law and right differ as much as obligation and liberty, which in one and the same matter are inconsistent.

And because the condition of man (as hath been declared in the precedent chapter) is a condition of war of every one against every one, in which case every one is governed by his own reason, and there is nothing he can make use of that may not be a help unto him in preserving his life against his enemies; it followeth that in such a condition every man has a right to every thing, even to one another's body. And therefore, as long as this natural right of every man to every thing endureth, there can be no security to any man, how strong or wise soever he be, of[1] living out the time which nature ordinarily alloweth men to live. And consequently it is a precept, or general rule of reason: *that every man ought to endeavour peace, as far as he has hope of obtaining it; and when he cannot obtain it, that he may seek and use all helps and advantages of war.* The first branch of which rule containeth the first and fundamental law of nature, which is: *to seek peace and follow it.* The second, the sum of the right of nature, which is: *by all means we can to defend ourselves.*

From this fundamental law of nature, by which men are commanded to endeavour peace, is derived this second law: *that **a man be willing, when others are so too, as far forth as for peace and defence of himself he shall think it necessary, to lay down this right to all things; and be contented with so much liberty against other men as he would allow other men against himself.*** For as long as every man holdeth this right, of doing anything he liketh; so long are all men in the condition of war. But if other men will not lay down their right, as well as he, then there is no reason for anyone to divest[2] himself of his: for that were to expose himself to prey, which no man is bound to, rather than to dispose himself to peace. This is that law of the gospel: *Whatsoever you require that others should do to you, that do ye to them.* And that law of all men, *quod tibi fieri non vis, alteri ne feceris*[3].

To *lay down* a man's *right* to anything is to divest himself of the *liberty* of hindering another of the benefit[4] of his own right to the same. For he that renounceth or passeth away his right giveth not to any other man a right which he had not before, because there is nothing to which every man had not right by nature, but only standeth out of his way that he may enjoy his own original right without hindrance from him, not without hindrance from another. So that the effect which redoundeth[5] to one man by another man's defect of right is but so much diminution of impediments to the use of his own right original.

---

1 **of:** security ... of
2 **divest:** take away from
3 *quod tibi fieri non vis, alteri ne feceris:* Namely, whatsoever you require that others should do to you, that do ye to them.
4 **hindering another of the benefit:** taking away the benefit from another
5 **redound:** increase

Heritage of Western Intellectual Tradition   A Sourcebook

Right is laid aside, either by simply renouncing it, or by transferring it to another. By *simply* renouncing, when he cares not to whom the benefit thereof redoundeth. By transferring, when he intendeth the benefit thereof to some certain person or persons. And when a man hath in either manner abandoned or granted away his right, then is he said to be obliged, or bound, not to hinder those to whom such right is granted, or abandoned, from the benefit of it: and that he *ought*, and it is duty, not to make void that voluntary act of his own: and that such hindrance is injustice, and injury, as being *sine jure*; the right being before renounced or transferred. So that *injury* or *injustice*, in the controversies of the world, is somewhat like to that which in the disputations[1] of scholars is called *absurdity*. For as it is there called an absurdity to contradict what one maintained in the beginning; so in the world it is called injustice, and injury voluntarily to undo that which from the beginning he had voluntarily done. The way by which a man either simply renounceth or transferreth his right is a declaration, or signification, by some voluntary and sufficient sign, or signs, that he doth so renounce or transfer, or hath so renounced or transferred the same, to him that accepteth it. And these signs are either words only, or actions only; or, as it happeneth most often, both words and actions. And the same are the bonds, by which men are bound and obliged: bonds that have their strength, not from their own nature (for nothing is more easily broken than a man's word), but from fear of some evil consequence upon the rupture.

Whensoever a man transferreth his right, or renounceth it, it is either in consideration of some right reciprocally transferred to himself, or for some other good he hopeth for thereby. For it is a voluntary act: and of the voluntary acts of every man, the object is some *good to himself*. And therefore there be some rights which no man can be understood by any words, or other signs, to have abandoned or transferred. As first a man cannot lay down the right of resisting them that assault him by force to take away his life, because he cannot be understood to aim thereby at any good to himself. The same may be said of wounds, and chains, and imprisonment, both because there is no benefit consequent to such patience, as there is to the patience of suffering another to be wounded or imprisoned, as also because a man cannot tell when he seeth men proceed against him by violence whether they intend his death or not. And lastly the motive and end for which this renouncing and transferring of right is introduced is nothing else but the security of a man's person, in his life, and in the means of so preserving life as not to be weary of it[2]. And therefore if a man by words, or other signs, seem to despoil[3] himself of the end for which those signs were intended, he is not to be understood as if he meant it, or that it was his will, but that he was ignorant of how such words and actions were to be interpreted.

The mutual transferring of right is that which men call contract.

...

---

1 **disputation:** academic debate
2 **preserving life as not to be weary of it:** protecting life so that it won't suffer from injury
3 **despoil:** deprive

If a covenant be made wherein neither of the parties perform presently, but trust one another, in the condition of mere nature (which is a condition of war of every man against every man) upon any reasonable suspicion[1], it is void: but if there be a common power set over them both, with right and force sufficient to compel performance, it is not void. For he that performeth first has no assurance the other will perform after, because the bonds of words are too weak to bridle[2] men's ambition, avarice, anger, and other passions, without the fear of some coercive power; which in the condition of mere nature, where all men are equal, and judges of the justness of their own fears[3], cannot possibly be supposed. And therefore he which performeth first does but betray himself to his enemy, contrary to the right he can never abandon[4] of defending his life and means of living.

But in a civil estate, where there is a power set up to constrain those that would otherwise violate their faith, that fear is no more reasonable; and for that cause, he which by the covenant is to perform first is obliged so to do.

...

Chapter XV   Of Other Laws of Nature

FROM that law of nature by which we are obliged to transfer to another such rights as, being retained, hinder the peace of mankind, there followeth a third; which is this: ***that men perform their covenants made*; without which covenants are in vain, and but empty words; and the right of all men to all things remaining, we are still in the condition of war.**

And in this law of nature consisteth the fountain and original of justice. For where no covenant hath preceded, there hath no right been transferred, and every man has right to everything and consequently, no action can be *unjust*. But when a covenant is made, then to break it is unjust and the definition of injustice is no other than *the not performance of covenant*. And whatsoever is not unjust is just.

But because covenants of mutual trust, where there is a fear of not performance on either part (as hath been said in the former chapter), are invalid, though the original of justice be the making of covenants, yet injustice actually there can be none[5] till the cause of such fear be taken away; which, while men are in the natural condition of war, cannot be done. Therefore before the names of just and unjust can have place, there must be some coercive power[6] to compel men

---

1   **If a covenant be made … any reasonable suspision:** namely, let whatever will happen if the covenant (contract) is violated
2   **bridle:** check, control
3   **judges of the justness of their own fears:** namely, all men are judges of their own deeds
4   **contrary to the right he can never abandon:** violate his most important right
5   **injustice actually there can be none:** i.e., everything can be justified
6   **coercive power:** compelling power by use of force or authority

equally to the performance of their covenants, by the terror of some punishment greater than the benefit they expect by the breach of their covenant, and to make good[1] that propriety which by mutual contract men acquire in recompense of[2] the universal right they abandon: and such power there is none before the erection of a Commonwealth. And this is also to be gathered out of the ordinary definition of justice in the Schools, for they say that *justice is the constant will of giving to every man his own*. And therefore where there is no own, that is, no propriety, there is no injustice; and where there is no coercive power erected, that is, where there is no Commonwealth, there is no propriety, all men having right to all things: therefore where there is no Commonwealth, there nothing is unjust. So that the nature of justice consisteth in keeping of valid covenants, but the validity of covenants begins not but with the constitution of a civil power sufficient to compel men to keep them: and then it is also that propriety begins.

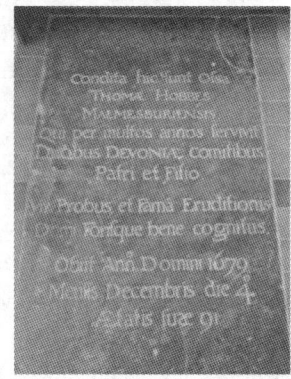

Hobbes' grave in England

...

Chapter XVII　Of the Causes, Generation, and Definition of a Commonwealth

The final cause, end, or design of men (who naturally love liberty, and dominion over others) in the introduction of that restraint upon themselves, in which we see them live in Commonwealths, is the foresight of their own preservation, and of a more contented life thereby; that is to say, of getting themselves out from that miserable condition of war which is necessarily consequent, as hath been shown, to the natural passions of men when there is no visible power to keep them in awe, and tie them by fear of punishment to[3] the performance of their covenants, and observation of those laws of nature set down in the fourteenth and fifteenth chapters.

For the laws of nature, *as justice, equity, modesty, mercy*, and, in sum, *doing to others as we would be done to*, of themselves, without the terror of some power to cause them to be observed, are contrary to our natural passions, that carry us to partiality, pride, revenge, and the like. And covenants, without the sword, are but words and of no strength to secure a man at all. Therefore, notwithstanding the laws of nature (which every one hath then kept, when he has the will to keep them, when he can do it safely), if there be no power erected, or not great enough for our security, every man will and may lawfully rely on his own strength and art for caution against all other men. And in all places, where men have lived by small families, to rob and spoil one another has been a trade, and so far from being reputed against the law of nature that the greater spoils they gained, the greater was their honour; and men observed no other laws therein but the laws of honour; that is, to abstain from cruelty, leaving to men their lives and instruments of husbandry.

---

1 **make good:** accomplish

2 **in recompense of:** as the compensation for

3 **tie them by fear of punishment to:** tie ... to

And as small families did then; so now do cities and kingdoms, which are but greater families (for their own security), enlarge their dominions upon all pretences of danger, and fear of invasion, or assistance that may be given to invaders; endeavour as much as they can to subdue or weaken their neighbours by open force, and secret arts, for want of other caution, justly; and are remembered for it in after ages with honour.

Nor is it the joining together of a small number of men that gives them this security; because in small numbers, small additions on the one side or the other make the advantage of strength so great as is sufficient to carry the victory, and therefore gives encouragement to an invasion. The multitude sufficient to confide in[1] for our security is not determined by any certain number, but by comparison with the enemy we fear; and is then sufficient when the odds of the enemy is not of so visible and conspicuous moment to determine the event of war, as to move him[2] to attempt.

And be there never so great a multitude; yet if their actions be directed according to their particular judgements, and particular appetites, they can expect thereby no defence, nor protection, neither against a common enemy, nor against the injuries of one another. For being distracted in opinions concerning the best use and application of their strength, they do not help, but hinder one another, and reduce their strength by mutual opposition to nothing[3]: whereby they are easily, not only subdued by a very few that agree together, but also, when there is no common enemy, they make war upon each other for their particular interests. For if we could suppose a great multitude of men to consent in the observation of justice, and other laws of nature, without a common power to keep them all in awe, we might as well suppose all mankind to do the same; and then there neither would be, nor need to be, any civil government or Commonwealth at all, because there would be peace without subjection.

Nor is it[4] enough for the security, which men desire should last all the time of their life, that they be governed and directed by one judgement for a limited time; as in one battle, or one war. For though they obtain a victory by their unanimous endeavour against a foreign enemy, yet afterwards, when either they have no common enemy, or he that by one part is held for an enemy is by another part held for a friend, they must needs[5] by the difference of their interests dissolve, and fall again into a war amongst themselves.

It is true that certain living creatures, as bees and ants, live sociably one with another (which are therefore by Aristotle numbered amongst political creatures), and yet have no other direction than their particular judgements and appetites; nor speech, whereby one of them can signify to another what he thinks expedient[6] for the common benefit: and therefore some man may perhaps desire to know why mankind cannot do the same. To which I answer,

---

1　**confide in:** have trust or faith in
2　**him:** enemy
3　**reduce their strength by mutual opposition to nothing:** reduce … to nothing
4　**it:** that they be governed and directed
5　**must needs:** must
6　**expedient:** advantageous

First, that men are continually in competition for honour and dignity, which these creatures are not; and consequently amongst men there ariseth on that ground, envy, and hatred, and finally war; but amongst these not so.

Secondly, that amongst these creatures the common good differeth not from the private; and being by nature inclined to their private, they procure[1] thereby the common benefit. But man, whose joy consisteth in comparing himself with other men, can relish nothing but what is eminent.

Leviathan the Monster

Thirdly, that these creatures, having not, as man, the use of reason, do not see, nor think they see, any fault in the administration of their common business: whereas amongst men there are very many that think themselves wiser and abler to govern the public better than the rest[2], and these strive to reform and innovate, one this way, another that way; and thereby bring it into distraction and civil war.

Fourthly, that these creatures, though they have some use of voice in making known to one another their desires and other affections, yet they want that art of words by which some men can represent to others that which is good in the likeness of evil; and evil, in the likeness of good; and augment or diminish the apparent greatness of good and evil, discontenting men and troubling their peace at their pleasure.

Fifthly, irrational creatures cannot distinguish between *injury* and *damage*; and therefore as long as they be at ease, they are not offended with their fellows: whereas man is then most troublesome when he is most at ease; for then it is that he loves to show his wisdom, and control the actions of them that govern the Commonwealth.

Lastly, the agreement of these creatures is natural; that of men is by covenant only, which is artificial: and therefore it is no wonder if there be somewhat else required, besides covenant, to make their agreement constant and lasting; which is a common power to keep them in awe and to direct their actions to the common benefit.

The only way to erect such a common power, as may be able to defend them from the invasion of foreigners, and the injuries of one another, and thereby to secure them in such sort as that by their own industry and by the fruits of the earth they may nourish themselves and live contentedly, is to confer[3] all their power and strength upon one man, or upon one assembly of

---

1 **procure:** obtain

2 **many that think themselves wiser ... the rest:** You may compare this statement with the discussion of wisdom by Socrates in Unit 2.

3 **The only way to erect such a common power ... is to confer:** The only way ... is to confer

men, that may reduce all their wills, by plurality of voices, unto one will: which is as much as to say, to appoint one man, or assembly of men, to bear their person; and every one to own and acknowledge himself[1] to be author of whatsoever he that so beareth their person shall act, or cause to be acted, in those things which concern the common peace and safety; and therein to submit their wills, every one to his will, and their judgements to his judgement. **This is more than consent, or concord; it is a real unity of them all in one and the same person, made by covenant of every man with every man, in such manner as if every man should say to every man:** *I authorise and give up my right of governing myself to this man, or to this assembly of men, on this condition; that thou give up thy right to him, and authorise all his actions in like manner.*

Leviathan as an analogy for the state

This done, the multitude so united in one person is called a COMMONWEALTH; in Latin, CIVITAS. This is the generation of that great LEVIATHAN, or rather, to speak more reverently, of that *mortal god* to which we owe, under the *immortal God*, our peace and defence. For by this authority, given him by every particular man in the Commonwealth, he hath the use of so much power and strength conferred on him that, by terror thereof, he is enabled to form the wills of them all, to peace at home, and mutual aid against their enemies abroad. And in him consisteth the essence of the Commonwealth; which, to define it, is: *one person, of whose acts a great multitude, by mutual covenants one with another, have made themselves every one the author, to the end he may use the strength and means of them all as he shall think expedient for their peace and common defence.*

And he that carrieth this person is called sovereign, and said to have *sovereign power*; and every one besides, his subject.

Key Concepts

artificial man	liberty
automata/covenant	natural condition
Commonwealth/state	Nature
contract/covenant	right of nature
every man against every man	royal prerogative
law of nature	sovereignty/sovereign right
Leviathan	three principal causes of quarrel

---

1 **himself:** that one man

John Locke: Of Civil Government

John Locke (1632–1704) is initiator of the Enlightenment in England and France, inspirer of the U. S. Constitution and philosopher who founded the school of empiricism. The English Civil War (1642 –46) began when Locke was 10. In 1652 he entered Christ Church, Oxford. Puritan reforms at Oxford had not yet altered the traditional Scholastic curriculum of rhetoric, grammar, moral philosophy, geometry, and Greek; Locke found the course insipid and interested himself in studies outside the traditional program, particularly experimental science and medicine. As a newly appointed tutor in his college, Locke enthusiastically welcomed the end of the turbulence by the Puritan Common-

wealth and the restoration of Charles II to the throne. In Restoration years, Locke stood firm for a constitutional monarchy, civil liberty, toleration in religion, and the rule of Parliament. In view of his opposition to the Roman Catholicism favored by the English monarchy, he found it expedient to re-main in the Continent. From 1683 to 1688 he lived in Holland for exile, and in 1685 his name appeared on the list sent to The Hague of 84 traitors wanted by the English government. Following the Glorious Revolution of 1688 and the restoration of Protestantism to favor, Locke returned to England. The new king, William III, appointed him to the Board of Trade in 1696. Locke's views, in his *Two Treatises of Government*, attacked the theory of divine right of kings and the nature of the state as conceived by the English political theorist Thomas Hobbes. He argued that sover-eignty did not reside in the state but with the people, and that the state is supreme, but only if it is bound by civil and what he called "natural" law. Many of Locke's political ideas, such as those relating to natural rights, property rights, the duty of the government to protect these rights, and the rule of the majority, found expression in the U.S. Constitution. Locke further held that revolution was not only a right but often an obligation, and he advocated a system of checks and balances in government, which was to comprise three branches, of which the legislative is more powerful than the executive or the judicial. These are the common talks of today, but in the times of John Locke were almost "treasonous."

I think it may not be amiss[1] to set down what I take to be political power. That the power of a magistrate over a subject may be distinguished from that of a father over his children, a master over his servant, a husband over his wife, and a lord over his slave. All which distinct powers happening sometimes together in the same man, if he be considered under these different relations,

---

1   **amiss:** inappropriate

it may help us to distinguish these powers one from another, and show the difference betwixt a ruler of a commonwealth, a father of a family, and a captain of a galley.[1]

Political power, then, I take to be a right of making laws, with penalties of death, and consequently all less penalties for the regulating and preserving of property, and of employing the force of the community in the execution of such laws, and in the defence of the Commonwealth from foreign injury, and all this only for the public good.[2]

Chapter 2   Of the State of Nature

To understand political power aright, and derive it from its original, we must consider what estate all men are naturally in, and that is, a state of perfect freedom to order their actions, and dispose of[3] their possessions and persons as they think fit, within the bounds of the law of Nature, without asking leave or depending upon the will of any other man.

A state also of equality, wherein all the power and jurisdiction is reciprocal[4], no one having more than another, there being nothing more evident than that creatures of the same species and rank, promiscuously[5] born to all the same advantages of Nature, and the use of the same faculties, should also be equal one amongst another, without subordination or subjection, unless the lord and master of them all should, by any manifest declaration of his will, set one above another, and confer on him, by an evident and clear appointment, an undoubted right to dominion and sovereignty. …

But though this be a state of liberty, yet it is not a state of licence[6]; though man in that state have an uncontrollable liberty to dispose of his person or possessions, yet he has not liberty to destroy himself, or so much as any creature in his possession, but where some nobler use than its bare preservation calls for it. **The state of Nature has a law of Nature to govern it, which obliges every one, and reason, which is that law, teaches all mankind who will but consult it, that being all equal and independent, no one ought to harm another in his life, health, liberty or possessions; for men being all the workmanship of one omnipotent and infinitely wise Maker; all the servants of one sovereign Master, sent into the world by His order and about His business; they are His property, whose workmanship they are made to last during His, not one another's pleasure.** And, being furnished with like faculties, sharing all in one community of Nature, there cannot be supposed any such subordination among us

---

1 **galley:** low, flat ship
2 **Political power, then … for the public good.:** To better understand what political power is, it might be beneficial to compare this Lockean definition with others proposed by people like Aristotle, Cicero, Machiavelli, and Hobbes.
3 **dispose of:** deal with
4 **reciprocal:** mutual
5 **promiscuously:** indiscriminately
6 **licence:** wrong use of freedom with no regard to law

Heritage of Western Intellectual Tradition   A Sourcebook

that may authorise us to destroy one another, as if we were made for one another's uses, as the inferior ranks of creatures are for ours. Every one as he is bound to preserve himself, and not to quit his station wilfully[1], so by the like reason, when his own preservation comes not in competition, ought he as much as he can to preserve the rest of mankind, and not unless it be to do justice on an offender, take away[2] or impair the life, or what tends to the preservation of life, the liberty, health, limb, or goods of another.

Cottage, long since destroyed, where Locke was born

And that all men may be restrained from invading others' rights, and from doing hurt to one another, and the law of Nature be observed, which willeth[3] the peace and preservation of all mankind, the execution of the law of Nature is in that state put into every man's hands, whereby every one has a right to punish the transgressors of that law to such a degree as may hinder its violation. For the law of Nature would, as all other laws that concern men in this world, be in vain if there were nobody that in the state of Nature had a power to execute that law, and thereby preserve the innocent and restrain offenders; and if any one in the state of Nature may punish another for any evil he has done, every one may do so. For in that state of perfect equality, where naturally there is no superiority or jurisdiction of one over another, what any may do in prosecution[4] of that law, every one must needs have a right to do.

And thus, in the state of Nature, "one man comes by a power over another," but yet no absolute or arbitrary power to use a criminal, when he has got him in his hands, according to the passionate heats or boundless extravagancy of his own will, but only to retribute[5] to him so far as calm reason and conscience dictate, what is proportionate[6] to his transgression, which is so much as may serve for reparation[7] and restraint. For these two are the only reasons why one man may lawfully do harm to another, which is that we call punishment. In transgressing the law of Nature, the offender declares himself to live by another rule than that of reason and common equity, which is that measure God has set to the actions of men for their mutual security, and so he becomes dangerous to mankind; the tie which is to secure them from injury and violence being slighted and broken by him, which being a trespass against the whole species, and the peace and safety of it, provided for by the law of Nature, every man upon this score[8], by the right he hath

---

1 **willfully:** intentionally

2 **not unless it be to do justice on an offender, take away:** not ... take away

3 **will:** intend, guarantee

4 **prosecution:** execution

5 **retribute:** punish

6 **retribute to him so far as ...what is proportionate:** retribute what is proportionate to him

7 **reparation:** compensation

8 **upon this score:** on this account

to preserve mankind in general, may restrain, or where it is necessary, destroy things noxious[1] to them, and so may bring such evil on any one who hath transgressed that law, as may make him repent the doing of it, and thereby deter[2] him, and, by his example, others from doing the like mischief. And in this case, and upon this ground, "every man hath a right to punish the offender, and be executioner of the law of Nature."

…

Chapter 3   Of the State of War

The state of war is a state of enmity and destruction; and therefore declaring by word or action, not a passionate and hasty, but sedate[3], settled design upon another man's life, puts him in a state of war with him against whom he has declared such an intention, and so has exposed his life to the other's power to be taken away by him, or any one that joins with him in his defence, and espouses[4] his quarrel; it being reasonable and just, I should have a right to destroy that which threatens me with destruction; for by the fundamental law of Nature, man being to be preserved as much as possible, when all cannot be preserved, the safety of the innocent is to be preferred, and one may destroy a man who makes war upon him, or has discovered an enmity to his being, for the same reason that he may kill a wolf or a lion, because they are not under the ties of the common law of reason, have no other rule but that of force and violence, and so may be treated as a beast of prey, those dangerous and noxious creatures that will be sure to destroy him whenever he falls into their power.

And hence it is that he who attempts to get another man into his absolute power does thereby put himself into a state of war with him; it being to be understood as a declaration of a design[5] upon his life. **For I have reason to conclude that he who would get me into his power without my consent would use me as he pleased when he had got me there, and destroy me too when he had a fancy[6] to it; for nobody can desire to have me in his absolute power unless it be to compel me by force to that which is against the right of my freedom — i.e. make me a slave.** To be free from such force is the only security of my preservation, and reason bids me look on him as an enemy to my preservation who would take away that freedom which is the fence to it; so that he who makes an attempt to enslave me thereby puts himself into a state

"Nobody can desire to have me in his absolute power"

---

1   **noxious:** harmful
2   **deter:** prevent, discourage
3   **sedate:** serious
4   **espouse:** give support to
5   **design:** plot, intention
6   **fancy:** desire

Heritage of Western Intellectual Tradition   A Sourcebook

of war with me. He that in the state of Nature would take away the freedom that belongs to any one in that state must necessarily be supposed to have a design to take away everything else, that freedom being the foundation of all the rest; as he that in the state of society would take away the freedom belonging to those of that society or commonwealth must be supposed to design to take away from them everything else, and so be looked on as in a state of war.

This makes it lawful for a man to kill a thief who has not in the least hurt him, nor declared any design upon his life, any farther than by the use of force, so to get him in his power as to take away his money, or what he pleases, from him; because using force, where he has no right to get me into his power, let his pretence be what it will, I have no reason to suppose that he who would take away my liberty would not, when he had me in his power, take away everything else. And, therefore, it is lawful for me to treat him as one who has put himself into a state of war with me — i.e., kill him if I can; for to that hazard does he justly expose himself whoever introduces a state of war[1], and is aggressor in it.

And here we have the plain "difference between the state of Nature and the state of war," which however some men have confounded[2], are as far distant as a state of peace, goodwill, mutual assistance, and preservation; and a state of enmity, malice, violence and mutual destruction are one from another. **Men living together according to reason without a common superior on earth, with authority to judge between them, is properly the state of Nature.** But force, or a declared design of force upon the person of another, where there is no common superior on earth to appeal to for relief, is the state of war; and it is the want of such an appeal gives a man the right of war even against an aggressor, though he be in society and a fellow-subject.

...

Chapter 4   Of Slavery

The natural liberty of man is to be free from any superior power on earth, and not to be under the will or legislative authority of man, but to have only the law of Nature for his rule. The liberty of man in society is to be under no other legislative power but that established by consent in the commonwealth, nor under the dominion of any will, or restraint of any law, but what that legislative shall enact according to the trust put in it. Freedom, then, is not what Sir Robert Filmer[3] tells us: "A liberty for every one to do what he lists[4], to live as he pleases, and not to be tied by any laws;" but freedom of men under government is to have a standing rule to live by, common to every one of that society, and made by the legislative power erected in it. **A liberty to follow my**

---

1   **for to that hazard does he ... a state of war:** namely, whoever introduces a state of war justly exposes himself to that hazard

2   **confound:** confuse

3   **Sir Robert Filmer (c. 1588 – 1653):** English political theorist known for an absolutist concept of kingship and the similarity he drew between the power of the father and the power of the king, and the argument that all authority trace back to the first man, Adam, who was granted authority by God the Father

4   **list:** please

own will in all things where that rule prescribes not, not to be subject to the inconstant, uncertain, unknown, arbitrary will of another man, as freedom of nature is to be under no other restraint but the law of Nature.

This freedom from absolute, arbitrary power is so necessary to, and closely joined with, a man's preservation, that he cannot part with it but by what forfeits[1] his preservation and life together.

…

Chapter 5   Of Property

God, who hath given the world to men in common, hath also given them reason to make use of it to the best advantage of life and convenience. The earth and all that is therein is given to men for the support and comfort of their being. And though all the fruits it naturally produces, and beasts it feeds, belong to mankind in common, as they are produced by the spontaneous hand of Nature, and nobody has originally a private dominion exclusive of the rest of mankind in any of them, as they are thus in their natural state, yet being given for the use of men, there must of necessity be a means to appropriate them some way or other before they can be of any use, or at all beneficial, to any particular men. The fruit or venison[2] which nourishes the wild Indian, who knows no enclosure[3], and is still a tenant in common, must be his, and so his — i.e., a part of him, that another can no longer have any right to it before it can do him any good for the support of his life.

Though the earth and all inferior creatures be common to all men, yet every man has a "property" in his own "person." This nobody has any right to but himself. **The "labour" of his body and the "work" of his hands, we may say, are properly his. Whatsoever, then, he removes out of the state that Nature hath provided and left it in, he hath mixed his labour with it, and joined to it something that is his own, and thereby makes it his property.** It being by him removed from the common state Nature placed it in, it hath by this labour something annexed to it that excludes the common right of other men. For this "labour" being the unquestionable property of the labourer, no man but he can have a right to what that is once joined to, at least where there is enough, and as good left in common for others.

He that is nourished by the acorns he picked up under an oak, or the apples he gathered from the trees in the wood, has certainly appropriated them to himself. Nobody can deny but the nourishment is his. I ask, then, when did they begin to be his? when he digested? or when he ate? or when he boiled? or when he brought them home? or when he picked them up? And it is plain,

---

1   **forfeit:** suffer the loss as punishment

2   **venison:** deer meat

3   **enclosure:** land enclosed as one's own

Heritage of Western Intellectual Tradition   A Sourcebook

if the first gathering made them not his, nothing else could. That labour put a distinction between them and common. That added something to them more than Nature, the common mother of all, had done, and so they became his private right. And will any one say he had no right to those acorns or apples he thus appropriated because he had not the consent of all mankind to make them his? Was it a robbery thus to assume to himself what belonged to all in common? If such a consent as that was necessary, man had starved, notwithstanding the plenty God had given him. We see in commons, which remain so by compact[1], that it is the taking any part of what is common, and removing it out of the state Nature leaves it in, which begins the property, without which the common is of no use. And the taking of this or that part does not depend on the express consent of all the commoners. Thus, the grass my horse has bit, the turfs my servant has cut, and the ore I have digged in any place, where I have a right to them in common with others, become my property without the assignation or consent of anybody. The labour that was mine, removing them out of that common state they were in, hath fixed my property in them.

...

Chapter 7   Of Political or Civil Society

...

Whenever ... any number of men so unite into one society as to quit every one his executive power[2] of the law of Nature, and to resign it to the public, there and there only is a political or civil society.[3] And this is done wherever any number of men, in the state of Nature, enter into society to make one people one body politic under one supreme government: or else when any one joins himself to, and incorporates with any government already made. For hereby he authorises the society, or, which is all one, the legislative thereof, to make laws for him as the public good of the society shall require, to the execution whereof his own assistance (as to his own decrees) is due[4]. And this puts men out of a state of Nature into that of a commonwealth, by setting up a judge on earth with authority to determine all the controversies and redress the injuries that may happen to any member of the commonwealth, which judge is the legislative or magistrates appointed by it. And wherever there are any number of men, however associated, that have no such decisive power to appeal to, there they are still in the state of Nature.

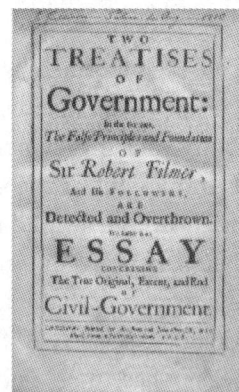

And hence it is evident that absolute monarchy, which by some men is counted for the only

---

1   **compact:** agreement

2   **quit every one his executive power:** every one quit his executive power

3   **Whenever ... any number of men ... or civil society.:** Compare this definition of civil society with that made by Aristotle, Cicero, Machiavelli and Hobbes.

4   **to the execution whereof his own assistance is due:** provide his own assistance to the execution of law

government in the world, is indeed inconsistent with civil society, and so can be no form of civil government at all. For the end of civil society being to avoid and remedy those inconveniences of the state of Nature which necessarily follow from every man's being judge in his own case, by setting up a known authority to which every one of that society may appeal upon any injury received, or controversy that may arise, and which every one of the society ought to obey. Wherever any persons are who have not such an authority to appeal to, and decide any difference between them there, those persons are still in the state of Nature. And so is every absolute prince in respect of those who are under his dominion.

For he being supposed to have all, both legislative and executive, power in himself alone, there is no judge to be found, no appeal lies open to any one, who may fairly and indifferently[1], and with authority decide, and from whence relief and redress may be expected of[2] any injury or inconveniency that may be suffered from him, or by his order. So that such a man, however entitled, Czar, or Grand Signior, or how you please, is as much in the state of Nature, with all under his dominion, as he is with the rest of mankind. For wherever any two men are, who have no standing[3] rule and common judge to appeal to on earth, for the determination of controversies of right betwixt them, there they are still in the state of Nature, and under all the inconveniencies of it, with only this woeful difference to the subject, or rather slave of an absolute prince. That whereas, in the ordinary state of Nature, he has a liberty to judge of his right, according to the best of his power to maintain it; but whenever his property is invaded by the will and order of his monarch, he has not only no appeal, as those in society ought to have, but, as if he were degraded from the common state of rational creatures, is denied a liberty to judge of, or defend his right, and so is exposed to all the misery and inconveniencies that a man can fear from one, who being in the unrestrained state of Nature, is yet corrupted with flattery and armed with power.

For he that thinks absolute power purifies men's blood, and corrects the baseness of human nature, need read but the history of this, or any other age, to be convinced of the contrary.

...

Chapter 8   Of the Beginning of Political Societies

Men being, as has been said, by nature all free, equal, and independent, no one can be put out of this estate and subjected to the political power of another without his own consent[4], which is done by agreeing with other men, to join and unite into a community for their comfortable, safe,

---

1 **indifferently:** equally
2 **relief and redress may be expected of:** relief and redress ... of
3 **standing:** established
4 **without his own consent:** Pay attention to the idea of "consent," which is crucial to the concept of social contract in Hobbes and Locke, and which is developed into more complex ideas by the 20th century thinkers, such as Antonio Gramsci and Michel Foucault.

and peaceable living, one amongst another, in a secure enjoyment of their properties, and a greater security against any that are not of it. This any number of men may do, because it injures not the freedom of the rest; they are left, as they were, in the liberty of the state of Nature. When any number of men have so consented to make one community or government, they are thereby presently incorporated, and make one body politic, wherein the majority have a right to act and conclude[1] the rest.

For, when any number of men have, by the consent of every individual, made a community, they have thereby made that community one body, with a power to act as one body, which is only by the will and determination of the majority. For that which acts[2] any community, being only the consent of the individuals of it, and it being one body, must move one way, it is necessary the body should move that way whither the greater force carries it, which is the consent of the majority, or else it is impossible it should act or continue one body, one community, which the consent of every individual that united into it agreed that it should; and so every one is bound by that consent to be concluded by the majority. And therefore we see that in assemblies empowered to act by positive laws where no number is set by that positive law which empowers them, the act of the majority passes for the act of the whole, and of course determines as having, by the law of Nature and reason, the power of the whole.

And thus every man, by consenting with others to make one body politic under one government, puts himself under an obligation to every one of that society to submit to the determination of the majority, and to be concluded by it; or else this original compact, whereby he with others incorporates into one society, would signify nothing, and be no compact if he be left free and under no other ties than he was in before in the state of Nature.

...

Chapter 9   Of the Ends of Political Society and Government

If man in the state of Nature be so free as has been said, if he be absolute lord of his own person and possessions, equal to the greatest and subject to nobody, why will he part with his freedom, this empire, and subject himself to the dominion and control of any other power? To which it is obvious to answer, that though in the state of Nature he hath such a right, yet the enjoyment of it is very uncertain and constantly exposed to the invasion of others; for all being kings as much as he, every man his equal, and the greater part no strict observers of equity and justice, the enjoyment of the property he has in this state is very unsafe, very insecure. This makes him willing to quit this condition which, however free, is full of fears and continual dangers; and it is not without reason that he seeks out and is willing to join in society with others who are already united, or have a mind to unite for the mutual preservation of their lives, liberties and estates, which I call by the general name — property.

1 **conclude:** decide
2 **act:** play the role of

The great and chief end, therefore, of men uniting into commonwealths, and putting themselves under government, is the preservation of their property; to which in the state of Nature there are many things wanting.

Firstly, there wants an established, settled, known law, received and allowed by common consent to be the standard of right and wrong, and the common measure to decide all controversies between them. For though the law of Nature be plain and intelligible to all rational creatures, yet men, being biased[1] by their interest, as well as ignorant for want of study of it, are not apt to allow of it as a law binding to them in the application of it to their particular cases.

Secondly, in the state of Nature there wants a known and indifferent judge, with authority to determine all differences according to the established law. For every one in that state being both judge and executioner of the law of Nature, men being partial to themselves, passion and revenge is very apt to carry them too far, and with too much heat[2] in their own cases, as well as negligence and unconcernedness, make them too remiss[3] in other men's.

Thirdly, in the state of Nature there often wants power to back and support the sentence when right, and to give it due execution. They who by any injustice offended will seldom fail where they are able by force to make good[4] their injustice. Such resistance many times makes the punishment dangerous, and frequently destructive to those who attempt it.

Thus mankind, notwithstanding all the privileges of the state of Nature, being but in an ill condition while they remain in it are quickly driven into society. Hence it comes to pass[5], that we seldom find any number of men live any time together in this state. The inconveniencies that they are therein exposed to by the irregular and uncertain exercise of the power every man has of[6] punishing the transgressions of others, make them take sanctuary[7] under the established laws of government, and therein seek the preservation of their property. It is this that makes them so willingly give up every one his single power of punishing to be exercised by such alone as shall be appointed to it amongst them, and by such rules as the community, or those authorised by them to that purpose, shall agree on[8]. And in this we have the original right and rise of both the legislative and executive power as well as of the governments and societies themselves.

…

Chapter 13   Of the Subordination of the Powers of the Commonwealth

---

1 **biased:** predisposed, affeeted

2 **heat:** concern, care

3 **remiss:** careless

4 **make good:** compensate for

5 **come to pass:** happen

6 **the power every man has of:** the power … of

7 **sanctuary:** protection

8 **as the community, or those authorised by them to that purpose, shall agree on:** as the community, or those authorised by them … shall agree on

Heritage of Western Intellectual Tradition   A Sourcebook

Though in a constituted commonwealth standing upon its own basis and acting according to its own nature — that is, acting for the preservation of the community, there can be but one supreme power, which is the legislative, to which all the rest are and must be subordinate, yet the legislative being only a fiduciary[1] power to act for certain ends, there remains still in the people a supreme power to remove or alter the legislative, when they find the legislative act contrary to the trust reposed[2] in them. For all power given with trust for the attaining an end being limited by that end, whenever that end is manifestly neglected or opposed, the trust must necessarily be forfeited[3], and the power devolve[4] into the hands of those that gave it, who may place it anew where they shall think best for their safety and security. And thus the community perpetually retains a supreme power of saving themselves from the attempts and designs of anybody, even of their legislators, whenever they shall be so foolish or so wicked as to lay and carry on designs against the liberties and properties of the subject. For no man or society of men having a power to deliver up their preservation, or consequently the means of it, to the absolute will and arbitrary dominion of another, whenever any one shall go about to bring them into such a slavish condition, they will always have a right to preserve what they have not a power to part with[5], and to rid themselves of those who invade this fundamental, sacred, and unalterable law of self-preservation for which they entered into society. And thus the community may be said in this respect to be always the supreme power.

...

Chapter 19   Of the Dissolution of Government

The reason why men enter into society is the preservation of their property; and the end while they choose and authorise a legislative is that there may be laws made, and rules set, as guards and fences to the properties of all the society, to limit the power and moderate the dominion of every part and member of the society. For since it can never be supposed to be the will of the society that the legislative should have a power to destroy that which every one designs to secure by entering into society, and

Locke's grave in England

for which the people submitted themselves to legislators of their own making[6]: whenever the legislators endeavour to take away and destroy the property of the people, or to reduce them to slavery

---

1 **fiduciary:** holding of something in trust for another
2 **repose:** put trust
3 **forfeit:** take back, lose
4 **devolve:** transfer
5 **what they have not a power to part with:** their preservation or life and property
6 **legislators of their own making:** legislators they selected

under arbitrary power, they put themselves into a state of war with the people, who are thereupon absolved from[1] any farther obedience, and are left to the common refuge which God hath provided for all men against force and violence. **Whensoever, therefore, the legislative shall transgress this fundamental rule of society, and either by ambition, fear, folly, or corruption, endeavour to grasp themselves, or put into the hands of any other, an absolute power[2] over the lives, liberties, and estates of the people, by this breach of trust they forfeit the power the people had put into their hands for quite contrary ends, and it devolves to the people, who have a right to resume their original liberty, and by the establishment of a new legislative (such as they shall think fit), provide for their own safety and security, which is the end for which they are in society.** What I have said here concerning the legislative in general holds true also concerning the supreme executor, who having a double trust put in him, both to have a part in the legislative and the supreme execution of the law, acts against both, when he goes about to set up his own arbitrary will as the law of the society. He acts also contrary to his trust when he employs the force, treasure, and offices of the society to corrupt the representatives and gain them to his purposes, when he openly pre-engages the electors, and prescribes[3], to their choice, such whom he has, by solicitation[4], threats, promises, or otherwise, won to his designs, and employs them to bring in such who have promised beforehand what to vote and what to enact[5]. Thus to regulate candidates and electors, and new model the ways of election, what is it but to cut up the government by the roots, and poison the very fountain of public security?

…

But it will be said this hypothesis lays a ferment[6] for frequent rebellion. To which I answer:

First: no more than[7] any other hypothesis. For when the people are made miserable, and find themselves exposed to the ill usage of arbitrary power, cry up[8] their governors as much as you will for sons of Jupiter[9], let them be sacred and divine, descended or authorised from Heaven; give them out[10] for whom or what you please, the same will happen. **The people generally ill**

---

1   **absolved from:** free from
2   **grasp themselves, or put into the hands of any other, an absolute power:** grasp … or put in the hands … an absolute power
3   **prescribe:** use
4   **solicitation:** request
5   **enact:** make law
6   **ferment:** excitement, potential danger
7   **no more than:** just as
8   **cry up:** sing praises
9   **Jupiter:** supreme god of Roman mythology, protector of Rome
10 **give them out:** make them known

Heritage of Western Intellectual Tradition — A Sourcebook

treated, and contrary to right, will be ready upon any occasion to ease themselves of a burden that sits heavy upon them. They will wish and seek for the opportunity, which in the change, weakness, and accidents of human affairs, seldom delays long to offer itself[1]. He must have lived but a little while in the world, who has not seen examples of this in his time; and he must have read very little who cannot produce examples of it in all sorts of governments in the world.[2]

Secondly: I answer, such revolutions happen not upon every little mismanagement in public affairs. Great mistakes in the ruling part, many wrong and inconvenient laws, and all the slips of human frailty will be borne by the people without mutiny[3] or murmur. But if a long train of abuses, prevarications[4], and artifices[5], all tending the same way, make the design visible to the people, and they cannot but feel what they lie under, and see whither they are going, it is not to be wondered that they should then rouse themselves, and endeavour to put the rule into such hands which may secure to them the ends for which government was at first erected.

...

Whosoever uses force without right — as every one does in society who does it without law — puts himself into a state of war with those against whom he so uses it, and in that state all former ties are cancelled, all other rights cease, and every one has a right to defend himself, and to resist the aggressor.

Key Concepts

absolute, arbitrary power	political society
freedom	preservation of property
Glorious Revolution	rule of the majority
law of Nature	system of checks and balances
legislative power	state of Nature
natural liberty of man	unquestionable property of the labourer
political power	

---

1   **itself:** opportunity
2   **he must have lived but … in the world:** he must have lived to see and read these examples
3   **mutiny:** open rebellion
4   **prevarication:** telling lies
5   **artifice:** deceitfulness

Heritage of Western Intellectual Tradition   A Sourcebook

Compare with China

1. *Confucianism and Human Dignity: Toward a Balanced View of Rights and Duty*

The following is an interesting discussion of human rights and duty in Confucianism as complementary, rather than detrimental, to the liberalism in Hobbes and Locke.

It is commonly asserted that the Chinese tradition in general and Confucianism in particular lacked clear conception of rights. While this appears to be apparently true from even a cursory[1] scan of classical Confucian works, it would be a mistake to infer that Confucianism is inherently opposed to individual rights, including basic political rights. I argue that the Confucian concept of human dignity can accommodate the notion of rights as a device for cultivating individual virtues.

1. The Primacy of Rights over Duty in Western Liberalism

Belief in human dignity is often implicitly assumed in modern liberalism, a dominant ideology in the Western liberal democracies. Yet, paradoxical enough, modern liberalism seems to be incapable of providing a solid philosophical foundation for its widely held belief in human dignity, given its basically negative view on human nature.

It is well known that the Western idea of individual rights is originally derived from the ideas of contract in Thomas Hobbes. In his *Leviathan*, Hobbes postulates a state of nature, in which egoistical individuals, with limited resources (including material goods and honor) and without mutual trust and a common government, find themselves trapped in "a war of all against all." To balance such a condition, every person rationally enters a compact with every other person to put themselves under a sovereign. From such a promise, enforced by the common power, is derived a set of natural laws which command each individual to keep peace and observe the terms of compact. The duties thus prescribed, however, is strictly conditioned upon the original purpose for which the compact was made in the first place: the preservation of individual life. This is indeed the "inalienable" natural right that Hobbes finds in every rational human being. Every government must work toward the preservation and security of life; failure to do so constitutes a fundamental breach by the sovereign, which brings back the state of nature, where every individual is absolved of all duties toward others and regains natural liberty. The primacy of natural right over duty is obvious, as there is no equivalent "natural duty", but only duties derived from rights. The notion of natural right is further extended by John Locke to include the right to liberty

---

1   **cursory:** quick

and property. Although, in Locke's theory, natural laws maintain their binding force in the state of nature, the fundamental asymmetry between rights and duty would remain if the biblical authority of God is left out.

Despite its wide acceptance today, the social contract theory of rights contains several difficulties. First, without presupposing a priori validity of transcendental divine command, the existence of human duty would depend entirely upon the prudential calculations of one's self-interest, and is thus made secondary to rights. Among other things, the Hobbesian theory can support only a weak notion of duty, that is, a person observes his duty not for its own sake, but only because it furthers his selfish interest, and his duty stops as soon as the cost of obeying it apparently outweighs the benefits. Prudential considerations, however, depend on the actors' foresight and circumstances in which they are situated, and the ensuing uncertainty necessarily undermines the binding force of basic duties. Second, without the sanction[1] of an external divine authority, which requires belief in a particular religion, the primacy of natural right of self-preservation in the Hobbesian theory makes it difficult to even accommodate other widely held rights, such as personal liberty and property. If human beings are by nature selfish, unjust, vile, and rapacious[2], it seems doubtful whether they are worthy of any rights other than bare preservation. Finally, and most significant for our purpose, it seems to be very difficult to consistently derive from this theory the widely held "recognition of the inherent dignity" in the *Preamble of the Universal Declaration of Human Rights*[3]. If everyone is, as Hobbes depicts, an egoistical animal preoccupied with his self-interest, and his apparent observance of law and duties arises only from the fear for the punishments of the sovereign power, then it is difficult to find any worth and dignity in human beings.

The basic problem with the modern liberal theory of rights is, then, its low estimation of human being contrary to the widely held practical beliefs. Such an initial assumption makes it difficult to derive the notion of innate dignity or worth, and makes basic duties too easily over-whelmed by the prudential concerns of self-interests. For this reason modern liberalism is criticized, perhaps with some justice, for adopting an unnecessarily dim view of human nature and for ignoring the inherent moral potential in a human being. By undermining social duty and legal constraints on personal gratification of desires, it is charged, the radical individualistic tendency in modern liberalism dehumanizes human beings. In this respect, Confucianism, while fundamentally a duty ethics and despite its own problems, provides a salutary[4] correction to such a tendency and, if properly construed, is capable of accommodating a better-balanced theory of rights.

2. From Universal Duty to Universal Rights: A Confucian Transformation?

As a consistent implication of the Confucian belief, the universal respect for human dignity

---

1   **sanction:** permission

2   **rapacious:** greedy

3   "The Universal Declaration of Human Rights," in view of the Nazi atrocity and based on principles expressed in the UN Charter, was adopted by the United Nations in 1948 to codify human rights in international law.

4   **salutary:** helpful

carries the demand that state and society must protect and help cultivate the innate virtues in every individual human being, and this task is probably best achieved by providing a constitutional system of basic rights. It is nevertheless true that such a system of rights has been conspicuously lacking throughout the Chinese history. It appears as if the traditional China, by emphasizing social duty, were diametrically opposed to the modern West. The reason for such a difference lies partly in the different conception of equality. The classical Chinese philosophers recognized only natural equality in the sense that everyone is born with innate virtues as unique human potentials, but denied actual equality that all men could in fact develop their nature to such an equal extent as to entitle them to equal respect. In Confucianism, this view had justified the hierarchical structure of society and the denial of popular participation in government. By focusing on the capacities people have developed through education, Confucianists had limited the participation in government to a small group of elites, and ignored the notion of innate moral rights developed in the West, which entitles every adult to some form of participation. As a result, Confucianism had never developed an explicit notion of "rights" — not modern political right to participation, not the Lockean right to property in virtue of one's labor, not even the Hobbesian natural right to self-preservation.

Similar to its classical and medieval counterparts in the West, Confucianism was decidedly duty-orientated. In what the Chinese view as a just society, one's "right" (that is, social, economic and political privileges) was to be made strictly proportional to the degree of actually developed worth and ability. The state and society must be run by the most virtuous and worthy, who almost always remain a small minority, and it seemed to them patently absurd to allow the ignorant, selfish, and morally immature mass to choose their own leaders. Confucius and his followers were simply concerned with how to make men virtuous and, at the same time, make the virtuous men rule.

In a sense the Confucianists were quite right. If one is truly incompetent in a certain vocation (e.g. political engagement), then both justice and common prudence require that he should refrain from getting involved in it, but leave it instead to those who are in a better position for it. And rights, freedom and participation are not the only things about which people ought to care; indeed these things alone are not sufficient to sustain social and political institutions. Rather, they presuppose something else as their foundation, that is, the development of virtues and the primary means by which these virtues are acquired, namely, proper education and upbringing. After all, hardly anyone wants to live in a society full of "rights" and "freedom," but bereft of basic norms, values, and a sense of duty — a society in which everyone feels free to do whatever s/he wants, without sufficient moral constraint. Such a society would be necessarily one of "littlemen," among whom numerous conflicts, strives, infringements and oppressions are bound to occur. On the other hand, a democracy worthy of its name presupposes a society of gentlemen who, having developed their virtues and become mature citizens, are capable of exercising their "rights" intelligently. Thus, for good reasons, self-cultivation has occupied the central position in Confucianism; it is the very path toward the making of virtuous and dignified citizens. (Adapted from Zhang Qianfan: *The Idea of Human Dignity in Classical Chinese Philosophy: A Recon-*

Heritage of Western Intellectual Tradition　A Sourcebook

struction of Confucianism)

2.　*Locke Talking about China and the Chinese*

The following two excerpts from Locke's essays touched upon China and the Chinese, and it might be interesting to read how this prominent thinker at the time was talking about the issues he was concerned by alluding to another people in the other end of the world, ignorantly and narrow-mindedly.

If any idea can be imagined innate, the idea of God may, of all others, for many reasons, be thought so; since it is hard to conceive how there should be innate moral principles, without an innate idea of a Deity[1]. Without a notion of a law-maker, it is impossible to have a notion of a law, and an obligation to observe it. Besides the atheists[2] taken notice of amongst the ancients, and left branded upon the records of history, hath not navigation discovered, in these later ages, whole nations, at the bay of Soldania, in Brazil, [in Boranday,] and in the Caribbee islands, & c., amongst whom there was to be found no notion of a God, no religion? ... These are instances of nations where uncultivated nature has been left to itself, without the help of letters and discipline, and the improvements of arts and sciences. But there are others to be found who have enjoyed these[3] in a very great measure, who yet, for want of a due application of their thoughts this way, want[4] the idea and knowledge of God. It will, I doubt not, be a surprise to others, as it was to me, to find the Siamites[5] of this number. But for this, let them consult the King of France's late envoy thither, who gives no better[6] account of the Chinese themselves. And if we will not believe La Loubere, the missionaries of China, even the Jesuits themselves, the great encomiasts[7] of the Chinese, do all to a man agree, and will convince us, that the sect of the literari, or learned, keeping to the old religion of China, and the ruling party there, are all of them atheists. ... And perhaps, if we should with attention mind the lives and discourses of people not so far off, we should have too much reason to fear, that many, in more civilized countries, have no very strong and clear impressions of a Deity upon their minds, and that the complaints of atheism made from the pulpit are not without reason. And though only some profligate[8] wretches own it too barefacedly[9] now; yet perhaps we should hear more than we do of it from others, did not the fear of the magistrate's

---

1　**since it is hard to conceive ... of a Deity:** Here Locke is using the same logic of argument Descartes used in his writing.

2　**atheists:** people who do not believe in God

3　**these:** the help of letters and discipline, and the improvements of arts and sciences

4　**want:** lack

5　**Siamites:** Siamese 暹罗（泰国）人

6　**better:** better than the Siamites

7　**encomiast:** one who praises

8　**profligate:** shamelessly immoral

9　**barefacedly:** shamelessly

sword, or their neighbour's censure, tie up people's tongues; which, were the apprehensions of punishment or shame taken away, would as openly proclaim their atheism as their lives do. (Adapted from John Locke, *An Essay Concerning Human Understanding*)

Others there are, the greatest part of whose business in this world is to be done with their tongues and with their pens; and to these it is convenient, if not necessary, that they should speak properly and correctly, whereby they may let their thoughts into other men's minds the more easily, and with the greater impression. Upon this account it is, that any sort of speaking, so as will make him be understood, is not thought enough[1] for a gentleman. He ought to study grammar amongst the other helps of speaking well, but it must be the grammar of his own tongue, of the language he uses, that he may understand his own country speech nicely, and speak it properly, without shocking the ears of those it is addressed to, with solecisms[2] and offensive irregularities. … Whether all gentlemen should not do this, I leave to be considered, since the want of propriety and grammatical exactness is thought very misbecoming[3] one of that rank, and usually draws on one guilty of such faults the censure of having had a lower breeding and worse company than suits with his quality. If this be so, (as I suppose it is) it will be matter of wonder why young gentlemen are forced to learn the grammars of foreign and dead languages, and are never once told of the grammar of their own tongues, they do not so much as know there is any such thing, much less is it made their business to be instructed in it. Nor is their own language ever proposed to them as worthy their care and cultivating, though they have daily use of it, and are not seldom, in the future course of their lives, judg'd of by their handsome or awkward way of expressing themselves in it. Whereas the languages whose grammars they have been so much employed in, are such as probably they shall scarce ever speak or write; or if, upon occasion, this should happen, they should be excused for the mistakes and faults they make in it. Would not a Chinese who took notice of this way of breeding, be apt to imagine that all our young gentlemen were designed to be teachers and professors of the dead languages of foreign countries, and not to be men of business in their own?

… Narrow breasts, short and stinking breath, ill lungs, and crookedness[4], are natural and almost constant effects of hard bodice[5], and clothes that pinch[6]. That way of making slender wastes, and fine shapes, serves but the more effectually to spoil them. Nor can there indeed but be disproportion in the parts, when the nourishment prepared in the several offices of the body cannot be distributed as nature designs. And therefore what wonder is it, if, it being laid where it can, on some part not so braced, it often makes a shoulder or hip higher or bigger than its just

---

1 **any sort of speaking, so as will make him be understand, is not thought enough:** any sort of speaking … is not thought enough
2 **solecism:** here improper requests
3 **misbecoming:** ill match
4 **crookedness:** dishonesty
5 **bodice:** woman's dress, very tight
6 **pinch:** hurt by being too tight

proportion? 'Tis generally known, that the women of China, (imagining I know not what kind of beauty in it) by bracing and binding them hard from their infancy, have very little feet. I saw lately a pair of China shoes, which I was told were for a grown woman: they were so exceedingly disproportion'd to the feet of one of the same age among us, that they would scarce have been big enough for one of our little girls. Besides this, 'tis observ'd, that their women are also very little, and short-liv'd; whereas the men are of the ordinary stature of other men, and live to a proportionable age. These defects in the female sex in that country, are by some imputed to the unreasonable binding of their feet, whereby the free circulation of the blood is hinder'd, and the growth and health of the whole body suffers. And how often do we see, that some small part of the foot being injur'd by a wrench or a blow, the whole leg or thigh thereby lose their strength and nourishment, and dwindle away? How much greater inconveniences may we expect, when the thorax[1], wherein is placed the heart and seat of life, is unnaturally compress'd, and hinder'd from its due expansion? (Adapted from John Locke, *Some Thoughts Concerning Education*, 1692)

Supplementary Reading

1. Political Controversies in the 17th Century England

The 17th century was one of the most tumultuous times in the English history, since the country witnessed three major political events which helped to lay the foundation of modern political institution of the country. The following are some of the important concepts relating to what was happening at the time.

European Enlightenment

There were, essentially, two responses to the political chaos of the seventeenth century, as many of the aspects of the Reformation began to be translated into political terms. On the one hand, a group of thinkers led initially by Hugo Grotius[2] believed that natural laws governed states and their relations. Drawing on the thought of Greek and Roman Stoicism[3], where the idea of

---

1   **thorax:** chest

2   **Hugo Grotius (or Huig de Groot, 1583–1645):** Dutch jurist, humanist, and statesman, whose legal writings laid the foundation for modern international law

3   **Stoicism:** school of philosophy, founded in ancient Greece, opposed to Epicureanism in its views of life and duty. It was the most influential philosophy in the Roman Empire during the period preceding the rise of Christianity. The four virtues of the Stoic philosophy are wisdom, courage, justice, and temperance, a classification derived from the teachings of Plato.

Heritage of Western Intellectual Tradition   A Sourcebook

"natural law" originates, Grotius and others believed that there were constant and immutable[1]

Death of the divine right theory, and birth of modern constitutional politics

rational laws which should be applied to all governments. In many ways, this concept is very similar to the Roman concept of the Law of Nations, which is also derived from Stoic principles. On the other hand, Jacques-Benigne Bossuet[2] reinforced medieval notions of kingship in his theory of the Divine Right of Kings, a theory which argued that certain kings ruled because they were chosen by God to do so and that these kings were accountable to no person except God.

Legitimation of Authority

The origin of this concept extends as far back into European, Middle Eastern, and Northern African history as the practice of monarchy does; as a legitimation of authority, the idea that monarchs are divinely chosen often carried much further than the assertion that the monarch is divine which leaves little room for argument. The problem for Europe, however, is the fundamentally anti-political nature of early Christianity. This anti-political aspect of foundational Christianity threw the institution of emperorship and kingship into question. If Christ rejects all political actions and institutions, how can one justify having a monarch? Saint Augustine in *The City of God* set out the theoretical framework for the institution of Christian monarchy in his concept of the Two Cities, the City of God, that is, the body of believers, and the City of Man, that is, the secular world. Although these two cities are in spiritual conflict, the City of Man was instituted by God, according to Augustine, in order to secure the safety and security of the members of the City of God. Therefore, monarchs are placed on their thrones by God for a specific purpose. Although they may be ungodly, to question their authority is in essence to question God's purpose for both the City of Man and the City of God. This, or some form of this, made up the foundation of medieval and Renaissance theories of monarchy.

Absolutism[3]

Bossuet, however, was reacting to an extreme situation and carried this argument to its farthest extent in his doctrine of the Divine Right of Kings. Not only did God bestow power on certain monarchs (and he argued that his king, Louis XIV of France, was one such monarch),

---

1   **immutable:** that cannot be changed
2   **Jacques-Benigne Bossuet (1627–1704):** French Roman Catholic clergyman and writer, best remembered for his *Funeral Orations* (1689)
3   **absolutism:** generally applied to political systems ruled by a single dictator with little legal, customary, or moral limit on its power; it can also be applied to seemingly democratic systems that grant sweeping powers to the legislature or executive.

but the bestowal of this power legitimated autocracy (rule by one person). The king ruled by virtue of God's authority; therefore he should be obeyed in all things. No group, whether they be nobles, or a parliament, or the people in the street, have a right to participate in this rule; to question or oppose the monarch was to rebel against God's purpose. This doctrine of absolutism would follow a tortured course through the eighteenth century culminating in the French Revolution of 1789 – 1792 and the beheading of Louis XVI, the king of France.

Divine Right of Kings

An ancient doctrine that sovereigns are representatives of God and derive their right to rule directly from God. The divine right of kings as a European doctrine was largely though not exclusively associated with the medieval era, based on contemporary Christian belief that a monarch owed his rule to the will of God, not to the will of people, parliament, the aristocracy or any other competing authority and that any attempt to depose a monarch or to restrict his powers ran contrary to the will of God. Though no longer believed in, its symbolism remains in the coronation of the British monarch, in which s/he is anointed with Holy oils by the Archbishop of Canterbury, supposedly ordaining them to monarchy.

Louis XVI of France executed in 1793 by parliament

The concept of Divine Right of Kings is different from a much broader concept of "royal god-given rights," which simply says that "the right to rule is anointed by god(s)" which is found in other cultures. Unlike the Chinese concept of the Mandate of Heaven which legitimized the overthrow of an oppressive or incompetent monarch, a European king could not lose the Divine Right by misrule. In addition, the concept of Mandate of Heaven required that the emperor properly carry out the proper rituals, consult his ministers, and made it extremely difficult to undo any acts carried out by an ancestor.

Japanese imperial theory based the legitimacy of the Emperor of Japan on his descent from Ameratsu[1], however unlike the European case, this divinity did not usually translate into political power.

In the Western world it came to be associated with Roman Catholicism and other Christian faiths in the Reformation period. The notion of divine right of kings was certainly in existence anterior to[2] the medieval period, however it was during this time that the notion became extensively used as a primarily political mechanism i.e. for increasing the power of kings within cen-

---

1　**Ameratsu:** full name Amaterasu-ō-mi-kami (天照大神, literally meaning "Great Goddess Who Shines in the Heavens"), a Shinto sun goddess, the mythical ancestress of the royal family of Japan

2　**anterior to:** prior to

tralized monarchies relative to their nobles and subjects. It was given its most comprehensive formulations by the French bishop Jacques-Benigne Bossuet and King James I of England, but it owes much to the earlier writings of St. Augustine of Hippo and St. Paul of Tarsus.

In the Epistle to the Romans, ch. 13, St. Paul wrote that earthly rulers, even though they may not be Christians, have been appointed by God to their places of power for the purpose of punishing evildoers. Some Biblical scholars believe that St. Paul was writing, in part, to reassure the Roman authorities who ruled his world that the Christian movement was not politically subversive. The difficulty posed for later Christians is that the New Testament contained no explicit plan for the government of a mostly Christian society. It assumed that Christians would always be a minority in a pagan world, and its political counsel was limited mostly to advising members to obey the law and stay out of the way of pagan government.

St. Augustine modified these emphases in his work *The City of God* for the purpose of a newly converted Roman Empire that was in serious political and military turmoil. While the City of Man and the City of God may stand at cross-purposes, both of them have been instituted by God and served His ultimate will. The City of Man — the world of secular government — may seem ungodly and be governed by sinners, even so, it has been placed on earth for the protection of the City of God. Therefore, monarchs have been placed on their thrones for God's purpose, and to question their authority is to question God.

During the early reign of Louis XIV of France, Bossuet took this argument to its furthest conclusion. Reviewing Old Testament precedents concerning the selection of kings, Bossuet concluded that kings were God's anointed representatives on earth. Each of them has been given his throne by God Himself, and to rebel against their authority is to rebel against God. No parliament, nobleman, nor the common people had a right to participate in that God-given authority, since it was conferred by providence through the right of primogeniture[1].

In fact, Bossuet wrote, not to justify the authority of an already autocratic monarchy, but to shore it up against further incidents of turmoil that had shaken the French throne, such as the series of Frondes[2], in which French noblemen had fought petty civil wars against the authority of Louis XIII, and against Louis XIV himself. Bossuet's teaching ultimately proved to be the cause of much turmoil and bloodshed in France; the notion of divine right was finally overthrown in the

---

1 **primogeniture:** the firstborn
2 **Frondes (1648–1653):** civil war in France. The original goal of the "revolutionaries" was to limit the king's power and discuss various grievances; however, the movement soon degenerated into factions, some of which were attempting to overthrow Mazarin. When Louis XIV became king in 1643, he was only a child. It is probable that Louis's later insistence on absolutist rule and depriving the high nobility of actual power was a result of these events in his childhood. The term frondeur was later used to refer to anyone who suggested that the power of the king should be limited, and has now passed into normal French usage to refer to anyone who will show insubordination or engage in criticism of the powers in place.

Heritage of Western Intellectual Tradition A Sourcebook

French Revolution.

These arguments are exemplified and taken further still in the following passages from Chapter 20 of James I's Works:

The state of monarchy is the supremest thing upon earth; for kings are not only God's lieutenants upon earth, and sit upon God's throne, but even by God himself are called gods. There be three principal similitudes[1] that illustrate the state of monarchy: one taken out of the word of God; and the two other out of the grounds of policy and philosophy. In the Scriptures kings are called gods, and so their power after a certain relation compared to the divine power. Kings are also compared to fathers of families: for a king is truly Parens patriae[2], the politique father of his people. And lastly, kings are compared to the head of this microcosm of the body of man.

Kings are justly called gods, for that they exercise a manner or resemblance of divine power upon earth: for if you will consider the attributes to God, you shall see how they agree in the person of a king. God hath power to create or destroy, make or unmake, at his pleasure, to give life or send death, to judge all and to be judged nor accountable to none; to raise low things and to make high things low at his pleasure, and to God are both souls and body due. And the like power have kings: they make and unmake their subjects, they have power of raising and casting down, of life and of death, judges over all their subjects and in all causes and yet accountable to none but God only.

I conclude then this point touching the power of kings with this axiom of divinity, That as to dispute what God may do is blasphemy[3], so is it sedition[4] in subjects to dispute what a king may do in the height of his power. But just kings will ever be willing to declare what they will do, if they will not incur the curse of God. I will not be content that my power be disputed upon; but I shall ever be willing to make the reason appear of all my doings[5], and rule my actions according to my laws. [...]

James's subjects were not willing to submit to these assertions. A contrary doctrine arose, formulated by judges such as Sir Edward Coke[6], that the King of England was the creation of the

---

1   **similitude:** resemblance
2   **Parens patriae:** The doctrine literally asserting that the king is the parent of the state was formulated in England in the 13th century to assert the state's role as guardian of those who were mentally incompetent.
3   **blasphemy:** irreverent remarks about God
4   **sedition:** rebellion
5   **reason appear of all my doings:** reason of all my doings appear
6   **Sir Edward Coke (1552–1634):** English jurist, considered one of the most eminent jurists in English history, known for his challenge to royal authority

law of England, and subject to that law. This doctrine found adherents in Parliament, spurred on by such anti-monarchical precedents such as the nobles' revolt that led to Magna Carta[1]. This conflict ultimately came to a head[2] in the English Civil War, which was won by the forces representing Parliament. The Parliamentary victory, confirmed by the Glorious Revolution of 1688, was the death knell[3] of the divine right of kings in England, and firmly established the principle of constitutional monarchy where the ultimate authority was Parliament, not the monarch.

Execution of Louis XVI of France in 1793

English opponents of divine right included the poet and prose writer John Milton[4], the republican leader Algernon Sidney[5], and the political theorist James Harrington[6]. The chief supporters of the doctrine were the English philosopher Thomas Hobbes, the French classical scholar Claudius Salmasius[7], and the English political writer Sir Robert Filmer[8], whose *Patriarcha, or The Natural Power of Kings Asserted* (1680) contains a complete exposition of the theory. The controversy terminated in 1689, following the Glorious Revolution when William III and Mary II were jointly crowned after agreeing to accept the Act of Toleration and the Declaration of Rights.

Regicide

Regicide is a term used to describe the deliberate killing of a king by one of his subjects. It has particular resonance within the concept of the Divine Right of Kings, whereby monarchs were presumed by decision of God to have a divinely anointed authority to rule. As such, an attack on a king by one of his own subjects was taken to amount a direct challenge to (i) the monarch, (ii) his Divine Right to Rule, and (iii) God's will. Even after the disappearance of the

---

1 **Magna Carta:** (Latin, "Great Charter") originally document sealed by King John of England on June 15, 1215, in which he made a series of promises to his subjects that he would govern England according to the feudal law. Over the course of centuries, these promises have required governments in England to follow the law in dealing with their citizens.

2 **come to a head:** culminate

3 **knell:** sound of bell

4 **John Milton (1608–1674):** English poet, whose rich, dense verse was a powerful influence on succeeding English poets, and whose prose was devoted to the defense of civil and religious liberty. He is best known for the three epic poems, *Paradise Lost* (1667), *Paradise Regained* (1671) and *Samson Agonistes* (1671).

5 **Algernon Sidney (1622–1683):** English statesman and writer, leader of the Whig opposition to King Charles II

6 **James Harrington (1611–1677):** English political philosopher, best known for his controversial work *Oceana*, an exposition of an ideal constitution

7 **Claudius Salmasius (1588–1653):** French classical scholar, best remembered for *Defensio regia pro Carolo I* against the Independents. Charles II paid the expense of printing, and presented the author with £100.

8 **Robert Filmer (1588–1653):** English political writer, known for his *Patriarcha, or the Natural Power of Kings*. John Locke singled him out as the most remarkable of the advocates of Divine Right.

Divine Right of Kings and the appearance of Constitutional Monarchies, the term continued and continues to be used to describe the murder of a king by one of his subjects or citizens.

Five famous historical regicides were the executions or deliberate assassinations of

Henry IV of France in 1610 assassinated by Ravaillac[1];

Charles I of England in 1649 after sentence of death by parliament;

Louis XVI of France in 1793 after sentence of death by parliament;

Umberto I of Italy in 1900 by an assassin;

ex-Tsar Nicholas II of Russia in 1918 by the revolutionary government.

More recently, King Birendra of Nepal was killed in the massacre of the Nepalese royal family in 2001 by his own son, the Crown Prince.

About 100 is the number of people excepted from the Act of Pardon of 6 June 1660. At the Restoration of the Monarchy, Charles II showed political adeptness[2] by quickly resolving past conflicts. He gave a general pardon that excluded those excepted by Parliament. About 100 men who were closely involved with the execution of his father and the establishment of Oliver Cromwell as Lord Protector were excepted. Charles II, who was 18 when his father was executed in 1649, could easily have been more vengeful, but he focused more on reuniting the nation. Most of those excepted secured pardons or prison sentences. Mercy was usually given to those who turned themselves in rather than wait to be arrested. The 13 who were executed could be called scapegoats, but it's remarkable that only 13 of the conspirators were executed in this effort to bring closure to the Civil Wars and seal the Restoration of the Monarchy.

Once the decision had been taken to put Charles on trial, the outcome was a foregone conclusion. On January 20th 1649, a High Court of Justice convened to try Charles for attempting to subvert England's ancient liberties and replace them with arbitrary, tyrannical government. 135 Parliamentary Commissioners participated in what was effectively a "show trial."

A believer in divine right monarchy, Charles refused to acknowledge the court's legitimacy or respond to the charges. Eventually he was removed from Court and the charges read out in his absence. After three days of internal consultation and private interview of witnesses, Charles returned to the Court on 27th January to hear the verdict — guilty. Realising too late what was happening, he protested his innocence but it was all in vain. The Parliamentary Commissioners then convened to sign the Death Warrant and when Richard Ingoldsby[3] proved unwilling to write,

---

1   **Ravaillac (1578–1610):** killer of Henry IV of France on May 14, 1610, soon sentenced to death by being pulled apart by four horses
2   **adeptness:** flexibility
3   **Richard Ingoldsby (1617–85):** officer in the New Model Army and a Regicide who as a Commisoner (Judge) at the trial of King Charles I signed his death warrant

Cromwell grabbed his hand and forced him to sign his name.

Bowing to the inevitable, Charles met his end with great fortitude[1]. On 30th January 1649, he climbed the specially-erected scaffold outside Banqueting House to face execution. Re-affirming his allegiance to Anglicanism and his innocence of the charges, executioner Brandon then severed his head with one clean blow.

2. *Charles I: Speech Before Execution (January 30, 1649)*

On January 27, 1649, Charles I, king of England, Scotland, and Ireland, was sentenced to death as a tyrant, murderer, and enemy of the nation. His trial and execution were unprecedented in Europe. Charles met his death with composure. Of the large crowd that had gathered to witness his last moments, only those nearest Charles heard his final speech.

I shall be very little heard of anybody here; I shall therefore speak a word unto you here; indeed I could hold my peace very well, if I did not think that holding my peace would make some men think that I did submit to the guilt, as well as to the punishment; but I think it is my duty to God first and then to my country for to clear myself both as an honest man and a good king and a good Christian. I shall begin first with my innocency. In troth[2] I think it not very needful for me to insist long upon this, for all the world knows that I never did begin a war with the two Houses

Execution of King Charles I

of Parliament, and I call God to witness, to whom I must shortly make my account, that I never did intend for to encroach[3] upon their privileges; they began upon me, it is the militia, they began upon, they contest that the militia was mine, but they thought it fit for to have it from me; and to be short, if anybody will look to the dates of the commissions, of their commissions and mine, and likewise to the declarations, will see clearly that they began these unhappy troubles, not I; so that as the guilt of these enormous crimes that are laid against me, I hope in God that God will clear me of it, I will not, I am in charity; God forbid that I should lay it upon the two Houses of Parliament; there is no necessity of either, I hope they are free of this guilt, for I do believe that ill instruments between them and me has been the chief cause of all this bloodshed; so that by way of speaking as I find myself clear of this, I hope (and pray God) that they may too[4]: yet for all this, God forbid that I should be so ill a Christian as not to say that God's judgements are just upon me: many times he does pay justice by an unjust sentence[1], that is

---

1 **fortitude:** calm, self-control

2 **in troth:** truly

3 **encroach:** force, take away

4 **clear of this, I hope (and pray God) that they may too:** I hope (and pray God) that they may too be clear of this

ordinary; I will only say this, that an unjust sentence that I suffered for to take effect is punished now, by an unjust sentence upon me; that is, so far I have said, to show you that I am an innocent man.

Now for to show you that I am a good Christian: I hope there is a good man that will bear me witness, that I have forgiven all the world; even those in particular that have been the chief causes of my death; who they are, God knows, I do not desire to know, I pray God forgive them. But this is not all; my charity must go farther, I wish that they may repent, for indeed they have committed a great sin in that particular; I pray God with Saint Stephen[2] that they may take the right way to the peace of the kingdom, for my charity commands me not only to forgive particular men, but my charity commands me to endeavour to the last gasp the peace of the kingdom: so, sirs, I do with all my soul, and I do hope (there is some here will carry it further) that they may endeavour the peace of the kingdom. Now, sirs, I must show you both how you are out of the way and will put you in a way; first, you are out of the way, for certainly all the way you ever had yet as I could find by anything is in the way of conquest; certainly this is an ill way, for conquest, sir, in my opinion is never just, except there be a good just cause, either for the matter of wrong or just title, and then if you go beyond it, the first quarrel that you have to it, that makes it unjust at the end, that was just as first: But if it be only matter of conquest, then it is a great robbery; as a pirate said to Alexander, that he was the great robber, he was but a petty robber[3]; and so, sir, I do think the way that you are in, is much out of the way.

Now, sir, for to put you in the way, believe it you will never do right, nor God will never prosper you, until you give God his due, the King his due (that is, my successor), and the people their due; I am as much for them as any of you; you must give God his due by regulating rightly his church according to his Scripture which is now out of order: for to set you in a way particularly now I cannot, but only this, a national synod[4] freely called, freely debating among themselves, must settle this, when that every opinion is freely and clearly heard.

For the King: the laws of the land will clearly instruct you for that; therefore, because it concerns my own particular, I only give you a touch of it.

For the people. And truly I desire their liberty and freedom, as much as anybody whomsoever; but I must tell you that their liberty and their freedom consists in having of government those laws by which their life and their goods may be most their own. It is not for having share in government, sir, that is nothing pertaining[5] to them. A subject and a sovereign are clean different

---

1 **pay justice by an unjust sentence:** do justice through an unjust sentence
2 **Saint Stephen:** first martyr of Christianity and a saint of the Roman Catholic Church, who upon the death of Jesus began to work hard to spread what was then called The Way (teachings of Jesus) for the conversion of Jews and Gentiles.
3 **he was the great robber, he ... a petty robber:** the first "he": Alexander; the second "he": pirate
4 **synod:** meeting
5 **pertaining:** relating, concerning

things; and therefore, until they do that, I mean, that you do put the people in that liberty as I say, certainly they will never enjoy themselves.

Sirs, it was for this that now I am come here: if I would have given way to an arbitrary way, for to have all laws changed according to the power of the sword, I needed not to have come here; and therefore, I tell you (and I pray God it be not laid to your charge) that I am the martyr of the people.

In troth, sirs, I shall not hold you much longer; for I will only say this to you, that in truth I could have desired some little time longer, because that I would have put this I have said in a little more order, and a little better digested, than I have done; and therefore I hope you will excuse me.

I have delivered my conscience, I pray God, that you do take those courses that are best for the kingdom, and your own salvation.

In troth, sirs, my conscience in religion, I think, is very well known to the world; and therefore I declare before you all that I die a Christian according to the profession of the church of England, as I found it left me by my father; ... Sirs, excuse me for this same. I have a good cause, and I have a gracious God; I will say no more. I go from a corruptible to an incorruptible crown, where no disturbance can be, no disturbance in the world.

Questions for Discussion

1. Why is man in danger if left alone? What is the remedy suggested by Hobbes?
2. How is the Contract to be observed?
3. Hobbes has been regarded as both reactionary and revolutionary: reactionary against the freedom of the renaissance and the reformation by arguing for returning to strong man and tight law, revolutionary in his insistence on the security and right of individual human beings. What is your opinion?
4. Do you agree with Hobbes (he seemed to be influenced in this matter by the determinism of the 17th century physics) that men, like material atoms in disordered mass, are controlled by a certain physical force?
5. What is the definition of political power and law of nature?
6. What is the relation between freedom and obligation?
7. Why does Locke argue for self-defense?
8. What is "consent" and why is it useful?
9. How are Hobbes and Locke different from Confucius in terms of "duty" and "rights"? What are the possible causes for such differences?

UNIT 10

Classical Liberalism

Pretest

- Quote from either Adam Smith or John Stuart Mill and comment.
- Discuss what you believe to be the most important idea of the two people.
- How is the concept "freedom" variously expressed in the two men?

What You Will Learn in This Unit

- Some more knowledge about the Age of Reason;
- Important sections from two last Enlightenment thinkers: Smith and Mill; and
- Western Images of China.

Learn to Pronounce

Adam Smith /smɪθ/ 亚当·斯密
authoritarianism /ˌɔːˈθɒrɪˈteərɪənɪzm/ 独裁做法
Bastille /bæsˈtiːl/ 巴士底狱
cosmopolitan /ˌkɒzməˈpɒlɪtən/ 世界性的
Denis Diderot /ˈdiːdərəʊ/ 狄德罗
despotism /ˈdespətɪzəm/ 专制统治
Edmund Burke /bɜːk/ 柏克
Jean-Jacques Rousseau /ˈruːsəʊ/ 卢梭

John Stuart Mill /mɪl/ 密尔
laissez-faire /leɪˈseɪˈfeə(r)/ 自由放任政策
mercantilism /ˈmɜːkəntaɪlɪzm/ 重商主义
monopoly /məˈnɒpəlɪ/ 专营，垄断
Suffrage /ˈsʌfrɪdʒ/ 选举权，参政权
Voltaire /ˈvɒlteə/ 伏尔泰

Introduction

Modern political science, or the systematic study of and reflection upon politics, paved the way for classical liberalism, "attitude, philosophy, or movement that has as its basic concern the development of personal freedom and social progress." Classical liberalism differs from the contemporary concept of democracy in that the past liberals often tended to view with suspicion the idea of "mass participation in politics." Therefore, when liberalism eventually became identified with "movements to change the social order through the further extension of democracy," this change is usually conceived of as gradual, flexible, and adaptive, rather than as bloody and fundamental as the French Revolution. Diversified as they are, classical liberals are generally marked by an argument for political, economic, and social reform: they opposed feudal restraints that prevent individuals from any change of social status, barriers such as censorship that limit free expression of opinion, and arbitrary power exercised over the individual by the state. In international affairs, they opposed the domination by military considerations and the exploitation of native colonial people, and argued instead for a cosmopolitan policy of international cooperation. In economics, liberals have attacked monopolies and mercantilist state policies[1] that subject the economy to state control. In religion, liberals have fought against church interference in the affairs of the state and attempts by religious pressure groups to influence public opinion. Although the tendency to resist and rebel in classical liberalism, or the "negative liberalism," found its critical parallel in the mid-19th-century "positive liberalism," one that stressed the constructive social activity of the state and advocating state action in the interests of the individual, and although governmental interference in many cases proves to be necessary and beneficial in the present day situation, the suspicion of "authoritarianism" keeps the intellectual vitality of classical liberalism, thanks to the ideas generated by the 18th and early 19th century liberals.

Adam Smith: An Inquiry into the Nature and Causes of the Wealth of Nations

Adam Smith (1723 – 1790), British philosopher and economist, "father of modern economics" whose *The Wealth of Nations* was the first serious study on the nature of capital and the historical development of industry and commerce among European nations. Smith was born in Kirkcaldy, Scotland. At 14 he went to the University of Glasgow and later with a fellowship to Oxford. From 1748 to 1751, he gave lectures on rhetoric and *belles-lettres* in Edinburgh, before being appointed professor of logic in 1751 at 27 and then professor of

---

1　**mercantilist state policies:** national policies of accumulating bullion, establishing colonies and a merchant marine, and developing industry and mining to attain a favorable balance of trade

Heritage of Western Intellectual Tradition — A Sourcebook

moral philosophy in 1752 at the University of Glasgow. His first major work, *Theory of Moral Sentiments* (1759), systematized his ethical teachings. In 1763 he resigned to be tutor to Henry Scott, 3rd duke of Buccleuch, whom he accompanied on an 18-month tour of France and Switzerland, where he met many leading Continental philosophers such as Voltaire, Turgot, Quesnay, and started writing *The Wealth of Nations*. Smith worked in London until 1767 when he was elected a fellow of the Royal Society. His intellectual circle included Edmund Burke, Samuel Johnson, Edward Gibbon, and perhaps Benjamin Franklin. From 1766 to 1776 he lived in Kirkcaldy preparing *The Wealth of Nations* (1776, the year for the birth of economics as a separate discipline, known as "English School of Classical Political Economy"). The treatise embodies a penetrating analysis of the processes whereby economic wealth is produced and distributed. The central thesis of the book is that capital is best employed for the production and distribution of wealth under conditions of governmental noninterference, or *laissez-faire*, and free trade. To explain this concept, Smith proclaimed the principle of the "invisible hand": every individual in pursuing his or her own good is led to achieve the best good for all. Individuals become socialized, market-oriented, class-bound. Therefore any interference with free competition by government is almost certain to be injurious. By the time *The Wealth of Nations* was published, Jefferson was signing the US Declaration of Independence, and the Industrial Revolution saw new techniques in iron production and invention of steam engine. Smith tried and succeeded in providing a comprehensive philosophical account for this spirit of the age.

Book IV, Chapter II

Of Restraints upon the Importation

from Foreign Countries of Such Goods

As Can Be Produced at Home

By restraining, either by high duties or by absolute prohibitions, the importation of such goods from foreign countries as can be produced at home, the monopoly of the home market is more or less secured to the domestic industry employed in producing them. Thus the prohibition of importing either live cattle or salt provisions[1] from foreign countries secures to the graziers[2] of Great Britain the monopoly of the home market for butcher's meat. The high duties upon the importation of corn, which in times of moderate plenty amount to a prohibition, give a like[3] advantage to the growers of that commodity. The prohibition of the importation of foreign woollens is equally favourable to the woollen manufacturers. The silk manufacture, though altogether employed upon foreign materials, has lately obtained the same advantage. The linen[4] manufacture has not yet obtained it, but is making great strides towards it. Many other sorts of manufacturers have, in the same manner, obtained in Great Britain, either altogether or very nearly, a monopoly

---

1 **provisions:** food supplies
2 **grazier:** person who feeds cattle for market
3 **like:** similar
4 **linen:** cloth, textile

against their countrymen. The variety of goods of which the importation into Great Britain is prohibited, either absolutely, or under certain circumstances, greatly exceeds what can easily be suspected by those who are not well acquainted with the laws of the customs.

That this monopoly of the home market frequently gives great encouragement to that particular species of industry which enjoys it, and frequently turns towards that employment a greater share of both the labour and stock of the society than would otherwise have gone to it, cannot be doubted. But whether it tends either to increase the general industry of the society, or to give it the most advantageous direction, is not, perhaps, altogether so evident.

The general industry of the society never can exceed what the capital of the society can employ. As the number of workmen that can be kept in employment by any particular person must bear a certain proportion to his capital, so the number of those that can be continually employed by all the members of a great society must bear a certain proportion to the whole capital of that society, and never can exceed that proportion. **No regulation of commerce can increase the quantity of industry in any society beyond what its capital can maintain. It can only divert a part of it into a direction into which it might not otherwise have gone; and it is by no means certain that this artificial direction is likely to be more advantageous to the society than that into which it would have gone of its own accord.**

Bank of England had decided to put Adam Smith's image on the reverse of the new £20 note.

Every individual is continually exerting himself to find out the most advantageous employment for whatever capital he can command. It is his own advantage, indeed, and not that of the society, which he has in view. But the study of his own advantage naturally, or rather necessarily, leads him to prefer that employment which is most advantageous to the society.

First, every individual endeavours to employ his capital as near home as he can, and consequently as much as he can in the support of domestic industry; provided always that he can thereby obtain the ordinary, or not a great deal less than the ordinary profits of stock.

Thus, upon equal or nearly equal profits, every wholesale merchant naturally prefers the home trade to the foreign trade of consumption, and the foreign trade of consumption to the carrying trade[1]. In the home trade his capital is never so long out of his sight as it frequently is in the foreign trade of consumption. He can know better the character and situation of the persons whom he trusts, and if he should happen to be deceived, he knows better the laws of the country

---

1 **carrying trade:** the business of transporting goods, etc., from one place or country to another by water or land

from which he must seek redress. ... Upon equal, or only nearly equal profits, therefore, every individual naturally inclines to employ his capital in the manner in which it is likely to afford the greatest support to domestic industry, and to give revenue[1] and employment to the greatest number of people of his own country.

Secondly, every individual who employs his capital in the support of domestic industry, necessarily endeavours so to direct that industry that its produce[2] may be of the greatest possible value.

The produce of industry is what it adds to the subject or materials upon which it is employed. In proportion as the value of this produce is great or small, so will likewise be the profits of the employer. But it is only for the sake of profit that any man employs a capital in the support of industry; and he will always, therefore, endeavour to employ it in the support of that industry of which the produce is likely to be of the greatest value, or to exchange for the greatest quantity either of money or of other goods.

But the annual revenue of every society is always precisely equal to the exchangeable value of the whole annual produce of its industry, or rather is precisely the same thing with that exchangeable value. As every individual, therefore, endeavours as much as he can both to employ his capital in the support of domestic industry, and so to direct that industry that its produce may be of the greatest value; every individual necessarily labours to render the annual revenue of the society as great as he can. He generally, indeed, neither intends to promote the public interest, nor knows how much he is promoting it. **By preferring the support of domestic to that of foreign industry, he intends only his own security; and by directing that industry in such a manner as its produce may be of the greatest value, he intends only his own gain, and he is in this, as in many other cases, led by an invisible hand to promote an end which was no part of his intention. Nor is it always the worse for the society that it was no part of it[3]. By pursuing his own interest he frequently promotes that of the society more effectually than when he really intends to promote it.** I have never known much good done by those who affected[4] to trade for the public good. It is an affectation, indeed, not very common among merchants, and very few words need be employed in dissuading them from it.

What is the species of domestic industry which his capital can employ, and of which the produce is likely to be of the greatest value, every individual, it is evident, can, in his local situation, judge much better than any statesman or lawgiver can do for him. The statesman who should attempt to direct private people in what manner they ought to employ their capitals would not only load[5] himself with a most unnecessary attention, but assume an authority which could safely be trusted, not only to no single person, but to no council or senate whatever, and which would nowhere be so dangerous as in the hands of a man who had folly and presump-

---

1 **revenue:** income
2 **produce:** that which is produced, product
3 **no part of it:** not part of his intention
4 **affect:** pretend
5 **load:** burden

tion enough to fancy himself fit to exercise it.

To give the monopoly of the home market to the produce of domestic industry, in any particular art or manufacture, is in some measure to direct private people in what manner they ought to employ their capitals, and must, in almost all cases, be either a useless or a hurtful regulation. If the produce of domestic can be brought there as cheap as that of foreign industry, the regulation is evidently useless. If it cannot, it must generally be hurtful. It is the maxim of every prudent master of a family never to attempt to make at home what it will cost him more to make than to buy. The tailor does not attempt to make his own shoes, but buys them of the shoemaker. The shoemaker does not attempt to make his own clothes, but employs a tailor. The farmer attempts to make neither the one nor the other, but employs those different artificers[1]. All of them find it for their interest to employ their whole industry in a way in which they have some advantage over their neighbours, and to purchase with a part of its produce, or what is the same thing, with the price of a part of it, whatever else they have occasion for.

...

The grave of Adam Smith, Canongate Churchyard, Edinburgh, Scotland

Even the free importation of foreign corn could very little affect the interest of the farmers of Great Britain. Corn is a much more bulky[2] commodity than butcher's meat. A pound of wheat at a penny is as dear as a pound of butcher's meat at fourpence. The small quantity of foreign corn imported even in times of the greatest scarcity may satisfy our farmers that they can have nothing to fear from the freest importation. The average quantity imported, one year with anothers, amount only, according to the very well informed author of the tracts upon the corn trade, to[3] twenty-three thousand seven hundred and twenty-eight quarters[4] of all sorts of grain, and does not exceed the five hundred and seventy-one part of the annual consumption. But as the bounty[5] upon corn occasions a greater exportation in years of plenty, so it must of consequence occasion a greater importation in years of scarcity than in the actual state of tillage[6] would otherwise take place. By means of it the plenty of one year does not compensate the scarcity of another, and as the average quantity exported is necessarily augmented by it, so must likewise, in the actual state of tillage, the average quantity imported[7]. If there were no bounty, as less corn

---

1 **artificers:** skilled workmen
2 **bulky:** of large quantity
3 **amounts only, according to the very well informed author of the tracts upon the corn trade, to:** amounts only … to
4 **quarter:** 8 bushels or 64 gallons
5 **bounty:** subsidy as award
6 **tillage:** cultivation, growth
7 **the average quantity imported:** The average quantity imported is also necessarily augmented by it.

would be exported, so it is probable that, one year with another, less would be imported than at present. The corn-merchants, the fetchers and carriers of corn between Great Britain and foreign countries would have much less employment, and might suffer considerably; but the country gentlemen and farmers could suffer very little. It is in the corn merchants accordingly, rather than in the country gentlemen and farmers, that I have observed the greatest anxiety for the renewal and continuation of the bounty.

Country gentlemen and farmers are, to their great honour, of all people, the least subject to the wretched spirit of monopoly. The undertaker of a great manufactory is sometimes alarmed if another work of the same kind is established within twenty miles of him. The Dutch undertaker of the woollen manufacture at Abbeville stipulated[1] that no work of the same kind should be established within thirty leagues[2] of that city. Farmers and country gentlemen, on the contrary, are generally disposed rather to promote than to obstruct the cultivation and improvement of their neighbours' farms and estates. They have no secrets such as those of the greater part of manufacturers, but are generally rather fond of communicating to their neighbours and of extending as far as possible any new practice which they have found to be advantageous. *Pius Questus*, says old Cato, *stabilissimusque, minimeque invidiosus; minimeque male cogitantes sunt, qui in eo studio occupati sunt.*[3] Country gentlemen and farmers, dispersed in different parts of the country, cannot so easily combine as merchants and manufacturers, who, being collected into towns, and accustomed to that exclusive corporation spirit which prevails in them, naturally endeavour to obtain against all their countrymen the same exclusive privilege which they generally possess against the inhabitants of their respective towns. They accordingly seem to have been the original inventors of those restraints upon the importation of foreign goods which secure to them the monopoly of the home market. It was probably in imitation of them, and to put themselves upon a level with those who, they found, were disposed to oppress them, that the country gentlemen and farmers of Great Britain so far forgot the generosity which is natural to their station as to demand[4] the exclusive privilege of supplying their countrymen with corn and butcher's meat. They did not perhaps take time to consider how much less their interest could be affected by the freedom of trade than that of the people whose example they followed.

To prohibit by a perpetual law the importation of foreign corn and cattle is in reality to enact that the population and industry of the country shall at no time exceed what the rude produce of its own soil can maintain.

...

---

1   **stipulate:** insist on, state as a condition

2   **league:** 3 miles

3   **Pius Questus ... studio occupati sunt.:** "On the other hand, it is from the farming class that the bravest men and the sturdiest soldiers come, their calling is most highly respected, their livelihood is most assured and is looked on with the least hostility, and those who are engaged in that pursuit are least inclined to be disaffected." Cato the Elder (or Marcus Porcius Cato, 234–149 BC), Roman statesman and writer known for his interested in agriculture and the simple life typical of Roman landholders of early Republican times.

4   **so far forgot the generosity ... as to demand:** so far forgot ... as to demand

The case in which it may sometimes be a matter of deliberation[1], how far, or in what manner, it is proper to restore the free importation of foreign goods, after it has been for some time interrupted, is, when particular manufactures, by means of high duties or prohibitions upon all foreign goods which can come into competition with them, have been so far extended as to employ a great multitude of hands.[2] Humanity may in this case require that the freedom of trade should be restored only by slow gradations, and with a good deal of reserve and circumspection[3]. Were those high duties and prohibitions taken away all at once, cheaper foreign goods of the same kind might be poured so fast into the home market as to deprive all at once many thousands of our people of[4] their ordinary employment and means of subsistence[5]. The disorder which this would occasion might no doubt be very considerable. It would in all probability, however, be much less than is commonly imagined, for the two following reasons:

First, all those manufactures, of which any part is commonly exported to other European countries without a bounty, could be very little affected by the freest importation of foreign goods. Such manufactures must be sold as cheap abroad as any other foreign goods of the same quality and kind, and consequently must be sold cheaper at home. They would still, therefore, keep possession of the home market, and though a capricious[6] man of fashion might sometimes prefer foreign wares, merely because they were foreign, to cheaper and better goods of the same kind that were made at home, this folly could, from the nature of things, extend to so few that it could make no sensible impression upon the general employment of the people. But a great part of all the different branches of our woollen manufacture, of our tanned leather, and of our hardware, are annually exported to other European countries without any bounty, and these are the manufactures which employ the greatest number of hands. The silk, perhaps, is the manufacture which would suffer the most by this freedom of trade, and after it the linen, though the latter much less than the former.

Secondly, though a great number of people should, by thus restoring the freedom of trade, be thrown all at once out of their ordinary employment and common method of subsistence, it would by no means follow that they would thereby be deprived either of employment or subsistence. By the reduction of the army and navy at the end of the late war, more than a hundred thousand soldiers and seamen, a number equal to what is employed in the greatest manufactures, were all at once thrown out of their ordinary employment; but, though they no doubt suffered some inconveniency, they were not thereby deprived of all employment and subsistence. The greater part of the seamen, it is probable, gradually betook themselves to[7] the merchant-service as they

---

1   **deliberation:** careful consideration
2   **The case in which it may ... multitude of hands.:** The case ... is ... when particular manufactures ... have been ...
3   **circumspection:** carefulness
4   **deprive all at once many thousands of our people of:** deprive ... of
5   **subsistence:** existence
6   **capricious:** changeable, unreliable
7   **betake oneself to:** go to

could find occasion, and in the meantime both they and the soldiers were absorbed in the great mass of the people, and employed in a great variety of occupations. Not only no great convulsion[1], but no sensible disorder arose from so great a change in the situation of more than a hundred thousand men, all accustomed to the use of arms, and many of them to rapine[2] and plunder. The number of vagrants[3] was scarce anywhere sensibly increased by it, even the wages of labour were not reduced by it in any occupation, so far as I have been able to learn, except in that of seamen in the merchant service. But if we compare together the habits of a soldier and of any sort of manufacturer, we shall find that those of the latter do not tend so much to disqualify him from being employed in a new trade, as those of the former from being employed in any. The manufacturer has always been accustomed to look for his subsistence from his labour only: the soldier to expect it from his pay. Application and industry have been familiar to the one; idleness and dissipation[4] to the other. But it is surely much easier to change the direction of industry from one sort of labour to another than to turn idleness and dissipation to any. To the greater part of manufactures besides, it has already been observed, there are other collateral[5] manufactures of so similar a nature that a workman can easily transfer his industry from one of them to another. The greater part of such workmen too are occasionally employed in country labour[6]. The stock[7] which employed them in a particular manufacture before will still remain in the country to employ an equal number of people in some other way. The capital of the country remaining the same, the demand for labour will likewise be the same, or very nearly the same, though it may be exerted in different places and for different occupations. Soldiers and seamen, indeed, when discharged from the king's service, are at liberty to exercise any trade, within any town or place of Great Britain or Ireland. Let the same natural liberty of exercising what species of industry they please, be restored to all his Majesty's subjects, in the same manner as to soldiers and seamen; that is, break down the exclusive privileges of corporations, and repeal[8] the Statute[9] of Apprenticeship, both which are real encroachments[10] upon natural liberty, and add to these the repeal of the Law of Settlements, so that a poor workman, when thrown out of employment either in one trade or in one place, may seek for it in another trade or in another place without the fear either of a prosecution or of a removal, and neither the public nor the individuals will suffer much more from the occasional disbanding[11] of some particular classes of manufacturers than from that of

---

1 **convulsion:** violent disturbance

2 **rapine:** robbery

3 **vagrant:** wandering poor person

4 **dissipation:** engagement in foolish behaviors

5 **collateral:** subordinate

6 **country labour:** people who work in a farm

7 **stock:** supply

8 **repeal:** revoke, annul

9 **statute:** law

10 **encroachment:** violation

11 **disband:** break up

soldiers. Our manufacturers have no doubt great merit with their country, but they cannot have more than those who defend it with their blood, nor deserve to be treated with more delicacy.

To expect, indeed, that the freedom of trade should ever be entirely restored in Great Britain is as absurd as to expect that an Oceana[1] or Utopia should ever be established in it. Not only the prejudices of the public, but what is much more unconquerable, the private interests of many individuals, irresistibly oppose it[2]. Were the officers of the army to oppose with the same zeal and unanimity any reduction in the numbers of forces with which[3] master manufacturers set themselves against every law that is likely to increase the number of their rivals in the home market; were the former to animate their soldiers in the same manner as the latter enflame their workmen to attack with violence and outrage the proposers of any such regulation, to attempt to reduce the army would be as dangerous as it has now become to attempt to diminish in any respect the monopoly which our manufacturers have obtained against us. **This monopoly has so much increased the number of some particular tribes of them that, like an overgrown standing army, they have become formidable[4] to the government, and upon many occasions intimidate[5] the legislature.** The Member of Parliament who supports every proposal for strengthening this monopoly is sure to acquire not only the reputation of understanding trade, but great popularity and influence with an order of men whose numbers and wealth render them of great importance. If he opposes them, on the contrary, and still more if he has authority enough to be able to thwart[6] them, neither the most acknowledged probity[7], nor the highest rank, nor the greatest public services can protect him from the most infamous[8] abuse and detraction[9], from personal insults, nor sometimes from real danger, arising from the insolent[10] outrage of furious and disappointed monopolists.

The undertaker of a great manufacture, who, by the home markets being suddenly laid open to the competition of foreigners, should be obliged to abandon his trade, would no doubt suffer very considerably. That part of his capital which had usually been employed in purchasing materials and in paying his workmen might, without much difficulty, perhaps, find another employment.

---

1 **Oceana:** a work by James Harrington (1611–1677, English political philosopher) where he describes an ideal constitution with "Oceana" being England, and the lawgiver Olphaus Megaletor representing Oliver Cromwell, with details carefully elaborated, right down to the salaries of officials. The book was originally banned by Oliver Cromwell, but eventually published in 1656.

2 **it:** free trade

3 **which:** zeal and unanimity

4 **formidable:** very powerful

5 **intimidate:** frighten

6 **thwart:** frustrate, defeat

7 **probity:** honesty

8 **infamous:** shameful, wicked

9 **detraction:** disparagement, devaluing

10 **insolent:** offensive, insulting

Heritage of Western Intellectual Tradition   A Sourcebook

But that part of it which was fixed in workhouses, and in the instruments of trade, could scarce be disposed of without considerable loss. The equitable[1] regard, therefore, to his interest requires that changes of this kind should never be introduced suddenly, but slowly, gradually, and after a very long warning. The legislature, were it possible that its deliberations could be always directed, not by the clamorous importunity[2] of partial interests, but by an extensive view of the general good, ought upon this very account, perhaps, to be particularly careful neither to establish any new monopolies of this kind, nor to extend further those which are already established. Every such regulation introduces some degree of real disorder into the constitution of the state, which it will be difficult afterwards to cure without occasioning another disorder.

Key Concepts

absolute prohibition	invisible hand
censorship	monopoly
freedom of trade	prohibition of importing
greatest possible value	revenue for government
high duties	tax
home market	wealth of nations
hurtful regulation	

John Stuart Mill: On Liberty*

John Stuart Mill (1806–1873) had a great impact on the 19th-century British thought, not only in philosophy and economics but also in areas of political science, logic, and ethics. Mill had an unusually early and extensive education by his father, the British historian, economist, and philosopher James Mill. He began Greek at 3, and by 8 he had read in the original Greek *Aesop's Fables*, Xenophon's *Anabasis*, and the whole of the historian Herodotus. Meanwhile he started Latin, the geometry of Euclid, and algebra and began to teach the younger children of the family. His main reading was history, but he went through all the Latin and Greek authors commonly read in the schools and universities. By 10 he could read Plato with ease. At about 12, he began a thorough

---

1 **equitable:** fair, reasonable
2 **clamorous importunity:** noisy, continuous and unreasonable request
* *On Liberty*, still a classic work in the field, best represents this "saint of rationalism" by laying emphasis on freedom of thought, discussion and conscience.

study of Scholastic logic, at the same time reading Aristotle's logical treatises in the original. In the following year he began to study Adam Smith. He could but didn't go to Oxford and Cambridge as they  were under ecclesiastical control. So he continued his study under his father's tutelage. At 17 he had completed advanced and thorough courses of study in Greek literature and philosophy, chemistry, botany, psychology, and law. But this childhood was a strain on his constitution and he suffered from the lack of natural, unforced development. Mill stands "as a bridge between the 18th-century concern for liberty, reason, and science and the 19th-century trend toward empiricism and collectivism." In political economy, Mill advocated the policies most consistent with individual liberty. He is probably most famous for his essay "On Liberty" (1859). In Parliament, Mill was considered a radical, because he supported public ownership of natural resources, equality for women, compulsory education, and birth control, and worked actively to improve the conditions of the working people. He supported the North in the U.S. Civil War in the struggle for the abolition of slavery. In 1867 he had been one of the founders of the first women's suffrage society, which developed into the National Union of Women's Suffrage Societies, and in 1869 he published *The Subjection of Women* (written 1861), the classical theoretical statement of the case for woman suffrage.

Chapter I   Introductory

The object of this Essay is to assert one very simple principle, as entitled to govern absolutely the dealings of society with[1] the individual in the way of compulsion and control, whether the means used be physical force in the form of legal penalties, or the moral coercion[2] of public opinion. **That principle is, that the sole end for which mankind are warranted[3], individually or collectively, in interfering with the liberty of action of any of their number, is self-protection. That the only purpose for which power can be rightfully exercised over any member of a civilized community, against his will, is to prevent harm to others.** His own good, either physical or moral, is not a sufficient warrant. He cannot rightfully be compelled to do or forebear[4] because it will make him happier, because, in the opinion of others, to do so would be wise, or even right. These are good reasons for remonstrating[5] with him, or reasoning with him, or persuading him, or entreating[6] him, but not for compelling him, or visiting him with any evil in case he do otherwise. To justify that, the conduct from which it is desired to deter him, must be calculated to produce evil to some one else. **The only part of the conduct of any**

---

1 **the dealings of society with:** dealings … with
2 **coercion:** forced obedience
3 **warrant:** guarantee, justify
4 **forebear:** here forbear, refrain from doing
5 **remonstrate:** argue on protest
6 **entreat:** ask earnestly

one, for which he is amenable[1] to society, is that which concerns others. In the part which merely concerns himself, his independence is, of right, absolute. Over himself, over his own body and mind, the individual is sovereign.

It is, perhaps, hardly necessary to say that this doctrine is meant to apply only to human beings in the maturity of their faculties. We are not speaking of children, or of young persons below the age which the law may fix as that of manhood or womanhood. Those who are still in a state to require being taken care of by others, must be protected against their own actions as well as against external injury. For the same reason, we may leave out of consideration those backward states of society in which the race itself may be considered as in its nonage[2]. The early difficulties in the way of spontaneous progress are so great, that there is seldom any choice of means for overcoming them; and a ruler full of the spirit of improvement is warranted in the use of any expedients that will attain an end, perhaps otherwise unattainable. **Despotism[3] is a legitimate mode of government in dealing with barbarians, provided the end be their improvement, and the means justified by actually effecting that end. Liberty, as a principle, has no application to any state of things anterior to the time when mankind have become capable of being improved by free and equal discussion.** Until then, there is nothing for them but implicit obedience to an Akbar[4] or a Charlemagne[5], if they are so fortunate as to find one. But as soon as mankind have attained the capacity of being guided to their own improvement by conviction or persuasion (a period long since reached in all nations with whom we need here concern ourselves), compulsion, either in the direct form or in that of pains and penalties for non-compliance, is no longer admissible as a means to their own good, and justifiable only for the security of others.

It is proper to state that I forego[6] any advantage which could be derived to my argument from the idea of abstract right, as a thing independent of utility, I regard utility as the ultimate appeal on all ethical questions; but it must be utility in the largest sense, grounded on the permanent interests of a man as a progressive being. Those interests, I contend, authorize the subjection of individual spontaneity to[7] external control, only in respect to those actions of each, which concern the interest of other people. If any one does an act hurtful to others, there is a *prima facie*[8] case for punishing him, by law, or, where legal penalties are not safely applicable, by general disapprobation[9]. There are also many positive acts for the benefit of others, which he may rightfully be compelled to perform; such as to give evidence in a court of justice; to bear his fair

---

1 **amenable:** responsible
2 **nonage:** immaturity
3 **despotism:** rule with unlimited powers, tyranny
4 **Akbar (1542–1605):** third Mughal emperor of India (1556–1605), founder of the Mughal Empire
5 **Charlemagne (c.742–814):** king of the Franks (768–814) and emperor of the Romans (800–814).
6 **forego:** give up
7 **the subjection of individual spontaneity to:** subjection … to
8 *prima facie*: evident without proof or reasoning, obvious
9 **disapprobation:** disapproval

share in the common defence, or in any other joint work necessary to the interest of the society of which he enjoys the protection; and to perform certain acts of individual beneficence[1], such as saving a fellow-creature's life, or interposing[2] to protect the defenceless against ill-usage, things which whenever it is obviously a man's duty to do, he may rightfully be made responsible to society for not doing. A person may cause evil to others not only by his actions but by his inaction, and in either case he is justly accountable to them for the injury. The latter case, it is true, requires a much more cautious exercise of compulsion than the former. To make any one answerable for doing evil to others, is the rule; to make him answerable for not preventing evil, is comparatively speaking, the exception. Yet there are many cases clear enough and grave enough to justify that exception. In all things which regard the external relations of the individual, he is *de jure*[3] amenable to those whose interests are concerned, and if need be, to society as their protector. There are often good reasons for not holding him to the responsibility; but these reasons must arise from the special expediences[4] of the case; either because it is a kind of case in which he is on the whole likely to act better, when left to his own discretion, than when controlled in any way in which society have it in their power to control him; or because the attempt to exercise control would produce other evils, greater than those which it would prevent. When such reasons as these preclude the enforcement of responsibility, the conscience of the agent himself should step into the vacant judgment seat, and protect those interests of others which have no external protection; judging himself all the more rigidly, because the case does not admit of his being made accountable to the judgment of his fellow-creatures.

But there is a sphere of action in which society, as distinguished from the individual, has, if any, only an indirect interest; comprehending all that portion of a person's life and conduct which affects only himself, or if it also affects others, only with their free, voluntary, and undeceived consent and participation. When I say only himself, I mean directly and in the first instance; for whatever affects himself, may affect others through himself; and the objection which may be grounded on this contingency[5], will receive consideration in the sequel. This, then, is the appropriate region of human liberty. It comprises, first, the inward domain of consciousness; demanding liberty of conscience, in the most comprehensive sense; liberty of thought and feeling; absolute freedom of opinion and sentiment on all subject, practical or speculative, scientific, moral or theological. The liberty of expressing and publishing opinions may seem to fall under a different principle, since it belongs to that part of the conduct of an individual which concerns other people; but, being almost of as much importance as the liberty of thought itself, and resting in great part on the same reasons, is practically inseparable from it[6]. Secondly, the principle requires liberty of tastes and pursuits; of framing the plan of our life to suit our own character; of doing as

---

1 **beneficence:** doing good
2 **interpose:** make an interruption
3 *de jure*: according to law, by right
4 **expedience:** suitability
5 **contingency:** uncertainty of occurrence
6 **it:** liberty of expressing and publishing

we like, subject to such consequences as may follow: without impediment from our fellow creatures, so long as what we do does not harm them, even though they should think our conduct foolish, perverse, or wrong. Thirdly, from this liberty of each individual, follows the liberty, within the same limits, of combination among individuals, freedom to unite, for any purpose not involving harm to others; the persons combining being supposed to be of full age, and not forced or deceived.

No society in which these liberties are not, on the whole, respected, is free, whatever may be its form of government; and none is completely free in which they[1] do not exist absolutely and unqualified. The only freedom which deserves the name, is that of pursuing our own good in our own way, so long as we do not attempt to deprive others of theirs[2], or impede their efforts to obtain it. Each is the proper guardian of his own health, whether bodily, or mental and spiritual. Mankind are greater gainers by suffering each other to live as seems good to themselves, than by compelling each to live as seems good to the rest.

Chapter II   Of the Liberty of Thought and Discussion

The time, it is to be hoped, is gone by, when any defence would be necessary of the "liberty of the press" as one of the securities against corrupt or tyrannical government. No argument, we may suppose, can now be needed, against permitting a legislature or an executive, not identified in interest with the people, to prescribe opinions to them, and determine what doctrines or what arguments they shall be allowed to hear. This aspect of the question, besides, has been so often and so triumphantly enforced by preceding writers, that it needs not be specially insisted on in this place. Though the law of England on the subject of the press, is as servile[3] to this day as it was in the time of the Tudors[4], there is little danger of its being actually put in force against political discussion, except during some temporary panic, when fear of insurrections[5] drives ministers and judges from their propriety; and, speaking generally, it is not, in constitutional countries, to be apprehended[6], that the government, whether completely responsible to the people or not, will often attempt to control the expression of opinion, except when in doing so it makes itself the organ of the general intolerance of the public. Let us suppose, therefore, that the government is entirely at one with the people, and never thinks of exerting any power of coercion unless in agreement with what it conceives to be their voice[7]. But I deny the right of the people to exercise such coercion, either by themselves, or by their government. **The power itself is**

---

1 **they:** these liberties
2 **theirs:** their good
3 **servile:** slavish
4 **Tudors:** the dynasty that occupied the throne of England from 1485 to 1603, followed in royal succession by the Stuart family
5 **insurrection:** rebellion
6 **apprehend:** fear
7 **unless in agreement with what it conceives to be their voice:** unless they ask for coercion

illegitimate. **The best government has no more title to it than the worst. It is as noxious, or more noxious, when exerted in accordance with public opinion, than when in opposition to it. If all mankind minus one, were of one opinion, and only one person were of the contrary opinion, mankind would be no more justified in silencing that one person, than he, if he had the power, would be justified in silencing mankind.** Were an opinion a personal possession of no value except to the owner; if to be obstructed[1] in the enjoyment of it were simply a private injury, it would make some difference whether the injury was inflicted only on a few persons or on many. But the peculiar evil of silencing the expression of an opinion is, that it is robbing the human race, posterity as well as the existing generation; those who dissent from the opinion, still more than those who hold it[2]. If the opinion is right, they are deprived of the opportunity of exchanging error for truth; if wrong, they lose, what is almost as great a benefit, the clearer perception and livelier impression of truth, produced by its collision with error.

Mill on Suffrage for Women

It is necessary to consider separately these two hypotheses, each of which has a distinct branch of the argument corresponding to it. **We can never be sure that the opinion we are endeavoring to stifle is a false opinion; and if we were sure, stifling it would be an evil still.**

...

Mankind can hardly be too often reminded, that there was once a man named Socrates, between whom and the legal authorities and public opinion of his time, there took place a memorable collision. Born in an age and country abounding in individual greatness, this man has been handed down to us by those who best knew both him and the age, as the most virtuous man in it; while *we* know him as the head and prototype of all subsequent teachers of virtue, the source equally of the lofty inspiration of Plato and the judicious utilitarianism of Aristotle, "*i maestri di color che sanno*[3]," the two headsprings[4] of ethical as of all other philosophy. This acknowledged master of all the eminent thinkers who have since lived — whose fame, still growing after more than two thousand years, all but overweighs the whole remainder of the names which make his native city illustrious — was put to death by his countrymen, after a judicial conviction, for impiety and immorality. Impiety, in denying the gods recognized by the State; indeed his accuser asserted that he believed in no gods at all. Immorality, in being, by his doctrines and instructions, a "corrupter of youth." Of these charges the tribunal, there is every ground for believing,

---

1 **obstruct:** block up
2 **it is robbing the human race ... who hold it:** it is robbing ... those who dissent from the opinion more than those who hold it
3 *i maestri di color che sanno*: the masters of those who know
4 **headspring:** pioneer

Heritage of Western Intellectual Tradition A Sourcebook

honestly found him guilty, and condemned the man who probably of all then born had deserved best of mankind, to be put to death as a criminal.

To pass from this to the only other instance of judicial iniquity[1], the mention of which, after the condemnation of Socrates, would not be an anti-climax: the event which took place on Calvary[2] rather more than eighteen hundred years ago. The man who left on the memory of those who witnessed his life and conversation, such an impression of his moral grandeur, that eighteen subsequent centuries have done homage to him as the Almighty in person, was ignominiously[3] put to death, as what? As a blasphemer[4]. Men did not merely mistake their benefactor; they mistook him for the exact contrary of what he was, and treated him as that prodigy[5] of impiety, which they themselves are now held to be, for their treatment of him. The feeling with which mankind now regard these lamentable transactions, especially the latter of the two, render them extremely unjust in their judgment of the unhappy actors. These were, to all appearance, not bad men — not worse than men commonly are, but rather the contrary; men who possessed in a full, or somewhat more than a full measure, the religious, moral, and patriotic feelings of their time and people: the very kind of men who, in all times, our own included, have every chance of passing through life blameless and respected. The high-priest who rent his garments when the words were pronounced[6], which according to all the ideas of his country, constituted the blackest guilt, was in all probability quite as sincere in his horror and indignation, as the generality of respectable and pious men now are in the religious and moral sentiments they profess; and most of those who now shudder at his conduct, if they had lived in his time, and been born Jews, would have acted precisely as he did. **Orthodox Christians who are tempted to think that those who stoned to death the first martyrs must have been worse men than they themselves are, ought to remember that one of those persecutors was Saint Paul[7].**

…

Before quitting the subject of freedom of opinion, it is fit to take some notice of those who say, that the free expression of all opinions should be permitted, on condition that the manner be temperate, and do not pass the bounds of fair discussion. Much might be said on the impossibility

---

1 **iniquity:** injustice, wickedness
2 **Calvary:** the hill outside ancient Jerusalem where the crucifixion of Jesus Christ took place
3 **ignominiously:** dishonorably
4 **blasphemer:** one who speaks irreverently about God
5 **prodigy:** a young person with unusual ability
6 **The high-priest who ... words were pronounced:** Biblical allusion: "Then Baruch answered them, He pronounced all these words unto me with his mouth, and I wrote them with ink in the book. ... Yet they were not afraid, nor rent their garments, neither the king, nor any of his servants that heard all these words (Jeremiah 36:18, 24).
7 **Saint Paul:** The Apostle Paul, originally called Saul of Tarsus, one of the early leaders of the Christian Church. Before his conversion to Christianity, his zeal for the Jewish Law led him to persecute the nascent Christian church and support the stoning of St. Stephen, the first Christian martyr.

of fixing where these supposed bounds are to be placed; for if the test be offence to those whose opinions are attacked, I think experience testifies that this offence is given whenever the attack is telling[1] and powerful, and that every opponent who pushes them[2] hard, and whom[3] they find it difficult to answer, appears to them, if he shows any strong feeling on the subject, an intemperate opponent[4]. ... The worst offence of this kind which can be committed by a polemic[5], is to stigmatize[6] those who hold the contrary opinion as bad and immortal men. To calumny[7] of this sort, those who hold any unpopular opinion are peculiarly exposed, because they are in general few and uninfluential, and nobody but themselves feels much interested in seeing justice done them; but this weapon is, from the nature of the case, denied to those who attack a prevailing opinion: they

MILL'S LOGIC; OR, FRANCHISE FOR FEMALES.

This punch cartoon mocks Mill's attempt to replace the term 'man' with 'person' in the second Reform Bill of 1867. His proposal was greeted with laughter in the House of Commons and defeated by 76 votes to 196.

can neither use it with safety to themselves, nor, if they could, would it do anything but recoil[8] on their own cause. In general, opinions contrary to those commonly received can only obtain a hearing by studied moderation of language, and the most cautious avoidance of unnecessary offence, from which they hardly ever deviate even in a slight degree without losing ground: while unmeasured vituperation[9] employed on the side of the prevailing opinion, really does deter people from professing contrary opinions, and from listening to those who profess them. For the interest, therefore, of truth and justice, it is far more important to restrain this employment of vituperative language than the other; and, for example, if it were necessary to choose, there would be much more need to discourage offensive attacks on infidelity than on religion. It is, however, obvious that law and authority have no business with restraining either, while opinion ought, in every instance, to determine its verdict by the circumstances of the individual case; condemning every one, on whichever side of the argument he places himself, in whose mode of advocacy either want of candor[10], or malignity, bigotry[11], or intolerance of feeling manifest themselves; but not

---

1 **telling:** effective
2 **them:** those whose opinions are attacked
3 **whom:** every opponent
4 **every opponent who pushes them ... an intemperate opponent:** every opponent ... appears to them ... an intemperate opponent
5 **polemic:** argument
6 **stigmatize:** describe scornfully
7 **calumny:** an untrue and unfair statement
8 **recoil:** draw back
9 **vituperation:** abusive language
10 **candor:** frankness
11 **bigotry:** holding strongly to an opinion

Heritage of Western Intellectual Tradition   A Sourcebook

inferring these vices from the side which a person takes, though it be the contrary side of the question to our own; and giving merited honor to every one, whatever opinion he may hold, who has calmness to see and honesty to state what his opponents and their opinions really are, exaggerating nothing to their discredit, keeping nothing back which tells, or can be supposed to tell, in their favor. This is the real morality of public discussion: and if often violated, I am happy to think that there are many controversialists[1] who to a great extent observe it, and a still greater number who conscientiously strive towards it.

...

Chapter III   Of Individuality, As One of the Elements of Well-Being

Such being the reasons which make it imperative that human beings should be free to form opinions, and to express their opinions without reserve; and such the baneful[2] consequences to the intellectual, and through that to the moral nature of man, unless this liberty is either conceded[3], or asserted in spite of prohibition; let us next examine whether the same reasons do not require that men should be free to act upon their opinions — to carry these out in their lives, without hindrance, either physical or moral, from their fellow-men, so long as it is at their own risk and peril. This last proviso[4] is of course indispensable. No one pretends that actions should be as free as opinions. On the contrary, even opinions lose their immunity[5], when the circumstances in which they are expressed are such as to constitute their expression a positive instigation[6] to some mischievous act. An opinion that corn-dealers are starvers of the poor, or that private property is robbery, ought to be unmolested[7] when simply circulated through the press, but may justly incur punishment when delivered orally to an excited mob assembled before the house of a corn-dealer, or when handed about among the same mob in the form of a placard[8]. Acts, of whatever kind, which, without justifiable cause, do harm to others, may be, and in the more important cases absolutely require to be, controlled by the unfavourable sentiments, and, when needful, by the active interference of mankind. The liberty of the individual must be thus far limited; he must not make himself a nuisance to other people. But if he refrains from molesting others in what concerns them, and merely acts according to his own inclination and judgment in things which concern himself, the same reasons which show that opinion should be free, prove also that he should be allowed, without molestation, to carry his opinions into practice at his own cost. That mankind are not infallible; that their truths, for the most part, are only half-truths; that unity of

---

1 **controversialists:** people who enjoy arguing with others
2 **baneful:** evil
3 **concede:** admit, grant
4 **proviso:** precondition
5 **immunity:** security, exemption
6 **instigation:** excitement, encouragement
7 **unmolested:** not being troubled or annoyed
8 **placard:** poster, notice

opinion, unless resulting from the fullest and freest comparison of opposite opinions, is not desirable, and diversity not an evil, but a good, until mankind are much more capable than at present of recognizing all sides of the truth, are principles applicable to men's modes of action, not less than to their opinions. As it is useful that while mankind are imperfect there should be different opinions, so is it that there should be different experiments of living; that free scope should be given to varieties of character, short of injury to others; and that the worth of different modes of life should be proved practically, when any one thinks fit to try them. It is desirable, in short, that in things which do not primarily concern others, individuality should assert itself. Where, not the person's own character, but the traditions of customs of other people are the rule of conduct, there is wanting one of the principal ingredients of human happiness, and quite the chief ingredient of individual and social progress.

    In maintaining this principle, the greatest difficulty to be encountered does not lie in the

John Stuart Mill and his wife Helen Tay

appreciation of means towards an acknowledged end, but in the indifference of persons in general to[1] the end itself. If it were felt that the free development of individuality is one of the leading essentials of well-being; that it is not only a co-ordinate[2] element with all that is designated by the terms civilization, instruction, education, culture, but is itself a necessary part and condition of all those things; there would be no danger that liberty should be undervalued, and the adjustment of the boundaries between it and social control would present no extraordinary difficulty. But the evil is, that individual spontaneity is hardly recognized by the common modes of thinking, as having any intrinsic worth, or deserving any regard on its own account. The majority, being satisfied with the ways of mankind as they now are (for it is they who make them what they are[3]), cannot comprehend why those ways should not be good enough for everybody; and what is more, spontaneity forms no part of the ideal of the majority of moral and social reformers, but is rather looked on with jealousy, as a troublesome and perhaps rebellious obstruction to the general acceptance of what these reformers, in their own judgment, think would be best for mankind. Few persons, out of Germany, even comprehend the meaning of the doctrine which Wilhelm Von Humboldt[4], so eminent both as a *savant*[5] and as a politician, made the text of a treatise — that "the end of man, or that which is prescribed by the eternal or immutable[6] dictates of reason, and not suggested by vague and transient desires, is the highest and most harmonious development of his powers to a complete and consistent whole;" that, therefore, the object "towards which every human being must cease-

---

1   **indifference of persons in general to:** indifference … to
2   **co-ordinate:** equal
3   **for it is they who make them what they are:** first "they", the majority; second "they", mankind
4   **Wilhelm Von Humboldt (1767 – 1835):** Prussian statesman, educational reformer, and philologist. Humboldt wrote on philology, political science and composed poetry and translated Greek classics.
5   *savant:* learned person, scholar
6   **immutable:** unchangeable

Heritage of Western Intellectual Tradition   A Sourcebook

lessly direct his efforts, and on which especially those who design to influence their fellow-men must ever keep their eyes, is the individuality of power and development;" that for this there are two requisites, "freedom, and variety of situations;" and that from the union of these arise "individual vigor and manifold diversity," which combine themselves in "originality."

Little, however, as people are accustomed to a doctrine like that of Von Humboldt, and surprising as it may be to them to find so high a value attached to individuality, the question one must nevertheless think, can only be one of degree. No one's idea of excellence in conduct is that people should do absolutely nothing but copy one another. No one would assert that people ought not to put into their mode of life, and into the conduct of their concerns, any impress[1] whatever of their own judgment, or of their own individual character. On the other hand, it would be absurd to pretend that people ought to live as if nothing whatever had been known in the world before they came into it; as if experience had as yet done nothing towards showing that one mode of existence, or of conduct, is preferable to another. Nobody denies that people should be so taught and trained in youth, as to know and benefit by the ascertained results of human experience. But it is the privilege and proper condition of a human being, arrived at the maturity of his faculties, to use and interpret experience in his own way. It is for him to find out what part of recorded experience is properly applicable to his own circumstances and character. The traditions and customs of other people are, to a certain extent, evidence of what their experience has taught *them*; presumptive evidence, and as such, have a claim to his deference[2]: but, in the first place, their experience may be too narrow; or they may not have interpreted it rightly. Secondly, their interpretation of experience may be correct, but unsuitable to him. Customs are made for customary circumstances, and customary characters; and his circumstances or his character may be uncustomary[3]. Thirdly, though the customs be both good as customs, and suitable to him yet to conform to custom, merely *as* custom, does not educate or develop in him any of the qualities which are the distinctive endowment of a human being. The human faculties of perception, judgment, discriminative feeling, mental activity, and even moral preference, are exercised only in making a choice. He who does anything because it is the custom, makes no choice. He gains no practice either in discerning or in desiring what is best. The mental and moral, like the muscular powers, are improved only by being used. The faculties are called into no exercise by doing a thing merely because others do it, no more than by believing a thing only because others believe it. If the grounds of an opinion are not conclusive to the person's own reason, his reason cannot be strengthened, but is likely to be weakened, by his adopting it: and if the inducements to an act are not such as are consentaneous[4] to his own feelings and character (where affection, or the rights of others, are not concerned) it is so much done towards rendering his feelings and character inert and torpid[5], instead of active and energetic.

---

1   **impress:** mark, impression
2   **deference:** courteous respect
3   **uncustomary:** not commonly practiced or based on tradition
4   **consentaneous:** agreeable
5   **torpid:** dull, slow, inactive

He who lets the world, or his own portion of it, choose his plan of life for him, has no need of any other faculty than the ape-like one of imitation. He who chooses his plan for himself, employs all his faculties. He must use observation to see, reasoning and judgment to foresee, activity to gather materials for decision, discrimination to decide, and when he has decided, firmness and self-control to hold to his deliberate decision. And these qualities he requires and exercises exactly in proportion as the part of his conduct which he determines according to his own judgment and feelings is a large one. It is possible that he might be guided in some good path, and kept out of harm's way, without any of these things. But what will be his comparative worth as a human being? It really is of importance, not only what men do, but also what manner of men they are that do it. Among the works of man, which human life is rightly employed in perfecting and beautifying, the first in importance surely is man himself. Supposing it were possible to get houses built, corn grown, battles fought, causes tried, and even churches erected and prayers said, by machinery — by automatons[1] in human form — it would be a considerable loss to exchange for these automatons even the men and women who at present inhabit the more civilized parts of the world, and who assuredly are but starved[2] specimens of what nature can and will produce. **Human nature is not a machine to be built after a model, and set to do exactly the work prescribed for it, but a tree, which requires to grow and develop itself on all sides, according to the tendency of the inward forces which make it a living thing.**

It will probably be conceded that it is desirable people should exercise their understandings, and that an intelligent following of custom, or even occasionally an intelligent deviation from custom, is better than a blind and simply mechanical adhesion to it. To a certain extent it is admitted, that our understanding should be our own: but there is not the same willingness to admit that our desires and impulses should be our own likewise; or that to possess impulses of our own, and of any strength, is anything but a peril and a snare. Yet desires and impulses are as much a part of a perfect human being, as beliefs and restraints: and strong impulses are only perilous when not properly balanced; when one set of aims and inclinations is developed into strength, while others, which ought to co-exist with them, remain weak and inactive. It is not because men's desires are strong that they act ill; it is because their consciences are weak. There is no natural connection between strong impulses and a weak conscience. The natural connection is the other way. To say that one person's desires and feelings are stronger and more various than those of another, is merely to say that he has more of the raw material of human nature, and is therefore capable, perhaps of more evil[3], but certainly of more good. Strong impulses are but another name for energy. Energy may be turned to bad uses; but more good may always be made of an energetic nature, than of an indolent[4] and impassive[5] one. Those who have most natural feeling, are always those whose cultivated feelings may be made the strongest. The same strong

---

1 **automaton:** self-operating machine or mechanism, such as a robot
2 **starved:** here most needed
3 **capable, perhaps of more evil:** capable … of more evil
4 **indolent:** inactive
5 **impassive:** motionless

susceptibilities[1] which make the personal impulses vivid and powerful, are also the source from whence are generated the most passionate love of virtue, and the sternest self-control. It is through the cultivation of these, that society both does its duty and protects its interests: not by rejecting the stuff of which heroes are made, because it knows not how to make them. A person whose desires and impulses are his own — are the expression of his own nature, as it has been developed and modified by his own culture — is said to have a character. One whose desires and impulses are not his own, has no character, no more than a steam-engine has a character. If, in addition to being his own, his impulses are strong, and are under the government of a strong will, he has an energetic character. Whoever thinks that individuality of desires and impulses should not be encouraged to unfold itself, must maintain that society has no need of strong natures — is not the better for containing many persons who have much character — and that a high general average of energy is not desirable.

... In our times, from the highest class of society down to the lowest, every one lives as under the eye of a hostile and dreaded censorship. Not only in what concerns others, but in what concerns only themselves, the individual or the family do not ask themselves — what do I prefer? or, what would suit my character and disposition? or, what would allow the best and highest in me to have fair play, and enable it to grow and thrive? They ask themselves, what is suitable to my position? what is usually done by persons of my station and pecuniary[2] circumstances? or (worse still) what is usually done by persons of a

Delacroix's "Liberty Leading the People" (1830). Mill's thinking reflects much of the 19th century liberalism.

station and circumstances superior to mine? I do not mean that they choose what is customary, in preference to what suits their own inclination. It does not occur to them to have any inclination, except for what is customary. Thus the mind itself is bowed to the yoke: even in what people do for pleasure, conformity is the first thing thought of; they like in crowds; they exercise choice only among things commonly done: peculiarity of taste, eccentricity of conduct, are shunned equally with crimes: until by dint of[3] not following their own nature, they have no nature to follow: their human capacities are withered and starved: they become incapable of any strong wishes or native pleasures, and are generally without either opinions or feelings of home growth, or properly their own. Now is this, or is it not, the desirable condition of human nature?

It is so, on the Calvinistic theory. According to that, the one great offence of man is self-will. All the good of which humanity is capable, is comprised in obedience. You have no choice;

---

1 **susceptibility:** feeling, sensitiveness
2 **pecuniary:** relating to money
3 **by dint of:** by means of

thus you must do, and not otherwise: "whatever is not a duty, is a sin." Human nature being radically corrupt, there is no redemption for any one until human nature is killed within him. To one holding this theory of life, crushing out any of the human faculties, capacities, and susceptibilities, is no evil: man needs no capacity, but that of surrendering himself to the will of God: and if he uses any of his faculties for any other purpose but to do that supposed will[1] more effectually, he is better without them[2]. This is the theory of Calvinism; and it is held, in a mitigated[3] form, by many who do not consider themselves Calvinists; the mitigation consisting in giving a less ascetic[4] interpretation to the alleged will of God; asserting it to be his will that mankind should gratify some of their inclinations; of course not in the manner they themselves prefer, but in the way of obedience, that is, in a way prescribed to them by authority; and, therefore, by the necessary condition of the case, the same for all.

...

It is not by wearing down into uniformity all that is individual in themselves, but by cultivating it, and calling it forth, within the limits imposed by the rights and interests of others, that human beings become a noble and beautiful object of contemplation[5]; and as the works partake[6] the character of those who do them, by the same process human life also becomes rich, diversified, and animating, furnishing more abundant aliment[7] to high thoughts and elevating feelings, and strengthening the tie which binds every individual to the race, by making the race infinitely better worth belonging to. In proportion to the development of his individuality, each person becomes more valuable to himself, and is therefore capable of being more valuable to others. There is a great fullness of life about his own existence, and when there is more life in the units there is more in the mass which is composed of them. As much compression[8] as is necessary to prevent the stronger specimens of human nature from encroaching on the rights of others, cannot be dispensed with; but for this there is ample compensation even in the point of view of human development. The means of development which the individual loses by being prevented from gratifying his inclinations to the injury of others, are chiefly obtained at the expense of the development of other people. And even to himself there is a full equivalent in the better development of the social part of his nature, rendered possible by the restraint put upon the selfish part. To be held to rigid rules of justice for the sake of others, develops the feelings and capacities which have the good of others for their object. But to be restrained in things not affecting their good by

---

1 **supposed will:** will of God
2 **them:** his faculties
3 **mitigate:** make less severe
4 **ascetic:** self-denying
5 **It is not by wearing down ... object of contemplation:** It is not by ... but by ... that ...
6 **partake:** involve
7 **aliment:** something that nourishes, supports or sustains
8 **compression:** putting together

Heritage of Western Intellectual Tradition   A Sourcebook

their mere displeasure, develops nothing valuable, except such force of character as may unfold itself in resisting the restraint. If acquiesced in[1], it dulls and blunts the whole nature. To give any fair play to the nature of each, it is essential that different persons should be allowed to lead different lives. In proportion as this latitude[2] has been exercised in any age, has that age been noteworthy to posterity. Even despotism does not produce its worst effects, so long as individuality exists under it; and whatever crushes individuality is despotism, by whatever name it may be called, and whether it professes to be enforcing the will of God or the injunctions[3] of men.

Key Concepts

compulsion and control

despotism

external control

freedom of opinion and sentiment

freedom to unite

human liberty

legal penalties

liberty of conscience

liberty of expressing and publishing

liberty of tastes and pursuits

liberty of thought and feeling

moral coercion of public opinion

subjection of individual spontaneity

Compare with China

It is difficult to pinpoint the exact time for Sino-Western cultural exchange, but it certainly reached a peak in the late 18th and early 19th centuries, evidenced by the liberalists' representations of the West made of China. The cultural exchange continues till today in, for instance, the dialogue between classical liberalism and Confucianism.

1. Western Images of China

Until the middle of the eighteenth century, China generally received favorable attention in the West. In large part this stemmed from the wide dissemination of books and published correspon-

---

1　**acquiesce in:** accept blindly
2　**latitude:** freedom in action and opinion
3　**injunction:** order

Heritage of Western Intellectual Tradition　A Sourcebook

dence by Catholics, especially the Jesuits, who saw in the huge population of China a potential harvest of souls for the Christian faith[1]. Although mindful of some of China's problems, most Catholic observers followed the example of the Jesuit missionary Matteo Ricci, who had lived in China from 1583 to 1610 and admired the industry of China's population, the sophistication of the country's bureaucracy, the philosophical richness of its cultural traditions, and the strength of its rulers.

The French Jesuits, who dominated the China missions late in Kangxi's reign, presented an even more laudatory[2] picture of the early Qing state, one deliberately designed to appeal to the "Sun King," Louis XIV, and to persuade him to back the missionaries with money and personnel. Central to these flattering presentations was the idea that the ethical content of the Confucian Classics proved the Chinese were a deeply moral nation and had once practiced a form of monotheism not so different from that found in the Judaeo-Christian tradition. With a little effort, therefore, the Chinese could be brought back to the true values they had once espoused[3], and did not have to be forced to convert.

Although the Jesuits rapidly lost influence in China during the last years of Kangxi's reign, and declined in prestige in Europe during the eighteenth century until suppressed altogether in 1773, their books on Chinese government and society remained so far the most detailed available. The German philosopher Gottfried Wilhelm von Leibnitz[4] read them and became deeply interested in the structure of the hexagrams[5] in the *Book of Changes*. Even the anticlerical philosopher Voltaire was intrigued by what he read about the Chinese. Since Voltaire was intent on attacking the power of the Catholic church in eighteenth-century France, he cleverly used the information about China provided by the Catholics to disprove their more extreme claims. If, argued Voltaire, the Chinese really were so moral, intelligent, ethical, and well governed, and if this was largely attributable to the influence of Confucius, it followed that since Confucius had not been a Christian it was obviously possible for a country to get along admirably without the presence of Catholic clerical power.

In a series of influential works written between 1740 and 1760, Voltaire expounded his ideas about China. In one novel he presented his views on the parallelism of moral values in different societies, European and Asian. In a play he suggested that the innate moral strength of the Chinese

---

1   **huge population of China a potential harvest of souls for the Christian faith:** Namely, this vast population is just waiting to be converted to Christianity.

2   **laudatory:** expressing or conferring praise

3   **espouse:** give loyalty or support to

4   **Gottfried Wilhelm von Leibnitz (1646 – 1716):** German philosopher and mathematician who invented differential and integral calculus independently of Newton and proposed an optimist metaphysical theory that included the notion that we live in "the best of all possible worlds"

5   **hexagram:** a figure of six lines or sides, here representing images making Xiangs（象）and Trigrams（卦）

Heritage of Western Intellectual Tradition   A Sourcebook

had been able to calm even the Mongol conquerors led by Genghis Khan[1]. And in an unusual historiographical gesture, Voltaire began his review of world history — *Essai sur les moeurs et l'esprit des nations* ("An Essay on the Customs and Spirit of Nations") — with a lengthy section on China. He did this to emphasize the values of differing civilizations and to put European arrogance in perspective: "The great misunderstanding over Chinese rites sprang from our judging their practices in light of ours: for we carry the prejudices that spring from our contentious nature to the ends of the world." Unable to find a "philosopher-king" in Europe to exemplify his views of religion and government, Voltaire believed Emperor Qianlong would fill the gap, and he wrote poems in the distant emperor's honor.

Voltaire's praise for Chinese institutions appeared in a cultural context that was intensely sympathetic to China. During this same brief period in the mid-eighteenth century, Europe was swept by a fascination with China that is usually described by the French word *chinoiserie*, an enthusiasm drawn more to Chinese decor[2] and design than to philosophy and government. In prints and descriptions of Chinese houses and gardens, and in Chinese embroidered silks, rugs, and colorful porcelains, Europeans found an alternative to the geometrical precision of their neoclassical architecture and the weight[3] of baroque[4] design. French rococo[5] was a part of this mood, which tended to favor pastel[6] colors, asymmetry, a calculated disorder, a dreamy sensuality. Its popular manifestations could be found everywhere in Europe, from the "Chinese" designs on the new wallpapers and furnishings that graced middle-class homes to the pagodas in public parks, the sedan chairs, in which people were carried through the streets, and the latticework[7] that surrounded ornamental gardens.

Yet this cult[8] of China, whether intellectual or aesthetic, faded swiftly as angry and sarcastic accounts like George Anson's[9] became available. Voltaire's very enthusiasms made him the object of sarcasm or mockery as other great figures among the French Enlightenment philosophers began to find his picture of China unconvincing. Jean-Jacques Rousseau and the Baron de Montesquieu worried that the Chinese did not seem to enjoy true liberty, that their laws were

---

1 **Genghis Khan (c. 1162 – 1227):** originally Temujin, Mongol conqueror who united the Mongol tribes and forged an empire stretching from China to the Danube River and into Persia. In 1206 he took the name Genghis Khan ("supreme conqueror").

2 **decor:** decorative style or scheme, as of a room

3 **weight:** importance, influence

4 **baroque:** a style in art and architecture developed in Europe from the early 17th to mid-18th century, emphasizing dramatic, often strained effect and typified by bold, curving forms, elaborate ornamentation, and overall balance of disparate parts

5 **rococo:** style of art, especially architecture and decorative art, that originated in France in the early 18th century and is marked by elaborate ornamentation, as with a profusion of scrolls, foliage, and animal forms

6 **pastel:** light

7 **latticework:** open and crisscross pattern

8 **cult:** worship

9 **George Anson (1797 – 1857):** British soldier, Commander-in-Chief in India early in 1856

based on fear rather than on reason, and that their elaborate educational system might lead to the corruption of Chinese morals rather than to their improvement. Other writers declared that China did not seem to be progressing, had indeed no notion of progress; from this it was but a short step to see the Chinese as, in fact, retrogressing[1]. In the somber words of the French historian Nicolas Boulanger[2], written in 1763 and translated from the French the following year by the English radical John Wilkes[3]:

Hegel the Philosopher

All the remains of her ancient institutions, which China now possesses, will necessarily be lost; they will disappear in the future revolutions; as what she hath already lost of them vanished in former ones; and finally, as she acquires nothing new, she will always be on the losing side.

Reflecting on these arguments concerning China and the Chinese, some leading European thinkers labored to assess the country's prospects. One of these was the Scottish philosopher Adam Smith, who wrote on China in *The Wealth of Nations*, first published in 1776. In his analysis of the productive capacities of different countries, Smith found China useful for comparative purposes, especially with the nations of Europe and the developing societies of North America. Examining population growth as an index of development, he concluded that in Europe, where countries doubled their populations every five hundred years, growth was steady if undramatic. In North America, where the population doubled every twenty or twenty-five years, there was instant employment for the entire new work force; the New World was therefore "much more thriving, and advancing with much greater rapidly to the further acquisition of riches."

China, however, "long one of the richest, that is, one of the most fertile, best cultivated, most industrious, and most populous countries in the world," had reached that stage in the cycle of growth where it had "acquired that full complement of riches which the nature of its laws and institutions permits it to acquire." In such a situation, continued population growth brought serious economic repercussions[4]: "If in such a country the wages of labour had ever been more than sufficient to maintain the labourer, and to enable him to bring up a family, the competition of the labourers and the interest of the masters would soon reduce them to this lowest rate which is consistent with common humanity." The result was that "the poverty of the lower ranks of people in China far surpasses that of the most beggarly nations in Europe" and infanticide[5] became an integral social practice. As Smith acidly phrased it: "Marriage is encouraged in China, not by the profitableness of children, but by the liberty of destroying them." China was

---

1 **retrogress:** go back to an earlier and worse state
2 **Nicolas Boulanger (1722–1759):** contemporary of Jean-Jacques Rousseau, Voltaire, and Diderot
3 **John Wilkes (1727–1797):** English radical, journalist and politician
4 **repercussion:** back driving, retreat
5 **infanticide:** practice of killing newborn infants

Heritage of Western Intellectual Tradition   A Sourcebook

exacerbating[1] these problems, according to Smith, by refusing to consider change. By staying aloof from the growth of the world economy, China was sealing its fate:[2] "A country which neglects or despises foreign commerce, and which admits the vessels of foreign nations into one or two of its ports only, cannot transact the same quantity of business which it might do with different laws and institutions."

In a famous series of lectures delivered by the German philosopher Georg Wilhelm Friedrich Hegel[3] in the early 1820s, the various critical analyses; explored by Boulanger, Rousseau, Montesquieu[4], and Smith were synthesized in such away that "Oriental Civilizations" — China pre-eminent among them — came to be seen as a nearly and now by-passed stage of history. The view of "Asiatic Society" synthesized by Hegel was to have a profound influence on the young Karl Marx and other later nineteenth-century thinkers. History, to Hegel, was the development of what he called the ideas and practices of freedom throughout the world. Freedom was the expression of the self-realization of the "World Spirit," and that spirit was reaching its fullest manifestations in the Christian states of Europe and North America. Optimistic about his own time, Hegel developed a theory that downplayed China's past. He described China as dominated by its emperors or despots[5], as typical of the "oriental nations" that saw only one man as free. In the West, the Greeks and Romans had come to see that some men were free; and, centuries later, Hegel's generation had come to see that all human were free. Lacking an understanding of the march of Spirit in the world, even the Chinese emperor's "freedom" was "caprice[6]," expressed as either "ferocity[7] — brutal recklessness of passion — or a mildness and tameness of the desires, which is itself only an accident of Nature."

Part of China's fate, Hegel wrote, turned on geographical factors: "The extensive tract of eastern Asia is severed from the general historical development." In a powerfully worded passage, Hegel explained that China had lacked the great boldness of the Europeans in exploring the seas and instead had stayed tied to the agricultural rhythms of her great plains. The soil presented only "an infinite multitude of dependencies," whereas the sea carried people "beyond these limited circles of thought and action. ... This stretching out of the sea beyond the limitations of the land, is wanting to the splendid political edifices[8] of Asiatic States, although they themselves border on

---

1 **exacerbate:** aggravate, become more serious

2 **seal its fate:** make something, especially something bad, sure to happen

3 **Georg Wilhelm Friedrich Hegel (1770 – 1831):** German idealist philosopher who interpreted nature and human history and culture as expressions of a dialectical process in which Spirit, or Mind, realizes its full potentiality. His major works include *The Phenomenology of Spirit* (1807) and *The Philosophy of Right* (1821).

4 **Montesquieu (1689 – 1755):** French philosopher and jurist. An outstanding figure of the early French Enlightenment, he wrote the influential *Parisian Letters* (1721), a veiled attack on the monarchy and the *ancien régime*, and *The Spirit of the Laws* (1748), a discourse on government.

5 **despot:** tyrant, ruler with unlimited powers

6 **caprice:** changeable, irregular

7 **ferocity:** cruelty

8 **edifice:** ambition, plan

the sea — as for example, China. For them the sea is only the limit, the ceasing of the land; they have no positive relation to it." Though such a statement would have startled the wealthy ocean-going merchants of Fujian had they seen it, Hegel was basically correct that the Qing state itself was not interested in maritime exploration.

In a series of bleak conclusions, Hegel consigned[1] the Chinese permanently to their space outside the development of the World Spirit. Although China had historians galore[2], they studied their country within their own limited preconceptions, not realizing that China itself lay "outside the World's History, as the mere presupposition of elements whose combination must be waited for to constitute their vital-progress." Although Chinese emperors may speak words of "majesty and paternal kindness and tenderness to the people," the Chinese people "cherish the meanest opinion of themselves, and believe that men are born only to drag the car of Imperial Power." In a passage that moved beyond anything Lord Macartney[3] had opined[4] about the fate of the Qing Dynasty, Hegel mourned for the Chinese people themselves: "The burden which presses them to the ground, seems to them to be their inevitable destiny: and it appears nothing terrible to them to sell themselves as slaves, and to eat the bitter bread of slavery."

Yet perhaps China was not caught forever in a metaphysical and geographical isolation. In one of his most ambiguous asides[5], Hegel added that "a relation to the rest of History could only exist in their case, through their being sought out, and their character investigated by others." The question of by whom or how that seeking out was to be done was left open by Hegel, but the Western powers, with their ships, their diplomatic missions, and their opium, were rapidly beginning to provide an answer. (Adapted from Jonathan D. Spence)

2. Qianlong Meets Macartney: Collision of Two World Views

On Sept. 14,1793, a British delegation led by Sir George Macartney arrived in Peking, bearing expensive gifts of telescopes, watches, globes, and astronomical instruments, to "celebrate" Qianlong's birthday and ask "freer trade". Macartney won an audience with the emperor who accepted the gifts as a sign of respect but declared that the Chinese had no need for foreign goods. The episode led finally to the First Opium War in 1842.

The Macartney mission of 1792–94 is a defining episode in the modern encounter between

---

1　**consign:** give up

2　**galore:** in plenty

3　**George Macartney (1737 – 1806):** 1st Earl Macartney, British statesman, colonial administrator. Appointed the first envoy of Britain to China (1792), he arrived in Beijing in 1793 with a large British delegation. He met the Emperor Qianlong, but failed in negotiating the British requests: relaxation of the restrictions on trade between Britain and China, acquisition by Britain of "a small unfortified island near Chusan for the residence of English traders, storage of goods, and outfitting of ships," and establishment of a permanent British embassy in Beijing.

4　**opine:** express the opinion

5　**asides:** words spoken aside on stage

China and the West. It is the first major event in which British diplomats well read in the ideas of the European Enlightenment came face to face with the leadership of the world's greatest and most populous land power. Before that time, educated Europeans had learned about China mainly through the writings of French Catholic missionaries. Eighteenth-century European philosophers, with the notable exception of Montesquieu, had rather liked what they perceived as the rationality and beneficence of Chinese Imperial government. In addition, a taste for Chinese art developed among the European aristocracy. Whole rooms in eighteenth-century European palaces and aristocratic estates were given over to *chinoiserie*. But this was contact at a distance. Outside of Russo-Chinese relations, no major diplomatic or political decision making had as yet been involved.

The Qing dynasty rulers, for their part, had developed an interest in the products of Western culture. The Qianlong emperor in particular took a fancy to European art and culture. During his long reign (1736–96) Italian artists produced scrolls and paintings depicting court life and ceremonies and trained Chinese court artists to paint using Western-style perspective. Numerous watches, clocks, and scientific utensils with Western art motifs made their way into the Court furnishings. The most notable access of Western style came with the construction of the old Summer Palace outside of Peking, which reproduced motifs from Versailles on Qing Imperial soil. In addition, several European missionaries resided in Beijing and were available to advise the Emperor on European matters.

But the Qing Court did not normally permit any concession to Western tastes in how it conducted its ritual ceremonies. These ceremonies, carried out in formal settings with casts of hundreds or thousands, represented the Emperor as Son of Heaven or as Chief Ruler, mediating with supranatural[1] or terrestrial powers to maintain cosmic and political harmony, through a process that the texts refer to as 'centering.'

The Emperor himself had to carry out ceremonies mediating with superior authority, such as Heaven, or his forbears, or even his living elders. For example, the Qianlong Emperor was exceedingly devoted to his mother and went to extraordinary lengths to exhibit his filiality. His Chinese subordinates carried out comparable rituals within their spheres of jurisdiction.

For Qing Manchu rulers, this ceremonial role was particularly important to establish their legitimacy with the Confucian bureaucracy as holders of Heaven's mandate. This was how 2-3 million Manchus were able to legitimize control over a population that grew to as much as a hundred times that size. In addition, as rulers who had extended their power over non-ethnic Chinese domains of southeast and inner Asia, the Qing rulers functioned as Buddhist redemptive sovereigns and intercessors, responsible for bringing peace to huge regions beyond the traditional Chinese domain.

---

1 **supranatural:** supra, above

The Qing emperors developed a large imperial domain at Rehe (Jehol), 200 kilometers north of Beijing and replete with Tibetan Buddhist temples, which they could use to greet missions from dependent rulers in their capacity as both Confucian and Buddhist sovereigns. As recently as 1791 (a year before the Macartney mission set out for China), Qing armies successfully defeated a Nepalese (尼泊尔) invasion of Tibet, once again demonstrating their power over the vast, mountainous and desert regions of Inner Asia. The Qing rulers also maintained a capital in Manchuria, where they could receive delegations from northeastern dependencies.

Lord George Macartney

When missions came from countries beyond the boundaries of the Qing empire, they were expected to fit in with the Confucian ceremonial system by which relations between the Qing emperor and lesser powers were formalised and Qing dynastic power manifested. Thus the role of foreign officials requesting admission to the Court was to come as representatives of lesser rulers seeking grace and favor from the Confucianized overlord[1] presiding over the Qing empire. Most missions were willing to take on this stance, including a Dutch mission which followed on the heels of Macartney's.

On the British side, the Macartney mission came armed with a series of goals appropriate to an industrializing nation that was rapidly developing a world-wide trading system. As Adam Smith had pointed out, the British were a nation of shopkeepers and traders, and trade was becoming the key to their access to power and prosperity. In the 1790s the British government of Pitt[2] and Dundas[3] was busy reconstructing the British mandate in India to reduce the political power of the East India Company and create a less mercantile and more open trading system. Because trade with China had become a significant factor in the development of British power in India, they wanted to cut through the restrictions of the Canton trading system imposed by the Qianlong

Arrival of the Emperor of China to meet Lord Macartney near Peking in 1793

government on European merchants in 1760 and negotiate a freer trade environment with China as a whole. They also wanted to establish a direct liaison — along European diplomatic lines — with the Qing Court. Because of his erudition, diplomatic experience, and familiarity with British policy in India, Macartney was in principle an ideal person to represent the British government on such a mission.

---

1 **overlord:** feudal lord or nobleman
2 **William Pitt (1759–1806):** prime minister of Great Britain (1783–1801 and 1804–1806)
3 **Henry Dundas (1742–1811):** Scottish lawyer and politician, War Secretary under Pitt (1794–1801) and First Lord of the Admiralty (1804).

Heritage of Western Intellectual Tradition   A Sourcebook

But beyond these goals, Macartney and his associates came to China with perceptions about trade and national intercourse which were certain to cause friction with their Chinese hosts. As heirs of Galileo, Newton, and Locke, and contemporaries of the French Enlightenment philosophers, they regarded themselves as representatives of a modern, rational and specifically scientific world outlook. Within their lifetimes British technicians had developed chronometers needed to determine longitude, which would greatly increase the power and profitability of British navigation. They lived in a world in which Adam Smith had worked out the advantages of trade, James Watt[1] had harnessed the power of steam, and Captain Cook[2] had explored vast reaches of the Pacific Ocean. Buoyed by such developments, the Macartney mission came to China not just to promote trade and diplomacy, but to assess China's status as a rational order and to collect data on matters of interest to scientific as well as political colleagues. These latter goals were to some extent achieved, although not in a manner favorable to China's reputation in Europe.

Approach of the Emperor of China to his tent in Tartary to Receive the British Ambassador: published London 1796

Once in China Macartney proved — or appeared to the Qing leadership to prove — unwilling to function within the parameters of Qing "Guest" ritual for ordering relations between the supreme ruler and subordinate dependencies. (The issue over the "kowtow" or three kneelings and nine prostrations is only one of various problems which surfaced.) This created a serious challenge for the Empire's ceremonial managers. Some of them recognized that Macartney was educated, worldly-wise and well-equipped with gifts for the Emperor. Why couldn't he conform to the vital ceremonials by which peace and harmony were maintained and dependent leaders brought into a fulfilling relationship with the Son of Heaven and Chief Ruler? And how could his dissonant conduct be managed so that it did not disrupt ceremonial order and cast doubt upon the efficacy of the Qing emperor?

This analysis, made possible by recent scholarship, suggests that the problems of the Macartney mission were not determined so much by restrictions in trade policy or by cross-cultural misunderstandings. Rather, they resulted from increasingly divergent global interpretive and managerial systems: Imperial Confucianism on the one hand with its theories about the Mandate of Heaven and their exercise by Manchu rulers to attain dominion over China and surrounding regions;

---

1 **James Watt (1736–1819):** Scottish inventor and mechanical engineer, renowned for his improvements of the steam engine

2 **Captain James Cook (1728–1779):** British explorer and navigator, famous for his three voyages of exploration in the South Pacific Ocean and the coastal waters of North America. Cook is believed to be the discoverer of the Hawaiian Islands and is known for his detailed, careful documentation of his discoveries.

and European Enlightenment ideas about law and rationality and their application by British leaders to the reorganization of British power in India and Asia. The encounter is undertaken by human beings who try hard to sort out what is going on. Indeed, few tried harder than Qianlong and Macartney to find ways to achieve their differing objectives. But the systems were, and to a certain extent still are, incompatible. Macartney was trying to introduce to China peaceful changes in trade and diplomatic practice, while at the same time assessing Qing capacity to resist enforced change. But the Manchu-controlled Chinese state system had its own goals for the management and control of foreign power, which Macartney's mission intentionally sought to change. Thus Qianlong and his aides ended up spending much of their time figuring out how to get Macartney and company out of China. (Adapted from John R. Watt)

Chinese in late 18th century in Guangdong taking opium produced in the British East India Company

Supplementary Reading

1. The Declaration of Independence

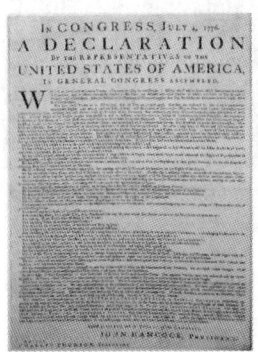

The Declaration of Independence refers to the document proclaiming the independence of the 13 British colonies, adopted by the Continental Congress on July 4, 1776. It marked the culmination of a political process that had begun as a protest against oppressive restrictions imposed by the mother country on colonial trade, manufacturing, and political liberty and had developed into a revolutionary struggle for establishing a new nation. On June 7, 1776, Richard Henry Lee, in the name of the Virginia delegates to the Continental Congress, moved that "These united colonies are and of right ought to be free and independent States, they are absolved from all allegiance to the British crown, and that all political connection between them and the State of Great Britain is and ought to be totally dissolved." This motion was seconded by John Adams of Massachusetts, and the resolution was passed on July 2. In the meantime, a committee (appointed June 11) comprising the delegates Thomas Jefferson, Benjamin Franklin, John Adams, Roger Sherman, and Robert R. Livingston was preparing a declaration in line with Lee's resolution. Jefferson prepared the draft, using "neither book nor pamphlet," as he later said. Adams and Franklin made a number of minor changes in Jefferson's draft before it was submitted to Congress, which, on July 4, made a number of additional small alterations, deleted several sections, including one condemning black slavery, incorporated Lee's resolution, and issued the whole as the

Declaration of Independence. The declaration was adopted by a unanimous vote of the delegates of 12 colonies. On July 9, the New York Provincial Congress voted to endorse the declaration. On August 2, it was signed by the 53 members present. The three absentees signed subsequently.

In Congress, July 4, 1776
The Unanimous Declaration of the Thirteen United States of America

When in the course of human events, it becomes necessary for one people to dissolve the political bands which have connected them with another, and to assume among the powers of the earth, the separate and equal station to which the Laws of Nature and of Nature's God entitle them[1], a decent respect to the opinions of mankind requires that they should declare the causes which impel them to the separation.

We hold these truths to be self-evident, that all men are created equal, that they are endowed by their Creator with certain unalienable[2] rights, that among these are life, liberty and the pursuit of happiness. That to secure these rights, governments are instituted among men, deriving their just powers from the consent of the governed. That whenever any form of government becomes destructive of these ends, it is the right of the people to alter or to abolish it, and to institute new government, laying its foundation on such principles and organizing its powers in such form, as to them shall seem most likely to effect[3] their safety and happiness. Prudence, indeed, will dictate that governments long established should not be changed for light and transient[4] causes; and accordingly all experience hath shown, that mankind are more disposed to suffer, while evils are sufferable[5], than to right[6] themselves by abolishing the forms to which they are accustomed. But when a long train of abuses and usurpations[7], pursuing invariably the same object evinces[8] a design to reduce them under absolute despotism, it is their right, it is their duty, to throw off such government, and to provide new guards for their future security. Such has been the patient sufferance of these Colonies; and such is now the necessity which constrains them to alter their former systems of government. The history of the present King of Great Britain is a history of re-

The Declaration Committee by Curries and Ives, 1876

peated injuries and usurpations, all having in direct object the establishment of an absolute tyr-

---

1   **assume among the powers ... God entitle them:** assume ... equal station to which the Laws ... entitle them
2   **unalienable:** not to be separated, given away, or taken away
3   **effect:** bring about, produce
4   **transient:** brief
5   **sufferable:** bearable
6   **right:** put in order or set right; correct
7   **usurpation:** wrongfully taking away other's rights, position, etc.
8   **evince:** show

anny over these States. To prove this, let facts be submitted to a candid[1] world.

He has refused his assent[2] to laws, the most wholesome and necessary for the public good.

He has forbidden his Governors to pass laws of immediate and pressing importance, unless suspended in their operation till his assent should be obtained; and when so suspended, he has utterly neglected to attend to them.

He has refused to pass other laws for the accommodation of large districts of people, unless those people would relinquish the right of representation in the Legislature, a right inestimable[3] to them and formidable to tyrants only.

He has called together legislative bodies at places unusual, uncomfortable, and distant from the depository[4] of their public records, for the sole purpose of fatiguing them into compliance with[5] his measures.

He has dissolved representative houses repeatedly, for opposing with manly firmness his invasions on the rights of the people.

He has refused for a long time, after such dissolutions, to cause others to be elected; whereby the legislative powers, incapable of annihilation, have returned to the people at large for their[6] exercise; the State remaining in the meantime exposed to all the dangers of invasion from without and convulsions[7] within.

He has endeavoured to prevent the population of these states; for that purpose obstructing[8] the laws of naturalization of foreigners; refusing to pass others to encourage their migration hither, and raising the conditions of new appropriations of lands.

Writing the Declaration: Jefferson, Franklin & Adams

He has obstructed the administration of justice, by refusing his assent to laws for establishing judiciary powers.

He has made judges dependent on his will alone, for the tenure[9] of their offices, and the amount and payment of their salaries.

---

1 **candid:** frank, straight-forward
2 **assent:** agreement
3 **inestimable:** very precious
4 **depository:** storehouse
5 **compliance with:** submission to
6 **their:** legislative powers'
7 **convulsion:** violent disturbance
8 **obstruct:** make difficult, prevent
9 **tenure:** holding

Heritage of Western Intellectual Tradition – A Sourcebook

He has erected a multitude of new offices, and sent hither swarms of officers to harass[1] our people, and eat out their substance.

He has kept among us, in times of peace, standing armies without the consent of our legislatures.

He has affected[2] to render the military independent of and superior to the civil power.

He has combined with others to subject us to a jurisdiction foreign to our constitution, and unacknowledged by our laws; giving his assent to their acts of pretended legislation:

Signing of the Declaration in Independence Hall, Philadelphia by J. Adams, R. Sherman, T. Jefferson (presenting the document), and B. Franklin, oil painting by John Trumbull, 1817

For quartering[3] large bodies of armed troops among us:

For protecting them, by a mock[4] trial, from punishment for any murders which they should commit on the inhabitants of these States:

For cutting off our trade with all parts of the world:

For imposing taxes on us without our consent:

For depriving us in many cases, of the benefits of trial by jury:

For transporting us beyond seas to be tried for pretended offences:

For abolishing the free system of English laws in a neighbouring Province, establishing therein an arbitrary government, and enlarging its boundaries so as to render it at once[5] an example and fit instrument for introducing the same absolute rule into these Colonies:

For taking away our Charters, abolishing our most valuable laws, and altering fundamentally the forms of our governments:

For suspending our own Legislatures, and declaring themselves invested with power to legislate for us in all cases whatsoever.

He has abdicated[6] government here, by declaring us out of his protection and waging war against us.

---

1 **harass:** trouble, disturb
2 **affect:** have an influence
3 **quarter:** place
4 **mock:** nor real
5 **at once:** at the same time
6 **abdicate:** give up

He has plundered our seas, ravaged our coasts, burnt our towns, and destroyed the lives of our people.

He is at this time transporting large armies of foreign mercenaries[1] to complete the works of death, desolation and tyranny, already begun with circumstances of cruelty and perfidy[2] scarcely paralleled in the most barbarous ages, and totally unworthy the head of a civilized nation.

He has constrained our fellow citizens taken captive on the high seas to bear arms against their country, to become the executioners of their friends and brethren, or to fall[3] themselves by their hands.

He has excited domestic insurrections[4] amongst us, and has endeavoured to bring on the inhabitants of our frontiers, the merciless Indian savages, whose known rule of warfare, is an undistinguished destruction[5] of all ages, sexes, and conditions.

In every state of these oppressions we have petitioned for redress in the most humble terms: our repeated petitions have been answered only by repeated injury. A prince whose character is thus marked by every act which may define a tyrant is unfit to be the ruler of a free people.

Nor have we been wanting in attention to our British brethren. We have warned them from time to time of attempts by their legislature to extend an unwarrantable[6] jurisdiction over us. We have reminded them of the circumstances of our emigration and settlement here. We have appealed to their native justice and magnanimity[7], and we have conjured[8] them by the ties of our common kindred[9] to disavow[10] these usurpations, which would inevitably interrupt our connections and correspondence. They too have been deaf to the voice of justice and of consanguinity[11]. We must, therefore, acquiesce in[12] the necessity, which denounces our separation, and hold them[13], as we hold the rest of mankind, enemies in war, in peace friends.

We, therefore, the Representatives of the United States of America, in General Congress assembled, appealing to the Supreme Judge of the world for the rectitude[14] of our intentions, do,

---

1 **mercenaries:** soldiers hired to fight in a foreign army
2 **perfidy:** treachery
3 **fall:** kill
4 **insurrection:** rebellion, revolt
5 **undistinguished destruction:** killing with no regards to
6 **unwarrantable:** not justifiable; inexcusable
7 **magnanimity:** generosity
8 **conjure:** appeal solemnly to
9 **kindred:** blood relationship
10 **disavow:** oppose, disapprove of
11 **consanguinity:** relationship by blood
12 **acquiesce in:** accept without protest
13 **them:** our British brethren
14 **rectitude:** honesty

Heritage of Western Intellectual Tradition   A Sourcebook

in the name, and by authority of the good people of these Colonies, solemnly publish and declare, That these United Colonies are, and of right ought to be Free and Independent States; that they are absolved[1] from all allegiance to the British Crown, and that all political connection between them and the State of Great Britain, is and ought to be totally dissolved; and that as Free and Independent States, they have full power to levy[2] war, conclude peace, contract alliances, establish commerce, and to do all other acts and things which Independent States may of right do. And for the support of this declaration, with a firm reliance on the protection of Divine Providence, we mutually pledge to each other our lives, our fortunes, and our sacred honor.

2. *United Nations Universal Declaration of Human Rights (1948)*

By the end of World War II it became widely known that there had been some terrible abuses of people during the war, in particular the attempted extermination[3] of the Jews in Europe by the German National Socialist (Nazi) Government. The United Nations declared that all people had certain rights that must never be violated. It listed these in its 1948 Universal Declaration of Human Rights, based on principles expressed in the UN Charter to affirm the dignity and rights of all human beings. The Declaration was prepared by the Commission on Human Rights of the Economic and Social Council (ECOSOC) of the United Nations. Eleanor Roosevelt, widow of US president Franklin D. Roosevelt, chaired the commission. French jurist and Nobel laureate René Cassin[4] was the declaration's principal author. In 1950 the United Nations General Assembly proclaimed December 10, the anniversary of the 1948 adoption of the declaration, as Human Rights Day.

Logo for the 50th anniversary of the Universal Declaration of Human Rights

All people everywhere have the same human rights which no one can take away. This is the basis of freedom, justice and peace in the world.

This Declaration affirms the dignity and worth of all people, and the equal rights of women and men. The rights described here are the common standard for all people everywhere. Every person and nation is asked to support the understanding and respect for these rights, and to take steps to make sure that they are recognised and observed everywhere, for all people.

---

1 **absolve:** declare free
2 **levy:** impose
3 **extermination:** complete destruction
4 **René Samuel Cassin (1887–1976):** French jurist and judge, served on the UN's Human Rights Commission and the Hague Court of Arbitration. He received the Nobel Peace Prize in 1968 for his work in drafting the Universal Declaration of Human Rights, adopted by the United Nations General Assembly on 10 December 1948.

Article 1   You have the same human rights as everyone else in the world because you are a human being. These rights cannot be taken away from you. Everybody ... should be treated with dignity.

Article 2   You should not be treated differently, or have your rights taken away because of your race [ethnicity], colour, sex, language, religion or political opinions. Your basic rights should be respected ... no matter how rich or poor you are.

Article 3   Everyone has the right to life, liberty and [to be safe].

Article 4   Human beings must not be owned, bought or sold. No one has the right to enslave anyone else. Slavery is a crime.

Article 5   Torture is forbidden ... No one should suffer treatment or punishment that is cruel or makes them feel less than human.

Article 6   Everyone has the right to be treated as a person in the eyes of the law.

Article 7   You have the right to be treated [and protected] by law in the same way as everyone else.

Article 8   If your rights under the law are violated ... you have the right to see justice done.

Article 9   You may not be arrested or [imprisoned] without good reason. You may not be kept out of your own country ...

Article 10   You have the right to a fair and public [trial] ... The courts must be independent from the government, qualified ... and free to make their own decisions.

Article 11   If accused of a crime, you have the right to be treated as innocent until you are proved guilty ... You have the right to ... defend yourself ...

Article 12   No one has the right to intrude in your private life ... without good reason. No one has the right to attack your good name without reason ... The law should protect you against such interference.

Eleanor Roosevelt, known for her humanitarian work, helped draft the Universal Declaration of Human Rights.

Article 13   You have the right to move about freely within your own country [and] to travel to and from your own country ...

Article 14   If you are forced to flee your country because of human rights abuses, you have the right to seek safety in another country. This right does not apply if you have committed a non-political crime ...

Article 15   You have the right to be treated as a citizen of the country you come from. No one can take away your citizenship or prevent you from changing your country without good reason.

Article 16   All adults have the right to marry ...

Both partners have equal rights in the marriage, and their full and free agreement is needed for the marriage to take place ...

Article 17   You have the right to own goods ... and other property ... No one has the right to take your property away without any good reason.

Article 18   You have the right to hold views on any issue ... without fear of punishment ... You also have the right to believe in any religion — or none at all ... and to practice and teach your religion and beliefs.

Article 19   You have the right to tell people your opinion ... [no matter how] unpopular [it may be].

Article 20   You have the right to peacefully gather together with other people, in public or in private. No one should force you to join any group if you do not wish to.

Article 21   You have the right to take part in the government of your country directly or by being represented ... free and fair elections should be held on a regular basis.

Article 22   You have the right to have your basic needs met. Everyone is entitled to live in economic, social and cultural conditions that allow them dignity ...

Article 23   You have the right to work in fair and safe conditions and to choose your job. You have the right to be paid enough for a decent standard of living ... You also have the right to form or join trade unions to protect your interests.

Article 24   You have the right to time off from work ... [and] to holidays with pay.

Article 25   Everyone has the right to a decent life, including enough food, clothing, housing, medical care and social services. Society should help those unable to work ... Mothers and children are entitled to special care ...

Article 26   Everyone has the right to an education. In the early years ... it should be free ... and compulsory ... at a higher level [it] should be equally available to everyone on the basis of merit ...

Article 27   No-one may stop you from participating in the cultural life of your community.

Article 28   Human beings have the right to live in the kind of world where their rights and freedoms are respected.

Article 29   We all have a responsibility to the people around us ... All the rights in [this declaration] can be limited only by law and then only if necessary to protect other people's rights, meet society's sense of right and wrong, maintain order, and look after the welfare of society as a whole.

Article 30   There is nothing [in this declaration] that justifies any person or state doing anything that takes away from the rights to which we are all entitled. (Simplified version)

Questions for Discussion

1. What is the "invisible hand" mentioned in the essay?
2. What are the advantages and disadvantages of "prohibition"?
3. Why does Smith oppose monopoly?
4. What is the "sole" excuse for interference?
5. How does Mill go about arguing for one's own individuality?

Heritage of Western Intellectual Tradition — A Sourcebook

Unit 11

Anti-Liberalism

Pretest

- Quote from either Jacques Rousseau or Nietzsche and comment.
- Discuss what you believe to be the most important idea of the two people.
- How is the concept "freedom" variously expressed in contradiction to what you find in other enlightenment thinkers?

What You Will Learn in This Unit

- Some more knowledge about the Age of Reason;
- Important sections from Rousseau and Nietzsche; and
- Western Liberalism vs. Asian Communitarianism.

Learn to Pronounce

aristocratism /ˌærɪsˈtɒkrətɪzəm/ 贵族气派
Diogenes /daɪˈɒdʒiniːz/ 第欧根尼
Dionysian spirit /ˌdaɪəˈnɪzɪən/ 酒神节的
Hume /hjuːm/ 休谟
iconoclast /aɪˈkɒnəklæst/ 偶像破坏者
Judaic /dʒu(ː)ˈdeɪɪk/ 犹太的
Nihilist /ˈnaɪɪlɪst, ˈniː-/ 虚无主义者
Denis Diderot /ˈdiːdərəʊ/ 狄德罗

Friedrich (Wilhelm) Nietzsche /ˈniːtʃə/ 尼采
Jean-Jacques Rousseau /ˈruːsəʊ/ 卢梭
Napoleon /nəˈpəʊljən/ 拿破仑
Orientalism /ˌɔ(ː)rɪˈentəlɪzəm/ 东方主义
Prussia /ˈprʌʃə/ 普鲁士
Schopenhauer /ˈʃəʊpənhaʊə/ 叔本华
Spinoza /spɪˈnəʊzə/ 斯宾诺莎
Wagner /ˈwægnə/ 瓦格纳

Introduction

The tradition of classical liberalism from high Renaissance in the 15th century was met with resistance now and then, marked by a distrust for the enlightenment ideals of reason and science, evidenced by romanticists' appeals in the 18th century to a return to the ideals of a simple, primitive society uncontaminated by modern civilization, culminated in a total rebuttal of the Judeo-Christian tradition and all its corrupting influences in the 19th century, though this anti-liberalist ideology was itself based on and a furtherance of the ideals of classical liberalism. Rousseau tried to trace the successive stages by which man has descended from primitive innocence to corrupt sophistication. His "noble savages" lived isolated, trouble-free lives where ethical and social problems would be more easily solved. Rousseau thus blamed society for the emergence of vices with the introduction of property. Thus the inequality between men was seen not as a separate problem but as one of the features of the long process by which men became alienated from nature and from innocence. The modern society for Nietzsche was one of passive nihilism which produced a "slave morality" marked by a virtue of meekness, poverty, and humility. Such an ethics undermined the human drives that had led to the greatest and most noble human achievements. Nietzsche suggested a "reevaluation of all values," to be replaced by a set of new values such as independence, creativity, and originality. The questioning of metaphysical and theological foundations of bourgeois morality was accompanied by a sharp critique of a more vehement type, as we shall see in this unit.

Jean-Jacques Rousseau:
A Discourse on the Moral Effects of the Arts and Sciences*

Jean-Jacques Rousseau (1712–1778), French philosopher, social and political theorist, one of the most eloquent writers of the Age of Enlightenment, marked the end of the Age of Reason and the birth of Romanticism. Rousseau was born in Geneva and was raised by an aunt and uncle after his mother died in childbirth. He was apprenticed at 13 to an engraver, but after three years he ran away to a monastery for conversion to Catholicism, where he became secretary and companion to Mme Louise de Warens, a wealthy woman. She furthered his education to turn him from a stammering apprentice who had never been to school into a man of letters. In 1742 Rousseau went to Paris, where he became

---

* This essay was written for a contest sponsored by the Academy of Dijon on the subject "Have the Arts and Sciences Benefited Mankind?" This prize-winning essay criticizes the "organized tyranny" of the educated few which led to the enslavement of the masses, and the essay established Rousseau as a genuine intellectual.

Heritage of Western Intellectual Tradition   A Sourcebook

a close friend of the French philosopher Denis Diderot. The two soon became the centre of a group of intellectuals who gathered round the *Encyclopédie*, an important organ of radical and anticlerical opinion with Diderot as its editor. Rousseau, the most original of them all in his thinking and the most  forceful and eloquent in his style of writing, was soon the most conspicuous. At 37 Rousseau, while walking to visit Diderot, had a "terrible flash" that modern progress had corrupted instead of improved men. Hence his first important work *A Discourse on the Moral Effects of the Arts and Sciences* (1750), followed by *Discourse on the Origin of Inequality Among Mankind* (1755) and *The Social Contract* (1762), in which he argues that science, art, and social institutions have corrupted humankind and that the natural, or primitive, state is morally superior to the civilized state. These writings helped prepare the ideological background of the French Revolution by defending the popular will against divine right. In 1770 he completed the manuscript of his most remarkable work, the autobiographical *Confessions* (1782), whose extreme emotional expression profoundly influenced romanticism in literature and philosophy in the early 19th century. The spirit and ideas of Rousseau's work "stand midway between the 18th-century Enlightenment, with its passionate defense of reason and individual rights, and early 19th-century romanticism, which defended intense subjective experience against rational thought." Rousseau died in 1778 in wretched poverty. In 1794 the Revolutionary Convention moved his body to the Pantheon, to lie near the remains of Voltaire, to honour the man who provided the rallying cry for the stormers of the Bastille.

The question before me is: "Whether the Restoration of the arts and sciences has had the effect of purifying or corrupting morals." Which side am I to take? That[1], gentlemen, which becomes an honest man, who is sensible of his own ignorance, and thinks himself none the worse for it.

I feel the difficulty of treating this subject fittingly, before the tribunal[2] which is to judge of what I advance. How can I presume to belittle the sciences before one of the most learned assemblies in Europe, to commend ignorance in a famous Academy[3], and reconcile my contempt for study with the respect due to the truly learned?

I was aware of these inconsistencies[4], but not discouraged by them. It is not science, I said to myself, that I am attacking; it is virtue that I am defending, and that before virtuous men — and goodness is ever dearer to the good than learning to the learned[5].

What then have I to fear? The sagacity[6] of the assembly before which I am pleading? That, I

---

1 **that:** that side
2 **tribunal:** place of judgment
3 **one of the most learned assemblies in Europe … a famous Academy:** i.e., the Academy of Dijon
4 **inconsistency:** criticism of science and respect for the scientists
5 **goodness is ever dearer to the good than learning to the learned:** That is, I shall give priority to virtue rather than to learning.
6 **sagacity:** wisdom

acknowledge, is to be feared; but rather on account of faults of construction than of the views I hold. Just sovereigns have never hesitated to decide against themselves in doubtful cases; and indeed the most advantageous situation in which a just claim can be, is that of being laid before a just and enlightened arbitrator, who is judge in his own case.

To this motive, which encouraged me, I may add another which finally decided me. And this is, that as I have upheld the cause of truth to the best of my natural abilities, whatever my apparent success, there is one reward which cannot fail me. That reward I shall find in the bottom of my heart.

The First Part

It is a noble and beautiful spectacle to see man raising himself, so to speak, from nothing by his own exertions; dissipating[1], by the light of reason, all the thick clouds in which he was by nature enveloped; mounting above himself; soaring in thought even to the celestial regions; like the sun, encompassing with giant strides the vast extent of the universe; and, what is still grander and more wonderful, going back into himself, there to study man and get to know his own nature, his duties and his end. All these miracles we have seen renewed within the last few generations.

Europe had relapsed into[2] the barbarism of the earliest ages; the inhabitants of this part of the world, which is at present so highly enlightened, were plunged, some centuries ago, in a state still worse than ignorance. A scientific jargon[3], more despicable[4] than mere ignorance, had usurped[5] the name of knowledge, and opposed an almost invincible[6] obstacle to its[7] restoration.

Things had come to such a pass, that it required a complete revolution to bring men back to common sense. This came at last from the quarter from which it was least to be expected. It was the stupid Mussulman[8], the eternal scourge[9] of letters, who was the immediate cause of their revival[10] among us. The fall of the throne of Constantine brought to Italy the relics of ancient Greece; and with these precious spoils France in turn was enriched. The sciences soon followed literature, and the art of thinking joined that of writing: an order which may seem strange, but is perhaps only too natural. The world now began to perceive the principal advantage of an inter-

---

1 **dissipate:** drive away
2 **relapse into:** fall back into
3 **jargon:** language full of technical terms
4 **despicable:** contemptible
5 **usurp:** take wrongfully
6 **invincible:** too strong to overcome
7 **its:** knowledge's
8 **Mussulman:** Turkish musulmân, probably alteration of Arabic Muslim
9 **scourge:** cause of suffering
10 **their revival:** revival of letters

Heritage of Western Intellectual Tradition — A Sourcebook

course with the Muses[1], that of rendering mankind more sociable by inspiring them with the desire to please one another with performances worthy of their mutual approbation[2].

The mind, as well as the body, has its needs: those of the body are the basis of society, those of the mind its ornaments.

So long as government and law provide for the security and well-being of men in their common life, the arts, literature, and the sciences, less despotic though perhaps more powerful[3], fling garlands of flowers over the chains which weigh them down. They stifle[4] in men's breasts that sense of original liberty, for which they seem to have been born; cause them to love their own slavery, and so make of them what is called a civilized people.

Portrait painted for Hume in March 1766, showing Rousseau in his Armenian costume

Necessity raised up thrones; the arts and sciences have made them strong. Powers of the earth cherish all talents and protect those who cultivate them. **Civilized peoples cultivate such pursuits: to them, happy slaves, you owe that delicacy and exquisiteness of taste, which is so much your boast, that sweetness of disposition and urbanity[5] of manners which make intercourse so easy and agreeable among you — in a word, the appearance of all the virtues, without being in possession of one of them.**

It was for this sort of accomplishment, which is so much the more captivating, as it seems less affected, that Athens and Rome were so much distinguished in the boasted times of their splendour and magnificence: and it is doubtless in the same respect that our own age and nation will excel all periods and peoples. An air of philosophy without pedantry[6]; an address at once natural and engaging, distant equally from Teutonic[7] clumsiness and Italian pantomime[8]; these are the effects of a taste acquired by liberal studies and improved by conversation with the world. What happiness would it be for those who live among us, if our external appearance were always a true mirror of our hearts; if decorum[9] were but virtue; if the maxims we professed were the rules of our conduct; and if real philosophy were inseparable from the title of a philosopher! But so many good qualities too seldom go together; virtue rarely appears in so

---

1 **Muses:** in Greek mythology, nine goddesses, daughters of the god Zeus, king of the gods, and of Mnemosyne, the goddess of memory, were believed to inspire all artists, especially poets, philosophers, and musicians

2 **approbation:** approval

3 **more powerful:** compared with government

4 **stifle:** suppress

5 **urbanity:** refinement, politeness

6 **pedantry:** unnecessary display of learning

7 **Teutonic:** of the Germanic (i.e Anglo-Saxon, Dutch, German and Scandinavian) peoples or their languages

8 **pantomime:** acting without words

9 **decorum:** dignified and socially acceptable manner

much pomp and state[1].

Richness of apparel[2] may proclaim the man of fortune, and elegance the man of taste; but true health and manliness are known by different signs. It is under the homespun of the labourer, and not beneath the gilt[3] and tinsel[4] of the courtier, that we should look for strength and vigour of body.

External ornaments are no less foreign to virtue, which is the strength and activity of the mind. The honest man is an athlete, who loves to wrestle stark naked; he scorns all those vile trappings, which prevent the exertion of his strength, and were, for the most part, invented only to conceal some deformity.

Before art had moulded our behaviour, and taught our passions to speak an artificial language, our morals were rude but natural; and the different ways in which we behaved proclaimed at the first glance the difference of our dispositions. Human nature was not at bottom better then than now; but men found their security in the ease with which they could see through one another, and this advantage, of which we no longer feel the value, prevented their having many vices.

In our day, now that more subtle study and a more refined taste have reduced the art of pleasing to a system, there prevails in modern manners a servile[5] and deceptive conformity; so that one would think every mind had been cast in the same mould. Politeness requires this thing; decorum that[6]; ceremony has its forms, and fashion its laws, and these we must always follow, never the promptings[7] of our own nature.

We no longer dare seem what we really are, but lie under a perpetual restraint; in the meantime the herd of men, which we call society, all act under the same circumstances exactly alike, unless very particular and powerful motives prevent them. Thus we never know with whom we have to deal; and even to know our friends we must wait for some critical and pressing occasion; that is, till it is too late; for it is on those very occasions that such knowledge is of use to us.

What a train of vices must attend this uncertainty! Sincere friendship, real esteem, and perfect confidence are banished from among men. Jealousy, suspicion, fear, coldness, reserve, hate, and fraud lie constantly concealed under that uniform and deceitful veil of politeness; that

---

1 **state:** rank, dignity
2 **apparel:** clothing
3 **gilt:** gold-like leaf
4 **tinsel:** glittering metallic substance
5 **servile:** submissive, slavish
6 **decorum that:** decorum requires that thing
7 **prompting:** action of our own initiative

Heritage of Western Intellectual Tradition   A Sourcebook

boasted candour[1] and urbanity[2], for which we are indebted to the light and leading of this age. We shall no longer take in vain by our oaths the name of our Creator; but we shall insult Him with our blasphemies[3], and our scrupulous[4] ears will take no offence. We have grown too modest to brag of our own deserts[5]; but we do not scruple to decry[6] those of others. We do not grossly outrage even our enemies, but artfully calumniate[7] them. Our hatred of other nations diminishes, but patriotism dies with it. Ignorance is held in contempt; but a dangerous scepticism has succeeded it. Some vices indeed are condemned and others grown dishonourable; but we have still many that are honoured with the names of virtues, and it is become necessary that we should either have, or at least pretend to have them. Let who will extol the moderation of our modern sages, I see nothing in it but a refinement of intemperance as unworthy of my commendation[8] as their artificial simplicity.

Such is the purity to which our morals have attained; this is the virtue we have made our own. Let the arts and sciences claim the share they have had in this salutary[9] work. I shall add but one reflection more; suppose an inhabitant of some distant country should endeavour to form an idea of European morals from the state of the sciences, the perfection of the arts, the propriety of our public entertainments, the politeness of our behaviour, the affability of our conversation, our constant professions of benevolence[10], and from those tumultuous[11] assemblies of people of all ranks, who seem, from morning till night, to have no other care than to oblige[12] one another. Such a stranger, I maintain, would arrive at a totally false view of our morality.

Where there is no effect, it is idle to look for a cause: but here the effect is certain and the depravity actual; our minds have been corrupted in proportion as the arts and sciences have improved. Will it be said, that this is a misfortune peculiar to the present age? No, gentlemen, the evils resulting from our vain curiosity are as old as the world. The daily ebb and flow of the tides are not more regularly influenced by the moon than the morals of a people by the progress of the arts and sciences. As their light has risen above our horizon, virtue has taken flight, and the same phenomenon has been constantly observed in all times and places.

...

---

1 **candour:** frankness, straightforwardness
2 **urbanity:** refined manners, smooth elegance and sophistication
3 **blasphemy:** irreverent talk about God
4 **scrupulous:** paying too much attention to small things
5 **desert:** merit
6 **decry:** blame, criticize
7 **calumniate:** slander
8 **commendation:** praise, approval
9 **salutary:** having a good effect
10 **benevolence:** wish to do good
11 **tumultuous:** noisy, violent
12 **oblige:** engage

Thus it is that luxury, profligacy[1], and slavery have been, in all ages, the scourge of the efforts of our pride to emerge from that happy state of ignorance, in which the wisdom of providence had placed us. That thick veil with which it has covered all its operations seems to be a sufficient proof that it never designed us for such fruitless researches. But is there, indeed, one lesson it has taught us, by which we have rightly profited, or which we have neglected with impunity[2]? Let men learn for once that nature would have preserved them from science, as a mother snatches a dangerous weapon from the hands of her child. Let them know that all the secrets she hides are so many evils from which she protects them, and that the very difficulty they find in acquiring knowledge is not the least of her bounty towards them. **Men are perverse; but they would have been far worse, if they had had the misfortune to be born learned.**

How humiliating are these reflections to humanity, and how mortified[3] by them our pride should be! What! it will be asked, is uprightness the child of ignorance? Is virtue inconsistent with learning? What consequences might not be drawn from such suppositions? But to reconcile these apparent contradictions, we need only examine closely the emptiness and vanity of those pompous[4] titles, which are so liberally bestowed on human knowledge, and which so blind our judgment. Let us consider, therefore, the arts and sciences in themselves. Let us see what must result from their advancement, and let us not hesitate to admit the truth of all those points on which our arguments coincide with the inductions we can make from history.

The Second Part

An ancient tradition passed out of Egypt into Greece, that some god, who was an enemy to the repose[5] of mankind, was the inventor of the sciences. What must the Egyptians, among whom the sciences first arose, have thought of them? And they beheld, near at hand, the sources from which they sprang. **In fact, whether we turn to the annals[6] of the world, or eke out[7] with philosophical investigations the uncertain chronicles of history, we shall not find for human knowledge an origin answering to the idea we are pleased to entertain of it at present.** Astronomy was born of superstition, eloquence of ambition, hatred, falsehood, and flattery; geometry of avarice[8]; physics of an idle curiosity; and even moral philosophy of human pride. Thus the arts and sciences owe their birth to our vices; we should be less doubtful of their advantages, if they had sprung from our virtues.

Their evil origin is, indeed, but too plainly reproduced in their objects. What would

---

1 **profligacy:** shameless immorality
2 **impunity:** freedom from punishment
3 **mortify:** humiliate, hurt
4 **pompous:** arrogant
5 **repose:** peace
6 **annal:** record of knowledge
7 **eke out:** seek, find out
8 **avarice:** greed

become of the arts, were they not cherished by luxury? If men were not unjust, of what use were jurisprudence[1]? What would become of history, if there were no tyrants, wars, or conspiracies? In a word who would pass his life in barren speculations, if everybody, attentive only to the obligations of humanity and the necessities of nature, spent his whole life in serving his country, obliging his friends, and relieving[2] the unhappy? Are we then made to live and die on the brink of that well at the bottom of which Truth lies hid? This reflection alone is, in my opinion, enough to discourage at first setting out[3] every man who seriously endeavours to instruct himself by the study of philosophy.

What a variety of dangers surrounds us! What a number of wrong paths present themselves in the investigation of the sciences! Through how many errors, more perilous than truth itself is useful[4], must we not pass to arrive at it? The disadvantages we lie under are evident; for falsehood is capable of an infinite variety of combinations; but the truth has only one manner of being. Besides, where is the man who sincerely desires to find it? Or even admitting his good will, by what characteristic marks is he sure of knowing it? Amid the infinite diversity of opinions where is the criterion by which we may certainly judge of it? Again, what is still more difficult, should we even be fortunate enough to discover it, who among us will know how to make right use of it?

If our sciences are futile in the objects they propose, they are no less dangerous in the effects they produce. Being the effect of idleness, they generate idleness in their turn; and an irreparable[5] loss of time is the first prejudice which they must necessarily cause to society. To live without doing some good is a great evil as well in the political as in the moral world; and hence every useless citizen should be regarded as a pernicious[6] person. Tell me then, illustrious philosophers, of whom we learn the ratios in which attraction acts in vacuo[7]; and in the revolution of the planets, the relations of spaces traversed[8] in equal times; by whom we are taught what curves have conjugate points, points of inflexion, and cusps; how the soul and body correspond, like two clocks, without actual communication; what planets may be inhabited; and what insects reproduce in an extraordinary manner. **Answer me, I say, you from whom we receive all this sublime information, whether we should have been less numerous, worse governed, less formidable, less flourishing, or more perverse, supposing you had taught us none of all these fine things.**

Reconsider therefore the importance of your productions; and, since the labours of the most enlightened of our learned men and the best of our citizens are of so little utility, tell us what we

---

1 **jurisprudence:** science or philosophy of law
2 **relieve:** bring relief to
3 **at first setting out:** at the very beginning
4 **more perilous than truth itself is useful:** danger overweighs the usefulness of truth
5 **irreparable:** unable to be restored
6 **pernicious:** harmful
7 **in vacuo:** in a vacuum
8 **traverse:** travel across

ought to think of that numerous herd of obscure writers and useless littérateurs[1], who devour without any return the substance of the State.

Useless, do I say? Would God they were! Society would be more peaceful, and morals less corrupt. But these vain and futile declaimers go forth on all sides, armed with their fatal paradoxes, to sap[2] the foundations of our faith, and nullify[3] virtue. They smile contemptuously at such old names as patriotism and religion, and consecrate[4] their talents and philosophy to the destruction and defamation of all that men hold sacred. Not that they bear any real hatred to virtue or dogma; they are the enemies of public opinion alone; to bring them to the foot of the altar, it would be enough to banish them to a land of atheists. What extravagancies will not the rage of singularity[5] induce men to commit!

The waste of time is certainly a great evil; but still greater evils attend upon literature and the arts. One is luxury, produced like them by indolence[6] and vanity. Luxury is seldom unattended by the arts and sciences; and they are always attended by luxury. I know that our philosophy, fertile in paradoxes, pretends, in contradiction to the experience of all ages, that luxury contributes to the splendour of States. But, without insisting on the necessity of sumptuary[7] laws, can it be denied that rectitude[8] of morals is essential to the duration of empires, and that luxury is diametrically opposed to such rectitude? Let it be admitted that luxury is a certain indication of wealth; that it even serves, if you will, to increase such wealth; what conclusion is to be drawn from this paradox, so worthy of the times? **And what will become of virtue if riches are to be acquired at any cost? The politicians of the ancient world were always talking of morals and virtue; ours speak of nothing but commerce and money.** One of them will tell you that in such a country a man is worth just as much as he will sell for at Algiers[9]: another, pursuing the same mode of calculation, finds that in some countries a man is worth nothing, and in others still less than nothing; they value men as they do droves[10] of oxen.

Rousseau longed for the pleasure of the simplicity in the earliest times.

…

---

1 **littérateur:** one devoted to the study or writing of literature
2 **sap:** weaken
3 **nullify:** make (sth.) ineffective
4 **consecrate:** devote or sacrifice for a special (esp. religious) purpose
5 **singularity:** trait marking one as distinct from others; peculiarity
6 **indolence:** laziness
7 **sumptuary:** limiting private expenditure
8 **rectitude:** honesty, upright behavior
9 **Algiers:** capital and largest city of Algeria
10 **drove:** large number of animals

We cannot reflect on the morality of mankind without contemplating with pleasure the picture of the simplicity which prevailed in the earliest times[1]. This image may be justly compared to a beautiful coast, adorned only by the hands of nature; towards which our eyes are constantly turned, and which we see receding with regret. While men were innocent and virtuous and loved to have the gods for witnesses of their actions, they dwelt together in the same huts; but when they became vicious, they grew tired of such inconvenient onlookers, and banished them to magnificent temples. Finally, they expelled their deities even from these[2], in order to dwell there themselves; or at least the temples of the gods were no longer more magnificent than the palaces of the citizens. This was the height of degeneracy; nor could vice ever be carried to greater lengths than when it was seen, supported, as it were, at the doors of the great, on columns of marble, and graven on Corinthian capitals[3].

As the conveniences of life increase, as the arts are brought to perfection, and luxury spreads, true courage flags[4], the virtues disappear; and all this is the effect of the sciences and of those acts which are exercised in the privacy of men's dwellings. When the Goths[5] ravaged Greece, the libraries only escaped the flames owing to an opinion that was set on foot[6] among them, that it was best to leave the enemy with a possession so calculated to divert their attention from military exercises, and keep them engaged in indolent and sedentary[7] occupations.

Charles the Eighth[8] found himself master of Tuscany and the kingdom of Naples, almost without drawing sword; and all his court attributed this unexpected success to the fact that the princes and nobles of Italy applied themselves with greater earnestness to the cultivation of their understandings than to active and martial pursuits. In fact, says the sensible person who records these characteristics, experience plainly tells us that in military matters and all that resemble them application to the sciences tends rather to make men effeminate[9] and cowardly than resolute and vigorous.

The Romans confessed that military virtue was extinguished among them, in proportion as

---

1 **contemplating with pleasure the picture of the simplicity which prevailed in the earliest times:** Rousseau, in criticizing the "noble savage," is recalling the "good old days." Voltaire was amused by his fuzzy romanticism and wrote to him caustically, "One longs in reading your book to walk on all fours. As, however, it is some sixty years since I gave up the practice, I feel that it is unfortunately impossible for me to resume it."

2 **these:** magnificent temples

3 **Corinthian capitals:** heads of Greek columns

4 **flag:** droop, become weak

5 **Goth:** German tribe that invaded the Roman Empire in the 3rd and 4th centuries

6 **set on foot:** start moving, become popular

7 **sedentary:** seating still

8 **Charles VIII (1470–1498):** king of France (1483–1498). The chief event of his reign was his invasion of Italy in 1494 and his temporary occupation of Naples in 1495.

9 **effeminate:** womanly, unmanly

they became connoisseurs[1] in the arts of the painter, the engraver, and the goldsmith, and began to cultivate the fine arts. Indeed, as if this famous country was to be for ever an example to other nations, the rise of the Medici and the revival of letters has once more destroyed, this time perhaps for ever, the martial reputation which Italy seemed a few centuries ago to have recovered.

The ancient republics of Greece, with that wisdom which was so conspicuous in most of their institutions, forbade their citizens to pursue all those inactive and sedentary occupations, which by enervating[2] and corrupting the body diminish also the vigour of the mind. With what courage, in fact, can it be thought that hunger and thirst, fatigues, dangers, and death, can be faced by men whom the smallest want overwhelms and the slightest difficulty repels[3]? With what resolution can soldiers support the excessive toils of war, when they are entirely unaccustomed to them? With what spirits can they make forced marches under officers who have not even the strength to travel on horseback? It is no answer to cite the reputed valour of all the modern warriors who are so scientifically trained. I hear much of their bravery in a day's battle; but I am told nothing of how they support excessive fatigue, how they stand the severity of the seasons and the inclemency[4] of the weather. A little sunshine or snow, or the want of a few superfluities[5], is enough to cripple and destroy one of our finest armies in a few days. Intrepid[6] warriors! permit me for once to tell you the truth, which you seldom hear. Of your bravery I am fully satisfied. I have no doubt that you would have triumphed with Hannibal[7] at Cannae, and at Trasimene: that you would

Rousseau's Emile, a treatise on education published in 1762

have passed the Rubicon[8] with Caesar, and enabled him to enslave his country; but you never would have been able to cross the Alps with the former[9], or with the latter[10] to subdue your own

---

1 **connoisseur:** good judge of artistic taste

2 **enervate:** cause to lose strength

3 **repel:** cause the feeling of dislike

4 **inclemency:** severity of weather

5 **superfluity:** things not necessarily needed

6 **intrepid:** fearless

7 **Hannibal (247–183 BC):** Carthaginian general, whose march on Rome from Spain across the Alps in 218–217 BC remains one of the greatest feats in military history. At the Battle of Cannae he almost completely annihilated a Roman army of more than 50,000 men; at Lake Trasimene he demolished a Roman army in 217 BC.

8 **the Rubicon:** In the 1st century BC, the Rubicon River in central Italy formed the boundary between Italy and the Roman province of Cisalpine Gaul. In 49 BC, Julius Caesar made his famous crossing of the Rubicon; as the Roman Senate had forbidden him to enter Italy with an army, this action initiated civil war between his forces and those of Pompey the Great. The phrase "to cross the Rubicon" has come to mean the taking of a step by which one is committed to a hazardous enterprise.

9 **the former:** Hannibal

10 **the latter:** Caesar

ancestors, the Gauls[1].

A war does not always depend on the events of battle: there is in generalship an art superior to that of gaining victories. A man may behave with great intrepidity under fire, and yet be a very bad officer. Even in the common soldier, a little more strength and vigour would perhaps be more useful than so much courage, which after all is no protection from death. And what does it matter to the State whether its troops perish by cold and fever, or by the sword of the enemy?

If the cultivation of the sciences is prejudicial[2] to military qualities, it is still more so to moral qualities. Even from our infancy an absurd system of education serves to adorn our wit and corrupt our judgment. We see, on every side, huge institutions, where our youth are educated at great expense, and instructed in everything but their duty. Your children will be ignorant of their own language, when they can talk others which are not spoken anywhere. They will be able to compose verses which they can hardly understand; and, without being capable of distinguishing truth from error, they will possess the art of making them unrecognizable by specious[3] arguments. But magnanimity[4], equity, temperance, humanity, and courage will be words of which they know not the meaning. The dear name of country will never strike on their ears; and if they ever hear speak of God, it will be less to fear than to be frightened of Him. I would as soon, said a wise man, that my pupil had spent his time in the tennis court as in this manner; for there his body at least would have got exercise.

Rousseau cherishes the simplicity of life.

I well know that children ought to be kept employed, and that idleness is for them the danger most to be feared. But what should they be taught? This is undoubtedly an important question. Let them be taught what they are to practice when they come to be men; not what they ought to forget.

Our gardens are adorned with statues and our galleries with pictures. What would you imagine these masterpieces of art, thus exhibited to public admiration, represent? The great men who have defended their country, or the still greater men who have enriched it by their virtues? Far from it. They are the images of every perversion of heart and mind, carefully selected from ancient mythology, and presented to the early curiosity of our children, doubtless that they may have before their eyes the representations of vicious actions, even before they are able to read.

---

1 **the Gauls:** inhabitants of Gaul, ancient Roman designation, bounded on the east by the Alps and the Rhine River
2 **prejudicial:** causing injury
3 **specious:** seeming right or true
4 **magnanimity:** generosity

Whence arise all those abuses, unless it be from that fatal inequality introduced among men by the difference of talents and the cheapening of virtue[1]? This is the most evident effect of all our studies, and the most dangerous of all their consequences. The question is no longer whether a man is honest, but whether he is clever. We do not ask whether a book is useful, but whether it is well written. Rewards are lavished on wit and ingenuity, while virtue is left unhonoured. There are a thousand prizes for fine discourses, and none for good actions. I should be glad, however, to know whether the honour attaching to the best discourse that ever wins the prize in this Academy is comparable with the merit of having founded the prize.

A wise man does not go in chase of fortune; but he is by no means insensible to glory, and when he sees it so ill distributed, his virtue, which might have been animated by a little emulation[2], and turned to the advantage of society, droops and dies away in obscurity and indigence[3]. It is for this reason that the agreeable arts must in time everywhere be preferred to the useful; and this truth has been but too much confirmed since the revival of the arts and sciences. We have physicists, geometricians, chemists, astronomers, poets, musicians, and painters in plenty; but we have no longer a citizen among us; or if there be found a few scattered over our abandoned countryside, they are left to perish there unnoticed and neglected. Such is the condition to which we are reduced, and such are our feelings towards those who give us our daily bread, and our children milk.

I confess, however, that the evil is not so great as it might have become. The eternal providence, in placing salutary simples[4] beside noxious[5] plants, and making poisonous animals contain their own antidote,[6] has taught the sovereigns of the earth, who are its ministers, to imitate its wisdom. It is by following this example that the truly great monarch, to whose glory every age will add new lustre[7], drew from the very bosom of the arts and sciences the very fountains of a thousand lapses[8] from rectitude, those famous societies, which, while they are depositaries[9] of the dangerous trust of human knowledge, are yet the sacred guardians of morals, by the attention they pay to their maintenance among themselves in all their purity, and by the demands which they make on every member whom they admit.

These wise institutions, confirmed by his august[10] successor and imitated by all the kings of

---

1 **cheapening of virtue:** i.e., cheap wit or shallow cleverness takes precedence over virtue
2 **emulation:** effort at doing better
3 **indigence:** poverty
4 **salutary simple:** healthy and beneficial medicinal plant
5 **noxious:** harmful
6 **antidote:** substance that acts against the effects of a poison or disease
7 **lustre:** glory, distinction
8 **lapse:** error
9 **depositary:** (or depository) storehouse
10 **august:** majestic, respectful

Heritage of Western Intellectual Tradition — A Sourcebook

Europe, will serve at least to restrain men of letters, who, all aspiring to the honour of being admitted into these Academies, will keep watch over themselves, and endeavour to make themselves worthy of such honour by useful performances and irreproachable morals. Those Academies also, which, in proposing prizes for literary merit, make choice of such subjects as are calculated to arouse the love of virtue in the hearts of citizens, prove that it prevails in themselves, and must give men the rare and real pleasure of finding learned societies devoting themselves to the enlightenment of mankind, not only by agreeable exercises of the intellect, but also by useful instructions.

An objection which may be made is, in fact, only an additional proof of my argument. So much precaution proves but too evidently the need for it. We never seek remedies for evils that do not exist. Why, indeed, must these bear all the marks of ordinary remedies, on account of their inefficacy[1]? The numerous establishments in favour of the learned are only adapted to make men mistake the objects of the sciences, and turn men's attention to the cultivation of them. One would be inclined to think, from the precautions everywhere taken, that we are overstocked with husbandmen, and are afraid of a shortage of philosophers. I will not venture here to enter into a comparison between agriculture and philosophy, as they would not bear it. I shall only ask: What is philosophy? What is contained in the writings of the most celebrated philosophers? What are the lessons of these friends of wisdom? To hear them, should we not take them for so many mountebanks[2], exhibiting themselves in public, and crying out, *Here, Here, come to me, I am the only*

Rousseau the botanist and naturalist

true doctor? One of them teaches that there is no such thing as matter, but that everything exists only in representation. Another declares that there is no other substance than matter, and no other God than the world itself. A third tells you that there are no such things as virtue and vice, and that moral good and evil are chimeras[3]; while a fourth informs you that men are only beasts of prey, and may conscientiously devour one another. Why, my great philosophers, do you not reserve these wise and profitable lessons for your friends and children? You would soon reap the benefit of them, nor should we be under the apprehension[4] of our own becoming your disciples.

Such are the wonderful men, whom their contemporaries held in the highest esteem during their lives, and to whom immortality has been attributed since their decease. Such are the wise

---

1 **inefficacy:** ineffectiveness
2 **mountebank:** one who persuades people into buying worthless medicine
3 **chimera:** wild fancy
4 **apprehension:** fear

maxims we have received from them, and which are transmitted, from age to age, to our descendants. Paganism, though given over to[1] all the extravagances of human reason, has left nothing to compare with the shameful monuments which have been prepared by the art of printing, during the reign of the gospel. The impious writings of Leucippus[2] and Diagoras[3] perished with their authors. The world, in their days, was ignorant of the art of immortalizing the errors and extravagances of the human mind. But thanks to the art of printing and the use we make of it, the pernicious reflections of Hobbes and Spinoza[4] will last for ever. Go, famous writings, of which the ignorance and rusticity[5] of our forefathers would have been incapable. Go to our descendants, along with those still more pernicious works which reek of[6] the corrupted manners of the present age! Let them together convey to posterity a faithful history of the progress and advantages of our arts and sciences. **If they are read, they will leave not a doubt about the question we are now discussing, and unless mankind should then be still more foolish than we, they will lift up their hands to Heaven and exclaim in bitterness of heart: "Almighty God! Thou who holdest in Thy hand the minds of men, deliver us from the fatal arts and sciences of our forefathers; give us back ignorance, innocence, and poverty, which alone can make us happy and are precious in Thy sight."**

Key Concepts

appearance of all the virtues	military virtue
artificial language	moral effects
civilized people	noble savage
complete revolution	perpetual restraint
Encyclopédie	sense of original liberty
external ornaments	servile and deceptive conformity
herd of men	urbanity of manners
man of taste	vigour of body

---

1 **give over to:** indulge in

2 **Leucippus (c. 450 – c. 370 BC):** Greek philosopher, credited with founding the atomic theory of matter, according to which all matter is constituted of identical indivisible particles called atoms

3 **Diagoras**, Greek poet and sophist, flourished in the second half of the 5th century BC. In consequence of his blasphemous speeches, and especially his criticism of the Mysteries, he was condemned to death at Athens. He fled to Corinth and died there.

4 **Spinoza (1632–1677):** Dutch rationalist philosopher and religious thinker, the most thoroughgoing moden exponent of pantheism

5 **rusticity:** rustic trait or country mannerism

6 **reek of:** be covered with

Friedrich Nietzsche: The Will to Power*

Friedrich (Wilhelm) Nietzsche (1844–1900), German philosopher, poet, and one of the most provocative and influential thinkers of the 19th century, was born in Prussia and studied classical philology at the University of Bonn and Leipzig. In Leipzig he came to appreciate Schopenhauer's criticism of traditional thinking in *The World As Will and Idea*. He also admired the composer Richard Wagner for this creative genius, though later he denounced him in *Nietzsche against Wagner* for his decadent virtues of humility. In 1869 the University of Leipzig conferred the doctor-

ate without examination or dissertation on the strength of his published writings, and the University of Basel appointed him extraordinary professor of classical philology. The following year Nietzsche was promoted to ordinary professor at 25. While serving as a volunteer medical orderly in the Franco-Prussian War, he contracted dysentery (瘫痪) and diphtheria (白喉), which prompted him to seek retirement in 1879. Ten years later he suffered a mental breakdown from which he never recovered. His first book *The Birth of Tragedy from the Spirit of Music* (1872) marks his emancipation from the trappings of classical scholarship by praising what he termed Dionysian spirit of unbridled passion and defying the Apollonian elements of measure, restraint, harmony. For this unbridled spirit of liberation he was variously called "nihilist," "iconoclast," or "destructionist," as Nietzsche thought himself as a gadfly, the 19th century Socrates. *Thus Spoke Zarathustra*, Nietzsche's acknowledged literary and philosophical masterpiece, published between 1883 and 1885, received little attention. But the 20th century saw gradual revival of interest in him. He is more and more viewed as primarily a moral philosopher, an "affirmer of life value," one who reached out beyond the confines of traditional mores for a new set of values in opposition to Judaic-Christian values. This is what the 20th century men of thought have been doing. Existentialism and deconstructionism owe much to him. Alfred Adler and Carl Jung were similarly influenced, as was Sigmund Freud, who said of Nietzsche that he had a more penetrating understanding of himself than any man who ever lived or was ever likely to live. So were poets and playwrights George Bernard Shaw and William Butler Yeats.

373. *The origin of moral values.* Egoism has as much value as the physiological worth of its

---

* The *will to power* is one of Nietzsche's central concepts. Due to his elusive style, we are left without a proper definition of what the phrase may mean. One possible interpretation is that it is a venting of creative energy as the basic driving force of nature. As such, it is "the driving force of all natural phenomena and the dynamic to which all other causal powers could be reduced." In that sense, *will to power* could be a "theory of everything."

bearer. Each individual constitutes the entire evolutionary lineage[1] (he is not, contrary to the mo-ralistic conception of him, merely something that begins with his birth). Should he represent the ascendancy of the human lineage, then his value is, in fact, exceptional, and great may be the concern over the maintenance and encouragement of his growth. (It is the concern over the promise of the future which he embodies that gives the fortunate individual so extraordinary aright[2] to egoism.) But should he represent the descending lineage, that of degeneration and chronic sickness, then little value accrues[3] to him; and it is a matter of elementary justice that he takes from the fortunate as little space, strength, and sunlight as possible. **In this instance society's task is the suppression of egoism** (it occasionally expresses itself in absurd, pathological[4], and rebel-lious forms), **be it a question of individuals or of entire degenerated, vestigial[5] strata of mankind. Among such strata, a dogma or religion of "love," of suppression of self-affirmation, of patience, suffering, and service, of mutuality in word and deed can be of highest value**, even from the point of view of their rulers. For it suppresses feelings of rivalry, resentment, and envy, — the all-too-natural feelings of the ill-begotten[6]; it even deifies[7] them by idealizing slavish humility and obedience, subordination, poverty, infirmity[8], and lowliness. Accordingly, we see why ruling classes (or races) and individuals have supported the cult[9] of unselfishness, the slave-gospel of the "God on the Cross."

The predominance of an altruistic[10] mode of the valuing is the consequence of an instinct-to-failure. At bottom, this value judgment affirms: "I am not worth much," — a mere physi-ological value judgment; plainer yet: the feeling of impotence[11], the dearth[12] of great yea-saying surges of power (in the muscles, nerves, limbs). In accordance with the particular culture of these strata, this value judgment translates itself into a moral or religious judgment (the pre-eminence of religious or moral judgments is always a mark of an inferior culture); it seeks to establish itself out of contexts in which the concept of "value" is already familiar. The interpre-tation by which the Christian sinner seeks to understand himself is an attempt to justify his lack of power and self-assurance: he would rather find himself guilty than feel himself to be bad for no reason; to have need of such interpretations in the first place is already a symptom of

---

1 **lineage:** Bear in mind the "lowly origin" of man Darwin tells us.
2 **aright:** rightly
3 **accrue:** come as a natural development
4 **pathological:** relating to sickness
5 **vestigial:** remaining trace
6 **begotten:** born
7 **deify:** worship
8 **infirmity:** weakness
9 **cult:** religious sect generally considered to be false
10 **altruistic:** unselfish
11 **impotence:** inability to act
12 **dearth:** scarcity, lacking

Heritage of Western Intellectual Tradition A Sourcebook

decadence[1]. In other instances the misbegotten[2] seeks the reason for it not in his own "guilt" (like the Christian does), but in society (the socialist, the anarchist[3], the nihilist[4]). Insofar as he feels his condition to be one for which someone ought to be guilty, however, he remains the next-of-kin[5] of the Christian, who also believes that he can better endure his negative self-discovery[6] and misbegottenness if he has found someone he can hold responsible for it. In both instances, the instinct for revenge and resentment appears as a means of bearing it, as an instinct of self-preservation, much the same as the predilection[7] for altruistic theory and practice. The hatred of egoism, be it directed against self (as with the Christian) or other (as with the socialist), reveals itself thereby as a value judgment under the aegis[8] of revenge; yet at the same time as the cunning of self-preservation on the part of the suffering, through an enhancing of their feelings of cooperation and solidarity. Basically, as already indicated, this discharge of resentment in the

Nietzsche with Mom

form of judging, condemning, and punishing egoism (one's own or another's) is nothing but an instinct of self preservation on the part of the misbegotten. In sum: the cult of altruism is a special form of egoism which, given certain physiological conditions, regularly appears.

When, in righteous indignation, the socialist demands "justice," "equality," "equal rights," he is under pressure of a substandard culture which cannot help him comprehend why he suffers; otherwise regarded, he is amusing himself, — were he better off, he would not dream of making such outcries: he would amuse himself in some other way. Likewise for the Christian: he condemns, calumniates, curses the world — and himself in the bargain[9]. But that is no reason to take his clamor seriously. In both instances we are in the midst of invalids crying benefits, for whom calumny affords relief.

...

464. ... But where might I look with any hope at all for my kind of philosophers, or at the very least for my kind of yearning[10] for new philosophers? Only where there prevails a noble turn of mind, one that believes in slavery and in many gradations of serfdom[11] as being the

---

1 **decadence:** falling to lower level

2 **misbegotten:** ill-born

3 **anarchist:** person who wishes to overthrow all government

4 **nihilist:** one who totally rejects religious and moral beliefs

5 **kin:** family, relation

6 **negative self-discovery:** self-elimination

7 **predilection:** preference

8 **aegis:** protection

9 **in the bargain:** as well, in addition

10 **yearn:** desire, long

11 **serfdom:** social system where serfs or slaves are being used, here slave mentality

preconditions of any higher culture; where there prevails a creative turn of mind, one that does not postulate[1] the bliss of eternal repose, the "Sabbath of Sabbaths[2]" as the world's destiny, but honors, even in peacetime, the means to new wars; a turn of mind that prescribes laws to the future, one that for the future's sake deals harshly and tyrannically with itself and its time; an unscrupulous[3], "immoral" turn of mind, determined to nourish towards greatness man's good and evil qualities in equal measure, entrusting itself with the power to give each its proper due, — proper in so far as each requires the other. But he who goes in quest of philosophers today, what are his prospects of finding what he seeks? Isn't it likely that even with the best lamp-of-Diogenes[4] to hand, he wanders about day and night in vain? This age has the contrary instinct: first and foremost, it wants comfort; secondly, it wants publicity, the bustle[5] and din[6] of the theatre and the dancehall, so congenial to its county-fair tastes; thirdly, it wants everybody to crawl on his belly in abject[7] submission before the greatest of all lies — its name is "equality of mankind" — and pay homage exclusively to the equalizing, the levelling[8] virtues. But therewith the advent[9] of the philosopher, as I understand him, is utterly precluded, even though in all innocence this age imagines itself to be conducive to him. Indeed, all the world presently bemoans[10] the evils earlier philosophers had to endure, caught as they were between the stake[11], their guilty conscience, and the presumptuous wisdom of the Church Fathers. But the truth is that just these circumstances afforded far more favorable conditions for a powerful, comprehensive, subtle, and audacious mentality than do the circumstances of present-day life. Today, conditions favor the appearance of another kind of spirit, that of the demagogue[12], the actor, perhaps that of the beaver-like, antlike scholar as well. The superior artists, on the other hand, are already in a bad way: aren't nearly all of them being ruined for want of inner discipline? They are no longer being tyrannized from without by Church- or Court-imposed tablets of absolute value; accordingly, they no longer learn to cultivate their

---

1 **postulate:** demand
2 **Sabbath of Sabbaths:** Sabbath, day of rest and worship, Sunday for most Christians. Cf. holy of holies
3 **unscrupulous:** not guided by conscience
4 **lamp-of-Diogenes:** Diogenes Laertius of Sinope (第欧根尼 c. 400–325 BC), better known as *Diogenes the Cynic*, Greek philosopher and founder of the Cynic school who advocated self-control and the pursuit of virtue through simple living. Diogenes is said to have once wandered through the streets of Athens with a lantern in daylight, searching for an honest man.
5 **bustle:** excitement
6 **din:** loud noise
7 **abject:** miserable
8 **level:** equalize, make mediocre. Nietzsch hated "leveling": "Everyone wants an equal share, everyone is equal: whoever feels otherwise voluntarily enters a madhouse."
9 **advent:** arrival
10 **bemoan:** show sorrow
11 **stake:** post to which a person is tied before being burned to death
12 **demagogue:** political leader good at stirring up people

"inner tyrant," their will. And what holds true for artists holds true in a higher and more ominous[1] sense for philosophers. **Where are the free spirits today? Show me a free spirit today!**

...

728. It is part of the very concept of life that it must grow that it must extend its power and consequently absorb alien forces. Befogged[2] by the narcotic[3] called morality, one speaks of the right of the individual to defend himself. By the same token, one ought to speak of the individual's right to attack, for both — and the second more than the first — are necessities for every living thing: aggressive and defensive egoism are not matters of choice (not to speak of "free will") but the fatality of life itself. In this context it makes no difference whether an individual or a living organism, an aspiring "society," is held in view. At bottom, the right to punish (society's self-defense) was arrived at only through a misuse of the word "right": a right is obtained only by contract, whereas self-defense and self-protection do not rest on a contractual basis[4]. At the very least, and with just as much show of reason, a people should describe its passion for conquest, its lust for power, be it force of arms, trade, commerce, or colonization, as a right. A society which, definitely and in accordance with its instinct, foreswears[5] war and conquest, is in a state of decline: it is ripe for democracy and rule by shopkeepers.

...

753. I am averse to socialism, because it dreams naively of "the Good, the True, the Beautiful" and "equal rights" (anarchism too pursues similar ideals, only in a more brutal way); parliamentarianism and the cult of the newspaper, because they are the means by which the herd[6]-animal becomes master.

...

854. In the era of "universal suffrage[7]," meaning that everyone is able to sit in judgment upon everyone and everything, I am constrained to reestablish the order of rank.

Nietzsche in sick-bed

---

1   **ominous:** threatening
2   **befogged:** obscured in fog, confused, muddle-headed
3   **narcotic:** producing sleep or other insensible condition
4   **self-defense and self-protection do not rest on a contractual basis:** Namely, social contracts are made for submission and give-up, not for self-defense and self-protection, even for attack (cf. Hobbes, Rousseau, Mill, etc.)
5   **foreswear:** forswear, give up
6   **herd:** here mass of common people
7   **suffrage:** right to vote

855. Power-quanta[1] and nothing but power-quanta determine and distinguish rank.

…

866. It is imperative to set forth a counterdirection to the ever-increasing economic exploitation of man and mankind, to the ever more tightly interlocked "machinery" of interests and output. I designate this counterdirection the extraction of man's luxury-surplus[2]: through it shall be brought to light a stronger kind, a higher type, whose conditions of origin and maintenance shall be other than those of the average man. My concept, my image for this type is, as one knows, the word "Overman[3]."

The first direction, which is now fully in view, is marked by conformity, levelling, higher Orientalism[4], modesty of instinct, contentment with the diminution of man — a kind of human standstill-level. Once we achieve, as is unavoidably imminent[5], collective economic[6] management of the earth, mankind can find its meaning as machinery in such service — as a colossal gearbox consisting of ever smaller and ever more finely "adaptable" wheels, characterized by an ever-increasing superfluousness of dominating and ruling elements; as an enormously powerful whole whose component parts represent minutiae[7] of power and value. **To counteract this shrinkage and adaptation of men to a specialized utility, one must go in the opposite direction: the production of the synoptic[8], the all-encompassing, the vindicating[9] man, for whom the mechanization of mankind is a precondition, a foundation upon which he can erect his higher form of being.**

He needs the antagonism[10] of the mass, of the "be-levelled" — the feeling of distance that comes from comparing himself with them. He stands on them, he lives off[11] them. This higher form of aristocratism is that of the future. **Morally speaking, the machine-collectivity, the solidarity**

---

1 **quanta:** singular quantum, amount required

2 **luxury-surplus:** more luxury than what is normally needed

3 **Overman:** German word "Übermensch," Über: above, over, or higher than ordinary. The metaphor imbodies the idea of self-overcoming (overcome the traditional life-denying self) and tends to be different from the "superman" with animalistic and destructive impulses, a prototype of the Nazi Aryan. This Overman is able to face reality of life "without sinking into either despair, nihilism, or pity."

4 **Orientalism:** qualities associated with the Orient, including submission, courtesy, conformity, loss of individuality, reticence, reserve, etc. which lead to the contemporary critique of Orientalism as a myth created by the West for maintaining East-West dichotomy

5 **imminent:** likely to happen

6 **economic:** practical

7 **minutiae:** typical details

8 **synoptic:** summarizing, here encompassing, inclusive

9 **vindicate:** show truth and validity

10 **antagonism:** active opposition

11 **live off:** live by consuming

of all wheels, represents a maximum of human exploitation; but it presupposes those for whose sake such exploitation would make sense. Otherwise it would indeed be nothing but the collective diminution, the value — diminution of the human type — a retrogression in high style. It should be apparent that what I am fighting is economic optimism: as though the increasing sacrifice of each were necessarily accompanied by an increasing advantage for all[1]. To me just the contrary seems the case: the sacrifice of each aggregates[2] into a collective loss; man is diminished, in such a way that one no longer knows what end this stupendous[3] process was meant to subserve[4]. A what-for? A new what-for? That's what mankind requires.

881. With reference to the order of rank: What is mediocre about the typical man? — That he fails to comprehend that things necessarily have a reverse side; that he combats evils as though they could be dispensed with; that he refuses to take the one with the other[5], that he would blur and efface[6] the typical character of a thing, a state of affairs, a period, a person by sanctioning[7] only part of their qualities and dismissing the rest. The "wishfulness" of the mediocre is what the others contend with: the Ideal conceived as something devoid of anything injurious, evil, dangerous, dubious[8], or destructive. Our conception is quite the contrary: that **with man's every growth his reverse side must also grow, that the highest man (granted such a concept is permitted) would be that man who would exhibit the antithetical[9] character of existence most vigorously, as his glory and sole vindication.** Ordinary men can allow themselves to exhibit this quality of nature only to the smallest degree: increase the manysidedness of the elements and the tension among antithesis — the preconditions of man's greatness — and they soon perish. That man must become better and worse: that is my formula for this inevitability.

Most men constitute mere bits and pieces of men; only when they are added together does a man emerge. In this sense there is something fragmentary about whole ages, whole peoples; perhaps it is inherent in the economy[10] of human evolution that man develops only piecemeal[11].

Napoleon Bonaparte, Nietzsche's hero

---

1 **as though the increasing sacrifice ... advantage for all:** This seems to be a counter argument of Adam Smith who believes the increasing advantage of each is necessarily accompanied by an increasing advantage for all. See Unit 10.

2 **aggregate:** amount to

3 **stupendous:** tremendous, amazing

4 **subserve:** serve to promote for an end

5 **take the one with the other:** take both "positive" and "negative" sides

6 **efface:** wipe out

7 **sanction:** approve, agree

8 **dubious:** doubtful

9 **antithetical:** opposing, contradictory

10 **economy:** structure, organization

11 **piecemeal:** piece by piece, part at a time

Precisely for this reason we must not fail to recognize that the emergence of the comprehensive man is all that matters, and that the inferior men, the vast majority, are nothing but preludes and rehearsals[1] — an ensemble[2] out of which here and there the whole man emerges, the milestoneman, the measure of how far mankind has thus far advanced. It does not advance in a straight line; frequently the already achieved type is lost again (for example, notwithstanding three hundred years' exertion, we have failed to measure up to[3] the men of the Renaissance — and Renaissance man in turn fell short of the men of Antiquity).

...

874. The deterioration of the rulers and the ruling classes has brought about the greatest mischief in history! Without the Roman Caesars and Roman society the madness of Christianity would never have come to the fore. When inferior men come to doubt whether there are higher men, then there is great danger! Ultimately one discovers that even the inferior, the subjugated[4], the spiritually impoverished[5] have virtues, and that before God all men are equal: than which no greater nonsense has ever existed on earth! For eventually the higher men themselves accept as their measure the slaves' standard of virtue — find themselves "prideful[6]," etc., find all their higher qualities to be reprehensible. It was when Nero[7] and Caracalla[8] sat on high that the paradox arose, "the lowest man is worth more than the one on high!" And the image of God became prevalent which was as remote as possible from the image of — the Almighty-God on the Cross!

877. The Revolution made possible Napoleon[9]: that is its justification. For a comparable prize one should long for the anarchic collapse of our entire civilization. Napoleon made possible nationalism: that is his excuse.

The value of man (leaving aside, and rightly so, morality and immorality, since these concepts do not even begin to touch a man's worth) is not to be found in his usefulness; for it persists even if there were no one to whom he could be useful. And why couldn't precisely the man who engenders the most destructive consequences be the summit of the entire human species — so

---

1 **preludes and rehearsals:** musical terms, introductory parts and practices, not the most important
2 **ensemble:** group of musicians playing together, general effect
3 **measure up to:** reach the standard of
4 **subjugated:** ruled, oppressed
5 **impoverish:** cause to be poor, take away good quality
6 **prideful:** Pride is one of the deadly sins for Christians.
7 **Nero:** Roman emperor (54–68). In 59 he murdered his mother and in 62, his wife Octavia. When half of Rome was burned in a fire in 64, he accused the Christians of starting it and began the first Roman persecution.
8 **Caracalla (188–217):** real name Marcus Aurelius Antoninus, Roman emperor (211–217), infamous for cruelty and bloodshed
9 **Napoleon Bonaparte (1769–1821):** general of the French Revolution, and ruler of the French Republic (1799 –1804), Emperor of the French and King of Italy under the name Napoleon I (1804–1814), and again (20 March–22 June 1815). Napoleon developed a number of innovative military strategies that led to many successful victories.

Heritage of Western Intellectual Tradition — A Sourcebook

grand, so superior that confronted by him everything would die of envy?[1]

957. It draws near, inexorable[2], trembling, as frightening as fate — the great task and question, How shall the earth as a whole be administered? And toward what end shall mankind as a whole — no longer a mere people, a race — be trained and cultivated?

Legislated morals are the chief means whereby one can cull[3] from man what is suitable to a creative and profound will: provided that such a high order artist — will has power in hand and is able to impose itself over long periods in the form of law-giving, religions, and moralities. To my mind, such men of great achievement, such authentically great men, will be pursued in vain today and probably for a long time to come. They are lacking, and will be, until finally, after much disappointment, one begins to understand why they are lacking, and that now and for a long time to come nothing impedes their genesis and development with greater hostility than what passes in Europe for "the morality" — as though there were and could be no other — the one heretofore described as herd morality, the one which strives with all its might for that common green pasture — land happiness on earth, i.e., security, absence of danger, coziness, ease of life, and, last but not least, "if all goes well," the pious hope of dispensing with all manner of shepherds and bellwethers[4]. Its two most broadly preached doctrines are called "equality of rights" and "compassion for all suffering" — and suffering itself is thought to be something which must by all means be got rid of. That such ideas can still be modern inclines one to a low opinion of modernity. But whoever ponders thoroughly the question where and how the plant Man has hitherto grown up most vigorously cannot help but suppose that this occurred under quite the contrary conditions: that the danger of its habitat[5] must be magnified[6] to frightful proportions, its powers of sensation and locomotion[7] must struggle against long hardship and constriction, its will to life must be intensified into an unconditioned will to power and predominance, and that, danger, harshness, violence, peril in the street as in the heart, inequality of rights, concealment, stoicism[8], the art of seduction, deviltry of every kind — in short, that the elevation of the species Man demands the very antithesis of all herdlike wish-fulfillment. Amorality[9] with such opposite intentions, seeking to nurture man upwards instead of into the cozy and the mediocre, a morality seeking to nurture a ruling caste — the future lords of the earth – must, before it can be promulgated[10], introduce itself as though in league with[11] prevalent moral law and

---

1 **And why couldn't precisely ... die of envy?:** cf. Machiavelli's prince, see Unit 5.
2 **inexorable:** relentless, unyielding
3 **cull:** select
4 **bellwether:** leading sheep of a flock
5 **habitat:** home, natural place of growth
6 **magnify:** enlarge
7 **locomotion:** movement from place to place
8 **stoicism:** patient enduring of suffering
9 **amorality:** paying no attention to morality, not to be confused with immorality
10 **promulgate:** made public
11 **in league with:** in line with, agreeable to

in the guise of the latter's words and shapes. But that accordingly a number of provisional and diversionary[1] tactics need be discovered and that, whereas the life-span of a man means next to nothing in face of the fulfillment of such protracted[2] tasks and aims, above all else a new species must be nurtured, in which the appropriate wills and instincts will be guaranteed duration through many generations — a new ruling species and caste: to envision all this is no easier than to comprehend the lengthy and hard-to-articulate Etcetera[3] of its underlying thought. To prepare a transvaluation[4] of values for a certain powerful species of men, endowed with the highest intellect and will-power, and to this end liberate him slowly and carefully from a host of repressed and vilified[5] instincts: who ponders this belongs to us, the free spirits ...

997. I teach that there are higher and lower men, and that in some cases the existence of entire millennia may be justified by a single individual — that is a fuller, richer, greater, more whole man, in contrast with countless incomplete, fragmentary men.

998. **The highest men live beyond rulers, free of all bonds; and in the rulers they find their instruments.**

999. Order of rank: **he who determines values and directs the will of millennia by directing the highest natures, is the highest man.**

1000. I think I have fathomed[6] something of what goes on in the soul of the highest man; perhaps anyone who fathoms him entire is doomed: but whoever has glimpsed him must help to make him possible.

Fundamental idea: we must take the future as the criterion for all our value appraisals — and not look behind us for the laws of our action.

1001. Not "mankind" but the Overman is the goal!

Key Concepts

Apollonian spirit	equality of mankind
collective diminution	free spirit
Dionysian spirit	higher Orientalism
Egoism	iconoclasm

---

1 **diversionary:** diverting, giving a different direction
2 **protract:** prolong, lengthen the time
3 **Etcetera:** miscellaneous unspecified objects, usually as "etc."
4 **transvaluation:** evaluation by a new standard or principle, especially by one that varies from conventional standards
5 **vilify:** slander, say evil things
6 **fathom:** measure

instinct-to-failure	Overman
machine-collectivity	self-assurance
milestoneman	yes-saying

Compare with China

From Western Liberalism to Asian Communitarianism

To understand what is at stake, let me articulate briefly the principles of Western liberalism and show how these contrast with East Asian principles of political and economic organization and social philosophy.

The first principle is that of *individualism*. The individual is prior to society. Each individual is morally autonomous, free to choose his or her own life goals, and to pursue these in any way the individual wants, so long as he or she does not interfere with another's pursuit of goals. Societies come into existence only because of voluntary contracts of individuals trying to pursue more effectively their individual goals.

A second assumption is *rationalism*. The individuals who constitute societies are rational agents. The rationality they possess is primarily instrumental — the capacity to calculate the most effective means to achieve their ends. The way to establish public order is to increase, through a secular scientific education, the capacity of each individual for this kind of rational action. That way, each individual will see that he or she needs to follow similar procedures.

The rational individual will recognize the need to organize the pursuit of his or her goals through entering into contracts. Thus *contractualism* is the third principal assumption of liberalism. Stable social relations are formed because individual parties enter into agreements to provide mutual benefits. Aggregated[1], all of these micro-level contracts constitute the social contract that is the basis of society itself.

Legitimate contracts must be based on voluntary, rational choice — the ability of the individual to choose what is best for him or herself from the widest set of alternatives, without having any alternative arbitrarily excluded. In other words, choice must be based — the fourth principal assumption of liberalism — on *universalistic* rather than *particularistic* criteria.

Government, according to these assumptions, should maximize the capacity of individuals to achieve their private goals. It should provide the basic security necessary for this pursuit, and it

---

1   **aggregate:** bring together

should establish the procedures necessary to make the pursuit orderly, but otherwise it should interfere as little as possible. When governments impose limitations on some of the freedoms of individuals for the sake of maximizing the overall possible freedom, these choices must be legitimated through democratic procedures, which are based on the aggregation of individuals' choices through voting.

These are the principles that govern relations between individuals and society in a liberal nation state. Scholars and statesmen working within the liberal tradition assume that the path to a peaceful and just global community is an expansion of these principles to the world order: the world system is made up of a set of nation states that are like individuals writ large, sovereign and self-determining. These nations enter into contractual relations with one another based on their perception of self-interest. A healthy world economy depends on the capacity of such nations to trade freely among each other in an unfettered open market. A healthy world political system entails the ability of such nations to make free contractual agreements — "open covenants, openly arrived at." Norms governing international trade and international security should ideally be established by an international deliberating body like the United Nations. (Realistically, they are established and backed up by the power and for the interests of the most powerful nations.)

These liberal assumptions are beginning to be called into question within the West because they correspond less and less to the experience of people anywhere in the modern world. As self-doubt deepens, East Asian societies are providing alternative models of the successful pursuit of wealth and power-models that challenge and may supplant[1] those of the faltering[2] West. For all of their differences, people in East Asia seem to share certain half-articulated, taken-for-granted general assumptions about how to pursue a good life, how the individual relates to society, and how societies should pursue wealth and power.

The first of these assumptions is that society is *prior to the individual* — that individuals cannot have any substantial identity apart from social relationships, especially familial but also (broadly conceived) political relationships. Although there would be enormous controversy over what this means in practice, Asians share a vaguely defined sense that the interests of society as a whole can, and sometimes should, take precedence over individuals' private interests.

A second assumption has to do with the nature of *reason*. The Confucian tradition stresses the rationality of humans, but it lays great emphasis on a moral rationality — not technical reason but the kind of reason that enables one to understand the rightness of the moral duties connected with one's role in society. In societies as different as Japan, China, and Malaysia, it is assumed that education should inculcate[3] moral values rather than simply teach techniques. Although the specific content of those values may differ from society to society, it is assumed that the best and the

---

1 **supplant:** take the place of
2 **faltering:** shaking, wavering
3 **inculcate:** fix (ideas, principles, etc.) firmly in mind, especially by repetition

brightest graduates of the educational system should be generalists with a firm grasp of the responsibilities that go with leadership rather than specialized technical experts.

Social relationships, it is widely assumed, are ultimately based not simply on voluntary contracts between individuals, but upon *responsibilities* toward the society as a whole. People need to share not merely common procedures to pursue their own private self-fulfillment, but common public goals, and a common commitment to the social relationships that anchor their individual identities. It is one of the government's more important responsibilities to create this consensus[1].The state is a paternalistic educator, not just a neutral referee. The government — as long as it is doing its job correctly and has not become corrupt — is a guardian of a moral order that makes citizenship possible.

Since East Asian societies have not had the capacity to play a truly global role for most of 20th century, it is less clear how Asian scholars and diplomats will translate the above principles for a good national society into global norms for international conduct. The attempt by China to mobilize other East Asian nations in an effort to change international human rights standards gives one indication. As their wealth and power increases, Asian regimes will try to insist that individual rights are less important than the right of whole societies to maintain order as the foundation for economic prosperity. Like Kishore Mahbubani, Singapore's Deputy Secretary of Foreign Affairs, they may argue that the West is foolishly destroying the foundations of its wealth and prosperity because of its obsession with "the idea of individual freedom."

Western social theory predicts that authoritarian societies will be less productive than ones that emphasize individual freedoms, because modern technologies require the kind of creativity and initiative that can only flourish in a free society. If authoritarian Asian societies continue their advances in productivity, they may force the theorists to modify their ideas. They may also push Western societies to modify the bases of their social contracts. Asian societies keep wages relatively low by restricting organization of independent labor unions. They provide limited social welfare benefits, expecting intact[2], mutually loyal families to take care of members in need. Thus labor costs there are low in comparison with most Western countries. In the name of keeping pace with "international competition," Western countries like the United States are breaking the power of labor unions, dismantling much of their welfare states, and "getting tough on crime" by suppressing previously accepted liberties. They are beginning to let Asian forms of social organization set the world standard for labor practices.[3]

Besides changing the international moral balance between rights and responsibilities, and individual and society, the Asian societies are shifting the balance between particularism and universalism. Businesses award contracts not simply on the basis of universalistic, open competi-

---

1   **consensus:** common agreement

2   **intact:** complete, undamaged

3   **They are beginning to … for labor practices.:** Here the author is more than "neutral" in his value judgment: one party is compelled by the other to change its principles, for better.

tive bidding, but because of long-standing particularistic relationships, sometimes based on near or distant kinship. Consumers, too, often base their buying decisions on long-standing loyalty, rather than simply on price. The result is the myriad[1] of informal barriers to open trade that so upsets American business interests. The Japanese, especially, are weaving these patterns into regional trading blocs[2].

If the United States and Western Europe were to become largely shut out of this latter day version of a "Greater East Asia Co-prosperity Sphere," they might have to concentrate their economic energies in their own regions, thus building on an expanded NAFTA[3] in the Americas and the EEU[4] in Europe. Expectations about what constitutes a good international economic system would change from a single open market to a regionalized world economy.

Changes in this economic "substructure" might generate changes in cultural-ideological superstructure. Economists might start to recast theories that assume that economic life everywhere follows a single set of universal laws. They might "discover" more contextualized economic principles. This would accelerate the move toward various forms of cultural relativism that has already begun in the other social sciences. The centrality of universalistic, instrumental rationality in education might change, as the philosophy of Western scientific education no longer set the standard for modern education throughout the world. (Adapted from Richard Madsen, "After Liberalism: What If Confucianism Becomes the Hegemonic Ethic of the Twenty-First Century?")

Supplementary Reading

1. Edmund Burke: Reflections on the Revolution in France

Edmund Burke (1729–1797), British statesman and orator, and sometimes "founder of conservatism," was born in Dublin and educated at Trinity College. He studied law in London after 1761 demonstrated aptitude for political service. Four years later he became private secretary to the new British prime minister Charles Watson-Wentworth. In 1766 he was elected as a Whig to Parliament. He urged justice

---

1 **myriad:** huge number
2 **bloc:** interest group
3 **NAFTA:** The North American Free Trade Agreement links Canada, the United States, and Mexico in a free trade sphere. NAFTA went into effect on January 1, 1994.
4 **EEU:** European Economic Union

Heritage of Western Intellectual Tradition — A Sourcebook

and conciliation toward the American colonies, and advocated a reversal of the British policy that allowed the East India Company to exploit the population of that country. With the publication of "Reflections on the Revolution in France" (1790), however, Burke appeared as the champion of the feudal order in Europe. In an eloquent expression of conservative principles, Burke urged gradual reform rather than rebellion as a means of correcting social and political problems. The text, which was read throughout Europe, encouraged European rulers in the aftermath of the French Revolution.

Kings, in one sense, are undoubtedly the servants of the people, because their power has no other rational end than that of the general advantage; but it is not true that they are, in the ordinary sense, (by our constitution at least,) anything like servants; the essence of whose situation is to obey the commands of some other, and to be removable at pleasure. But the king of Great Britain obeys no other person; all other persons are individually, and collectively too, under him, and owe to him a legal obedience. The law, which knows neither to flatter nor to insult, calls this high magistrate, not our servant, as this humble divine calls him, but *"our sovereign Lord the king*;" and we, on our parts, have learned to speak only the primitive language of the law, and not the confused jargon[1] of their Babylonian pulpits[2].

As he is not to obey us, but as we are to obey the law in him, our constitution has made no sort of provision towards rendering him, as a servant, in any degree responsible. Our constitution knows nothing of a magistrate like the *Justicia* of Arragon[3]; nor of any court legally appointed, nor of any process legally settled, for submitting the king to the responsibility belonging to all servants. In this he is not distinguished from the Commons and the Lords, who, in their several public capacities, can never be called to an account[4] for their conduct; although the Revolution Society chooses to assert in direct opposition to one of the wisest and most beautiful parts of our constitution, that "a king is no more than the first servant of the public, created by it, *and responsible to it.*"

Ill would our ancestors at the Revolution have deserved their fame for wisdom, if they had found no security for their freedom, but in rendering their government feeble in its operations and precarious[5] in its tenure;[6] if they had been able to contrive[7] no better remedy against arbitrary power than civil confusion. Let these gentlemen state who that *representative* public is to whom

---

1 **jargon:** meaningless talk
2 **pulpit:** elevated platform for preaching
3 *Justicia* **of Arragon:** office founded early in the twelfth century and noted for its defence of popular rights. The Justicia's functions were in theory similar to those of the Lord Chief Justice of England, but in practice more important and extensive.
4 **call to an account:** question
5 **precarious:** unsteady, unsafe
6 **tenure:** office holding
7 **contrive:** invent, design

they will affirm the king, as a servant, to be responsible. It will then be time enough for me to produce to them the positive statute law[1] which affirms that he is not.

Storming of the Bastille

The ceremony of cashiering[2] kings, of which these gentlemen talk so much at their ease, can rarely, if ever, be performed without force. It then becomes a case of war, and not of constitution. Laws are commanded to hold their tongues amongst arms; and tribunals[3] fall to the ground with the peace they are no longer able to uphold. The Revolution of 1688 was obtained by a just war, in the only case in which any war, and much more a civil war, can be just. "Justa bella quibus necessaria.[4]" The question of dethroning or, if these gentlemen like the phrase better "cashiering kings," will always be, as it has always been an extraordinary question of state, and wholly out of the law; a question (like all other questions of state) of dispositions, and of means, and of probable consequences, rather than of positive rights. As it was not made for common abuses, so it is not to be agitated by common minds. The speculative line of demarcation[5], where obedience ought to end, and resistance must begin, is faint, obscure, and not easily definable. It is not a single act, or a single event, which determines it. Governments must be abused and deranged[6] indeed, before it can be thought of; and the prospect of the future must be as bad as the experience of the past. When things are in that lamentable condition, the nature of the disease is to indicate the remedy to those whom nature has qualified to administer in extremities this critical, ambiguous, bitter potion[7] to a distempered[8] state. Times, and occasions, and provocations, will teach their own lessons. The wise will determine from the gravity of the case; the irritable, from sensibility to oppression; the high-minded, from disdain and indignation at abusive power in unworthy hands; the brave and bold, from the love of honorable danger in a generous cause; but, with or without right, a revolution will be the very last resource of the thinking and the good.

The third head of right, asserted by the pulpit of the Old Jewry, namely, the "right to form a government for ourselves," has, at least, as little countenance[9] from anything done at the Revolution, either in precedent or principle, as the two first of their claims. The Revolution was made to preserve our *ancient*, indisputable laws and liberties, and that *ancient* constitution of government which is our only security for law and liberty. If you are desirous of knowing the spirit of our

---

1 **statute law:** all the statutes as a group（成文法）
2 **cashier:** dismiss from office
3 **tribunal:** seat or court of justice
4 **Justa bella quibus necessaria.:** Wars are just to those to whom they are necessary.
5 **demarcation:** division
6 **derange:** disrupt
7 **potion:** drink of medicine, poison or a liquid used in magic
8 **distempered:** mentally disturbed
9 **countenance:** support or approval

Heritage of Western Intellectual Tradition A Sourcebook

constitution and the policy which predominated in that great period which has secured it to this hour, pray look for both in our histories, in our records, in our acts of parliament, and journals of parliament, and not in the sermons of the Old Jewry and the after-dinner toasts of the Revolution Society. In the former you will find other ideas and another language. Such a claim is as ill-suited to our temper and wishes as it is unsupported by an appearance of authority. The very idea of the fabrication[1] of a new government is enough to fill us with disgust and horror. We wished at the period of the Revolution, and do now wish, to derive all we possess as *an inheritance from our forefathers*. Upon that body and stock of inheritance we have taken care not to inoculate[2] any scion[3] alien to the nature of the original plant. All the reformations we have hitherto made have proceeded upon the principle of reverence to antiquity: and I hope, nay I am persuaded, that all those which possibly may be made hereafter will be carefully formed upon analogical precedent, authority, and example.

…

Our oldest reformation is that of Magna Charta[4]. You will see that Sir Edward Coke[5], that great oracle of our law, and indeed all the great men who follow him, to Blackstone[6], are industrious to prove the pedigree[7] of our liberties. They endeavor to prove that the ancient charter, the Magna Charta of King John, was connected with another positive charter from Henry I, and that both the one and the other were nothing more than a re-affirmance of the still more ancient standing law of the kingdom. In the matter of fact, for the greater part, these authors appear to be in the right; perhaps not always; but if the lawyers mistake in some particulars, it proves my position still the more strongly, because it demonstrates the powerful prepossession[8] toward antiquity, with which the minds of all our lawyers and legislators, and of all the people whom they wish to influence, have been always filled, and the stationary[9] policy of this kingdom in considering their most sacred rights and franchises[10] as an *inheritance*.

…

France, by the perfidy[11] of her leaders, has utterly disgraced the tone of lenient[12] council in

---

1 **fabrication:** making, formation

2 **inoculate:** introduce

3 **scion:** detached shoot or twig from a woody plant used in grafting

4 **Magna Charta:** charter of English political and civil liberties granted by King John at Runnymede in June 1215

5 **Edward Coke (1552 – 1634):** early English colonial entrepreneur and jurist whose writings on the English common law were the definitive legal texts for some 300 years

6 **Sir William Blackstone (1723 – 1780):** English jurist known for his treatise on the common law called *Commentaries on the Laws of England*, first published in four volumes over 1765 – 1769

7 **pedigree:** a line of ancestors

8 **prepossession:** favourable feelings

9 **stationary:** fixed in position

10 **franchise:** right or privilege

11 **perfidy:** treachery

12 **lenient:** merciful, generous

the cabinets of princes, and disarmed it of its most potent topics. She has sanctified the dark, suspicious maxims of tyrannous distrust, and taught kings to tremble at (what will hereafter be called) the delusive plausibilities of moral politicians. Sovereigns will consider those who advise them to place an unlimited confidence in their people as subverters of their thrones, as traitors who aim at their destruction by leading their easy good-nature, under specious[1] pretenses, to admit combinations of bold and faithless men into a participation of their power. This alone (if there were nothing else) is an irreparable calamity[2] to you and to mankind. Remember that your parliament of Paris told your king that, in calling the states together, he had nothing to fear but the prodigal[3] excess of their zeal in providing for the support of the throne. It is right that these men should hide their heads. It is right that they should bear their part in the ruin which their counsel has brought on their sovereign and their country. Such sanguine[4] declarations tend to lull

Guillotining of Louis XVI of France on January 21, 1793 terrified conservatives in Europe

authority asleep; to encourage it rashly to engage in perilous adventures of untried policy; to neglect those provisions, preparations, and precautions which distinguish benevolence from imbecility[5], and without which no man can answer for the salutary effect of any abstract plan of government or of freedom. For want of these, they have seen the medicine of the state corrupted into its poison. They have seen the French rebel against a mild and lawful monarch with more fury, outrage, and insult than ever any people has been known to rise against the most illegal usurper or the most sanguinary[6] tyrant. Their resistance was made to concession, their revolt was from protection, their blow was aimed at a hand holding out graces, favors, and immunities[7].

This was unnatural. The rest is in order. They have found their punishment in their success: laws overturned; tribunals subverted; industry without vigor; commerce expiring; the revenue unpaid, yet the people impoverished; a church pillaged[8], and a state not relieved; civil and military anarchy made the constitution of the kingdom; everything human and divine sacrificed to the idol of public credit, and national bankruptcy the consequence; and, to crown all, the paper securities of new, precarious, tottering[9] power, the discredited paper securities of impoverished fraud and

---

1   **specious:** seeming right or true but actually wrong or false
2   **calamity:** disaster
3   **prodigal:** wastefully extravagant
4   **sanguine:** optimistic
5   **imbecility:** stupidity or foolishness
6   **sanguinary:** bloodthirsty
7   **immunity:** exemption
8   **pillage:** rob by force
9   **totter:** shake

Heritage of Western Intellectual Tradition   A Sourcebook

beggared rapine[1], held out as a currency for the support of an empire in lieu of[2] the two great recognized species that represent the lasting, conventional credit of mankind, which disappeared and hid themselves in the earth from whence they came, when the principle of property, whose creatures and representatives they are, was systematically subverted.

Were all these dreadful things necessary? Were they the inevitable results of the desperate struggle of determined patriots, compelled to wade through blood and tumult to the quiet shore of a tranquil and prosperous liberty? No! nothing like it. The fresh ruins of France, which shock our feelings wherever we can turn our eyes, are not the devastation of civil war; they are the sad but instructive monuments of rash and ignorant counsel in time of profound peace. They are the display of inconsiderate and presumptuous, because unresisted and irresistible, authority. The persons who have thus squandered away the precious treasure of their crimes, the persons who have made this prodigal and wild waste of public evils (the last stage reserved for the ultimate ransom of the state) have met in their progress with little or rather with no opposition at all. Their whole march was more like a triumphal procession than the progress of a war. Their pioneers have gone before them and demolished and laid everything level at their feet. Not one drop of *their* blood have they shed in the cause of the country they have ruined. They have made no sacrifices to their projects of greater consequence than their shoe-buckles, whilst they were imprisoning their king, murdering their fellow citizens, and bathing in tears and plunging in poverty and distress thousands of worthy men and worthy families. Their cruelty has not even been the base result of fear. It has been the effect of their sense of perfect safety, in authorizing treasons, robberies, rapes, assassinations, slaughters, and burnings throughout their harassed land. But the cause of all was plain from the beginning.

2. *Declaration of the Rights of Man and of the Citizen*

Declaration of the Rights of Man and of the Citizen is a revolutionary manifesto adopted on August 26, 1789, by the National Assembly of France. Written principally by Abbé Mmanuel Sieyès, the declaration enumerated a number of rights described as inalienable with which "all men" were held to be endowed and nullified the age-old divine right of kings to rule. These inalienable rights included participation, through chosen representatives, in the making of laws; equality of all persons before the law; equitable taxation; protection against loss of property through arbitrary action by the state; freedom of religion, speech, and the press; and protection against arbitrary arrest and punishment. The political origins of the declaration were

multifold, which may include the influence of the U.S. *Declaration of Independence* and the bills of rights of a number of state constitutions in the United States, English principles of democratic rights,

---

1 **rapine:** plunder
2 **in lieu of:** instead of

and even the Calvinistic doctrine of freedom of conscience. But the declaration was first of all a product of the current of ideas known as the Age of Enlightenment and expounded by the French philosopher Jean Jacques Rousseau in *Social Contract.* The declaration had great influence on political thought and institutions. It was a model for most of the declarations of political and civil rights adopted by European states in the 19th century and for the bill of rights of the constitution of the Weimar Republic of Germany (1919–1933).

Approved by the National Assembly of France, August 26, 1789

The representatives of the French people, organized as a National Assembly, believing that the ignorance, neglect, or contempt of the rights of man are the sole causes of public calamities and of the corruption of governments, have determined to set forth in a solemn declaration the natural, unalienable, and sacred rights of man, in order that this declaration, being constantly before all the members of the social body, shall remind them continually of their rights and duties; in order that the acts of the legislative power, as well as those of the executive power, may be compared at any moment with the objects and purposes of all political institutions and may thus be more respected, and, lastly, in order that the grievances of the citizens, based hereafter upon simple and incontestable[1] principles, shall tend to the maintenance[2] of the Constitution and redound[3] to the happiness of all. Therefore the National Assembly recognizes and proclaims, in the presence and under the auspices of[4] the Supreme Being, the following rights of man and of the citizen:

Articles:

1. Men are born and remain free and equal in rights. Social distinctions may be founded only upon the general good.

2. The aim of all political association is the preservation of the natural and inalienable rights of man. These rights are liberty, property, security, and resistance to oppression.

3. The principle of all sovereignty resides essentially in the nation. No body nor individual may exercise any authority which does not proceed directly from the nation.

4. Liberty consists in the freedom to do everything which injures no one else; hence the exercise of the natural rights of each man has no limits except those[5] which assure to the other members of the society the enjoyment of the same rights. These limits can only be determined by law.

5. Law can only prohibit such actions as are hurtful to society. Nothing may be prevented which is not forbidden by law, and no one may be forced to do anything not provided for by law.

6. Law is the expression of the general will. Every citizen has a right to participate personally,

---

1 **incontestable:** indisputable
2 **maintenance:** continuation, support
3 **redound:** contribute greatly
4 **under the auspices of:** favoured by
5 **those:** limits

or through his representative, in its foundation. It must be the same for all, whether it protects or punishes. All citizens, being equal in the eyes of the law, are equally eligible[1] to all dignities[2] and to all public positions and occupations, according to their abilities, and without distinction except that of their virtues and talents.

7. No person shall be accused, arrested, or imprisoned except in the cases determined and according to the forms prescribed by law. Any one soliciting[3], transmitting, executing, or causing to be executed, any arbitrary order, shall be punished. But any citizen summoned or arrested in virtue of the law shall submit without delay, as resistance constitutes an offense.

8. The law shall provide for such punishments only as are strictly and obviously necessary, and no one shall suffer punishment except it be legally inflicted in virtue of a law passed and promulgated[4] before the commission of the offense.

9. As all persons are held innocent until they shall have been declared guilty, if arrest shall be deemed indispensable, all harshness not essential to the securing of the prisoner's person shall be severely repressed by law.

10. No one shall be disquieted[5] on account of his opinions, including his religious views, provided their manifestation does not disturb the public order established by law.

11. The free communication of ideas and opinions is one of the most precious of the rights of man. Every citizen may, accordingly, speak, write, and print with freedom, but shall be responsible for such abuses of this freedom as shall be defined by law.

12. The security of the rights of man and of the citizen requires public military forces. These forces are, therefore, established for the good of all and not for the personal advantage of those to whom they shall be entrusted.

13. A common contribution is essential for the maintenance of the public forces and for the cost of administration. This should be equitably[6] distributed among all the citizens in proportion to their means.

14. All the citizens have a right to decide, either personally or by their representatives, as to the necessity of the public contribution, to grant this freely, to know to what uses it is put, and to fix the proportion, the mode of assessment and of collection and the duration of the taxes.

15. Society has the right to require of every public agent an account of his administration.

16. A society in which the observance of the law is not assured, nor the separation of powers defined, has no constitution at all.

17. Since property is an inviolable and sacred right, no one shall be deprived thereof except where public necessity, legally determined, shall clearly demand it, and then only on condition that the owner shall have been previously and equitably indemnified[7].

---

1 **eligible:** suitable

2 **dignity:** high post

3 **solicit:** make request

4 **promulgate:** make public announcement officially

5 **disquiet:** make uneasy, trouble

6 **equitably:** fairly, justly

7 **indemnify:** protect against damage, loss, or injury; insure

Questions for Discussion

1. Why is Rousseau critical of modern arts and sciences?

2. "The philosophy of Rousseau was a mixture of Lao-Tse's return to nature, Buddha's compassion for the poor, Isaiah's search for social justice, St. Augustine's progress from licentiousness to love, and Locke's blueprint for a better world. In addition … Rousseau brought to his work the imagination of a poet and the sympathy of a gentle soul." Do you agree?

3. What is meant by "Will to Power"? What is implied in the concept of "Overman"?

4. Nietzsche in his last major book *Ecce Homo* asks his readers, "Have you understood me…?" Discuss why he is so much misunderstood.

5. *The Will to Power* contends that traditional values (represented primarily by Christianity) had lost their power in the lives of individuals. This contention finds expression in the proclamation "God is dead," perhaps the most widely repeated Nietzschean aphorism. Comment.

6. Not all countries share the Western view of individual rights. The United Nations in 1948 was basically a Western organisation. Many Asian and African countries were their colonies, or were very weak economically and therefore not very influential. Does the Universal Declaration of Human Rights apply to them?

7. According to Confucius five relationships are central to happiness and well-being: the ruler should be obeyed and respected by all; loyalty on the part of subjects should be repaid with benevolence on the part of the ruler; a son must respect his parents and parents must love their son; younger brothers must respect older brothers, who have a responsibility to look after them; a wife must respect her husband; and a person must respect all his friends. How do the rules listed above agree or conflict with the United Nations list of rights? How might a belief in Confucianism affect a person's attitude to some of the individual rights claimed by the Western tradition? Is there a situation where the two sets of principles will find the other complementary?

Heritage of Western Intellectual Tradition   A Sourcebook

UNIT 12

Evolutionists

Pretest

- Comment on the concept of "survival of the fittest."
- What do you know about "social Darwinism"?
- Why should Nietzsche propose the concept of an "Overman"?

What You Will Learn in This Unit

- Some knowledge about Darwinism;
- Important sections from *An Essay on the Principle of Population*, *On the Origin of Species*, and *The Descent of Man*; and
- Social Darwinism in Early 20th Century China.

Learn to Pronounce

catastrophist theory /kəˈtæstrəfɪst/ 突变论

Charles Darwin /ˈdɑːwɪn/ 达尔文

embryology /ˌembrɪˈɒlədʒɪ/ 胚胎学

Herbert Spencer /ˈspensə/ 斯宾塞

hereditary /hɪˈredɪtərɪ/ 遗传的

humanitarianism /ˌhjuːmænɪˈteərɪənɪzm/ 人道主义

iconoclast /aɪˈkɒnəklæst/ 偶像破坏者

Noah /ˈnəʊə/ 诺亚

species /ˈspiːʃɪz/ 物种

Thomas Huxley /ˈhʌkslɪ/ 赫胥黎

Thomas Malthus /mælˈθəs/ 马尔萨斯

Introduction

The 18th and early 19th century liberalism goes hand in hand with other intellectual movements. Three powerful tendencies of thought, among others, influenced almost all the social sciences in the 19th century and afterwards. The first is a positivism that was not merely an appeal to but almost reverence for science; the second, humanitarianism; and the third, the philosophy of evolution. The positivist appeal of science was to be seen everywhere. The spirit of Age of Reason saw a fruition in the 19th century science, with the virtual institutionalization of this ideal. The ambition was that of dealing with moral values, institutions, and all social phenomena through the fundamental methods of physics and biology. In the 19th century, the distinction between philosophy and science became an overwhelming one. Virtually every area of man's thought and behavior was thought to be amenable to scientific investigation. The idea of a *science* of society manifests itself in humanitarianism, for the ultimate purpose of "social science" was the welfare of society and the improvement of its moral and social condition. Here is the beginning of the institutionalization of compassion, the extension of welfare and succour from family and village to society at large. Contrary to humanitarianism is the intellectual influence of evolution. Evolution generally means the "complex process by which the characteristics of living organisms change over many generations as traits are passed from one generation to the next." The science of evolution seeks to understand the forces that caused ancient organisms to develop into the ever-changing variety of life on earth today. Throughout history, philosophers, religious thinkers, and scientists have attempted to explain the history and variety of life on earth. A modern theory of evolution came in the mid-19th century when Charles Darwin described the evolution of life as a process of natural selection, a competitive struggle to survive. Certain individuals possess characteristics that make them more likely to survive and reproduce. The idea of "survival of the fittest," when applied to humanity, leads to Social Darwinism which advocates a *laissez-faire* political and economic system that favors competition and self-interest and rejects compassion and social responsibility. Although Social Darwinists try to deny the idea of "law of the jungle," they openly justify imbalances of power between individuals, races, and nations, which most people believe is a rationalization behind racism, imperialism, and capitalism.

Thomas Malthus: An Essay on the Principle of Population*

Thomas Robert Malthus (1766 – 1834), British economist, was educated at Jesus College, Univer-

---

* In 1793 English political philosopher William Godwin (1756 – 1836) published *Enquiry Concerning Political Justice and Its Influence on Morals and Happiness* to call for "maximum individual and collective efforts" in total disregard of government interference. A similar claim was made by the French philosopher Marquis de Condorcet (1743 – 94) in 1794. Daniel Malthus the father supported these people, but Thomas disagreed. Hence the essay he had promised his father to publish, anonymously, *An Essay on the Principle of Population As It Affects the Future Improvement of Society, with Remarks on the Speculations of Mr. Godwin, M. Condorcet, and Other Writers* (1798).

sity of Cambridge. He was ordained in 1797 in charge of a shall parish in his native county of Surrey.

In childhood Malthus saw the terrible condition of a large portion of the population — the grinding poverty and squalor. In manhood he was to make known the reasons for such a misery and suggest ways to improve the situation. From 1805 until his death, he was professor of political economy and modern history at the college of the East India Company at Haileybury. His main contribution to economics was the theory of population, published in *An Essay on the Principle of Population* (1798). According to this theory, population tends to increase faster than the supply of food available for its needs. Whenever a relative gain occurs in food production over population growth, a higher rate of population increase is stimulated; on the other hand, if population grows too much faster than food production, the growth is to be checked by famine, disease, and war. This theory contradicts Adam Smith's optimistic view that everything will work out fine if laws of economics are allowed to function with a minimum of interference, an optimistic belief prevailing in the early 19th century that a society's fertility would lead to economic progress. The writings of Malthus initiated the science of population study or demography. They also influenced subsequent economists and policy makers — Prime Minister William Pitt (1759 – 1806) withdrew a proposed law for the relief of the poor in 1800 because, according to Malthus, this only tended to aggravate the situation by encouraging additional births, and he was conductive to the first census in England in 1801. As "that black and terrible demon that is always ready to stifle the hopes of humanity," he was extremely unpopular among the poor in his own day, though he as a person was characteristically kind, mild, cheerful, and affectionate.

Book I　Of the Checks to Population
in the Less Civilized Parts of the World and in Past Times

Chapter I　Statement of the Subject.
Ratios of the Increase of Population and Food

In an inquiry concerning the improvement of society, the mode of conducting the subject which naturally presents itself, is,

1. To investigate the causes that have hitherto impeded[1] the progress of mankind towards happiness; and,

2. To examine the probability of the total or partial removal of these causes in future.

To enter fully into this question, and to enumerate all the causes that have hitherto influenced human improvement, would be much beyond the power of an individual. **The principal object of the present essay is to examine the effects of one great cause intimately united with the very nature of man; which, though it has been constantly and powerfully operating since**

1　**impede:** hinder

the commencement[1] of society, has been little noticed by the writers who have treated this subject. The facts which establish the existence of this cause have, indeed, been repeatedly stated and acknowledged; but its natural and necessary effects have been almost totally overlooked; though probably among these effects may be reckoned[2] a very considerable portion[3] of that vice and misery, and of that unequal distribution of the bounties of nature, which it has been the unceasing object of the enlightened philanthropist[4] in all ages to correct.

It can be seen from this portrait of the young Malthus (1833) that there is a slight twist to the mouth, which is believed to be the hair lip from which Malthus suffered.

The cause to which I allude, is the constant tendency in all animated[5] life to increase beyond the nourishment prepared for it.

It is observed by Dr. Franklin, that there is no bound to the prolific[6] nature of plants or animals, but what is made by their crowding and interfering with each other's means of subsistence. Were the face of the earth, he says, vacant of other plants, it might be gradually sowed and overspread with one kind only, as for instance with fennel[7]: and were it empty of other inhabitants, it might in a few ages be replenished[8] from one nation only, as for instance with Englishmen.

This is incontrovertibly[9] true. Through the animal and vegetable kingdoms Nature has scattered the seeds of life abroad with the most profuse[10] and liberal hand; but has been comparatively sparing[11] in the room and the nourishment necessary to rear them. The germs of existence contained in this earth, if they could freely develop themselves, would fill millions of worlds in the course of a few thousand years. Necessity, that imperious[12], all-pervading law of nature, restrains them within the prescribed bounds. The race of plants and the race of animals shrink under this great restrictive law; and man cannot by any efforts of reason escape from it.

In plants and irrational animals, the view of the subject is simple. They are all impelled by a

---

1 **commencement:** beginning
2 **reckon:** find out
3 **though probably among these ... considerable portion:** i.e., a very considerable portion of ... may be reckoned among these effects
4 **philanthropist:** people who help those in trouble
5 **animated:** living
6 **prolific:** producing offspring
7 **fennel:** yellow-flowered herb（茴香）
8 **replenish:** fill up
9 **incontrovertibly:** absolutely
10 **profuse:** plentiful, abundant
11 **sparing:** frugal, not wasteful
12 **imperious:** commanding

powerful instinct to the increase of their species; and this instinct is interrupted by no doubts about providing for their offspring. Wherever therefore there is liberty, the power of increase is exerted; and the superabundant effects are repressed afterwards by want of room and nourishment.

The effects of this check on man are more complicated. Impelled to the increase of his species by an equally powerful instinct, reason interrupts his career, and asks him whether he may not bring beings into the world, for whom he cannot provide the means of support. If he attend[1] to this natural suggestion, the restriction too frequently produces vice. If he hear it not, the human race will be constantly endeavoring to increase beyond the means of subsistence. But as, by that law of our nature which makes food necessary to the life of man, population can never actually increase beyond the lowest nourishment capable of supporting it, a strong check on population, from the difficulty of acquiring food, must be constantly in operation. This difficulty must fall somewhere, and must necessarily be severely felt in some or other of the various forms of misery, or the fear of misery, by a large portion of mankind.

That population has this constant tendency to increase beyond the means of subsistence, and that it is kept to its necessary level by these causes, will sufficiently appear from a review of the different states of society in which man has existed. But, before we proceed to this review, the subject will, perhaps, be seen in a clearer light, if we endeavour to ascertain what would be the natural increase of population, if left to exert itself with perfect freedom; and what might be expected to be the rate of increase in the productions of the earth, under the most favourable circumstances of human industry.

It will be allowed that no country has hitherto been known, where the manners were so pure and simple, and the means of subsistence so abundant, that no check whatever has existed to early marriages from the difficulty of[2] providing for a family, and that no waste of the human species has been occasioned[3] by vicious customs, by towns, by unhealthy occupations, or too severe labour. Consequently in no state that we have yet known, has the power of population been left to exert itself with perfect freedom.

Whether the law of marriage be instituted, or not, the dictate of nature and virtue seems to be an early attachment to one woman[4]; and where there were no impediments of any kind in the way of an union to which such an attachment would lead, and no causes of depopulation afterwards, the increase of the human species would be evidently much greater than any increase which has been hitherto known.

In the northern states of America, where the means of subsistence have been more ample, the manners of the people more pure, and the checks to early marriages fewer, than in any of the

---

1 **If he attend:** subjunctive mood here
2 **no check whatever has existed to early marriages from the difficulty of:** no check ... from the difficulty of ...
3 **occasioned:** caused
4 **early attachment to one woman:** here early marriage

modern states of Europe, the population has been found to double itself, for above a century and a half successively, in less than twenty-five years. Yet, even during these periods, in some of the towns, the deaths exceeded the births, a circumstance which clearly proves that, in those parts of the country which supplied this deficiency, the increase must have been much more rapid than the general average.

In the back settlements, where the sole employment is agriculture, and vicious customs and unwholesome occupations are little known, the population has been found to double itself in fifteen years. Even this extraordinary rate of increase is probably short of[1] the utmost power of population. Very severe labour is requisite[2] to clear a fresh country; such situations are not in general considered as particularly healthy; and the inhabitants, probably, are occasionally subject to the incursions[3] of the Indians, which may destroy some lives, or at any rate diminish the fruits of industry.

According to a table of Euler[4], calculated on a mortality of 1 in 36, if the births be to the deaths in the proportion of 3 to 1, the period of doubling will be only 12 years and $4/5$ ths[5]. And this proportion is not only a possible supposition, but has actually occurred for short periods in more countries than one.

Sir William Petty[6] supposes a doubling possible in so short a time as ten years.

But, to be perfectly sure that we are far within the truth, we will take the slowest of these rates of increase, a rate in which all concurring[7] testimonies agree, and which has been repeatedly ascertained to be from procreation[8] only.

It may safely be pronounced, therefore, that population, when unchecked, goes on doubling itself every twenty-five years, or increases in a geometrical ratio.

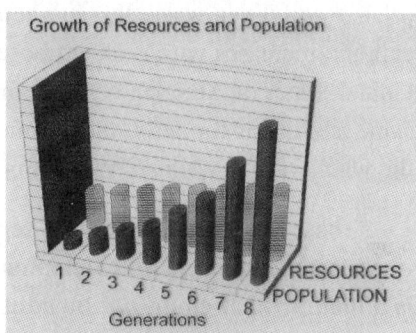

Growth of Resources and Population

The Malthusian Delemma

The rate according to which the productions of the earth may be supposed to increase, it

---

1 **short of:** less than the expected result of
2 **requisite:** needed, required
3 **incursion:** sudden attack, invasion
4 **Leonhard Euler (1707 – 1783):** Swiss mathematician and physicist, considered to be one of the greatest mathematicians
5 **$4/5$ths:** 0.8
6 **Sir William Petty (1737 – 1805):** English economist, scientist and philosopher, best remembered for his theories on economics and his methods of *political arithmetic.*
7 **concurring:** happening together
8 **procreation:** production, generation

will not be so easy to determine. Of this, however, we may be perfectly certain, that the ratio of their increase in a limited territory must be of a totally different nature from the ratio of the increase of population. A thousand millions are just as easily doubled every twenty-five years by the power of population as a thousand[1]. But the food to support the increase from the greater number will by no means be obtained with the same facility. Man is necessarily confined in room. When acre has been added to acre till all the fertile land is occupied, the yearly increase of food must depend upon the melioration[2] of the land already in possession. This is a fund; which, from the nature of all soils, instead of increasing, must be gradually diminishing. But population, could it be supplied with food, would go on with unexhausted vigour; and the increase of one period would furnish the power of a greater increase the next, and this without any limit.

From the accounts we have of China and Japan, it may be fairly doubted, whether the best-directed efforts of human industry could double the produce[3] of these countries even once in any number of years. There are many parts of the globe; indeed, hitherto uncultivated, and almost unoccupied; but the right of exterminating[4], or driving into a corner where they must starve, even the inhabitants[5] of these thinly-peopled regions, will be questioned in a moral view. The process of improving their minds and directing their industry would necessarily be slow; and during this time, as population would regularly keep pace with the increasing produce, it would rarely happen that a great degree of knowledge and industry would have to operate at once upon rich unappropriated[6] soil. Even where this might take place, as it does sometimes in new colonies, a geometrical ratio increases with such extraordinary rapidity, that the advantage could not last long. If the United States of America continue increasing, which they certainly will do, though not with the same rapidity as formerly, the Indians will be driven further and further back into the country, till the whole race is ultimately exterminated, and the territory is incapable of further extension.

These observations are, in a degree, applicable to all the parts of the earth, where the soil is imperfectly cultivated. **To exterminate the inhabitants of the greatest part of Asia and Africa, is a thought that could not be admitted for a moment. To civilise and direct the industry of the various tribes of Tartars[7] and Negroes, would certainly be a work of considerable time, and of variable and uncertain success.**

Europe is by no means so fully peopled as it might be. In Europe there is the fairest chance that human industry may receive its best direction. The science of agriculture has been much studied in England and Scotland; and there is still a great portion of uncultivated land in these

---

1   **as a thousand:** as a thousand are easily doubled every twenty-five years by the power of population
2   **melioration:** improvement
3   **produce:** here food
4   **exterminate:** destroy completely
5   **inhabitants:** native people
6   **unappropriated:** unoccupied
7   **Tartars:** Turkic and Mongolian peoples of central Asia who invaded western Asia and eastern Europe in the Middle Ages

countries. Let us consider at what rate the produce of this island might be supposed to increase under circumstances the most favourable to improvement.

If it be allowed that by the best possible policy, and great encouragements to agriculture, the average produce of the island could be doubled in the first twenty-five years, it will be allowing, probably, a greater increase than could with reason be expected[1].

In the next twenty-five years, it is impossible to suppose that the produce could be quadrupled[2]. It would be contrary to all our knowledge of the properties of land. The improvement of the barren parts would be a work of time and labour; and it must be evident to those who have the slightest acquaintance with agricultural subjects, that in proportion as cultivation extended, the additions that could yearly be made to the former average produce must be gradually and regularly diminishing. That we may be the better able to compare the increase of population and food, let us make a supposition, which, without pretending to accuracy, is clearly more favourable to the power of production in the earth, than any experience we have had of its qualities will warrant[3].

Let us suppose that the yearly additions which might be made to the former average produce, instead of decreasing, which they certainly would do, were to remain the same; and that the produce of this island might be increased every twenty-five years, by a quantity equal to what it at present produces. The most enthusiastic speculator cannot suppose a greater increase than this. In a few centuries it would make every acre of land in the island like a garden.

If this supposition be applied to the whole earth, and if it be allowed that the subsistence for man which the earth affords might be increased every twenty-five years by a quantity equal to what it at present produces, this will be supposing a rate of increase much greater than we can imagine that any possible exertions of mankind could make it.

It may be fairly pronounced, therefore, that, considering the present average state of the earth, the means of subsistence, under circumstances the most favourable to human industry, could not possibly be made to increase faster than in an arithmetical ratio.

The necessary effects of these two different rates of increase, when brought together, will be very striking. Let us call the population of this island eleven millions; and suppose the present produce equal to the easy support of such a number. In the first twenty-five years the population would be twenty-two millions, and the food being also doubled, the means of subsistence would be equal to this increase. In the next twenty-five years, the population would be forty-four millions, and the means of subsistence only equal to the support of thirty-three millions. In the next period the population would be eighty-eight millions, and the means of

---

1 **could with reason be expected:** could be expected with reason
2 **quadruple:** double once again
3 **any experience we have had of its qualities will warrant:** any experience of its qualities we have had will warrant

Heritage of Western Intellectual Tradition   A Sourcebook

subsistence just equal to the support of half that number. And, at the conclusion of the first century, the population would be a hundred and seventy-six millions, and the means of subsistence only equal to the support of fifty-five millions, leaving a population of a hundred and twenty-one millions totally unprovided for.

Taking the whole earth, instead of this island, emigration would of course be excluded; and, supposing the present population equal to a thousand millions, **the human species would increase as the numbers, 1, 2, 4, 8, 16, 32, 64, 128, 256, and subsistence as 1, 2, 3, 4, 5, 6, 7, 8, 9. In two centuries the population would be to the means of subsistence as 256 to 9; in three centuries as 4096 to 13, and in two thousand years the difference would be almost incalculable.**

In this supposition no limits whatever are placed to the produce of the earth. It may increase for ever and be greater than any assignable quantity; yet still the power of population being in every period so much superior, the increase of the human species can only be kept down to the level of the means of subsistence by the constant operation of the strong law of necessity, acting as a check upon the greater power[1].

Chapter II   Of the General Checks to Population, and the Mode of Their Operation.

The ultimate check to population appears then to be a want of food, arising necessarily from the different ratios according to which population and food increase. But this ultimate check is never the immediate check, except in cases of actual famine.

The immediate check may be stated to consist in all those customs, and all those diseases, which seem to be generated by a scarcity of the means of subsistence; and all those causes, independent of this scarcity, whether of a moral or physical nature, which tend prematurely[2] to weaken and destroy the human frame.

Malthusian Poor Law Amendment Act of 1834 to deal with the poor population

These checks to population, which are constantly operating with more or less force in every society, and keep down the number to the level of the means of subsistence, may be classed under two general heads — the preventive, and the positive checks.

The preventive check, as far as it is voluntary, is peculiar to man, and arises from that distinctive superiority in his reasoning faculties, which enables him to calculate distant consequences. The checks to the indefinite increase of plants and irrational animals are all either positive, or, if preventive, involuntary. But man cannot look around him, and

---

1   **the greater power:** the power of population

2   **prematurely:** before human being reach maturity

see the distress which frequently presses upon those who have large families; he cannot contemplate his present possessions or earnings, which he now nearly consumes himself, and calculate the amount of each share, when with very little addition they must be divided, perhaps, among seven or eight, without feeling a doubt whether, if he follow the bent of his inclinations, he may be able to support the offspring which he will probably bring into the world. In a state of equality, if such can exist, this would be the simple question. In the present state of society other considerations occur. Will he not lower his rank in life, and be obliged to give up in great measure his former habits? Does any mode of employment present itself by which he may reasonably hope to maintain a family? Will he not at any rate subject himself to greater difficulties, and more severe labour, than in his single state? Will he not be unable to transmit to his children the same advantages of education and improvement that he had himself possessed? Does he even feel secure that, should he have a large family, his utmost exertions can save them from rags and squalid[1] poverty, and their consequent degradation in the community? And may he not be reduced to the grating[2] necessity of forfeiting[3] his independence, and of being obliged to the sparing hand of Charity for support?

These considerations are calculated to prevent, and certainly do prevent, a great number of persons in all civilized nations from pursuing the dictate of nature in an early attachment to one woman.

If this restraint do not produce vice, it is undoubtedly the least evil that can arise from the principle of population. Considered as a restraint on a strong natural inclination, it must be allowed to produce a certain degree of temporary unhappiness; but evidently slight, compared with the evils which result from any of the other checks to population; and merely of the same nature as many other sacrifices of temporary to permanent gratification, which it is the business of a moral agent continually to make.

When this restraint produces vice, the evils which follow are but too conspicuous[4]. A promiscuous[5] intercourse to such a degree as to prevent the birth of children, seems to lower, in the most marked manner, the dignity of human nature. It cannot be without its effect on men, and nothing can be more obvious than its tendency to degrade the female character, and to destroy all its most amiable and distinguishing characteristics. Add to which, that among those unfortunate females, with which all great towns abound, more real distress and aggravated misery are, perhaps, to be found, than in any other department of human life.

When a general corruption of morals, with regard to the sex, pervades all the classes of society, its effects must necessarily be, to poison the springs of domestic happiness, to

---

1 **squalid:** mean, uncared for
2 **grate:** make harsh sound
3 **forfeit:** suffer the loss of
4 **conspicuous:** remarkable, easily seen
5 **promiscuous:** mixed, disorderly

weaken conjugal[1] and parental affection, and to lessen the united exertions and ardour of parents in the care and education of their children; — effects which cannot take place without a decided diminution of the general happiness and virtue of the society; particularly as the necessity of art in the accomplishment and conduct of intrigues, and in the concealment of their consequences necessarily leads[2] to many other vices.

...

The positive checks to population are extremely various, and include every cause, whether arising from vice or misery, which in any degree contributes to shorten the natural duration of human life. Under this head, therefore, may be enumerated all unwholesome occupations, severe labour and exposure to the seasons, extreme poverty, bad nursing of children, great towns, excesses of all kinds, the whole train of common diseases and epidemics, wars, plague, and famine.

On examining these obstacles to the increase of population which I have classed under the heads of preventive and positive checks, it will appear that they are all resolvable into moral restraint, vice, and misery.

Of the preventive checks, the restraint from marriage which is not followed by irregular gratifications may properly be termed moral restraint.[3]

Promiscuous intercourse, unnatural passions, violations of the marriage bed, and improper arts to conceal the consequences of irregular connections, are preventive checks that clearly come under the head of vice.

Of the positive checks, those which appear to arise unavoidably from the laws of nature, may be called exclusively misery; and those which we obviously bring upon ourselves, such as wars, excesses, and many others which it would be in our power to avoid, are of a mixed nature. They are brought upon us by vice, and their consequences are misery.[4]

---

1   **conjugal:** marriage, wedded life

2   **the necessity of art ... leads:** the necessity of art ... necessarily leads

3   [Malthus' note] It will be observed, that I here use the term *moral* in its most confined sense. By moral restraint I would be understood to mean a restraint from marriage, from prudential motives, with a conduct strictly moral during the period of this restraint; and I have never intentionally deviated from this sense. ...

4   [Malthus' note] As the general consequence of vice is misery, and as this consequence is the precise reason why an action is termed vicious, it may appear that the term misery alone would be here sufficient, and that it is superfluous to use both. But the rejection of the term vice would introduce a considerable confusion into our language and ideas. We want it particularly to distinguish those actions, the general tendency of which is to produce misery, and which are therefore prohibited by the commands of the Creator, and the precepts of the moralist, although, in their immediate or individual effects, they may produce perhaps exactly the contrary. The gratification of all our passions in its immediate effect is happiness, not misery; and, in individual instances, even the remote consequences (at least in this life) may possibly come under the same denomination. ...

The sum of all these preventive and positive checks, taken together, forms the immediate check to population; and it is evident that, in every country where the whole of the procreative[1] power cannot be called into action, the preventive and the positive checks must vary inversely as each other; that is, in countries either naturally unhealthy, or subject to a great mortality, from whatever cause it may arise, the preventive check will prevail very little. In those countries, on the contrary, which are naturally healthy, and where the preventive check is found to prevail with considerable force, the positive check will prevail very little, or the mortality be very small.

In every country some of these checks are, with more or less force, in constant operation; yet, notwithstanding their general prevalence, there are few states in which there is not a constant effort in the population to increase beyond the means of subsistence. This constant effort as constantly tends to subject the lower classes of society to distress, and to prevent any great permanent melioration of their condition.

These effects, in the present state of society, seem to be produced in the following manner. We will suppose the means of subsistence in any country just equal to the easy support of its inhabitants. The constant effort towards population, which is found to act even in the most vicious societies, increases the number of people before the means of subsistence are increased. The food, therefore, which before supported eleven millions, must now be divided among eleven millions and a half. The poor consequently must live much worse, and many of them be reduced to severe distress. The number of labourers also being above the proportion of work in the market, the price of labour must tend to fall, while the price of provisions would at the same time tend to rise. The labourer therefore must do more work, to earn the same as he did before. During this season of distress, the discouragements to marriage and the difficulty of rearing a family are so great, that the progress of population is retarded[2]. In the mean time, the cheapness, of labour, the plenty of labourers, and the necessity of an increased industry among them, encourage cultivators to employ more labour upon their land, to turn up fresh soil, and to manure[3] and improve more completely what is already in tillage, till ultimately the means of subsistence may become in the same proportion to the population, as at the period from which we set out. The situation of the labourer being then again tolerably comfortable, the restraints to population are in some degree loosened; and, after a short period, the same retrograde[4] and progressive movements, with respect to happiness, are repeated.

This sort of oscillation[5] will not probably be obvious to common view; and it may be difficult even for the most attentive observer to calculate its periods. Yet that, in the generality[6] of old states, some alternation of this kind does exist though in a much less marked, and in a much more

---

1   **procreative:** productive, generative
2   **retard:** check, hinder
3   **manure:** fertilize
4   **retrograde:** backward, deteriorating
5   **oscillation:** backward and forward movement
6   **generality:** an observation or principle having general application

irregular manner, than I have described it, no reflecting man, who considers the subject deeply, can well doubt.

One principal reason why this oscillation has been less remarked, and less decidedly confirmed by experience than might naturally be expected, is, that the histories of mankind which we possess are, in general, histories only of the higher classes. We have not many accounts that can be depended upon, of the manners and customs of that part of mankind, where these retrograde and progressive movements chiefly take place. **A satisfactory history of this kind, of one people and of one period, would require the constant and minute attention of many observing minds in local and general remarks on the state of the lower classes of society, and the causes that influenced it; and to draw accurate inferences upon this subject, a succession of such historians for some centuries would be necessary.**[1] This branch of statistical knowledge has, of late years, been attended to in some countries, and we may promise ourselves a clearer insight into the internal structure of human society from the progress of these inquiries. But the science may be said yet to be in its infancy, and many of the objects, on which it would be desirable to have information, have been either omitted or not stated with sufficient accuracy. Among these, perhaps, may be reckoned the proportion of the number of adults to the number of marriages; the extent to which vicious customs have prevailed in consequence of the restraints upon matrimony[2]; the comparative mortality among the children of the most distressed part of the community, and of those who live rather more at their ease; the variations in the real price of labour; the observable differences in the state of the lower classes of society, with respect to ease and happiness, at different times during a certain period; and very accurate registers of births, deaths, and marriages, which are of the utmost importance in this subject.

A faithful history, including such particulars, would tend greatly to elucidate[3] the manner in which the constant check upon population acts; and would probable prove the existence of the retrograde and progressive movements that have been mentioned; though the times of their vibration must necessarily be rendered irregular from the operation of many interrupting causes; such as, the introduction or failure of certain manufactures; a greater or less prevalent spirit of agricultural enterprise; years of plenty, or years of scarcity; wars, sickly seasons, poor-laws, emigrations and other causes of a similar nature.

A circumstance which has, perhaps, more than any other, contributed to conceal this oscillation from common view, is the difference between the nominal[4] and real price of labour. It very rarely happens that the nominal price of labour universally falls; but we well know that it frequently remains the same, while the nominal price of provisions has been gradually rising.

---

1 Malthus is talking about a science of population study, or "demography" as what it is known today.
2 **matrimony:** marriage
3 **elucidate:** explain, throw light on
4 **nominal:** existing in name

This, indeed, will generally be the case, if the increase of manufactures and commerce be sufficient to employ the new labourers that are thrown into the market, and to prevent the increased supply from lowering the money-price. But an increased number of labourers receiving the same money-wages will necessarily, by their competition, increase the money-price of corn. This is, in fact, a real fall in the price of labour; and, during this period, the condition of the lower classes of the community must be gradually growing worse. But the farmers and capitalists are growing rich from the real cheapness of labour. Their increasing capitals enable them to employ a greater number of men; and, as the population had probably suffered some check from the greater difficulty of supporting a family, the demand for labour, after a certain period, would be great in proportion to the supply, and its price would of course rise, if left to find its natural level; and thus the wages of labour, and consequently the condition of the lower classes of society, might have progressive and retrograde movements, though the price of labour might never nominally fall.

In savage life, where there is no regular price of labour, it is little to be doubted that similar oscillations took place. When population has increased nearly to the utmost limits of the food, all the preventive and the positive checks will naturally operate with increased force. Vicious habits with respect to the sex will be more general, the exposing[1] of children more frequent, and both the probability and fatality of wars and epidemics will be considerably greater; and these causes will probably continue their operation till the population is sunk below the level of the food; and then the return to comparative plenty will again produce an increase, and, after a certain period, its further progress will again be checked by the same causes.

But without attempting to establish these progressive and retrograde movements in different countries, which would evidently require more minute histories than we possess, and which the progress of civilization naturally tends to counteract, the following propositions are intended to be proved:

1. Population is necessarily limited by the means of subsistence.

2. Population invariably increases where the means of subsistence increase, unless prevented by some very powerful and obvious checks.

3. These checks, and the checks which repress the superior power of population, and keep its effects on a level with the means of subsistence, are all resolvable into moral restraint, vice and misery.

The first of these propositions scarcely needs illustration. The second and third will be sufficiently established by a review of the immediate checks to population in the past and present state of society.

---

1   **expose:** leave (young children) in the open to die of cold or hunger

Key Concepts

arithmetical ratio

check on population

geometrical ratio

humanitarianism

immediate check

instinct to increase

law of the jungle

means of subsistence

natural selection

philosophy of evolution

positive checks

preventive check

Social Darwinism

superabundant effects

ultimate check

Charles Darwin: The Origin of Species (1859)

Charles Robert Darwin (1809 – 1882), British scientist, is known for his evolutionary theory of all forms of life developing through the slow process of natural selection. Darwin was born in Shrewsbury, England, the fifth child of a wealthy family. After graduating from the elite school at Shrewsbury in 1825, the young Darwin went to the University of Edinburgh to study medicine. In 1827 he dropped out of medical school and entered the University of Cambridge in preparation for a clergyman. There he met John Stevens Henslow, a naturalist who taught him to be a meticulous and painstaking observer of natural phenomena and collector of specimens. After graduation, the 22-year-old Darwin was taken aboard the survey ship HMS *Beagle,* largely on Henslow's recommendation, as an unpaid naturalist on a scientific expedition around the world. This gave him the opportunity to observe the various geological formations along the way, and he was most impressed with the effect natural forces had on shaping the earth's surface. At the time, most geologists held the so-called catastrophist theory: that the earth had experienced a succession of creations of animal and plant life, and that each creation had been destroyed by a sudden catastrophe, the most recent one being Noah's flood. In this catastrophist theory, species were individually created and unchangeable for all time. Aboard the *Beagle,* Darwin found that some of his own observations run counter to this theory. After returning to England in 1836, Darwin began recording his ideas about changeability of species, enlightened by Malthus' *An Essay on the Principle of Population* (1798). His theory was first announced in 1858 and published in 1859 as *On the Origin of Specie,* often referred to as the "book that shook the world." Darwin's theory of evolution by natural selection is essentially that, because of the food-supply problem, the young born to any species intensely compete for survival. Those that survive to produce the next generation tend to embody favorable natural variations and pass them on to their offspring hereditarily. Therefore, each generation will improve adaptively over the preceding generations, and this gradual and continuous process is the source of the evolution of all species.

Nothing is easier than to admit in words the truth of the universal struggle for life, or more difficult — at least I have found it so — than constantly to bear this conclusion in mind. Yet unless it be thoroughly engrained[1] in the mind, I am convinced that the whole economy of nature, with every fact on distribution, rarity, abundance, extinction, and variation, will be dimly seen or quite misunderstood. We behold the face of nature bright with gladness, we often see superabundance of food; we do not see, or we forget, that the birds which are idly singing round us mostly live on insects or seeds, and are thus constantly destroying life; or **we forget how largely these songsters[2], or their eggs, or their nestlings are destroyed by birds and beasts of prey; we do not always bear in mind, that though food may be now superabundant, it is not so at all seasons of each recurring year.**

...

A struggle for existence inevitably follows from the high rate at which all organic beings tend to increase. Every being, which during its natural lifetime produces several eggs or seeds, must suffer destruction during some period of its life, and during some season or occasional year, otherwise, on the principle of geometrical increase, its numbers would quickly become so inordinately[3] great that no country could support the product. Hence, as more individuals are produced than can possibly survive, there must in every case be a struggle for existence, either one individual with[4] another of the same species, or with the individuals of distinct species, or with the physical conditions of life. It is the doctrine of Malthus applied with manifold force to the whole animal and vegetable kingdoms; for in this case there can be no artificial increase of food, and no prudential restraint from marriage. Although some species may be now increasing, more or less rapidly, in numbers, all cannot do so, for the world would not hold them.

M.H.S. Beagle in Straits of Magellan

There is no exception to the rule that every organic being naturally increases at so high a rate that, if not destroyed, the earth would soon be covered by the progeny[1] of a

---

1 **engrain:** or ingrain, fix deeply or indelibly
2 **songster:** songbird
3 **inordinately:** excessively, not properly restrained
4 **either one individual with:** either one individual struggle with

Heritage of Western Intellectual Tradition · A Sourcebook

single pair. Even slow-breeding man has doubled in twenty-five years, and at this rate, in a few thousand years, there would literally not be standing room for his progeny. Linneaus[2] has calculated that if an annual plant produced only two seeds — and there is no plant so unproductive as this — and their seedlings next year produced two, and so on, then in twenty years there would be a million plants. The elephant is reckoned[3] to be the slowest breeder of all known animals, and I have taken some pains to estimate its probable minimum rate of natural increase: it will be under the mark[4] to assume that it breeds when thirty years old, and goes on breeding till ninety years old, bringing forth three pairs of young in this interval, and surviving until one hundred years old; if this be so, after a period of from 740 to 750 years there would be nearly nineteen millions elephants alive, descended from the first pair.

But we have better evidence on this subject than mere theoretical calculations, namely, the numerous recorded cases of the astonishingly rapid increase of various animals in a state of nature, when circumstances have been favourable to them during two or three following seasons. Still more striking is the evidence from our domestic animals of many kinds which have run wild in several parts of the world: if the statements of the rate of increase of slow-breeding cattle and horses in South America, and latterly in Australia, had not been well authenticated[5], they would have been quite incredible. So it is with plants: cases could be given of introduced plants which have become common throughout whole islands in a period of less than ten years, several of the plants now most numerous over the wide plains of La Plata[6], such as the cardoon and a tall thistle, clothing square leagues[7] of surface almost to the exclusion of all other plants, have been introduced from Europe; and there are plants which now range in India, as I hear from Dr Falconer, from Cape Comorin[8] to the Himalaya, which have been imported from America since its discovery. In such cases, and endless instances could be given, no one supposes that the fertility of these animals or plants has been suddenly and temporarily increased in any sensible degree. The obvious explanation is that the conditions of life have been very favourable, and that there has consequently been less destruction of the old and young, and that nearly all the young have been enabled to breed. In such cases the geometrical ratio of increase, the result of which never fails to be surprising, simply explains the extraordinarily rapid increase and wide diffusion of naturalized productions in their new homes.

1 **progeny:** children, offspring
2 **Carolus Linnaeus (1707–1778):** Swedish botanist and physician who laid the foundations for the modern scheme of taxonomy(分类学) and modern ecology
3 **reckon:** regard
4 **under the mark:** below the normal
5 **authenticate:** prove to be true
6 **La Plata:** city of east-central Argentina
7 **league:** distance about three miles
8 **Cape Comorin:** Kanyakumari is a town and a cape at the southernmost tip of the Indian peninsula, located in the state of Tamil Nadu. During British rule, it was known as Cape Comorin.

In a state of nature almost every full-grown plant annually produces seed, and amongst animals there are very few which do not annually pair[1]. **Hence we may confidently assert, that all plants and animals are tending to increase at a geometrical ratio, that all would most rapidly stock[2] every station in which they could anyhow exist, and that the geometrical tendency to increase must be checked by destruction at some period of life.** Our familiarity with the larger domestic animals tends, I think, to mislead us: we see no great destruction falling on them, and we forget that thousands are annually slaughtered for food, and that in a state of nature an equal number would have somehow to be disposed of.

...

In looking at Nature, it is most necessary to keep the foregoing considerations always in mind — never to forget that every single organic being around us may be said to be striving to the utmost to increase in numbers; that each lives by a struggle at some period of its life; that heavy destruction inevitably falls either on the young or old, during each generation or at recurrent intervals. Lighten any check, mitigate[3] the destruction ever so little, and the number of the species will almost instantaneously increase to any amount. The face of Nature may be compared to a yielding surface, with ten thousand sharp wedges[4]

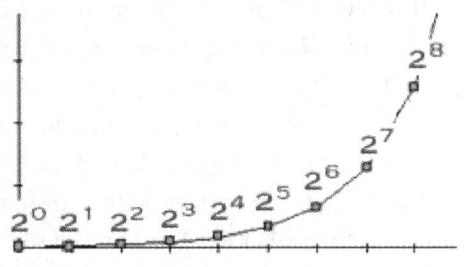

A single pair of elephants producing 19 million in 750 years

packed close together and driven inwards by incessant blows, sometimes one wedge being struck, and then another with greater force.

What checks the natural tendency of each species to increase in number is most obscure. Look at the most vigorous species; by as much as it swarms in numbers, by so much will its tendency to increase be still further increased. We know not exactly what the checks are in even one single instance. Nor will this surprise any one who reflects how ignorant we are on this head[5], even in regard to mankind, although so incomparably better known than any other animal. This subject has been ably treated by several authors, and I shall, in my future work, discuss some of the checks at considerable length, more especially in regard to the feral[6] animals of South America. Here I will make only a few remarks, just to recall to the reader's mind some of the chief points. Eggs or very young animals seem generally to suffer most, but this is not invariably the case. With plants there is a vast destruction of seeds, but, from some observations which I

---

1   **pair:** form pairs, mate
2   **stock:** multiply, fill up, breed
3   **mitigate:** make less severe and painful
4   **wedge:** V-shaped piece used to force into something to split it up（楔子）
5   **head:** group of a flock
6   **feral:** wild, brutal

have made, I believe that it is the seedlings which suffer most from germinating[1] in ground already thickly stocked with other plants. Seedlings, also, are destroyed in vast numbers by various enemies; for instance, on a piece of ground three feet long and two wide, dug and cleared, and where there could be no choking from other plants, I marked all the seedlings of our native weeds as they came up, and out of the 357 no less than 295 were destroyed, chiefly by slugs[2] and insects. If turf[3] which has long been mown, and the case would be the same with turf closely browsed by quadrupeds[4], be let to grow, the more vigorous plants gradually kill the less vigorous, though fully grown, plants: thus out of twenty species growing on a little plot of turf (three feet by four) nine species perished from the other species being allowed to grow up freely.

The amount of food for each species of course gives the extreme limit to which each can increase; but very frequently it is not the obtaining food, but the serving as prey to other animals, which determines the average numbers of a species. Thus, there seems to be little doubt that the stock of partridges[5], grouse[6], and hares on any large estate depends chiefly on the destruction of vermin[7]. If not one head of game were shot during the next twenty years in England, and, at the same time, if no vermin were destroyed, there would, in all probability, be less game[8] than at present, although hundreds of thousands of game animals are now annually killed. On the other hand, in some cases, as with the elephant and rhinoceros[9], none are destroyed by beasts of prey: even the tiger in India most rarely dares to attack a young elephant protected by its dam[10].

…

If under changing conditions of life, organic beings vary at all in the several parts of their organization, and I think this cannot be disputed; if there be, owing to the high geometrical powers of increase of each species, at some age, season, or year, a severe struggle for life, and this certainly cannot be disputed; then, considering the infinite complexity of the relations of all organic beings to each other and to their conditions of existence, causing an infinite diversity in structure, constitution, and habits, to be advantageous to them, I think it would be a most extraordinary fact if no variation ever had occurred useful to each being's own welfare, in the same way as so many variations have occurred useful to man. **But if variations useful to any or-**

---

1 **germinate:** start growing
2 **slug:** snail-like creature destructive to seedlings
3 **turf:** grassland
4 **quadruped:** four-footed animals
5 **partridge:** long-tailed bird, pheasant（雉）
6 **grouse:** 松鸡
7 **vermin:** animals harmful to birds（害虫）
8 **game:** birds and animals hunted for sports
9 **rhinoceros:** 犀牛
10 **dam:** mother of four-footed animal

ganic being do occur, assuredly individuals thus characterized will have the best chance of being preserved in the struggle for life; and from the strong principle of inheritance, these will tend to produce offspring similarly characterized. **This principle of preservation, or the survival of the fittest, I have called, Natural Selection.** It leads to the improvement of each creature in relation to its organic and inorganic conditions of life; and consequently, in most cases, to what must be regarded as an advance in organization. Nevertheless, low and simple forms will long endure[1] if well fitted for their simple conditions of life.

Natural selection, on the principle of qualities being inherited at corresponding ages, can modify the egg, seed, or young, as easily as the adult. Amongst many animals, sexual selection will give its aid to ordinary selection, by assuring to the most vigorous and best adapted males the greatest number of offspring. Sexual selection will also give characters useful to the males alone, in their struggles or rivalry with other males; and these characters will be transmitted to one sex or to both sexes, according to the form of inheritance which prevails.

Whether natural selection has really thus acted in nature, in modifying and adapting the various forms of life to their several[2] conditions and stations, must be judged of by the general tenor[3] and balance of evidence given in the following chapters. But we already see how it entails[4] extinction; and how largely extinction has acted in the world's history, geology[5] plainly declares. Natural selection, also, leads to divergence of character; for more living beings can be supported on the same area the more they diverge in structure, habits, and constitution, of which we see proof by looking at the inhabitants of any small spot or at naturalized productions. Therefore during the modification of the descendants of any one species, and during the incessant[6] struggle of all species to increase in numbers, the more diversified these descendants become, the better will be their chance of succeeding in the battle of life. Thus the small differences distinguishing varieties of the same species, will steadily tend to increase till they come to equal the greater differences between species of the same genus, or even of distinct genera[7].

Complex chain of being that shocked Darwin's contemporaries

We have seen that it is the common, the widely-diffused, and widely-ranging species, belonging to the larger genera, which vary most; and these will tend to transmit to their modified

---

1 **low and simple forms will long endure:** Namely, competition is not that fierce for low and simple forms, and variations do not occur so often.

2 **several:** respective

3 **tenor:** general direction, meaning

4 **entail:** make necessary

5 **geology:** science of the earth's history as shown by its rocks, crust, etc.

6 **incessant:** continuous

7 **genera:** singular form of genus, group of animals or plants within a family

Heritage of Western Intellectual Tradition   A Sourcebook

offspring that superiority which now makes them dominant in their own countries. **Natural selection, as has just been remarked, leads to divergence of character and to much extinction of the less improved and intermediate forms of life. On these principles, I believe, the nature of the affinities[1] of all organic beings may be explained.** It is a truly wonderful fact — the wonder of which we are apt to overlook from familiarity — that all animals and all plants throughout all time and space should be related to each other in group, subordinate to group, in the manner which we everywhere behold — namely, varieties of the same species most closely related together, species of the same genus less closely and unequally related together, forming sections and sub-genera, species of distinct genera much less closely related, and genera related in different degrees, forming sub-families, families, orders, sub-classes, and classes. The several subordinate groups in any class cannot be ranked in a single file, but seem rather to be clustered round points, and these round other points, and so on in almost endless cycles. On the view that each species has been independently created, I can see no explanation of this great fact in the classification of all organic beings; but, to the best of my judgment, it is explained through inheritance and the complex action of natural selection, entailing extinction and divergence of character, as we have seen illustrated in the diagram.

...

I see no good reason why the views given in this volume should shock the religious feelings of any one. It is satisfactory, as showing how transient such impressions are, to remember that the greatest discovery ever made by man, namely, the law of the attraction of gravity, was also attacked by Leibnitz, "as subversive[2] of natural, and inferentially[3] of revealed, religion." A celebrated author and divine[4] has written to me that "he has gradually learnt to see that it is just as noble a conception of the Deity to believe that He created a few original forms capable of self-development into other and needful forms, as to believe[5] that He required a fresh act of creation to supply the voids caused by the action of His laws."

Why, it may be asked, have all the most eminent living naturalists and geologists rejected this view of the mutability[6] of species? It cannot be asserted that organic beings in a state of nature are subject to no variation; it cannot be proved that the amount of variation in the course of long ages is a limited quantity; no clear distinction has been, or can be, drawn between species and well-marked varieties. It cannot be maintained that species when intercrossed[7] are invariably sterile[8],

---

1 **affinity:** close connection, resemblance
2 **subversive:** overthrowing, destructive
3 **inferentially:** consequently
4 **divine:** one learned in theology
5 **it is just as noble a conception ... as to believe:** it is just as noble a conception of the Deity to believe ... as to believe
6 **mutability:** liability to change
7 **intercross:** interbreed
8 **sterile:** unable to produce seeds

and varieties invariably fertile[1]; or that sterility is a special endowment and sign of creation. The belief that species were immutable productions was almost unavoidable as long as the history of the world was thought to be of short duration; and now that we have acquired some idea of the lapse of time, we are too apt to assume, without proof, that the geological record is so perfect that it would have afforded us plain evidence of the mutation of species, if they had undergone mutation.

But the chief cause of our natural unwillingness to admit that one species has given birth to other and distinct species, is that we are always slow in admitting any great change of which we do not see the intermediate steps. The difficulty is the same as that felt by so many geologists, when Lyell[2] first insisted that long lines of inland cliffs had been formed, and great valleys excavated[3], by the slow action of the coast-waves. The mind cannot possibly grasp the full meaning of the term of a hundred million years; it cannot add up and perceive the full effects of many slight variations, accumulated during an almost infinite number of generations.

Although I am fully convinced of the truth of the views given in this volume under the form of an abstract, I by no means expect to convince experienced naturalists whose minds are stocked with a multitude of facts all viewed, during a long course of years, from a point of view directly opposite to mine. It is so easy to hide our ignorance under such expressions as the "plan of creation," "unity of design," & c.[4], and to think that we give an explanation when we only restate a fact. Any one whose disposition leads him to attach more weight to unexplained difficulties than to the explanation of a certain number of facts will certainly reject my theory. A few naturalists, endowed with much flexibility of mind, and who have already begun to doubt on the immutability of species, may be influenced by this volume; but I look with confidence to the future, to young and rising naturalists, who will be able to view both sides of the question with impartiality. Whoever is led to believe that species are mutable will do good service by conscientiously expressing his conviction; for only thus can the load of prejudice by which this subject is overwhelmed be removed.

...

The other and more general departments of natural history will rise greatly in interest. The terms used by naturalists of[5] affinity,[6] relationship, community of type, paternity, morphology,[7] adaptive characters, rudimentary and aborted organs, & c., will cease to be metaphorical, and will have a plain signification. When we no longer look at an organic being as a savage looks at a ship, as at something wholly beyond his comprehension; when we regard every production of nature as one which has had a history; when we contemplate every complex structure and

---

1 **fertile:** able to produce offspring
2 **Sir Charles Lyell (1797 – 1875):** British geologist and a founder of modern geology, whose *Principles of Geology* (1830 – 1833) opposed the catastrophic theory of geologic change
3 **excavate:** uncover by digging
4 **& c.:** Et cetera or etc.
5 **The terms used by naturalists of:** terms ... of, split proposition
6 **affinity:** structural resemblance
7 **morphology:** scientific study of the form and structure of animals and plants

Heritage of Western Intellectual Tradition   A Sourcebook

instinct as the summing up of many contrivances[1], each useful to the possessor, nearly in the same way as when we look at any great mechanical invention as the summing up of the labour, the experience, the reason, and even the blunders[2] of numerous workmen; when we thus view each organic being, how far more interesting, I speak from experience, will the study of natural history become!

Cartoon in Punch
magazine, 1862

A grand and almost untrodden field of inquiry will be opened, on the causes and laws of variation, on correlation of growth, on the effects of use and disuse, on the direct action of external conditions, and so forth. The study of domestic productions will rise immensely in value. A new variety raised by man will be a far more important and interesting subject for study than one more species added to the infinitude[3] of already recorded species.

Our classifications will come to be, as far as they can be so made, genealogies[4]; and will then truly give what may be called the plan of creation. The rules for classifying will no doubt become simpler when we have a definite object in view. We possess no pedigrees[5] or armorial bearings[6]; and we have to discover and trace the many diverging lines of descent in our natural genealogies, by characters of any kind which have long been inherited. Rudimentary organs will speak infallibly with respect to the nature of long-lost structures. Species and groups of species, which are called aberrant[7], and which may fancifully be called living fossils, will aid us in forming a picture of the ancient forms of life. Embryology will reveal to us the structure, in some degree obscured, of the prototypes of each great class.

When we can feel assured that all the individuals of the same species, and all the closely allied species of most genera, have within a not very remote period descended from one parent, and have migrated from some one birthplace; and when we better know the many means of migration, then, by the light which geology now throws, and will continue to throw, on former changes of climate and of the level of the land, we shall surely be enabled to trace in an admirable manner the former migrations of the inhabitants of the whole world. Even at present, by comparing the differences of the inhabitants of the sea on the opposite sides of a continent, and the nature of the various inhabitants of that continent in relation to their apparent means of immigration, some light can be thrown on ancient geography.

The noble science of Geology loses glory from the extreme imperfection of the record. The crust of the earth with its embedded remains must not be looked at as a well-filled museum, but

---

1   **contrivance:** invention, design
2   **blunder:** careless mistake
3   **infinitude:** infinite number
4   **genealogy:** science of the development of plants and animals
5   **pedigree:** line of ancestors
6   **armorial bearing:** a coat of arms
7   **aberrant:** abnormal

as a poor collection made at hazard and at rare intervals. The accumulation of each great fossiliferous[1] formation will be recognized as having depended on an unusual concurrence of circumstances, and the blank intervals between the successive stages as[2] having been of vast duration. But we shall be able to gauge[3] with some security the duration of these intervals by a comparison of the preceding and succeeding organic forms. We must be cautious in attempting to correlate as strictly contemporaneous two formations, which include few identical species, by the general succession of their forms of life. As species are produced and exterminated by slowly acting and still existing causes, and not by miraculous acts of creation and by catastrophes[4]; and as the most important of all causes of organic change is one which is almost independent of altered and perhaps suddenly altered physical conditions, namely, the mutual relation of organism to organism, — the improvement of one being entailing the improvement or the extermination of others; it follows, that the amount of organic change in the fossils of consecutive formations probably serves as a fair measure of the lapse of actual time. A number of species, however, keeping in a body might remain for a long period unchanged, whilst within this same period, several of these species, by migrating into new countries and coming into competition with foreign associates, might become modified; so that we must not overrate the accuracy of organic change as a measure of time.

In the future I see open fields for far more important researches. Psychology will be based on a new foundation, that of the necessary acquirement of each mental power and capacity by gradation. Light will be thrown on the origin of man and his history.

Authors of the highest eminence seem to be fully satisfied with the view that each species has been independently created. To my mind it accords better with what we know of the laws impressed on matter by the Creator, that the production and extinction of the past and present inhabitants of the world should have been due to secondary causes, like those determining the birth and death of the individual. When I view all beings not as special creations, but as the lineal descendants of some few beings which lived long before the first bed of the Silurian system[5] was deposited（积淀）, they seem to me to become ennobled. Judging from the past, we may safely infer that not one living species will transmit its unaltered likeness to a distant futurity. And of the species now living very few will transmit progeny of any kind to a far distant futurity; for the manner in which all organic beings are grouped, shows that the greater number of species of each genus, and all the species of many genera, have left no descendants, but have become utterly extinct. We can so far take a prophetic glance into futurity as to foretell that it will be the common and widely-spread species, belonging to the larger and dominant groups, which will ultimately prevail and procreate[6] new and dominant species. As all the living forms of life are the lineal descendants of those which lived long before the Silurian epoch, we may feel certain that

---

1　**fossiliferous:** containing fossils
2　**as:** will be recognized as
3　**gauge:** measure accurately
4　**not by miraculous acts of creation and by catastrophes:** evolution by catastrophes rather than by natural selection
5　**Silurian system:** belonging to the geologic time or sedimentary deposits of the third period of the Paleozoic Era, characterized by the development of jawed fishes, early invertebrate land animals, and land plants
6　**procreate:** reproduce offspring sexually

Heritage of Western Intellectual Tradition — A Sourcebook

the ordinary succession by generation has never once been broken, and that no cataclysm[1] has desolated[2] the whole world. **Hence we may look with some confidence to a secure future of equally inappreciable[3] length. And as natural selection works solely by and for the good of each being, all corporeal[4] and mental endowments will tend to progress towards perfection.**

It is interesting to contemplate an entangled[5] bank, clothed with many plants of many kinds, with birds singing on the bushes, with various insects flitting[6] about, and with worms crawling through the damp earth, and to reflect that these elaborately constructed forms, so different from each other, and dependent on each other in so complex a manner, have all been produced by laws acting around us. These laws, taken in the largest sense, being Growth with Reproduction; inheritance which is almost implied by reproduction; Variability from the indirect and direct action of the external conditions of life, and from use and disuse; a Ratio of Increase so high as to lead to a Struggle for Life, and as a consequence to Natural Selection, entailing Divergence of Character and the Extinction of less-improved forms. Thus, from the war of nature, from famine and death, the most exalted object which we are capable of conceiving, namely, the production of the higher animals, directly follows[7]. There is grandeur in this view of life, with its several powers, having been originally breathed into a few forms or into one; and that, whilst this planet has gone cycling on according to the fixed law of gravity, from so simple a beginning endless forms most beautiful and most wonderful have been, and are being, evolved[8].

Charles Darwin: The Descent of Man*

Chapter XXI   General Summary and Conclusion

The main conclusion here arrived at, and now held by many naturalists who are

---

1 **cataclysm:** sudden and violent change
2 **desolate:** make destroyed
3 **inappreciable:** not worth consideration, too short
4 **corporeal:** physical
5 **entangled:** twisted together in a tangled mass
6 **flit:** move quickly
7 **the most exalted object which ... directly follows:** Namely, the most exalted object ... directly follows from ...
8 **from so simple a beginning ... evolved:** i.e., endless forms most beautiful and most wonderful have been, and are being, evolved from so simple a beginning
* Darwin's writing on human evolution came twelve years after his work on *Origin*. As such, the book is a response to various debates of Darwin's time far more wide-ranging than the questions he raised in *Origin*, especially through that of sexual selection. The book was not the first to elaborate on human evolution and common descent, because Darwin had already alluded to the subject in the *Origin*. But no doubt *The Descent of Man* as a concentrated study of human evolution is his most controversial work.

well competent to form a sound judgment is that man is descended from some less highly-organized form. The grounds upon which this conclusion rests will never be shaken, for the close similarity between man and the lower animals in embryonic (胚胎的) development, as well as in innumerable points of structure and constitution, both of high and of the most trifling importance — the rudiments which he retains, and the abnormal reversions to which he is occasionally liable — are facts

The close affinity of man with ape shocked all.

which cannot be disputed. They[1] have long been known, but until recently they told us nothing with respect to the origin of man. Now when viewed by the light of our knowledge of the whole organic world, their meaning is unmistakable. The great principle of evolution stands up clear and firm, when these groups or facts are considered in connection with others, such as the mutual affinities of the members of the same group, their geographical distribution in past and present times, and their geological succession. It is incredible that all these facts should speak falsely. **He who is not content to look, like a savage, at the phenomena of nature as disconnected, cannot any longer believe that man is the work of a separate act of creation. He will be forced to admit that the close resemblance of the embryo of man to that, for instance, of a dog** — the construction of his skull, limbs and whole frame on the same plan with that of other mammals, independently of the uses to which the parts may be put — the occasional reappearance of various structures, for instance, of several distinct muscles, which man does not normally possess, but which are common to the Quadrumana[2] — **and a crowd of analogous facts — all point in the plainest manner to the conclusion that man is the co-descendant with other mammals of a common progenitor[3].**

...

The main conclusion arrived at in this work, namely, that man is descended from some lowly-organized form, will, I regret to think, be highly distasteful to many persons. But there can hardly be a doubt that we are descended from barbarians[4]. The astonishment which I felt on first seeing a party of Fuegians[5] on a wild and broken shore will never be forgotten by me, for the reflection at once rushed into my mind — such were our ancestors. These men were absolutely naked and bedaubed[6] with paint, their long hair was tangled, their mouths frothed[7] with excitement, and their expression was wild, startled, and distrustful. They possessed hardly any arts, and like

1 **they:** facts
2 **Quadrumana:** 灵长类动物，四足构造皆如手的脊椎动物
3 **progenitor:** ancestor
4 **barbarian:** uncivilized man
5 **Fuegian:** inhabitant of Tierra del Fuego, islands divided between Chile and Argentina
6 **bedaub:** smear, cover
7 **froth:** have foam in mouth

wild animals lived on what they could catch; they had no government, and were merciless to every one not of their own small tribe. **He who has seen a savage in his native land will not feel much shame, if forced to acknowledge that the blood of some more humble creature flows in his veins.** For my own part I would as soon be descended from that heroic little monkey, who braved[1] his dreaded enemy in order to save the life of his keeper, or from that old baboon[2], who descending from the mountains, carried away in triumph his young comrade from a crowd of astonished dogs — as from a savage who delights to torture his enemies, offers up bloody sacrifices, practices infanticide[3] without remorse, treats his wives like slaves, knows no decency, and is haunted by the grossest[4] superstitions.

Gorilla, "That man wants to claim my Pedigree. He says he is one of my Descendants." Mr. Bergh, "Now, Mr. Darwin, how could you insult him so?" (Satirical cartoon from Harper's Weekly, August 19,1871)

Man may be excused for feeling some pride at having risen, though not through his own exertions, to the very summit of the organic scale; and the fact of his having thus risen, instead of having been aboriginally[5] placed there, may give him hope for a still higher destiny in the distant future. **But we are not here concerned with hopes or fears, only with the truth as far as our reason permits us to discover it; and I have given the evidence to the best of my ability. We must, however, acknowledge, as it seems to me, that man with all his noble qualities, with sympathy which feels for the most debased[6], with benevolence which extends not only to other men but to the humblest living creature, with his god-like intellect which has penetrated into the movements and constitution of the solar system — with all these exalted powers — Man still bears in his bodily frame the indelible[7] stamp of his lowly origin.**

Key Concepts

catastrophist theory   geometrical ratio
common progenitor   grossest superstitions

---

1   **brave:** meet without fear
2   **baboon:** large monkey with dog-like face（狒狒）
3   **infanticide:** killing infants
4   **gross:** vulgar, coarse
5   **aboriginally:** living as native
6   **debased:** poorer in quality and lower in character
7   **indelible:** of marks not easily removable

less highly-organized form

lowly origin

mammals of a common progenitor

natural selection

natural variations

origin of man

principle of evolution

sexual selection

struggle for existence

struggle for life

survival of the fittest

Compare with China

Darwin's evolutionary ideas were indeed revolutionary, and when it reached China around 1900 it brought about a "cultural shock," among the Chinese, at the time when intellectuals in China were debating possible ways to save the country from deterioration. The situation was discussed by a Yale historian in the following essay, which provides a connection from his perspective between Darwin and modern China.

The Warning Voice of Social Darwinism in Early 20th Century China

The fragmentation of authority under Yuan Shikai, the failure of fledgling[1] republic, and the betrayal of Versailles[2] — all served to deepen a fear that had been latent among Chinese since the late Qing: that China was about to be dismembered, that it would cease to exist as a nation, and that the four thousand years of its recorded history would come to a jolting[3] end. At the same time, analytical tools for probing China's plight[4] had been made available by the spreading popularity of Western Social Darwinism; and even if the theories gave little solace[5] to Chinese thinkers, these ideas nevertheless helped to bring some senses of method into a despairing debate.

The evolutionary theories of Charles Darwin, whose *Origin of Species* was first published in England in 1859, explained how the adaptive processes of natural selection determined which

---

1 **fledgling:** young

2 **The Treaty of Versailles of 1919:** the peace treaty which officially ended World War I between the Allies and Germany. After six months of negotiations which took place at the Paris Peace Conference of 1919, the treaty required that Germany pay large amounts of compensation (war reparations) to the Allies. Germany also lost territory to many surrounding countries, had its military forces severely limited and was stripped of its overseas and African colonies.

3 **jolt:** shake up

4 **plight:** serious condition

5 **solace:** relief, comfort

species managed to thrive and which were doomed to extinction. From the huge range of observations that he had made while sailing on the Beagle to the Cape Verde Islands, Chile, the Galapagos Islands, New Zealand, and Australia, Darwin came to realize that those organisms that were best fitted to survive in the constant struggle for the limited resources that made existence possible were the ones that did survive, and that in doing so they slowly ousted[1] those less well fitted. Through the laws of heredity, furthermore, the degree of adaptation achieved by a species would be maintained or improved.

The British sociologist Herbert Spencer[2] made his own creative adaptation of these theories. In *The Study of Sociology*, published in 1873, Spencer applied Darwinian theories to the development of human societies, arguing that the "survival of the fittest," a phrase Spencer coined in 1864, governed social as well as biological evolution. He declared that human societies evolved from the homogeneous[3] to the heterogeneous[4] and hence to a stage of increasing individuation. Societies were further divided between military ones obtaining cooperation by force and industrial societies in which voluntarism and spontaneity rose from the acknowledgment of individual consciousness. Spencer's theories were then reanalyzed and contested by the scientist Thomas Huxley[5], and encapsulated[6] in 1893 in his book *Evolution and Ethics*. Yan Fu, a product of China's naval school system during the self-strengthening period and later a student in England, read Huxley's book at the time of the Sino-Japanese War and translated it into Chinese in 1896 — with his own added commentary and interpretations — under the title *On Evolution*. Partly because Yan Fu chose to give the work a nationalistic emphasis not evident in the original, it had an immense impact on Chinese scholars in the late Qing and early republic.

The message that came across from Yan Fu was that Spencer's sociological writings were not merely analytical and descriptive, but prescriptive as well, offering means to transform and strengthen society. Yan Fu summarized Darwin as follows:

> Peoples and living things struggle for survival. At first, species struggle with species; then as [people] gradually progress, there is a struggle between one social group and another. The weak invariably become the prey of the strong, the stupid invariably become subservient to the clever.

---

1   **oust:** drive or push out
2   **Herbert Spencer (1820 – 1903):** English philosopher and sociologist, most prominently known as the father of Social Darwinism, a school of thought that applied natural selection or survival of the fittest (a phrase coined by Spencer) to sociological concerns of education and class struggle
3   **homogeneous:** made up of the same kind
4   **heterogeneous:** made up of different kinds
5   **Thomas Huxley (1825 – 1895):** English biologist and leading exponent of Darwin's theory of evolution, known as "Darwin's Bulldog" for his defence of natural selection
6   **encapsulate:** express in a brief summary, epitomize

Spencer, Yan Fu continues, "based himself on the theory of evolution to explain the origins of human relations and of civilization." Other late Qing thinkers were quick to see the significance of these ideas. In advocating the 1898 reforms, Liang Qichao observed hopefully that evolutionary theories allowed "the possibility of influence and change that can cause the species to steadily improve." Liang noted how heredity and education acted on human "thought, intelligence, physique and habits," and that the Chinese could strengthen their race to engage in the struggle for survival: "All countries that wish to have strong soldiers insure that all their women engage in calisthenics[1], for they believe that only thus will the sons they bear be full in body and strong of muscle."

Manuscript of Yan Fu's translation of On Evolution

Social Darwinism inevitably led the Chinese to ponder problems of race and racial strength, and many Chinese combined the new theories from the West with the writings of seventeenth-century anti-Manchu nationalists like Wang Fuzhi. Writers reflected on whether there was an inherent Chinese essence and, if so, when it had developed. If all Chinese were descendants of the Yellow Emperor, had that noble progenitor sprung from peoples who had migrated to what was now China from somewhere else? Was their past history, therefore, one of creative adaptation that had only recently slowed because of the Manchus, perhaps, or the savage force of the foreign powers? China might well be doomed to extinction unless the nation evolved new strengths; a measure of hope lay in the belief that with will power and awareness that task could be achieved. "A nation with spirit will survive," a Chinese scholar wrote just before the 1911 Wuhan uprising; "a nation without it will perish. But where does the 'national spirit' lie? In national studies."

For those who saw a danger that national studies might lead in a reactionary direction, the translation of foreign literature seemed to offer the best chance of preparing Chinese consciousness for the bitter struggles ahead. This was the goal of the young Lu Xun when he gave up his medical studies in Japan in order to translate fiction and poetry, especially Russian, Eastern European, and German works. Lu Xun hoped to evoke "super human will power" in his readers, for "when the individual is exalted to develop his full capacity, the country will be strengthened and will arise." But the reception of Lu Xun's translations was dismal. When published, after years of work, in Tokyo and Shanghai during 1908, they sold a grand total[2] of twenty copies in each city.

Thomas Huxley, "Darwin's Bulldog"

---

1 **calisthenics:** exercises for developing strong bodies
2 **a grand total:** everything included

Heritage of Western Intellectual Tradition — A Sourcebook

The 1911 revolution briefly raised hopes that Social Darwinist ideas of harsh social competition were now discredited. Just before the 1912 elections were won by his reorganized Guomindang, Sun Yat-sen wrote:

> Before the twentieth century, the nations of Europe invented a newfangled[1] struggle-for-existence theory, which for a time influenced everything. Every nation assumed that "the survival of the fittest" and "the weak are the meat of the strong" were the vital laws on which to establish a state. They even went so far as to say that "might is the only right, there is no reason." This kind of theory in the early days of the evolution of European civilization had its uses. But, from the vantage point of today, it appears a barbaric form of learning.

But by 1913, Sun was writing sadly of a world dominated by struggles for survival from which no government or industrial enterprise could be exempt. Yan Fu, too, lost his enthusiasm for the theories he had so much helped to popularize in China, writing that the failures of the Chinese republic and the bloodshed of World War I in Europe showed that "three hundred years of evolutionary progress have all come down to nothing but four words: selfishness, slaughter, shamelessness, and corruption."

Such pessimism might well lead to a refusal to strive anymore for social change, as indeed happened among Social Darwinists in the United States. This possibility lent added urgency to China's radical thinkers. As Chen Duxiu, later a cofounder of the Chinese Communist party, wrote to a friend just after Yuan Shikai's death: "The majority of our people are lethargic[2] and do not know that not only our morality, politics and technology but even common commodities for daily use are all unfit for struggle and are going to be eliminated in the process of natural selection." If that happened, China would die.

Herbert Spencer, father of Social Darwinism

Elements of these strains of thought came together in the mind of another future leader of the Chinese Communist party, Mao Zedong. In 1917, when he published his first essay, Mao was twenty-four years old. He had rebelled against his father, rejecting both the rural life on the family farm in Hunan province and the marriage his parents had arranged for him with the daughter of a neighboring family. Instead, after serving briefly in the anti-Qing army in 1911, he had plunged into a life of study in Changsha, haphazard[3] and eclectic[4]. Having made his own way through Yan Fu's translations of Mill, Montesquieu, Rousseau, and Spencer, as well as a wide range of Chinese political philosophers, Mao was accepted as a student at the well-known First Normal School in Changsha, where he studied ethics as his major field. This deepened his knowledge of the works

---

1   **newfangled:** latest, the most fashionable
2   **lethargic:** lacking in energy, tired, sleepy
3   **haphazard:** accidental
4   **eclectic:** borrowing freely from various sources

of Spencer and Rousseau, and introduced him to Kant, as well as to the ways that such thinkers could be usefully compared to figures from China's own past.

Mao's first approach to the problems of China's weakness was a literal-minded one. If China was weak, it was because the Chinese were weak. If the Chinese were weak, it was because their culture concentrated on building up the mind and neglected strengthening the body. Mao tempered his own physique by swimming and exercising; in his essay "A Study of Physical Education," published in the journal *New Youth* in April 1917, he urged his countrymen to do the same. "Physical education not only harmonizes the emotions, it also strengthens the will," he wrote. The trouble was that the Chinese traditionally hated violent exertion and cultivated "flowing garments, a slow gait[1], a grave, calm gaze." All that must change: "Exercise should be savage and rude. To be able to leap on horseback and to shoot at the same time; to go from battle to battle; to shake the mountains by one's cries, and the colors of the sky by one's roars of anger" — that was what Chinese should strive for.

In another essay, written two years later for a Hunan provincial journal and entitled "To the Glory of the Han People," Mao urged collective action on the Chinese race as a whole, using some of the rhetorical flourishes that had made Zou Rong's anti-Manchu diatribes[2] in *The Revolutionary Army* so effective fifteen years before. If only the Chinese could truly combine, Mao wrote, if they could form a "union of the popular masses," then they could join the great tide of world change. This tide was "rolling ever more impetuously[3]" and "he who conforms to it shall survive, he who resists it shall perish." If the Chinese people could so adapt, concluded Mao, "we should not fear the dead. We should not fear the bureaucrats. We should not fear the militarists. We should not fear the capitalists."

Finally, in a series of nine articles he wrote for a local Changsha newspaper in November 1919, Mao showed that he had combined his thinking on the need for collective struggle with the kinds of reflections on women and their rights that had been advocated by Liang Qichao, Qiu Jin, and others in the late Qing. They had argued that the energy of China's women should be harnessed to strengthen the state, enabling China to face the world with its full complement of 400 million people, rather than with the political resources of only its 200 million males. Mao's newspaper articles "On the Suicide of Miss Zhao" addressed an event that had occurred in Changsha that same month. A young woman from the Zhao family had been betrothed[4] without her consent to a young man from the Wu family. Such arranged marriages were the norm in China, but what was unusual about Miss Zhao was that she objected so violently to the marriage that she slit[5] her own throat inside the sedan chair carrying her to the marriage ceremonies in her future husband's

----

1　**gait:** manner of walking
2　**diatribe:** violent verbal attack
3　**impetuously:** moving quickly and violently
4　**betroth:** engage in contract of marriage
5　**slit:** cut

home. Her death was followed by a grim tussle[1] between the Wu and Zhao families as each tried to give the other responsibility for burying the corpse.

Writing with both passion and acuteness, Mao observed that this tragedy could have been avoided if any of three conditions had been different: if Miss Zhao's family had been more sympathetic, if the Wu family had not insisted on the letter of their marriage contract, and if the society of Changsha (and, by implication, of all China) had been more brave and open. Miss Zhao's death mattered, wrote Mao. "It happened because of the shameful system of arranged marriages, because of the darkness of the social system, the negation of the individual will, and the absence of the freedom to choose one's own mate." Yet Mao could not condone[2] the act of suicide, even in such a state of despair. If the Chinese were to refuse to confront reality, they would achieve nothing. People commit suicide because society has deprived them of all hope, Mao argued; but even in a position of complete hopelessness, "we should struggle against society in order to regain the hope that we have lost. ... We should die fighting."

"We should die fighting." The words were bold ones, but the real difficulty lay in deciding who was the main enemy. Was it just an apathetic[3] local society? Was it the local warlords who controlled Hunan? Was it corrupt politicians in Peking? Was it the gunboats of the foreign powers, or the foreign businesses that were making ever further inroads[4] into China? Or was it perhaps something even more complex: the whole structure of Chinese beliefs, and the economic system that went with it? For the young men and women of Mao's generation, the problems were baffling, but they had somehow to come up with a program for solving these difficulties if China were not to succumb to despair. (Adapted from Jonathan D. Spence, *The Search for Modern China*)

Supplementary Reading

1. Autobiography of Charles Darwin

Some biologists argued that Darwin could not prove his hypothesis, or that he could not explain the origin of variations. The most publicized attacks on Darwin, however, came not from scientists but

---

1   **tussle:** hard fight
2   **condone:** forgive
3   **apathetic:** indifferent, unsympathetic
4   **inroad:** invasion

from religious opponents for his denial of special creation of humankind, which led to serious contradictions to orthodox theological opinion. Darwin himself was torn between his rationalism and the religious atmosphere around him. A skeptical agnostic[1], he participated in church functions that were part of village life where he lived. When he died on April 19, 1882, he was buried in Westminster Abbey. The following excerpt describes some of his doubts and dilemmas.

During these two years I was led to think much about religion. Whilst on board the Beagle I was quite orthodox, and I remember being heartily laughed at by several of the officers (though themselves orthodox) for quoting the Bible as an unanswerable authority[2] on some point of morality. I suppose it was the novelty of the argument that amused them. But I had gradually come, by this time, to see that the Old Testament from its manifestly false history of the world, with the Tower of Babel, the rainbow at sign, etc., etc., and from its attributing to God the feelings of a revengeful tyrant, was no more to be trusted than the sacred books of the Hindus, or the beliefs of any barbarian. The question then continually rose before my mind and would not be banished, — is it credible that if God were now to make a revelation to the Hindoos[3], would he permit it to be connected with the belief in Vishnu[4], Siva[5], & c., as Christianity is connected with the Old Testament. This appeared to me utterly incredible.

By further reflecting that the clearest evidence would be requisite to make any sane man believe in the miracles by which Christianity is supported, — that the more we know of the fixed laws of nature the more incredible do miracles become, — that the men at that time were ignorant and credulous[6] to a degree almost incomprehensible by us, — that the Gospels cannot be proved to have been written simultaneous with the events, — that they differ in many important details, far too important as it seemed to me to be admitted as the usual inaccuracies of eyewitnesses; — by such reflections as these, which I give not as having the least novelty or value, but as they influenced me, I gradually came to disbelieve in Christianity as a divine revelation. The fact that many false religions have spread over large portions of the earth like wild-fire had some weight on me. Beautiful as is the morality of the New Testament, it can hardly be denied that its perfection depends in part on the interpretation which we now put on metaphors and allegories[7].

But I was very unwilling to give up my belief; — I feel sure of this for I can well remember often and often inventing day-dreams of old letters between distinguished Romans and manu-

---

1　**agnostic:** person who believes that nothing can be known about the existence of God or of anything except material things（不可知论者）

2　**unanswerable authority:** authority against which no good argument can possibly be brought

3　**Hindoo:** believers of Hinduism in north India

4　**Vishnu:** one of the greatest gods of Hinduism, also called Narayana

5　**Siva:** one of the principal Hindu deities, worshiped as the destroyer and restorer of worlds

6　**credulous:** ready to believe

7　**metaphors and allegories:** rhetorical devices, not to be confused with actual reality

Heritage of Western Intellectual Tradition　A Sourcebook

scripts being discovered at Pompeji[1] or elsewhere which confirmed in the most striking manner all that was written in the Gospels. But I found it more and more difficult, with free scope given to my imagination, to invent evidence which would suffice to convince me. Thus disbelief crept over me at very slow rate, but was at last complete. The rate was so slow that I felt no distress, and have never since doubted even for a single second that my conclusion was correct. I can indeed hardly see how anyone ought to wish Christianity to be true; for if so the plain language of the text seems to show that the men who do not believe, and this would include my Father, Brother and almost all of my friends, will be everlasting punished.

And this is a damnable doctrine

Although I did not think much about the existence of a personal God until a considerably later period of my life, I will here give the vague conclusions to which I have been driven. The old argument of design in nature, as given by Paley[2], which formerly seemed to me so conclusive, fails, now that the law of natural selection has been discovered. We can no longer argue that, for instance, the beautiful hinge of a bivalve[3] shell must have been made by an intelligent being, like the hinge of a door by man. There seems to be no more design in the variability of organic beings and in the action of natural selection, than in the course the wind blows. Everything in nature is the result of fixed laws. But I have discussed this subject at the end of my book on the Variation of Domestic Animals and Plants, and the argument there given has never, as far as I can see, been answered.

But passing over the endless beautiful adaptations which we everywhere meet with, it may be asked how can the generally beneficent arrangement of the world be accounted for? Some writers indeed are so much impressed with the amount of suffering in the world that they doubt if we look to all sentiment beings, whether there is more of misery or of happiness; — whether the world as a whole is a good or a bad one. According to my judgment happiness decidedly prevails, though this would be very difficult to prove. If the truth of this conclusion be granted, it harmonises well with the effects which we might expect from natural selection. If all the individuals of any species were habitually to suffer to an extreme degree they would neglect to propagate[4] their kind; but we have no reason to believe that this have[5] ever or at least often occurred. Some other considerations, moreover, lead to the belief that all sentiment beings have been formed so as to enjoy, as a general rule, happiness.

Everyone who believes, as I do, that all the corporeal[6] and mental organs (excepting those

---

1   **Pompeji:** or Pompeii, a ruined Roman city near modern Naples, destroyed during a catastrophic eruption of the volcano Mount Vesuvius in 79 AD

2   **William Paley (1743 – 1805):** English divine, Christian apologist and philosopher

3   **bivalve:** water animal with a hinged double shell（双壳贝类）

4   **propagate:** increase the number of (plants, animals, etc.) by a natural process

5   **have:** should have

6   **corporeal:** bodily

which are neither advantageous or disadvantageous to the possessor) of all beings have been developed through natural selection, or the survival of the fittest, together with use or habit, will admit that these organs have formed so that their possessors may compete successfully with other beings, and thus increase in number. Now an animal may be led to pursue that course of action which is the most beneficial to the species by suffering, such as pain, hunger, thirst, and fear, — or by pleasure, as in eating and drinking and in the propagation of the species, & c. or by both means combined, as in the search for food. But pain or suffering of any kind, if long continued, causes depression and lessens the power of action; yet is well adapted to make a creature guard itself against any great or sudden evil. Pleasurable sensations, on the other hand, may be long continued without any depressive effect; on the contrary they stimulate the whole system to increase action. Hence it has come to pass that most or all sentiment beings have been developed in such a manner through natural selection, that pleasurable sensations serve as their habitual guides. We see this in the pleasure from exertion, even occasionally from great exertion of the body or mind, — in the pleasure of our daily meals, and especially in the pleasure derived from sociability and from loving our families. The sum of such pleasures as these, which are habitual or frequently recurrent, give, as I can hardly doubt, to most beings an excess of happiness over misery, although many occasionally suffer much. Such suffering is quite compatible with the belief in Natural Selection, which is not perfect in its action, but tends only to render each species as successful as possible in the battle for life with other species, in wonderfully complex and changing circumstances.

That there is much suffering in the world no one disputes. Some have attempted to explain this in reference to man by imagining that it serves for his moral improvement. But the number of men in the world is as nothing compared with that of all other sentiment beings, and these often suffer greatly without any moral improvement. A being so powerful and so full of knowledge as a God who could create the universe, is to our finite minds omnipotent and omniscient[1], and it revolts our understanding to suppose that his benevolence is not unbounded, for what advantage can there be in the suffering of millions of the lower animals throughout almost endless time? This very old argument from the existence of suffering against the existence of an intelligent first cause seems to me a strong one; whereas, as just remarked, the presence of much suffering agrees well with the view that all organic beings have been developed through variation and natural selection.

At the present day the most usual argument for the existence of an intelligent God is drawn from the deep inward conviction and feelings which are experienced by most persons. But it cannot be doubted that Hindoos, Mahomadans[2] and others might argue in the same manner and with equal force in favour of the existence of one God, or of many Gods, or as with the Buddhists of no God. There are also many barbarian tribes who cannot be said with any truth to believe in what we call God: they believe indeed in spirits or ghosts, and it can be explained, as Tyler and

---

1 **omnipotent:** having unlimited power; omniscient: knowing everything
2 **Mahomadans:** Mohammedans, followers of Mohammed, Prophet of Islam

Herbert Spencer have shown, how such a belief would be likely to arise.

Formerly I was led by feelings such as those just referred to (although I do not think that the religious sentiment was ever strongly developed in me), to the firm conviction of the existence of God, and of the immortality of the soul. In my journal I wrote that whilst standing in the midst of the grandeur of a Brazilian forest, "it is not possible to give an adequate idea of the higher feelings of wonder, admiration, and devotion which fill and elevate the mind." I well remember by conviction that there is more in man than the mere breath of his body. But now the grandest scenes would not cause any such convictions and feelings to rise in my mind. It may be truly said that I am like a man who has become colour-blind, and the universal belief by men of the existence of redness makes my present loss of perception of not the least value as evidence[1]. This argument would be a valid one if all men of all races had the same inward conviction of the existence of one God; but we know that this is very far from being the case. Therefore I cannot see that such inward convictions and feelings are of any weight as evidence of what really exists. The state of mind which grand scenes formerly excited in me, and which was intimately connected with a belief in God, did not essentially differ from that which is often called the sense of sublimity; and however difficult it may be to explain the genesis of this sense, it can hardly be advanced as an argument for the existence of God, any more than the powerful though vague and similar feelings excited by music.

With respect to immortality, nothing shows me how strong and almost instinctive a belief is, as the consideration of the view now held by most physicist, namely that the sun with all the planets will in time grow too cold for life, unless indeed some great body dashes into the sun and thus gives it fresh life. — Believing as I do that man in the distant future will be a far more perfect creature than he now is, it is an intolerable thought that he and all other sentiment beings are doomed to complete annihilation[2] after such long-continued slow progress. To those who fully admit the immortality of the human soul, the destruction of our world will not appear so dreadful.

Another source of conviction in the existence of God connected with the reason and not the feelings, impresses me as having much more weight. This follows from the extreme difficulty or rather impossibility of conceiving this immense and wonderful universe, including man with his capability of looking far backwards and far into futurity, as the result of blind chance or necessity. When thus reflecting I feel compelled to look at a first cause having an intelligent mind in some degree analogous to that of man; and I deserve to be called a theist[3].

This conclusion was strong in my mind about the time, as far I can remember, when I wrote the *Origin of Species*; and it is since that time that it has very gradually with many

---

1   **the universal belief by men ... least value as evidence:** Darwin is being a bit sarcastic here: everyone else sees the redness (God) but I do not see such "evidence" with "great value."

2   **annihilation:** destruction

3   **theist:** believer in theism, or existence of one god

fluctuations[1] become weaker. But then arises the doubt — can the mind of man, which has, as I fully believe, been developed from a mind as low as the mind possessed by the lowest animal, be trusted when it draws such a grand conclusions? May not these be the result of the connection between cause and effect which strikes us as a necessary one, but probably depends merely on inherited experience? Nor must we overlook the probability of the constant inculcation[2] in a belief in God on the minds of children producing so strong and perhaps an inherited effect on their brains not yet fully developed, that it would be as difficult for them to throw off their belief in God, as for a monkey to throw off its instinctive fear and hatred of a snake.

I cannot pretend to throw the least light on such abstruse[3] problems. The mystery of the beginning of all things is insoluble to us; and I for one[4] must be content to remain an Agnostic[5].

2. Piltdown Man Forgery

One of the most interesting indications of the inspiration the theory of evolution offered to British imperialism was the Piltdown man scandal.

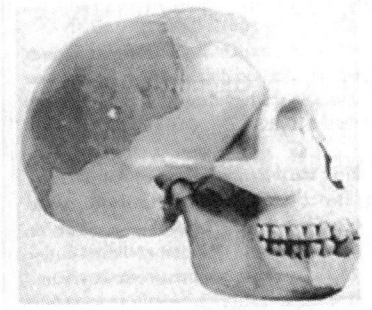

This fake fossil was actually produced by assembling an ape's jaw to a human skull.

In 1912, a strange skull was found in Piltdown, England. Charles Dawson, the scientist who found the skull together with his team, declared that it belonged to a creature which was half ape-half human. Arthur Keith, the renowned evolutionist anatomist examined the fossil and confirmed the results.

However, Dawson and Keith emphasised an important point. The brain of the fossil was as big as that of modern man. The jawbone, however, had ape-like features.

Suddenly the brain of Piltdown man became a matter of pride for the British. Since this skull was found in England, it had to be the ancestor of the British. According to the British people, the greater volume of the brain indicated that British had evolved before other races, and were thus superior to other races.

That is why the discovery of Piltdown man aroused great excitement in England. Newspapers ran headlines and crowds joyously celebrated the discovery. The British government, on the other hand, granted a knighthood to Arthur Keith for his famous discovery.

The famous evolutionist paleontologist[6], Don Johanson, describes the relationship between

---

1 **fluctuation:** irregularity, up and down movement
2 **inculcation:** firm fixation by repetition
3 **abstruse:** profound
4 **for one:** as for me
5 **Agnostic:** person who believes that nothing can be known about God or anything else except material things
6 **paleontologist:** expert in paleontology, science of fossils

the Piltdown fossil and English imperialism:

> The Piltdown discovery was very Eurocentric[1]. Not only did the brain have pre-eminence, but the English had pre-eminence, too.

The inspiration the English derived from Piltdown man lasted only until 1953, when Kenneth Oakley, a scientist who re-examined the fossil in detail, revealed it to be the greatest forgery[2] of the 20th century. The fossil had been produced by affixing an orang-utan[3] jaw to a human skull. (Adapted from http://www.update.uu.se/~fbendz/library/cd_relig.htm)

Questions for Discussion

1. Comment on Malthus' concept of population growth. Why do you agree / disagree with him?
2. Why does Malthus oppose greater equality, welfare, and relief payment to the poor?
3. Soon after Malthus's theory came into being, it received attacks from every aspect. Engels was against his theory on population as he believed that this theory was the cruelest one that ever existed in the world, a desperate system that destroyed the notion of love and mankind as a result of the Malthusian population control. Despite all the attacks, can you tell anything that is positive in this theory?
4. Does the theory of Malthus have anything in common with Darwin's?
5. Why does Darwinism look so "radical" to his contemporaries?
6. In what sense is Darwin's theory against the belief of Christianity?
7. How does Darwin argue for the "survival of the fittest"?
8. What is the rationale behind social Darwinism? Why is it dangerous, judging from the history of the 20th century?

---

1 **Eurocentric:** racist assumption that Europeans are racially superior to other peoples
2 **forgery:** something counterfeit, copy for deception
3 **orang-utan:** orangutan, often simply orang, arboreal anthropoid ape, now an endangered species（猩猩）

Heritage of Western Intellectual Tradition A Sourcebook

UNIT 13

Socialism and Communism

Pretest

- What do you know about Karl Marx and Friedrich Engels?
- Name a few important concepts in the "Communist Manifesto" and explain.
- Tell the major differences between Marx/Engels and Bernstein.

What You Will Learn in This Unit

- Ideas about the "Communist Manifesto";
- Important selections from the "Communist Manifesto";
- Comparison between Marx/Engels and Eduard Bernstein; and
- Karl Marx on China.

Learn to Pronounce

Brussels /ˈbrʌslz/ 布鲁塞尔

bourgeoisie /ˌbuəʒwɑːˈziː/ 资产阶级

Eduard Bernstein /ˈbɜːnstaɪn/ 伯恩斯坦

Friedrich Engels /ˈeŋəls/ 恩格斯

Karl Marx /mɑːks/ 马克思

proletarian /ˌprəuleˈteəriən/ 无产阶级的

Robert Owen /ˈəuɪn/ 欧文

bourgeois /buəʒˈwɑː/ 资产阶级的

Comte de Saint-Simon /seɪntˈsaɪmən/ 圣西门

Fabian Society /ˈfeɪbjən/ 费边式的

Hegel /ˈheɪgl/ 黑格尔

Manifesto /ˌmænɪˈfestəu/ 宣言

proletariat /ˌprəuleˈteəriət/ 无产阶级

Introduction

It is necessary to distinguish at the outset what is discussed here as "socialism" and what is often meant by communism. The socialism at the time referred to ideas from people like Robert Owen and Comte de Saint-Simon, called by Marx as "utopian socialists" as they tried, in vain, to reform existing political, economic, social institutions. Communism or "scientific socialism," on the contrary, designates theories and movements that, in accordance with Marx and Engels, advocate the "abolition of capitalism and all private profit by means of violent revolution if necessary." The first international forum for the promulgation of Marxian concept of Communism was the congress of the International Workingmen's Association met at Geneva in 1866, or the First International. The Marxian concept was later developed by Lenin, who defined a socialist society as one in which the workers, free from capitalist exploitation, became the masters of the product of their own labor. Meanwhile the "utopian socialism" went on as a social doctrine and political movement demanding state ownership and reconstruction of the existing capitalist system through "peaceful, democratic, and parliamentary means." It specifically advocates nationalization of natural resources, basic industries, banking and credit facilities, and public utilities. Smaller and less vital enterprises, however, are left under private ownership. Such a view was held by the founders of the Fabian Society, organized in 1884 by a group of middle-class intellectuals, and was most expressive in the revisionist movement of the late 19th century. Its followers doubted the indispensability of revolution and began to revise the basic tenets of Marxism. Led by Eduard Bernstein, they declared that socialism could best be attained by reformist, parliamentary, and evolutionary methods, including the support of the bourgeoisie. Marx's contribution was to give a definite purpose and a clear rationale to the disorganized and ineffective socialist movement at the time. His theory of scientific socialism, though largely unheard of in the 19th century, was to take root in the minds of millions and took definite shapes in the 20th century. It is still a forceful ideology today worldwide.

Karl Marx and Friedrich Engels:
Manifesto of the Communist Party*

Karl Marx (1818–1883), German political philosopher and cofounder, with Friedrich Engels, of scientific socialism or modern Communism. Marx was educated at the University of Bonn, Berlin, and Jena. In 1842 he became editor of the Cologne newspaper *Rheinische Zeitung* and wrote to criticize contemporary political and social conditions. This embroiled him in controversy with the authorities,

---

* The draft of *The Communist Manifesto* (1848) was first prepared by Friedrich Engels, and elaborated and finalized by Karl Marx. Of all the socialist and communist tracts published in the early and mid-19th century, this one is the single most succinct expression of modern socialist ideas propounded by Marx and Engels.

and in 1843 he was compelled to resign his editorial post, and before long the *Rheinische Zeitung*

was forced to discontinue publication. Marx then went to Paris, and there furthered studies in philosophy, history, and political science. In 1844 when Engels visited him, the two men began a lifelong friendship. Their first major collaboration was to elucidate systematically the theoretical principles of communism and to organize an international working class movement dedicated to those principles. After 1848 when again banished from France, Marx spent the remaining 30 years in London, in the library of British Museum. During this period he wrote his greatest work, *Das Kapital* (volume 1, 1867; volumes 2 and 3, edited by Engels and published posthumously in 1885 and 1894, respectively), a systematic and historical analysis of the economy of the capitalist system and society. Marx's ideas and theories came to be known as Marxism, or scientific socialism, which constitutes one of the principal currents of contemporary political thought. His analysis of capitalist economy and his theories of historical materialism, class struggle, and surplus value have become the basis of modern socialist doctrine.

In 1845 Marx settled in Brussels and began organizing and directing Communist Correspondence Committees in a number of European cities. In 1847 these committees were consolidated to

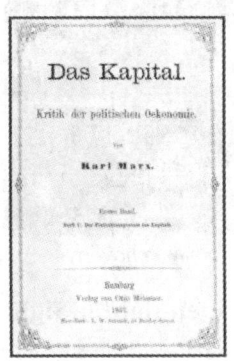

form the Communist League, and Marx and Engels were commissioned to formulate a statement of principles. The program they submitted, known throughout the world as the *Communist Manifesto* declares principles and objectives of the Communist League shortly before the February Revolution in Paris. Marx outlines his theory of history and prophesies an end to exploitation. Identifying class struggle as the primary dynamic in history, he characterizes the modern world as the stage for a dramatic confrontation between the ruling bourgeoisie[1] (the capitalists) and the downtrodden proletariat[2] (the working class). Driven by the logic of capitalism to seek ever greater profit, the bourgeoisie constantly revolutionizes the means of economic production, the fulcrum of history. In so doing, it unwittingly sets in motion sociohistorical forces that it can no longer control, thus ironically calling into existence the class destined to end its rule — the proletariat. As the proletariat increases in number and political awareness, heightened class antagonism will generate a revolution and the inevitable defeat of the bourgeoisie. Marx identifies the Communists as vanguard of the proletariat. He emphasizes the necessity of abolishing private property, a fundamental change in material existence that will unmask bourgeois culture, the ideological expression of capitalism. After the revolution, economic production will be in the hands of the state, that is, of the proletariat, organized as the ruling class. The *Manifesto* is the most concise and intelligible statement of Marx's materialist view of history. Hence, although it produced little immediate effect, it has since become the most widely read of his works and the single most influential document in the socialist canon.

---

1 **bourgeoisie:** class of modern capitalists, owners of the means of social production and employers of wage labourers

2 **proletariat:** class of modern wage labourers who, having no means of production of their own, are reduced to selling their labor power in order to live

Heritage of Western Intellectual Tradition   A Sourcebook

A specter[1] is haunting Europe — the specter of communism. All the powers of old Europe have entered into a holy alliance to exorcise[2] this specter: Pope and Tsar, Metternich[3] and Guizot[4], French Radicals and German police-spies.

Where is the party in opposition that has not been decried[5] as communistic by its opponents in power? Where is the opposition that has not hurled back the branding[6] reproach of communism, against the more advanced opposition parties, as well as against its reactionary adversaries[7]?

Two things result from this fact:

I. Communism is already acknowledged by all European powers to be itself a power.

II. It is high time that Communists should openly, in the face of the whole world, publish their views, their aims, their tendencies, and meet this nursery tale of the specter of communism with a manifesto of the party itself.

To this end, Communists of various nationalities have assembled in London and sketched the following manifesto, to be published in the English, French, German, Italian, Flemish[8] and Danish languages.

I. Bourgeois and Proletarians

The history of all hitherto existing society is the history of class struggles.

Freeman and slave, patrician[9] and plebeian[10], lord and serf[11], guild-master[12] and journeyman[13], in a word, **oppressor and oppressed, stood in constant opposition to one another, carried on an uninterrupted, now hidden, now open fight, a fight**

The working class family in poverty

---

1 **specter:** It is a famous analogy, both threatening and exciting.

2 **exorcise:** drive out

3 **Klemens Wenzel von Metternich (1773 – 1859):** Austrian politician who helped form the Quadruple Alliance that ultimately defeated Napoleon I

4 **François Pierre Guillaume Guizot (1787 – 1874):** French historian and premier (1847 – 1848) who advocated a constitutional monarchy

5 **decry:** criticize, devalue

6 **brand:** give a bad name

7 **adversary:** enemy

8 **Flemish:** language of the Flanders, now Dutch dialects spoken in the southwestern Netherlands, northwest Belgium, and parts of northern France

9 **patrician:** people of noble birth

10 **plebeian:** people of low social class

11 **serf:** slave

12 **guild-master:** head of trade society

13 **journeyman:** skilled workers

that each time ended, either in a revolutionary re-constitution of society at large[1], or in the common ruin of the contending classes.

In the earlier epochs of history, we find almost everywhere a complicated arrangement of society into various orders, a manifold gradation of social rank. In ancient Rome we have patricians, knights, plebeians, slaves; in the Middle Ages, feudal lords, vassals[2], guild-masters, journeymen, apprentices, serfs; in almost all of these classes, again, subordinate gradations.

The modern bourgeois society that has sprouted from the ruins of feudal society has not done away with class antagonisms. It has but established new classes, new conditions of oppression, new forms of struggle in place of the old ones.

Our epoch, the epoch of the bourgeoisie, possesses, however, this distinct feature: it has simplified class antagonisms: Society as a whole is more and more splitting up into two great hostile camps, into two great classes, directly facing each other — bourgeoisie and proletariat.

From the serfs of the Middle Ages sprang the chartered[3] burghers[4] of the earliest towns. From these burgesses the first elements of the bourgeoisie were developed.

The discovery of America, the rounding of the Cape[5], opened up fresh ground for the rising bourgeoisie. The East-Indian and Chinese markets, the colonization of America, trade with the colonies, the increase in the means of exchange and in commodities generally, gave to commerce, to navigation, to industry, an impulse never before known, and thereby, to the revolutionary element in the tottering[6] feudal society, a rapid development.

The feudal system of industry, in which industrial production was monopolized by closed guilds, now no longer suffices for the growing wants of the new markets. The manufacturing system took its place. The guild-masters were pushed aside by the manufacturing middle class; division of labor between the different corporate guilds vanished in the face of division of labor in each single workshop.

Meantime, the markets kept ever growing, the demand ever rising. Even manufacturers no longer sufficed. Thereupon, steam and machinery revolutionized industrial production. The place of manufacture was taken by the giant, MODERN INDUSTRY; the place of the industrial middle class by industrial millionaires, the leaders of the whole industrial armies, the modern bourgeois.

---

1 **society at large:** whole society
2 **vassal:** a person holding a fief
3 **charter:** grant a privilege
4 **burgher:** citizen
5 **rounding of the Cape:** Cape of Good Hope was first rounded by Portuguese navigator Bartolomeu Dias in 1488, who named it "Cape of Storms." It was later renamed by John II of Portugal as "Cape of Good Hope" because of the opening of a route to the east.
6 **totter:** shake, almost fall

Heritage of Western Intellectual Tradition   A Sourcebook

Modern industry has established the world market, for which the discovery of America paved the way. This market has given an immense development to commerce, to navigation, to communication by land. This development has, in turn, reacted on the extension of industry; and in proportion as industry, commerce, navigation, railways extended, in the same proportion the bourgeoisie developed, increased its capital, and pushed into the background every class handed down from the Middle Ages.

We see, therefore, how the modern bourgeoisie is itself the product of a long course of development, of a series of revolutions in the modes of production and of exchange.

Each step in the development of the bourgeoisie was accompanied by a corresponding political advance in that class. An oppressed class under the sway[1] of the feudal nobility, an armed and self-governing association in the medieval commune; here independent urban republic (as in Italy and Germany); there taxable "third estate" of the monarchy (as in France); afterward, in the period of manufacturing proper, serving either the semi-feudal or the absolute monarchy as a counterpoise[2] against the nobility, and, in fact, corner-stone of the great monarchies in general — the bourgeoisie has at last, since the establishment of Modern Industry and of the world-market, conquered for itself, in the modern representative State, exclusive political sway. The executive of the modern State is but a committee for managing the common affairs of the whole bourgeoisie.

The house where Marx was born in Trier, Germany

The bourgeoisie, historically, has played a most revolutionary part.

The bourgeoisie, wherever it has got the upper hand, has put an end to all feudal, patriarchal[3], idyllic[4] relations. It has pitilessly torn asunder[5] the motley[6] feudal ties that bound man to his "natural superiors," and has left no other nexus[7] between people than naked self-interest, than callous[8] "cash payment." It has drowned out the most heavenly ecstasies[9] of religious fervor, of chivalrous[10] enthusiasm, of philistine[11] sentimentalism, in the icy water of egotistical[12] calculation. It has resolved personal worth

1 **sway:** control, rule
2 **counterpoise:** weight for balance, equilibrium
3 **patriarchal:** of male head of a family or tribe
4 **idyllic:** simple and pleasant
5 **asunder:** into pieces
6 **motley:** of various character
7 **nexus:** connection, bond
8 **callous:** unfeeling
9 **ecstasy:** great joy
10 **chivalrous:** knight-like
11 **philistine:** uncultured people
12 **egotistical:** self-centered, selfish

into exchange value, and in place of the numberless indefeasible[1] chartered freedoms, has set up that single, unconscionable[2] freedom — Free Trade. In one word, for[3] exploitation, veiled by religious and political illusions, it has substituted naked, shameless, direct, brutal exploitation.

The bourgeoisie has stripped of its halo[4] every occupation hitherto honored and looked up to with reverent awe. It has converted the physician, the lawyer, the priest, the poet, the man of science, into its paid wage laborers.

The bourgeoisie has torn away from the family its sentimental veil, and has reduced the family relation into a mere money relation.

The bourgeoisie has disclosed how it came to pass[5] that the brutal display of vigor in the Middle Ages, which reactionaries so much admire, found its fitting complement in the most slothful indolence[6]. It has been the first to show what man's activity can bring about. It has accomplished wonders far surpassing Egyptian pyramids, Roman aqueducts[7], and Gothic cathedrals; it has conducted expeditions that put in the shade[8] all former exoduses of nations and crusades.

The bourgeoisie cannot exist without constantly revolutionizing the instruments of production, and thereby the relations of production, and with them the whole relations of society. Conservation of the old modes of production in unaltered form, was, on the contrary, the first condition of existence for all earlier industrial classes. Constant revolutionizing of production, uninterrupted disturbance of all social conditions, everlasting uncertainty and agitation distinguish the bourgeois epoch from all earlier ones. All fixed, fast frozen relations, with their train of ancient and venerable prejudices and opinions, are swept away, all new-formed ones become antiquated[9] before they can ossify[10]. All that is solid melts into air, all that is holy is profaned[11], and man is at last compelled to face with sober senses his real condition of life and his relations with his kind.

The need of a constantly expanding market for its products chases the bourgeoisie over the entire surface of the globe. It must nestle everywhere, settle everywhere, establish connections everywhere.

The bourgeoisie has, through its exploitation of the world market, given a cosmopolitan[12]

---

1 **indefeasible:** not liable to being voided or undone
2 **unconscionable:** unreasonable
3 **for:** in place of
4 **halo:** circle of light around the sun or sacred people
5 **come to pass:** happen
6 **slothful indolence:** inactive laziness
7 **aqueduct:** artificial channel for supplying water
8 **put in the shade:** make inconsequential, belittle
9 **antiquated:** old-fashioned
10 **ossify:** become rigid, fixed, unprogressive
11 **profane:** treat holy things with contempt
12 **cosmopolitan:** global

Heritage of Western Intellectual Tradition A Sourcebook

character to production and consumption in every country. To the great chagrin[1] of reactionaries, it has drawn from under the feet of industry the national ground on which it stood. All old-established national industries have been destroyed or are daily being destroyed. They are dislodged by new industries, whose introduction becomes a life and death question for all civilized nations, by industries that no longer work up indigenous raw material, but raw material drawn from the remotest zones; industries whose products are consumed, not only at home, but in every quarter of the globe. In place of the old wants, satisfied by the production of the country, we find new wants, requiring for their satisfaction the products of distant lands and climes[2]. In place of the old local and national seclusion[3] and self-sufficiency, we have intercourse in every direction, universal inter-dependence of nations. And as in material, so also in intellectual production. The intellectual creations of individual nations become common property. National one-sidedness and narrow-mindedness become more and more impossible, and from the numerous national and local literatures, there arises a world literature.

The bourgeoisie, by the rapid improvement of all instruments of production, by the immensely facilitated means of communication, draws all, even the most barbarian, nations into civilization. The cheap prices of commodities are the heavy artillery with which it batters[4] down all Chinese walls, with which it forces the barbarians' intensely obstinate[5] hatred of foreigners to capitulate[6]. It compels all nations, on pain of[7] extinction, to adopt the bourgeois mode of production; it compels them to introduce what it calls civilization into their midst, i.e., to become bourgeois themselves. In one word, it creates a world after its own image.

The bourgeoisie has subjected the country to the rule of the towns. It has created enormous cities, has greatly increased the urban population as compared with the rural, and has thus rescued a considerable part of the population from the idiocy[8] of rural life. Just as it has made the country dependent on the towns, so it has made barbarian and semi-barbarian countries dependent on the civilized ones, nations of peasants on nations of bourgeois, the East on the West.

The bourgeoisie keeps more and more doing away with the scattered state of the population, of the means of production, and of property. It has agglomerated[9] population, centralized the means of production, and has concentrated property in a few hands. The necessary consequence of this was political centralization. Independent, or but loosely connected provinces, with separate interests, laws, governments, and systems of taxation, became lumped together into one nation,

---

1 **chagrin:** feeling of disappointment
2 **clime:** climate
3 **seclusion:** isolation
4 **batter:** strike hard
5 **obstinate:** stubborn
6 **capitulate:** surrender
7 **on pain of:** at the risk of, as punishment
8 **idiocy:** extreme stupidity
9 **agglomerate:** gather into a mass, make concentrated

with one government, one code of laws, one national class interest, one frontier, and one customs tariff.

The bourgeoisie, during its rule of scarce one hundred years, has created more massive and more colossal productive forces than have all preceding generations together. Subjection of nature's forces to man, machinery, application of chemistry to industry and agriculture, steam navigation, railways, electric telegraphs, clearing of whole continents for cultivation, canalization or rivers, whole populations conjured[1] out of the ground — what earlier century had even a presentiment[2] that such productive forces slumbered in the lap of social labor?

We see then: the means of production and of exchange, on whose foundation the bourgeoisie built itself up, were generated in feudal society. At a certain stage in the development of these means of production and of exchange, the conditions under which feudal society produced and exchanged, the feudal organization of agriculture and manufacturing industry, in one word, the feudal relations of property became no longer compatible with the already developed productive forces; they became so many fetters[3]. They had to be burst asunder[4]; they were burst asunder.

Into their place stepped free competition, accompanied by a social and political constitution adapted in it, and the economic and political sway of the bourgeois class.

A similar movement is going on before our own eyes. **Modern bourgeois society**, with its relations of production, of exchange and of property, a society that has conjured up such gigantic means of production and of exchange, **is like the sorcerer[5] who is no longer able to control the powers of the nether[6] world whom he has called up by his spells**. For many a decade past, the history of industry and commerce is but the history of the revolt of modern productive forces against modern conditions of production, against the property relations that are the conditions for the existence of the bourgeois and of its rule. It is enough to mention the commercial crises that, by their periodical return, put the existence of the entire bourgeois society on its trial, each time more threateningly. In these crises, a great part not only of the existing products, but also of the previously created productive forces, are periodically destroyed. In these crises, there breaks out an epidemic[7] that, in all earlier epochs, would have seemed an absurdity — the epidemic of over-production. Society suddenly finds itself put back into a state of momentary barbarism; it appears as if a famine, a universal war of devastation, had cut off the supply of every means of subsistence; industry and commerce seem to be destroyed. And why? Because there is too much civilization, too much means of subsistence, too much industry, too much commerce. The productive forces

---

1 **conjured:** magically performed

2 **presentiment:** feeling that something is about to happen

3 **fetter:** chain for prisoners

4 **burst asunder:** split apart

5 **sorcerer:** magician assisted by evil spirit

6 **nether:** lower

7 **epidemic:** disease widespread among many people in the same place for a certain time

Heritage of Western Intellectual Tradition A Sourcebook

at the disposal of society no longer tend to further the development of the conditions of bourgeois property; on the contrary, they have become too powerful for these conditions, by which they are fettered, and so soon as they overcome these fetters, they bring disorder into the whole of bourgeois society, endanger the existence of bourgeois property. The conditions of bourgeois society are too narrow to comprise[1] the wealth created by them. And how does the bourgeoisie get over these crises? On the one hand, by enforced destruction of a mass of productive forces; on the other, by the conquest of new markets, and by the more thorough exploitation of the old ones. That is to say, by paving the way for more extensive and more destructive crises, and by diminishing the means whereby crises are prevented.

Karl Marx, his daughters Jenny, Laura and Eleanor, and F. Engels, 1864

The weapons with which the bourgeoisie felled feudalism to the ground are now turned against the bourgeoisie itself.

But not only has the bourgeoisie forged the weapons that bring death to itself; it has also called into existence the men who are to wield those weapons — the modern working class — the proletarians.

In proportion as the bourgeoisie, i.e., capital, is developed, in the same proportion is the proletariat, the modern working class, developed — a class of laborers, who live only so long as they find work, and who find work only so long as their labor increases capital. These laborers, who must sell themselves piecemeal, are a commodity, like every other article of commerce, and are consequently exposed to all the vicissitudes[2] of competition, to all the fluctuations of the market.

Owing to the extensive use of machinery, and to the division of labor, the work of the proletarians has lost all individual character, and, consequently, all charm for the workman. He becomes an appendage[3] of the machine, and it is only the most simple, most monotonous, and most easily acquired knack[4], that is required of him. Hence, the cost of production of a workman is restricted, almost entirely, to the means of subsistence that he requires for maintenance, and for the propagation[5] of his race. But the price of a commodity, and therefore also of labor, is equal to its cost of production. In proportion, therefore, as the repulsiveness of the work increases, the wage decreases. What is more, in proportion as the use of machinery and division of labor increases, in the same proportion the burden of toil also increases, whether by prolongation of the working hours, by the increase of the work exacted[6] in a given time, or by increased speed of machinery, etc.

---

1 **comprise:** include
2 **vicissitude:** change
3 **appendage:** something fastened to a larger piece
4 **knack:** skill, cleverness
5 **propagation:** increase
6 **exact:** demand

Modern Industry has converted the little workshop of the patriarchal master into the great factory of the industrial capitalist. Masses of laborers, crowded into the factory, are organized like soldiers. As privates[1] of the industrial army, they are placed under the command of a perfect hierarchy of officers and sergeants. Not only are they slaves of the bourgeois class, and of the bourgeois state; they are daily and hourly enslaved by the machine, by the overlooker[2], and, above all, in the individual bourgeois manufacturer himself. The more openly this despotism[3] proclaims gain to be its end and aim, the more petty, the more hateful and the more embittering it is.

Marx died March 14, 1883 and buried at Highgate Cemetery in North London.

...

But with the development of industry, the proletariat not only increases in number; it becomes concentrated in greater masses, its strength grows, and it feels that strength more. The various interests and conditions of life within the ranks of the proletariat are more and more equalized, in proportion as machinery obliterates[4] all distinctions of labor, and nearly everywhere reduces wages to the same low level. The growing competition among the bourgeois, and the resulting commercial crises, make the wages of the workers ever more fluctuating. The increasing improvement of machinery, ever more rapidly developing, makes their livelihood more and more precarious[5]; the collisions between individual workmen and individual bourgeois take more and more the character of collisions between two classes. Thereupon, the workers begin to form combinations (trade unions) against the bourgeois; they club[6] together in order to keep up the rate of wages; they found permanent associations in order to make provision beforehand for these occasional revolts. Here and there, the contest breaks out into riots.

Now and then the workers are victorious, but only for a time. The real fruit of their battles lie not in the immediate result, but in the ever-expanding union of the workers. This union is helped on by the improved means of communication that are created by Modern Industry, and that place the workers of different localities in contact with one another. It was just this contact that was needed to centralize the numerous local struggles, all of the same character, into one national struggle between classes. But every class struggle is a political struggle. And that union, to attain which the burghers of the Middle Ages, with their miserable highways, required centuries, the modern proletarian, thanks to railways, achieve in a few years.[7]

---

1 **private:** private soldier

2 **overlooker:** supervisor

3 **despotism:** tyranny

4 **obliterate:** wipe out

5 **precarious:** uncertain

6 **club:** join together for a common purpose

7 **And that union ... advieve in a few years.:** Here means the efficiency of transportation (from highways to railways) greatly facilitates the modern solidarity of working class.

Heritage of Western Intellectual Tradition   A Sourcebook

This organization of the proletarians into a class, and, consequently, into a political party, is continually being upset again by the competition between the workers themselves. But it ever rises up again, stronger, firmer, mightier. It compels legislative recognition of particular interests of the workers, by taking advantage of the divisions among the bourgeoisie itself. Thus, the Ten-Hours Bill[1] in England was carried.

Altogether, collisions between the classes of the old society further in many ways the course of development of the proletariat. The bourgeoisie finds itself involved in a constant battle. At first with the aristocracy; later on, with those portions of the bourgeoisie itself, whose interests have become antagonistic to the progress of industry; at all time with the bourgeoisie of foreign countries. In all these battles, it sees itself compelled to appeal to the proletariat, to ask for help, and thus to drag it into the political arena[2]. **The bourgeoisie itself, therefore, supplies the proletariat with its own elements of political and general education, in other words, it furnishes the proletariat with weapons for fighting the bourgeoisie.**

Further, as we have already seen, entire sections of the ruling class are, by the advance of industry, precipitated[3] into the proletariat, or are at least threatened in their conditions of existence. These also supply the proletariat with fresh elements of enlightenment and progress.

Finally, in times when the class struggle nears the decisive hour, the progress of dissolution going on within the ruling class, in fact within the whole range of old society, assumes such a violent, glaring character, that a small section of the ruling class cuts itself adrift[4], and joins the revolutionary class, the class that holds the future in its hands. Just as, therefore, at an earlier period, a section of the nobility went over to the bourgeoisie, so now a portion of the bourgeoisie goes over to the proletariat, and in particular, a portion of the bourgeois ideologists, who have raised themselves to the level of comprehending theoretically the historical movement as a whole.

Of all the classes that stand face to face with the bourgeoisie today, the proletariat alone is a genuinely revolutionary class. The other classes decay and finally disappear in the face of Modern Industry; the proletariat is its special and essential product.

The lower middle class, the small manufacturer, the shopkeeper, the artisan, the peasant, all these fight against the bourgeoisie, to save from extinction their existence as fractions of the middle class. They are therefore not revolutionary, but conservative. Nay more, they are reactionary, for they try to roll back the wheel of history. If, by chance, they are revolutionary, they are only

---

1   **Ten-Hours Bill:** Lord Ashley introduced a Ten Hours bill in January 1846 which was eventually defeated after he had resigned his seat. After the fall of Sir Robert Peel's administration John Fielden took charge of a new bill in 1847 which passed with large majorities through both houses. From May 1848 the daily hours of work for women and young persons in mills and factories were restricted to ten (58 in the week).
2   **arena:** central stage for games or fights in a Roman amphitheatre
3   **precipitate:** throw violently into a condition
4   **adrift:** driven away by wind

so in view of their impending[1] transfer into the proletariat; they thus defend not their present, but their future interests; they desert their own standpoint to place themselves at that of the proletariat.

The "dangerous class", the social scum[2], that passively rotting mass thrown off by the lowest layers of the old society, may, here and there, be swept into the movement by a proletarian revolution; its conditions of life, however, prepare it far more for the part of a bribed tool of reactionary intrigue[3].

In the condition of the proletariat, those of old society at large are already virtually swamped. The proletarian is without property; his relation to his wife and children has no longer anything in common with the bourgeois family relations; modern industry labor, modern subjection to capital, the same in England as in France, in America as in Germany, has stripped him of every trace of national character. Law, morality, religion, are to him so many bourgeois prejudices, behind which lurk[4] in ambush just as many bourgeois interests.

All the preceding classes that got the upper hand sought to fortify[5] their already acquired status by subjecting society at large to their conditions of appropriation[6]. The proletarians cannot become masters of the productive forces of society, except by abolishing their own previous mode of appropriation, and thereby also every other previous mode of appropriation. They have nothing of their own to secure and to fortify; their mission is to destroy all previous securities for, and insurances of, individual property.

All previous historical movements were movements of minorities, or in the interest of minorities. The proletarian movement is the self-conscious, independent movement of the immense majority, in the interest of the immense majority. The proletariat, the lowest stratum of our present society, cannot stir, cannot raise itself up, without the whole superincumbent[7] strata of official society being sprung into the air.

Though not in substance, yet in form, the struggle of the proletariat with the bourgeoisie is at first a national struggle. The proletariat of each country must, of course, first of all settle matters with its own bourgeoisie.

In depicting the most general phases of the development of the proletariat, we traced the more or less veiled civil war, raging within existing society, up to the point where that war breaks out into open revolution, and where the violent overthrow of the bourgeoisie lays the foundation for the sway of the proletariat.

---

1 **impending:** about to happen
2 **scum:** froth, worthless part
3 **intrigue:** secret plotting
4 **behind which lurk:** behind which lurk … bourgeois interest; **lurk:** lie in wait, wait in hiding to attack
5 **fortify:** strengthen
6 **appropriation:** a delicate act of acquisition
7 **superincumbent:** lying or resting on and exerting pressure on something else

Heritage of Western Intellectual Tradition   A Sourcebook

Hitherto, every form of society has been based, as we have already seen, on the antagonism of oppressing and oppressed classes. But in order to oppress a class, certain conditions must be assured to it under which it can, at least, continue its slavish existence. The serf, in the period of serfdom, raised himself to membership in the commune, just as the petty bourgeois, under the yoke of the feudal absolutism, managed to develop into a bourgeois. The modern laborer, on the contrary, instead of rising with the process of industry, sinks deeper and deeper below the conditions of existence of his own class. He becomes a pauper[1], and pauperism develops more rapidly than population and wealth. And here it becomes evident that the bourgeoisie is unfit any longer to be the ruling class in society, and to impose its conditions of existence upon society as an overriding[2] law. It is unfit to rule because it is incompetent to assure an existence to its slave within his slavery, because it cannot help letting him sink into such a state, that it has to feed him, instead of being fed by him. Society can no longer live under this bourgeoisie, in other words, its existence is no longer compatible with society.

The essential conditions for the existence and for the sway of the bourgeois class is the formation and augmentation of capital; the condition for capital is wage labor. Wage labor rests exclusively on competition between the laborers. The advance of industry, whose involuntary promoter is the bourgeoisie, replaces the isolation of the laborers, due to competition, by the revolutionary combination, due to association. The development of Modern Industry, therefore, cuts from under its feet the very foundation on which the bourgeoisie produces and appropriates products. **What the bourgeoisie therefore produces, above all, are its own grave-diggers. Its fall and the victory of the proletariat are equally inevitable.**

Key Concepts

bourgeois/proletarians	money relation
class struggles/class antagonisms	paid wage labourers
collisions between classes	periodical return
commercial crises	productive forces
commodity	relations of production
division of labour	revolutionary reconstitution of society
epidemic of over-production	social conditions
exploitation	specter of communism
modes of production and of exchange	world market

---

1   **pauper:** person without any means of livelihood
2   **overriding:** more important than any other considerations

Eduard Bernstein: Evolutionary Socialism*

Eduard Bernstein (1850 – 1932), German Social Democratic leader, political theorist, and historian, was born in Berlin into a Jewish family, his father a railroad engineer and his uncle editor of the *Berliner Volks-Zeitung* (Berlin People's Newspaper), a working-class newspaper. Educated at Berlin University, he joined the Social Democratic Party in 1872, and from 1881 to 1890 he and the Social Democratic leader August Bebel jointly edited the newspaper *Sozialdemokrat* (Social Democrat). While living in exile in London from 1888 to 1901, Bernstein became acquainted with Friedrich Engels, and studied the theories developed by Marx and Engels dealing with the nature of capitalist society and the establishment of socialism. Rejecting the labour theory of value, economic determinism, and the significance of the class struggle, Bernstein argued that capitalism was not on the verge of collapse, capital not being amassed by fewer and fewer persons, the middle class not disappearing, and the working class not afflicted by "increasing misery." He no longer regarded the bourgeoisie as exclusively parasitic and oppressive. Citing such reforms as factory legislation, he pointed out that, under pressure from the socialist movement, a reaction had set in against the exploitive inclinations of capital. In 1902 Bernstein was elected a member of the *Reichstag*, or Parliament, to which he was reelected several times. He regarded the bloody outrages of the Nazis as thoughtless actions of unbalanced minds, but was powerless to prevent its seizure of power. Less than six weeks after his death, the democratic state on which he had set all his hopes was to give way to the dictatorship of Adolf Hitler.

Preface

It has been maintained in a certain quarter that the practical deductions[1] from my treatises would be the abandonment of the conquest of political power by the proletariat organised politically and economically. That is quite an arbitrary deduction, the accuracy of which I altogether deny.

I set myself against the notion that we have to expect shortly a collapse of the bourgeois economy, and that social democracy should be induced by the prospect of such an

---

* This is taken from a letter Bernstein wrote to the German Social Democratic Party assembled at Stuttgart from October 3rd to October 8th , 1898, which is included in the "Preface" to *Evolutionary Socialism* published in 1899.

1 **deduction:** process of making judgments

imminent[1], great, social catastrophe to adapt its tactics to that assumption. That I maintain most emphatically.

The adherents of this theory of a catastrophe base it especially on the conclusions of the *Communist Manifesto.* This is a mistake in every respect.

The theory which the *Communist Manifesto* sets forth of the evolution of modern society

was correct as far as it characterised the general tendencies of that evolution. But it was mistaken in several special deductions, above all in the estimate of the time the evolution would take.[2] The last has been unreservedly acknowledged by Friedrich Engels, the joint author with Marx of the *Manifesto,* in his preface to the *Class War in France.* But it is evident that if social evolution takes a much greater period of time than was

Socialists differed on how Marxism was to be interpreted. Karl Kautsky (left), Rosa Luxemburg (middle), and Eduard Bernstein (right) held divergent ideas.

assumed, it must also take upon itself forms and lead to forms that were not foreseen and could not be foreseen then.

Social conditions have not developed to such an acute opposition of things and classes as is depicted in the *Manifesto.* It is not only useless, it is the greatest folly to attempt to conceal this from ourselves. The number of members of the possessing classes is today not smaller but larger. The enormous increase of social wealth is not accompanied by a decreasing number of large capitalists but by an increasing number of capitalists of all degrees. The middle classes change their character but they do not disappear from the social scale.

The concentration in productive industry is not being accomplished even today in all its departments with equal thoroughness and at an equal rate. In a great many branches of production it certainly justifies the forecasts of the socialist critic of society; but in other branches it lags even today behind them. The process of concentration in agriculture proceeds still more slowly. Trade statistics show an extraordinarily elaborated graduation of enterprises in regard to size. No rung[3] of the ladder is disappearing from it. The significant changes in the inner structure of these enterprises and their interrelationship cannot do away with this fact.

In all advanced countries we see the privileges of the capitalist bourgeoisie yielding step by step to democratic organisations. Under the influence of this, and driven by the

---

1 **imminent:** impending, about to happen
2 **But it was mistaken … evolution would take.:** Note here Bernstein is appropriating the *Communist Manifesto* as the word "evolution" does not appear there.
3 **rung:** step of a ladder

movement of the working classes which is daily becoming stronger, a social reaction has set in against the exploiting tendencies of capital, a counteraction which, although it still proceeds timidly and feebly, yet does exist and is always drawing more departments of economic life under its influence. Factory legislation, the democratising of local government, and the extension of its area of work, the freeing of trade unions and systems of co-operative trading from legal restrictions, the consideration of standard conditions of labour in the work undertaken by public authorities — all these characterise this phase of the evolution.

But the more the political organisations of modern nations are democratised the more the needs and opportunities of great political catastrophes are diminished.[1] He who holds firmly to the catastrophic theory of evolution must, with all his power, withstand and hinder the evolution described above, which, indeed, the logical defenders of that theory[2] formerly did. **But is the conquest of political power by the proletariat simply to be by a political catastrophe? Is it to be the appropriation and utilisation of the power of the State by the proletariat exclusively against the whole non-proletarian world?**[3]

He who replies in the affirmative must be reminded of two things. In 1872 Marx and Engels announced in the preface to the new edition of the *Communist Manifesto* that the Paris Commune had exhibited a proof that "the working classes cannot simply take possession of the ready made State machine and set it in motion for their own aims." And in 1895 Friedrich Engels stated in detail in the preface to *War of the Classes* that the time of political surprises, of the "revolutions of small conscious minorities at the head of unconscious masses" was today at an end, that a collision on a large scale with the military would be the means of checking the steady growth of social democracy and of even throwing it back for a time — in short, that **social democracy would flourish far better by lawful than by unlawful means and by violent revolution**. And he points out in conformity with this opinion that **the next task of the party should be "to work for an uninterrupted increase of its votes"** or to carry on a slow *propaganda of parliamentary activity*.[4]

Thus Engels, who, nevertheless, as his numerical examples show, still somewhat overestimated the rate of process of the evolution! Shall we be told that he abandoned the conquest of political power by the working classes, because he wished to avoid the steady growth of social democracy

---

1 **But the more the political ... catastrophes are diminished.:** Namely, the more ... democratised, the more ... diminished.

2 **that theory:** theory of evolution

3 **Is it to be the appropriation ... non-proletarian world?:** Is it the appropriation and utilisation ... to be exclusively against ...?

4 **And in 1895 Friedrich Engels stated ...** *of parliamentary activity*.: Here, as elsewhere, Bernstein is appropriating Engels.

secured by lawful means being interrupted by a political revolution?

If not, and if one subscribes to his conclusions, one cannot reasonably take any offence if it is declared that for a long time yet the task of social democracy is, instead of speculating on a great economic crash, "to organise the working classes politically and develop them as a democracy and to fight for all reforms in the State which are adapted to raise the working classes and transform the State in the direction of democracy."

In short, Engels is so thoroughly convinced that the tactics based on the presumption of a catastrophe have had their day[1], that he even considers a revision of them necessary in the Latin countries[2] where tradition is much more favourable to them than in Germany. "If the conditions of war between nations have altered," he writes, "no less have those for the war between classes." Has this already been forgotten?

No one has questioned the necessity for the working classes to gain the control of government. The point at issue[3] is between the theory of a social cataclysm[4] and the question whether with the given social development in Germany and the present advanced state of its working classes in the towns and the country, a sudden catastrophe would be desirable in the interest of the social democracy. I have denied it and deny it again, because in my judgment a greater security for lasting success lies in a steady advance than in the possibilities offered by a catastrophic crash.

B. E. Laermans: Evening of Strike: The Red Flag. 1893, oil painting

And as I am firmly convinced that important periods in the development of nations cannot be leapt over **I lay the greatest value on the next tasks of social democracy, on the struggle for the political rights of the working man, on the political activity of working men in town and country for the interests of their class, as well as on the work of the industrial organisation of the workers.**

In this sense I wrote the sentence that the movement means everything for me and that what is *usually* called "the final aim of socialism" is nothing; and in this sense I write down again today. Even if the word "usually" had not shown that the proposition was only to be understood conditionally, it was obvious that it could not express indifference concerning the final carrying out of socialist principles, but only indifference — or, as it would be better expressed, careless-

---

1   **have had their day:** become dated, useless
2   **Latin countries:** nations and areas that speak a Romance language and have a culture based on the Roman culture, a civilization part of Latin Civilization
3   **at issue:** in consideration or under discussion
4   **cataclysm:** sudden and violent change

ness — as to the form of the final arrangement of things. I have at no time had an excessive interest in the future beyond general principles; I have not been able to read to the end any picture of the future[1]. My thoughts and efforts are concerned with the duties of the present and the nearest future, and I only busy myself with the perspectives beyond so far as they give me a line of conduct for suitable action now.

The conquest of political power by the working classes, the expropriation[2] of capitalists, are no ends themselves but only means for the accomplishment of certain aims and endeavours. As such they are demands in the programme of social democracy and are not attacked by me. Nothing can be said beforehand as to the circumstances of their accomplishment; we can only fight for their realisation. But the conquest of political power necessitates the possession of political *rights;* and the most important problem of tactics which German social democracy has at the present time to solve appears to me to be to devise the best ways for the extension of the political and economic rights of the German working classes.

Key Concepts

acute opposition	possessing class
capitalist bourgeoisie	social cataclysm
Communist Manifesto	social democracy
conquest of political power	social/political catastrophe
democratising of local government	slow *propaganda of parliamentary activity*
factory legislation	standard conditions of labour
middle class	trade union
political and economic right	

Compare with China

1. Karl Marx on China[3]

Already in the *Communist Manifesto* the significance of the East Indian and Chinese mar-

---

1 **read ... picture of the future:** predict
2 **expropriation:** dispossession, taking away property
3 **David Riazanov (1870–1938),** Russian Marxist scholar, founder of the Institute of Marxism-Leninism in Moscow, whose reputation rests mainly on his being the editor of the Marx-Engels Works. This summary of Marx's view of China represents, actually, how the revolutionary Chinese intellectuals viewed their own country at the time.

Heritage of Western Intellectual Tradition   A Sourcebook

ket is pointed out as a factor in the development of European capitalism. It was, indeed, from East India that British capitalism began its offensive against China. The East India Company used its trade monopoly with China to make the latter a market for the sale of Indian opium. Since, however, all English traders were equally interested in the intoxication[1] of the Chinese people, the monopoly was removed in 1833. The attempt of the Chinese Government in 1839 to forbid the import of opium produced the so-called opium war against China, which Marx characterises in *Capital* as one of the chief links in the long chain of trade wars in which since the sixteenth century, even in the East, the European nations were engaged. After the English had cruelly destroyed a whole series of Chinese towns and had slaughtered thousands of Chinese for the honour of Christianity and European civilisation, they forced on China in 1842 the treaty of Nanking, which provided for the opening of the five Treaty Ports — Kanton, Amoy, Ningpo, Shanghai and Foochow, the payment of what was at that time an enormous indemnity[2], and the surrender of the island of Hong Kong, which forms the chief base for British Imperialism in the Far East. Following the treaty of Nanking came treaties with the United States and with France.

The defeat in battle with the Europeans was a hard blow for the prestige of the Manchu dynasty which had been supreme in China since the seventeenth century. Among the peasant masses, groaning under the burden of taxation and the pressure of the bureaucracy, and who reacted at times to their subjection by sporadic[3] revolts, there now began to ripen a ferment of dissatisfaction which was especially strong in the South East where the destructive influence of foreign capital most made itself felt[4]. To this was added the fermentation among the Chinese "intelligentsia[5]" of that time, the teachers and the lower officials, as well as among the craftsmen ruined by foreign competition.

Just at the time when in West Europe the waves of the 1848 revolution reached their height, the activity of the secret societies in China also became stronger and propaganda for new religious sects developed among the peasants. The European missionaries against their will played the part of hens with a brood[6] of ducklings[7]. They remarked with terror that the drawing-room Christianity preached by them had taken root among the rebellious peasantry in the only militant form of Christianity, which demands equality in this world. Europe learnt of this for the first time through

---

1 **intoxication:** loss of self-control because of poisoning
2 **indemnity:** compensation for the loss in war
3 **sporadic:** occasional
4 **most made itself felt:** was severest
5 **intelligentsia:** collectively, intellectuals
6 **brood:** all the young birds in the nest
7 **duckling:** young duck

the well-known German missionary and sinologist[1], Gutzlaff[2], who also was the first to make a Chinese translation of the Bible.

In the same international review (January, 1850) in which Marx investigated the influence of the discovery of the Californian gold mines on the development of the world market, and in which he prophesied for the Pacific Ocean the same role that the Mediterranean had once played in the ancient world, and which had then passed to the Atlantic Ocean, Marx also refers to the interesting communications of Gutzlaff. He wrote:

Taiping soldiers fighting Qing troops

"The slow but regularly increasing over-population of the country long ago made the social relations there very oppressive for the great majority of the nation. Then came the English and enforced free trade for themselves in the five ports. Thousands of British and American vessels sailed towards China, and in a short time the country was filled to excess[3] with cheap British and American factory wares. The Chinese industry based on hand labour was subjected to the competition of the machines. The hitherto unshakeable Central Empire experienced a social crisis. Taxes ceased to come in, the State fell to the edge of bankruptcy, the population sank in masses into pauperism, broke out in revolts, maltreated[4] and killed the Emperor's mandarins[5] and the priests of the Fohis. The country came to the verge of ruin, and is already threatened with a mighty revolution. And there is even worse. Among the masses and in the insurrection[6] there appeared people who pointed to the poverty on the one side and the riches on the other, and who demanded, and are still demanding, a different division of property and even the entire abolition of private property. When Mr. Gutzlaff, after twenty years' absence, returned once more to civilised people and Europeans, he heard talk of Socialism, and asked what that was. When it was explained to him he exclaimed in consternation[7], 'Shall I then never escape this pernicious[8] doctrine? The very same thing has been preached for some time by

---

1 **sinologist:** expert on China

2 **Karl Friedrich August Gützlaff, anglicized as Charles Gutzlaff (1803–1851):** German missionary, the Netherlands Missionary Society sent him to Java in 1826, where he learned Chinese. In 1834 he published *Journal of Three Voyages along the Coast of China in 1831, 1832 and 1833*. In Hong Kong, he worked on a Chinese translation of the Bible, published a Chinese-language magazine, and wrote Chinese-language books on practical subjects.

3 **to excess:** much more than is needed

4 **maltreat:** treat cruelly

5 **mandarin:** high Chinese government official

6 **insurrection:** uprising, revolt

7 **consternation:** surprise, dismay

8 **pernicious:** vicious, wicked

many people among the mobs in China.'"

"Chinese Socialism," continues Marx, "bears much the same relation to European Socialism as Chinese philosophy does to Hegelian philosophy. It is, in any case, an intriguing[1] fact that the oldest and the most unshakable empire in the world has in eight years by the cannon-balls of the English bourgeoisie been brought to the eve of a social revolution which will certainly have the most important results for civilisation. When our European reactionaries in their immediately coming flight across Asia finally come up against the Great Wall of China, who knows whether they will not find on the gates which lead to the home of ancient reaction and ancient conservatism the inscription[2], 'Chinese Republic — liberty, equality, fraternity'." (*Literary Remains*, vol.3, pages 444–5)

The movement on which the good missionary Gutzlaff, the apostle of China, as the Germans called him, gave information to the Europeans was the forerunner of the great Taiping rebellion. The leader of this movement, Hung, had become acquainted with Christianity through the Gutzlaff translations of the old and new Testaments. As early as 1851 he became the leader of the revolting peasants. The Taipings took one town after another. Finally, in March, 1853, even Nanking was taken, which for a long time remained the capital of the celestial empire founded by Hung. At that time it appeared as if the Taipings within a few months would also take possession of Peking. The entry into Nanking, however, remained the highest point in the rebellion.

It was at this period that there was written the article of Marx which appeared in the *New York Tribune* on June 14, 1853. At that time reaction was triumphant in Europe. The Communist League was in dissolution, the Mailand [Milan] revolt (February 1853) which was organised by Mazzini[3] and his followers ended in defeat. Marx had greeted it as the symptom of an approaching revolutionary crisis. With even greater fervour, therefore, he greeted the beginning of the revolutionary movement in the Far East. The contrast between petrified[4] Europe and the movement in China, where movement had so long been absent, forcibly impressed itself. Civilised Europe, where thrones and altars had been stormed, was now diligently occupied with table turning[5], a fashion of American origin. "One is reminded of the fact," wrote Marx later in *Capital*, referring to these events, "that China and the tables began to dance when all the remaining world appeared to be standing still — *pour encourager les autres*[6]."

---

1 **intriguing:** capable of arousing interest or curiosity
2 **whether they will not find ... the inscription:** whether they will not find ... the inscription
3 **Giuseppe Mazzini (1805–1872):** Italian patriot who spurred the movement for an independent, unified Italy with his political writings and machinations, conducted mostly from exile in London
4 **petrified:** horrified, scared
5 **table turning:** change/revert the situation
6 *pour encourager les autres*: to encourage the others

The State founded by Hung or Tjan-Wang[1] was of a purely theocratic[2] character. After the Taipings and their leaders had renounced all hope of the conquest of Northern China, they sought to assure themselves of the South-East, utilising for this purpose the antagonism between the Manchus and the English. When in 1856 a new Chinese war broke out with England, and later also with France, the Taipings allowed themselves to be taken in tow[3] by the British Imperialists. While they owed their first victories precisely to the circumstance that they had risen against the yoke of the strangers, against the Manchus, they now — in order to save their theocratic state – made common cause with the much more revengeful and treacherous foreigners. Thus the Taiping movement which in the beginning had borne a revolutionary character, became a reactionary movement which lost the sympathy of the peasant masses. After the English, in union with the Taipings, had subdued Northern China, they helped Peking to drown in blood the Taiping insurrection.

Marx followed attentively the further development of these events in China and not only stigmatised[4], in a series of articles in the *New York Tribune* during 1857–1859, all the crimes of the "civilised seafarers," but also subjected to a new analysis the statistics of Anglo-Chinese trade. Although Marx in the article mentioned begins with the fact of the rapid destruction of the "Asiatic mode of production" under the influence of the penetration of English capitalism, and although he still hoped that the imminent European revolution would find the requisite support in the awakened East, nevertheless he comes to the conclusion that he had at first over-estimated the extent and tempo[5] of the destructive influences of English capitalism.

"The real task of bourgeois society," wrote Marx in 1858 in a letter to Engels, "is the creation, at least in outline, of a world market, and of a type of production resting on this basis. Since the world is round, this task seems to have been brought to a conclusion with the colonisation of California and Australia and the inclusion of China and Japan. The difficult question for us is as follows. Revolution is imminent on the Continent and will at once assume a Socialist character. But will it not necessarily be crushed in this little corner, since over a much greater territory the movement of bourgeois society is still in the ascendant[6]? As far as China is especially concerned, I have assured myself by a close analysis of the movement of trade since 1836, firstly that the soaring of English and American exports in 1844–1846 revealed itself in 1847 as a sheer delusion, and that also in the ten years following the average has remained practically stationary while

---

1 **Tjan-Wang:** 天王
2 **theocratic:** governed by priests
3 **in tow:** tied together
4 **stigmatise:** describe scornfully
5 **tempo:** speed
6 **in the ascendant:** rising in power and influence

Chinese exports to England and America increased enormously, and secondly that the opening of the five ports and the occupation of Hongkong only resulted in the trade of Canton passing to Shanghai. The other 'emporiums[1]' do not count. The chief cause of the failure of this market seems to be the opium trade, to which in fact all increase in the export trade to China is continually limited; and, after that, the internal organisation of the country, its minute agriculture, & c., which will cost an enormous time to break down." (*Correspondence of Marx and Engels*, vol. 2, pages 292–3.)

When Marx in 1862 renewed his writing on the Taiping movement (*Press*, July 7, 1862) he was already much more condemnatory[2]. As already mentioned, this movement was in a stage of complete dissolution. Marx says:

"A little while before the tables began to turn, China, this living fossil, began to become revolutionary. In itself there was nothing extraordinary in this phenomenon, for Oriental empires continually exhibit an immutability in social sub-structure with restless permutations of the persons and races who have possessed themselves of the political super-structure. China is ruled by a foreign dynasty. After three hundred years why should not a movement develop for the overthrow of this dynasty? The movement had from the beginning a religious complexion, but that was a feature it had in common with all Oriental movements. The immediate motives for the appearance of the movement were obvious — European interference, opium wars, and consequent disruption of the existing Government, the flow of silver out of the country, disturbance of the economic equilibrium[3] through the introduction of foreign manufactures, & c. What seemed to me a paradox was that the opium animated[4] instead of stupefying[5]. As a matter of fact the only original part of this revolution was its leaders. They are conscious of their task, quite apart from the change of dynasty. They have no slogans. They represent a still greater torment for the masses of the people than for the old rulers. Their motive seems to be nothing else than to bring into play against the conservative marasmus[6] grotesquely repulsive forms of destruction, destruction without any germ of regeneration."

In many respects, indeed, the Taiping insurrection was reminiscent of the European peasant wars, if only in as much as the participation in it of the town proletariat was equally non-existent.

In regard to India, also, as in regard to China, Marx was compelled to come to the conclusion

---

1   **emporium:** center of commerce
2   **condemnatory:** critical, blaming
3   **equilibrium:** balance
4   **animate:** give life to
5   **stupefy:** make dull or stupid or muddle with drunkenness or infatuation
6   **marasmus:** extreme malnutrition and emaciation, weakness

that the tempo of development, measured in terms of world history, took place at a much slower rate from the point of view of the individual than might have been anticipated. In the third volume of *Capital* he wrote:

"The obstacle presented by the internal solidity and articulation of pre-capitalistic national modes of production to the corrosive[1] influence of commerce is strikingly shown in the intercourse of the English with India and China. The broad basis of the mode of production is here formed by the unity of small agriculture and domestic industry, to which is added in India the form of communes resting upon common ownerships of the land, which, by the way, was likewise the original form in China. In India, the English created simultaneously their direct political and economic power as rulers and landlords, for the purpose of disrupting these small economic organisations. The English commerce exerts a revolutionary influence on these organisations and tears them apart only to the extent that it destroys by the low prices of its goods the spinning and weaving industries, which are an archaic and integral part of this unity. And even so this work of dissolution is proceeding very slowly. It proceeds still more slowly in China where it is not backed up by any direct political power on the part of the English." (*Capital*, vol.iii, English translation, C. H. Kerr & Co., pages 392–3.)

The power of resistance of the "Asiatic mode of production" proved itself so great that several decades passed before European capitalism succeeded in shattering this "Great Wall of China." To the assistance of the economic factor, the low prices of industrial goods, came the political factor, a new series of wars, in which the youthful Japanese imperialism played no small part. The indivisible union of agriculture and industry, the main secret of the immobility of the "Asiatic mode of production," was burst asunder. The Chinese peasantry separated from itself great masses of "coolies," and fell ever deeper into dissolution. Emigration, which for a period had acted as a safety valve[2], soon proved itself powerless in the struggle with the "plague spot of the proletariat."

Attracted by cheap labour power in China, Japanese and British capitalists began to bring into existence a "national" big industry. In effect they produced an organised and disciplined industrial proletariat, which is now preparing to assume the leadership of all the exploited poor, rural as well as urban.

The question which Marx formulated sixty years ago has been given a positive answer by history. No danger threatens the European revolution from the East. There, also, capitalism is finding its grave-diggers. And even if ancient Europe still has the appearance of stability, "immobile" China on the other hand, following the example of Soviet Russia, is already dancing the

---

1 **corrosive:** worn away
2 **safety valve:** 安全阀

Heritage of Western Intellectual Tradition   A Sourcebook

revolutionary Carmagnole[1]— *Ca ira, Ca ira*! (Excerpt from David Riazanov, 1926)

2.《共产党宣言》在中国的早期翻译、出版和传播

从 1899 年《共产党宣言》的片段文字传入中国到 1920 年 8 月陈望道翻译的《共产党宣言》完整译本出版，可视为该书的最初传入阶段。

1899 年 2 月到 4 月，上海广学会主办的《万国公报》连续刊载了由李提摩太[2]节译、蔡尔康撰文题为《大同学》的文章，在汉文刊物中首次提到了 "马克思"、"安民新学"（即 "社会主义" socialism）及《共产党宣言》的一段文字："马克思之言曰：'纠股办事之人，其权笼罩五洲，突过于君相之范围一国'"，援引的就是《共产党宣言》中的一段话，现在的译文是："资产阶级，由于开拓了世界市场，使一切国家的生产和消费都成为世界性的了。"

李提摩太系英国威尔士人，1870 年来中国传教，在中国度过 45 年，曾任天津《时报》主笔。1877 年，上海成立基督教在华第一个文化机构 "广学会"，1891 年李提摩太任广学会总干事，直到 1916 年回国。在他的策动下，广学会出版了许多传播西方文化的书籍、刊物，对当时先进人士影响颇大。1895 年，康有为与他通信，讨论社会改革问题。李氏还聘用梁启超为中文秘书。光绪皇帝曾购买西学书籍 129 种，其中的 89 种由广学会出版。孙中山早年也与李提摩太有过交往。由此可见，李提摩太在传教的同时，将流行于欧美的社会改良主义和各种流派的社会主义学说传到中国，以迎合当时的改良运动。

孙中山 1896 年伦敦蒙难[3]之后在英国留居近一年，其间常到大英博物馆研究欧洲社会主义运动。正是在这里，他第一次知道了马克思和恩格斯的名字及其活动情况，第一次读到了《共产党宣言》、《资本论》等马克思主义著作，对他形成三民主义思想影响深远。

1904 年 10 月，《共产党宣言》一书在日本由英文译成日文。1905 年 8 月，孙中山从欧洲回来后，在东京建立中国同盟会；同年 11 月，同盟会机关报《民报》创刊。当时在日本留学的同盟会成员朱执信撰写了《德意志社会革命家小传》一文，署名蛰伸，发表于 1905 年 11 月 26 日的《民报》第 2 号上，第一次扼要介绍了《共产党宣言》的写作背景、基本思想和历史意义，还依据《共产党宣言》的日文本并参照英文本摘译了该书的五段文字和第二章的十大纲领全文。作者将该书的书名译为《共产主义宣言》。

随着 1917 年俄国十月革命的胜利，《共产党宣言》在中国的翻译、研究和传播进入一个

---

1 **Carmagnole:** a song and dance of unknown authorship popular during the "Reign of Terror" which took place during the French Revolution. It criticized the King and Queen of the time, Louis XVI of France and Marie Antoinette.

2 **李提摩太 (Timothy Richard, 1845–1919):** 英国浸礼会传教士，在山东、山西、上海等地传教达 20 余年，是有名的中国通，曾代表英方接受山西 "庚子赔款" 白银 50 万两，主持翻译过一些书籍，对中国社会的影响很大。

3 1896 年 9 月 30 日，孙中山由纽约乘船抵达利物浦，10 月 1 日到伦敦，与他的老师康德黎晤面，后被清朝侦探跟踪，将他挟持至清朝驻伦敦使馆软禁起来。康德黎发动舆论力量，将他拯救出来。这就是有名的 "伦敦蒙难记"。孙中山伦敦蒙难获国际关注，成为国际公认的中国革命领导者。

新阶段。最早介绍《共产党宣言》并成为马克思主义者的是李大钊。1918 年 12 月，李大钊

和陈独秀一起创办《每周评论》，1919 年 4 月 6 日《每周评论》第 16 号发表了《共产党宣言》第二章的最后几段文字，包括十大纲领全文，标题是《共产党宣言》，译者是成舍我（署名舍）。译文和按语都采用白话文，译文更为准确，如按语说："这个宣言是马克思和恩格斯最先最大的意见……其要者是主张阶级战争，要求各地劳动的联合，则表示新时代的文书。"

1936 年 10 月，陶行知去英国伦敦出席世界反侵略大会，凭吊马克思墓后留影，并留诗一首："光明照万世，宏论醒天下。二四七四八（马克思墓号），小坟葬伟大。"

1919 年 5 月 5 日至 8 日，由李大钊主编的北京《晨报》副刊连载日本河上肇著、渊泉译的《马克思的唯物史观》一文，《新青年》同时于第 6 卷第 5 号转载。文章摘译了《共产党宣言》第一章，首句被译为"一个妖怪，徘徊欧洲——共产主义的妖怪"。

1919 年 11 月，北京《国民》杂志第 2 卷第 1 号刊载了北京大学经济系学生李泽彰从英文译出的《共产党宣言》第一章的全文，译名是《马克斯和昂格斯共产党宣言》。据许德珩回忆，译者已将《宣言》全文译出，准备分期发表，但在第一章发表后，因受胡适威胁和利诱，译者取回译稿，《国民》杂志未再刊载。

《共产党宣言》1899 年初在中国的报刊上被首次提到，1920 年第一个完整的中译本出版，历经 20 多年。在此期间，有两次传播高潮，即辛亥革命前和五四运动后。此时中国新纪元曙光已现，《共产党宣言》的完整中文译本也应运而生。

陈望道，浙江义乌人，早年曾留学日本早稻田大学，结识日本早期社会主义者河上肇、山川均等人并阅读他们翻译的马克思主义著作，1919 年 6 月应五四运动感召回国。途经杭州时受浙江第一师范校长聘请，陈望道任该校语文教员，浙一师是当时浙江省最高学府，鲁迅、沈均儒、李叔同、俞平伯、叶圣陶、朱自清等人先后在此任教。陈望道与几个青年教师发起国文教育改革，提倡白话文和教学内容的思想性、艺术性，遭省教育厅诽谤和迫害，校长也被撤换，师生抗议，招军警包围，酿闻名全国的"一师风潮"流血事件。之后陈望道回到家乡，在义乌县分水塘村的一间小柴屋内，干了一件惊天动地的大事，这就是翻译了影响 20 世纪中国命运的《共产党宣言》。

陈望道那时翻译《共产党宣言》是应上海《星期评论》杂志的约稿，所依据的日文本和英文本《共产党宣言》分别由《星期评论》编辑戴季陶和《新青年》主编陈独秀提供。

1920 年 3—4 月份，陈望道将《共产党宣言》译完，即携译稿到上海，准备在《星期评论》刊载。但他抵沪第二日该刊便停刊了。此时《新青年》编辑部也适到上海不久，应陈独秀之邀，陈望道参加了《新青年》编辑工作。当时的"马克思主义研究会"（内部也叫共产党，陈独秀是书记）对陈望道译出的《共产党宣言》很重视，想出版，又无经费。恰在这时，共产国际代表维经斯基和杨明斋经李大钊介绍来上海与陈独秀联系并商谈中国建党问题。维经斯基知道后非常重视，便资助研究会（即后来的上海共产主义小组）在上海拉斐德路（今复

兴中路)成裕里 12 号建起了名叫"又新"的小印刷所。不久,《共产党宣言》的第一个中文全译本就在这里问世了,时间是 1920 年 8 月。(改写自杨金海,胡永钦)

Supplementary Reading

1. Study Guide for *The Communist Manifesto*

The following is a helpmate for the reading of *The Communist Manifesto*, in the form of questions leading, hopefully, to a better understanding of this important document.

The Communist Manifesto, first published in 1848 for the Communist League, had little influence in its own day. Only after Karl Marx and Friedrich Engels' other writings had made their views on socialism widely known did it become a standard text. For about a century it was one of the most widely read documents in the world.

The manifesto is meant to achieve two major goals: to convert the proletarians and their allies to Marx's version of socialism and to put the ruling class on notice as to the revolutionaries' intentions. So it expresses both hopes and warnings.

1. The opening words of the *Manifesto* are famous. Marx taunts[1] his adversaries, saying they are terrified of communism without understanding in the slightest what it is. Since communism is such a threat, it must be important, and worth understanding. Hence the *Manifesto*.

2. Marx felt that the revolutions of 1848 marked a major turning point, as is now undisputed. He sets out to trace the patterns which have run through all of preceding history. Unsurprisingly, he considers exclusively European societies, beginning with the classical world. He explains how the bourgeoisie (literally dwellers in towns) originated out of the old medieval peasant class, in opposition to the medieval titled aristocracy (kings, dukes, knights, etc.).

3. These people derived their wealth from trade rather than agriculture. Why was the age of exploration and colonization important to them? What caused the old guild system to collapse? What have the major effects of the ensuing industrial revolution been? What are the major achievements caused by the extension (expansion) of industry? As the bourgeoisie grew in power, what happened to the other old feudal classes like the aristocracy and the peasants? Did the bourgeoisie create capitalism or did capitalism create the bourgeoisie, according to Marx?

1　**taunt:** criticize, attack

Heritage of Western Intellectual Tradition　A Sourcebook

4. What does this famous phrase mean: "The executive of the modern state is but a committee for managing the common affairs of the whole bourgeoisie?" Note that he praises the bourgeoisie for having abolished the feudal system and prepared the way for socialism; but he does so ironically. How has capitalism's emergence changed "human nature?" "Exchange value" is a typical Marxist term which does not exactly mean "price," but in this context that is close enough. What does he say is the limit of bourgeois freedom? Can you think of examples to illustrate his point about the reduction of "the family relation to a mere money relation"? Keep in mind that he is speaking here mainly of the effects of capitalism on workers, not on the bourgeoisie.

5. To what cause does he attribute the bourgeoisie's energy in creating railways, factories, etc.? Why do owners need constantly to create new ways of manufacturing and processing goods? How does competition drive this process? Can you think of modern examples, or counter-examples? How does the very essence of bourgeois production (capitalism, used interchangeably with "bourgeois society" below) make it by definition a revolutionary force? Why does capitalism have to spread worldwide? What tendencies

Midday meal in factory in 1856

undermine the independence of nation-states? What forces generate expanded markets for capitalism? Can you think of examples of "new wants being created"?

6. What effects does he say international trade has on "intellectual production" such as literature, philosophy, music, etc.? Is literature more or less international now than in the Middle Ages? Has nationalism been weakened as a force in the last hundred years, as Marx expected? Why or why not? He argues that all societies tend to become civilized (drawn into the social patterns of European civilization). To what extent is this true? What is the process by which he says the bourgeois society creates a world after its own image? How has capitalism altered the relationship between cities and the countryside? Has that process continued since Marx's time? What does he mean by the "idiocy of rural life?" Farmers a hundred years ago were considered much less sophisticated than city dwellers. Is that still true? What analogy is he drawing between the city/country relationship and the "civilized"/"barbarian" relationship? How has capitalism tended to create large countries with uniform laws?

7. What have been the main creations of capitalism during the preceding 100 years? Having described how the emergence of capitalism from mercantilism destroyed the old feudal system, Marx proclaims that a similar transformation is now taking place. How has capitalism created forces which work against its continued existence? A "commercial crisis" would more likely be called a depression or recession today. What pattern does he feel there is in these crises?

8. Why does capitalism tend to over-produce goods, unlike any previous form of economy? How does an over-abundance of goods produce an apparent "famine" (depression)? Is it possible

to produce too much? How do economists today relate manufacturers' inventories[1] to the health of the economy? How could such over-production be prevented? What are some of the irrational contradictions that he sees in capitalism? What three methods does the bourgeoisie use to solve such a crisis? Why do these methods not really solve the ultimate problem? How have the bourgeoisie created the force which will destroy them? Why are laborers forced to sell their services for the lowest possible wages? In fact, in the century after the writing of the *Manifesto* the wages of workers tended generally to rise (though with many fluctuations and crises), until most workers under capitalism were much too prosperous to be enemies of the system which produced their wages. What forces do you think caused this result, contradicting Marx's expectation?

9. Besides low wages, what other evils does Marx trace to modern industrialism? How could these evils be avoided? To what extent is hard work not rewarded with more wealth? How is work made harder? Why has industrialism resulted in the entry into the workplace of more and more women and children? What effects does Marx thinks this has had on society?

10. What happens to the "lower strata of the middle class" (what Marx elsewhere calls the "petit" [small] or "petty" bourgeoisie)? What are the major stages in the class struggle as the proletariat develops? As the struggle is becoming sharpened, what forces continually strengthen the proletariat?

11. What unstable forces inherent in capitalism cause the workers to seek organizations which will help them stabilize their wages? Since most strikes and riots are failures, what is the "real fruit" of these struggles? Why can modern workers organize so much more easily than their medieval predecessors? What is the next step after the proletarians have become conscious of themselves as a class rather than as isolated individuals, and become organized?

12. How does the need of the bourgeoisie to seek allies among the proletariat help to strengthen the latter? Which of these two classes — bourgeoisie and proletariat — tends to grow the most? When Marx says that "a small section of the ruling class cuts itself adrift, and joins the revolutionary class" he is thinking primarily of intellectuals like himself and Engels, who allied themselves with the workers despite their bourgeois background. The relationship of such idealistic Marxists to working class movements has been a troubled one. What problems might these two groups have in relating to one another? Why does he call peasants reactionaries? Was Marx right? Can you think of an important modern Communist revolution which was created primarily among and for peasants?

13. To what extent has modern capitalism stripped workers of their national character? Are proletarians less nationalistic than the bourgeoisie? Why does he believe that proletarians will be motivated to destroy the whole system of individual private property? What fact makes the proletarian movement different from all previous movements? Does Marx believe that the struggle of the proletariat with the bourgeoisie can be carried out internationally, all at once? What might be

---

1 **inventory:** stock of goods

the weaknesses of carrying it out country by country? (Adapted from http://www.wsu.edu/~brians/hum_303/manifesto.html)

2. V. I. Lenin: Marxism and Revisionism[1]

There is a well-known saying that if geometrical axioms[2] affected human interests attempts would certainly be made to refute them. Theories of natural history which conflicted with the old prejudices of theology provoked, and still provoke, the most rabid[3] opposition.

No wonder, therefore, that the Marxian doctrine, which directly serves to enlighten and organise the advanced class in modern society, indicates the tasks facing this class and demonstrates the inevitable replacement (by virtue of economic development) of the present system by a new order — no wonder that this doctrine has had to fight for every step forward in the course of its life.

Needless to say, this applies to bourgeois science and philosophy, officially taught by official professors in order to befuddle[4] the rising generation of the propertied classes and to "coach" it against internal and foreign enemies. This science will not even hear of Marxism, declaring that it has been refuted and annihilated. Marx is attacked with equal zest by young scholars who are making a career by refuting socialism, and by decrepit[5] elders who are preserving the tradition of all kinds of outworn "systems." The progress of Marxism, the fact that its ideas are spreading and taking firm hold among the working class, inevitably increase the frequency and intensity of these bourgeois attacks on Marxism, which becomes stronger, more hardened and more vigorous every time it is "annihilated" by official science.

But even among doctrines connected with the struggle of the working class, and current mainly among the proletariat, Marxism by no means consolidated its position all at once. In the first half-century of its existence (from the 1840s on) Marxism was engaged in combating theories fundamentally hostile to it. In the early forties Marx and Engels settled accounts with[6] the radical Young Hegelians whose viewpoint was that of philosophical idealism. At the end of the forties the struggle began in the field of economic doctrine, against Proudhonism[7]. The fifties saw

---

1 This article was written no later than April 3, 1908.

2 **axiom:** a rule or principle that is generally considered to be true

3 **rabid:** mad

4 **befuddle:** confuse; perplex, stupefy

5 **decrepit:** weak by old age

6 **settle accounts with:** criticize

7 **Pierre Joseph Proudhon (1809 – 1865):** French anarchist who believed that human moral development would ultimately eliminate the need for laws and government

the completion of this struggle in criticism of the parties and doctrines which manifested themselves in the stormy year of 1848. In the sixties the struggle shifted from the field of general theory to one closer to the direct labour movement: the ejection[1] of Bakuninism[2] from the International. In the early seventies the stage in Germany was occupied for a short while by the Proudhonist Muhlberger, and in the late seventies by the positivist Dühring[3]. But the influence of both on the proletariat was already absolutely insignificant. Marxism was already gaining an unquestionable victory over all other ideologies in the labour movement.

By the nineties this victory was in the main completed. Even in the Latin countries, where the traditions of Proudhonism held their ground longest of all, the workers' parties in effect built their programmes and their tactics on Marxist foundations. The revived international organisation of the labour movement — in the shape of periodical international congresses — from the outset, and almost without a struggle, adopted the Marxist standpoint in all essentials. But after Marxism had ousted all the more or less integral[4] doctrines hostile to it, the tendencies expressed in those doctrines began to seek other channels. The forms and causes of the struggle changed, but the struggle continued. And the second half-century of the existence of Marxism began (in the nineties) with the struggle of a trend hostile to Marxism within Marxism itself.

Lenin speaking to a crowd

Bernstein, a one-time orthodox Marxist, gave his name to this trend by coming forward with the most noise and with the most purposeful expression of amendments to Marx, revision of Marx, revisionism[5]. Even in Russia where — owing to the economic backwardness of the country and the preponderance[6] of a peasant population weighed down[7] by the relics of serfdom — non-Marxist socialism has naturally held its ground longest of all, it is plainly passing into revisionism before our very eyes. Both in the agrarian[8] question (the programme of the municipalisation[9] of all

---

1   **ejection:** expeling, forcing to leave
2   **Mikhail Aleksandrovich Bakunin (1814 – 1876):** Russian anarchist and political theorist, imprisoned and later exiled to Siberia for his revolutionary activities, escaped to London (1861), where he opposed Karl Marx with his theories of anarchy.
3   **Eugen Karl Dühring (1833 – 1921):** philosopher and economist, and supporter of capitalism. He was once lecturer in Berlin, but lost his position at the university as a result of a conflict with the authorities.
4   **integral:** complete, systematic by its own
5   **revisionism:** Here it refers to the revisionism proposed by Eduard Bernstein who sought to *revise* the teachings of Karl Marx by claiming that a violent revolution was not necessary to achieve socialism. The later "guilt by association" comes from this initial intent of Bernstein in opposing violent revolution.
6   **preponderance:** majority
7   **weigh down:** bring down by heavy weight, make troubled, tired
8   **agrarian:** of land
9   **municipalisation:** the transfer of corporations or other assets from private ownership to municipal ownership (usually by purchase)

land) and in general questions of programme and tactics, our Social-Narodniks[1] are more and more substituting "amendments" to Marx for the moribund[2] and obsolescent[3] remnants of their old system, which in its own way was integral and fundamentally hostile to Marxism.

Pre-Marxist socialism has been defeated. It is continuing the struggle, no longer on its own independent ground, but on the general ground of Marxism, as revisionism. Let us, then, examine the ideological content of revisionism.

...

In the sphere of politics, revisionism did really try to revise the foundation of Marxism, namely, the doctrine of the class struggle. Political freedom, democracy and universal suffrage remove the ground for the class struggle — we were told — and render untrue the old proposition of the *Communist Manifesto* that the working men have no country. For, they said, since the "will of the majority" prevails in a democracy, one must neither regard the state as an organ of class rule, nor reject alliances with the progressive, social-reform bourgeoisie against the reactionaries.

It cannot be disputed that these arguments of the revisionists amounted to a fairly well-balanced system of views, namely, the old and well-known liberal-bourgeois views.

Last Paris Commune members being shot

The liberals have always said that bourgeois parliamentarism[4] destroys classes and class divisions, since the right to vote and the right to participate in the government of the country are shared by all citizens without distinction. The whole history of Europe in the second half of the nineteenth century, and the whole history of the Russian revolution in the early twentieth, clearly show how absurd such views are. Economic distinctions are not mitigated[5] but aggravated and intensified under the freedom of "democratic" capitalism. Parliamentarism does not eliminate, but lays bare the innate character even of the most democratic bourgeois republics as organs of class oppression. By helping to enlighten and to organise immeasurably wider masses of the population than those which previously took an

---

1   **Narodniks:** name for Russian revolutionaries of the 1860s and 1870s. Their movement was known as "Narodnichestvo" (Narodism). The term derives from the Russian expression and means in English, *Going into the people*.

2   **moribund:** dying

3   **obsolescent:** becoming out of date

4   **parliamentarism:** or parliamentary system, distinguished by the executive branch of government being dependent on the direct or indirect support of the parliament, often expressed through a vote of confidence

5   **mitigate:** make less severe and painful

Heritage of Western Intellectual Tradition — A Sourcebook

active part in political events, parliamentarism does not make for the elimination of crises and political revolutions, but for the maximum intensification of civil war during such revolutions. The events in Paris in the spring of 1871[1] and the events in Russia in the winter of 1905[2] showed as clearly as could be how inevitably this intensification comes about. The French bourgeoisie without a moment's hesitation made a deal with the enemy of the whole nation, with the foreign army which had ruined its country, in order to crush the proletarian movement. Whoever does not understand the inevitable inner dialectics of parliamentarism and bourgeois democracy — which leads to an even sharper decision of the argument by mass violence than formerly — will never be able on the basis of this parliamentarism to conduct propaganda and agitation consistent in principle, really preparing the working-class masses for victorious participation in such "arguments." The experience of alliances, agreements and blocs with the social-reform liberals in the West and with the liberal reformists (Cadets[3]) in the Russian revolution, has convincingly shown that these agreements only blunt the consciousness of the masses, that they do not enhance but weaken the actual significance of their struggle, by linking fighters with elements who are least capable of fighting and most vacillating[4] and treacherous. Millerandism[5] in France — the biggest experiment in applying revisionist political tactics on a wide, a really national scale — has provided a practical appraisal of revisionism that will never be forgotten by the proletariat all over the world.

Questions for Discussion

1. Why is the *Communist Manifesto* so important to so many for so long?
2. What do you think are the things Marx and the *Manifesto* can still teach us?
3. In the 1872 German edition of *The Communist Manifesto*, Marx and Engels, while believing that "However much that state of things may have altered during the last twenty-five years, the general principles laid down in the Manifesto are, on the whole, as correct today as ever," also saw the necessity of change. "Here and there, some detail might be improved. The practical application of the principles will depend, as the

---

1 **Paris in the spring of 1871:** Paris Commune, armed rebellion of the workers in Paris from March 18 to May 28, 1871

2 **Russian revolution of 1905:** A massive demand for social and political reform forced Russian emperor Nicholas II to concede to major changes in the autocratic system of government, including freedom of speech and the creation of a popularly elected assembly, or Duma.

3 **Cadets:** students in military colleges

4 **vacillate:** hesitate, waver

5 **Millerandism:** socialists who take office in bourgeois governments, named after the French Socialist Millerand who joined the bourgeois French government of Waldeck-Rousseau in 1899

Manifesto itself states, everywhere and at all times, on the historical conditions for the time being existing ..." How will you comment on this statement?

4. Compare Karl Marx and Eduard Bernstein and comment.

5. What is meant by "Revisionism"?

6. Why should Bernstein say that the final "collapse" of capitalism may not happen at all?

UNIT 14

Early 20th Century: Man & Society

Pretest

- What do you know about Sigmund Freud and John Dewey?
- How did the situation at the beginning of the century affect the development of intellectual thoughts?
- Dewey went to China around the May Fourth Movement. What relevance can you find of Dewey to the modern education system in China?

What You Will Learn in This Unit

- Some knowledge about Freudianism and liberalism in the early years of the 20th century;
- Ideas about psychology and education which were affecting China in the early years of the 20th century; and
- John Dewey as both teacher and learner in China.

Learn to Pronounce

Albert Einstein /ˈaɪnstaɪn/ 爱因斯坦
Austrian /ˈɔːstrɪən/ 奥地利的
experimentalism /ɪkˌsperɪˈmentəlɪzəm/ 经验主义
neuropathology /ˌnjʊərəʊpəˈθɒlədʒɪ/ 神经病理学
pedagogy /ˈpedəgɒgɪ/ 教授法
psychoanalytic /ˈsaɪkəʊˌænəˈlɪtɪk/ 心理分析的
Vienna /vɪˈenə/ 维也纳

anti-Semitism /ˈsemɪtɪzəm/ 反犹太主义
Edmund Husserl /ˈhʊsəl/ 胡塞尔
John Dewey /ˈdju(ː)ɪ/ 杜威
Oedipus /ˈiːdɪpəs, ˈedɪpəs/ (希神)俄狄浦斯
pragmatism /ˈprægmətɪzəm/ 实用主义
Sigmund Freud /frɔɪd/ 弗洛伊德

-452-

Introduction

For most Europeans, the turn of the century witnessed the most violent period in human history. The days of *La Belle Epoque* ("the beautiful times") were over, and many believed that Europe was "dancing on a volcano." The industrial working class, growing in number and organized strength, pressured European governments to improve working conditions and demanded more rights and opportunities. National rivalries were exacerbated by imperial competition, and a new and virulent strain of anti-Semitism infected the political life of Austria-Hungary, Russia, and France. The crisis at the turn of the century eventually led to the outbreak of the imperialist world war, and the death of over 10 million men in combat left a gaping chasm in the social and economic life of the Western world. The survivors returned home physically and mentally disabled, and widows and orphans had to cope with severe economic hardship and emotional loss. Worst of all, the war profoundly disrupted the cultural tradition of the West. Optimism about human nature and about the glorious future of civilization was discredited. It is out of this caution against a facile optimism and dismissal of the liberal conception of rational humanity that intellectuals began to question and tried to find answers. Sigmund Freud explored the darker side of man's inner world for an explanation of the slaughter, Edmund Husserl tried to secure an order in philosophy in the decadence of civilization, and John Dewey suggested that signs of hope for the declining West might be best found in education. It is also roughly the late 19th and early 20th centuries that the disillusioned Western intellectuals turned to the oriental wisdom to balance their intellectual lost. Meanwhile the Chinese also started to ponder over the strengths and weaknesses of the Western aliens and themselves.

Sigmund Freud: An Outline of Psychoanalysis*

Sigmund Freud (1856 – 1939), Austrian physician, neurologist, and founder of modern psychoanalysis, one of the three Jews who have, as is said, changed the 20th century (the other two being Karl Marx and Albert Einstein). Oldest of the 7 children, Freud's childhood ambition had been a career in law, but he became a medical student shortly before he entered University of Vienna in 1873. He was so engaged in research on the nervous system that he neglected the prescribed courses and remained in medical school three years longer than other students. In 1885, he was appointed lecturer in neuropathology. Causes of mental disorders were attributed at that time exclusively to the nervous system, and the study was conducted mainly in anatomical and physiological labs. Freud was to change the whole situation. In identifying the "real" causes, Freud found evidence for the mental mechanisms of repres-

---

* This "outline" is one of the popular essays Freud wrote to describe the Freudian theory to the laymen, where we find some of the most important concepts, such as id, ego, super-ego, and the mechanism by which dream works.

sion and resistance, based on clinical observations. He described repression as a device operating unconsciously to make the memory of painful or threatening events inaccessible to the conscious mind. Resistance was defined as the unconscious defense against awareness of repressed experiences in order to avoid anxiety. He established a private practice in Vienna in 1886, and during 1895 to 1900 developed many of the concepts to be incorporated into psychoanalytic practice and doctrine. He used free associations to guide the patient in the interpretation of dreams. Dream analysis led to his discoveries of infantile sexuality and of the so-called Oedipus complex. Then appeared Freud's most important work, *The Interpretation of Dreams* (1900). When the Germans occupied Austria in 1938, Freud, a Jew, escaped with his family to England and died in London. Although never accorded full recognition during his lifetime, Freud is generally acknowledged as one of the greatest creative minds of modern times. He created an entirely new approach to the understanding of human personality, and formulated basic therapeutic procedures that are still being applied widely in the present-day treatment of neuroses and psychoses. What is most important of Freud is that he opened up enormous areas for humanities and social sciences. "Psychological man," along with political, religious, or economic man, has become the dominant self-image in the 20th century.

Chapter One   The Psychical Apparatus

Psychoanalysis makes a basic assumption, the discussion of which is reserved to philosophical thought but the justification for which lies in its results[1]. **We know two kinds of things about what we call our psyche (or mental life): firstly, its bodily organ and scene of action, the brain (or nervous system) and, on the other hand, our acts of consciousness, which are immediate data and cannot be further explained by any sort of description. Everything that lies between is unknown to us, and the data do not include any direct relation between these two terminal points of our knowledge.** If it existed, it would at the most afford an exact localization of the processes of consciousness and would give us no help towards understanding them.

Sigmund and Anna Freud on holiday in Italy, 1913

Our two hypotheses start out from these ends or beginnings[2] of our knowledge. The first is concerned with localization. We assume that mental life is the function of an apparatus to which we ascribe the characteristics of being extended in space and of being made up of several portions — which we imagine, that is, as being like a telescope or microscope or something of the sort. The consistent carrying through of a conception of this kind is a scientific novelty, even though some attempts in that direction have been made previously.

---

1   **justification for which lies in its results:** Freud is saying this is the work of a psychologist or psychiatrist, such as Freud himself.

2   **these ends or beginnings:** the "two terminal points" mentioned above

We have arrived at our knowledge of this psychical apparatus by studying the individual development of human beings. To the oldest of these psychical provinces or agencies we give the name of id. It contains everything that is inherited, that is present at birth, that is laid down in the constitution — above all, therefore, the instincts, which originate from the somatic[1] organization and which find a first psychical expression here (in the id) in forms unknown to us.

Under the influence of the real external world around us, one portion of the id has undergone a special development. From what was originally a cortical[2] layer, equipped with the organs for receiving stimuli and with arrangements for acting as a protective shield against stimuli, a special organization has arisen which henceforward acts as an intermediary between the id and the external world. To this region of our mind we have given the name of ego.

Here are the principal characteristics of the ego. In consequence of the pre-established connection between sense perception and muscular action, the ego has voluntary movement at its command. It has the task of self-preservation. As regards external events, it performs that task by becoming aware of stimuli from without[3], by storing up experiences about them (in the memory), by avoiding excessively strong stimuli (through flight), by dealing with moderate stimuli (through adaptation) and finally by learning to bring about expedient[4] changes in the external world to its own advantage (through activity). As regards internal events, in relation to the id, it performs that task by gaining control over the demands of the instincts, by deciding whether they are to be allowed satisfaction, by postponing that satisfaction to times and circumstances favourable in the external world or by suppressing their excitations entirely. It is guided in its activity by consideration of the tensions produced by stimuli, whether these tensions are present in it or introduced into it. The raising of these tensions is in general felt as unpleasure and their lowering[5] as pleasure. It is probable, however, that what is felt as pleasure or unpleasure is not the absolute height of this tension but something in the rhythm of the changes in them. The ego strives after pleasure and seeks to avoid unpleasure. An increase in unpleasure that is expected and foreseen is met by a signal of anxiety; the occasion of such an increase, whether it threatens from without or within, is known as a danger. From time to time the ego gives up its connection with the external world and withdraws into the state of sleep, in which it makes far-reaching changes in its organization. It is to be inferred from the state of sleep that this organization consists in a particular distribution of mental energy.

The long period of childhood, during which the growing human being lives in dependence on

*Birth House of Freud,
Zamecnicka Ulice 117,
Pribor, Czech Republic*

1　**somatic:** relating to or affecting the body
2　**cortical:** relating to a cortex（皮层的）
3　**without:** outside
4　**expedient:** likely to be useful and helpful
5　**lowering:** lowering of these tensions

Heritage of Western Intellectual Tradition　A Sourcebook

his parents, leaves behind it as a precipitate[1] the formation in his ego of a special agency in which this parental influence is prolonged. It has received the name of super-ego. In so far as this super-ego is differentiated from the ego or is opposed to it, it constitutes a third power which the ego must take into account.

An action by the ego is as it should be if it satisfies simultaneously the demands of the id, of the super-ego and of reality that is to say, if it is able to reconcile their demands with one another. The details of the relation between the ego and the super-ego become completely intelligible when they are traced back to the child's attitude to its parents. This parental influence of course includes in its operation not only the personalities of the actual parents but also the family, racial and national traditions handed on through them, as well as the demands of the immediate social milieu which they represent. In the same way, the super-ego, in the course of an individual's development, receives contributions from later successors and substitutes of his parents, such as teachers and models in public life of[2] admired social ideals. It will be observed that, for all their fundamental difference, the id and the super-ego have one thing in common: they both represent the influences of the past — the id the influence[3] of heredity, the super-ego the influence, essentially, of what is taken over from other people — whereas the ego is principally determined by the individual's own experience, that is by accidental and contemporary events.

This general pattern of a psychical apparatus may be supposed to apply equally to the higher animals which resemble man mentally. A superego must be presumed to be present whenever, as in the case of man, there is a long period of dependence in childhood. The assumption of a distinction between ego and id cannot be avoided.

Animal psychology has not yet taken in hand[4] the interesting problem which is here presented.

Chapter Two   The Theory of the Instincts

The power of the id expresses the true purpose of the individual organism's life. This consists in the satisfaction of its innate needs. No such purpose as that of keeping itself alive or of protecting itself from dangers by means of[5] anxiety can be attributed to the id. That is the task of the ego, whose business it also is to discover the most favorable and least perilous[6] method of obtaining satisfaction, taking the external world into account. The super-ego may bring fresh needs to the fore, but its main function remains

Interpretation of dreams

---

1 **precipitate:** condensation, accumulation
2 **models in public life of:** models ... of
3 **the id the influence:** the id represents the influence
4 **take in hand:** deal with
5 **by means of:** through, caused by
6 **perilous:** dangerous

the limitation of satisfactions.

The forces which we assume to exist behind the tensions caused by the needs of the id are called instincts. They represent the somatic demands upon the mind. Though they are the ultimate cause of all activity, they are of a conservative nature; the state, whatever it may be, which an organism has reached gives rise to a tendency to reestablish that state so soon as it has been abandoned. It is thus possible to distinguish an indeterminate number of instincts, and in common practice this is in fact done.[1] For us, however, the important question arises whether it may not be possible to trace all these numerous instincts back to a few basic ones. We have found that instincts can change their aim (by displacement) and also that they can replace one another — the energy of one instinct passing over to another. This latter process is still insufficiently understood. After long hesitancies and vacillations[2] we have decided to assume the existence of only two basic instincts, Eros and the destructive instinct. (The contrast between the instincts of self-preservation and the preservation of the species, as well as the contrast between ego-love and object-love, fall within Eros.) The aim of the first of these basic instincts is to establish ever greater unities and to preserve them thus — in short, to bind together; the aim of the second is, on the contrary, to undo connections and so to destroy things. In the case of the destructive instinct we may suppose that its final aim is to lead what is living into an inorganic state[3]. For this reason we also call it the death instinct. If we assume that living things came later than inanimate ones and arose from them, then the death instinct fits in with the formula we have proposed to the effect that instincts tend towards a return to an earlier state[4]. In the case of Eros (or the love instinct) we cannot apply this formula. To do so would presuppose that living substance was once a unity which had later been torn apart and was now striving towards reunion.

In biological functions the two basic instincts operate against each other or combine with each other. Thus, the act of eating is a destruction of the object with the final aim of incorporating it, and the sexual act is an act of aggression with the purpose of the most intimate union. This concurrent[5] and mutually opposing action of the two basic instincts gives rise to the whole variegation[6] of the phenomena of life. The analogy of our two basic instincts

Freud next to his analytic couch in a summer residence, 1932

extends from the sphere of living things to the pair of opposing forces — attraction and repulsion — which rule in the inorganic world.

...

1 **It is thus possible to … in fact done.:** Namely, in practice we do distinguish an indeterminate number of instincts.
2 **vacillation:** hesitation
3 **inorganic state:** state of dissolution, death
4 **earlier state:** death, before life starts. So death here is a necessary beginning stage of life, dialectically. In this sense, death instinct is also life instinct.
5 **concurrent:** existing together, cooperating
6 **variegation:** irregularity, variety

Chapter Six   The Technique of Psychoanalysis

A dream, then, is a psychosis[1], with all the absurdities, delusions, and illusions of a psychosis. No doubt it is a psychosis which has only a short duration, which is harmless and even performs a useful function, which is brought about with the subject's consent and is ended by an act of his will. **Nevertheless it is a psychosis, and we learn from it that even so deep-going a modification of mental life as this can be undone and can give place to normal functioning. Is it too bold, then, to hope that it must also be possible to submit the dreaded spontaneous illnesses of the mind to our control and bring about their cure?**

We already possess much knowledge preliminary to such an undertaking. We have postulated that it is the ego's task to meet the demands of the three forces upon which it is dependent — reality, the id, and the superego — and meanwhile to preserve its own organization and maintain its own autonomy. The necessary condition for the pathological[2] states we have mentioned can only be a relative or absolute weakening of the ego which prevents it from performing its tasks. The severest demand upon the ego is probably the keeping down of the instinctual claims of the id, and for this end the ego is obliged to maintain great expenditures of energy upon anti-cathexes[3]. But the claims made by the superego, too, may become so powerful and so remorseless[4] that the ego may be crippled, as it were, for its other tasks. We may suspect that, in the economic conflicts which now arise, the id and the superego often make common cause[5] against the hard pressed ego, which, in order to retain its normal state, clings on to reality. But if the other two are too strong, they may succeed in loosening the organization of the ego and altering it so that its proper relation to reality is disturbed or even abolished. We have seen it happen in dreams: when the ego is detached from the reality of the external world, then, under the influence of the external world, it slips down into psychosis.

Our plan of cure is based upon these views. The ego has been weakened by the internal conflict; we must come to its aid. The position is like a civil war which can only be decided by the help of an ally from without. The analytical physician and the weakened ego of the patient, basing themselves upon the real external world, are to combine against the enemies, the instinctual demands of the id, and the moral demands of the superego. **We form a pact with each other. The patient's sick ego promises us the most complete candor[6], promises, that is, to put at our disposal all of the material which his self-perception provides; we, on the other hand, assure him of the strictest discretion[7] and put at his service our experience in interpreting material that has been influenced by the unconscious. Our knowledge shall compensate for his ignorance and shall give his ego once more mastery over the lost provinces of his**

1   **psychosis:** abnormal or unusual mental state
2   **pathological:** of or relating to pathology; relating to or caused by disease
3   **cathexes:** concentration of emotional energy on an object or idea
4   **remorseless:** without regret
5   **make common cause:** ally, fight together
6   **candor:** straightforwardness, frankness
7   **discretion:** prudence, carefulness

mental life. This pact constitutes the analytic situation.

No sooner have we taken this step than we meet with a first disappointment, a first warning against complacency[1]. If the patient's ego is to be a useful ally in our common work, it must, however hard it may be pressed by the hostile powers, have retained a certain degree of coherence, a fragment at least of understanding for the demands of reality. But this is not to be expected from the ego of a psychotic[2]; it cannot carry out a pact of this sort, indeed it can scarcely engage in it. It will very soon toss us away and the help we offer it, to join the portions of the external world that no longer mean anything to it. Thus we learn that we must renounce the idea of trying our plan of cure upon psychotics — renounce it forever, perhaps, of only for the moment, until we have discovered some other plan better suited for that purpose.

But there is another class of psychological patients who evidently resemble the psychotics very closely, the immense number of sufferers from severe neuroses[3]. The causes as well as the pathogenic[4] mechanisms of their illness must be the same or at least very similar. Their ego, however, has proved more resistant and has become less disorganized. Many of them, in spite of their troubles and of their consequent inadequacy, are none the less able to maintain their position in real life. It may be that these neurotics will show themselves ready to accept our help. We will confine our interest to them and see how far and by what means we can "cure" them.[5]

Psyche, in Roman mythology, the beautiful princess is loved by Cupid, god of love, a suggestion of the union of love and the soul, or the yearning of the soul for immortality.

We conclude our pact then with the neurotics: complete candor on one side, strict discretion on the other. This looks as though we were aiming at the post of a secular father confessor. But there is a great difference, for what we want to hear from our patient is not only what he knows and conceals from other people, but what he does not know. With this end in view we give him a more detailed definition of what we mean by candor. We impose upon him the fundamental rule of analysis, which is henceforward to govern his behavior to us. He must tell us not only what he can say intentionally and willingly, what will give him relief like a confession, but everything else besides that his self-observation presents him with — everything that comes into his head, even if it is disagreeable

---

1   **complacency:** contentment, self-satisfaction
2   **psychotic:** person affected by psychosis（精神病患者）
3   **neuroses:** disorder of the mind
4   **pathogenic:** capable of causing disease
5   **We will confine our interest … can "cure" them.:** Namely, we can only talk about patients who will accept, to varying degrees, our help — there are patients who reject totally outside aid, and we can do nothing about them. Freud knows there are cases his psychoanalysis cannot deal with. In fact his success rate is very low. He is, therefore, more interesting as a theorist than a practitioner.

Heritage of Western Intellectual Tradition   A Sourcebook

to say it, even if it seems unimportant or positively meaningless. If he can succeed after this injunction in putting his self-criticism[1] out of action, he will provide us with a mass of material — thoughts, ideas, recollections — which already lie under the influence of the unconscious, which are often its direct derivatives, and which thus put us in a position to conjecture the nature of his repressed unconscious material and to extend, by the information we give him, his ego's knowledge of his unconscious.

Key Concepts

analytic situation	mental life
basic instincts	nervous system
brain	protective shield
conservative nature	psyche
death instinct	psychoanalysis
demands of reality	satisfaction of innate needs
Eros	self-preservation
free association	stimuli
id/ego/superego	unconscious

John Dewey: Liberalism and Social Action*

John Dewey (1859 – 1952), American philosopher, psychologist, educator, and a founder of the philosophical school of pragmatism, received B.A. from University of Vermont in 1879 and Ph.D. from Johns Hopkins University in 1884. He taught at University of Michigan, University of Minnesota, University of Chicago and Columbia University until his retirement in 1931. He lectured and studied educational systems in China, Japan, Mexico, Turkey, and the Soviet Union. Dewey tested his edu-

---

1   **self-criticism:** This is super-ego at work. Freud is asking his patient to totally reject social conventions so that he can tell all his "secrets." But in reality this is no easy job for a patient. It needs pre-training.

*   This essay was one of the lectures Dewey gave at the University of Virginia in 1935. Dewey criticized the early liberalism based on "laissez-faire" economics and possessive individualism, and called for a radical liberalism, a cooperatively controlled economy, which would promote freedom and cultural development. This essay best summarizes Dewey's philosophy: a. pragmatism (thinking toward definite ends and practical effects); b. instrumentalism (ideas as instruments in the construction of experience); c. radical empiricism (experience is all); and d. experimentalism (verification of results).

cational principles at the famous experimental Laboratory School, the so-called Dewey School, the "most important experimental venture in the whole history of American education," established in 1896. These principles emphasized the student-centred rather than the subject-centred pedagogy,

education through activity rather than through formal learning, and laboratory, workshop, or occupational education rather than the mastery of traditional subjects. He insisted that the educational process must begin with and build upon the interests of the child, that the teacher should be a guide and coworker with the pupils, rather than a taskmaster assigning a fixed set of lessons and recitations, and that the school's goal is the growth of the child in all aspects of its being. Thousands of fascinated people flocked to Chicago to visit Dewey's classrooms. Dewey felt, moreover, that education should not merely be a preparation for future life but a full life in itself. Dewey's philosophical orientation has been labeled a form of pragmatism, though Dewey himself seemed to favour the term "instrumentalism," or "experimentalism." He conceived of democracy not as a mere form of government, but rather as a mode of association which provides the members of a society with the opportunity for maximum experimentation and personal growth. During the last two decades of Dewey's life, his philosophy of education was blamed for the failure of American school systems to train pupils adequately in the liberal arts and for their neglect of such basic subjects as mathematics and science. Furthermore, critics blamed Dewey for insufficient emphasis on discipline in the schools, for turning schools into an "Alice-in-Wonderland world of madness." However, this is largely due to his over enthusiastic followers. Although Dewey opposed authoritarian methods, he did not advocate lack of guidance and control. He criticized, as well as education that was oriented toward pure vocational training education that emphasized formal and rigid learning.

Nothing is blinder than the supposition that we live in a society and world so static that either nothing new will happen or else it will happen because of the use of violence. Social change is here as a fact, a fact having multifarious[1] forms and marked in intensity. Changes that are revolutionary in effect are in process in every phase of life. Transformations in the family, the church, the school, in science and art, in economic and political relations, are occurring so swiftly that imagination is baffled[1] in attempt to lay hold of them. Flux[3] does not have to be created. But it does have to be directed. It has to be so controlled that it will move to some end in accordance with the principles of life, since life itself is development. **Liberalism is committed to an end that is at once enduring and flexible: the liberation of individuals so that realization of their capacities may be the law of their life. It is committed to the use of freed intelligence as the method of directing change.** In any case, civilization is faced with the problem of uniting the changes that are going on into a coherent pattern of social organization. **The liberal spirit is**

---

1   **multifarious:** various

2   **baffle:** puzzle

3   **flux:** continuous succession of changes

marked by its own picture of the pattern that is required: a social organization that will make possible effective liberty and opportunity for personal growth in mind and spirit in all individuals. Its present need is recognition that established material security is a prerequisite of the ends which it cherishes, so that, the basis of life being secure, individuals may actively share in the wealth of cultural resources that now exist and may contribute, each in his own way, to their further enrichment.

The fact of change has been so continual and so intense that it overwhelms our minds. We are bewildered by the spectacle of its rapidity, scope and intensity. It is not surprising that men have protected themselves from the impact of such vast change by resorting to what psycho-analysis has taught us to call rationalizations, in other words, protective fantasies. The Victorian idea that change is a part of an evolution that necessarily leads through successive stages to some preordained[1] divine far-off event is one rationalization. The conception of a sudden, complete, almost catastrophic, transformation, to be brought about by the victory of the proletariat over the class now dominant, is a similar rationalization. But men have met the impact of change in the realm of actuality, mostly by drift[2] and by temporary, usually incoherent, improvisations[3]. **Liberalism, like every theory of life, has suffered from the state of confused uncertainty that is the lot of a world suffering from rapid and varied change for which there is no in-tellectual and moral preparation.**

In 1916 John Dewey publishes Democracy and Education

Because of this lack of mental and moral preparation the impact of swiftly moving changes produced, as I have just said, confusion, uncertainty and drift. Change in patterns of belief, desire and purpose has lagged behind the modification of the external conditions under which men associate. Industrial habits have changed most rapidly; there has followed at considerable distance, change in political relations[4]; alterations in legal relations and methods have lagged even more, while changes in the institutions that deal most directly with patterns of thought and belief have taken place to the least extent[5]. This fact defines the primary, though not by any means the ultimate, responsibility of a liberalism that intends to be a vital force. **Its work is first of all education, in the broadest sense of that term. Schooling is a part of the work of education, but education in its full meaning includes all the influences that go to form the attitudes and dispositions (of de-sire as well as of belief), which constitute dominant habits of mind and character.**

...

---

1 **preordained:** predetermined
2 **drift:** state of being carried along by current, instability
3 **improvisation:** an unplanned performance
4 **there has followed at considerable distance, change in political relations:** change in political relations has followed at considerable distance (falling behind)
5 **changes in the institutions ... to the least extent:** change in institutions (such as education) has been quite slow

When, then, I say that the first object of a renascent[1] liberalism is education, I mean that its task is to aid in producing the habits of mind and character, the intellectual and moral patterns, that are somewhere near even with the actual movements of events. It is, I repeat, the split between the latter as they have externally occurred and the ways of desiring, thinking, and of putting emotion and purpose into execution that[2] is the basic cause of present confusion in mind and paralysis in action. The educational task cannot be accomplished merely by working upon men's minds, without action[3] that effects actual change in institutions. The idea that dispositions and attitudes can be altered by merely "moral" means conceived of as something that goes on wholly inside of persons is itself one of the old patterns that has to be changed. Thought, desire and purpose exist in a constant give and take of interaction with environing[4] conditions. But resolute thought is the first step in that change of action that will itself carry further the needed change in patterns of mind and character.

In short, liberalism must now become radical, meaning by "radical" perception of the necessity of thoroughgoing changes in the set-up[5] of institutions and corresponding activity to bring the changes to pass. For the gulf between what the actual situation makes possible and the actual state itself is so great that it cannot be bridged by piecemeal policies undertaken *ad hoc*[6]. The process of producing the changes will be, in any case, a gradual one. But "reforms" that deal now with this abuse and now with that without having a social goal based upon an inclusive plan, differ entirely from effort at re-forming, in its literal sense, the institutional scheme of things. The liberals of more than a century ago were denounced in their time as subversive radicals, and only when the new economic order was established did they become apologists[7] for the *status quo* or else content with social patchwork. If radicalism be defined as perception of need for radical change, then today any liberalism which is not also radicalism is irrelevant and doomed.

"Playhouse" built by children at Dewey's Laboratory School in Chicago, 1901

But radicalism also means, in the minds of many, both supporters and opponents, dependence upon use of violence as the main method of effecting drastic changes. Here the liberal parts company[8]. For he is committed to the organization of intelligent action as the chief method. Any

---

1 **renascent:** reviving

2 **It is … that …:** Emphatic structure. Education can play the role of a bridge to close the split.

3 Dewey believes in education which leads to action and produces actual effect on man and society, or as Wang Yangming puts it, "a combination of knowledge and action"（知行合一）.

4 **environing:** surrounding

5 **set-up:** organization

6 *ad hoc*: for that special purpose

7 **apologist:** person who defends a doctrine by logical arguments

8 **part company:** depart from others

Heritage of Western Intellectual Tradition   A Sourcebook

frank discussion of the issue must recognize the extent to which those who decry[1] the use of any violence are themselves willing to resort to violence and are ready to put their will into operation. Their fundamental objection is to change in the economic institution that now exists, and for its maintenance they resort to the use of the force that is placed in their hands by this very institution. They do not need to advocate the use of force; their only need is to employ it. Force, rather than intelligence, is built into the procedures of the existing social system, regularly as coercion[2], in times of crisis as overt violence. The legal system, conspicuously in its penal aspect, more subtly in civil practice, rests upon coercion. Wars are the methods recurrently used in settlement of disputes between nations. One school of radicals dwells upon the fact that in the past the transfer of power in one society has either been accomplished by or attended with violence. But what we need to realize is that physical force is used, at least in the form of coercion, in the very set-up of our society[3]. That the competitive system, which was thought of by early liberals as the means by which the latent abilities of individuals were to be evoked and directed into socially useful channels, is now in fact a state of scarcely disguised battle hardly needs to be dwelt upon. That the control of the means of production by the few in legal possession operates as a standing agency of coercion of the many, may need emphasis in statement, but is surely evident to one who is willing to observe and honestly report the existing scene. It is foolish to regard the political state as the only agency now endowed with coercive power. Its exercise of this power is pale in contrast with that exercised by concentrated and organized property interests.

It is not surprising in view of our standing[4] dependence upon the use of coercive force that at every time of crisis coercion breaks out into open violence. In this country, with its tradition of violence fostered by frontier conditions and by the conditions under which immigration went on during the greater part of our history, resort to violence is especially recurrent on the part of those who are in power. In times of imminent change, our verbal and sentimental worship of the Constitution, with its guarantees of civil liberties of expression, publication and assemblage[5], readily goes overboard[6]. Often the officials of the law are the worst offenders, acting as agents of some power that rules the economic life of a community. What is said about the value of free speech as a safety value is then forgotten with the utmost of ease: a comment, perhaps, upon the weakness of the defense of freedom of expression that[7] values it[8] simply as a means of blowing-off steam[9].

---

1 **decry:** make less valuable

2 **coercion:** use force to make obedient

3 **very set-up of our society:** Dewey is concerned not so much with the use of force as with the production of force within the social institution itself. Similar ideas about use of coercion and power may be found in his Italian contemporary Antonio Gramsci and in the late 20th century French philosopher Michael Foucault.

4 **standing:** existing

5 **assemblage:** gathering

6 **overboard:** over the boat into the water, here become ineffective

7 **that:** defense of freedom of expression

8 **it:** free speech

9 **blowing-off steam:** something that helps get rid of strong feelings or energy

It is not pleasant to face the extent to which, as matter of fact, coercive and violent force is relied upon in the present social system as a means of social control. It is much more agreeable to evade the fact. **But unless the fact is acknowledged as a fact in its full depth and breadth, the meaning of dependence upon intelligence as the alternative method of social direction will not be grasped. Failure in acknowledgment signifies, among other things, failure to realize that those who propagate the dogma of dependence upon force have the sanction[1] of much that is already entrenched[2] in the existing system.** They would but turn the use of it to opposite ends. The assumption that the method of intelligence already rules and that those who urge the use of violence are introducing a new element into the social picture may not be hypocritical but it is unintelligently unaware of what is actually involved in intelligence as an alternative method of social action.[3]

…

John Dewey, c. 1890

Intelligence in politics when it is identified with discussion means reliance upon symbols. The invention of language is probably the greatest single invention achieved by humanity. The development of political forms that promote the use of symbols in place of arbitrary power was another great invention. The nineteenth-century establishment of parliamentary institutions, written constitutions and the suffrage as means of political rule, is a tribute to the power of symbols. But symbols are significant only in connection with realities behind them. No intelligent observer can deny, I think, that they are often used in party politics[4] as a substitute for realities instead of as means of contact with them[5]. Popular literacy, in connection with the telegraph, cheap postage and the printing press, has enormously multiplied the number of those influenced. That which we term education has done a good deal to generate habits that put symbols in the place of realities. The forms of popular government make necessary the elaborate use of words to influence political action. "Propaganda" is the inevitable consequence of the combination of these influences and it extends to every area of life. Words not only take the place of realities but are themselves debauched[6]. Decline in the prestige of suffrage and of parliamentary government are intimately associated with the belief, manifest in practice even if not expressed in words, that intelligence is an individual possession to be reached by means of verbal persuasion.

This fact suggests, by way of contrast, the genuine meaning of intelligence in connection with public opinion, sentiment and action. The crisis in democracy demands the substitution of the intelligence that is exemplified in scientific procedure for the kind of intelligence that is now

---

1   **sanction:** power, permission
2   **entrench:** establish firmly
3   **The assumption that ... of social action.:** The assumption … may not be hypocritical but …
4   **party politics:** politics played by a certain party, used in a derogative sense here
5   **as a substitute for realities instead of as means of contact with them:** Namely, they are taken as realities, rather than as representation or understanding of realities.
6   **debauch:** turn away from good taste or judgment

accepted. The need for this change is not exhausted in the demand for greater honesty and impartiality, even though these qualities be now corrupted by discussion carried on mainly for purposes of party supremacy and for imposition of some special but concealed interest. These qualities need to be restored. But the need goes further. The social use of intelligence would remain deficient even if these moral traits were exalted[1], and yet intelligence continued to be identified simply with discussion and persuasion, necessary as are these things. Approximation to use of scientific method in investigation and of the engineering mind in the invention and projection of far-reaching social plans is demanded. The habit of considering social realities in terms of cause and effect and social policies in terms of means and consequences is still inchoate[2]. The contrast between the state of intelligence in politics and in the physical control of nature is to be taken literally. What has happened in this latter is the outstanding demonstration of the meaning of organized intelligence. The combined effect of science and technology has released more productive energies in a bare hundred years than stands to the credit[3] of prior human history in its entirety. Productively it has multiplied nine million times in the last generation alone. The prophetic vision of Francis Bacon of subjugation of the energies of nature through change in methods of inquiry has well-nigh[4] been realized. The stationary engine, the locomotive, the dynamo[5], the motor car, turbine[6], telegraph, telephone, radio and moving picture are not the products of either isolated individual minds nor of the particular economic regime called capitalism. They are the fruit of methods that first penetrated to the working causalities of nature and then utilized the resulting knowledge in bold imaginative ventures of invention and construction.

We hear a great deal in these days about class conflict. The past history of man is held up to us as almost exclusively a record of struggles between classes, ending in the victory of a class that had been oppressed and the transfer of power to it. It is difficult to avoid reading the past in terms of the contemporary scene. Indeed, fundamentally it is impossible to avoid this course. With a certain proviso[7], it is highly important that we are compelled to follow this path. **For the past as past is gone, save for esthetic enjoyment and refreshment, while the present is with us. Knowledge of the past is significant only as it deepens and extends our understanding of the present.** Yet there is a proviso. We must grasp the things that are most important in the present when we turn to the past and not allow ourselves to be misled by secondary phenomena no matter how intense and immediately urgent they are. Viewed from this standpoint, the rise of scientific method and of technology based upon it is the genuinely active force in producing the vast complex of changes the world is now undergoing, not the class struggle whose spirit and

---

1 **exalt:** praise highly
2 **inchoate:** only partly in existence; imperfectly formed
3 **to the credit:** owing to the achievement
4 **well-nigh:** nearly. For Bacon's discussion of the importance of method, see Unit 7.
5 **dynamo:** electricity generator
6 **turbine:** engine driven by current
7 **proviso:** limitation, condition

Heritage of Western Intellectual Tradition A Sourcebook

method are opposed to science[1]. If we lay hold upon the causal force exercised by this embodiment of intelligence we shall know where to turn for the means of directing further change.

When I say that scientific method and technology have been the active force in producing the revolutionary transformations society is undergoing, I do not imply no other forces have been at work to arrest, deflect[2] and corrupt their[3] operation. Rather this fact is positively implied. At this point, indeed, is located the conflict that underlies the confusions and uncertainties of the present scene. The conflict is between institutions and habits originating in the pre-scientific and pre-technological age and the new forces generated by science and technology. The application of science, to a considerable degree, even its own growth, has been conditioned by the system to which the name of capitalism is given, a rough designation of a complex of political and legal arrangements centering about a particular mode of economic relations. Because of the conditioning of science and technology by this setting, the second and humanly most important part of Bacon's prediction has so far largely missed realization. The conquest of natural energies has not accrued[4] to the betterment of the common human estate in anything like the degree he anticipated.

Because of conditions that were set by the legal institutions and the moral ideas existing when the scientific and industrial revolutions came into being, the chief usufruct[5] of the latter has been appropriated by a relatively small class. Industrial entrepreneurs have reaped out of all proportion to what they sowed[6]. By obtaining private ownership of the means of production and exchange they deflected a considerable share of the results of increased productivity to their private pockets. This appropriation was not the fruit of criminal conspiracy or of sinister intent. It was sanctioned not only by legal institutions of age-long standing but by the entire prevailing moral code. The institution of private property long antedated[7] feudal times. It is the institution with which men have lived, with few exceptions, since the dawn of civilization. Its existence has deeply impressed itself upon mankind's moral conceptions. Moreover, the new industrial forces tended to break down many of the rigid class barriers that had been in force, and to give to millions a new outlook and inspire a new hope; — especially in this country with no feudal background and no fixed class system.

...

The ultimate place of economic organization in human life is to assure the secure basis for an ordered expression of individual capacity and for the satisfaction of the needs

---

1 **not the class struggle whose spirit and method are opposed to science:** So Dewey's radicalism took another direction for the solution of social conflicts at the time of radical changes (around 1935).

2 **deflect:** cause to turn aside

3 **their:** transformations'

4 **accrue:** come as a natural development

5 **usufruct:** right of suing another one' property

6 **reaped out of all proportion to what they sowed:** i.e., got much more than what they deserved

7 **antedate:** come before in date

Heritage of Western Intellectual Tradition A Sourcebook

of man in non-economic directions. The effort of mankind in connection with material production belongs, as I said earlier, among[1] interests and activities that are, relatively speaking, routine in character, "routine" being defined as that which, without absorbing attention and energy, provides a constant basis for liberation of the values of intellectual, esthetic and companionship life. Every significant religious and moral teacher and prophet has asserted that the material is instrumental to the good life. Nominally at least, this idea is accepted by every civilized community. The transfer of the burden of material production from human muscles and brain to steam, electricity and chemical processes now makes possible the effective actualization of this idea. Needs, wants and desires are always the moving force in generating creative action. When these wants are compelled by force of conditions to be directed for the most part, among the mass of mankind, into obtaining the means of subsistence[2], what should be a means becomes perforce[3] an end in itself. Up to the present the new mechanical[4] forces of production, which are the means of emancipation from this state of affairs[5], have been employed to intensify and exaggerate the reversal of the true relation between means and ends[6]. Humanly speaking, I do not see how it would have been possible to avoid an epoch having this character. But its perpetuation is the cause of the continually growing social chaos and strife. Its termination cannot be effected by preaching to individuals that they should place spiritual ends above material means. It can be brought about by organized social reconstruction that puts the results of the mechanism of abundance at the free disposal of individuals. The actual corrosive[7] "materialism" of our times does not proceed from science. It springs from the notion, sedulously[8] cultivated by the class in power, that the creative capacities of individuals can be evoked and developed only in a struggle for material possessions and material gain. We either should surrender our professed belief in the supremacy of ideal and spiritual values and accommodate our beliefs to the predominant material orientation, or we should through organized endeavor institute the socialized economy of material security and plenty that will release human energy for pursuit of higher values.

Since liberation of the capacities of individuals for free, self-initiated expression is an essential part of the creed[9] of liberalism, liberalism that is sincere must will[10] the means that condition the achieving of its ends. Regimentation of material and mechanical forces is the only way by which the mass of individuals can be released from regimentation and consequent

---

1 **belong ... among:** belong in, belong to
2 **subsistence:** existence
3 **perforce:** of necessity, necessarily
4 **mechanical:** relating to machines
5 **this state of affairs:** the means of subsistence
6 **intensify and exaggerate ... means and ends:** Namely, the pursuit of material wealth is taken as an end rather than a means for pursuit of "higher values," or spiritual elevation.
7 **corrosive:** that which destroys slowly
8 **sedulously:** perseveringly, persistently
9 **creed:** belief
10 **will:** choose, desire

suppression of their cultural possibilities. The eclipse[1] of liberalism is due to the fact that it has not faced the alternatives and adopted the means upon which realization of its professed aims depends. Liberalism can be true to its ideals only as it takes the course that leads to their attainment. The notion that organized social control of economic forces lies outside the historic path of liberalism shows that liberalism is still impeded by remnants of its earlier laissez faire phase, with its opposition of society and the individual.[2] The thing which now dampens[3] liberal ardor and paralyzes its efforts is the conception that liberty and development of individuality as ends exclude the use of organized social effort as means. Earlier liberalism regarded the separate and competing economic action of individuals as the means of social well-being as the end[4]. We must reverse the perspective and see that socialized economy is the means of free individual development as the end.

John Dewey at his 90th birthday, 1949

That liberals are divided in outlook and endeavor while reactionaries are held together by community of interests and the ties of custom is well-nigh a commonplace. Organization of standpoint and belief among liberals can be achieved only in and by unity of endeavor. Organized unity of action attended by consensus of beliefs will come about in the degree in which social control of economic forces is made the goal of liberal action. The greatest educational power, the greatest force in shaping the dispositions and attitudes of individuals, is the social medium in which they live. The medium that now lies closest to us is that of unified action for the inclusive end of a socialized economy. The attainment of a state of society in which a basis of material security will release the powers of individuals for cultural expression is not the work of a day. But by concentrating upon the task of securing a socialized economy as the ground and medium for release of the impulses and capacities men agree to call ideal, the now scattered and often conflicting activities of liberals can be brought to effective unity.

It is no part of my task to outline in detail a program for renascent liberalism. But the question of "what is to be done" cannot be ignored. Ideas must be organized, and this organization implies an organization of individuals who hold these ideas and whose faith is ready to translate itself into action. Translation into action signifies that the general creed of liberalism be formulated as a concrete program of action. It is in organization for action that liberals are weak, and without this organization there is danger that democratic ideals may go by default[5]. Democracy has been a fighting faith. When its ideals are reinforced by those of scientific method and experimental

---

1   **eclipse:** loss of power and reputation
2   **The notion that organized ... and the individual.:** Dewey is here criticizing the traditional laissez faire liberalism and prefers "organized social control." For the "laissez faire liberalism," see Adam Smith in Unit 10.
3   **dampen:** make dull or weak
4   **regarded the seperate ... as the end:** regarded ... as the end
5   **by default:** not present

Heritage of Western Intellectual Tradition   A Sourcebook

intelligence, it cannot be that it is incapable of evoking discipline, ardor and organization. To narrow the issue for the future to a struggle between Fascism and Communism[1] is to invite a catastrophe that may carry civilization down in the struggle. Vital and courageous democratic liberalism is the one force that can surely avoid such a disastrous narrowing of the issue. I for one do not believe that Americans living in the tradition of Jefferson and Lincoln will weaken and give up without a whole-hearted effort to make democracy a living reality. This, I repeat, involves organization.

The question cannot be answered by argument. Experimental method means experiment, and the question can be answered only by trying, by organized effort[2]. The reasons for making the trial are not abstract or recondite[3]. They are found in the confusion, uncertainty and conflict that mark the modern world. The reasons for thinking that the effort if made will be successful are also not abstract and remote. They lie in what the method of experimental and cooperative intelligence has already accomplished in subduing to potential human use the energies of physical nature[4]. In material production, the method of intelligence is now the established rule; to abandon it would be to revert to savagery. The task is to go on, and not backward, until the method of intelligence and experimental control is the rule in social relations and social direction. Either we take this road or we admit that the problem of social organization in behalf of human liberty and the flowering of human capacities is insoluble[5].

It would be fantastic folly to ignore or to belittle the obstacles that stand in the way. But what has taken place, also against great odds[6], in the scientific and industrial revolutions, is an accomplished fact; the way is marked out. It may be that the way will remain untrodden. If so, the future holds the menace[7] of confusion moving into chaos, a chaos that will be externally masked for a time by an organization of force, coercive and violent, in which the liberties of men will all but disappear. Even so, the cause of liberty of the human spirit, the cause of opportunity of human beings for full development of their powers, the cause for which liberalism enduringly stands, is too precious and too ingrained in the human constitution to be forever obscured. Intelligence after millions of years of errancy[8] has found itself as a method, and it will not be lost forever in the blackness of night. The business of liberalism is to bend[9] every energy and exhibit every courage

---

1   **To narrow the issue … between Fascism and Communism:** Here we see Dewey's own political position as a "liberal bourgeois."

2   **by trying, by organized effort:** This is Dewey's pragmatism and experimentalism, namely act upon deeds rather than words — empty argument will lead to nowhere.

3   **recondite:** profound, out of the way

4   **subduing to potential human use the energies of physical nature:** i.e., subduing the energies of physical nature to potential human use

5   **insoluble:** (problems) that can not be solved

6   **against … odds:** in spite of difficulties

7   **menace:** threat

8   **errancy:** state of making mistakes

9   **bend:** direct

so that these precious goods may not even be temporarily lost but be intensified and expanded here and now.

Key Concepts

confused uncertainty	new social orientation
crisis in democracy	ordered expression of individual capacity
education	organized intelligence
far-reaching social plans	organized social control
free intelligence	social action
habits of mind	social change
liberalism	social direction
liberation of the capacities of individuals	

Compare with China

John Dewey as a Learner in China

The decade of the 1920s marks an important period in the life of John Dewey: his trips to Japan, China, Russia, Mexico, and Turkey undoubtedly broadened his horizons and enriched his understanding of international politics. Of all the foreign nations Dewey visited, China is where he stayed the longest and about which he wrote the most extensively. Dewey's two-year visit[1] (1919 – 1921) marks a geographical and cultural transition from the West to the East.

A Timely Visit

Dewey arrived in China on May 1, 1919. Excited about this adventure, Dewey wrote, "We are going to see more of the dangerous daring side of life here I predict," and he added, "Nothing worries us. ... We ought to have a very good time." Interestingly, Dewey was right about the "dangerous daring side of life" in China. Three days after he made this remark, Dewey learned of

---

1   **Dewey's two-year visit:** Shortly after the end of the First World War, Dewey and his wife, Alice, decided to travel to Japan. Dewey hoped that this trip could help eliminate Alice's depression, while allowing himself a temporary break from postwar politics. Their initial plan for a short vacation in Japan led to an unexpectedly long sojourn in China: from May 1919 to July 1921. Even though Dewey agreed to his former students' invitation to lecture in China while traveling there, he initially saw himself more as a tourist than a lecturer and did not plan to stay in China beyond the summer of 1919 [writer's note].

a serious student revolt, which came to be known as the May Fourth Movement. Dewey's response to the May Fourth Movement was more than enthusiastic; he was galvanized[1] by the social energies being released. As Dewey wrote to his children in June 1919, "never in our lives had we begun to learn as much as in the last four months. And the last month particularly, there has been too much food to be digestible." The May Fourth Movement was China's gift to Dewey. It kept him excited, interested, involved, anxious, puzzled, and, at times, frustrated. It was also an intellectual bait that enticed[2] Dewey to stay in China for a full year, and later, to extend his stay to a second year.

Dewey as a Political Commentator: The May Fourth Movement

Dewey's timely presence in May-Fourth China provided a great opportunity for his own learning and gave him a vantage[3] point to witness the unfolding of the event. It also put him in a unique position to serve as a political commentator for the *New Republic*. During his stay, Dewey published dozens of essays about China. Dewey first interpreted the meaning of the May Fourth Movement for his American readers by saying that "[t]he possibilities of organization independent of government, but capable in the end of controlling government, have been demonstrated." He felt so hopeful that he even predicted, "It would be highly surprising if a new constitutionalist movement were not set going. The combination of students and merchants that has proved so effective will hardly be allowed to become a mere memory." Dewey believed that these events embodied the power of public opinion. As he later indicated, "the most impressive single feature of my stay in China was witnessing the sure and rapid growth of an enlightened and progressive public opinion." This experience was reassuring to Dewey because he had always believed that public opinion as a moral and intellectual force *should and would* triumph over the forces of coercion and violence.

However, Dewey's hope that the impact of the May Fourth Movement would effect significant political change was thwarted[4]. It did not accomplish much other than prevent China's signing of the Versailles peace treaty. This "relative political failure," as Dewey analyzed retrospectively, was due to "the youth and inexperience of the students," "the fear of excess," "the difficulty in maintaining continuous organized cooperation with the mercantile guilds," and "the natural waning of enthusiasm when crisis was past." Nonetheless, it was a mistake, as Dewey said, to think that the movement proved to be of no avail. "In the Sequel of the Student Revolt," Dewey turned to emphasize its intellectual implications: "It was the manifestation of a new consciousness, an intellectual awakening in the young men and young women who through their schooling had been aroused to the necessity of a new order of belief, a new method of thinking."

---

1 **galvanize:** shock
2 **entice:** persuade
3 **vantage:** advantage
4 **thwart:** frustrate, prevent

Dewey as a Goodwill Ambassador

While Dewey's stay in China proved to be a rare opportunity for him to gain an insider perspective on Oriental conditions, it also entailed a moral responsibility. Throughout the course of Dewey's writing about China, one senses Dewey's ongoing concern about the role of the United States in the Far East. Like his views of the May Fourth Movement, Dewey's suggestions for American diplomacy in China also underwent significant changes.

Early in his stay, Dewey noticed a pro-American sentiment, especially prevailing in the intellectual circles of China. In the eyes of many Chinese, Japan was the despoiler[1], whereas America was the rescuer. Resentment toward Japan had contributed to a "pathetic affection for America." As Dewey put it, "China in her despair has created an image of a powerful democratic, peace-loving America, devoted to securing international right and justice, especially for weak nations." He insisted that China's idealization of America should impose "humility rather than self-glorification upon Americans." Even though he applauded the American influence "in the educational line," he cautioned: "this success is not of a kind to be impressive when it comes to determination of international affairs." The key to peace in the Far East, Dewey claimed, lay in the relationship between Japan and America. In his own writings, Dewey tried to influence American policy toward China by attacking Japanese propaganda. He urged American politicians not to be bought off[2] by Japan or be taken in by their façade[3] of liberalism. After learning more about the status of Japan in international politics and its predatory[4] attitude toward China, Dewey perceived the seed of a future war being deeply implanted in China. He cautioned American readers that "every appeal to American sympathy on the ground of the growing liberalism of Japan should meet with neither credulity nor cynicism, but with a request to know what this liberalism is doing, especially what it is doing about China and Siberia."

Apart from informing his American readers of the reality of Japanese imperialism, Dewey also gave suggestions concerning what America should do to help China overcome its current crisis and to embark on the path of normal development. In his earlier writings, Dewey asked America to "sympathetically comprehend the Chinese situation," to be "patient and persistent" in its foreign policies, and to realize "the enormous power which is now in her hands." Dewey advised that the American government assist China in important practical tasks such as improving agriculture, constructing railways and inland waterway systems, and regulating currency systems. He hoped that such potential on the part of the United States won't be "thrown away by reason of stupidity and ignorance."

Dewey's sense of obligation as a close witness of China's predicaments and his deep convictions about the interconnectedness of international affairs propelled him initially to espouse[5] an

---

1   **despoiler:** robber, plunderer
2   **buy off:** bribe
3   **façade:** face, appearance
4   **predatory:** (for the purpose of) plundering
5   **espouse:** support

activist, paternalistic[1] approach toward China. However, as his understanding of Chinese history, culture, and psychology deepened, his initial activism mellowed[2]. In his response to whether the U.S. should join the alliance with Great Britain to resolve the Far Eastern crisis, Dewey said, "There is an obligation upon us not to engage too much or too readily with them until there is assurance that we shall not make ourselves worse." Experience had taught Dewey much about the dark realities of international politics — that professed ideals for democracy and peace could turn out to serve imperialistic ends.

The shift in Dewey's thinking was most evident in an article written shortly after his return as a response to the upcoming Pacific Conference in Washington. Dewey advised against exogenous[3] intervention in China's domestic affairs and suggested instead a "hands-off" policy:

> The hope of the world's peace, as well as China's freedom, lies in adhering to a policy of Hands Off. Give China a chance. Give her time. The danger lies in being in a hurry, in impatience, possibly in the desire of Americans to show that we are a power in international affairs and that we too have a positive foreign policy. And a benevolent policy from without, instead of promoting her aspirations from within, may in the end do China about as much harm as a policy conceived in malevolence[4].

Dewey's earlier paternalistic impulses gave way to a deep respect for the self-determination and self-government of the Chinese people. His earlier enthusiasm gave way to a healthy skepticism that kept him suspicious of any proposal to place China under international tutelage[5]. Dewey's non-interventionist approach was the result not of cold indifference but of a profound respect for China's capacity for self-governance. In addition, Dewey realized that "China will not be saved from outside herself," for she "is used to taking time for her problems: she can neither understand nor profit by the impatient methods of the Western world which are profoundly alien to her genius."

In an article written a few years after his return, Dewey reiterated[6] his opposition to the paternal attitude of the United States in its interaction with China, particular in light of the increasing resentment toward missionary efforts in China. He said,

> We have gone there with ideas and ideals, with sentiments and aspirations; we have presented a certain type of culture to China as a model to be imitated. As far as we have gone at all, we have gone in *loco parentis*[7], with advice, with instruction, with example and precept. Like a good parent we would have brought up China in the way in which she should go. There is a genial[8] and generous aspect to all this. But nonetheless it has

---

1 **paternalistic:** like father to son, condescending
2 **mellow:** become wide and sympathetic
3 **exogenous:** derived or developed from outside the body; originating externally
4 **malevolence:** wish to do evil
5 **tutelage:** guardianship
6 **reiterate:** say again
7 **in *loco parentis*:** in the position or place of a parent
8 **genial:** kind, sympathetic

created a situation, and that situation is fraught with[1] danger.

The danger lay in the resentment on the part of the Chinese toward the "the air of superiority" assumed by foreign guardians, such as American missionaries, and in the consequent charges on the part of the foreign helpers that the Chinese were ungrateful. Dewey urged the United States to alter its "traditional parental attitude, colored as it has been by a temper of patronage, conscious or unconscious, into[2] one of respect and esteem for a cultural equal."

Dewey as a Cultural Anthropologist

One major purpose of Dewey's trip was to "get some acquaintance" with what was happening on the other side of the world. Soon after he arrived on the scene, he became interested in more than collecting exotic stories that might impress his grandchildren. His mind was set on an intelligent inquiry into China's predicaments and his heart on the destiny of its people.

As a reflective thinker, Dewey soon realized that the history of contact between the West and China was characterized by grave misunderstandings. The reason was that many of the political and economic conceptions of the Western world did not apply to Chinese situations. In other words, Dewey was realizing that a non-Eurocentric[3] point of view — a concept alien to Dewey's time but quite in keeping with[4] his pragmatic sensibility — was key to an accurate and sympathetic understanding of China. Dewey summarized this unusual cultural experience to a former student of philosophy: "This is really 'the other side of the world' in every sense, and it [is] most interesting to see a culture where so many of our prepossessions are reversed. It has a tendency to make academic affairs including [academic] philosophy shrink. [It's] a good thing we can't [visit] the rest of the universe in space; our [own] habits and beliefs would shrink too much."

On a different occasion, Dewey wrote, "The visitor spends his time learning, if he learns anything about China, not to think of what he sees in terms of the ideas he uses as a matter of course[5] at home." For Dewey, the need to cultivate a culturally sensitive perspective is what gave China its "overpowering intellectual interest for an observer of the affairs of humanity." Given that the Western world view in the early twentieth century was predominantly Eurocentric, one finds remarkable intellectual farsightedness and open-mindedness in Dewey's reflections on the problem of Eurocentrism. A tyro[6] in Chinese history, Dewey inevitably made a few mistakes in his judgments about current events, but he was quick to correct them and continued to learn along the way.

One of Dewey's misjudgments pertains to his overzealous attitude toward the May Fourth

---

1   **fraught with:** filled with or attended with
2   **alter its "traditional ... into:** ... alter ... into
3   **Eurocentric:** focused on Europe and the Europeans
4   **in keeping with:** agreeable with
5   **a matter of course:** something which is taken for granted
6   **tyro:** tiro, beginner

Heritage of Western Intellectual Tradition   A Sourcebook

student movement, which was largely grounded in his own political desires. As mentioned earlier, Dewey was fascinated by the power of public opinion and grassroots activism demonstrated in the student movement. His spontaneous enthusiasm kept him, as he put it, "always on the alert to see what is coming next"; he admitted that it was hard "to repress one's desire for a [little] more [direct] western energy to tackle things before they get to the toppling over point[1]." However, everything seemed to have returned to normalcy[2] after a few weeks of heated agitation, leaving Dewey's high hopes for significant change unfulfilled. The disappointed Dewey sometimes found the ingrained passivity of the Chinese people baffling. As Dewey wrote to his children one month after the outbreak of the student demonstration:

> Status quo is China's middle name, most status and a little quo. I have one more motto to add to "You Never Can Tell" and "Let George Do It." It is, "That is very bad." Instead of concealing things, they expose all their weak and bad points very freely, and after setting them forth most calmly and objectively, say 'That is very bad.'"

北京大学第一批七名女学生和杜威家人合影

Dewey observed that the Chinese "talk more easily than they act — especially in politics," and they love "finding substitutes for positive action, of avoiding entering upon a course of action which might be irrevocable[3]." Dewey later came to realize that "China has never been anything but apathetic[4] towards governmental questions. The Student Revolt marked a temporary exception only in appearance."

Implying his own error, Dewey wrote, "The new comer in China in observing and judging usually makes the mistake of attaching too much significance to current happenings." He even remarked in a tongue-in-cheek[5] manner, "After a few months in China, a visitor will take an oath, if he is wise, never to indulge in prediction." Refraining from making predictions may be easy for others but difficult for Dewey, whose lifelong project is to make practice intelligent through anticipation of consequences and application of foresight. Dewey still allowed himself to make a few more predictions in his later articles on China, but a few more in Dewey's eyes probably wouldn't count as indulgence. On one occasion, Dewey posed the question, "Is it possible for a Westerner to understand Chinese political psychology?" He quickly answered, "certainly not without a prior knowledge of the historic customs and institutions of China, for institutions have shaped the mental habits, not the mind the social habits."

---

1 **toppling over point:** turning point, climax
2 **normalcy:** state of being normal
3 **irrevocable:** final and unalterable
4 **apathetic:** indifferent, lack of interest
5 **tongue-in-cheek:** not intended seriously; ironical or joking

As a committed and diligent learner about China, Dewey undertook to read Chinese history; he read local English newspapers to keep abreast of the latest political developments; he conversed with local foreigners to share and exchange views with them; and he even took Chinese language lessons from a tutor. Dewey could have made the same comment as his wife when she said, "Since reading of their history I can see why they have always been in a state much like this." Dewey's exposure to Chinese history, coupled with his own observations, led him to remark: "China can be understood only in terms of the institutions and ideas which have been worked out in its own historical evolution."

To be more specific, Chinese politics "has to be understood in terms of itself, not translated over into the classification of an alien political morphology." According to Dewey, Westerners who pigeonholed Chinese facts into Western conceptions misconstrued China as a nation with a single centralized government in full operation. Dewey argued that China was not a nation, but, at best, a nation-to-be. In his view, China was more like older Europe than contemporary France. Patriotism, Dewey observed, took a special form in China; it was not allegiance to a political state but an attachment to soil and birthplace. The Western conception of the nation-state could not be universalized across cultures.

Moreover, Western economic terms do not fit the Chinese context. He said, "When we turn from political to economic affairs, our habitual western ideas are even less applicable. Their irrelevancy makes it impossible intelligently to describe the Chinese conditions or even grasp them intelligently."

Dewey insisted that China was politically and economically a different world and should be understood and treated as such. Not only is China a politically and economically different world, it is socially different as well. An example of Dewey's penetrating insights into Chinese social psychology is his analysis of China's "crowd psychology" that contributed to her conservatism and passivity. As he observed,

It is beyond question that many traits of the Chinese mind are the products of an extraordinary and long-continued density of populations. Psychologists have discovered, or possibly invented, a "psychology of the crowd" to account for the way men act in masses, as a mob at a lynching bee. They have not inquired as to the effect upon the mind of constant living in close contact with large numbers, of continual living in a crowd. ... I wonder whether even the Anglo-Saxons would have developed or retained initiative if they had lived for centuries under conditions that gave them no room to stir about, no relief from the unremitting surveillance of their fellows? Possibly they would then have acquired a habit of thinking of their "face" before they thought of the thing to be done. Perhaps when they thought of a new thing they would have decided discretion and hesitation to be the better part of invention.

Dewey may not have been a great prophet in a world that was constantly changing, in a world that operated under habits of mind often contrary to his own. However, he proved to be a remarkable learner whose intellectual humility and open-mindedness were exemplary. His perseverance in learning led him to the ultimate understanding that China was not only a politically, economically and socially different world but more importantly, a philosophically different world, a world that could be understood only in its own philosophical terms. (Adapted from Jessica Ching-Sze Wang)

Supplementary Reading

1. Freud on the Couch

Sigmund Freud is now discredited as a scientist and vilified[1] for intellectual dishonesty. But the author argues that, despite his flaws, Freud was a genius whose influence on human self-awareness is still being felt today.

Sigmund Freud was born 150 years old this week, and his stock[2] has never been lower. Almost no intellectual or character fault has not been ascribed to him. It is now as fashionable to revile[3] him as it once was to revere him; he is regarded as little better than a charlatan[4] who would have been more accurately named Fraud[5] than Freud.

His theories have been thoroughly exploded[6] and his life's work undermined to the point of complete destruction by conclusive historical and biographical research. And yet almost everyone suspects that, despite all that has been written against him, despite the myriad[7] books debunking[8] him, he remains a greater man than any of his critics. For if he were quite as negligible a figure as he is now accounted, why would it be necessary to throw so many stones at him for so long?

Of course, historical importance and intellectual merit are not quite the same thing. A man's ideas may be utterly worthless yet highly influential, or brilliant but without significant echo. With Freud, it is not easy to say precisely what his achievement was; but a man who created a climate of opinion the world over must have been out of the ordinary.

---

1   **vilify:** criticize, slander
2   **stock:** personal reputation or status
3   **revile:** call bad names
4   **charlatan:** person who pretends to have medical knowledge
5   **fraud:** person who deceives
6   **explode:** destroy, overthrow
7   **myriad:** great number
8   **debunk:** reveal truth by stripping away false tradition

The charges against him are many and serious. Far from having been the lone pioneer of the unconscious mind that he claimed to have been, he was a continuer and follower of the ideas of other men, whose influence he dishonestly failed to acknowledge. In short, Freud was a mythomaniac[1] of gigantic proportions who had no hesitation in rewriting the past.

He was intellectually dishonest. He was well aware that his patients were not cured in the way that his published case histories claimed that they were, and that therefore the claims he made for his method were false; hence all his theorising about the structure of the mind was based on no scientific evidence whatsoever. He claimed to be a natural scientist but in fact had little appreciation of scientific method and acted more as the leader of a cult or new religion than as a disinterested[2] searcher after truth.

Whenever a disciple, such as Jung[3] or Adler[4], disagreed with him, he did not so much refute his ideas as seek to ruin him by excommunication[5] from the "true church" of psychoanalysis, which was a reaction to criticism more appropriate to a theocrat[6] than to a real scientist. Freud wanted uncritical admiration and agreement from his followers, or rather disciples, not honest criticism, which he believed (or pretended to believe) was the consequence of an unresolved Oedipus complex[7].

The influence of his ideas, albeit in vulgarised[8] and simplified versions, has been culturally baleful[9] and even catastrophic. For example, the notion that dysfunctional[10] behaviour in adulthood has its origin in infantile or childhood traumas[11] has led to a general belief in the existence of buried psychological treasure which, once unearthed and expressed in clear terms, automatically, in and of itself, causes the dysfunctional behaviour to cease, without any further conscious effort to control it on the patient's part. Freud thus strengthened a tendency for people to place the blame for their vices first on their parents and secondly on the doctors who failed to "cure" them of those vices. He was one of the most powerful modern destroyers of the concept of personal responsibility.

---

1 **mythomaniac:** compulsion to embroider the truth, engage in exaggeration, or tell lies
2 **disinterested:** not influenced by personal feelings
3 **Carl Gustav Jung (1875 – 1961):** Swiss psychiatrist who founded analytical psychology, known for the concepts of extraversion and introversion and the notion of the collective unconscious
4 **Alfred Adler (1870 – 1937):** Austrian psychiatrist who rejected Sigmund Freud's emphasis on sexuality and theorized that neurotic behavior is an overcompensation for feelings of inferiority
5 **excommunication:** exclusion from the Christian community
6 **theocrat:** believer in theocracy or government ruled by or subject to religious authority
7 **Oedipus complex:** in Freudian psychoanalysis, a subconscious sexual desire in a child, especially a male child, for the parent of the opposite sex, the mother, usually accompanied by hostility to the parent of the same sex, the father
8 **vulgarised:** popularized
9 **baleful:** evil
10 **dysfunctional:** abnormal or impaired functioning, especially of a bodily system or social group
11 **trauma:** psychological injury, shock

Heritage of Western Intellectual Tradition   A Sourcebook

His view that the repression of childhood sexuality caused, or could cause, neuroses or even psychoses resulted in the crude sexualisation of culture, for it implied that attempts to control oneself were not merely unhealthy but dangerous. Freud was thus the principal intellectual influence behind our current libertinism[1]. He also weakened the place of rational argument in human affairs. He made it possible for people always to argue that those with whom they disagreed were not so much mistaken about the evidence or logic of the matter as motivated by neuroses of which they were unaware. Thus Freud was one of the patron saints of the *ad hominem*[2] argument, which leads inevitably to intellectual laziness and dishonesty. Freud argued that those who disagreed with him were blinded by their neuroses — which only psychoanalysis, as prescribed by him, could cure. Psychoanalysis, therefore, is "reinforced dogmatism" because its attempts at refutation are taken by believers as being confirmation of their truth.

Even if many of the charges against Freud are true, however, a man is not necessarily responsible for the uses to which his ideas are put. Moreover, Freud clearly was exceptionally gifted.

Starting out to study neuroanatomy[3] and neurophysiology[4], to which he made considerable contributions, he became a neurologist for a time and wrote a classic work on cerebral palsy[5]. He also came near to discovering the local anaesthetic[6] effects of cocaine (the first such anaesthetic ever discovered), though instead he went off at an unfortunate tangent[7] and recommended it as a cure for opiate[8] addiction, in the process ruining the life of an addicted colleague, Dr Fleischl-Marxow. Nevertheless, it is clear that from the start he was a very brilliant man, and not only in the black art of self-promotion.

He was possessed of exceptional literary gifts. There can be no question that he was a great writer: to read him is to be beguiled[9] by him. Just as with Sherlock Holmes[10], one is inclined to overlook the faults of his logic and lacunae[11] in the evidence for his conclusions because of the sheer brio[12] involved. His imaginative leaps dazzle; his ability to find significance in small details — for example, slips of the tongue (and who among us does not use the concept of the Freudian slip?) — leave us feeling that we have been in the presence of a genius.

---

1 **libertinism:** the behavior characteristic of a libertine, one who defies established religious precepts, a freethinker; or one who acts without moral restraint
2 *ad hominem*: appealing to personal considerations rather than to logic or reason
3 **neuroanatomy:** branch of anatomy dealing with the nervous system
4 **neurophysiology:** branch of physiology dealing with the functions of the nervous system
5 **cerebral palsy:** disorder usually caused by brain damage occurring at or before birth and marked by muscular impairment, involving speech and learning difficulties
6 **anaesthetic:** producing insensibility to pain
7 **tangent:** sudden digression or change of course
8 **opiate:** drug containing opium
9 **beguile:** amuse, pass time pleasantly
10 **Sherlock Holmes:** fictitious detective in stories by A. Conan Doyle
11 **lacuna:** blank, missing part
12 **brio:** vigor, excitement

Freud was a deeply cultivated man, too. He was a good linguist and his knowledge of literature, especially Shakespeare (which he read and memorised), was vast. Highly intelligent men, such as the great Austrian writer Stefan Zweig[1], were deeply impressed by him; when Freud arrived in England as a refugee after the Anschluss[2] in 1938, the Royal Society immediately conferred an exceptional honour on him. The Royal Society is not composed of fools. If Freud's errors are quite so obvious as they now seem to his detractors, why were they not spotted much sooner? Something akin to a psychoanalytical explanation would be necessary to explain it. Thus we cannot dispose of Freud's mode of thinking as easily as we should like.

Freud's views were not simplistic. Indeed, his view of human life was tragic rather than optimistic in any facile[3] way. Contrary to the uses to which his writings and ideas have sometimes been put, he was no advocate of libertinism. Indeed, he was notably reticent[4] in his public behaviour. He certainly did not believe that if only a man could give practical expression to all his instincts, whenever and however they prompted him, he would lead a life permanently free of frustration and sorrow.

Oedipus and the Sphinx (1808) in the Louvre Museum

On the contrary, as a deeply civilised Viennese bourgeois intellectual, he believed that frustration was part of the price mankind had to pay for civilisation: but it was a price well worth paying. He believed that we were but a veneer's[5] thickness away from barbarism — and in the light of subsequent events in the 20th century, who can say that he was not prescient[6]?

Although his writings were not scientific in any rigorous sense, and although he was not the lone pioneer that he claimed to be, supposedly charting a completely unknown psychological continent, there is no doubt that it was he who made us aware, in a straightforward and coherent fashion, just how hidden and contorted[7] human motivation could be, how little reliance we could place on our consciously avowed intentions, and how important, though also how difficult, it is for us to know ourselves.

Freud was not a great scientist, nor did he discover anything in the sense that Robert Koch[8]

---

1 **Stefan Zweig (1881–1942):** Austrian writer
2 **Anschluss:** political union, especially the one unifying Nazi Germany and Austria in 1938
3 **facile:** easily obtained
4 **reticent:** reserved
5 **veneer:** thin layer
6 **prescient:** able to see into the future
7 **contorted:** twisted
8 **Robert Koch (1843 – 1910):** German bacteriologist who isolated the anthrax bacillus and the tubercle bacillus and the cholera bacillus

Heritage of Western Intellectual Tradition   A Sourcebook

discovered the germ that causes tuberculosis, and Watson and Crick[1] discovered the double helix[2]. He did not contribute any store of positive facts to human knowledge. Science would be deprived of practically nothing had he not lived. His theories are now universally dismissed, either as having been disproved or, somewhat contradictorily, as being incapable of disproof and therefore not scientific theories in the first place.

Yet his influence on all of us was enormous, and it would be as impossible to return to a pre-Freudian way of thinking as to return to a pre-heliocentric[3] theory of the solar system. Freud is a little like Nature in Horace's[4] famous line: though you may throw him out with a pitchfork[5], yet he returns. It is as if he enunciated[6] deep if unprovable truths about ourselves that had never been so clearly enunciated before. He did not arrive at these by scientific means but instinctively, in the manner of a great writer.

If I may be allowed a little instinct of my own, I don't think it is possible to look at photographs of Freud and doubt that he was a very considerable human being. And the two words that he wrote in his diary when the Gestapo[7] came to turn him out of Vienna (he was too world-famous for them to lay a finger on him) have a poignant[8], moving and infinitely dignified greatness about them: *Finis Austriae*[9]. (Adapted from Anthony Daniels, *Times* May 05, 2006)

2. Early Education in China

In February of 1916, Teachers College Dean James Earl Russell received a letter from a man known then as Tao Wen Tsing[10], who wrote to acknowledge his award of a Livingston Scholarship, which was money granted primarily to foreign missionaries engaged in important educational work. "After seeing the serious defects of the sudden birth of our Republic," Tao wrote, "I was convinced that no genuine republic could exist without a genuine public education."

With that in mind, Tao Wen Tsing, whose name meant "academic elite professional," set out to create just such an educational system for China. "I wish to assure you and the donors of the Livingston Scholarships," he wrote, "that after two more years' preparation ... I shall go back to

---

1   **James D. Watson and Francis Crick:** who together discovered the structure of DNA in the 1950s, for which they were awarded the 1962 Nobel Prize for Physiology or Medicine, along with Maurice Wilkins

2   **helix:** spiral form or structure

3   **heliocentric:** relating to a reference system based at the center of the sun

4   **Horace:** Quintus Horatius Flaccus (65 – 8 BC), Roman lyric poet, whose *Odes* and *Satires* have exerted a major influence on English poetry

5   **pitchfork:** long-handled fork for lifting hay

6   **enunciate:** express clearly

7   **Gestapo:** German secret state police during Nazi period

8   **poignant:** deeply moving

9   *Finis Austriae*: death of Austria. See note to Anschluss.

10 **Tao Wen Tsing:** the original name of Tao Xingzhi was (陶文睿)

cooperate with other educators to organize an efficient system of public education for our people ..." Tao's preparation continued at Teachers College, where he took graduate studies under the tutelage of such professors as John Dewey, Paul Monroe and William Heard Kilpatrick. He returned to China in 1917 and worked as a professor and administrator at Nanjing Teachers College.

It wasn't until John Dewey journeyed to China in 1919 to present his educational philosophy to a republic in the making[1] that Tao realized the tragic conditions of Chinese education — over 77 percent of the population was illiterate — and that he had been negligent in identifying with the needs of the ordinary working person in China. Thereafter, Tao devoted his efforts to putting Dewey's philosophy to work in his homeland. He realized that, "what we need now is a new type of education ... which will enlighten the people ... and mould them into citizens for the republic and for the modern world."

Like Dewey, Tao believed that school must be closely connected to society to play a vital role in social reform and that education is an active, constructive process in real-life experiences rather than one of telling and being told. Yet, when Tao applied Dewey's methods to Chinese education, he found that Chinese students were limited by what the schools were offering them.

Expanding on Dewey's ideas, Tao did what he termed a "half somersault[2]" with Dewey's philosophy. Instead of "school as society," Tao looked at "society as school"; instead of "education as life," he saw "life as education"; and, instead of "learning by doing," he proposed "unity of teaching, learning, and reflective acting." Tao's most famous experiment was to create the Morning Village Normal School in Nanjing（南京晓庄师范学校）, which not only was designed to train rural teachers in his philosophy, but was also designed to become the center of all political, social and economic activity in an effort to renew the village itself. The experiment was a success, resulting in the improvement of production, living standards, education, economics and security.

Though John Dewey never visited the Morning Village Normal School, William H. Kilpatrick did in 1929. Writing in his diary, he described a coordinated effort between the school and community where the students were taught by attacking actual life problems. He commented, "It seemed particularly good that so excellent an enterprise should succeed so well, cost so little, and be so completely Chinese."

Classroom Building of the Nanking Morning Village Normal School, 1927

As part of his dedication to his ideas, Tao changed his name twice to reflect his beliefs. From

---

1   **in the making:** just taking shape
2   **somersault:** 翻筋斗

Tao Wen Tsing, the name his parents gave to reflect their hopes for him, he became Tao Zhixing, which means, "knowing then doing." Finally, he became Tao Xingzhi, which means, "doing then knowing," because he believed that one should do first, then one will know.

陶行知破 "女禁" 1920 年在南高师（后来 的南京大学）招收第一批女大学生

The Morning Village Normal School was shut down in 1930 by Nationalist troops, and was reopened after the establishment of the People's Republic of China in 1949 with a commitment to improving teacher education, reforming rural education and establishing Tao's principles. Today, it is one of the four normal schools in Nanjing Metropolitan for training elementary school teachers for rural and city schools.

Tao's principles of education have gone from the creation of an experimental school to a national education reform movement. There is a Tao Museum and 18 branches throughout The People's Republic of China of the Tao Research Association, which focuses on his life, his educational thoughts and practices. Today, Tao Xingzhi is still regarded as a hero for his implementation of the theories he developed through his contact with John Dewey and Teachers College.

Questions for Discussion

1. What is the structure of the "Psyche"?
2. According to Freud, what causes psychosis and how to combat psychosis?
3. Why is Freud still popular, in spite of the fact that many of his assumptions turn out to be either limited or even completely wrong?
4. What is Dewey's idea concerning democracy and education?
5. How has Dewey influenced modern education, positively as well as negatively, according to your own experience?
6. Discuss strengths and weaknesses of Dewey's "instrumentalism."

UNIT 15

Science & Religion

Pretest

- What do you know about the social context of the first half of the 20th century?
- How did this context affect the development of the intellectual thought of the time?
- Do you have any idea about Bertrand Russell and A. N. Whitehead?

What You Will Learn in This Unit

- Trends of humanities in the first half of the 20th century;
- Selected readings from Bertrand Russell and A. N. Whitehead; and
- Russell's contrast between Chinese and Western Civilizations.

Learn to Pronounce

Alfred North Whitehead /'(h)waɪthed/ 怀特海

Bertrand Russell /'rʌsəl/ 罗素

Cassandra /kəˈsændrə/ 卡珊德拉

Mephistopheles /ˌmefɪsˈtɒfɪliːz/ 麦裴斯托裴利

Militarism /'mɪlɪtərɪzəm/ 黩武；军国主义

Moloch /'məʊlɒk/ 摩洛神

Nobel laureate /'lɔːrɪɪt/ 月桂树叶（授予竞赛的优胜者）

Promethean /prəˈmiːθɪən/ 普罗米修斯的

Thomas Carlyle /kɑːˈlaɪl/ 卡莱尔

Heritage of Western Intellectual Tradition　A Sourcebook

-485-

Introduction

The crises and wars in the first half of the 20th century threw humanity into one of its worst chaos. In face of the glooming reality, intellectuals felt called upon, once again, to fight the encroaching dangers. Like Jean Jacques Rousseau some 200 years ago, Bertrand Russell had to find an answer to the question of "whether the arts and sciences have contributed to the improvement of morals." Unlike Rousseau, however, Russell did this with his long-standing social activism and his popularizations of technical writings in philosophy and the natural sciences. Others, such as John Dewey and Alfred North Whitehead however, sought to redress the situation through science and education, since for them, as for many Chinese intellectuals at the time as well, science and education seemed to be the best solution to the numerous problems they found in society, and to affect man's mentality seemed to be the best way to affect a change in society. The age of education continues into the present day, although it is still doubtful what type of education we need and if it could be the final remedy for the problems of humanity.

Bertrand Russell: A Free Man's Worship*

Bertrand Arthur William Russell (1872–1970), British philosopher, mathematician, and Nobel laureate, whose emphasis on logical analysis influenced the course of 20th-century philosophy. Born in Trelleck, Wales, Russell questioned Euclid at 11. After obtaining a First Class with distinction in philosophy at Trinity College, Cambridge, he was elected a fellow in 1895. From an early age he involved himself in the study of logical and mathematical questions and lectured at many institutions throughout the world, including China. He achieved prominence with *The Principles of Mathematics* (1902), in which he attempted to give mathematics a precise scientific framework. Russell then collaborated for eight years with A. Whitehead to produce the monumental work *Principia Mathematica* (1910–1913). In *The Problems of Philosophy* (1912) he borrowed from sociology, psychology, physics, and mathematics to refute the tenets of idealism, the dominant philosophical school of the period, which held that all objects and experiences are the product of the intellect. Russell, a realist, believed that objects perceived by the senses have an inherent reality independent of the mind. Russell condemned both sides in World War I (1914–1918). After his college deprived him of his lectureship in 1916, he was offered a post at Harvard University, but was refused a passport. In 1918 he was sentenced to six months' imprisonment for a pacifistic article. After the war he visited the USSR, but expressed his disappointment in *Practice and Theory of Bolshevism* (1920). He taught at Peking University on philosophy during 1921 and 1922. He was barred from teaching at the City University of New York by

---

*   First published in Dec. 1903, this is perhaps Russell's best known and most reprinted essay. As a historical landmark of early-20th-century European thought, its mood and language have often been explained, even by Russell himself, as reflecting a particular time in his life.

the state supreme court because of his attacks on religion in *What I Believe* (1925) and his advocacy of sexual freedom in *Manners and Morals* (1929). Russell supported the Allied cause in World War II, but he became an ardent opponent of nuclear weapons. As a bridge between the intellectual circles of the two centuries, he visited W. Whitman in his home, interviewed Lenin, exchanged numerous letters with D.H. Lawrence, and taught L. Wittgenstein at Trinity College. His friends included A. Einstein, J. Keynes and T. S. Eliot. He received the 1950 Nobel Prize for Literature and was cited as "the champion of humanity and freedom of thought." At 89 he was imprisoned after an antinuclear demonstration. At 90, he said of himself, and of humanity, "Like Cassandra[1], I am doomed to prophesy evil and not be believed. Her promises came true. I desperately hope that mine will not."

To Dr. Faustus in his study, Mephistopheles[2] told the history of the Creation, saying:

"The endless praises of the choirs[3] of angels had begun to grow wearisome; for, after all, did he not deserve their praise? Had he not given them endless joy? Would it not be more amusing to obtain undeserved praise, to be worshipped by beings whom he tortured? He smiled inwardly, and resolved that the great drama should be performed.

"For countless ages the hot nebula[4] whirled aimlessly through space. At length it began to take shape, the central mass threw off planets, the planets cooled, boiling seas and burning mountains heaved and tossed, from black masses of cloud hot sheets of rain deluged[5] the barely solid crust. And now the first germ[6] of life grew in the depths of the ocean, and developed rapidly in the fructifying[7]

Mephistopheles flying over Wittenberg

warmth into vast forest trees, huge ferns springing from the damp mould, sea monsters breeding, fighting, devouring, and passing away. And from the monsters, as the play unfolded itself, Man was born, with the power of thought, the knowledge of good and evil, and the cruel thirst for worship. And Man saw that all is passing in this mad, monstrous world, that all is struggling to snatch, at any cost, a few brief moments of life before Death's inexorable[8] decree. And Man said: 'There is a hidden purpose, could we but fathom it, and the purpose is good; for we must reverence[9] something, and in the visible world there is nothing worthy of reverence.' And Man

---

1　**Cassandra:** in Greek mythology daughter of Priam, king of Troy, endowed with the gift of prophecy but fated by Apollo never to be believed

2　**Mephistopheles:** name frequently used as an alternative form of Satan or the Devil. It appears most prominently in the legend of Faustus, a man who sells his soul to the Devil. This legend was famously recorded in Christopher Marlowe's play *The Tragical History of Doctor Faustus*, and in drama *Faust* by Goethe.

3　**choirs:** group singing

4　**nebula:** mass of stars in the night sky

5　**deluge:** flood

6　**germ:** portion of living organism becoming new organism（胚芽）

7　**fructify:** make fruitful

8　**inexorable:** relentless

9　**reverence:** worship

Heritage of Western Intellectual Tradition　A Sourcebook

stood aside from the struggle, resolving that God intended harmony to come out of chaos by human efforts. And when he followed the instincts which God had transmitted to him from his ancestry of beasts of prey, he called it Sin, and asked God to forgive him. But he doubted whether he could be justly forgiven, until he invented a divine Plan by which God's wrath was to have been appeased[1]. And seeing the present was bad, he made it yet worse, that thereby the future might be better. And he gave God thanks for the strength that enabled him to forgo[2] even the joys that were possible. And God smiled; and when he saw that Man had become perfect in renunciation[3] and worship, he sent another sun through the sky, which crashed into Man's sun; and all re-turned (returned) again to nebula.

"'Yes,' he murmured, 'it was a good play; I will have it performed again.'"

Such, in outline, but even more purposeless, more void of meaning, is the world which Science presents for our belief. Amid such a world, if anywhere, our ideals henceforward must find a home. That Man is the product of causes which had no prevision of the end they were achieving; that his origin, his growth, his hopes and fears, his loves and his beliefs, are but the outcome of accidental collocations[4] of atoms; that no fire, no heroism, no intensity of thought and feeling, can preserve an individual life beyond the grave; that all the labours of the ages, all the devotion, all the inspiration, all the noonday brightness of human genius, are destined to extinction in the vast death of the solar system, and that the whole temple of Man's achievement must inevitably be buried beneath the debris[5] of a universe in ruins — all these things, if not quite beyond dispute, are yet so nearly certain, that no philosophy which rejects them can hope to stand. Only within the scaffolding[6] of these truths, only on the firm foundations of unyielding despair, can the soul's habitations henceforth be safely built.

How, in such an alien and inhuman world, can so powerless a creature as Man preserve his aspirations untarnished[7]? **A strange mystery it is that Nature, omnipotent[8] but blind, in the revolutions of her secular hurryings through the abysses[9] of space, has brought forth at last a child, subject still to her power, but gifted with sight, with knowledge of good and evil, with the capacity of judging all the works of his unthinking Mother. In spite of Death, the mark and seal of the parental control, Man is yet free, during his brief years,**

---

1   **appease:** make calm
2   **forgo:** give up
3   **renunciation:** self-denial
4   **collocation:** arrangement, grouping together
5   **debris:** broken pieces
6   **scaffolding:** a scaffold or a system of scaffolds (脚手架)
7   **untarnished:** not losing brightness
8   **omnipotent:** all-powerful
9   **abyss:** bottomless hole

to examine, to criticise, to know, and in imagination to create. To him alone, in the world with which he is acquainted, this freedom belongs; and in this lies his superiority to the resistless forces that control his outward life.

The savage, like ourselves, feels the oppression of his impotence[1] before the powers of Nature; but having in himself nothing that he respects more than Power, he is willing to prostrate[2] himself before his gods, without inquiring whether they are worthy of his worship. Pathetic and very terrible is the long history of cruelty and torture, of degradation and human sacrifice, endured in the hope of placating[3] the jealous gods: surely, the trembling believer thinks, when what is most precious has been freely given, their[4] lust for blood must be appeased, and more will not be required. The religion of Moloch[5] — as such creeds may be generically called — is in essence the cringing[6] submission of the slave, who dare not, even in his heart, allow the thought that his master deserves no adulation[7]. Since the independence of ideals is not yet acknowledged, Power may be freely worshipped, and receive an unlimited respect, despite its wanton[8] infliction of pain.

But gradually, as morality grows bolder, the claim of the ideal world begins to be felt; and worship, if it is not to cease, must be given to gods of another kind than those created by the savage. Some, though they feel the demands of the ideal, will still consciously reject them[9], still

Bertrand Russell at the Nobel Award dinner

urging that naked Power is worthy of worship. Such is the attitude inculcated[10] in God's answer to Job out of the whirlwind: the divine power and knowledge are paraded, but of the divine goodness there is no hint. Such also is the attitude of those who, in our own day, base their morality upon the struggle for survival, maintaining that the survivors are necessarily the fittest. But others, not content with an answer so repugnant[11] to the moral sense, will adopt the position which we have become accustomed to regard as specially religious, maintaining that, in some hidden manner, the world of fact is really harmonious with the world of ideals. Thus Man creates God, all-powerful and all-good, the mystic unity of what is and what should be.

---

1 **impotence:** powerlessness, hopelessness
2 **prostrate:** yield to
3 **placate:** pacify, soothe, please
4 **their:** gods'
5 **Moloch:** god to whom children are sacrificed
6 **cringing:** humble, fearful
7 **adulation:** excessive flattery or admiration
8 **wanton:** irresponsible, wilful
9 **them:** demands
10 **inculcate:** fix firmly by repetition
11 **repugnant:** distasteful

But the world of fact, after all, is not good; and, in submitting our judgment to it, there is an element of slavishness from which our thoughts must be purged. For in all things it is well to exalt the dignity of Man, by freeing him as far as possible from the tyranny of non-human Power. **When we have realised that Power is largely bad, that man, with his knowledge of good and evil, is but a helpless atom in a world which has no such knowledge, the choice is again presented to us: Shall we worship Force, or shall we worship Goodness? Shall our God exist and be evil, or shall he be recognised as the creation of our own conscience?**

The answer to this question is very momentous[1], and affects profoundly our whole morality. The worship of Force, to which Carlyle[2] and Nietzsche and the creed of Militarism[3] have accustomed us, is the result of failure to maintain our own ideals against a hostile universe: it is itself a prostrate submission to evil, a sacrifice of our best to Moloch. If strength indeed is to be respected, let us respect rather the strength of those who refuse that false "recognition of facts" which fails to recognise that facts are often bad. Let us admit that, in the world we know, there are many things that would be better otherwise, and that the ideals to which we do and must adhere are not realised in the realm of matter. Let us preserve our respect for truth, for beauty, for the ideal of perfection which life does not permit us to attain, though none of these things meet with the approval of the unconscious universe. **If Power is bad, as it seems to be, let us reject it from our hearts. In this lies Man's true freedom: in determination to worship only the God created by our own love of the good, to respect only the heaven which inspires the insight of our best moments. In action, in desire, we must submit perpetually to the tyranny of outside forces; but in thought, in aspiration, we are free, free from our fellow-men, free from the petty planet on which our bodies impotently crawl, free even, while we live, from the tyranny of death.** Let us learn, then, that energy of faith which enables us to live constantly in the vision of the good; and let us descend, in action, into the world of fact, with that vision always before us.

When first the opposition of fact and ideal grows fully visible, a spirit of fiery revolt, of fierce hatred of the gods, seems necessary to the assertion of freedom. To defy with Promethean constancy a hostile universe, to keep its evil always in view, always actively hated, to refuse no pain that the malice[4] of Power can invent, appears to be the duty of all who will not bow before the inevitable. But indignation is still a bondage, for it compels our thoughts to be occupied with an evil world; and in the fierceness of desire from which rebellion springs there is a kind of self-assertion which it is necessary for the wise to overcome. Indignation is a submission of our thoughts, but not of our desires; the Stoic freedom in which wisdom consists is found in the submission of our desires, but not of our thoughts. From the submission of our desires springs

---

1 **momentous:** important, serious
2 **Thomas Carlyle (1795–1881):** Scottish essayist, satirist, and historian, whose work was hugely influential during the Victorian era
3 **Militarism:** belief that the foundation of a society's security is its military capacity, and that the development and maintenance of the military to ensure that capacity is the most important goal for that society
4 **malice:** ill will, desire to harm others

Heritage of Western Intellectual Tradition   A Sourcebook

the virtue of resignation[1]; from the freedom of our thoughts springs the whole world of art and philosophy, and the vision of beauty by which, at last, we half reconquer the reluctant world. **But the vision of beauty is possible only to unfettered contemplation, to thoughts not weighted by the load of eager wishes; and thus Freedom comes only to those who no longer ask of life that it shall yield them any of those personal goods that are subject to the mutations[2] of Time.**

Although the necessity of renunciation is evidence of the existence of evil, yet Christianity, in preaching it, has shown a wisdom exceeding that of the Promethean philosophy of rebellion. It must be admitted that, of the things we desire, some, though they prove impossible, are yet real goods; others, however, as ardently longed for, do not form part of a fully purified ideal. The belief that what must be renounced is bad, though sometimes false, is far less often false than untamed passion supposes; and the creed of religion, by providing a reason for proving that it is never false, has been the means of purifying our hopes by the discovery of many austere[3] truths. But there is in resignation a further good element: even real goods, when they are

The Nobel Award for Literature awarded to Bertrand Russell in 1950

unattainable, ought not to be fretfully[4] desired. To every man comes, sooner or later, the great renunciation. For the young, there is nothing unattainable; a good thing desired with the whole force of a passionate will, and yet impossible, is to them not credible. Yet, by death, by illness, by poverty, or by the voice of duty, we must learn, each one of us, that the world was not made for us, and that, however beautiful may be the things we crave, Fate may nevertheless forbid them. It is the part of courage, when misfortune comes, to bear without repining[5] the ruin of our hopes, to turn away our thoughts from vain regrets. This degree of submission to Power is not only just and right: it is the very gate of wisdom.

But passive renunciation is not the whole of wisdom; for not by renunciation alone can we build a temple for the worship of our own ideals. Haunting foreshadowings[6] of the temple appear in the realm of imagination, in music, in architecture, in the untroubled kingdom of reason, and in the golden sunset magic of lyrics, where beauty shines and glows, remote from the touch of sorrow, remote from the fear of change, remote from the failures and disenchantments[7] of the world of fact. In the contemplation of these things the vision of heaven will shape itself in our hearts, giving at once a touchstone to judge the world about us, and an inspiration by which to

---

1　**resignation:** endurance, acceptance of life as what it is
2　**mutation:** change
3　**austere:** plain, simple
4　**fretfully:** discontentedly, irritably
5　**repine:** be discontented
6　**foreshadowing:** warning
7　**disenchantment:** disillusion

fashion to our needs whatever[1] is not incapable of serving as a stone in the sacred temple.

Except for those rare spirits that are born without sin, there is a cavern[2] of darkness to be traversed before that temple can be entered. The gate of the cavern is despair, and its floor is paved with the gravestones of abandoned hopes. There Self must die; there the eagerness, the greed of untamed desire must be slain, for only so can the soul be freed from the empire of Fate. But out of the cavern the Gate of Renunciation leads again to the daylight of wisdom, by whose radiance a new insight, a new joy, a new tenderness, shine forth to gladden the pilgrim's heart.

When, without the bitterness of impotent rebellion, we have learnt both to resign ourselves to the outward rules of Fate and to recognise that the non-human world is unworthy of our worship, it becomes possible at last so to transform and refashion the unconscious universe, so to transmute[3] it in the crucible[4] of imagination, that a new image of shining gold replaces the old idol of clay. In all the multiform facts of the world — in the visual shapes of trees and mountains and clouds, in the events of the life of man, even in the very omnipotence of Death — the insight of creative idealism can find the reflection of a beauty which its[5] own thoughts first made. In this way mind asserts its subtle mastery over the thoughtless forces of Nature. The more evil the material with which it deals, the more thwarting[6] to untrained desire, the greater is its achievement in inducing the reluctant rock to yield up its hidden treasures[7], the prouder its victor in compelling the opposing forces to swell the pageant[8] of its triumph. Of all the arts, Tragedy is the proudest, the most triumphant; for it builds its shining citadel[9] in the very centre of the enemy's country, on the very summit of his highest mountain; from its impregnable[10] watchtowers, his camps and arsenals, his columns and forts, are all revealed; within its[11] walls the free life continues, while the legions of Death and Pain and Despair, and all the servile[12] captains of tyrant Fate, afford the burghers[13] of that dauntless city new spectacles of beauty. Happy those sacred ramparts[14], thrice happy the dwellers on that all-seeing eminence. Honour to those brave warriors who, through countless ages of warfare, have preserved for us the priceless heritage of liberty, and

---

1 **fashion to our needs whatever:** i.e., fashion whatever ... to our needs

2 **cavern:** cave

3 **transmute:** change the shape or nature

4 **crucible:** pot in which metals are melted

5 **its:** creative idealism's

6 **thwarting:** frustrating, defeating

7 **rock to yield up its hidden treasures:** an allusion to the tale of The Forty Thieves in the Arabian Nights, where the door of the robbers' cave flew open at the password "sesame"

8 **pageant:** public celebration

9 **citadel:** fortress

10 **impregnable:** that which cannot be seized or taken

11 **its:** citadel's or Tragedy's

12 **servile:** slavish

13 **burgher:** citizen

14 **rampart:** defence work

have kept undefiled by the sacrilegious[1] invaders the home of the unsubdued[2].

But the beauty of Tragedy does but make visible a quality which, in more or less obvious shapes, is present always and everywhere in life. In the spectacle of Death, in the endurance of intolerable pain, and in the irrevocableness[3] of a vanished past, there is a sacredness, an overpowering awe, a feeling of the vastness, the depth, the inexhaustible mystery of existence, in which, as by some strange marriage of pain, the sufferer is bound to the world by bonds of sorrow. In these moments of insight, we lose all eagerness of temporary desire, all struggling and striving for petty ends, all care for the little trivial things that, to a superficial view, make up the common life of day by day; we see, surrounding the narrow raft[4] illumined by the flickering light of human comradeship, the dark ocean on whose rolling waves we toss for a brief hour; from the great night without, a chill blast breaks in upon our refuge; all the loneliness of humanity amid hostile forces is concentrated upon the individual soul, which must struggle alone, with what of courage it can command, against the whole weight of a universe that cares nothing for its[5] hopes and fears. Victory, in this struggle with the powers of darkness, is the true baptism into the glorious company of heroes, the true initiation into the overmastering[6] beauty of human existence. From that awful encounter of the soul with the outer world, renunciation, wisdom, and charity are born; and with their birth a new life begins. To take into the inmost shrine of the soul the irresistible forces whose puppets we seem to be — Death and change, the irrevocableness of the past, and the powerlessness of man before the blind hurry of the universe from vanity to vanity — to feel these things and know them is to conquer them.

This is the reason why the Past has such magical power. The beauty of its motionless and silent pictures is like the enchanted[7] purity of late autumn, when the leaves, though one breath would make them fall, still glow against the sky in golden glory. The Past does not change or strive; like Duncan[8], after life's fitful fever it sleeps well; what was eager and grasping, what was petty and transitory, has faded away, the things that were beautiful and eternal shine out of it[9] like stars in the night. Its beauty, to a soul not worthy of it, is unendurable; but to a soul which has conquered Fate it is the key of religion.

The life of Man, viewed outwardly, is but a small thing in comparison with the forces

---

1 **sacrilegious:** disrespectful to the sacred
2 **kept undefiled by … of the unsubdued:** i.e., kept the home of the unsubdued undefiled by the sacrilegious invaders
3 **irrevocableness:** final, unchangeableness, inalterability
4 **raft:** floating structure of timber
5 **its:** the individual soul's
6 **overmaster:** too strong to be defeated
7 **enchanted:** under a magic spell
8 **Duncan I (1001–1040):** King of the Scots, chiefly known today through his dispute with Macbeth over the succession to the throne, and Duncan was slain in battle by Macbeth, which has been immortalized by Shakespeare
9 **it:** the Past

Heritage of Western Intellectual Tradition   A Sourcebook

of Nature. The slave is doomed to worship Time and Fate and Death, because they are greater than anything he finds in himself, and because all his thoughts are of things which they devour. But, great as they are, to think of them greatly, to feel their passionless splendour, is greater still. And such thought makes us free men; we no longer bow before the inevitable in Oriental subjection[1], but we absorb it, and make it a part of ourselves. To abandon the struggle for private happiness, to expel all eagerness of temporary desire, to burn with passion for eternal things — this is emancipation, and this is the free man's worship. And this liberation is effected by a contemplation of Fate; for Fate itself is subdued by the mind which leaves nothing to be purged by the purifying fire of Time.

United with his fellow-men by the strongest of all ties, the tie of a common doom, the free man finds that a new vision is with him always, shedding over every daily task the light of love. The life of Man is a long march through the night, surrounded by invisible foes, tortured by weariness and pain, towards a goal that few can hope to reach, and where none may tarry[2]

Bertrand Russell tearing up his Labour Party membership card in October 1965 in protest of the Labour Government's support for the Vietnam war

long. One by one, as they march, our comrades vanish from our sight, seized by the silent orders of omnipotent Death. Very brief is the time in which we can help them, in which their happiness or misery is decided. Be it ours[3] to shed sunshine on their path, to lighten their sorrows by the balm of sympathy, to give them the pure joy of a never-tiring affection, to strengthen failing courage, to instill faith in hours of despair. Let us not weigh in grudging[4] scales their merits and demerits, but let us think only of their need — of the sorrows, the difficulties, perhaps the blindnesses, that make the misery of their lives; let us remember that they are fellow-sufferers in the same darkness, actors in the same tragedy with ourselves. And so, when their day is over, when their good and their evil have become eternal by the immortality of the past, be it ours[5] to feel that, where they suffered, where they failed, no deed of ours was the cause; but whenever a spark of the divine fire kindled in their hearts, we were ready with encouragement, with sympathy, with brave words in which high courage glowed.

Brief and powerless is Man's life; on him and all his race the slow, sure doom falls pitiless and dark. Blind to good and evil, reckless of destruction, omnipotent matter rolls on its relentless way; for Man, condemned to-day to lose his dearest, to-morrow himself[6] to pass through the

---

1   **Oriental subjection:** the image of the Orient described by the Western Orientalist as meek and submissive
2   **tarry:** stay, remain
3   **Be it ours:** May it be our time
4   **grudge:** unwilling to give
5   **ours:** our day
6   **to-morrow himself:** to-morrow to lose himself

gate of darkness, it remains only to cherish, ere[1] yet the blow falls, the lofty thoughts that ennoble his little day; disdaining the coward terrors of the slave of Fate, to worship at the shrine that his own hands have built; undismayed by the empire of chance, to preserve a mind free from the wanton tyranny that rules his outward life; proudly defiant of the irresistible forces that tolerate, for a moment, his knowledge and his condemnation, to sustain alone, a weary but unyielding Atlas[2], the world that his own ideals have fashioned despite the trampling[3] march of unconscious power.

Key Concepts

emancipation	passive renunciation
free man's worship	Promethean philosophy of rebellion
freedom of thoughts	slave of Fate
God/Mephistopheles	submission of desires
ideal world	unfettered contemplation
Nature	virtue of resignation
Oriental subjection	wisdom
outside forces	

Alfred North Whitehead: Science and the Modern World (1925)

Alfred North Whitehead (1861–1947), British mathematician and philosopher, was taught by his father at home until he was 14 as his parents considered him too frail for school. Whitehead received a classical education, showing a special gift for mathematics. Despite his over-protected childhood, he showed potential of a leader. In his last year at school, he was head prefect, responsible for all discipline outside the classroom, and was a highly successful captain of games. He was then sent to Trinity College, University of Cambridge. He taught mathematics there from 1885 to 1911, mathematics and mechanics at the University of London from 1911 to 1924,

---

1 **ere:** before
2 **Atlas:** a collection of maps, traditionally bound into book form, with geographic features and political boundaries
3 **trample:** crush under feet

and was professor of philosophy at Harvard from 1924 until his death. He was also a fellow of the Royal Society and a member of the British Academy. A brilliant mathematician, Whitehead also had a deep knowledge of philosophy and literature. He collaborated with Bertrand Russell for the three-volume *Principia Mathematica* (1910–1913), one of the world's greatest works on logic and mathematics. In 1916, as president of the Mathematical Association, he delivered the notable address "The Aims of Education: A Plea for Reform," where he argues that the purpose of education was not to pack knowledge into the pupils but to stimulate and guide their self-development: "Culture is activity of thought, and receptiveness to beauty and humane feeling. Scraps of information have nothing to do with it." Whitehead's address became a classic in virtue of its unequalled clarity, vigour, and realism and its reconciliation of general with special education.

Requisites for Social Progress

It has been the purpose of these lectures to analyse the reactions of science in forming that background of instinctive ideas which control the activities of successive generations. Such a background takes the form of a certain vague philosophy as to the last word about things, when all is said. The three centuries, which form the epoch of modern science, have revolved round the ideas of God, mind, matter, and also of space and time in their characters of expressing simple location for matter. Philosophy has on the whole emphasised mind, and has thus been out of touch with science during the two latter centuries. But it is creeping back into its old importance owing to the rise of psychology and its alliance with physiology. Also, this rehabilitation[1] of philosophy has been facilitated by the recent breakdown of the seventeenth century settlement of the principles of physical science. But, until that collapse, science seated itself securely upon the concepts of matter, space, time, and latterly, of energy. Also there were arbitrary laws of nature determining locomotion[2]. They were empirically observed, but for some obscure reason were known to be universal. Anyone who in practice or theory disregarded them was denounced with unsparing[3] vigour. This position on the part of scientists was pure bluff[4], if one may credit them with believing their own statements. For their current philosophy completely failed to justify the assumption that the immediate knowledge inherent in any present occasion throws any light either on its past, or its future.

I have also sketched an alternative philosophy of science in which organism takes the place of matter. For this purpose, the mind involved in the materialist theory dissolves into a function of organism. The psychological field then exhibits what an event is in itself. Our bodily event is an unusually complex type of organism and consequently includes cognition[5]. Further, space and

---

1 **rehabilitation:** restoration
2 **locomotion:** moving from place to place
3 **unsparing:** abundant
4 **bluff:** deception
5 **cognition:** knowing, awareness

time, in their most concrete signification, become the locus[1] of events. An organism is the realisation of a definite shape of value. The emergence of some actual value depends on limitation which excludes neutralising cross-lights. Thus an event is a matter of fact which by reason of its limitation is a value for itself; but by reason of its very nature it also requires the whole universe in order to be itself.

Importance depends on endurance. Endurance is the retention through time of an achievement of value. What endures is identity of pattern, self-inherited. Endurance requires the favourable environment. The whole of science revolves round this question of enduring organisms.

The general influence of science at the present moment can be analysed under the headings: General Conceptions Respecting the Universe, Technological Applications, Professionalism in Knowledge, Influence of Biological Doctrines on the Motives of Conduct. I have endeavoured in the preceding lectures to give a glimpse of these points. It lies within the scope of this concluding lecture to consider the reaction of science upon some problems confronting civilised societies.

The general conceptions introduced by science into modern thought cannot be separated from the philosophical situation as expressed by Descartes. I mean the assumption of bodies and minds as independent individual substances, each existing in its own right apart from any necessary reference to each other. Such a conception was very concordant[2] with the individualism which had issued from the moral discipline of the Middle Ages. But, though the easy reception of the idea is thus explained, the derivation in itself rests upon a confusion, very natural but none the less unfortunate. The moral discipline had emphasised the intrinsic value of the individual entity. This emphasis had put the notions of the individual and of its experiences into the foreground of thought. At this point the confusion commences. The emergent individual value of each entity is transformed into the independent substantial existence of each entity, which is a very different notion.

I do not mean to say that Descartes made this logical, or rather illogical transition, in the form of explicit reasoning. Far from it. What he did was first to concentrate upon his own conscious experiences, as being facts within the independent world of his own mentality. He was led to speculate in this way by the current emphasis upon the individual value of his total self. He implicitly transformed this emergent individual value, inherent in the very fact of his own reality, into a private world of passions, or modes, of independent substance.

Also the independence ascribed to bodily substances carried them away from the realm of values altogether. They degenerated into a mechanism entirely valueless, except as suggestive of an external ingenuity[3]. The heavens had lost the glory of God. This state of mind is illustrated in

---

1 **locus:** exact place

2 **concordant:** harmonious

3 **ingenuity:** cleverness, originality

Heritage of Western Intellectual Tradition   A Sourcebook

Heritage of Western Intellectual Tradition   A Sourcebook

the recoil[1] of Protestantism from aesthetic effects dependent upon a material medium. It was taken to lead to an ascription of value to what is in itself valueless. This recoil was already in full strength antecedently[2] to Descartes. Accordingly, the Cartesian scientific doctrine of bits of matter, bare of intrinsic value, was merely a formulation, in explicit terms, of a doctrine which was current before its entrance into scientific thought or Cartesian philosophy. Probably this doctrine was latent in the scholastic philosophy, but it did not lead to its consequences till it met with the mentality of northern Europe in the sixteenth century. But science, — as equipped by Descartes, gave stability and intellectual status to a point of view which has had very mixed effects upon the moral presuppositions of modern communities. Its good effects arose from its efficiency as a method for scientific researches within those limited regions which were then best suited for exploration. The result was a general clearing of the European mind away from the stains left upon it by the hysteria[3] of remote barbaric ages. This was all to the good, and was most completely exemplified in the eighteenth century.

But in the nineteenth century, when society was undergoing transformation into the manu-facturing system, the bad effects of these doctrines have been very fatal. The doctrine of minds, as independent substances, leads directly not merely to private worlds of experience, but also to private worlds of morals. The moral intuitions can be held to apply only to the strictly private world of psychological experience. Accordingly, self-respect, and the making the most of your own individual opportunities, together constituted the efficient morality of the leaders among the industrialists of that period. The Western world is now suffering from the limited moral outlook of the three previous generations.

Also the assumption of the bare valuelessness of mere matter led to a lack of reverence in the treatment of natural or artistic beauty. Just when the urbanisation of the Western world was entering upon its state of rapid development, and when the most delicate, anxious consideration of the aesthetic qualities of the new material environment was requisite[4], the doctrine of the irrelevance of such ideas was at its height. **In the most advanced industrial countries, art was treated as a frivolity[5]. A striking example of this state of mind in the middle of the nine-teenth century is to be seen in London where the marvellous beauty of the estuary[6] of the Thames, as it curves through the city, is wantonly defaced[7] by the Charing Cross railway bridge, constructed apart from any reference to aesthetic values.**

The two evils are: one, the ignoration of the true relation of each organism to its environment; and the other, the habit of ignoring the intrinsic worth of the environment which must be allowed

---

1   **recoil:** jumping back, reaction
2   **antecedently:** previously, before
3   **hysteria:** outburst of uncontrollable emotions
4   **requisite:** necessary, needed
5   **frivolity:** lightness of character
6   **estuary:** river mouth
7   **deface:** spoil the appearance of

its weight in any consideration of final ends.

Another great fact confronting the modern world is the discovery of the method of training professionals, who specialise in particular regions of thought and thereby progressively add to the sum of knowledge within their respective limitations[1] of subject. In consequence of the success of this professionalising of knowledge, there are two points to be kept in mind, which differentiate our present age from the past. In the first place, the rate of progress is such that an individual human being, of ordinary length of life, will be called upon to face novel situations which find no parallel in his past. The fixed person for the fixed duties, who in older societies was such a godsend[2], in the future will be a public danger. In the second place, the modern professionalism in knowledge works in the opposite direction so far as the intellectual sphere is concerned. The modern chemist is likely to be weak in zoology, weaker still in his general knowledge of the Elizabethan drama, and completely ignorant of the principles of rhythm in English versification. It is probably safe to ignore his knowledge of ancient history. Of course I am speaking of general tendencies; for chemists are no worse than engineers, or mathematicians, or classical scholars. **Effective knowledge is professionalised knowledge, supported by a restricted acquaintance with useful subjects subservient[3] to it.**

This situation has its dangers. It produces minds in a groove[4]. Each profession makes progress, but it is progress in its own groove. Now to be mentally in a groove is to live in contemplating a given set of abstractions. The groove prevents straying[5] across country, and the abstraction abstracts from something to which no further attention is paid. But there is no groove of abstractions which is adequate for the comprehension of human life. Thus in the modern world, the celibacy[6] of the medieval learned class has been replaced by a celibacy of the intellect which is divorced from the concrete contemplation of the complete facts. Of course, no one is merely a mathematician, or merely a lawyer. People have lives outside their professions or their businesses. But the point is the restraint of serious thought within a groove. The remainder of life is treated superficially, with the imperfect categories of thought derived from one profession.

The dangers arising from this aspect of professionalism are great, particularly in our democratic societies. The directive force of reason is weakened. The leading intellects lack balance. They see this set of circumstances, or that set; but not both sets together. The task of coordination is left to those who lack either the force or the character to succeed in some definite career, in short, the specialised functions of the community are performed better and more progressively, but the generalised direction lacks vision. The progressiveness in detail only adds to the danger produced by the feebleness of coordination.

---

1 **limitation:** scope
2 **godsend:** gift of God
3 **subservient:** useful as a means or an instrument, supportive of
4 **groove:** habitual way of living
5 **stray:** wander, travel
6 **celibacy:** state of living unmarried

This criticism of modern life applies throughout, in whatever sense you construe[1] the meaning of a community. It holds[2] if you apply it to a nation, a city, a district, an institution, a family, or even to an individual. There is a development of particular abstractions, and a contraction[3] of concrete appreciation. The whole is lost in one of its aspects. It is not necessary for my point that I should maintain that our directive wisdom, either as individuals or as communities, is less now than in the past. Perhaps it has slightly improved. But the novel pace of progress requires a greater force of direction if disasters are to be avoided. The point is that the discoveries of the nineteenth century were in the direction of professionalism, so that we are left with no expansion of wisdom and with greater need of it.

Wisdom is the fruit of a balanced development. It is this balanced growth of individuality which it should be the aim of education to secure. The most useful discoveries for the immediate future would concern the furtherance[4] of this aim without detriment[5] to the necessary intellectual professionalism.

My own criticism of our traditional educational methods is that they are far too much occupied with intellectual analysis, and with the acquirement of formularised[6] information. What I mean is, that we neglect to strengthen habits of concrete appreciation of the individual facts in their full interplay of emergent[7] values, and that we merely emphasise abstract formulations which ignore this aspect of the interplay of diverse values.

In every country the problem of the balance of the general and specialist education is under consideration. I cannot speak with first-hand knowledge of any country but my own. I know that there, among practical educationalists, there is considerable dissatisfaction with the existing practice. Also, the adaptation of the whole system to the needs of a democratic community is very far from being solved. I do not think that the secret of the solution lies in terms of the antithesis between thoroughness in special knowledge and general knowledge of a slighter character. The make-weight[8] which balances the thoroughness of the specialist intellectual training should be of a radically different kind from purely intellectual analytical knowledge. **At present our education combines a thorough study of a few abstractions, with a slighter study of a larger number of abstractions. We are too exclusively bookish[9] in our scholastic routine. The general training should aim at eliciting[10] our concrete apprehensions, and should**

---

1 **construe:** explain, analyze
2 **It holds:** It holds true
3 **contraction:** becoming smaller
4 **furtherance:** the act of furthering, advancing, or helping forward
5 **detriment:** damage, harm
6 **formularise:** express in the form of a formula, here restricted
7 **emergent:** emerging, coming out
8 **make-weight:** small quality added to make the weight right, something that supplies a deficiency
9 **bookish:** here giving too much weight to the books of a specialized subject
10 **elicit:** cause to come out

satisfy the itch[1] of youth to be doing something. There should be some analysis even here, but only just enough to illustrate the ways of thinking in diverse spheres. In the Garden of Eden Adam saw the animals before he named them; in the traditional system, children named the animals before they saw them.

There is no easy single solution of the practical difficulties of education. We can, however, guide ourselves by a certain simplicity in its general theory. The student should concentrate within a limited field. Such concentration should include all practical and intellectual acquirements requisite for that concentration. This is the ordinary procedure; and, in respect to it, I should be inclined even to increase the facilities for concentration rather than to diminish them. With the concentration there are associated certain subsidiary[2] studies, such as languages for science. Such a scheme of professional training should be directed to a clear end congenial to[3] the student. It is not necessary to elaborate the qualifications of these statements. Such a training must, of course have the width requisite for its end. But its design should not be complicated by the consideration of other ends. This professional training can only touch one side of education. Its centre of gravity lies in the intellect, and its chief tool is the printed book. The centre of gravity of the other side of training should lie in intuition[4] without an analytical divorce from the total environment.[5] Its object is immediate apprehension with the minimum of eviscerating[6] analysis. The type of generality, which above all is wanted, is the appreciation of variety of value. I mean an aesthetic growth. There is something between the gross[7] specialised values of the mere practical man, and the thin specialised values of the mere scholar. Both types have missed something; and if you add together the two sets of values, you do not obtain the missing elements. What is wanted is an appreciation of the infinite variety of vivid values achieved by an organism in its proper environment. **When you understand all about the sun and all about the atmosphere and all about the rotation of the earth, you may still miss the radiance of the sunset. There is no substitute for the direct perception of the concrete achievement of a thing in its actuality. We want concrete fact with a high light thrown on what is relevant to its preciousness.**

What I mean is art and aesthetic education. It is, however, art in such a general sense of the term that I hardly like to call it by that name. Art is a special example. What we want is to draw out habits of aesthetic apprehension. According to the metaphysical doctrine which I have been developing, to do so is to increase the depth of individuality. The analysis of reality indicates the two factors, activity emerging into individualised aesthetic value. Also the emergent value is the

---

1   **itch:** restless desire, longing

2   **subsidiary:** supporting, helpful

3   **congenial to:** suited to sb's character or tastes

4   **intuition:** immediate understanding without conscious reasoning

5   **The centre of gravity … the total environment.:** Whitehead here seems to be advocating an education that combines analytical training and cultivation of the power of intuition and imagination.

6   **eviscerating:** disembowel, here thorough

7   **gross:** general, popular

measure of the individualisation of the activity. We must foster[1] the creative initiative towards the maintenance of objective values. You will not obtain the apprehension without the initiative, or the initiative without the apprehension. As soon as you get towards the concrete, you cannot exclude action. Sensitiveness without impulse spells[2] decadence, and impulse without sensitiveness spells brutality. I am using the word "sensitiveness" in its most general signification, so as to include apprehension of what lies beyond oneself; that is to say, sensitiveness to all the facts of the case. Thus "art" in the general sense which I require is any selection by which the concrete facts are so arranged as to elicit attention to particular values which are realisable by them. For example, the mere disposing of the human body and the eyesight so as to get a good view of a sunset is a simple form of artistic selection. The habit of art is the habit of enjoying vivid values.

But, in this sense, art concerns more than sunsets. A factory, with its machinery, its community of operatives[3], its social service to the general population, its dependence upon organising and designing genius, its potentialities as a source of wealth to the holders of its stock is an organism exhibiting a variety of vivid values. What we want to train is the habit of apprehending such an organism in its completeness. It is very arguable that the science of political economy, as studied in its first period after the death of Adam Smith (1790), did more harm than good. It destroyed many economic fallacies, and taught how to think about the economic revolution then in progress. But it riveted[4] on men a certain set of abstractions which were disastrous in their influence on modern mentality. It dehumanised industry. This is only one example of a general danger inherent in modern science. Its methodological procedure is exclusive and intolerant, and rightly so. It fixes attention on a definite group of abstractions, neglects everything else, and elicits every scrap[5] of information and theory which is relevant to what it has retained. This method is triumphant, provided that the abstractions are judicious[6]. But, however triumphant, the triumph is within limits. The neglect of these limits leads to disastrous oversights[7]. The anti-rationalism of science is partly justified, as a preservation of its useful methodology; it is partly mere irrational prejudice. **Modern professionalism is the training of minds to conform to the methodology. The historical revolt of the seventeenth century, and the earlier reaction towards naturalism[8], were examples of transcending the abstractions which fascinated educated society in the Middle Ages.** These early ages had an ideal of rationalism, but they failed in its pursuit. For they neglected to note that the methodology of reasoning requires the limitations involved in the abstract. Accordingly, the true rationalism must always transcend itself by recurrence to the concrete in search of inspiration. A self-satisfied rationalism is in effect a

---

1   **foster:** develop, cultivate
2   **spell:** result in, lead to
3   **operatives:** workers
4   **rivet:** fasten, fix
5   **scrap:** small piece
6   **judicious:** having or showing good sense
7   **oversight:** failure to notice
8   **naturalism:** study of nature, here it probably refers to the abstract speculations of scholasticism

form of antirationalism. It means an arbitrary halt[1] at a particular set of abstractions. This was the case with science.

Modern science has imposed on humanity the necessity for wandering. Its progressive thought and its progressive technology make the transition through time, from generation to generation, a true migration into uncharted seas of adventure. The very benefit of wandering is that it is dangerous and needs skill to avert evils. We must expect, therefore, that the future will disclose[2] dangers. It is the business of the future to be dangerous; and it is among the merits of science that it equips the future for its duties. The prosperous middle classes, who ruled the nineteenth century, placed an excessive value upon placidity[3] of existence. They refused to face the necessities for social reform imposed by the new industrial system, and they are now refusing to face the necessities for intellectual reform imposed by the new knowledge. The middle class pessimism over the future of the world comes from a confusion between civilisation and security. In the immediate future there will be less security than in the immediate past, less stability. It must be admitted that there is a degree of instability which is inconsistent with civilisation. But, on the whole, the great ages have been unstable ages.

I have endeavoured in these lectures to give a record of a great adventure in the region of thought. It was shared by all the races of Western Europe. It developed with the slowness of a mass movement. Half a century is its unit of time. The tale is the epic of an episode in the manifestation of reason. It tells how a particular direction of reason emerges in a race by the long preparation of antecedent epochs, how after its birth its subject-matter gradually unfolds itself, how it attains its triumphs, how its influence moulds the very springs[4] of action of mankind, finally how at its moment of supreme success its limitations disclose themselves and call for a renewed exercise of the creative imagination. The moral of the tale is the power of reason, its decisive influence on the life of humanity. The great conquerors, from Alexander to Caesar, and from Caesar to Napoleon, influenced profoundly the lives of subsequent generations. But the total effect of this influence shrinks to insignificance, if compared to the entire transformation of human habits and human mentality produced by the long line of men of thought from Thales[5] to the present day, men individually powerless, but ultimately the rulers of the world.

Key Concepts

aesthetic values   balance of the general and specialist education

---

1 **halt:** pause, stop
2 **disclose:** allow to be seen, show
3 **placidity:** calmness
4 **spring:** actuating force or factor; a motive
5 **Thales (624 c.–546 c. BC):** Greek philosopher who is traditionally considered the first Western philosopher and a founder of geometry and abstract astronomy

Heritage of Western Intellectual Tradition   A Sourcebook

concrete appreciation/fact

formularised information

influence of science

interplay of diverse values

limited moral outlook

necessity for wandering

professionalising of knowledge

professionalism

purely intellectual analytical knowledge

Compare with China

Bertrand Russell: Chinese and Western Civilization Contrasted [1]

There is at present in China a close contact between our civilization and that which is native to this country. It is still a doubtful question whether this contact will breed a new civilization better than either of its parents, or whether it will merely destroy the native culture and replace it by that of America. Contacts between different civilizations have often in the past proved to be landmarks in human progress. Greece learned from Egypt, Rome from Greece, the Arabs from the Roman Empire, medieval Europe from the Arabs, a Renaissance Europe from the Byzantines. In many of these cases, the pupils proved better than their masters. In the case of China, if we regard the Chinese as the pupils, this may be the case again. In fact, we have quite as much to learn from them as they from us, but there is far less chance of our learning it. If I treat the Chinese as our pupils, rather than vice versa, it is only because I fear we are unteachable.

With the exception of Spain and America in the sixteenth century, I cannot think of any instance of two civilizations coming into contact after such a long period of separate development as has marked those of China and Europe. Considering this extraordinary separateness, it is surprising that mutual understanding between Europeans and Chinese is not more difficult. In order to make this point clear, it will be worthwhile to dwell for a moment on the historical origins of the two civilizations.

Western Europe and America have a practically homogeneous[2] mental life, which I should trace to three sources: (1) Greek culture; (2) Jewish religion and ethics; (3) modern industrialism, which itself is an outcome of modern science. We may take Plato, the Old Testament, and Galileo as representing these three elements, which have remained singularly separable down to

---

1   This is taken from Bertrand Russell's 1922 book *The Problem of China*, written from his experience of 9-month-stay in China.

2   **homogeneous:** of the same kind

the present day. From the Greek we derive literature and the arts, philosophy and pure mathematics; also the more urbane[1] portions of our social outlook. From the Jews we derive

fanatical belief, which its friends call "faith;" moral fervor[2], with the conception of sin; religious intolerance, and some part of our nationalism. From science, as applied in industrialism, we derive power and the sense of power, the belief that we are as gods, and may justly be the arbiters[3] of life and death for unscientific races. We derive also the empirical method, by which almost all real knowledge has been acquired. These three elements, I think, account for the most of our mentality.

Bertrand Russell, Edith Russell and Y. R. Chao (foreground), a Chinese-American scholar and Russell's interpreter in China

No one of these three elements has had any applicable part in the development of China, except that Greece indirectly influences Chinese painting, sculpture, and music. China belongs, in the dawn of its history, to the great river empires, of which Egypt and Babylonia contributed to our origins, by the influence which they had upon the Greeks and Jews. Just as these civilizations were rendered possible by the rich alluvial[4] soil of the Nile, the Euphrates and the Tigris, so the original civilization of China was rendered possible by the Yellow River. Even in the time of Confucius, the Chinese Empire did not stretch far either to south or north of the Yellow River. But in spite of this similarity in physical and economic circumstances, there was very little in common between the mental outlook of the Chinese and that of the Egyptians and Babylonians. Lao-tze and Confucius, who both belong to the sixth century before Christ, have already the characteristics which we should regard as distinctive of the modern Chinese. People who attribute everything to economic causes would be hard put to it[5] to account for the differences between the ancient Chinese and the ancient Egyptians and Babylonians. For my part, I have no alternative theory to offer. I do not think science can, at present, account wholly for national character. Climate and economic circumstances account for part, but not the whole. Probably a great deal depends upon the character of dominant individuals who happen to emerge at a formative period[6], such as Moses, Mohammed, and Confucius.

The oldest known Chinese sage is Lao-tze, the founder of Taoism. "Lao-tze" is not really a proper name, but merely means "the old philosopher." He was (according to tradition) an older contemporary of Confucius, and his philosophy is to my mind far more interesting. He held that every person, every animal, and every thing has a certain way or manner of behaving which is natural to him, or her, or it, and that we ought to conform to this way ourselves and encourage

---

1 **urbane:** polite, polished
2 **fervor:** earnestness, strength
3 **arbiter:** person with complete control
4 **alluvial:** made up of earth left by river
5 **be hard put to it:** find difficult
6 **formative period:** period when something takes a definite shape

others to conform to it. "Tao" means "way," but used in a more or less mystical sense, as in the text: "I am the Way and the Truth and the Life." I think he fancied that death was due to departing from the "way," and that if we all live strictly according to nature we should be immortal, like the heavenly bodies. In later times Taoism degenerated into mere magic, and was largely concerned with the search for the elixir[1] of life. But I think the hope of escaping from death was an element in Taoist philosophy from the first.

Lao-tze's book, or rather the book attributed to him, is very short, but his ideas were developed by his disciple Chuang-tze, who is more interesting than his master. The philosophy which both advocated was one of freedom. They thought ill of government, and of all interferences with nature. They complained of the hurry of modern life, which they contrasted with the calm existence of those whom they called the "pure men of old." There is a flavor of mysticism in the doctrine of the Tao, because in spite of the multiplicity of living things the Tao is in some sense one, so that if all live according to it there will be no

Taoism is always an attraction to Western philosophers.

strife in the world. But both sages have already the Chinese characteristics of humor, restraint, and understatement[2]. Their humor is illustrated by Chuang-tze's account of Po-lo, who "understood the management of horses," and trained them till five out of every ten died. Their restraint and understatement are evident when they are compared with Western mystics. Both characteristics belong to all Chinese literature and art, and to the conversation of cultivated Chinese in the present day. All classes in China are fond of laughter, and never miss a chance of a joke. In the educated classes, the humor is sly and delicate, so that Europeans often fail to see it, which adds to the enjoyment of the Chinese. Their habit of understatement is remarkable. I met one day in Peking a middle-aged man who told me he was academically interested in the theory of politics; being new to the country, I took his statement at its face value, but I afterward discovered that he had been governor of a province, and had been for many years a very prominent politician. In Chinese poetry there is an apparent absence of passion, which is due to the same practice of understatement. They consider that a wise man should always remain calm, and, though they have their passionate moment (being in fact a very excitable race), they do not wish to perpetuate them in art, because they think ill of them. Our romantic movement, which led people to like vehemence[3], has, so far as I know, no analogue[4] in their literature. Their old music, some of which is very beautiful, makes so little noise that one can only just hear it. In art they aim at being exquisite[5], and in life at being reasonable. There is no admiration for the ruthless strong man, or

---

1   **elixir:** medicine that prolongs life indefinitely
2   **understatement:** expression that is intentionally restrained
3   **vehemence:** strong feeling
4   **analogue:** equivalence
5   **exquisite:** flawless; excellent

Heritage of Western Intellectual Tradition   A Sourcebook

for the unrestrained expression of passion. After the more blatant[1] life of the West, one misses at first all the effects at which they are aiming; but gradually the beauty and dignity of their existence become visible, so that the foreigners who have lived longest in China are those who love the Chinese best.

The Taoists, though they survive as magicians, were entirely ousted from the favor of the educated classes by Confucianism. I must confess that I am unable to appreciate the merits of Confucius. His writings are largely occupied with trivial points of etiquette[2], and his main concern is to teach people how to behave correctly on various occasions. When one compares him, however, with the traditional religious teachers of some other ages and races, one must admit that he has great merits, even if they are mainly negative. His system, as developed by his followers, is one of pure ethics, without religious dogma; it has not given rise to a powerful priesthood, and it has not led to persecution. It certainly has succeeded in producing a whole nation possessed of exquisite manners and perfect courtesy. Nor is Chinese courtesy merely conventional; it is quite as reliable in situation for which no precedent has been provided. And it is not confined to one class; it exists even in the humblest coolie. It is humiliating to watch the brutal insolence[3] of white men received by the Chinese with a quiet dignity which cannot demean[4] itself to answer rudeness with rudeness. Europeans often regard this as weakness, but it is really strength, the strength by which the Chinese have hitherto conquered all their conquerors.

There is one, and only one, important foreign element in the traditional civilization of China, and that is Buddhism. Buddhism came to China from India in the early centuries of the

Lao-tze heading for hermitage

Christian era, and acquired a definite place in the religion of the country. We, with the intolerant outlook which we have taken over from the Jews, imagine that if a man adopts one religion he cannot adopt another. The dogmas of Christianity and Mohammedanism, in their orthodox forms, are so framed that no man can accept both. But in China this incompatibility does not exist; a man may be both a Buddhist and a Confucian, because nothing in either is incompatible with the other. In Japan, similarly, most people are both Buddhists and Shintoists[5]. Nevertheless, there is a temperamental difference between Buddhism and Confucianism, which will cause any individual to lay stress on one or the other even if he accepts both. Buddhism is a religion in the sense in which we understand the word. It has mystic doctrines and a way of salvation and a future life. It has a message to the world intended to cure the despair which it re-

---

1   **blatant:** noisy and rough
2   **etiquette:** rules for formal behaviour
3   **insolence:** offence, insult
4   **demean:** lower oneself in dignity, condescend
5   **Shintoism:** a religion native to Japan, characterized by veneration of nature spirits and ancestors and by a lack of formal dogma

gards as natural to those who have no religious faith. It assumes an instinctive pessimism, only to be cured by some gospel. Confucianism has nothing of all this. It assumes people fundamentally at peace with the world, wanting only instruction as to how to live, not encouragement to live at all. And this ethical instruction is not based upon any metaphysical or religious dogmas; it is purely mundane. The result of the coexistence of these two religions in China has been that the more religious and contemplative natures turned Buddhism, while the active administrative type was content with Confucianism, which was always the official teaching, in which candidates for the civil service were examined. The result is that for many ages the government of China has been in the hands of literary skeptics, whose administration has been lacking in those qualities of energy and destructiveness which Western nations demand of their rulers. In fact, they have conformed very closely to the maxims of Chuang-tze. The result has been that the population has been happy except where civil war brought misery; that subject nations have been allowed autonomy; and that foreign nations have had no need to fear China, in spite of its immense population and resources.

Comparing the civilization of China with that of Europe, one finds in China most of what was to be found in Greece, but nothing of the other two elements of our civilization — namely, Judaism and science. China is practically destitute[1] of religion, not only in the upper classes, but throughout the population. There is very definite ethical code, but it is not fierce or persecuting, and does not contain the notion "sin." Except quite recently, through European influence, there has been no science and no industrialism.

What will be the outcome of the contact of this ancient civilization with the West? I am not thinking of the political or economic, but of the effect on the Chinese mental outlook. It is difficult to dissociate the two questions altogether, because of course the cultural contact with the West must be affected by the nature of the political and economic contact. Nevertheless, I wish to consider the cultural question as far as I can in isolation.

There is, in China, a great eagerness to acquire Western learning, not simply in order to acquire national strength and be able to resist Western aggression, but because a very large number of people consider learning a good thing in itself. It is traditional in China to place a high value on knowledge, but in old days the knowledge sought was only of[2] the classical literature. Nowadays it is generally realized that Western knowledge is more useful. Many students go every year to universities in Europe, and still more to America, to learn science or economics or law or political theory. These men, when they return to China, mostly become teachers or civil servants or journalists or politicians. They are rapidly modernizing the Chinese outlook, especially in the educated classes.

The traditional civilization of China had become unprogressive, and had ceased to produce much of value in the way of art and literature. This was not due, I think, to any decadence[3] in the

---

1 **destitute:** lacking

2 **of:** that of

3 **decadence:** falling to a lower level

race, but merely to lack of new material. The influx of Western knowledge provides just the stimulus that was needed. Chinese students are able and extraordinarily keen. Higher education suffers from lack of funds and absence of libraries, but does not suffer from any lack of the finest human material. Although Chinese civilization has hitherto been deficient in science, it never contained anything hostile to science, and therefore the spread of scientific knowledge encounters no such obstacles as the church put in its way in Europe. I have no doubt that if the Chinese could get a stable government and sufficient funds, they would, within the next thirty years, begin to produce remarkable work in science. It is quite likely that they might outstrip[1], because they come with fresh zest and with all the ardor of a renaissance. In fact, the enthusiasm for learning in Young China reminds one constantly of the renaissance spirit in fifteenth-century Italy.

It is remarkable, as distinguishing the Chinese from the Japanese, that the things they wish to learn from us are not those that bring wealth or military strength, but rather those that have either an ethical and social value, or a purely intellectual interest. They are not by any means uncritical of our civilization. Some of them told me that they were less critical before 1914, but that the war made them think there must be imperfection in the Western manner of life. The habit of looking to the West for wisdom was, however, very strong, and some of the younger ones thought that Bolshevism could give what they were looking for. The Japanese adopted our faults and kept their own, but it is possible to hope that the Chinese will make the opposite selection, keeping their own merits and adopting ours.

The distinctive merits of our civilization, I should say, is the scientific method; the distinctive merits of the Chinese is a just conception of the ends of life. It is these two that one must hope to see gradually uniting.

Lao-tze describes the operation of the Tao as "production without possession, action without self-assertion, development without domination[2]." I think one could derive from these words a conception of the ends of life as reflective Chinese see them, and it must be admitted that they are very different from the ends which most white men set before themselves. Possession, self-assertion, domination, are eagerly sought, both nationally and individually. They have been erected into a philosophy by Nietzsche and Nietzsche's disciples are not confined to Germany.

But, it will be said, you have been comparing Western practice with Chinese theory; if you had compare Western theory with Chinese practice, the balance would have come out quite differently. There is, of course, a great deal of truth in this. Possession, which is one of the three things that Lao-tze wishes us to forgo, is certainly dear to the heart of the average Chinaman. As a race, they are tenacious[3] of money — not perhaps more so than the French. But certainly more

---

1 **outstrip:** do better than others
2 **production without possession … development without domination:** 生而不有，为而不恃，功成而弗居（《道德经》第二章）
3 **tenacious:** holding tightly

than the English or the Americans. Their politics are corrupt, and their powerful men[1] make money in disgraceful ways. All this it is impossible to deny.

Nevertheless, as regards the other two evils, self-assertion and domination, I notice a definite superiority to ourselves in Chinese practice. There is much less desire than among the white races to tyrannize over other people. The weakness of China internationally is quite as much due to this virtue as to the vices of corruption and so on which are usually assigned as the sole reason. If any nation in the world could ever be "too proud to fight," that nation would be China. The natural Chinese attitude is one of tolerance and friendliness, showing courtesy and expecting it in return. If the Chinese chose, they could be the most powerful nation in the world. But they only desire freedom, not domination. It is not improbable that other nations may compel them to fight for their freedom, and if so, they may lose their virtues and acquire a taste for empire[2]. But at present, though they have been an imperial race for two thousand years, their love of empire is extraordinarily slight.

Although there have been many wars in China, the natural outlook of the Chinese is very pacifistic[3]. I do not know of any other country where a poet would have chosen, as Po Chu-i[4] did in one of the poems translated by Mr. Waley, called by him "The Old Man with the Broken Arm," to make a hero of a recruit who maimed[5] himself to escape military service. Their pacifism is rooted in their contemplative outlook, and in the fact that they do not desire to change whatever they see. They take a pleasure — as their pictures show — in observing characteristic manifestations of different kinds of life, and they have no wish to reduce everything to a preconceived pattern. They have not the ideal of progress which dominate the Western nations, and affords a rationalization of our active impulses. Progress is, of course, a very modern ideal even with us; it is part of what we owe to science and industrialism. The cultivated conservative Chinese of the present day talk exactly as their earliest sages write. If one points to them that this shows how little progress there has been, they will say: "Why seek progress when you already enjoy what is excellent?" At first, this point of view seems to a European unduly indolent[6]; but gradually doubts as to one's own wisdom grow up, and one begins to think that much of what we call progress is only restless change bringing us no nearer to any desirable goal.

It is interesting to contrast what the Chinese have sought in the West with what the West has sought in China. The Chinese in the West seek knowledge, in the hope — which I fear is usually vain — that knowledge may prove a gateway to wisdom. White men have gone to China with three motives: to fight, to make money, and to convert the Chinese to our religion. The last of

---

1   **powerful men:** the warlords in the 20s

2   **empire:** supreme political power, here as a reference to the British Empire as the most powerful colonial power at the time

3   **pacifistic:** anti-war, peace-loving

4   **Po Chu-i:** 白居易

5   **maim:** injure so that part of the body is useless; the poem is 《新丰折臂翁》

6   **indolent:** lazy, inactive

these motives has the merit of being idealistic and has inspired many heroic lives. But the soldiers, the merchant, and the missionary are alike concerned to stamp our civilization upon the world; they are all three, in a certain sense, pugnacious[1]. The Chinese have no wish to convert us to Confucianism; they say "religions are many, but reason is one," and with that they are content to let us go our way. They are good merchants, but their methods are quite different from those of European merchants in China, who are perpetually seeking concessions, monopolies, railways, and mines, and endeavouring to get their claims supported by gunboats. The Chinese are not, as a rule, good soldiers, because the causes for which they are asked to fight are not worth fighting for, and they know it. But that is only proof of their reasonableness.

I think the tolerance of the Chinese is in excess of anything that Europeans can imagine from their experience at home. We imagine ourselves tolerant, because we are more so than our ancestors. But we still practice political and social persecution, and what is more, we are firmly persuaded that our civilization and our way of life are immeasurably better than any other, so that when we come across a nation like the Chinese, we are convinced that the kindest thing we can do to them is to take them like ourselves. I believe this to be a profound mistake. It seems to me that the average Chinese, even if he is miserably poor, is happier than the average Englishman, and is happier because the nation is built upon a more humane and civilized outlook than our own. Restlessness and pugnacity not only cause obvious evils, but fill our lives with discontent, incapacitate us for the enjoyment of beauty, and make us almost incapable of the contemplative virtues. In this respect we have grown rapidly worse during the last hundred years. I do not deny that the Chinese go too far in the other direction; but for that very reason I think contact between East and West is likely to be fruitful to both parties. They may learn from us the indispensable minimum of practical efficiency, and we may learn from them something of that contemplative wisdom which has enabled them to persist while all the other nations of antiquity have perished.

When I went to China, I went to teach; but every day that I stayed I thought less of what I had to teach them and more of what I had to learn from them. Among Europeans who had lived a long time in China, I found this attitude not uncommon; but among those whose stay is short, or who go only to make money, it is sadly rare. It is rare because the Chinese do not excel in the things we really value — military prowess[2] and industrial enterprise. But those who value wisdom or beauty, or even the simple enjoyment of life, will find more of these things in China than in the distracted and turbulent West, and will be happy to live where such things are valued. I wish I could hope that China, in return for our scientific knowledge, may give us something of her large tolerance and contemplative peace of mind.

---

1   **pugnacious:** fond of fighting
2   **prowess:** bravery

Supplementary Reading

Alfred North Whitehead on Education

Education is the acquisition of the art of the utilisation of knowledge. (A. E. p. 6)

It must never be forgotten that education is not a process of packing articles in a trunk. Such a simile is entirely inapplicable. It is, of course, a process completely of its own peculiar genus[1]. Its nearest analogue is the assimilation of food by a living organism: and we all know how necessary to health is palatable[2] food under suitable conditions. (A. E. p. 51)

Knowledge does not keep any better than fish. You may be dealing with knowledge of the old species, with some old truth; but somehow or other it must come to the students, as it were, just drawn out of the sea and with the freshness of its immediate importance. (A. E. p. 147)

There is only one subject matter for education, and that is Life in all its manifestations. Instead of this single unity, we offer children — Algebra, from which follows; Geometry, from which nothing follows; Science, from which nothing follows; History, from which nothing follows; a Couple of Languages, never mastered; and lastly, most dreary of all, Literature, represented by plays of Shakespeare, with philological notes and short analyses of plot and character to be in substance committed to memory. (A. E. p. 10)

A narrow convention as to learning, and as to the procedures of institutions connected with it, has developed. ... Thus, to a really learned man, matter exists in test tubes, animals in cages, art in museums, religion in churches, knowledge in libraries. (Harvard p. 265)

First hand knowledge is the ultimate basis of intellectual life. To a large extent book-learning conveys second-hand information, and as such can never rise to the importance of immediate practice. Our goal is to see the immediate events of our lives as instances of our general ideas. What the learned world tends to offer is one second-hand scrap of information illustrating ideas derived from another second-hand scrap of information. The secondhandedness of the learned world is the secret of its mediocrity. It is tame because it has never been scared by facts. (A. E. p. 79)

Whenever a textbook is written of real educational worth, you may be quite certain that some reviewer will say that it will be difficult to teach from it. Of course it will be difficult to

---

1 **genus:** kind

2 **palatable:** agreeable to the taste

teach from it. If it were easy, the book ought to be burned; for it cannot be educational. In education as elsewhere, the broad primrose path[1] leads to a nasty place. This evil path is represented by a book or a set of lectures which will practically enable the student to learn by heart all the questions likely to be asked at the next external examination. (A. E. pp. 6–7)

The fading of ideals is sad evidence of the defeat of human endeavour. In the schools of antiquity philosophers aspired to impart wisdom, in modern colleges our humbler aim is to teach subjects. (A. E. p. 45)

In order to acquire learning, we must first shake ourselves free of it. (M. T. 7 pp. 7–8)

The history of human thought in the past is a pitiful tale of self-satisfaction with a supposed adequacy of knowledge in respect to factors of human existence. We now know that in the past such self-satisfaction was a delusion. (Imm. p. 683)

Learning preserves the errors of the past, as well as its wisdom. For this reason, dictionaries are public dangers, although they are necessities. (Imm. p. 691)

The Greeks and the Romans at their best period have been taken as the standard of civilisation. ... The particular example of an ancient society sets too static an ideal, and neglects the whole range of opportunity. It is really not sufficient to direct attention to the best that has been said and done in the ancient world. The result is static, repressive, and promotes a decadent habit of mind. ... The most un-Greek thing that we can do is to copy the Greeks. For emphatically they were not copyists. (A. I. pp. 352-3)

To this day I cannot read *King Lear,* having had the advantage of studying it accurately at school. (Atlantic, Vol. 138, p. 197)

Whatever be the detail with which you cram your student, the chance of his meeting in after life exactly that detail[2] is almost infinitesimal[3]; and if he does meet it, he will probably have forgotten what you taught him about it. The really useful training yields a comprehension of a few general principles with a thorough grounding in the way they apply to a variety of concrete details. In subsequent practice the men will have forgotten your particular details; but they will remember by an unconscious common sense how to apply principles to immediate circumstances. Your learning is useless to you till you have lost your textbooks, burnt your lecture notes, and forgotten the minutiae[4] which you learned by heart for the examination. What, in the way of detail, you continually require will stick in your memory as obvious facts like the sun and the moon; and what you casually require can be looked up in any work of reference. The function of a University is to enable you to shed[5] details in favor of principles. When I speak of principles I

---

1   **primrose path:** pursuit of pleasure
2   **his meeting in after life exactly that detail:** his meeting exactly that detail later on
3   **infinitesimal:** small
4   **minutiae:** trivial details
5   **shed:** get rid of

am hardly even thinking of verbal formulations. A principle which has thoroughly soaked into you is rather a mental habit than a formal statement. It becomes the way the mind reacts to the appropriate stimulus in the form of illustrative circumstances. Nobody goes about with his knowledge clearly and consciously before him. Mental cultivation is nothing else than the satisfactory way in which the mind will function when it is poked up[1] into activity. (A.19. pp. 41–2)

I am sure that one secret of a successful teacher is that he has formulated quite clearly in his mind what the pupil has got to know in precise fashion. He will then cease from half-hearted attempts to worry his pupils with memorising a lot of irrelevant stuff of inferior importance. (A. E. p. 57)

There are three main methods which are required in a national system of education, namely, the literary curriculum, the scientific curriculum, the technical curriculum. But each of these curricula should include the other two. What I mean is, that every form of education should give the pupil a technique, a science, an assortment of general ideas, and aesthetic appreciation, and that each of these sides of his training should be illuminated by the others. (A. E. p. 75)

Mere literary knowledge is of slight importance. The only thing that matters is, how it is known. The facts related are nothing. Literature only exists to express and develop the imaginative world which is our life, the kingdom which is within us. It follows that the literary side of a technical education should consist in an effort to make the pupils enjoy literature. It does not matter what they know, but the enjoyment is vital. The great English Universities, under whose direct authority school children are examined in plays of Shakespeare, to the certain destruction of their enjoyment, should be prosecuted for soul murder. (A. E. pp. 88–9)

The antithesis between a technical and a liberal education is fallacious[2]. There can be no adequate technical education which is not liberal, and no liberal education which is not technical; that is, no education which does not impart both technique and intellectual vision. In simpler language, education should turn out the pupil with something he knows well and something he can do well. This intimate union of practice and theory aids both. The intellect does not work best in a vacuum. (A. E. p. 74)

The human mind was not evolved in bygone ages for the sake of reasoning, but merely to enable mankind with more art to hunt between meals for fresh food supplies. Accordingly few people can follow close reasoning without considerable practice. (A. E. pp. 127–8)

In the past, classics reigned throughout the whole sphere of higher education. ... All this is gone, and gone forever. Humpty Dumpty[3] was a good egg so long as he was on top of the wall, but you can never set him up again. (A. E. pp. 93–4)

---

1 **poke up:** push up
2 **fallacious:** misleading
3 **Humpty Dumpty:** a character in a *Mother Goose* rhyme, portrayed as an anthropomorphized egg, also in Lewis Carroll's *Through the Looking-Glass* discussing semantics with Alice

The function of Latin literature is its expression of Rome. When to England and France your imagination can add Rome in the background, you have laid firm the foundations of culture. The understanding of Rome leads back to the Mediterranean civilisation of which Rome was the last phase, and it automatically exhibits the geography of Europe, and the functions of seas and rivers and mountains and plains. The merit of this study in the education of youth is its concreteness, its inspiration to action, and the uniform greatness of persons, in their characters and their staging. Their aims were great, their virtues were great, and their vices were great. They had the saving merit of sinning with cart ropes. (A. E. p. 106)

The task of a University is the creation of the future, so far as rational thought, and civilized modes of appreciation, can affect the issue. The future is big with every possibility of achievement and of tragedy. (M. T. p. 233)

The careful shielding of a university from the activities of the world around is the best way to chill interest and to defeat progress. Celibacy does not suit a university. It must mate itself with action. (Harvard p. 267)

The tragedy of the world is that those who are imaginative have but slight experience, and those who are experienced have feeble imaginations. Fools act on imagination without knowledge; pedants[1] act on knowledge without imagination. The task of a university is to weld together imagination and experience. (A. E. p. 140)

During the school period the student has been mentally bending over his desk; at the University he should stand up and look around. For this reason it is fatal if the first year at the University be frittered[2] away in going over the old work in the old spirit. At school the boy painfully rises from the particular towards glimpses at general ideas; at the University he should start from general ideas and study their applications to concrete cases. (A. E. p. 41)

In my own work at universities I have been much struck by the paralysis of thought induced in pupils by the aimless accumulation of precise knowledge, inert and unutilised. It should be the chief aim of a university professor to exhibit himself in his own true character — that is, as an ignorant man thinking, actively utilising his small share of knowledge. (A. E. p. 58)

Nothing is more difficult than to distinguish between a loud voice and vigour, or a flow of words and originality, or mental instability and genius; or a big book and fruitful learning. Also the work requires dependable men. But if you are swayed too heavily by this admirable excellence, you will gather a faculty which can be depended upon for being commonplace. (Harvard p. 266)

---

1   **pedant:** one who lays too much stress on book-learning and rules

2   **fritter:** waste

Imagination is a contagious disease. It cannot be measured by the yard, or weighed by the pound, and then delivered to the students by members of the faculty. It can only be communicated by a faculty whose members themselves wear their learning with imagination. (A. E. p. 145)

The university imparts information, but it imparts it imaginatively. At least, this is the function which it should perform for society. A university which fails in this respect has no reason for existence. This atmosphere of excitement, arising from imaginative consideration, transforms knowledge. A fact is no longer a bare fact: it is invested with all its possibilities. It is no longer a burden on the memory: it is energising as the poet of our dreams, and as the architect of our purposes. (A. E. p. 139)

The history of ideas is a history of mistakes. But through all mistakes it is also the history of the gradual purification of conduct. (A. I. p. 30)

The middle class pessimism over the future of the world comes from a confusion between civilisation and security. In the immediate future there will be less security than in the immediate past, less stability. It must be admitted that there is a degree of instability which is inconsistent with civilisation. But, on the whole, the great ages have been unstable ages. (S. M. W. p. 299)

Nothing does more harm in unnerving[1] men for their duties in the present than the attention devoted to the points of excellence in the past as compared with the average failure of the present day. (S. M. W. p. 294)

The ultimate motive power, alike in science, in morality, and in religion, is the sense of value, the sense of importance. It takes the various forms of wonder, of curiosity, of reverence, or worship, of tumultuous desire for merging personality in something beyond itself. This sense of value imposes on life incredible labours, and apart from it life sinks back into the passivity of its lower types. (A. E. pp. 62–3)

Abbreviations:
A. E. — *The Aims of Education,* The Macmillan Co., New York, 1929.
M. T. — *Modes of Thought,* The Macmillan Co., New York, 1938.
A. I. — *Adventures of Ideas,* Cambridge University Press, 1933.
S. M. W. — *Science and the Modern World,* The Macmillan Co., New York, 1929.
P. R. — *Process and Reality,* The Macmillan Co., New York, 1929.
Harvard — "Harvard: The Future," *Atlantic Monthly,* Vol. 158.
F. R. — *The Function of Reason,* Princeton University Press, 1929.
Intro. Math. — *An Introduction to Mathematics,* Williams and Norgate, London, 1911.
Symb. — *Symbolism Its Meaning and Effect,* The Macmillan Co., New York, 1929.
Imm. — "Immortality," *The Philosophy of Alfred North Whitehead,* 1941.

---

1   **unnerve:** cause to lose power of decision and courage

Heritage of Western Intellectual Tradition   A Sourcebook

Questions for Discussion

1. What, according to Russell, is a freeman and how does this freeman worship?
2. What do you think is the intellectual freedom Russell advocates? Do you think Russell is being too idealistic here?
3. What conclusions you might be able to draw from Russell's pursuit of truth and Whitehead's aims of education?
4. What is Russell's idea about East West interaction?
5. Comment on the following famous statement made by Whitehead in his notable address "The Aims of Education: A Plea for Reform":

   Culture is activity of thought, and receptiveness to beauty and humane feeling. Scraps of information have nothing to do with it.
6. How is Whitehead comparable to John Dewey in their concepts of education?
7. If Russell and Whitehead still live today, what do you think they would say about intellectual pursuit and education?

Heritage of Western Intellectual Tradition   A Sourcebook

UNIT 16

Man & Woman: Modern Existence

Pretest

- What is existence and how is it related to existentialism?
- How does existentialism contribute to early feminist movement of the 20th century?
- Do you have any idea about Sartre and de Beauvoir?

What You Will Learn in This Unit

- Existentialism as humanistic movement in the first half of the 20th century;
- Selected readings from Sartre and de Beauvoir; and
- Sartre and de Beauvoir in China.

Learn to Pronounce

antiauthoritarian /ˌæntiɔːˈθɒrɪˈteərɪən/ 反独裁
Dostoyevsky /ˌdɒstəˈjefskiː/ 陀思妥耶夫斯基
Existentialist /ˌegzɪsˈtenʃəlist/ 存在主义的 / 者
Jean-Paul Sartre /ˈsɑːtrə/ 萨特
Prix Goncourt /gonˈgɒr/ 龚固尔文学奖
Simone de Beauvoir /bɒvvwˈaːr/ 波伏娃

anxiety /æŋgˈzaɪətɪ/ 焦虑
epistemology /ˌepɪstɪˈmɒlədʒɪ/ 认识论
Heidegger / ˈhaɪdegər/ 海德格尔
Kant /kɑːnt/ 康德
Proust /pruːst/ 普鲁斯特
Zola / ˈzoʊlə/ 左拉

Introduction

The spiritual chaos in the mid 20th century forced intellectuals to find ways to address it. "Anxiety" is the word for the existentialists to refer to the individual's confrontation with the "nothingness" or the impossibility of finding ultimate justification for the choices he must make faced with the pure contingency of the universe. By stressing concrete individual existence, subjectivity and choice, existentialists argued that one must choose one's own way without following morally perfect individuals or relying on universal standards. In this sense, "existence precedes essence." By arguing that freedom of choice entails risks and responsibility, the existentialists called for commitment and positive actions. The whole situation applies to women's movement, which saw an unprecedented development in the first half of the 20th century. The historical implication of "feminism" (movements for recognition of the claims of women for rights (legal, political, familial, etc.) equal to those possessed by men) saw its fulfillment in the 20th century as women have gained most of these political and legal rights. The feminism starting in the 1960s had been concerned not so much with the traditional women's rights as with issues more deeply rooted than those for the previous liberation movement, leading to the theoretical speculations on women and women related subjects. The turning point of this influential intellectual movement came with people like Simone De Beauvoir, who have helped to turn it into a social critique whose impact is felt everywhere today.

Jean Paul Sartre (1905 – 80), French philosopher, dramatist, novelist, and leading exponent of existentialism, lost his father at an early age and grew up in the home of his maternal grandfather. The boy, who wandered in the Luxembourg Gardens of Paris in search of playmates, was small in stature and cross-eyed. Educated at University of Fribourg in Switzerland, and the French Institute in Berlin, he taught philosophy from 1929 until the outbreak of World War II, when he was called into military service.

In 1940 – 41 he was imprisoned by the Germans; after his release, he was active in the French Resistance. The German authorities, unaware of his underground activities, permitted the production of his antiauthoritarian play *The Flies* (1943) and the publication of *Being and Nothingness* (1943). Sartre was an independent Socialist, critical of both the USSR and the United States in the cold war years. Most of his writing of the 1950s deals with literary and political problems. Sartre's other works include the novel *Nausea* (1938) and his autobiography, *The Words* (1964), for which he was awarded the 1964 Nobel Prize for Literature. Sartre rejected it, explaining that the award would compromise his integrity as a writer: "A writer must refuse to allow himself to be transformed into an institution, even if it takes place in the most honorable form." He resisted the "bourgeois marriage" and formed a settled partnership in life with Simone de Beauvoir, "mother of modern feminism." In *Being and Nothingness,* Sartre places human consciousness, or no-thingness, in opposition to being, or thingness. His consciousness is not-matter and escapes all determinism, hence having the capacity to negate and rebel. Freedom in *Existentialism and Humanism* (1946) implies social responsibility. Freedom and acceptance of personal responsibility are the main values in life and individuals must rely on their creative powers unaided by society, traditional morality, or religious faith. He died of a lung tumour, and some 25,000 ordinary people attended his funeral, reminiscent of the burial of Victor Hugo, "but without the official recognition that his illustrious predecessor had received."

Jean-Paul Sartre: Existentialism*

Existentialism, a philosophical interpretation of human existence stressing its concreteness and problematic character. Existentialism may be seen as an irrationalist revolt against traditional Western philosophy, idealism in particular, as it rejects epistemology and the attempt to ground human knowledge. First, human beings have no essence and are not even primarily knowers; rather they care, desire, manipulate, and, above all, choose and act, which makes them what they are. Secondly, the self or ego is not a "basic feature of the prereflective experience," but emerges from one's experience of other people. Finally, man is not a detached observer of the world, but "in the world." Since man's choices are not rationally grounded, Existentialists do not presuppose any set rules or values, but propose a framework in which action and choice are to be viewed. This framework does not tell one what to choose, but once the choice has been made, man has to be responsible for all its consequences.

What is meant by the term *existentialism*? Most people who use the word would be rather embarrassed if they had to explain it, since, now that the word is all the rage[1], even the work of a musician or painter is being called existentialist. A gossip columnist in *Clartes*[2] signs himself The Existentialist, so that by this time the word has been so stretched and has taken on so broad a meaning, that it no longer means anything at all. It seems that for want of an advanced-guard doctrine, analogous[3] to surrealism[4], the kind of people who are eager for scandal[5] and flurry[6] turn to this philosophy which in other respects does not at all serve their purposes in this sphere.

---

* This is Sartre's best known philosophic work (originally "Existentialism Is a Humannism"), which was delivered as a lecture in 1946 as an answer to critics who saw in his ideas a resignation, despair and "nothingness."

1 **rage:** something very fashionable, having widespread enthusiasm

2 *Clartes:* periodical published by a non-partisan socialist students' organisation in Sweden, which underwent a process of radicalisation in the 1970s.

3 **analogous:** similar or parallel to

4 **surrealism:** artistic and literary movement, officially launched in Paris in 1924 by French writer André Breton (1896–1966) who wrote the first surrealist manifesto, that explored and celebrated the realm of dreams and the unconscious mind through the creation of visual art, poetry and motion pictures

5 **scandal:** harmful gossip

6 **flurry:** short, sudden rush of wind, here gossip

Actually, it is the least scandalous, the most austere[1] of doctrines. It is intended strictly for specialists and philosophers. Yet it can be defined easily. What complicates matters is that there are two kinds of existentialists; first, those who are Christian, among whom I would include Jaspers[2] and Gabriel Marcel[3], both Catholic; and on the other hand the atheistic existentialists among whom I class Heidegger[4], and then the French existentialists and myself. What they have in common is that they think that existence precedes essence, or, if you prefer, that subjectivity must be the starting point.

Just what does that mean? Let us consider some object that is manufactured, for example, a book or a papercutter: here is an object which has been made by an artisan whose inspiration came from a concept. He referred to the concept of what a papercutter is and likewise to a known method of production, which is part of the concept, something which is, by and large, a routine. Thus, the papercutter is at once an object produced in a certain way and, on the other hand, one leaving a specific use; and one can not postulate[5] a man who produces a papercutter but does not know what it is used for. **Therefore, let us say that, for the papercutter, essence — that is, the ensemble[6] of both the production routines and the properties which enable it to be both produced and defined — precedes existence.** Thus, the presence of the papercutter or book in front of me is determined. Therefore, we have here a technical view of the world whereby it can be said that production precedes existence.

When we conceive God as the Creator, He is generally thought of as a superior sort of artisan. Whatever doctrine we may be considering, whether one like that of Descartes or that of Leibniz, we always grant that will more or less follows understanding or, at the very least, accompanies it, and that when God creates He knows exactly what he is creating. Thus, the concept of man in the mind of God is comparable to the concept of a papercutter in the mind of the manufacturer, and, following certain techniques and a conception, God produces man, just as the artisan, following a definition and a technique, makes a papercutter. Thus, the individual man is the realization of a certain concept in the divine intelligence.

Sartre at work

In the eighteenth century, the atheism of the philosophers discarded the idea of God, but not

---

1 **austere:** serious, moral, strict
2 **Karl Jaspers (1883–1969):** German philosopher, one of the originators of existentialism
3 **Gabriel Marcel (1889–1973):** French existentialist philosopher, dramatist, and critic, known for the idea that individuals can only be understood as embodied and involved in specific situations
4 **Martin Heidegger (1889–1976):** German philosopher, whose existential phenomenology is widely regarded as the most original and influential of the 20th century philosophy.
5 **postulate:** take as a basis for reasoning
6 **ensemble:** general effect

Heritage of Western Intellectual Tradition   A Sourcebook

so much for the notion that essence precedes existence. To a certain extent, this idea is found everywhere; we find it in Diderot[1], in Voltaire[2], and even in Kant[3]. Man has a human nature; this human nature, which is the concept of the human, is found in all men, which means that each man is a particular example of a universal concept, man. In Kant, the result of this universality is that the wild-man, the natural man, as well as the bourgeois, are circumscribed[4] by the same definition and have the same basic qualities. Thus, here too the essence of man precedes the historical existence that we find in nature.

Atheistic existentialism, which I represent, is more coherent. It states that if God does not exist, there is at least one being in whom existence precedes essence, a being who exists before he can be defined by any concept, and that this being is man, or, as Heidegger says, human reality. **What is meant here by saying that existence precedes essence? It means that, first of all, man exists, turns up, appears on the scene, and, only afterwards, defines himself. If man, as the existentialist conceives him, is indefinable, it is because at first he is nothing. Only afterward will he be something, and he himself will have made what he will be. Thus, there is no human nature, since there is no God to conceive it. Not only is man what he conceives himself to be, but he is also only what he wills himself to be after this thrust toward existence.**

Man is nothing else but what he makes of himself. Such is the first principle of existentialism. It is also what is called subjectivity, the name we are labeled with when charges are brought against us. But what do we mean by this, if not[5] that man has a greater dignity than a stone or table? For we mean that man first exists, that is, that man first of all is the being who hurls himself toward a future and who is conscious of imagining himself as being in the future. Man is at the start a plan which is aware of itself, rather than a patch of moss, a piece of garbage, or a cauliflower, as nothing exists prior to this plan; there is nothing in heaven; man will be what he will have planned to be. Not what he will want to be. Because by the word "will" we generally mean a conscious decision, which is subsequent to what we have already made of ourselves. I may want to belong to a political party, write a book, get married; but all that is only a manifestation of an earlier, more spontaneous choice that is called "will." But if existence really does precede essence, man is responsible for what he is. Thus, existentialism's first move is to make every man aware of what he is and to make the full responsibility of his existence rest on him. And when we say that a man is responsible for himself, we do not only mean that he is responsible for his own individuality, but that he is responsible for all men.

...

---

1   **Denis Diderot (1713–84):** French Encyclopedist and philosopher
2   **Voltaire (1694–1778):** French writer and philosopher, one of the leaders of the Enlightenment
3   **Immanuel Kant (1724–1804):** German philosopher, considered by many the most influential thinker of modern times
4   **circumscribe:** mark the limits
5   **if not:** namely, if it means more than

Heritage of Western Intellectual Tradition   A Sourcebook

Thus, our responsibility is much greater than we might have supposed, because it involves all mankind. If I am a workingman and choose to join a Christian trade-union rather than be a communist, and if by being a member I want to show that the best thing for man is resignation[1], that the kingdom of man is not of this world, I am not only involving my own case — I want to be resigned for everyone. As a result, my action has involved all humanity. To take a more individual matter, if I want to marry, to have children; even if this marriage depends solely on my own circumstances or passion or wish, I am involving all humanity in monogamy[2] and not merely myself. Therefore, I am responsible for myself and for everyone else. I am creating a certain image of man of my own choosing. In choosing myself, I choose man.

This helps us understand what the actual content is of[3] such rather grandiloquent[4] words as anguish, forlornness[5], despair. As you will see, it's all quite simple.

First, what is meant by anguish? **The existentialists say at once that man is anguish. What that means is this: the man who involves himself and who realizes that he is not only the person he chooses to be, but also a lawmaker who is, at the same time, choosing all mankind as well as himself, cannot help escaping the feeling of his total and deep responsibility.** Of course, there are many people who are not anxious; but we claim that they are hiding their anxiety, that they are fleeing from it. Certainly, many people believe that when they do something, they themselves are the only ones involved, and when someone says to them, "What if everyone acted that way?" they shrug their shoulders and answer, "Everyone doesn't act that way." But really, one should always ask himself, "What would happen if everybody looked at things that way?" There is no escaping this disturbing thought except by a kind of double-dealing[6]. A man who lies and makes excuses for himself by saying "not everybody does that," is someone with an uneasy conscience, because the act of lying implies that a universal value is conferred upon the lie.

Sartre and Beauvoir selling newspaper

Anguish is evident even when it conceals itself. This is the anguish that Kierkegaard[7] called

---

1   **resignation:** being ready to accept and endure whatever one finds oneself in
2   **monogamy:** marriage to one person at a time
3   **what the actual content is of:** what the actual content of … is
4   **grandiloquent:** full of pompous words
5   **forlornness:** loneness, unhappiness, forsakenness
6   **double-dealing:** deceit
7   **Søren Aabye Kierkegaard (1813–1855):** Danish philosopher, who was concerned with individual existence, choice, and commitment, and profoundly influenced modern theology and philosophy, especially existentialism

the anguish of Abraham. You know the story: an angel has ordered Abraham to sacrifice his son; if it really were an angel who has come and said, "You are Abraham, you shall sacrifice your son," everything would be all right. But everyone might first wonder, "Is it really an angel, and am I really Abraham? What proof do I have?"

Sartre in uniform, 1939

There was a madwoman who had hallucinations[1]; someone used to speak to her on the telephone and give her orders. Her doctor asked her, "Who is it who talks to you?" She answered, "He says it's God." What proof did she really have that it was God? If an angel comes to me, what proof is there that it's an angel? And if I hear voices, what proof is there that they come from heaven and not from hell, or from the subconscious, or a pathological condition? What proves that they are addressed to me? What proof is there that I have been appointed to impose my choice and my conception of man on humanity? I'll never find any proof or sign to convince me of that. **If a voice addresses me, it is always for me to decide that this is the angel's voice; if I consider that such an act is a good one, it is I who will choose to say that it is good rather than bad.**

Now, I'm not being singled out as an Abraham, and yet at every moment I'm obliged to perform exemplary[2] acts. For every man, everything happens as if all mankind had its eyes fixed on him and were guiding itself[3] by what he does. And every man ought to say to himself, "Am I really the kind of man who has the right to act in such a way that humanity might guide itself by my actions?" And if he does not say that to himself, he is masking his anguish.

There is no question here of the kind of anguish which would lead to quietism, to inaction. It is a matter of a simple sort of anguish that anybody who has had responsibilities is familiar with. For example, when a military officer takes the responsibility for an attack and sends a certain number of men to death, he chooses to do so, and in the main[4] he alone makes the choice. Doubtless, orders come from above, but they are too broad; he interprets them, and on this interpretation depend the lives of ten or fourteen or twenty men. In making a decision he cannot help having a certain anguish. All leaders know this anguish. That doesn't keep them from acting; on the contrary, it is the very condition of their action. For it implies that they envisage a number of possibilities, and when they choose one, they realize that it has value only because it is chosen. We shall see that this kind of anguish, which is the kind that existentialism describes, is explained, in addition, by a direct responsibility to the other men whom it involves. It is not a curtain separating us from action, but is part of action itself.

----

1 **hallucination:** illusion
2 **exemplary:** serving as example
3 **itself:** all mankind
4 **in the main:** for the most part

When we speak of forlornness, a term Heidegger was fond of, we mean only that God does not exist and that we have to face all the consequences of this. The existentialist is strongly opposed to a certain kind of secular ethics which would like to abolish God with the least possible expense. About 1880, some French teachers tried to set up a secular ethics which went something like this: God is a useless and costly hypothesis; we are discarding it; but, meanwhile, in order for there to be an ethics, a society, a civilization, it is essential that certain values be taken seriously and that they be considered as having an a priori[1] existence. It must be obligatory, a priori, to be honest, not to lie, not to beat your wife, to have children, etc., etc. **So we're going to try a little device which will make it possible to show that values exist all the same, inscribed in a heaven of ideas, though otherwise God does not exist.** In other words — and this, I believe, is the tendency of everything called reformism in France — nothing will be changed if God does not exist. We shall find ourselves with the same norms of honesty, progress, and humanism, and we shall have made of God an outdated hypothesis which will peacefully die off by itself.

The existentialist, on the contrary, thinks it very distressing that God does not exist, because all possibility of finding values in a heaven of ideas disappears along with Him; there can no longer be an a priori Good, since there is no infinite and perfect consciousness to think it. Nowhere is it written that the Good exists, that we must be honest, that we must not lie; because the fact is we are on a plane where there are only men. Dostoyevsky[2] said, "If God didn't exist, everything would be possible." That is the very starting point of existentialism. Indeed, everything is permissible if God does not exist, and as a result man is forlorn, because neither within him nor without does he find any-thing to cling to. He can't start making excuses for himself.

If existence really does precede essence, there is no explaining things away by reference to a fixed and given human nature. In other words, there is no determinism, man is free, man is freedom. On the other hand, if God does not exist, we find no values or commands to turn to which legitimize our conduct. So, in the bright realm of values, we have no excuse behind us, nor justification before us. We are alone, with no excuses.

Sartre with Simone de Beauvoir, Berlin, 1947

That is the idea I shall try to convey when I say that man is condemned to be free. Condemned, because he did not create himself, yet, in other respects is free; because, once thrown into the world, he is responsible for everything he does. **The existentialist does not believe in the power of passion. He will never agree that a sweeping passion is a ravaging torrent which fatally leads a man to certain acts and is therefore an excuse. He thinks that man is responsible for his passion.**

---

1   **a priori:** derived by reasoning without reference to particular facts or experience
2   **Fyodor Mikhaylovich Dostoyevsky (1821–1881):** Russian writer, one of the world's greatest novelists, whose works (*Crime and Punishment*, 1866, *The Idiot*, 1868–1869, and *The Brothers Karamazov*, 1879–1880) dramatize religious, moral, political, and psychological issues

Heritage of Western Intellectual Tradition   A Sourcebook

The existentialist does not think that man is going to help himself by finding in the world some omen[1] by which to orient himself. Because he thinks that man will interpret the omen to suit himself. Therefore, he thinks that man, with no support and no aid, is condemned every moment to invent man.

…

Now, for the existentialist there is really no love other than one which manifests itself in a person's being in love. There is no genius other than one which is expressed in works of art; the genius of Proust[2] is the sum of Proust's works; the genius of Racine[3] is his series of tragedies. Outside of that, there is nothing. Why say that Racine could have written another tragedy, when he didn't write it? A man is involved in life, leaves his impress on it, and outside of that there is nothing. To be sure, this may seem a harsh thought to someone whose life hasn't been a success. But, on the other hand, it prompts people to understand that reality alone is what counts, that dreams, expectations, and hopes warrant no more than to define a man as a disappointed dream, as miscarried[4] hopes, as vain expectations. In other words, to define him negatively and not positively. However, when we say, "You are nothing else than your life," that does not imply that the artist will be judged solely on the basis of his works of art; a thousand other things will contribute toward summing him up. What we mean is that **a man is nothing else than a series of undertakings, that he is the sum, the organization, the ensemble of the relationships which make up these undertakings.**

When all is said and done, what we are accused of, at bottom, is not our pessimism, but an optimistic toughness. If people throw up to us our works of fiction in which we write about people who are soft, weak, cowardly, and sometimes even downright bad, it's not because these people are soft, weak, cowardly, or bad; because if we were to say, as Zola[5] did, that they are that way because of heredity, the workings of environment, society, because of biological or psychological determinism, people would be reassured.

Sartre's funeral on April 19, 1980, Paris

---

1   **omen:** sign of fortune
2   **Marcel Proust (1871 –1922):** French writer, most famous for the 16-volume *à la recherche du temps perdu* (1913 –1927), or *Remembrance of Things Past*, regarded as one of the greatest achievements in world literature
3   **Jean Baptiste Racine (1639 –1699):** French dramatist, greatest writer of French classical tragedy
4   **miscarried:** failed
5   **Émile Zola (1840 –1902):** French novelist, essayist, and critic, chief advocate and practitioner in France of literary naturalism

They would say, "Well, that's what we're like, no one can do anything about it." But when the existentialist writes about a coward, he says that this coward is responsible for his cowardice. He's not like that because he has a cowardly heart or lung or brain; he's not like that on account of his physiological make-up; but he's like that because he has made himself a coward by his acts. There's no such thing as a cowardly constitution; there are nervous constitutions; there is poor blood, as the common people say, or strong constitutions. But the man whose blood is poor is not a coward on that account, for what makes cowardice is the act of renouncing or yielding. A constitution is not an act; the coward is defined on the basis of the acts he performs. People feel, in a vague sort of way, that this coward we're talking about is guilty of being a coward, and the thought frightens them. What people would like is that a coward or a hero be born that way.

Existentialism is nothing else than an attempt to draw all the consequences of a coherent atheistic position. It isn't trying to plunge man into despair at all. But if one calls every attitude of unbelief despair, like the Christians, then the word is not being used in its original sense. **Existentialism isn't so atheistic that it wears itself out[1] showing that God doesn't exist. Rather, it declares that even if God did exist, that would change nothing.** There you've got our point of view. Not that we believe that God exists, but we think that the problem of His existence is not the issue. In this sense existentialism is optimistic, a doctrine of action, and it is plain dishonesty for Christians to make no distinction between their own despair and ours and then to call us despairing.

Key Concepts

anguish	existentialism
atheistic existentialism	forlornness
conscious decision	nothingness
deep responsibility	optimistic toughness
despair	quietism
determinism	subjectivity
existence precedes essence	

---

1 **wear out:** become exhausted

Simone de Beauvoir: The Second Sex*

Simone De Beauvoir (1908 – 1986), French writer and social activist, one of the most influential feminist theorists of the 20th century. Beauvoir got a degree in philosophy in 1929 from the école Normale Supérieure and the Sorbonne, where she met Jean-Paul Sartre to begin a free, lifelong association with him. Beauvoir and Sartre remained in Paris during World War II, and were active in the resistance movement against the German occupation. During these years they refined the principles of existentialism. After the war Beauvoir became a committed writer, her writings including the novel *Les Mandarins* (*The Mandarins* 1954) which received the Prix Goncourt[1], a prestigious French literary award. She collaborated with Sartre on the political and literary journal *Les temps modernes* (*Modern Times*) and traveled with him throughout Europe, Asia and America. Beauvoir is known primarily for her treatise *The Second Sex* (*Le deuxième sexe* 1949), a scholarly and passionate plea for the abolition of what she called the myth of the "eternal feminine." It became a classic of feminist literature during the 1960s, and the existential analysis of the situation of women was extremely influential in the formation of feminist theory. In these writings she revealed herself as a woman of formidable courage and integrity: the basic options of an individual made on the premises of an equal vocation for man and woman founded on a common structure of their being, independent of their sexuality. For this and many others, she has often been referred to as "Grandmother" of 20th century feminism

For a long time I have hesitated to write a book on woman. The subject is irritating, especially to women; and it is not new. Enough ink has been spilled in quarrelling over feminism, and perhaps we should say no more about it. It is still talked about, however, for the voluminous nonsense uttered during the last century seems to have done little to illuminate the problem. **After all, is there a problem? And if so, what is it? Are there women, really?** Most assuredly the theory of the eternal feminine[2] still has its adherents who will whisper in your ear: "Even in Russia

---

* This book was first conceived, as Beauvoir later told, by chance. She wanted to talk about herself, but then she became aware that to do so she would have to talk first about the condition of woman in *general*. While putting the seemingly "completely incoherent" things together, she began to see that "it is both strange and stimulating to discover suddenly, after forty, an aspect of the world that has been staring you in the face all the time which somehow you have never noticed." ("On the publication of *The Second Sex*", 1963) Part of these ideas appeared in *Les Temps Modernes*, and when *The Second Sex* came out, it was well received: 22,000 copies were sold in the first week. Readers were shocked. Nobel laureate Albert Camus (1913 – 60), for instance, accused her of "making the French male look ridiculous." But others, especially women, hailed it as a monument of the feminist movement.

1　**Edmond Louis Antoine Huot de Goncourt (1822 – 1896):** French writer who collaborated with his brother Jules Alfred Huot de Goncourt (1830 – 1870) on numerous works, most notably naturalistic novels such as *Madame Gervaisais* (1869)

2　**eternal feminine:** or the essence of femininity. Today the argument still goes on as to what it is that makes women what they are, between essentialists and anti-essentialists.

women still are women;" and other erudite[1] persons — sometimes the very same — say with a sigh: "Woman is losing her way, woman is lost." **One wonders if women still exist, if they will always exist, whether or not it is desirable that they should, what place they occupy in this world, what their place should be.** "What has become of women?" was asked recently in an ephemeral[2] magazine.

But first we must ask: what is a woman? "*Tota mulier in utero*," says one, "woman is a womb." But in speaking of certain women, connoisseurs[3] declare that they are not women, although they are equipped with a uterus[4] like the rest. All agree in recognising the fact that females exist in the human species; today as always they make up about one half of humanity. And yet we are told that femininity is in danger; we are exhorted[5] to be women, remain women, become women. **It would appear, then, that every female human being is not necessarily a woman; to be so considered she must share in that mysterious and threatened reality known as femininity.** Is this attribute something secreted[6] by the ovaries[7]? Or is it a Platonic essence, a product of the philosophic imagination?

Simone de Beauvior at work

Is a rustling[8] petticoat[9] enough to bring it down to earth? Although some women try zealously to incarnate[10] this essence, it is hardly patentable[11]. It is frequently described in vague and dazzling terms that seem to have been borrowed from the vocabulary of the seers, and indeed in the times of St Thomas it was considered an essence as certainly defined as the somniferous[12] virtue of the poppy.[13]

But conceptualism has lost ground. The biological and social sciences no longer admit the existence of unchangeably fixed entities that determine given characteristics, such as those ascribed to woman, the Jew, or the Negro. Science regards any characteristic as a reaction dependent in part upon a *situation*. If today femininity no longer exists, then it never existed. But does the word *woman*, then, have no specific content? This is stoutly[14] affirmed by those who hold to

---

1 **erudite:** learned, scholarly

2 **ephemeral:** short lived

3 **connoisseur:** people having good taste

4 **uterus:** womb

5 **exhort:** advise earnestly

6 **secrete:** produce

7 **ovary:** female reproductive organs to produce ova

8 **rustling:** sound made by rustles

9 **petticoat:** woman's underskirt

10 **incarnate:** put in real form, actualize

11 **patentable:** easily recognized

12 **somniferous:** inducing sleep

13 **poppy:** 罌粟

14 **stoutly:** strongly

Heritage of Western Intellectual Tradition — A Sourcebook

the philosophy of the enlightenment, of rationalism, of nominalism[1]; women, to them, are merely the human beings arbitrarily designated by the word *woman*. Many American women particularly are prepared to think that there is no longer any place for woman as such; if a backward individual still takes herself for a woman, her friends advise her to be psychoanalysed and thus get rid of this obsession. In regard to a work, *Modern Woman: The Lost Sex*, which in other respects has its irritating features, Dorothy Parker[2] has written: "I cannot be just to books which treat of woman as woman ... My idea is that all of us, men as well as women, should be regarded as human beings." But nominalism is a rather inadequate doctrine, and the antifeminists have had no trouble in showing that women simply *are* not men. Surely woman is, like man, a human being; but such a declaration is abstract. The fact is that every concrete human being is always a singular, separate individual. To decline to accept such notions as the eternal feminine, the black soul, the Jewish character, is not to deny that Jews, Negroes, women exist today — this denial does not represent a liberation for those concerned, but rather a flight from reality. Some years ago a well-known woman writer refused to permit her portrait to appear in a series of photographs especially devoted to women writers; she wished to be counted among the men. But in order to gain this privilege she made use of her husband's influence! Women who assert that they are men lay claim none the less to masculine consideration and respect. I recall also a young Trotskyite[3] standing on a platform at a boisterous[4] meeting and getting ready to use her fists, in spite of her evident fragility. She was denying her feminine weakness; but it was for love of a militant male whose equal she wished to be. The attitude of defiance of many American women proves that they are haunted by a sense of their femininity. In truth, to go for a walk with one's eyes open is enough to demonstrate that humanity is divided into two classes of individuals whose clothes, faces, bodies, smiles, gaits, interests, and occupations are manifestly different. Perhaps these differences are superficial, perhaps they are destined to disappear. What is certain is that they do most obviously exist.

If her functioning as a female is not enough to define woman, if we decline also to explain her through "the eternal feminine," and if nevertheless we admit, provisionally[5], that women do exist, then we must face the question "what is a woman"?

To state the question is, to me, to suggest, at once, a preliminary answer. The fact that I ask it is in itself significant. A man would never set out to write a book on the peculiar situation of the human male. But if I wish to define myself, I must first of all say: "I am a woman;" on this truth

---

1   **nominalism:** doctrine holding that abstract concepts, general terms, or universals have no independent existence but exist only as names

2   **Dorothy Parker (1893 – 1967):** U.S. writer noted for her caustic wit, wisecracks, and sharp eye for 20th century urban foibles

3   **Trotskyite:** radicals who support Trotsky's theory that socialism must be established throughout the world by continuing revolution. Leon Trotsky (1879 – 1940): leader of the Bolshevik Revolution (1917), later expelled from the Communist Party (1927), banished in 1929 and murdered while in exile in Mexico.

4   **boisterous:** noisy, violent

5   **provisionally:** temporarily

must be based all further discussion. A man never begins by presenting himself as an individual of a certain sex; it goes without saying that he is a man. The terms *masculine* and *feminine* are used symmetrically[1] only as a matter of form, as on legal papers. In actuality the relation of the two sexes is not quite like that of two electrical poles, for man represents both the positive and the neutral, as is indicated by the common use of *man* to designate human beings in general; whereas woman represents only the negative, defined by limiting criteria, without reciprocity[2]. In the midst of an abstract discussion it is vexing to hear a man say: "You think thus and so because you are a woman;" but I know that my only defence is to reply: "I think thus and so because it is true," thereby removing my subjective self from the argument. It would be out of the question to reply: "And you think the contrary because you are a man," for it is understood that the fact of being a man is no peculiarity. A man is in the right in being a man; it is the woman who is in the wrong. It amounts to this: just as for the ancients there was an absolute vertical with reference to which the oblique[3] was defined, so there is an absolute human type, the masculine. Woman has ovaries, a uterus: these peculiarities imprison her in her subjectivity, circumscribe her within the limits of her own nature. It is often said that she thinks with her glands[4]. Man superbly ignores the fact that his anatomy also includes glands, such as the

Celebrating Sartre's 74th birthday, 1979

testicles[5], and that they secrete hormones. He thinks of his body as a direct and normal connection with the world, which he believes he apprehends objectively, whereas he regards the body of woman as a hindrance, a prison, weighed down by everything peculiar to it. "The female is a female by virtue of a certain lack of qualities," said Aristotle; "we should regard the female nature as afflicted with a natural defectiveness." And St Thomas for his part pronounced woman to be an "imperfect man," an "incidental[6]" being. This is symbolised in Genesis where Eve is depicted as made from what Bossuet called "a supernumerary[7] bone" of Adam.

Thus humanity is male and man defines woman not in herself but as relative to him; she is not regarded as an autonomous being. Michelet[8] writes: "Woman, the relative being ..." And Benda[9] is most positive in his *Rapport d'Uriel*: "The body of man makes sense in itself quite

---

1   **symmetrically:** in pairs
2   **reciprocity:** give-and-take, producing mutual effect
3   **oblique:** any angle that is not a right angle（斜角）
4   **gland:** an organ that produces a secretion for use elsewhere in the body
5   **testicles:** male sex glands for producing fertilizing element（睾丸）
6   **incidental:** small, unimportant
7   **supernumerary:** additional (to the normal number)
8   **Jules Michelet (1798–1874):** French historian noted for his lively 17-volume Histoire de France (1833–1867)
9   **Julien Benda (1867–1956):** French philosopher and novelist, remembered for his 1927 book *La Trahison des Clercs* (*The Treason of the Intellectuals*)

Heritage of Western Intellectual Tradition   A Sourcebook

apart from that of woman, whereas the latter seems wanting in significance by itself ... Man can think of himself without woman. She cannot think of herself without man." And she is simply what man decrees; thus she is called "the sex," by which is meant that she appears essentially to the male as a sexual being. **For him she is sex — absolute sex, no less. She is defined and differentiated with reference to man and not he with reference to her; she is the incidental, the inessential as opposed to the essential. He is the Subject, he is the Absolute — she is the Other.**

The category of the *Other* is as primordial[1] as consciousness itself. In the most primitive societies, in the most ancient mythologies, one finds the expression of a duality — that of the Self and the Other. This duality was not originally attached to the division of the sexes; it was not dependent upon any empirical facts. It is revealed in such works as that of Granet[2] on Chinese thought and those of Dumézil[3] on the East Indies and Rome. The feminine element was at first no more involved in such pairs as Varuna-Mitra[4], Uranus[5]-Zeus, Sun-Moon, and Day-Night than it was in the contrasts between Good and Evil, lucky

Sartre and Beauvoir visited China, 1955

and unlucky auspices[6], right and left, God and Lucifer[7]. Otherness is a fundamental category of human thought.

Thus it is that no group ever sets itself up as the One without at once setting up the Other over against itself. If three travellers chance to occupy the same compartment, that is enough to make vaguely hostile "others" out of all the rest of the passengers on the train. In small-town eyes all persons not belonging to the village are "strangers" and suspect; to the native of a country all who inhabit other countries are "foreigners;" Jews are "different" for the anti-Semite[8], Negroes are 'inferior' for American racists, aborigines[9] are 'natives' for colonists, proletarians are

---

1 **primordial:** primeval, very old

2 **Marcel Granet (1884–1940):** French sociologist, follower of Emile Durkheim, known also as an ethnologist and sinologist

3 **Georges Dumézil (1898–1986):** French comparative philologist best known for his analysis of sovereignty and power in Indo-European religion and society

4 **Varuna-Mitra:** Varuna, Hindu god of the dead; Mitra, god of the sun. As the heaven was imagined as made from a light and a dark half, Varuna may either correspond or rule over the dark half, or represent the "dark" side of the Sun as it travels back from West to East during the night.

5 **Uranus:** in Greek mythology the earliest supreme god, a personification of the sky, who was the son and consort of Gaea and the father of the Cyclopes and Titans

6 **auspices:** or auspex, in ancient Rome a religious official who interpreted omens to guide public policy

7 **Lucifer:** archangel cast from heaven for leading the revolt of the angels, Satan

8 **Semite:** races including Jews, Arabs, Phoenicians and Assyrians

9 **aborigine:** natives

Heritage of Western Intellectual Tradition   A Sourcebook

the 'lower class' for the privileged.

Lévi-Strauss[1], at the end of a profound work on the various forms of primitive societies, reaches the following conclusion: "Passage from the state of Nature to the state of Culture is marked by man's ability to view biological relations as a series of contrasts; duality, alternation, opposition, and symmetry, whether under definite or vague forms, constitute not so much phenomena to be explained as fundamental and immediately given data of social reality." These phenomena would be incomprehensible if in fact human society were simply a *Mitsein*[2] or fellowship based on solidarity and friendliness. Things become clear, on the contrary, if, following Hegel, we find in consciousness itself a fundamental hostility towards every other consciousness; the subject can be posed only in being opposed — he sets himself up as the essential, as opposed to the other, the inessential, the object.

But the other consciousness, the other ego, sets up a reciprocal claim. The native travelling abroad is shocked to find himself in turn regarded as a "stranger" by the natives of neighbouring countries. **As a matter of fact, wars, festivals, trading, treaties, and contests among tribes, nations, and classes tend to deprive the concept** *Other* **of its absolute sense and to make manifest its relativity; willy-nilly[3], individuals and groups are forced to realize the reciprocity of their relations.** How is it, then, that this reciprocity has not been recognised between the sexes, that one of the contrasting terms is set up as the sole essential, denying any relativity in regard to its correlative and defining the latter as pure otherness? Why is it that women do not dispute male sovereignty? No subject will readily volunteer to become the object, the inessential; it is not the Other who, in defining himself as the Other, establishes the One. **The Other is posed as such by the One in defining himself as the One. But if the Other is not to regain the status of being the One, he must be submissive enough to accept this alien point of view.** Whence comes this submission in the case of woman?

There are, to be sure, other cases in which a certain category has been able to dominate another completely for a time. Very often this privilege depends upon inequality of numbers — the majority imposes its rule upon the minority or persecutes it. But women are not a minority, like the American Negroes or the Jews; there are as many women as men on earth. Again, the two groups concerned have often been originally independent; they may have been formerly unaware of each other's existence, or perhaps they recognised each other's autonomy. But a historical event has resulted in the subjugation of the weaker by the stronger. The scattering of the Jews, the introduction of slavery into America, the conquests of imperialism are examples in point. In these cases the oppressed retained at least the memory of former days; they possessed in common a past, a tradition, sometimes a religion or a culture.

---

1   **Claude Lévi-Strauss (1908–):** French social anthropologist and leading exponent of the theory of structuralism. His works include *Structural Anthropology* (1958) and *Totemism* (1962).

2   *Mitsein:* togetherness

3   **willy-nilly:** without having a choice

Heritage of Western Intellectual Tradition   A Sourcebook

The parallel drawn by Bebel[1] between women and the proletariat is valid in that neither ever formed a minority or a separate collective unit of mankind. And instead of a single historical event it is in both cases a historical development that explains their status as a class and accounts for the membership of *particular individuals* in that class. But proletarians have not always existed, whereas there have always been women. They are women in virtue of their anatomy and physiology. Throughout history they have always been subordinated to men, and hence their dependency is not the result of a historical event or a social change — it was not something that *occurred*. The reason why otherness in this case seems to be an absolute is in part that it lacks the contingent[2] or incidental nature of historical facts. A condition brought about at a certain time can be abolished at some other time, as the Negroes of Haiti and others have proved: but it might seem that natural condition is beyond the possibility of change. In truth, however, the nature of things is no more immutably[3] given, once for all, than is historical reality. If woman seems to be the inessential which never becomes the essential, it is because she herself fails to bring about this change.

Burial, with Sartre, April 14, 1986

Proletarians say "We;" Negroes also. Regarding themselves as subjects, they transform the bourgeois, the whites, into "others." But women do not say "We," except at some congress of feminists or similar formal demonstration; men say "women," and women use the same word in referring to themselves. They do not authentically assume a subjective attitude. **The proletarians have accomplished the revolution in Russia, the Negroes in Haiti, the Indo-Chinese are battling for it in Indo-China; but the women's effort has never been anything more than a symbolic agitation[4]. They have gained only what men have been willing to grant; they have taken nothing, they have only received.**

The reason for this is that women lack concrete means for organising themselves into a unit which can stand face to face with the correlative unit. They have no past, no history, no religion of their own; and they have no such solidarity of work and interest as that of the proletariat. They are not even promiscuously herded together in the way that creates community feeling among the American Negroes, the ghetto[5] Jews, the workers of Saint-Denis[6], or the factory hands of Renault[7].

---

1 **August Ferdinand Bebel (1840–1913):** German social democrat and one of the founders of the Social Democratic Party of Germany

2 **contingent:** uncertain

3 **immutably:** unchangeably

4 **agitation:** excitement of feeling

5 **ghetto:** Jewish quarter of a town

6 **Saint-Denis:** an industrial suburb North of Paris for metals, chemicals, machinery, electronics, and food products

7 **Renault:** France's largest motor-vehicle manufacturer, founded in 1898 by Louis Renault (1877–1944) who formed the company with his brothers Fernand and Marcel. In 1899 they began motor racing and produced tanks for the French army in both world wars.

They live dispersed among the males, attached through residence, housework, economic condition, and social standing to certain men — fathers or husbands — more firmly than they are to other women. If they belong to the bourgeoisie, they feel solidarity with men of that class, not with proletarian women; if they are white, their allegiance is to white men, not to Negro women. The proletariat can propose to massacre the ruling class, and a sufficiently fanatical[1] Jew or Negro might dream of getting sole possession of the atomic bomb and making humanity wholly Jewish or black; but woman cannot even dream of exterminating the males. The bond that unites her to her oppressors is not comparable to any other. The division of the sexes is a biological fact, not an event in human history. Male and female stand opposed within a primordial *Mitsein*, and woman has not broken it. The couple is a fundamental unity with its two halves riveted[2] together, and the cleavage[3] of society along the line of sex is impossible. Here is to be found the basic trait of woman: she is the Other in a totality of which the two components are necessary to one another.

One could suppose that this reciprocity might have facilitated the liberation of woman. When Hercules[4] sat at the feet of Omphale[5] and helped with her spinning, his desire for her held him captive; but why did she fail to gain a lasting power? To revenge herself on Jason, Medea[6] killed their children; and this grim legend would seem to suggest that she might have obtained a formidable influence over him through his love for his offspring. In *Lysistrata* Aristophanes[7] gaily depicts a band of women who joined forces to gain social ends through the sexual needs of their men; but this is only a play. In the legend of the Sabine women, the latter

At a women's lib celebration, 1974

---

1   **fanatical:** wild, mad

2   **rivet:** fasten

3   **cleavage:** split, division

4   **Hercules:** in Greek & Roman mythology, son of Zeus and Alcmene, a hero of extraordinary strength who won immortality by performing 12 labors demanded by the Argive king Eurystheus

5   **Omphale:** Hercules killed Iphitus, son of the king of Oichalia, because the king would not give him his daughter Iole. When Neleus, king of Pylos, refused him absolution for that crime, Hercules sacked his kingdom and killed all his sons except Nestor. For that outrage the Delphic oracle bade him serve Omphale, queen of Lydia, who, in some legends, dressed him in women's clothes and had him work with her maids spinning wool. He later was her lover, but after he finished his servitude he returned to Oichalia and carried off Iole.

6   **Medea:** in Greek mythology, princess and sorceress of Colchis who helped Jason, husband of Medea and leader of the Argonauts, obtain the Golden Fleece, lived as his consort, and killed their children as revenge for his infidelity

7   *Lysistrata*: anti-war comedy by Greek comic dramatist Aristophanes (c. 448 – 380 BC), written in 411 BC, where female characters, led by the eponymous Lysistrata, withhold consensual sex from their husbands to secure peace and end the Peloponnesian War. In doing so, Lysistrata engages the support of women from Sparta, Boeotia, and Corinth, whom, at first aghast at the suggestion of withholding sex, finally agree and swear an oath to support each other.

Heritage of Western Intellectual Tradition   A Sourcebook

soon abandoned their plan of remaining sterile[1] to punish their ravishers[2]. In truth woman has not been socially emancipated through man's need — sexual desire and the desire for offspring — which makes the male dependent for satisfaction upon the female.

Master and slave, also, are united by a reciprocal need, in this case economic, which does not liberate the slave. In the relation of master to slave the master does not make a point of the need that he has for the other; he has in his grasp the power of satisfying this need through his own action; whereas the slave, in his dependent condition, his hope and fear, is quite conscious of the need he has for his master. Even if the need is at bottom equally urgent for both, it always works in favour of the oppressor and against the oppressed. That is why the liberation of the working class, for example, has been slow.

Burial cite of Sartre and de Beauvoir at the cemetery of Monpanasse

Now, woman has always been man's dependant, if not his slave; the two sexes have never shared the world in equality. And even today woman is heavily handicapped, though her situation is beginning to change. Almost nowhere is her legal status the same as man's, and frequently it is much to her disadvantage. Even when her rights are legally recognised in the abstract, long-standing custom prevents their full expression in the mores[3]. In the economic sphere men and women can almost be said to make up two castes[4]; other things being equal, the former hold the better jobs, get higher wages, and have more opportunity for success than their new competitors. In industry and politics men have a great many more positions and they monopolise the most important posts. In addition to all this, they enjoy a traditional prestige that the education of children tends in every way to support, for the present enshrines the past — and in the past all history has been made by men. At the present time, when women are beginning to take part in the affairs of the world, it is still a world that belongs to men — they have no doubt of it at all and women have scarcely any. To decline to be the Other, to refuse to be a party to the deal — this would be for women to renounce all the advantages conferred upon them by their alliance with the superior caste. Man-the-sovereign will provide woman-the-liege[5] with material protection and will undertake the moral justification of her existence; thus she can evade at once both economic risk and the metaphysical risk of a liberty in which ends and aims must be contrived without assistance. Indeed, along with the ethical urge of each individual to affirm his subjective existence, there is also the temptation to forgo liberty and become a thing. This is an inauspicious[6] road, for he who

1   **sterile:** not producing offspring
2   **ravishers:** people who rape them
3   **mores:** accepted traditional customs and usages of a particular social group
4   **caste:** fixed social class in India
5   **liege:** loyal subject to a monarch
6   **inauspicious:** unfavourable, not prosperous

takes it — passive, lost, ruined — becomes henceforth the creature of another's will, frustrated in his transcendence and deprived of every value. But it is an easy road; on it one avoids the strain involved in undertaking an authentic existence. When man makes of woman the Other, he may, then, expect to manifest deep-seated tendencies towards complicity. **Thus, woman may fail to lay claim to the status of subject because she lacks definite resources, because she feels the necessary bond that ties her to man regardless of reciprocity, and because she is often very well pleased with her role as the Other.**

Key Concepts

absolute sex	Platonic essence
eternal feminine	reciprocity of relations
femininity	the Self
the inessential/the essential	socially emancipated
liberation of woman	symbolic agitation
masculine/feminine	unchangeably fixed entities
the Other	woman is a womb

Compare with China

The First Glimpses of China

The Long March
published in 1957

Sartre and de Beauvoir were invited by premier Zhou Enlai to visit China in September, 1955, and they stayed for 45 days going around a large portion of the country. The travel notes she collected in The Long March, published shortly after she returned to Paris, presents a lively new China from her feminist perspective, though there were naïve readings here and there.

The old China Hands chuckle at those they call "the travelers," who go and explore China unequipped with any comprehensive knowledge of China's past and none at all of her language. The anti-communists apply themselves to discrediting eyewitness accounts which, in their virtual unanimity, are favorable to the regime. Fano, who does not know Chinese, recounts how at Hong Kong friends of his split their sides when one of these visitors conceded that he had indeed only talked with the Chinese through the intermediary of an interpreter; lest we continue to abuse ourselves, Fano explains that no Chinese would under any circumstances, even in privacy, have dared to open up sincerely with a foreigner. Guillain[1] finds that, in present conditions, no meaningful observations can be fetched home by any observer, unless he be Guillain; having paid his own way there and back, he further insinuates that spending six weeks at a government's expense is tantamount to winding up in its hire — which is to set a rather low price on his own honesty and on the honesty of others. Had I been hostile to China beforehand I would have declined China's invitation; but in accepting it, I contracted no engagement; China takes chances, and I have at no moment felt myself under any obligation to her except to be fair. As for the lack of a thorough background and the particularly serious drawback of my ignorance of Chinese, these are handicaps which I am by no means prone to underestimate; they did most certainly limit my experience; I deny that they robbed it of all value. If anti-Communists reject it a priori, they do so in the name of a curious thesis: that which one sees with one's own eyes, they hold, is necessarily sheer mirage. So it was that Martinet[2] who did not attend the Vienna Congress could declare that Sartre, owing to the very fact that he was present at it, had been unable to understand a word of what went on there; and Guillain spots a piece of Machiavellian cunning in Chou Enlai's "Come and see." For these initiates the world is mystery, conjuration, conspiracy, everything happens in smoke-filled back rooms; the naive spectator, dazzled by superficial appearances, is blinded to the underlying truths. More alert, more adroit, when ever they want to know whether the sun is shining, our clairvoyants look not out of the window but into their crystal ball. Guillain admits that the authorities are not very well able to fake a country over thousands of miles and for an entire year—although struggling with might and main, he was often reduced to believing his eyes: he saw properly dressed peasants, highways, factories, a hygiene, an order, achievements which amazed him: but in his fortuneteller's instrument he discovered famines, forced-labor camps. I confess not to have had any suck talisman in my traveling kit. On the other hand. I am perfectly willing to admit that mere eyesight is not enough to bring out everything an object may contain; nevertheless, I have very often found that eyes are not useless and that objects when looked at disclose something. To walk down a street is an immediate, irrecusable experience for which no hypothesis about a city, however ingenious, can be a substitute or as instructive . With its avidity for the arcane low-down the inside-track-on-China elite is too apt to forget that appearances also have their reality. Every fact requires to be interpreted, of course; but why need seeing prevent one from finding out and formulating opinions and criticisms? Let me give full details of the conditions under which the elements of this account were established.

The menu is in English and the service amazingly quick; young women in white jackets, a bow of ribbon in their short hair, bring on everything and remove the last crumb all inside less than twenty-five minutes. Tsai told me that when traveling abroad with his friends they were exasperated by the amount of time meals absorbed. My room is also done in the twinkling of an eye: I go down for a cup of tea, return to find everything in order. One morning, noticing in the hallway that I'd gone out without my bag, I retraced my steps and discovered a foursome in the

---

1   **Robert Guillain:** *Le Monde's* special correspondent and expert on China.

2   **Gilles Martinet:** member of the editorial committee of *France-Observateur*, a Paris weekly review of political affairs.

midst of sweeping, dusting, tidying. But the number does not provide the whole explanation; I have observed that, without being in any apparent haste, the Chinese work in a remarkably efficient manner. The enlarged Peking Hotel is today the Times Square cross roads of the cosmopolitan activity that goes on at a great rate from April to December and reaches its pitch toward the start of October; not long ago, existing only as the old wing, it was one of the centers of Occidental life. Built by the French, it later belonged to the Japanese: the bald old elevator man kept imperturbably at his post throughout these several avatars. Flanked by a wide roof garden, the tenth-floor salons were the headquarters of an Anglo-French Club where the white elite used to dance and drink their boredom away; and, when drunk, another of their distractions was to go down and urinate on the corner policeman — who, though in uniform, a patched and very dirty uniform, was only a Chinaman underneath it all. In those days, the main avenue was half its present width: on the other side extended a polo field, bordering on the diplomatic section that was surrounded by a wall studded with machine-gun nests. As for the esplanade, a French man named Casseville in about 1934 used these terms to describe it: "At the foot of this palatial establishment, heaps of ungodly rubbish litter vague banks of flowers; filthy beggars swarming amidst an army of coolies, whose rickshaws new development or achievement of exceptional importance, we were told so; we made impromptu entries into houses. In Shanghai and Canton, among other places, without our having asked, we were shown through overcrowded and poor sections the equivalents of which are passed over in delicate silence by the Baedekers to bourgeois countries. No, they did not hide China behind their backs, they had not daubed hundreds of villages with stage paint or draped camouflage nets over thousands of miles of countryside; they had us see China.

Concerning the method they adopted, I learned to put up in patience with certain of its defects. There some fifteen hundred of us delegates roaming the length and breadth of China and almost all of us stayed a good while in Peking too; to us all, which is normal, they showed the same vestiges of the past, the same new achievements: to prevent us from trouping all at once

Sartre and de Beauvoir at the Summer Palace

into factories or theaters, those in charge must have had to work out a system as complicated as the ones that regulate the movements of railway trains: it would have been too much to insist that a logical order be observed in the "program." It included a few pretty exhausting items. I remember how irritated I was over a trip to the Kwanting Reservoir. From eight a.m. till noon the train rolled through tunnels: this was a newly constructed line, inaugurated in July 1995, and the Chinese are proud of it for the good reason that it tunnels through mountains seventy-five time; they are also proud of the reservoir and dam which controls the once dreaded rising of the Hwai River. But while munching sandwiches in a hut with a delegation of Danes I thought about the four hours of darkness and soot ahead of me and asked myself just why they had sent me all the way out here. I could have got along very nicely with photographs and magazine articles. Later on I understood their stubborn desire to show me public works, hospitals, factories, laboratories which, when I saw them, did not seem at all extraordinary to me: what is extraordinary is that these things exist in China today. Westerners and Japanese had outvied each other repeating that, thrown on her own, China was capable of nothing beyond growing kaoliang: every tunnel blasted, every machine manufactured is a lofty reply to that challenge. The Chinese do not have the familiarity with the products of their labor which in Europe makes us take electric power plants as much for granted as we do highways; over and above its practical use, a telephone, like a railroad, represents a victory won against the past, a stride ahead toward a new future. They want the visitor to bear witness to his conquest: that is why he must ascertain it, verify it in person and on the spot; if he just relies on photographs, takes the word of reports, once home again doubting interlocutors may suspect him of having been the dupe of are lined up as though for a review, spit, pluck at their lice, and bowl their lamentations." The esplanade is a parking lot today. Taxis do not exist in Peking, neither do private automobiles; all these cars belong to departments of the government. There are Russian Pobiedas, Czech Skodas, some British cars — China buys cars from England — and a fleet of sleek American cars, a bequest of Chiang Kai-shek's administration. The chauffeurs are at it early in the morning: equipped with red, long-handled feather dusters, they whisk every speck of dust from the gleaming cars, inside and out.

Two or three times a day we go off for a drive in one of them. Tsai accompanies us. He is thirty, wears glasses, has a youthful and engaging look, but he is very reserved. At nine every morning, at two o'clock every afternoon he rings up from the lobby: "I'm ready," He takes us to see temples, palaces, parks, or else craft cooperatives, universities, hospitals, depending on a program mapped out somewhere up above. We are free by five. But if it is to be theater in the evening, one must dine at six thirty: curtains rise at half past seven in China. By eleven the streets are deserted. Peking is asleep.

Sartre's article published in the People's Daily on Nov. 2, 1955

The disadvantages of this sort of organizing are obvious. But I wish right away to state that, notwithstanding the allegations of the Fanos and the Guillains, in China an interpreter is not a detective. Guillain neglected to point out that it had been proposed to him that he bring along an interpreter of his own. If Tsai accompanies me, it is because, without him, I am deaf, dumb, lost: he is a necessity to me. But he is not under instructions to erect fences around me or to sieve the remarks made by people I meet. Never once was my freedom of movement hindered. I took walks by myself, as many and whenever I wanted. In Peking we frequently went out, unescorted, with L —, a French newspaperman who speaks Chinese. When, in Shanghai, we expressed the wish to meet some French who happen to be notoriously hostile to the regime, our desire was immediately satisfied. Only our ignorance of the language made it impossible to have contacts between ourselves and the man in the street, L —, who has been living in Peking for a long time, while out gathering material for a story stops in whatever villages he pleases, talks freely with the peasants; in all of this the authorities find nothing to object to. A Sinologist who left Peking in 1953, who spent a few days there again in 1955, told me he had sensed no awkwardness when chatting with the shopkeepers whose customer he had formerly been. However Guillain may choose to interpret the fact, we talked at length, alone, with Chinese who know English or French. When our visits were prepared in advance, this was not concealed from us; each time we were to be shown some propaganda; he must therefore to be able to say: I saw these things with my own eyes.

Supplementary Reading

1. Existentialism

This short article traces the development of existentialism as a humanistic movement and then presents a Marxist critique of existentialism.

Post-structuralism[1], the philosophical rationale[2] of contemporary "post-modernist discourse", presents itself as a radically new view of the world. However, in many ways it is simply a reincarnation of existentialism, which conceives of nature and society as dominated by accident and chance and stresses the meaningless of human existence.

The Origins of Existentialism

Existentialism was born as a bourgeois philosophical response to the crisis that World War I and its aftermath[3] dealt to the superficially optimistic world-view and belief in progressive development of capitalist society inherent in middle-class liberalism. Its most prominent figure was Martin Heidegger.

A philosopher of irrationalism, Heidegger maintained that the chief impediment to human self-development was reason and science, which, he claimed, led to a view of humans only as objects of impersonal investigation and practical manipulation. According to Heidegger, human existence could not be understood through rational-scientific thinking or through social practice, but only by an inward-turning orientation to one's self, particularly in the contemplation of death.

Heidegger was strongly influenced by the 19th century irrationalist philosophers Soren Kierkegaard and Friedrich Nietzsche, and was the disciple of the German idealist philosopher Edmund Husserl[4].

Edmund   Husserl (1859 – 1938), German philosopher, founder of phenomenology

---

1   **post-structuralism:** an umbrella term used to refer to all the philosophical and cultural theories after structuralism of the 60s, such as deconstruction, feminism, post-colonialism, and cultural studies

2   **rationale:** logical bases, fundamental reason

3   **aftermath:** consequence

4   **Edmund Husserl (1859 – 1938):** German philosopher who developed phenomenology

Kierkegaard previewed[1] many of the themes of 20th century existentialism, though in an explicitly religious context. In opposition to Hegelian determinism, Kierkegaard interpreted human existence in terms of chance and possibility. He believed that growing awareness of truth led to despair owing to the contrast between the brevity of individual human life compared to the "infinity of God". Nietzsche developed an anti-rationalist, atheistic humanism based on an extreme individualism that distrusted all group action.

Husserl founded the philosophy of phenomenology[2], which he claimed superseded[3] both materialism and idealism by rejecting all "presuppositions". He sought to eliminate any theory of knowledge and called for suspending belief about any previously known fact in the study of a particular phenomenon. The internal logic of a phenomenon was to be reconstructed from the appearances of it available to the observer. Thus far the method appeared to parallel empiricism, but Husserl then asserted that the aim of such investigation was to intuitively grasp the real essence of the phenomenon under observation. During the period of study, no consideration was to be given to the reality or non-reality of the object under examination. Thus, dreams, fantasies, and illusions were to be examined with a seriousness equal to that given to objectively indisputable existences. By 1907 Husserl had become an avowed[4] subjective idealist, asserting that objects had no existence outside of human consciousness.

In 1928 Husserl was stripped of his university post in Freiburg, Germany, because of his Jewish origins. He spent the last years of his life as a pariah[5] in Nazi Germany, although he was not arrested.

Martin Heidegger accepted the chair of philosophy at the University of Freiburg after his mentor was forced to relinquish it by the growing Nazi movement. Heidegger was himself a political reactionary. He supported Hitler, which led to his disgrace at the end of World War II, and his retirement in 1951 after a life of rural seclusion[6].

Heidegger's existentialist ideas, however, deeply influenced the French philosopher Jean-Paul Sartre, who was to become the best known populariser of the ideas of existentialism.

Sartrean Existentialism

In his early theoretical writings, culminating in *Being and Nothingness* (1943) Sartre summed up existentialism's deeply pessimistic view of life in the phrases "life is hell" and "hell is other

---

1 **preview:** be the forerunner of

2 **phenomenology:** philosophy or method, originated about 1905 by Edmund Husserl, of inquiry based on the premise that reality consists of objects and events as they are perceived or understood in human consciousness and not of anything independent of human consciousness

3 **supersede:** take the place of

4 **avow:** admit openly

5 **pariah:** social outcast

6 **seclusion:** the condition of being cut off from others, or from other places, retirement

Heritage of Western Intellectual Tradition A Sourcebook

people." By 1947, however, Sartre had begun to evolve away from the gloom and despair this view implied. He now argued that while the world was "hell" it was human beings who created the world. This implied a move away from passive self-contemplation toward an active striving for freedom, in which human action could overcome both "hells"[1]. However, this shift was still confined to a subjectivist and individualistic framework — a demand for absolute personal freedom.

From the late 1950s on, Sartre tried to marry his existentialist philosophy with the revolutionary doctrine of Marxism. In his 1960 philosophical treatise *The Critique of Dialectical Reason*, for example, Sartre declared that existentialism was a subordinate branch of Marxism which aspired to "renew" and "enrich" it.

But this "enriching" involved discarding the materialist, sociohistorical outlook of Marxism in favour of a subjectivist, individualistic approach to philosophy, sociology, morality and politics.

The whole of Sartre's philosophy revolved around the absolute primacy of the individual subject over everything objective, whether natural or social. The truth and value of human existence are to be sought exclusively within the existence of the isolated individual. "If we refuse to see the original dialectical movement in the individual and in his enterprise of producing his life, of objectifying himself, then we shall have to give up dialectic or else make[2] of it as the immanent law of history", Sartre wrote in the lengthy preface to his *Critique*. That is, Sartre located dialectical development exclusively within human practice. Moreover, he considered that the dialectical development of society proceeds from the actions of the isolated individual, rather from the objective realities, laws and necessities of social life.

Marxism takes a diametrically opposite point of view: the thoughts and actions of the individual are determined by the dialectical development of society. The isolated individual — so central to existentialism's world view — is an abstraction. As Marx himself observed in his "Theses on Feuerbach" (1845): "The human essence is no abstraction inherent in each single individual. In its reality it is the ensemble of the social relations." That is, the individual, with his or her own particular personality, is the product of society. Everything distinctive about humans, from tool-making, speech and abstract thinking, to the latest products of art and technology, is the result of millions of years of social practice. Human social practice in turn is a historical outgrowth of the dialectical development of nature; the organic developing out of the inorganic; the human from the animal.

Nature, humanity, social life and labour are inseparably interconnected. What separated humanity from the rest of animal life was the practice of labour — the regular, collective production of means of subsistence through the use and fashioning of tools. Through labour prehuman primates[3] began to transform their natural environment to serve their needs, and in the process they

---

1 **both "hells":** life and other people
2 **make:** way a thing is made
3 **primate:** highest order of mammals（灵长类）

transformed themselves and their descendants into a qualitatively new species.

Fundamental changes in the organisation of the labour process are the basis for the dialectical development of society. Subjective components of this development — individual psychology, for example — are integral and subordinate elements of this objective historical process. Thus society is more than the sum of its individuals because it is a product of collective activity. It is only in and through society that we develop as individuals.

Existentialism, on the other hand, pictures the individual as essentially divorced from other people, confronted by an inert[1], irrational and hostile social environment. It champions[2] the spontaneity of the individual against any established institution or organised movement. It is equally hostile to the social institutions of bourgeois society and to the working class's collective struggle against them. Rather than being a guide to revolutionary action, it is a philosophy that justifies the individualistic non-conformism of middle-class intellectuals.

2. *Virginia Woolf: A Room of One's Own*

Let me imagine, since facts are so hard to come by, what would have happened had Shakespeare had a wonderfully gifted sister, called Judith, let us say. Shakespeare himself went, very probably, — his mother was an heiress — to the grammar school, where he may have learnt Latin — Ovid[3], Virgil[4] and Horace[5] — and the elements of grammar and logic. He was, it is well known, a wild boy who poached[6] rabbits, perhaps shot a deer, and had, rather sooner than he should have done, to marry a woman in the neighbourhood, who bore him a child rather quicker than was right. That escapade[7] sent him to seek his fortune in London. He had, it seemed, a taste for the theatre; he began by holding horses at the stage door. Very soon he got work in the theatre, became a successful actor, and lived at the hub[8] of the universe, meeting everybody, knowing everybody, practising his art on the boards, exercising his wits in the streets, and even getting access to the palace of the queen. Meanwhile his extraordinarily gifted sister, let us suppose, remained at home. She was as adventurous, as imaginative, as agog[9] to see

---

1 **inert:** inactive, powerless
2 **champion:** support, defend
3 **Ovid (43 BC–17 AD):** Roman poet known for his explorations of love, especially the *Art of Love* (c. 1 BC) and *Metamorphoses* (c. 8 AD)
4 **Virgil (70–19 BC):** Roman poet whose greatest work is the epic poem *Aeneid*, which tells of the wanderings of Aeneas after the sack of Troy
5 **Horace (65–8 BC):** Roman lyric poet whose *Odes and Satires* have exerted a major influence on English poetry
6 **poach:** hunt illegally
7 **escapade:** mischievous act
8 **hub:** center
9 **agog:** eager

the world as he was. But she was not sent to school. She had no chance of learning grammar and logic, let alone of reading Horace and Virgil. She picked up a book now and then, one of her brother's perhaps, and read a few pages. But then her parents came in and told her to mend the stockings or mind the stew[1] and not moon about[2] with books and papers. They would have spoken sharply but kindly, for they were substantial[3] people who knew the conditions of life for a woman and loved their daughter — indeed, more likely than not she was the apple of her father's eye. Perhaps she scribbled some pages up in an apple loft[4] on the sly[5] but was careful to hide them or set fire to them. Soon, however, before she was out of her teens, she was to be betrothed[6] to the son of a neighbouring woolstapler[7]. She cried out that marriage was hateful to her, and for that she was severely beaten by her father. Then he ceased to scold her. He begged her instead not to hurt him, not to shame him in this matter of her marriage. He would give her a chain of beads or a fine petticoat, he said; and there were tears in his eyes. How could she disobey him? How could she break his heart? The force of her own gift alone drove her to it. She made up a small parcel of her belongings, let herself down by a rope one summer's night and took the road to London. She was not seventeen. The birds that sang in the hedge were not more musical than she was. She had the quickest fancy, a gift like her brother's, for the tune of words. Like him, she had a taste for the theatre. She stood at the stage door; she wanted to act, she said. Men laughed in her face. The manager — a fat, looselipped man — guffawed[8]. He bellowed[9] something about poodles[10] dancing and women acting—no woman, he said, could possibly be an actress. He hinted — you can imagine what. She could get no training in her craft. Could she even seek her dinner in a tavern or roam the streets at midnight? Yet her genius was for fiction and lusted to feed abundantly upon the lives of men and women and the study of their ways. At last — for she was very young, oddly like Shakespeare the poet in her face, with the same grey eyes and rounded brows — at last Nick Greene the actor-manager took pity on her; she found herself with child by that gentleman and so — who shall measure the heat and violence of the poet's heart when caught and tangled[11] in a woman's body? — killed herself one winter's night and lies buried at some cross-roads where the omnibuses[12] now stop outside the Elephant and Castle.

   That, more or less, is how the story would run, I think, if a woman in Shakespeare's day had had Shakespeare's genius. But for my part, I agree with the deceased bishop, if such he was — it

---

1 **stew:** cooking
2 **moon about:** waste time
3 **substantial:** practical, well-to-do
4 **loft:** room for storing things under the roof
5 **on the sly:** secretly
6 **betrothed:** engaged
7 **woolstapler:** merchant of wool
8 **guffaw:** laugh noisily
9 **bellow:** make a deep noise
10 **poodle:** dog with thick and curling hair
11 **tangle:** exist in a confused state
12 **omnibus:** bus

Heritage of Western Intellectual Tradition   A Sourcebook

is unthinkable that any woman in Shakespeare's day should have had Shakespeare's genius. For genius like Shakespeare's is not born among labouring, uneducated, servile[1] people. It was not born in England among the Saxons and the Britons. It is not born to-day among the working classes. How, then, could it have been born among women whose work began, according to Professor Trevelyan, almost before they were out of the nursery, who were forced to it by their parents and held to it by all the power of law and custom? Yet genius of a sort must have existed among women as it must have existed among the working classes. Now and again an Emily Brontë[2] or a Robert Burns[3] blazes out and proves its presence. But certainly it never got itself on to paper. When, however, one reads of a witch being ducked[4], of a woman possessed by devils, of a wise woman selling herbs, or even of a very remarkable man who had a mother, then I think we are on the track of a lost novelist, a suppressed poet, of some mute and inglorious Jane Austen, some Emily Brontë who dashed her brains out on the moor or mopped and mowed about the highways crazed with the torture that her gift had put her to. Indeed, I would venture to guess that Anon[5], who wrote so many poems without singing them, was often a woman. It was a woman Edward Fitzgerald, I think, suggested who made the ballads and the folk-songs, crooning[6] them to her children, beguiling[7] her spinning with them, or the length of the winter's night.

This may be true or it may be false — who can say? — but what is true in it, so it seemed to me, reviewing the story of Shakespeare's sister as I had made it, is that any woman born with a great gift in the sixteenth century would certainly have gone crazed, shot herself, or ended her days in some lonely cottage outside the village, half witch, half wizard[8], feared and mocked at. For it needs little skill in psychology to be sure that a highly gifted girl who had tried to use her gift for poetry would have been so thwarted and hindered by other people, so tortured and pulled asunder by her own contrary instincts, that she must have lost her health and sanity to a certainty[9]. No girl could have walked to London and stood at a stage door and forced

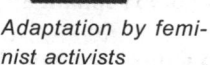

Adaptation by feminist activists

Famous WWII poster

---

1 **servile:** slave like

2 **Emily Brontë (1818 – 1848):** British novelist and poet, second (and some would say the finest) among the Brontë sisters and best remembered for *Wuthering Heights*, now an acknowledged classic of English literature

3 **Robert Burns (1759 – 1796):** best known of the poets who have written in Scots, whose poems include *Auld Lang Syne*, *Scots Wha Hae* (serving for a long time as an unofficial National anthem of the country) and *A Red, Red Rose*

4 **duck:** envade or avoid

5 **Anon:** or Anonymity, derived from the greek word "ανωνυμία," meaning without a name or nameless

6 **croon:** hum and sing gently

7 **beguile:** cause time to pass pleasantly

8 **wizard:** magician, person with amazing abilities

9 **to a certainty:** certainly

her way into the presence of actor-managers without doing herself a violence and suffering an anguish which may have been irrational — for chastity may be a fetish[1] invented by certain societies for unknown reasons — but were none the less inevitable. Chastity had then, it has even now, a religious importance in a woman's life, and has so wrapped itself round with nerves and instincts that to cut it free and bring it to the light of day demands courage of the rarest. To have lived a free life in London in the sixteenth century would have meant for a woman who was poet and playwright a nervous stress and dilemma which might well have killed her. Had she survived, whatever she had written would have been twisted and deformed, issuing from a strained and morbid[2] imagination. And undoubtedly, I thought, looking at the shelf where there are no plays by women, her work would have gone unsigned. That refuge she would have sought certainly. It was the relic[3] of the sense of chastity that dictated anonymity to women even so late as the nineteenth century. Currer Bell[4], George Eliot[5], George Sand[6], all the victims of inner strife as their writings prove, sought ineffectively to veil themselves by using the name of a man. Thus they did homage to the convention, which if not im-

Death of Ophelia in Hamlet, a talented girl like Shakespeare's sister

planted by the other sex was liberally encouraged by them (the chief glory of a woman is not to be talked of, said Pericles[7], himself a much-talked-of man) that publicity in women is detestable. Anonymity runs in their blood. The desire to be veiled still possesses them. They are not even now as concerned about the health of their fame as men are, and, speaking generally, will pass a tombstone or a signpost without feeling an irresistible desire to cut their names on it, as Alf, Bert or Chas must do in obedience to their instinct, which murmurs if it sees a fine woman go by, or even a dog, *Ce chien est a moi*. And, of course, it may not be a dog, I thought, remembering Parliament Square, the Sieges Allee and other avenues; it may be a piece of land or a man with curly black hair. It is one of the great advantages of being a woman that one can pass even a very fine negress[8] without wishing to make an Englishwoman of her.

1 **fetish:** something excessively worshipped and respected
2 **morbid:** diseased
3 **relic:** things that have survived from the past
4 **Currer Bell:** Emily Brontë, when the Brontë sisters decided to have their verses published, it appeared, at their own expense, as *Poems by Currer, Ellis and Acton Bell* (1846), each sister using her own initials in these pseudonyms. Two copies were sold.
5 **George Eliot (1819–1880):** English novelist whose work influenced the 19th century French naturalism, but her real name is Marry Ann.
6 **George Sand (1804–1876):** pseudonym of Amandine Aurore Lucile, Baronne Dudevant, French novelist of the romantic movement
7 **Pericles (c. 495–429 BC):** Athenian statesman, so influential in Athenian history that the period of his power is called the Age of Pericles
8 **negress:** negro woman

Heritage of Western Intellectual Tradition   A Sourcebook

...

But for women, I thought, looking at the empty shelves, these difficulties were infinitely more formidable. In the first place, to have a room of her own, let alone a quiet room or a sound-proof room, was out of the question, unless her parents were exceptionally rich or very noble, even up to the beginning of the nineteenth century. Since her pin money, which depended on the goodwill of her father, was only enough to keep her clothed, she was debarred[1] from such allevia-tions[2] as came even to Keats[3] or Tennyson[4] or Carlyle[5], all poor men, from a walking tour, a little journey to France, from the separate lodging which, even if it were miserable enough, sheltered them from the claims and tyrannies of their families. Such material difficulties were formidable; but much worse were the immaterial. The indifference of the world which Keats and Flaubert[6] and other men of genius have found so hard to bear was in her case not indifference but hostility. The world did not say to her as it said to them, Write if you choose; it makes no difference to me. The world said with a guffaw, Write? What's the good of your writing? Here the psychologists of Newnham and Girton might come to our help, I thought, looking again at the blank spaces on the shelves. For surely it is time that the effect of discouragement upon the mind of the artist should be measured, as I have seen a dairy company measure the effect of ordinary milk and Grade A milk upon the body of the rat. They set two rats in cages side by side, and of the two one was furtive[7], timid and small, and the other was glossy[8], bold and big. Now what food do we feed women as artists upon? I asked, remembering, I suppose, that dinner of prunes[9] and custard[10]. To answer that question I had only to open the evening paper and to read that Lord Birkenhead[11] is of opinion — but really I am not going to trouble to copy out Lord Birkenhead's opinion upon the writing of women. What Dean Inge[12] says I will leave in peace. The Harley Street[13] specialist may be allowed to rouse the echoes of Harley Street with his vociferations[14] without raising a

---

1 **debar:** prevent by convention

2 **alleviation:** making less painful

3 **John Keats (1795 – 1821):** major English poet for the beauty of the natural world and art as the vehicle for poetic imagination, despite his early death from tuberculosis at the age of 25

4 **Alfred Tennyson (1809 – 1892):** English poet, one of the great representative figures of the Victorian Age

5 **Thomas Carlyle (1795 – 1881):** Scottish essayist and historian, influential social critic

6 **Gustave Flaubert (1821 – 1880):** French writer, known for his novels *Madame Bovary* (1857) and *L'éducation sentimentale* (1869 *Sentimental Education*), considered by many to be the father of realistic fiction

7 **furtive:** done secretly so as not to cause any attention

8 **glossy:** shiny

9 **prune:** dried plum

10 **custard:** baked mixture of egg and milk

11 **Lord Birkenhead:** probably Frederick Edwin Smith, 1st Earl of Birkenhead (1872 – 1930), British Conserva-tive statesman, a skilled orator noted for his staunch opposition to Irish nationalism

12 **Dean Inge:** probably William Ralph Inge (1860 – 1954), English author and professor of divinity at Cambridge, and in 1911 Dean of St. Paul's Cathedral in London

13 **Harley Street:** road in the City of Westminster in London, noted for its large number of private dentists, surgeons, and doctors

14 **vociferation:** shouting, yelling

hair on my head. I will quote, however, Mr Oscar Browning[1], because Mr Oscar Browning was a great figure in Cambridge at one time, and used to examine the students at Girton and Newnham. Mr Oscar Browning was wont to declare "that the impression left on his mind, after looking over any set of examination papers, was that, irrespective of the marks he might give, the best woman was intellectually the inferior of the worst man." After saying that Mr Browning went back to his rooms — and it is this sequel[2] that endears him and makes him a human figure of some bulk and majesty — he went back to his rooms and found a stable-boy[3] lying on the sofa — "a mere skeleton, his cheeks were cavernous[4] and sallow, his teeth were black, and he did not appear to have the full use of his limbs. That's Arthur" [said Mr Browning]. "He's a dear boy really and most high-minded. — The two pictures always seem to me to complete each other. And happily in this age of biography the two pictures often do complete each other, so that we are able to interpret the opinions of great men not only by what they say, but by what they do.

But though this is possible now, such opinions coming from the lips of important people must have been formidable enough even fifty years ago. Let us suppose that a father from the highest motives did not wish his daughter to leave home and become writer, painter or scholar. "See what Mr Oscar Browning says," he would say; and there so was not only Mr Oscar Browning; there was the SATURDAY REVIEW; there was Mr Greg — the "essentials of a woman's being," said Mr Greg emphatically, "are that THEY ARE SUPPORTED BY, AND THEY MINISTER TO, MEN" — there was an enormous body of masculine opinion to the effect that nothing could be expected of women intellectually. Even if her father did not read out loud these opinions, any girl could read them for herself; and the reading, even in the nineteenth century, must have lowered her vitality, and told[5] profoundly upon her work. There would always have been that assertion — you cannot do this, you are incapable of doing that — to protest against, to overcome. Probably for a novelist this germ is no longer of much effect; for there have been women novelists of merit. But for painters it must still have some sting in it; and for musicians, I imagine, is even now active and poisonous in the extreme. The woman composer stands where the actress stood in the time of Shakespeare. Nick Greene, I thought, remembering the story I had made about Shakespeare's sister, said that a woman acting put him in mind of a dog dancing. Johnson repeated the phrase two hundred years later of women preaching. And here, I said, opening a book about music, we have the very words used again in this year of grace, 1928, of women who try to write music. Of Mlle. Germaine Tailleferre[6] one can only repeat Dr Johnson's dictum[7] concerning a woman preacher,

---

1   **Oscar Browning (1837–1923):** English writer, historian and educational reformer
2   **sequel:** consequent event
3   **stable-boy:** boy employed in the stable to take care of the horses
4   **cavernous:** cavern or cavelike
5   **tell:** influence
6   **Mlle. Germaine Tailleferre (1892–1983):** French composer and the only female member of the famous Group Les Six, a group of six composers working in Montparnasse whose music is a reaction against Wagnerism and Impressionism
7   **dictum:** Saying. Samuel Johnson (1709–1784), poet, essayist, biographer, lexicographer and a critic of English Literature, a great wit and prose stylist, well known for his *aphorisms*. Dr Johnson is the most quoted of English writers after Shakespeare.

transposed into terms of music. "Sir, a woman's composing is like a dog's walking on his hind legs. It is not done well, but you are surprised to find it done at all." So accurately does history repeat itself.

Questions for Discussion

1. What is existentialism? Why do you think it has stirred up so much response in the West in the mid-20th century and after?
2. How is existentialism related to man's life?
3. What does "God" mean as an Existentialist concept? Nietzsche said that "God is dead" while Satre declared that "God does not exist". What is the difference between the two ideas? What is your opinion?
4. Compared with "essence precedes existence," what makes Satre's "existence precedes essence" special in modern philosophy?
5. What makes Existentialism the target of public criticism? Is it the weakness of this theory? Why?
6. What do you know about feminism? What are the differences between the feminism in Beauvoir's time and that in our own?
7. Do you think this women as "Other" still exists today?
8. Comment on the story about Shakespeare's sister. Do you think this sister still lives today? If she does, how can we come to her assistance?
9. de Beauvoir makes a comparison between the proletariat and woman. What are the differences and similarities?